The
Miracles and Parables of
Christ

The Miracles and Parables of Christ

by Richard Chenevix Trench, M.A.

THE MIRACLES
AND PARABLES OF CHRIST

ISBN 0-529-10633-7

Printed in the United States of America

Contents

Notes on the Parables
INTRODUCTORY REMARKS

THE PARABLES

Contents   vii

I.

On the Names of the Miracles

E very discussion about a thing will best proceed from an investigation of the name or names which it bears; for the name ever seizes and presents the most distinctive features of the thing, embodying them for us in a word. In the name we have the true declaration of the innermost nature of the thing; we have a witness to that which the universal sense of men, finding its utterance in language, has ever felt thus to lie at its heart; and if we would learn to know the thing, we must start with seeking accurately to know the name which it bears. In the discussion upon which we are now entering, the names are manifold; for it is a consequence of this, that, where we have to do with anything which in many ways is significant, that will have inevitably many names, since no one will exhaust its meaning. Each of these will embody a portion of its essential qualities, will present it upon a single side, and not from the exclusive contemplation of anyone, but only of these altogether, will any adequate apprehension of that which we desire to know be obtained. Thus what we commonly call miracles, are in the Sacred Scriptures termed sometimes "wonders," sometimes "signs," sometimes "powers" sometimes, simply, "works." These titles they have in addition to some others of rarer occurrence, and which easily range themselves under one or other of these—on each of which I would fain say a few words, before attempting to make any further advance in the subject.

1. To take then first the name *"wonder,"* in which the effect of astonishment which the work produces upon the beholder is transferred to the work itself, an effect often graphically portrayed by the Evangelists, when relating our Lord's miracles (Mark 2:12; 4:41; 6:51; 8:37; Acts 3:10, 11) it will at once be felt that this does but touch the matter on the outside. The ethical meaning of the miracle

1

would be wholly lost, were blank astonishment or gaping wonder *all* which they aroused; since the same effect might be produced by a thousand meaner causes. Indeed it is not a little remarkable, rather is it singularly characteristic of the miracles of the New Testament, that this name "wonders" is never applied to them but in connection with other names. They are continually "signs *and* wonders," or "signs" or "powers" alone, but never "wonders" alone. Not that the miracle, considered simply as a wonder, as an astonishing event which the beholders can reduce to no law with which they are acquainted, is even as such without its meaning and its purpose; that purpose being that it should forcibly startle from the mere dream of a sense-bound existence, and, however it may not be itself an appeal to the spiritual in man, should yet be a summons to him that he should open his eyes to the spiritual appeal which is about to be addressed to him.

2. But the miracle, besides being a "wonder," is also a *"sign,"* a token and indication of the near presence and working of God. In this word the ethical end and purpose of the miracle comes out the *most* prominently, as in "wonder" the least. They are signs and pledges of something more than and beyond themselves (Is. 7:11; 38:7); they are valuable, not so much for what they are, as for what they indicate of the grace and power of the doer, or of the connection in which he stands with a higher world. Oftentimes they are thus seals of power set to the person who accomplishes them ("the Lord confirming the word by *signs* following," Mark 16:20; Acts 14:3; Heb. 2:4) legitimating acts, by which he claims to be attended to as a messenger from God. We find the word continually used in senses such as these, Thus, "What *sign* showest thou?" (John 2:18) was the question which the Jews asked, when they wanted the Lord to justify the things which he was doing, by showing that he had especial authority to do them. Again they say, "We would see a *sign* from thee" (Matt. 12:38); "Show us a *sign* from heaven" (Matt. 16:1). St. Paul speaks of himself as having "the *signs* of an apostle" (2 Cor. 12:12), in other words, the tokens which should mark him out as such. Thus, too, in the Old Testament, when God sends Moses to deliver Israel he furnishes him with two "signs." He warns him that Pharaoh will require him to legitimate his mission, to produce his credentials that he is indeed God's ambassador, and equips him with the powers which shall justify him as

such, which, in other words, shall be his "signs" (Ex. 7:9, 10). He "gave *a sign*" to the prophet whom he sent to protest against the will-worship of Jeroboam (1 Kgs. 13:3).

At the same time it may be as well here to observe that the "sign" is not of necessity a miracle, although only as such it has a place in our discussion. Many a common matter, for instance any foretold coincidence or event, may be to a believing mind a sign, a seal set to the truth of a foregoing word. Thus the angels give to the shepherds for "a sign" their finding the child wrapped in the swaddling clothes (Luke 2:12). Samuel gives to Saul three "signs" that God has indeed appointed him king over Israel, and only the last of these is linked with aught supernatural (1 Sam. 10:1–9). The prophet gave Eli the death of his two sons as "a sign" that his threatening word should come true (1 Sam. 2:34). God gave to Gideon a sign in the camp of the Midianites of the victory which he should win (Judg. 7:9–15), though it does not happen that the word occurs in that narration. Or it is possible for a man, under a strong conviction that the hand of God is leading him, to set such and such a contingent event as a sign to himself, the falling out of which in this way or in that he will accept as an intimation from God of what he would have him to do. Examples of this also are not uncommon in Scripture (Gen. 24:16; Judg. 6:36–40; 1 Sam. 14:8–13).

3. Frequently also the miracles are styled *"powers"* or *"mighty works,"* that is, of God. As in the term "wonder" or "miracle," the effect is transferred and gives a name to the cause, so here the cause gives its name to the effect. The *"power"* dwells originally in the divine Messenger (Acts 6:8; 10:38; Rom. 15:9); is one with which he is himself equipped of God. Christ is thus in the highest sense that which Simon blasphemously suffered himself to be named, "The great *Power* of God" (Acts 8:10). But then by an easy transition the word comes to signify the exertions and separate puttings forth of this power. These are "powers" in the plural, although the same word is now translated in our version, "wonderful works" (Matt. 7:22), and now, "mighty works" (Matt 11:20; Mark 6:14: Luke 10:13), and still more frequently, "miracles" (Acts 2:22; 19:11; 1 Cor. 12:10, 28; Gal. 3:5); in this last case giving sometimes such tautologies as this, "miracles *and* wonders" (Acts 2:22; Heb. 2:4); and always causing to be lost something of the express force of the

word—how it points to new *powers* which have come into, and are working in, this world of ours.

These three terms, of which we have hitherto sought to unfold the meaning, occur thrice together (Acts 2:22; 2 Cor. 12:12; 2 Thess. 2:9), although each time in a different order. They are all, as has already been noted in the case of two of them, rather descriptive of different sides of the same works, than themselves different classes of works. An example of one of our Lord's miracles may show how it may at once be all these. The healing of the paralytic, for example (Mark 2:1–12), was a wonder, for they who beheld it "were all amazed"; it was a power, for the man at Christ's word "arose, took up his bed, and went out before them all"; it was a sign, for it gave token that one greater than men deemed was among them; it stood in connection with a higher fact of which it was the sign and seal (cf. 1 Kgs. 13:3; 2 Kgs. 1:10); being wrought that they might "know that the Son of man hath power on earth to forgive sins."

4. A further term which St. John very frequently names the miracles is eminently significant. They are very often with him simply "*works*," (5:36; 7:21; 10:25, 32, 38; 14:11, 12; 15:24; see also Matt. 11:2). The wonderful is in his eyes only the natural form of working for him who is dwelt in by all the fullness of God; he must, out of the necessity of his higher being, bring forth these works greater than man's. They are the periphery of that circle whereof he is the center. The great miracle is the Incarnation; all else, so to speak, follows naturally and of course. It is no wonder that he whose name is "Wonderful" (Is. 9:6), does works of wonder; the only wonder would be if he did them not. The sun in the heavens is itself a wonder, but not that, being what it is, it rays forth its effluences of light and heat. These miracles are the fruit after its kind, which the divine tree brings forth; and may, with a deep truth, be styled "works" of Christ, with no further addition or explanation.

II.

The Miracles and Nature

Wherein, it may be asked, does the miracle differ from any step in the ordinary course of nature? For that too is wonderful; the fact that it is a marvel of continual recurrence may rob it, subjectively, or our admiration; we may be content to look at it with a dull incurious eye, and to think we find in its constant repetition the explanation of its law, even as we often find in this a reason for excusing ourselves altogether from wonder and reverent admiration; yet it does not remain the less a marvel still.

To this question it has been replied by some, that since all is thus marvelous, since the grass growing, the seed springing, the sun rising, are as much the result of powers which we cannot trace or measure, as the water made wine, or the sick healed, or the blind restored to vision, there is therefore no such thing as a miracle eminently so called. We have no right, they say, in the mighty and complex miracle of nature which encircles us on every side, to separate off in this arbitrary manner some certain facts, and to say that this and that are wonders, and all the rest ordinary processes of nature; but that rather we must confine ourselves to one language or the other, and entitle all or nothing miracle.

But this, however at first sight it may seem very deep and true, is indeed most shallow and fallacious. There is quite enough in itself and in its purposes to distinguish that which we name by this name from all with which it is thus attempted to be confounded, and in which to be lost. The distinction indeed which is sometimes made, that in the miracle God is immediately working, and in other events is leaving it to the laws which he has established, to work, cannot at all be admitted: for it has its root in a dead mechanical view of the universe which lies altogether remote from the truth. The clock-maker makes his clock and leaves it; the shipbuilder builds and launches his ship, and others navigate it; but the world is no curious piece of mechanism which its Maker makes and then dismisses from his hands, only from time to time reviewing and repairing it; but as our Lord says, "My Father worketh hitherto, and I work" (John 5:17); he "upholdeth all things by the word of his power" (Heb. 1:3). And to speak of "laws of God," "laws of nature," may become to us a language altogether deceptive, and hiding the deeper reality from our eyes. *Laws* of God exist only for us. It is a *will* of God for himself. That will indeed, being the will of highest wisdom and love, excludes all willfulness—is a will upon which we can securely count; from the past expressions of it we can presume its future, and so we rightfully call it a law. But still from moment to moment it is a will; each law, as we term it, of nature is only that which we have learned concerning this will in that particular region of its activity. To say then that there is more of the will of God in a miracle than in any other work of his, is insufficient. Such an affirmation grows out of that lifeless scheme of the world, of which we should ever be seeking to rid ourselves, but which such a theory will only help to confirm and to uphold.

For while we deny the conclusion, that since all is wonder, therefore the miracle commonly so called is in no other way than the ordinary processes of nature, the manifestation of the presence and power of God, we must not with this deny the truth which lies in this statement. All *is* wonder; to make a man is at least as great a marvel as to raise a man from the dead. The seed that multiplies in the furrow is as marvelous as the bread that multiplied in Christ's hands. The miracle is not a *greater* manifestation of God's power than those ordinary and ever-repeated processes; but it is a *different* manifestation. By those other God is speaking at all times and to all the world; they are a vast revelation of him. "The invisible things of him are clearly seen, being understood by the things that are made, even his eternal power and Godhead" (Rom. 1:20). Yet from the very circumstance that nature is thus speaking unto all, that this speaking is diffused over all time, addressed unto all men, from the very vastness and universality of this language, it may miss its aim. It cannot be said to stand in nearer relation to one man than to another, to confirm one man's word more than that of others, to address one man's conscience more than that of every other man. However it may sometimes have, it must often lack, a peculiar and personal significance. But in the miracle wrought in the sight of some certain men, and claiming their special attention, there is a speaking to them in particular. There is then a voice in nature which addresses itself directly to them, a singling of them out from the crowd. It is plain that God has now a peculiar word which they are to give heed to, a message to which he is bidding them to listen.

An extraordinary divine causality belongs, then, to the essence of the miracle; more than that ordinary, which we acknowledge in everything; powers of God other than those which have always been working; such, indeed, as most seldom or never have been working until now. The unresting activity of God, which at other times hides and conceals itself behind the veil of what we term natural laws, does in the miracle unveil itself; it steps out from its concealment, and the hand which works is laid bare. Beside and beyond the ordinary operations of nature, higher powers (higher, not as coming from a higher source, but as bearing upon higher ends), intrude and make themselves felt even at the very springs and sources of her power.

Yet when we say that it is of the very essence of the miracle that it should be thus "a new thing," it is not with this denied that the natural itself may become miraculous *to us* by the way in which it is timed, by the ends which it is made to serve. It is indeed true that aught which is perfectly explicable from the course of nature and history, is assuredly no miracle in the most proper sense of the word. Yet still the finger of God may be so plainly discernible in it, there may be in it so remarkable a convergence of many unconnected causes to a single end, it may so meet a crisis in the lives of men, or in the onward march of the kingdom of God, may stand in such noticeable relation with God's great work of redemption, that even while it is plainly deducible from natural causes, while there were such perfectly adequate to produce the effects, we yet may be entirely justified in terming it a miracle, a *providential*, although not an absolute, miracle. Absolute it cannot be called, since there were known causes perfectly capable of bringing it about, and, these existing, it would be superstition to betake ourselves to others, or to seek to break it loose from these. Yet the natural lifts itself up into the miraculous, by the moment at which it falls out, by the purposes which it is made to fulfill. It is a subjective wonder, a wonder *for us*, though not an objective, not a wonder in itself.

Thus many of the plagues of Egypt were the natural plagues of the land—these it is true raised into far direr than their usual activity. But in itself it was nothing miraculous that grievous swarms of flies should infest the houses of the Egyptians, or that flights of locusts should spoil their fields, or that a murrain should destroy their cattle. None of these visitations were or are unknown in that land; but the intensity of *all* these plagues, the manner in which they followed hard on one another, their connection with the word of Moses which went before, with Pharaoh's trial which was proceeding, with Israel's deliverance which they helped onward, the manner of their coming and going, all these do entirely justify us in calling them "the signs and wonders of Egypt," even as such is the Scriptural language about them (Ps. 78:43; Acts 7:36). It is no absolute miracle to find a coin in a fish's mouth (Matt 17:27), or that a lion should meet a man and slay him (1 Kgs. 13:24), or that a thunderstorm should happen at an unusual period of the year (1 Sam. 12:16–19); and yet these circumstances may be so timed for strengthening faith, for punishing disobedience, for awakening repentance, they may serve such high purposes in God's moral government, that we at once range them in the catalogue of miracles, without seeking to make an anxious discrimination between the miracle absolute and providential. Especially have they a right to their place among these, when (as in each of the instances alluded to above), the final event is a sealing of a foregoing word from the Lord; for so, as prophecy, as miracles of his foreknowledge, they claim that place, even if not as miracles of his power. Of course concerning these more than any other it will be true that they exist only for the religious mind, for the man who believes that God ruleth, and not merely in power, but in wisdom, in righteousness, and in love; for him they will be eminently *signs,* signs of a present working God. In the case of the more absolute miracle it will be sometimes possible to extort from the ungodly, as of old from the magicians of Egypt, the unwilling confession, "This is the finger of God," (Ex. 8:19); but in the case of these this will be well nigh impossible; since there is always the natural solution in which they may take refuge, beyond which they will refuse, and beyond which it will be impossible to compel them, to proceed.

But while the miracle is not thus nature, so neither is it *against* nature. That language, however commonly in use, is yet wholly unsatisfactory, which speaks of these wonderful works of God as *violations* of a natural law. *Beyond* nature, *beyond* and *above* the nature which we know, they are, but not contrary to it. Nor let it be said that this distinction is an idle one; so far from being so, Spinoza's whole assault upon the miracles (not his objections, for they lie much deeper, but his assault), turns upon the advantage which he has known how to take of this faulty statement of the truth, and, that being stated rightly, it becomes at once beside the mark. The miracle is not thus unnatural, nor can it be; since the unnatural, the contrary to order, is of itself the ungodly, and can in no way therefore be affirmed of a divine work such as that with which we have to do. The very idea of the world, as more than one name which it bears testifies, is that of an order; that which comes in then to enable it to realize this idea which it has lost, will scarcely itself be a disorder. So far from this, the true miracle is a higher and a purer nature, coming down out of the world of untroubled harmonies into this world of ours, which so many discords have jarred and disturbed, and bringing this back again, though it be but for one prophetic moment, into harmony with that higher. The healing of the sick can in no way be termed against nature, seeing that the sickness which was healed was against the true nature of man—that it is sickness which is abnormal, and not health. The healing is the restoration of the primitive order. We should term the miracle not the infraction of a law, but behold in it the lower law neutralized, and for the time put out of working by a higher; and of this abundant analogous examples are evermore going forward before our eyes. Continually we behold in the world around us lower laws held in restraint by higher, mechanic by dynamic, chemical by vital, physical and moral; yet we say not when the lower thus gives place in favor of the higher, that there was any violation of law—that anything contrary to nature came to pass—rather we acknowledge the law of a greater freedom swallowing up the law of a lesser. Thus, when I lift my arm, the law of gravitation is not, as far as my arm is concerned, denied or annihilated; it exists as much as ever, but is held in suspense by the higher law of my will. The chemical laws which would bring about decay in animal substances still subsist, even when they are hemmed in and hindered by the salt which keeps those substances from corruption. The law of sin in a regenerate man is held in continual check by the law of the spirit of life; yet is it in his members still, not indeed working, for a mightier law has stepped in and now holds it in check, but still there, and ready to work, did that higher law cease from its more effectual operation. What in each of these cases is wrought may be against one particular law, that law being contemplated in its isolation, and rent away from the complex of laws, whereof it forms only a part. But no law does stand thus alone, and it is not against, but rather in entire harmony with, the system of laws; for the law of those laws is, that where powers come into conflict, the weaker shall give place to the stronger, the lower to the higher. In the miracle, this world of ours is drawn into and within a higher order of things; laws are then at work in the world, which are not the laws of its fallen condition, for they are laws of mightier range and higher perfection; and as such they claim to make themselves felt, and to have the pre-eminence which is rightly their own. To make this clearer I might take a familiar illustration borrowed from our own church-system of feasts and fasts. It is the rule here that if the festival of the Nativity fall on a day which was designated in the ordinary calendar for a fast, the former shall displace the latter, and the day shall be observed as a festival. Shall we therefore say that the Church has awkwardly contrived two systems which here may, and sometimes do, come into collision with one another? And not rather admire her more complex law, and note how in the very concurrence of the two, with the displacement of the poorer by the richer, she brings out her idea that holy joy is a higher thing even than holy sorrow, and shall at last swallow it up altogether

It is with these wonders which have been, exactly as it will be with those wonders which we look for in regard of our own mortal bodies, and this physical universe. We do not speak of these changes which are in store for this and those, as violations of law. We should not speak of the resurrection of the body as something contrary to nature, as unnatural; yet no power now working in the world could bring it about; it must be wrought by some power not yet displayed, which God has kept in reserve. So, too, the great change which is in store for the outward world, and out of which it shall issue as a new heaven and a new earth, far exceeds any energies now working in the world, to bring it to pass (however there may be predispositions for it now, starting points from which it will proceed), yet it so belongs to the true idea of the world, not so imperfectly realized, that when it does take place, it will be felt to be the truest nature, which only then at length shall have come perfectly to the birth.

The miracles, then, not being against nature, however they may be beside and beyond it, are in no respect slights cast upon its ordinary and everyday workings; but rather, when contemplated aright, are an honoring of these, in the witness which they render to the source from which these also originally proceed. For Christ, healing a sick man with his word, is in fact claiming in this to be the lord and author of all the healing powers which have ever exerted their beneficent influence on the bodies of men, and saying, "I will prove this fact, which you are ever losing sight of, that in me the fontal power which goes forth in a thousand gradual cures resides, by this time only speaking a word, and bringing back a man unto perfect health"—not thus cutting off those other and more gradual healings from his person, but truly linking them to it. So again when he multiplies the bread, when he changes the water into wine, what does he but say, "It is I and no other who, by the sunshine and the shower, by the seed-time and the harvest, give food for the use of man; and you shall learn this, which you are always in danger of unthankfully forgetting, by witnessing for once or for twice, or if not actually witnessing, yet having it rehearsed in your ears forever, how the essences of things are mine, how the bread grows in my hands, how the water, not drawn up into the vine, nor slowly transmuted into the juices of the grape, nor from thence expressed in the vat, but simply at my bidding, changes into wine. You burn incense to your drag, but it is I who, giving you in a moment the draught of fishes which you had yourselves long labored for in vain, will remind you *who* guides them through the ocean paths, and suffers you either to toil long and to take nothing, or crowns your labors with a rich and unexpected harvest of the sea." Even the single miracle which wears an aspect of severity, that of the cursed fig-tree, speaks the same language, for in that the same gracious Lord is declaring, "These scourges of mine, wherewith I punish your sins, and summon you to repentance, continually miss their purpose altogether, or need to be repeated again and again, and this mainly because you see in them only the evil accidents of a blind nature; but I will show you that it is I and no other who smite the earth with a curse, who both can and do send these strokes for the punishing of the sins of men."

And we can quite perceive how all this should have been necessary. For if in one sense the orderly workings of nature reveal the glory of God (Ps. 19:1–6), in another they hide that glory from our eyes, if they ought to make us continually to remember him, yet there is danger that they lead us to forget him, until this world around us shall prove—not a translucent medium, through which we look to him, but a thick impenetrable veil, concealing him wholly from our sight. Were there no other purpose in the miracles than this, namely to testify the liberty of God, and to affirm the will of God, which, however it habitually shows itself *in* nature, is yet more than and above nature, were it only to break a link in that chain of cause and effect, which else we should come to regard as itself God, as the iron chain of an inexorable necessity, binding heaven no less than earth, they would serve a great purpose, they would not have been wrought in vain. But there are other purposes than these, and purposes yet more nearly bearing on the salvation of men, to which they serve, and to the consideration of these we have now arrived.

III.

The Authority of the Miracle

Is the miracle to command absolutely and without further question the obedience of those in whose sight it is done, or to whom it comes as an adequately attested fact, so that the doer and the doctrine, without any more debate, shall be accepted as from God? It cannot be so, for side by side with the miracles which serve for the furthering of the kingdom of God, runs another line of wonders, counterworks of him, who is ever the ape of the Most High, who has still his caricatures of the holiest; and who knows that in no way can he so realize his character of Satan, or the Hinderer, as by offering that which shall either be accepted instead of the true, or, being discovered false, shall bring the true into like discredit with itself. For that it is meant in Scripture to attribute real wonders to him there is to me no manner of doubt. They are "lying wonders" (2 Thess. 2:9), not because in themselves frauds and illusions, but because they are wrought to support the kingdom of lies.

Thus I cannot doubt that, according to the intention of Scripture we are meant to understand of the Egyptian magicians, that they stood in relation with a spiritual kingdom as truly as did Moses and Aaron. Indeed only so does the conflict between those and these come out in its true significance. It loses the chiefest part of this significance if we think of their wonders as mere conjurers' tricks, dexterous sleights of hands, with which they imposed upon Pharaoh and his servants; making believe, and no more, that their rods turned into serpents, that they also changed water into blood. Rather was this a conflict not merely between the might of Egypt's king and the power of God; but the gods of Egypt, the spiritual powers of wickedness which underlay, and were the soul of, that dark and evil kingdom, were in conflict with the God of Israel. In this conflict, it is true, their nothingness very soon was apparent;

but yet most truly the two unseen kingdoms of light and darkness did then in presence of Pharaoh do open battle, each seeking to win the king for itself, and to draw him into its own element. Else, unless it had been such a conflict as this, what meaning would such passages have as that in Moses' Song, "Who is like unto thee, O Lord, among the gods?" (Ex. 15:11); or that earlier, "Against all the gods of Egypt I will execute judgment; I am the Lord" (Ex. 12:12; cf. Num. 33:4). As it was *then*, so probably was it again at the Incarnation, for Satan's open encounter of our Lord in the wilderness was but one form of his manifold opposition; and we seem to have a hint of a resistance similar to that of the Egyptian magicians in the withstanding of Paul which is attributed to Elymas (Acts 13:8; cf. 2 Tim. 3:8). But whether then it was so, or not, so will it be certainly at the end of the world (Matt. 24:24; 2 Thess. 2:9; Rev. 13:13). Thus it seems that at each great crisis and epoch of the kingdom, the struggle between the light and the darkness, which has ever been going forward, comes out into visible manifestation.

Yet while the works of Antichrist and his organs are not mere tricks and juggleries, neither are they miracles in the very highest sense of the word; they only partake, in part, of the essential elements of the miracle. This they have, indeed, in common with it, that they are real works of a power which is suffered to extend thus far, and not merely dexterous sleights of hand; but this, also, which is most different, that they are abrupt, isolated, parts of no organic whole; not the highest harmonies, but the deepest discords, of the universe; not the omnipotence of God wielding his own world to ends of grace, and wisdom, and love, but evil permitted to intrude into the hidden springs of things just so far as may suffice for its own deeper confusion in the end, and in the meanwhile, for the needful trial and perfecting of God's saints and servants.

This fact, however, that the kingdom of lies has its wonders no less than the kingdom of truth, would be alone sufficient to convince us that miracles cannot be appealed to absolutely and simply, in proof of the doctrine which the worker of them proclaims; and God's word expressly declares the same (Deut. 13:1–5). A miracle does not prove the truth of a doctrine, or the divine mission of him that brings it to pass. That which alone it claims for him at the first is a right to be listened to: it puts him in the alternative of being from heaven or from hell. The doctrine must first commend itself to the conscience as being *good*, and only then can the miracle seal it as *divine*. But the first appeal is from the doctrine to the conscience, to the moral nature in man. For all revelation presupposes in man a power of recognizing the truth when it is shown him— that it will find an answer in him—that he will trace in it the linea- ments of a friend, though of a friend from whom he has been long estranged, and whom he has well nigh forgotten. It is the finding of a treasure, but of a treasure which he himself and no other had lost. The denial of this, that there is in man any organ by which truth may be recognized, opens the door to the most boundless skepticism, is indeed the denial of all that is godlike in man. But "he that is of God, heareth God's word," and knows it for that which it proclaims itself to be.

It may be objected, indeed. If this be so, if there be this inward witness of the truth, what need then of the miracle? To what does it serve, when the truth as accredited itself already? It has, indeed, accredited itself as good, as *from* God in the sense that all which is good and true is from him, as whatever was precious in the teach- ing even of heathen sage or poet was from him—but not as yet as a new word directly from him—a new speaking on his part to man. The miracles are to be the credentials for the bearer of that good word, signs that he has a special mission for the realization of the purposes of God in regard of humanity. When the truth has found a receptive heart, has awoke deep echoes in the innermost soul of man, he who brings it may thus show that he stands yet nearer to God than others, that he is to be heard not merely as one that is true, but as himself the Truth (see Matt. 11:4, 5; John 5:36), or if not this, as an immediate messenger standing in direct connection with him who is the Truth (1 Kgs. 13:3), claiming unreserved submis- sion, and the reception, upon his authority, of other statements which transcend the mind of man, mysteries, which though, of course, not *against* that measure and standard of truth which God has given unto every man, yet which cannot be weighed or mea- sured by it.

To ask such a sign from anyone who comes professing to the ut- terer of a new revelation, the bringer of a direct message from God, to demand this, even when the word already commends itself as in itself good, is no mark of unbelief, but on the contrary is a duty upon his part to whom the message is brought. Else might he lightly be persuaded to receive that as from God, which, indeed, was only the word of man. Thus it was no impiety on the part of Pharaoh to say to Moses and Aaron, "Show a miracle for you," (Ex. 7:9, 10), on the contrary, it was altogether right for him to require this. They came saying they had a message for him from God: it was his duty to put them to the proof. On the other hand, it was a mark of unbelief in Ahaz (Is. 7:10–13), however he might disguise it, that he would not ask a sign from God in confirmation of the prophet's word. Had that word been more precious to him, he would not have been satisfied till the seal was set to it; and that he did not care for the seal was a sure evidence that he did not truly care for the promise which with that was to be sealed.

But the purpose of the miracle being, as we have seen, to confirm that which is good, so, upon the other hand, where the mind and conscience witness against the doctrine, not all the miracles in the world have a right to demand submission to the word which they seal. On the contrary, the great act of faith is to believe, in the face, and in despite, of them all, in what God has revealed to, and implanted in, the soul, of the holy and the true; not to believe another Gospel, though an angel from heaven, or one transformed into such, should bring it (Deut. 13:3; Gal. 1:8); and instead of compelling assent, miracles are then rather warnings to us that we keep aloof, for they tell us that not merely lies are here, for to that the conscience bore witness already, but that he who utters them is more than a common deceiver, is eminently "a liar and an antichrist," a false prophet, standing in more immediate connection than other deceived and evil men to the kingdom of darkness, so that Satan has given him his power (Rev. 13:2), is using him to be an especial organ of his, and to do a signal work for him.

But in these things, if they are so, there might seem a twofold danger to which the simple and unlearned Christian would be exposed—the danger first of not receiving that which indeed comes from God, or secondly, of receiving that which comes from an evil source. But indeed these dangers do not beset the unlearned and the simple more than they beset and are part of the trial and temptation of every man—the safeguard from either of these fatal errors lying altogether in men's moral and spiritual, and not at all in their intellectual, condition. They only find the witness which the truth bears to itself to be no witness, they only believe the lying wonders, in whom the moral sense is already perverted; they have not before received the love of the truth that they might be saved from believing a lie. Thus, then, their believing this lie and rejecting that truth is, in fact, but the final judgment upon them that have had pleasure in unrighteousness. With this view exactly agree the memorable words of St. Paul (2 Thess. 2:9–12), wherein he declares that it is the anterior state of every man which shall decide whether he shall receive the lying wonders of Antichrist or reject them (cf. John 5:43). For while they come "with all deceivableness of unrighteousness" to them whose previous condition has fitted them to embrace them, who have been ripening themselves for this extreme judgment, there is ever something in these wonders, something false, or immoral, or ostentatious, or something merely idle, which detects and lays them bare to a simple faith, and for that at once broadly differences them from those which belong to the kingdom of the truth.

These differences have been often brought out. They are immoral; or if not so, yet futile, without consequences, leading to and ending in nothing. For as the miracle, standing as it does in connection with highest moral ends, must not be itself an immoral act, so may it not be in itself an act merely futile, issuing in vanity and nothingness. This is the argument which Origen continually uses, when he is plied with the alleged miracles of heathen saints and sages. He counts, and rightly, that he has sufficiently shown their emptiness, when he has asked, and obtained no answer to, this question, "What came of these? In what did they issue? Where is the society which has been founded by their help? What is there in the world's history which they have helped forward, to show that they lay deep in the mind and counsel of God? The miracles of Moses issued in a Jewish polity; those of the Lord in a Christian Church; whole nations were knit together through their help. What have your boasted Apollonius of Esculapius to show as the fruit of theirs? What traces have they left behind them?" And not merely, he goes on to say, were Christ's miracles effectual, but effectual for good—and such good was their distinct purpose and aim; for this is the characteristic distinction between the dealer in false shows of power and the true worker of divine works, that the latter has ever the reformation of men in his eye, and seeks always to forward this; while the first, whose own work is built upon fraud and lies, can have no such purpose of destroying that very kingdom out of which he himself grows.

These, too, are marks of the true miracles, and marks very nearly connected with the foregoing, that they are never mere freaks and plays of power, done as in wantonness, and for their own sakes, with no need compelling, for show and ostentation. With good right in that remarkable religious romance of earliest Christian times, *The Recognitions of Clement* and in the cognate

Clementine Homilies, Peter is made to draw a contrast between the wonderful works of Christ and those alleged by the followers of Simon Magus to have been wrought by him. What profit, what significance, was there, he asks, in his dogs of brass or stone that barked, his talking statues, his flights through the air, his transformations of himself now into a serpent, now into a goat, his putting on of two faces, his rolling of himself unhurt upon burning coals, and the like? Which even if he had done, the works possessed no meaning; they stood in relation to nothing; they were not, what each true miracle is always more or less, *redemptive* acts; in other words, works not merely of power but of grace, each one an index and a prophecy of the inner work of man's deliverance, which it accompanies and helps forward. But, as we should justly expect, it was preeminently thus with the miracles of Christ. Each of these is in small, and upon one side or another, a partial and transient realization of the great work which he came that in the end he might accomplish perfectly and forever. They are all pledges, in that they are themselves first-fruits, of his power; in each of them the word of salvation is incorporated in an act of salvation. Only when regarded in this light do they appear not merely as illustrious examples of his might, but also as glorious manifestations of his holy love.

It is worthwhile to follow this a little in detail. The evils what are they, which hinder man from reaching the true end and aim of his creation, and from which he needs a redemption? It may briefly be answered that they are sin in its moral and in its physical manifestations. If we regard its moral manifestations, the darkness of the understanding, the wild discords of the spiritual life, none were such fearful examples of its tyranny as the demoniacs; they were special objects, therefore, of the miraculous power of the Lord. Then if we ask ourselves what are the physical manifestations of sin; they are sicknesses of all kinds, fevers, palsies, leprosies, blindness, each of these death beginning, a partial death—and finally, the death absolute of the body. This region therefore is fitly another, as it is the widest region, of his redemptive grace. In the conquering and removing of these evils, he eminently bodied forth the idea of himself as the Redeemer of men. But besides these, sin has its manifestations more purely physical; it reveals itself and its consequences in the tumults and strife of the elements among themselves, as in the rebellion of nature against man; for the destinies of the natural world were linked to the destinies of man, and when he fell, he drew after him his whole inheritance, which became subject to the same vanity as himself. Therefore do we behold the Lord, him in whom the lost was recovered, walking on the stormy waves, or quelling the menace of the sea with his word; incorporating in these acts the deliverance of man from the rebel powers of nature, which had risen up against him, and instead of being his willing servants, were oftentimes now his tyrants and his destroyers. These also were redemptive acts. Even the two or three of his works which seem not to range themselves so readily under any of these heads, yet are not indeed exceptions. For instance, the multiplying of the bread easily shows itself as such. The original curse of sin was the curse of barrenness—the earth yielding hard-won and scanty returns to the sweat and labor of man; but here this curse is removed, and in its stead the primeval abundance for a moment reappears. All scantness and scarceness, such as this lack of bread in the wilderness, such as that failing of the wine at the marriage-feast, belonged not to man as his portion at the first; for all the earth was appointed to serve him, and to pour the fullness of its treasure into his lap. That he ever should hunger or thirst, that he should have need of anything, was a consequence of Adam's fall—fitly, therefore, removed by him, the second Adam, who came to give back all which had been forfeited by the first.

But the miracle being, then, this ethical act, and only to be received when it is so, and when it seals doctrines of holiness, the forgetting or failing to bring forward that the divine miracle must, of necessity, move in this sphere of redemption only, that the doctrine also is to try the miracle, as well as the miracle to seal the doctrine, is a most dangerous omission on the part of many who, in modern times, have written so-called "Evidences of Christianity," and have found in the miracles wrought by its Founder, and in those mainly as acts of power, the exclusive argument for its reception as a divine revelation. On the place which these works should take in the array of proofs for the things which we believe there will be occasion, by and bye, to speak. For the present it may be sufficient to observe, that if men are taught that they should believe in Christ upon no other grounds than because he attested his claims by works of wonder, and that simply on this score they shall do so, how shall they consistently refuse belief to any other, who shall come attesting his claims by the same? We have here a paving of the way of Antichrist, for as we know that he will have his signs and wonders, so, if this argument is good, he will have right on the score of these to claim the faith and allegiance of men. But no; the miracle must witness for itself, and the doctrine must witness for itself, and then the first is capable of witnessing for the second; and those books of Christian evidences are utterly maimed and imperfect, fraught with the most perilous consequences, which reverence in the miracle little else but its power, and see in that alone what gives either to it its attesting worth, or to the doctrine its authority as an adequately attested thing.

IV.

The Evangelical Compared with Other Cycles of Miracles

1. The Miracles of the Old Testament

The miracles of our Lord and those of the Old Testament afford many interesting points of comparison, and of a comparison equally instructive, whether we trace the points of likeness, or of unlikeness, which exist between them. Thus, to note first a remarkable difference, we find oftentimes the holy men of the old covenant bringing, if one may venture so to speak, hardly and with difficulty the wonder-work to the birth; there is sometimes a momentary pause, a seeming uncertainty about the issue; while the miracles of Christ are always accomplished with the highest ease; he speaks and it is done. Thus Moses must plead and struggle with God, "Heal her now, O God, I beseech thee," ere the plague of leprosy is removed from his sister, and not even so can he instantly win the boon (Num. 12:13–15); but Christ heals a leper by his touch (Matt. 8:3), or ten with even less than this, merely by the power of his will and at a distance (Luke 17:14). Elijah must pray long, and his servant go up seven times, before tokens of the rain appear (1 Kgs. 18:42–44); he stretches himself thrice on the child and cries unto the Lord, and painfully wins back its life (1 Kgs. 17:21, 22); and Elisha, with yet more of effort and only after partial failure (2 Kgs. 4:31–35), restores the child of the Shunammite to life. Christ, on the other hand, shows himself the Lord of the living and the dead, raising the dead with as much ease as he performed the commonest transactions of life. In the miracles wrought by men, glorious acts of faith as they are, for they are ever wrought in reliance on the strength and faithfulness of God, who

21

will follow up and seal his servant's word, it is yet possible for human impatience and human unbelief to break out. Thus Moses, God's organ for the work of power, speaks hastily and acts unbelievingly (Num. 20:11). It is needless to say of the Son, that his confidence ever remains the same that his Father heareth him always; that no admixture of even the slightest human infirmity mars the completeness of his work.

Where the miracles are similar in kind, his are larger and freer and more glorious. Elisha feeds a hundred men with twenty loaves (2 Kgs. 4:42–44), but he five thousand with five. They have continually their instrument of power to which the wonder-working power is linked. Moses has his rod, his staff of wonder, to divide the Red Sea, and to accomplish his other mighty acts, without which his is nothing (Ex. 7:19; 8:5, 16; 9:23; 10:13; 14:16 etc.), his tree to heal the bitter waters (Ex. 15:25); Elijah divides the waters with his mantle (2 Kgs. 2:8); Elisha heals the spring with a cruse of salt (2 Kgs. 2:20). But Christ accomplishes his miracles simply by the agency of his word, or by a touch (Matt. 20:34), or if he takes it, channel of his healing power, it is from himself he takes it (Mark 7:33; 8:23), or should he, as once he does, use any foreign medium (John 4:6), yet by other miracles of like kind, in which he has recourse to no such extraneous helps, he declares plainly that this was of free choice and not of any necessity. And, which is but another side of the same truth, while their miracles and those of the apostles are ever done in the name of, and with the attribution of the glory to, another, "Stand still and see the salvation of the Lord, which *he* will show you" (Ex. 19:13), "In the name of Jesus Christ of Nazareth rise up and walk" (Acts 3:6), "Eneas, Jesus Christ maketh thee whole" (Acts 9:34; cf. Mark 16:17; Luke 10:17; John 14:10), his are ever wrought in his own name and as in his own power: "*I will*, be thou clean" (Matt. 8:3), "Thou deaf and dumb spirit, *I* charge thee come out of him" (Mark 9:25); "Young man, *I* say unto thee, Arise" (Luke 7:14). Even where he prays, being about to perform one of his mighty works, his disciples shall learn even from his prayer itself that herein he is not asking for a power which he had not indwelling in him, but indeed is only testifying thus to the unbroken oneness of his life with his Father's (John 11:41, 42), just as on another occasion he will not suffer his disciples to suppose that it is for any but for their sakes that the testimony from heaven is borne unto him (John 12:30). Thus needful was it for them, thus needful for all, that they should have great and exclusive thoughts of him, and should not class him with any other, even the greatest and holiest of the children of men.

These likenesses and unlikenesses seem equally such as beforehand we should have naturally expected. We should have expected the mighty works of either covenant to be like, since the old and new form parts of one organic whole; and it is ever God's law that the lower should contain the germs and prophetic intimations of the higher. We should expect them to be unlike, since the very idea of God's kingdom is that of progress, of a gradually fuller communication and larger revelation of himself to men, so that he who in times past spoke unto the fathers by the prophets, did at length speak unto us by his Son; and it was only meet that this Son should be clothed with mightier powers than theirs, and powers which he held not from another, but such rather as were his own in fee.

And this, too, explains a difference in the character of the miracles of the two covenants, and how it comes to pass that those of the old wear oftentimes a far severer aspect than the new. They are miracles, indeed, of God's grace, but yet also miracles of the Law, of that Law which worketh wrath, which will teach, at all costs, the lesson of the awful holiness of God, his hatred of the sinner's sin— a lesson which men had all need thoroughly to learn, lest they should mistake and abuse the new lesson which a Savior taught, of God's love at the same time toward the sinner himself. Miracles of the Law, they preserve a character that accords with the Law; being oftentimes fearful outbreaks of God's anger against the unrighteousness of men; such for instance are the signs and wonders in Egypt, many of those in the desert (Num. 16:31; Lev. 10:2), and some which the later prophets wrought (2 Kgs. 1:10–12; 2:23–25); though of these also there are far more which wear a milder aspect, and are works, as *all* our lord's are, of evident grace and mercy. I say *all* of our Lord's for that single one, which seems an exception, the cursing of the barren fig-tree, has no right really to be considered such. Indeed it is difficult to see how our blessed Lord could more strikingly have shown his purpose of preserving throughout for his miracles their character of beneficence, or have witnessed for himself that he was come not to destroy men's lives but to save them, than in this circumstance—that when he needed in this very love to declare, not in word only but in act, what would be the consequences of an obstinate unfruitfulness and resistance to his grace, and thus to make manifest the severe side of his ministry, he should have chosen for the showing out of this, not one among all the sinners who were about him, but should rather have displayed his power upon a tree, which, itself incapable of feeling, might yet effectually serve as a sign and warning to men. He will not allow even a single exception to the rule of grace and love. When he blesses, it is men; but when he smites, it is an unfeeling tree. More upon this matter must be deferred till the time comes for treating that miracle in its order.

It is also noticeable that the region in which the miracles of the Old Testament chiefly move, is that of external nature; they are the cleaving of the sea (Ex. 14:21), or of a river (Josh. 3:14), yawnings of the earth (Num. 16:31), fire falling down from heaven (2 Kgs. 1:10, 12), furnaces which have lost their power to consume (Dan. 3), wild beasts which have laid aside their inborn fierceness (Dan. 6), and such as these: not of course these exclusively, but this nature is the haunt and main region of the miracle in the Old Testament, as in the New it is mainly the sphere of man's life in which it is at home. And consistently with this, the earlier miracles, done as the greater number of them were, in the presence of the giant powers of heathendom, have oftentimes a colossal character: those powers of the world are strong, but the God of Israel will show himself to be stronger yet. Thus is it with the miracles of Egypt, the miracles of Babylon: they are miracles eminently of strength; for under the influence of the great nature-worships of those lands, all religion had assumed a colossal grandeur. Compared with our Lord's works wrought in the days of his flesh, those were the whirlwind and the fire, and his as the still small voice which followed. In that old time God was teaching his people; he was teaching also the nations with whom his people were brought wonderfully into contact, that he who had entered into covenant with one among all the nations was not one God among many, the God of the hills or the God of the plains (1 Kgs. 20:23), but that the God of Israel was the Lord of the whole earth.

But Israel at the time of the Incarnation had thoroughly learned that lesson, much else as it had left unlearned: and the whole civilized world had practically outgrown polytheism, however it may have lingered still as the popular superstition. And thus the works of our Lord, though they bear not on their front the imposing character which did those of old, yet contain higher and deeper truths. They are eminently miracles of the Incarnation—of the Son of God, who had taken our flesh, and taking, would heal it. They have predominantly a relation to man's body and his spirit. Miracles of nature take now altogether a subordinate place: they still survive, even as we could have ill afforded wholly to have lost them, for this region of nature must still be claimed as part of Christ's dominion, though not its chiefest or its noblest province. Man, and not nature, is now the main subject of these mighty powers; and thus it comes to pass that, with less of outward pomp, less to startle and amaze, the new have a yet deeper inward significance than the old.

2. The Miracles of the Apocryphal Gospels

The apocryphal gospels, abject productions as, whether contemplated in a literary or moral point of view, they must be allowed to be, are yet instructive in this respect, that they show us what manner of gospels were the result, when men drew from their own fancy, and devised Christs of their own, instead of resting upon the basis of historic fact, and delivering faithfully to the world true records of him who indeed had lived and died among them. Here, as ever, the glory of the true comes out into strongest light by comparison with the false. But in nothing, perhaps, are these apocryphal gospels more worthy of note, than in the difference between the main features of their miracles and those of the canonical Gospels. Thus in the canonical, the miracle is indeed essential, yet, at the same time, ever subordinated to the doctrine which it confirms—a link in the great chain of god's manifestation of himself to men; its ethical significance never falls into the background, but the act of grace and power has, in every case where this can find room, nearer or remoter reference to the moral condition of the person or persons in whose behalf it is wrought. The miracles ever lead us off from themselves to their Author; they appear as emanations from the glory of the Son of God; but it is in him we rest, and not in them—they are but the halo round him; having their worth from him, not contrariwise, he from them. They are held, too, together by his strong and central personality, which does not leave them a conglomerate of marvelous anecdotes accidentally heaped together, but parts of a great organic whole, of which every part is in vital coherence with every other. But it is altogether otherwise in these apocryphal narratives. To say that the miracles occupy in them the foremost place would very inadequately express the facts of the case. They are everything. Some of these so-called histories are nothing else but a string of these;

which yet (and this too is singularly characteristic) stand wholly disconnected from the ministry of Christ. Not one of them belongs to the period after his Baptism, but they are all miracles of the Infancy—in other words, of that time whereof the canonical Gospels relate no miracle, and not merely do not relate any, but are remarkably at pains to tell us that during it no miracle was wrought, that in Cana of Galilee being his first (John 2:11).

It follows of necessity that they are never seals of a word and doctrine which has gone before; they are never "signs," but at the best wonders and portents. Any high purpose and aim is clearly altogether absent from them. It is never felt that the writer is writing out of any higher motive than to excite and feed a childish love of the marvelous—never that he could say, "These are written that ye might believe that Jesus is the Christ the Son of God, and that believing ye might have life through his name" (John 20:31). Indeed, so far from having a *religious*, they are often wanting in a *moral* element. The Lord Jesus appears in them as a wayward, capricious, passionate child, to be feared indeed, seeing that he is furnished with such formidable powers of avenging every wrong or accidental injury which he meets; and so bearing himself, that the request which the parents of some other children are represented as making, that he may be kept within the house, for he brings harm and mischief wherever he comes, is perfectly justified by the facts.

It may be well to cite a few examples in proof, however harshly some of them may jar on the Christian ear. Thus some children refuse to play with him, hiding themselves from him; he pursues and turns them into kids. Another child by accident runs against him and throws him down; whereupon he, being exasperated, exclaims, "As thou hast made me to fall, so shalt thou fall and not rise"; at the same hour the child fell down and expired. He has a dispute with the master who is teaching him letters, concerning the order in which he shall go through the Hebrew alphabet, and his master strikes him; whereupon Jesus curses him, and straightway his arm is withered, and he falls on his face and dies. This goes on, till at length Joseph says to Mary, "Henceforward let us keep him within doors, for whosoever sets himself against him, perishes." His passionate readiness to avenge himself shows itself at the very earliest age. At five years old he has made a pool of water, and is molding sparrows from the clay. Another child, the son of a scribe, displeased that he should do this on the Sabbath, opens the sluices of his pool and lets out the water. On this Jesus is indignant, gives him many injurious names, and causes him to wither and wholly dry up with his curse.

Such is the image which the authors of these books give us of the holy child Jesus—and no wonder; for man is not only unable to realize the perfect, he is unable to conceive it. The idea is as much a gift, as the power to realize that idea. Even the miracles which are not of this revolting character are childish, tricks like the tricks of a conjurer, never solemn acts of power and love. Jesus enters the shop of a dyer, who has various cloths from various persons, to be dyed of diverse colors. In the absence of the master, he throws them all into the dying vat together, and when the dyer returns and remonstrates, draws them out of the vat each dyed according to the color which was enjoined. He and some other children make birds and animals of clay; while each is boasting the superiority of his work, Jesus says, "I will cause those which I have made to go," which they do, the animals leaping and the birds flying, and at his bidding returning, and eating and drinking from his hand. While yet an infant at his mother's breast, he bids a palm-tree to stoop that she may pluck the fruits; it obeys, and only returns to its position at his command. Another time his mother sends him to the well for water; the pitcher breaks, and he brings the water in his cloak. And as the miracles which he does, so those that are done in regard of him, are idle or monstrous; the ox and ass worshiping him, a newborn infant in the crib, may serve for an example.

In all these, as will be observed, the idea of redemptive acts altogether falls out of sight; they are none of them the outward clothing of the inward facts of man's redemption. Of course it is not meant to be said that miracles of healing and of grace are altogether wanting in these books; that would evidently have been incompatible with any idea of a Redeemer; but only that they do not present to us any clear and consistent image of a Savior full of grace and power, but an image rather continually defaced by lines of passion, and caprice, and anger. The most striking, perhaps, of the miracles related in regard of the child Jesus, is that of the falling down of the idols of Egypt at his presence in the land; for it has in it something of a deeper significance, as a symbol and prophecy of the overthrow of the idol worship of the world by him who was now coming into the world. The lions and the leopards gathering harmlessly round him as he passed through the desert on the way to Egypt, is again not alien to the true spirit of the Gospel, and has its analogy in the words of St. Mark, that he "was with the wild beasts" (1:13); words which certainly are not introduced merely to enhance the savageness of the wilderness where he spent those forty days of temptation, but are meant as a hint to us that in him, the new head of the race, the second Adam, the Paradisaical state was once more given back (Gen. 1:28). But with a very few such partial exceptions as these, the apocryphal gospels are a barren and dreary waste of wonders without object or aim; and only instructive as making us strongly to feel, more strongly than but for these examples we might have felt, how needful it is that there should be other factors besides power for producing a true miracle; that wisdom and love must be there also; that where men conceive of power as its chiefest element, they give us only a hateful mockery of the divine. Had a Christ such as these gospels paint actually lived upon the earth, he had been no more than a potent and wayward magician, from whom all men would have shrunk with a natural instinct of distrust and fear.

3. The Later, or Ecclesiastical, Miracles.

It would plainly lead must too far form the subject in hand to enter into any detailed examination of the authority upon which the later, or, as they may be conveniently termed, the ecclesiastical miracles, come to us. Yet a few words must of necessity find place concerning the permanent miraculous gifts which have been claimed for the Church as her rightful heritage, equally by some who have gloried in their presumed presence, as by others who have lamented their absence—by those alike who have seen in the presence of such, evidences of her sanctity, or in their absence, of her degeneracy and fall. It is not my belief that she has this gift of working miracles, nor yet that she was intended to have, and only through her own unfaithfulness has lost, it; nor that her Lord has abridged her of aught that would have made her strong and glorious in not endowing her with powers such as these. With reasons enough for humbling herself, yet I do not believe that among those reasons is to be accounted her inability to perform these works that should transcend nature. So many in our own day have arrived at a directly opposite conclusion, that it will be needful shortly to justify the opinion here expressed.

And first, as a strong presumption against the intended continuance of these powers in the Church, may be taken the analogies derived from the earlier history of God's dealings with his people. We do not find the miracles sown broadcast over the whole Old Testament history, but they all cluster round a very few eminent persons, and have reference to certain great epochs and crises of the kingdom of God. Abraham, the father of the faithful—David, the great theocratic king—Daniel, the "man greatly beloved," are alike entirely without them; that is, they *do* no miracles; such may be accomplished in behalf of them, but they themselves accomplish none. In fact there are but two great outbursts of these; the first, at the establishing of the kingdom under Moses and Joshua, on which occasion it is at once evident that they could not have been wanting; the second in the time of Elijah and Elisha; and then also there was utmost need, when it was a question whether the court religion which the apostate kings of Israel had set up, should not quite overbear the true worship of Jehovah, when the Levitical priesthood was abolished, and the faithful were but a scattered few among the ten tribes. Then, in that decisive epoch of the kingdom's history, the two great prophets, they too in a subordinate sense the beginners of a new period, arose, equipped with powers which should witness that he whose servants *they* were, was the God of Israel, however Israel might refuse to acknowledge *him*. There is here in all this an entire absence of prodigality in the use of miracles; they are ultimate resources, reserved for the great needs of God's kingdom, not its daily incidents; they are not cheap off-hand expedients, which may always be appealed to, but come only into play when nothing else would have supplied their room. How unlike this moderation to the wasteful expenditure of miracles in the church-history of the middle ages! There no perplexity can occur so trifling that a miracle will not be brought in to solve it; there is almost no saint, certainly no distinguished one, without his *nimbus* of miracles around his head; they are adorned with these in rivalry with one another, in rivalry with Christ himself; no acknowledgment like this, "John did no miracle" (John 10:41), in any of the records of their lives finding place.

We must add to this the declarations of Scripture, which I have already entered on at large, concerning the object of miracles, that they are for the confirming the word by signs following, for authenticating a message as being from heaven—that signs are for the unbelieving (1 Cor. 14:22). What do they then in a Christendom? It may indeed be answered, that in it are unbelievers still; yet not in the sense in which St. Paul uses the word, for he would designate not the positively unbelieving, not those that in heart and will are estranged from the truth, but the negatively, and that, because the truth has never yet sufficiently accredited itself to them. Signs are not for the positively unbelieving, since as we have seen, they will exercise no power over those who harden themselves against the truth; such will resist them as surely as they will resist every other witness of God's presence in the world; but for the unbelieving who are such by no fault of their own—for them to whom the truth is now coming for the first time. And if not even for them now—as they exist, for instance, in a heathen land—we may sufficiently account for this by the fact, that the Church of Christ, with its immense and evident superiorities of all kinds over everything with which it is brought in contact, and some portions of which superiority every man must recognize, is itself now the great witness and proof of the truth which it delivers. That truth, therefore, has no longer need to vindicate itself by an appeal to something else; but the position which it has won in the very forefront of the world is itself its vindication now—is sufficient to give it a first claim on every man's attention.

And then further, all that we might ourselves beforehand presume from the analogy of external things leads us to the same conclusions. We find all beginning to be wonderful—to be under laws different from, and higher than, those which regulate ulterior progress. Thus the powers evermore at work for the upholding the natural world are manifestly insufficient for its first creation; there were other which must have presided at its birth, but which now, having done their work, have fallen back, and left it to its ordinary development. The multitudinous races of animals which people this world, and of plants which clothe it, needed infinitely more for their first production than suffices for their present upholding. It is only according to the analogies of that which thus everywhere surrounds us, to presume that it was even so with the beginnings of the spiritual creation—the Christian Church. It is unquestionably so in the beginning of that new creation in any single heart. Then, in the regeneration, the strongest tendencies of the old nature are overborne; the impossible has become possible, in some measure easy; by a mighty wonder-stroke of grace the polarity in the man is shifted; the flesh, that was the positive pole, has become the negative, and the spirit, which was before the negative, is henceforth the positive. Shall we count it strange, then, that the coming in of a new order, not into a single heart, but into the entire world—a new order bursting forcibly through the bonds and hindrances of the old, should have been wonderful? It had been inexplicable if it had been otherwise. The son of Joseph might have lived and died and done no miracles; but the Virgin-born, the Son of the Most Highest, himself the middle point of all wonder—for him to have done none, herein, indeed, had been the most marvelous thing of all.

But this new order, having not only declared but constituted itself, having asserted that it is not of any inevitable necessity bound by the heavy laws of the old, henceforth submits itself in outward things, and for the present time, to those laws. All its true glory, which is its inward glory, it retains; but these powers, which are not the gift—for Christ himself is the gift—but the signs of the gift, it forgoes. They were as the proclamation that the king was mounting his throne; yet the king is not proclaimed every day, but only at this accession: when he sits acknowledged on his throne, the proclamation ceases. They were as the bright clouds which gather round, and announce the sun at his first appearing; his midday splendor, though as full, and indeed fuller, of light and heat, knows not those bright heralds of his rising. That is *has had* these wonders—that its first birth was, like that of its wondrous Founder, wonderful—of this the Church preserves a record and attestation in its Scriptures of truth. The miracles recorded there live for the Church; they are as much present witnesses for Christ to us now as to them who actually saw them with their eyes. For they were done once, that they might be believed always—that we, having in the Gospels the living representation of our Lord's life portrayed for us, might as surely believe that he was the ruler of nature, the healer of the body, the Lord of life and of death, as though we had actually ourselves seen him allay a storm, or heal a leper, or raise one dead.

Moreover, a very large proportion of the later miracles presented to our belief bear inward marks of spuriousness. The miracles of Scripture—and among these, not so much the miracles of the Old Covenant as the miracles of Christ and his apostles, being the miracles of that highest and latest dispensation under which we live, we have a right to consider as normal, in their chief features at least, for all future miracles, if such were to continue in the Church. The details, the local coloring, may be different, and there were no need to be perplexed at such a difference appearing; yet the later must not be, in their inner spirit, totally unlike the earlier, or they carry the sentence of condemnation on their front. They must not, for instance, lead us back under the bondage of the senses, while those other were ever framed to release from that bondage. They must not be aimless and objectless, fantastic freaks of power, while those had every one of them a meaning, and distinct ethical aim—were bridges by which Christ found access from men's bodies to their souls—manifestations of his glory, that men might be drawn to the glory itself. They must not be ludicrous and grotesque, saintly jests, while those were evermore reverend and solemn and awful. And lastly, they must not be seals and witnesses to aught which the conscience, enlightened by the Word and Spirit of God—whereunto is the ultimate appeal, and which stands above the miracle, and not beneath it—protests against as untrue (the innumerable Romish miracles which attest transubstantiation), or as error largely mingling with the truth (the miracles which go to uphold the whole Romish system), those other having set their seal only to the absolutely true. Miracles such as any of these, we are bound, by all which we hold most sacred, by all which the Word of God has taught us, to reject and to refuse. It is for the reader, tolerably acquainted with the church-history of the middle ages, to judge how many of its miracles will, if these tests be acknowledged and applied, at once fall away, and come no more even into consideration.

Very interesting is it to observe how the men who in some sort fell in with the prevailing tendencies of their age (for, indeed, who escapes them?), yet did ever, in their higher moods, with a truest Christian insight, witness against those very tendencies by which they, with the rest of their contemporaries, were more or less borne away. Thus was it with regard to the over-valuing of miracles, the counting them the only evidences of an exalted sanctity. Against this what a continual testimony in all ages of the Church was borne; not, indeed, sufficient to arrest the progress of an error, into which the sense-bound generations of men only too naturally fall, yet showing that the Church herself was ever conscious that the holy life was in the sight of God of higher price than the wonderful works—that love is the greatest miracle of all—that to overcome the world, this is the greatest manifestation of the power of Christ in his servants.

One passage from Chrysostom, in the place of the many that might be quoted, and even that greatly abridged, must suffice. He is rebuking the faithful, that now, when their numbers were so large, they did so little to leaven the world, and this, when the apostles, who were but twelve, effected so much; and he puts aside the excuse, "But they had miracles at command," not with the answer, "So have we"; but in this language; "How long shall we use their miracles as a pretext for our sloth? And what was it then, you say, which made the apostles so great? I answer, This, that they contemned money; that they trampled on vain-glory; that they renounced the world. If they had not done thus, but had been slaves of their passions, though they had raised a thousand dead, they would not merely have profited nothing, but would have been counted as impostors. What miracle did John, who reformed so many cities, of whom yet it is expressly said, that he did no sign? And thou, if thou hadst thy choice, to raise the dead in the name of Christ, or thyself to die for his name, which wouldst thou choose? Would it not be plainly the latter? And yet that were a *miracle,* and this is but a *work.* And if one gave thee the choice of turning all grass into gold, or being able to despise all gold as grass, wouldst thou not choose the last? And rightly; for by this last wouldst thou most effectually draw men to the truth. This is not my doctrine, but the blessed Paul's: for when he had said, 'Covet earnestly the best gifts,' and then added, 'yet show I unto you a more excellent way'; he did not adduce miracles, but love, as the root of all good things."

Few points present greater difficulties than the attempt to fix accurately the moment when these miraculous powers departed from the Church, and it entered into its permanent state, with only its miracles of grace and the record of its miracles of power; instead of having actually going forward in the midst of it those miracles of power as well, with which it first asserted itself in the world. This is difficult, because it is difficult to say at what precise moment the Church was no longer in the act of *becoming,* but contemplated in the mind of God as now actually *being;* when to the wisdom of God it appeared that he had adequately confirmed the word with signs following, and that these props and strengthenings of the infant plant might safely be removed from the hardier tree.

That their retrocession was gradual, that this mighty tide of power should have ebbed only by degrees, this was what was to be looked for in that spiritual world which, like God's natural world, is free from all harsh and abrupt transitions, in which each line melts imperceptibly into the next. We can conceive the order of retrocession to have been in this way; that divine power which dwelt in all its fullness and intensity in Christ, was first divided

among his apostles, who, therefore, individually brought forth
fewer and smaller works than he. It was again from them further
subdivided among the ever-multiplying numbers of the Church,
who, consequently, possessed not these gifts in the same intensity
and plenitude as did the twelve. Yet must it always be remembered
that these receding gifts were ever helping to form that which
should be their own substitute; that if they were waning, that
which was to supply their room was ever waxing, that they only
waned as that other waxed; the flower dropped off only as the fruit
was being formed. If those wonders of a first creation have left us,
yet this was not so, till they could bequeath in their stead the standing wonder of a Church, itself a wonder, and embracing manifold
wonders in its bosom. For are not the laws of the spiritual world,
as they are ever working in the midst of us, a continual wonder?
What is the new birth in Baptism, and the communion of Christ's
body and blood in the Holy Eucharist, and the life of God in the
soul, and a kingdom of heaven in the world, what are these but
every one of them wonders? Wonders in this like the wonders of
ordinary nature, as distinguished from those which accompany a
new in-coming of power, that they are under a law which we can
anticipate; that they conform to an absolute order, the course of
which we can understand—but therefore the less divine. How
meanly do we esteem of a Church, of its marvelous gifts, of the
powers of the coming world which are working within it, of its
Word, of its Sacraments, when it seems to us a small thing that in it
men are new born, raised from the death of sin to the life of righteousness, the eyes of their understanding enlightened, and their
ears opened, unless we can also tell of more visible and sensuous
wonders. It is as though the heavens should not declare to us the
glory of God, nor the firmament show us his handiwork, except at
some single moment such as that when the sun was standing still
upon Gibeon, and the moon in Ajalon.

While then it does not greatly concern us to know *when* this
power was withdrawn, what does vitally concern us is, that we
suffer not these carnal desires after miracles, as if they were necessarily saints who had them, and they but ordinary Christians who
were without them, as though the Church were incomplete and
spiritually impoverished which could not show them, to rise up in
our hearts, as they are ever ready to rise up in the natural heart of
man, to which power is so much dearer than holiness. There is no
surer proof than the utterance of feelings such as these, that the

true glory of the Church is hidden from our eyes—no sadder sign that some of its outward trappings and ornaments have caught our fancy; and not the fact that it is all glorious within, taken possession of our hearts and minds. It is, indeed, ill with us, for it argues little which we ourselves have known of the miracles of grace, when *they* seem to us poor and pale, and only the miracles of power have any attraction in our eyes.

V.

The Assaults on the Miracles

1. The Jewish.

A rigid monotheistic religion like the Jewish, left but one way of escape from the authority of miracles, which once were acknowledged to be indeed such, and not mere collusions and sleights of hand. There remained nothing to say but that which we find in the New Testament the adversaries of the Lord continually did say, namely, that these works were works of hell: "This fellow doth not cast out devils but by Beelzebub, the prince of the devils" (Matt. 12:24; cf. Mark 3:22–27; Luke 11:15–22). We have our Lord's own answer to the deep malignity of this assertion; his appeal namely, to the whole tenor of his doctrine and his miracles—whether they were not altogether for the overturning of the kingdom of evil—whether such a lending of power to him on the part of Satan would not be wholly inconceivable, since it were merely and altogether suicidal. For though it would be quite intelligible that Satan should bait his hook with some good, should array himself as an angel of light, and do for a while deeds that might appear as deeds of light, that so he might the better carry through some mighty delusion—

> "Win men with honest trifles, to betray them
> In deepest consequence,"

just as Darius was willing that a small portion of his army should perish, that so the mighty deceit which Zopyrus was practicing against Babylon might succeed—yet a lasting, unvarying, unrelaxing assault on his kingdom is unintelligible as being furthered by himself: his kingdom thus in arms against itself, could not stand, but hath an end. He who came, as all his words and his deeds testified, to destroy the works of the Devil, could not have come armed with *his* power, and helped onward by his aid. It is not a pact with the Evil one which this tells of, but of one mightier than that Evil one having entered with power into his stronghold, and who, having bound him, is now spoiling his goods. Our Lord does in fact repel the accusation, and derive authority to his miracles, not on account of the power which they display, however that may be the first thing that brings them into consideration, but on account of the ethical ends which they serve. He appeals to every man's conscience whether the doctrine to which they bear witness, and which bears witness to them, be not from above and not from beneath: and if so, then the power with which he accomplished them could not have been lent him from beneath, since the kingdom of lies would never so contradict itself as seriously to help forward the establishment of the kingdom of truth.

There is indeed at first sight a difficulty in the argument which our Savior draws from the oneness of the kingdom of Satan—namely, that it seems the very idea of this kingdom, that it should be this anarchy—blind rage and hate not merely against God, but each part of it warring against every other part. And this is most deeply true, that hell is as much in arms against itself as against heaven; neither does our Lord deny that *in respect of itself* that kingdom is infinite contradiction and division: only he asserts that *in relation to the kingdom of goodness* it is at one: there is one life in it and one soul in relation to that. Just as a nation or kingdom may embrace within itself infinite parties, divisions, discords, jealousies, and heart-burnings; yet if it is to subsist as a nation at all, it must not, *as regards other nations,* have lost its sense of unity; when it does so, of necessity it falls to pieces and perishes. To the Pharisees he says: "This kingdom of evil subsists; by your own confession it does so: it cannot therefore have denied the one condition of its existence, which is, that it should not lend its powers to the overthrowing of itself—that it should not side with its own foes; I am its foe; it cannot therefore be siding with me."

This accusation against the miracles of Christ, that they were done by the power of an evil magic, the heathen also sometimes used; but evidently having borrowed it from the Jewish adversaries of the Christian faith. Yet in their mouths, who had no such earnest idea of the kingdom of God upon one side, and the kingdom of evil on the other, and the fixed limits which divide the two, who had peopled the intermediate space with middle powers, some good, some evil, some mingled of both, the accusation was not at all so deeply malignant as in the mouth of a Jew. It was little more than a stone which they found conveniently at hand to fling, and with them is continually passing over into the charge that those works were wrought by trick—that they were conjurer's arts; the line between the two charges is continually disappearing. The heathen, however, had a method more truly their own of evading the Christian miracles, which is now to consider.

2. The Heathen. (Celsus, Hierocles, Porphyry.)

A religion like the Jewish, which, besides God, and the angels who were in direct and immediate subordination to him, left no spirits conceivable but those in rebellion against him, the absolutely and entirely evil, this, as has been observed, allowed no choice, when once the miracle was adjudged to be not from God, but to attribute it to Satan. There was nothing between; it was from heaven, or if not from heaven, from hell. But it was otherwise in the heathen world, and with the "gods many" of polytheism. So long as these lived in the minds of men, the argument from the miracles was easily evaded. For, what did they prove at the uttermost with regard to the author of them? What but that *a* god it might be one of the higher, or it might be one of the middle powers, the δαίμονες, the intermediate deities, was with him? What was there, men replied, in this, which justified the demand of an absolute obedience upon their parts? Wherefore should they yield exclusive allegiance to him that wrought these works? The gods had spoken often by others also—had equipped them with powers equal to or greater than those claimed by his disciples for Jesus; yet no man therefore demanded for them that they should be recognized as absolute lords of the destinies of men. Esculapius performed wonderful cures; Apollonius went about the world healing the sick, expelling demons, raising the dead; Aristeas disappeared from the earth in as marvelous a way as the author of the Christian faith: yet no man built upon these wonders a superstructure such as that which the Christians built upon the wonders of Christ.

Thus Celsus, as we learn from more than one passage in Origen's reply, brings forward now the mythic personages of antiquity, now the magicians of a later date, though apparently with no very distinct purpose in his mind, but only with the feeling that somehow or other he can play them off against the divine Author of our religion, and undermine his claims to the allegiance of men. For it certainly remains a question how much credence he gave himself to the miracles which he adduced; and whether, sharing the almost universal skepticism of the educated classes of his day, he did not rather mean that all should fall, than that all should stand, together. Hierocles again, governor of Bithynia, who is accused of being a chief instigator of the cruelties under Diocletian, and who, if the charge be just, wielded arms of unrighteousness on both hands against the Christian faith, the persecutor's sword, and the libeller's pen—followed in the same line. His book we know from the extracts in the answer of Eusebius, and the course of his principal arguments. From this answer it appears that, having recounted various miracles wrought, as he affirms, by Apollonius, he proceeds thus: "Yet do we not account him who has done such things for a god, only for a man beloved of the gods: while the Christians, on the contrary, on account of a few insignificant wonder-works, proclaim their Jesus for a god." He presently, it is true, shifts his arguments, and no longer allows the miracles, denying only the conclusions drawn from them; but rather denies that they have any credible attestation: in his blind hate setting them in this respect beneath the miracles of Apollonius, which this "lover of truth," for under that name he writes, declares to be far more worthily attested.

This Apollonius (of Tyana in Cappadocia), whose historical existence there does not seem any reason to call in question, was probably born about the time of the birth of Christ, and lived as far as into the reign of Nerva, A.D. 97. Save two or three isolated notices of an earlier date, the only record which we have of him is a Life written by Philostratus, a rhetorician of the second century, professing to be founded on contemporary documents, yet everywhere betraying its unhistoric character. It is in fact a philosophic romance, in which the revival and re-action of paganism in the second century is portrayed. Yet was not that Life written, I believe, with any directly hostile purpose against Christianity, but only to prove that they of the old faith had their mighty wonder-worker as well. It was composed indeed, as seems to me perfectly clear, with an eye to the life of our Lord; the parallels are too remarkable to have been the effect of chance; in a certain sense also in emulation and rivalry; yet not in hostile opposition, not as implying this was the Savior of men, and not that; nor yet, as some of Lucian's works, in a mocking irony of the things which are written concerning the

Lord. This later use which has often been made of the book, must not be confounded with its original purpose, which was certainly different. The first, I believe, who *so* used it, was Charles Blount, one of the earlier English Deists. And passing over some other insignificant endeavors to make the book tell against revealed religion, endeavors in which the feeble hand, however, inspired by hate, yet wanted strength and skill to launch the dart, we come to Wieland's *Agathodoemon,* in which neither malice nor dexterity were wanting, and which, professing to explain upon natural grounds the miracles of Apollonius, yet unquestionably points throughout at one greater than the wonder-worker of Tyana, with a hardly suppressed *de te fabula narratur* running through the whole.

The arguments drawn from these parallels, as far as they were adduced in good faith and in earnest, have, of course, perished with the perishing of polytheism from the minds of men, even the minds of those who have not submitted themselves to the faith of Christ. Other miracles can no longer be played off against his miracles; the choice remains between these or none.

3. The Pantheistic. (Spinoza.)

These two classes of assailants of the Scripture miracles, the Jewish and the heathen, allowed the miracles themselves to stand unquestioned as facts, but either challenged their source, or denied the consequences which were drawn from them by the Church. Not so the pantheistic deniers of the miracles, who assailed them not as being of the devil, not as insufficient proofs of Christ's absolute claims of lordship; but cut at their very root, denying that any miracle was possible, since it was contrary to the idea of God. For these opponents of the truth Spinoza may be said, in modern times, to bear the word; the view is so connected with his name, that it will be well to hear the objection as he has uttered it. That objection is indeed only the necessary consequence of his philosophical system. Now the first temptation on making acquaintance with that system is to contemplate it as a mere and sheer atheism; and such has ever been the ordinary charge against it; nor in studying his works is it always easy to persuade oneself that it is anything higher, or that the various passages in which he himself assumes it as something different, are more than inconsequent statements, with which he seeks to blind the eyes of others, and to avert the odium of this charge of atheism from himself. And yet atheism it is not, not is it even a material, however it may be a formal, pantheism. All justice requires it to be acknowledged that he does not bring down and resolve God into nature, but rather takes up and loses nature in God. It is only man whom he submits to a blind fate, and for whom he changes, as indeed for him he does, all ethics into physics. But the idea of freedom, as regards God, is saved; since, however he affirms him immanent in nature and not transcending it, this is only because he has himself chosen these laws of nature as the one unchangeable manner of his working, and constituted them in his wisdom so elastic, that they shall prove under every circumstance and in every need, the *adequate* organs and servants of his will. He is not bound to nature otherwise than by that, his own will; the laws which limit him are of his own imposing; the necessity which binds him to them is not the necessity of any absolute fate, but of the highest fitness. Still, however, Spinoza does affirm such a necessity, and thus excludes the possibility of any revelation, whereof the very essence is that it is a new beginning, a new unfolding by God of himself to man, and especially excludes the miracle, which is itself at once the accompaniment, and itself a constituent part, of a revelation.

It would not be profitable to say here more than a few words on the especial charges which he brings against the miracle, as lowering, and unworthy of, the idea of God. They are but an application to a particular point of the same charges which he brings against all revelation, namely, that to conceive any such is a dishonoring, and a casting a slight upon, God's great original revelation of himself in nature and in man; an arguing that of such imperfection and incompleteness, as that it needed the author of the world's laws to interfere in aid of those laws, lest they should prove utterly inadequate to his purposes. And thus, as regards the miracle in particular, he finds fault with it as a bringing in of disorder into that creation, of which the only idea worthy of God is that of an unchangeable order; it is a making God to contradict himself, for the law which was violated by the miracle is as much God's law as the miracle which violated it. The answer to this objection has been already anticipated; it has been already sought to be shown that the miracle is not a discord in nature, but the coming in of a higher harmony; not disorder, but instead of the order of earth, the order of heaven; not the violation of law, but that which continually, even in this natural world, is taking place, the comprehension of a lower law by a higher; in this case the comprehension of a lower natural, by a higher spiritual law; with only the modifications of the lower, necessarily consequent upon this.

Then, again, when he charges the miracle with resting on a false assumption of the position which man occupies in the universe, as flattering the notion that nature is to serve him, he not to bow to nature, it is most true that it does rest on this assumption. But this were only a charge which would tell *against* it, supposing that true, which so far from being truth, is indeed his first great falsehood of all, namely, the substitution of a God of nature, in place of a God of men. If God be indeed only or chiefly the God of nature, and not in a paramount sense the God of grace, the God of men, if nature be indeed the highest, and man only created as furniture for this planet, it were indeed absurd and inconceivable that the higher should serve, or give place to, or fall into the order of, the lower. But if, upon the other hand, man is the end and object of all, if he be indeed the vicegerent of the Highest, the image of God, if this world and all that belongs to it be but a workshop for the training of men, only having a worth and meaning when so considered, then that the lower should serve, and, where need was, give way to the highest, this were only beforehand to be expected.

Here, as is so often the case, something much behind the miracle, something much earlier in our view of the relations between God and his creatures, has already determined whether we should accept or reject it, and this, long before we have arrived at the consideration of this specific matter.

4. The Skeptical. (Hume.)

While Spinoza rested his objection to the miracles on the ground that the everlasting laws of the universe left no room for such, and while the form therefore which the question in debate assumed in his hands was this, Are miracles (objectively) possible? Hume, a legitimate child and pupil of the empiric philosophy of Locke, started his objection in altogether a different shape, namely, in this, Are miracles (subjectively) credible? He is in fact the skeptic, which—taking the word in its more accurate sense, not as a denier of the truths of Christianity, but a doubter of the possibility of arriving at any absolute truth—the other is as far as possible from being. To this question his answer is in the negative; or rather, in the true spirit of the philosophy which leaves everything in uncertainty, It is always more probably that a miracle is false than true; it can therefore in no case prove anything else, since it is itself incapable of proof—which thus he proceeds to show. In every case, he observes, of conflicting evidence we weigh the evidence for and against the alleged facts, and give our faith to that side upon which the evidence preponderates, with an amount of confidence proportioned, not to the whole amount of evidence in its favor, but to the difference which remains after subtracting the evidence against it. Thus, if the evidence on the side of A might be set as = 20, and that on the side of B as = 15, then our faith in A would remain $20 - 15 = 5$; we give our faith upon the side on which a balance of probabilities remain. But every miracle is a case of conflicting evidence. In its favor is the evidence of the attesting witnesses; against it the testimony of all experience which has gone before, and which witnesses for an unbroken order of nature. When we come to balance these against one another, the only case in which the evidence for the miracle could be admitted as prevailing, would be that *in which the falseness or error of the attesting witnesses would be a greater miracle than the miracle which they affirm.* But no such case can occur. The evidence against a miracle having taken place is as complete as can be conceived; even were the evidence in its favor as complete, it would only be proof against proof, and absolute suspension of judgment would be the wise man's part. But further, the evidence in favor of the miracle never makes claim to any such completeness. It is always more likely that the attesting witnesses were deceived, or were willing to deceive, than that the miracle took place. For, however many they may be, they are always but a few compared with the multitudes who attest a fact which excludes their fact, namely, the uninterrupted succession of a natural order in the world, and those few submitted to diverse warping influences, from which the others, nature's witnesses, are altogether free. Therefore there is no case in which the evidence for any one miracle is able to outweigh the *á priori* evidence which is against all miracles. Such is the conclusion at which he arrives. The argument, it will be seen, is skeptical throughout. Hume does not, like Spinoza, absolutely deny the miracle, only that we can ever be convinced of one. Of two propositions or assertions that *may be* true which has the least evidence to support it; but according to the necessary constitution of our being, we must give our adherence to that which presents itself to us with the largest amount of evidence in its favor.

Here again, as on a former occasion, so long as we abide in the region of nature, miraculous and improbable, miraculous and incredible, may be allowed to remain convertible terms. But once lift up the whole discussion into a higher region, once acknowledge aught higher than nature, a kingdom of God, and men the intended denizens of it, and the whole argument loses its strength and the force of its conclusions. Against the argument from experience which tells against the miracle, is to be set, not, as Hume asserts, the evidence of the witnesses, which it is quite true can in no case itself be complete and of itself sufficient, but this, *plus* the anterior probability that God, calling men to live above nature and sense, would in this manner reveal himself as the Lord paramount of nature, the breaker through and slighter of the apparitions of sense; *plus* also the testimony which the particular miracle by its nature, its fitness, the glory of its circumstances, its intimate coherence as a redemptive act with the personality of the doer, in Coleridge's words, "its exact accordance with the ideal of a true miracle is the reason," gives to the conscience that it is a divine work. The *moral* probabilities Hume has altogether overlooked and left out of account, and when they are admitted—dynamic in the midst of his merely mechanic forces—they disturb and indeed utterly overbear and destroy them. His argument is as that fabled giant, unconquerable so long as it is permitted to rest upon the earth out of which it sprung; but easily destroyed when once it is lifted into a higher world. It is not, as Hume would fain have us to believe, solely an intellectual question; but it is in fact the moral condition of men which will ultimately determine whether they will believe the Scripture miracles or not—this, and not the exact balance of argument on the one side or the other, which will cause this scale or that to kick the beam.

He who already counts it likely that God will interfere for the higher welfare of men—who believes that there is a nobler world-order than that in which we live and move, and that it would be the blessing of blessings for that nobler to intrude into and to make itself felt in the region of this lower, who has found that here in this world we are bound by heavy laws of nature, of sin, of death, which no powers that we now possess can break, yet which must be broken if we are truly to live—he will not find it hard to believe the great miracle, the coming of the Son of God in the flesh, and his declaration as the Son of God with power by the resurrection from the dead; because all the deepest desires and longings of his heart have yearned after such a deliverer, however little he may have

been able even to dream of so glorious a fulfillment of those longings. And as he believes that greatest miracle, so will he believe all
other miracles, which, as satellites of a lesser brightness, naturally
wait on and cluster round and draw their luster from the central
brightness of that one. He, upon the other hand, to whom this
world is all, who has lost all sense of a higher world with which it
must once have stood connected, who is disturbed with no longings for aught nobler than it gives, to whom "the kingdom of God'
is an unintelligible phrase, he will resist, by an intellectual theory if
he can, or if not by that, by instinct, the miracle. Everything that is
in him predisposes him to disbelieve it, and the doctrines which it
seals. To him who denies thus any final causes, who does not believe that humanity is being carried forward under a mightier leading than its own to a certain and that a glorious end, to whom the
history of the world and of man is but the history of a bark, storm-
tossed long, and to be wrecked at last, these moral probabilities are
no probabilities; and this being so, we should learn betimes how
futile it is to argue with men about *our* faith, who are the deniers of
all upon which *any* faith can be built.

5. The Miracles Only Relatively Miraculous. (Schleiermacher.)

Another way of getting rid of the miraculous element in the
miracle, and one often united with Spinoza's *á priori* argument
against it, explaining the phenomenon of an apparent miracle after
that has shown that a real one was impossible, has been the following. These works it has been said were *relative* miracles—miracles, in other words, for those in regard of whom they were first
done—as when a savage believes that a telescope has the power of
bringing the far instantaneously near—but no miracles in themselves, being but in truth the anticipation of discoveries in the kingdom of nature, the works of one who had penetrated deeper into
her mysteries than the men of his own age, and therefore could
wield powers which were unknown, and bring about results which
were inexplicable, to them. It must be evident to the least thoughtful, that however the fact may be sought to be disguised, the miracle does thus become no miracle, and the doer of it can no longer
be recognized as one commanding nature in a way specifically different from other men, but only as one who has a clearer or earlier
insight than others into her laws and the springs of her power. It is

strange that any should ever have been satisfied with this statement, which is indeed only a decently veiled denial of the miracle
altogether. For thus it has no longer an eternal significance; it is no
longer a halo which is to surround the head of its worker forever;
with each enlargement of men's knowledge of nature a star in his
crown of glory is extinguished, till at length it fades altogether into
the light of common day—nay, rather declares that it was never
any more than a deceitful and meteor fire. For it implies a serious
moral charge against the doer of these works, if he vents them as
wonders, as acts of a higher power than nature's, or allows others
so to receive them, when indeed they are wrought but according to
her ordinary laws. It was well enough, according to the spirit in
which he was working, for one of the conquerors of the New World
to make the Indians, whom he wished to terrify, believe that in his
displeasure with them he would at a certain hour darken the moon,
when indeed he was but foreknowing an eclipse of that orb: but in
the kingdom of truth to use artifices like these were but by lies to
seek to overturn the kingdom of lies.

Schleiermacher endeavors so to guard this view that it shall not
appear an entire denial of the miracles, to dress it out and prevent
its bareness from being seen, but he does not in fact lift himself
above it. Christ, he says, had not merely this deeper acquaintance
with nature than any other that ever lived, but stands in a more inward connection with nature. He is able to evoke, as from her hidden recesses, her most inward sanctuary, powers which none other
could; although still powers which lay in her already. These facts,
which seem exceptional, were deeply laid in the first constitution
of the law; and now, at this turning point of the world's history, by
the providence of God, who had arranged all things from the beginning of the world for the glory of his Son, did at his bidding
emerge. Yet single and without analogy as they were, they belonged to the law as truly as when the aloe puts forth its flower, or
is said to put it forth, once in its hundred years, it yet does this according to its own innermost nature. For ninety and nine years it
would have seemed to men not to be the nature of the plant to
flower, yet the flowering of the hundredth year is only the coming
out of its truest nature.

We see in this scheme that attempt to reconcile and atone between revelation and science, which was the great purpose of all
Schleiermacher's writings, Yet is it impossible to accept the reconciliation which he offers; as it is really made, however the sacrifice

may be concealed, altogether at the expense of the miracle—which, in fact, is no miracle, if it lay in nature already, if it was not a new thing, it if was only the evoking of old and latent forces in nature, not the bringing in of the new powers of a higher world, if the mysterious processes and powers by which those works were brought about, are only undiscovered, not undiscoverable, by the efforts of human inquiry.

Augustine has sometimes been quoted as maintaining this scheme of the relatively miraculous, but altogether with injustice. It is quite true that, in arguing with the heathen, he does demand why they refuse to give credence to the Scripture miracles, when they believe so much that can in no way be explained by any laws which their experience gave them, and adduces some curious but actual, and some also entirely fabulous, phenomena of the natural world, such as fountains cold by night and hot by day—others which extinguished a lighted torch, but set on fire an extinguished one—stones which, once kindled, could not be quenched—magnets which attracted iron, and other wonders, to which he and they gave credence alike. But it is not herein his meaning to draw down the miracles to a level with natural appearances, hitherto unexplained, but capable of and waiting their explanation. Rather in these natural appearances he sees direct interpositions of the Divine Power; he does not reckon that any added knowledge will bring them under laws of human experience, and therefore he lifts them up to a level with the miracles. He did not merge the miracles in nature, but drew up a portion of nature into the region of the miraculous. However greatly as a natural philosopher he may have been here at fault, yet all extenuating of the miracle was far from him; indeed he ever refers it to the omnipotence of God as to its ultimate ground.

When he affirms that much *seems* to be against nature, but nothing truly is, this may sound at first like the same statement of the miraculous being what it is merely in relation to certain persons and certain stages of our knowledge of this outward world. But it is only in sound that it is similar. He has quite a different thought of nature from any that will allow such to be his meaning. Nature is for him but the outward expression of the will of God; and all which he affirms is, that God never can be contrary to God; that there can be no collision of his wills; that whatever comes in is as true an order, the result of as real a law, as that which gives place to it; and this must needs be, since it has come in according to the will of God, which will is itself the highest order, and law, and harmony.

6. The Rationalistic. (Paulus.)

The rise of rationalism—which term I use for convenience sake, and without at all consenting to its fitness, for it is as absurd a misnomer as when that in the last century was called *free*-thinking, which was assuredly to end in the slavery of all thought—the rise of rationalism seems to have been in this manner—that it was an escape from the conclusions of mere Deists concerning Christ's person and his Word, upon the part of those who had indeed abandoned the true faith of the Church concerning its Head; yet were not willing to give up the last lingering vestiges of their respect for Holy Scripture and for him of whom Scripture testified. They with whom this system grew up could no longer believe the miracles, they could no longer believe the great miracle in which all other are easily included, a Son of God, in the Church's sense of the words; they, too, were obliged to fall in with the first principles of the infidel adversary, that any who professed to accomplish miracles was either self-deceived or a deceiver, even as they who recorded such as having happened stood in the same dilemma.

But what if it could be shown that Christ never professed to do any miracles, nor the sacred historians to record any? If it could be shown that the sacred narratives, rightly read, were against any such supposition, and that it was only the lovers of, and cravers after, the marvelous, who had found any miracles there—the books themselves having been intended to record merely natural events? Were not this an escape from the whole difficulty? The divine, it is true, in these narratives would disappear; that however they did not desire to save; that they had already given up: but the human would be vindicated; the good faith, the honesty, the entire credibility of the Scripture historians, would stand fast. And in Christ himself there would be still that to which they could look up with reverence and love; they could still believe in him as the truthful founder of a religion which they did not desire to renounce altogether. No longer being, as the Church declared him, the worker of wonders, clothed with power from on high, nor professing to be that which he was not, as the blasphemers affirmed, he would still

abide for them in the fullness of his beneficent activity, as he went
up and down the world, healing and blessing, though with only
the same means which other men had at command.

Their attempt was certainly a bold one; to suffer the sacred text
to stand, and yet to find no miracles in it, did appear a hopeless
task; for this is that which altogether distinguishes this system
from later mythic theories, that it does accept the New Testament
as entirely historic; it does appeal to the word of Scripture as the
ground and proof of its assertions; its great assertion being that the
Evangelists did not intend to relate miracles, but ordinary facts of
everyday experience, works done by Jesus, now of friendship and
humanity, now of medical skill, now also of chance and good fortune, or other actions which from one cause or other seemed to
them of sufficient significant to be worth recording. Thus Christ,
they say, did not heal an impotent man at Bethesda, but only detected an impostor; he did not change water into wine at Cana, but
brought in a new supply of wine when that of the house was exhausted; he did not multiply the loaves, but, distributing his own
and his disciples' little store set an example of liberality, which was
quickly followed by others who had like stores, and in this way
there was sufficient for all. He did not cure blindness otherwise
than any skillful oculist might do it—which indeed, they observe,
is clear; for with his own lips he declared that he needed light for
so delicate an operation—"I must work the works of him that sent
me, while it is day; the night cometh when no man can work" (John
9:4); he did not walk on the sea, but on the shore; he did not tell
Peter to find a piece of money in the fish's mouth, but to catch as
many fish as would sell for that money; he did not raise Lazarus
from the dead, but guessed from the nature of his disease that he
was only in a swoon, and happily found it so.

This entire scheme, which many had already tried here and
there, but which first appeared full blown and consistently carried
through in the *Commentary* of Dr. Paulus did not long survive in its
first vigor. It perished under blows received from many quarters;
for, not to speak of a reviving faith in the hearts of many, that God
could do more than man could understand, even the children of
this world directed against it the keenest shafts of their ridicule.
Every philologist, nay every man who believed that language had
any laws, was its natural enemy, for it stood only by the violation
of all these laws. Even the very advance of unbelief was fatal to is,
for in it there was a slight lingering respect to the Word of God;

moved by which respect it sought forcibly to bring that Word into harmony with its theory, as a better alternative than the renouncing the authority of that Word altogether. But when men arose, who did not shrink from the other alternative, who had no desire to hold by that Word at all, then there was nothing to hinder them from at once coming back to the common-sense view of the subject, and one which no art could long succeed in concealing, namely that these Evangelists did intend to record supernatural events. Those to whom the Scriptures were *no* authority had at least this advantage, that they were not under the temptation to twist and pervert them, so to bring them into apparent accordance with their systems.

This scheme of interpretation, thus assailed from so many sides, and being merely artificial, quickly succumbed. And now, even in the land of its birth, it has entirely perished; on the one side a deeper faith, on the other a more rampant unbelief, have encroached on and wholly swallowed up the territory which it occupied. It is indeed so little the form in which an assault on Revelation will ever again clothe itself, and may be so entirely regarded as one of the cast-off garments of unbelief, now despised and trodden underfoot even of those who once glorified themselves in it, that I have not alluded, save very slightly and passingly, to it in the body of my book. Once or twice I have noticed its curiosities of interpretation, its substitutions, as they have been happily termed, of *philological* for *historical* wonders. The reader who is curious to see how Dr. Paulus and his compeers arrived at the desired result of exhausting the narrative of its miraculous element, will find specimens in the notes upon feeding of the five thousand, and the finding of the stater in the fish's mouth.

7. The Historico-Critical. (Woolston, Strauss.)

The last assault upon the miracles is that which may be not unfitly termed the historico-critical. It affirms that they are so full of contradictions, psychological and other improbabilities, discrepancies between the accounts of one Evangelist and another, that upon close handling they crumble to pieces, and are unable to stand as history. Among the English deists of the last century, Woolston especially addressed himself in this way to the undermining the historic credit of these narratives. He was brought to this evil work in a singular way, and abides a mournful example of the extremes wither spite and mortified vanity would carry a weak man, though, as all testimonies concur in acknowledging, at one time of estimable conversation, and favorably known for his temperate life, his charity to the poor, and other evidences of an inward piety. Born in 1669, and educated at Cambridge, where he became a fellow of Sidney, he first attracted unfavorable notice by a certain crack-brained enthusiasm for the allegorical interpretation of Scripture, which he carried to all lengths. Whether he owed this to the works of Philo and Origen, or whether he only strengthened and nourished an already existing predilection by the study of their writings, is not exactly clear; but it had become a sort of "fixed idea" in his mind. At first, although just offense was taken at more than one publication of his, in which his allegorical system was carried out at the expense apparently of the historic truth of the Scripture, yet as it was not considered that he meant any mischief, as it was not likely that he would exert any very wide influence, he was suffered to follow his own way, unvisited by any serious censures from the higher authorities of the Church. Meeting however with opposition in many quarters, and unable to carry the clergy with him, he broke out at last in unmeasured invectives against them, and in a virulent pamphlet styled them "slaves of the letter," "Baal-priests," "blind leaders of the blind," and was on account of this pamphlet deprived of his fellowship (1721).

From this time it seemed as if an absolute fury possessed him: not merely the Church, but Christianity itself, was the object of his attack. Whether his allegorical system of interpretation had indeed ended, as it was very likely to do, in depriving him of all faith in God's Word, and he retained his professed veneration for its spiritual meaning only that he might, under shelter of that, more securely advance to the assault of its historical foundations, or whether he did still retain this in truth, it was now at any rate only subordinate and subservient to his purposes of revenge. To these he was ready to offer up every other consideration. When then in that great controversy which was raging in the early part of the last century, the defenders of revealed religion entrenched themselves behind the miracles, as defenses from which they could never be driven, as being irrefragable proofs of the divine origin of Christianity. Woolston undertook, by the engines of his allegorical interpretation, to dislodge them from these also, and with this aim published his notorious *Letters on the Miracles*. It is his manner in these to take certain miracles which Christ did, or which were wrought in relation of him, two or three in a letter, and he then seeks to show that, understood in their literal sense, they contain such extravagancies, contradictions, and the like, that we can never suppose that Christ actually did them, or that the Evangelists, as honest men, men who had the credit of their Lord at heart, intended to record them as having been actually wrought, or desired us to receive them otherwise than as allegories, spiritual truths clothed in the form of historic events. The enormous difference between himself and those early Church writers, to whom he appeals, and whose views he professes to be only reasserting—a difference of which it is impossible that he could have been ignorant—is this: they said, This history, being real, has also a deeper ideal sense; he upon the contrary, Since it is impossible that this history can be real, therefore it must have a spiritual significance. They build upon the establishment of the historic sense, he upon its ruins.

When he wants to utter grosser blasphemies than in his own person he dares, or than would befit the standing point which he has assumed from whence to assault Revelation, he introduces a Jewish rabbi, and suffers him to speak without restraint, himself only observing, "This is what an adversary might say; to these accusations we Christians expose ourselves so long as we cleave to the historic letter; we only can escape from thence by forsaking that, and holding fast the allegorical meaning alone." I shall not (as it is not needful) offend the Christian reader by the reproduction of any of his coarser ribaldry, which has sufficient cleverness to have made it mischievous enough, but will endeavor to show by a single example the manner in which he seeks to make weak points in the Scripture narratives. He is dealing with the miracle of the man sick of the palsy, who was let through the broken roof of the house where Jesus was, and thereupon healed (Mark 2:1–12). But how, he asks, should there have been such a crowd to hear Jesus preach at Capernaum, where he was so well known and so little admired? And then, if there was that crowd, what need of such urgent haste? It was but waiting an hour or two, till the multitude had dispersed; "I should have thought their faith might have worked patience." Why did not Jesus tell the people to make way? Would they not have done so readily, since to see a miracle was the very thing they wanted? How should the pulleys, ropes, and ladder have been at hand to haul him up? How, strange that they should have had hatchets and hammers ready to break through the spars and rafters of the roof, and stranger still that the good man of the house should have endured, without a remonstrance, his property to be so injured! How did those below escape without injury from the falling tiles and plaster? And if there were a door in the roof, as some, to mitigate the difficulty, tell us, why did not Jesus go up to the roof, and there speak the healing word, and so spare all this trouble and damage and danger!

But enough—it is evident that this style of objection could be infinitely multiplied in regard of any history. There is always something else that might have been done besides the thing that was done. It is after this taking to pieces of the narrative, this triumphant showing, as he affirms, that it cannot stand in the letter, that he proceeds, as a sort of salvo, to say it may very well stand in its spirit, as an allegory and symbol of something else; and that so, and so only it was intended. This is what he offers by way of this higher meaning in the present case: By the palsy of this man is signified "a dissoluteness of morals and unsteadiness of faith and principles, which is the condition of mankind at present, who want Jesus' help for the cure of it." The four bearers are the four Evangelists, "on whose faith and doctrine mankind is to be carried unto Christ." The house to the top of which he is to be carried is "the intellectual edifice of the world, otherwise called Wisdom's house." But "to the sublime sense of the Scriptures, called the top of the house, is man to be taken; he is not to abide in the low and literal sense of them." Then if he dare to "open the house of wisdom, he will presently be admitted to the presence and knowledge of Jesus."

Not very different is Strauss's own method of proceeding. He wields the same weapons of destructive criticism, thinking to show how each history will crumble at his touch—will remain a heap of improbabilities, which no one can any longer maintain. It needs not to say that he is a more accomplished adversary than Woolston, with far ampler resources at command—more, if not of his own, yet of other men's learning; inheriting as he does all the negative criticism of the last hundred years, of an epoch, that is, which has been sufficiently fruitful in this kind. Here indeed is in great part the secret of the vast sensation which his work for a season caused: all that was scattered up and down in many books he has brought together and gathered into a single focus; all which other men had spoken faintly and with reserve, he with a greater boldness has spoken out; he has dared to give utterance to all which was trembling upon the lips of numbers, but which, from one cause or another, they had shrunk from openly declaring. Yet as regards the treatment of the miracles—for with that only we have now to do—there are differences between him and Woolston. He unites in his own person the philosophical and the critical assailant of these; for he starts from the philosophic ground of Spinoza, that the miracle is impossible, since the laws of nature are the only and the necessary laws of God; and he then proceeds to the critical examination of the Gospel miracles in detail; but of course in each case to the trial of that which is already implicitly tried and condemned. Thus, if he is ever at a loss—if any of them give him trouble—if they oppose a stubborn resistance to the powerful solvents which he applies, threatening to stand in despite of all, he immediately falls back on his philosophic ground, and exclaims, "But if we admit it was thus, then we should have here a miracle, and we have started from the first principle, that such is inconceivable." This mockery in every case he repeats, trying them one by one, which have all been condemned by him beforehand in the gross.

There is, too, this further difference, that while Woolston professed to consider the miracles as the conscious clothing of spiritual truth, allegories devised artificially, and, so to speak, in cold blood, for the setting forth truths of the kingdom, Strauss gives them a freer birth and a somewhat nobler origin. They are the halo of glory with which the infant Church gradually and without any purposes of deceit clothed its Founder and its Head. His mighty personality, of which it was livingly conscious, caused it ever to surround him with new attributes of glory. All which men had ever craved and longed for—deliverance from physical evil, dominion over the crushing powers of nature, victory over death itself—all which had ever in a lesser measure been attributed to any—they lent in larger abundance, in unrestrained fullness, to him whom they felt greater than all. The system may be most fitly characterized as the Church making its Christ, and not Christ his Church.

With one only observation I will pass on, and not detain the reader any longer from more pleasant and more profitable portions of the subject. It is this, that here, as so often, we find the longings and cravings of men after a redemption, in the widest sense of that word, made to throw suspicion upon him in whom these longings and cravings are affirmed to have been satisfied. But if we believe a divine life stirring at the root of our humanity, the depth and universality of such longings is a proof rather that they were meant some day to find their satisfaction—that they were not always to be hopes and dreams; and if so, in whom, but in him whom we preach—in whom, but in Christ? What other besides him could, with the slightest show of reason, be put forward as the fulfiller of the world's hopes? If we do not believe in this divine life, nor in a divine leading of our race—if we hold a mere brutal theory about man, it were then better altogether to leave discussing miracles and Gospels, which indeed have no meaning for, as they stand in no relation to, us.

VI.

The Apologetic Worth
of the Miracles

A most interesting question remains; namely this, What is the place which those who are occupied with marshaling and presenting the evidences of Revelation should give to the miracles? What is the service which they may render here? The circumstances have been already noticed which were sufficient to hinder them from taking a very prominent place in the early Apologies for Christianity. The Christian miracles had not sufficiently extricated themselves from the multitude of false miracles—nor was Christ sufficiently discerned and distinguished from the various wonder-workers of his own and of past ages; so that, even if men had admitted his miracles to be true and godlike, they would have been hardly nearer to the acknowledging of Christianity as the one faith, or of him as "the way, the truth, and the life."

But a different and far more important position has been assigned them in later times, especially during the last two hundred years; and the tone and temper of modern theology abundantly explains the greater prominence, sometimes, I believe, the undue, because the exclusive, prominence, which in this period they have assumed. The apologetic literature of this time, partook, as was inevitable, in the general depression of all its theology. There is no one, I think, who would now be satisfied with the general tone and spirit in which the defenses of the faith, written during the two last centuries, and beginning with the memorable work of Grotius, are composed. Much as this and many others contain of admirable, yet

in well nigh all that great truth of the Italian poet seems to have
been forgotten,

"They struggle vainly to preserve a part,
Who have not courage to contend for all."

These apologists, on the contrary, would seem very often to have
though that Deism was best to be resisted by reducing Christianity
to a sort of revealed Deism. Like men that had renounced the hope
of defending all, their whole endeavor was to save something, and
when their pursuers pressed them hard, they were willing to delay
the pursuit by casting to them as a prey much that ought to have
been the dearest to themselves. It has been well observed that they
were like men, who should cry "Thieves and robbers!" who were
yet themselves all the while throwing out of the windows the most
precious things of the house; and thus it sometimes happened that
the good cause suffered quite as much from its defenders as its assailants: for that enemies should be fierce and bitter, this was only
to be looked for; but that friends, those in whose keeping was the
citadel, should be timid and half-hearted and ready for a compromise, this was indeed an augury of ill. Now this, which caused so
much to be thrown greatly out of sight, as generally the mysteries
of our faith, which brought about a slight of the inner arguments
for revelation, caused that from the miracles to assume a disproportionate magnitude. A value too exclusive was set on them; they
were rent away from the truths for which they witnessed, and
which witnessed for them—only too much like seals torn off from
the document which at once *they* rendered valid, and which gave
importance to them. And thus, in this unnatural isolation, separated from Christ's person and doctrine, the whole burden of proof
was laid on them. *They* were the apology for Christianity, the reason which men were taught they should give for the faith which
was in them.

It is not hard to see the motives which led to this; they were
chiefly the desire to get an *absolute* demonstration of the Christian
faith—one which objectively should be equally good for every
man: it was the wish to bring the matter to the same sort of proof
as exists for a proposition in mathematics or in logic. And consistently with this we see the whole argument cast exactly into the
same forms of definitions, postulates, axioms, and propositions.
But at the same time the state of mind which made men to desire

either to find for themselves, or to furnish others with, proofs of this nature, was not altogether healthy. It was plain that their faith had become very much an external historic one, when they thus eagerly looked round for outward evidences, and found a value only in such; instead of turning in upon themselves as well, for evidence that they had "not followed cunningly devised fables," and saying, "We *know* the things which we believe—they are to us truer than aught else can be, for we have the witness of the Spirit for their truth. We have found these things to be true, for they have come to us in demonstration of the Spirit and in power." Instead of an appeal to those mighty influences which Christ's words and doctrine exercise on every heart that receives them, to their transforming, transfiguring power, to the miracles of grace which are the heritage of every one who had believed to salvation, instead of an addressing of the gainsayers in the very language of the Lord, "If any man will do his will, he shall know of the doctrine whether it be of God" (John 7:17), this all as mystical and uncertain (instead of being seen to be, as it truly was, the most certain thing of all), was thrown into the background. Men were afraid to trust themselves and their cause to arguments like these, and would know of no other statement of the case than this barren and hungry one: Christianity is a divine revelation, and this the miracles which accompanied its promulgation prove. What must first be found fault with in this is the willful abandonment of such large regions of proof, which the Christian apologist ought triumphantly to have occupied as his proper domain—the whole region, mainly and chiefly, of the inner spiritual life; his foregoing an appeal to the mysterious powers of regeneration and renewal, which are ever found to follow on a true adherence to him who is the Giver of this faith, and who has pledged himself to these very results.

On such he might at least have ventured, when he was seeking not to convince an unbeliever, but, as would be often his aim, to carry one that already believed round the whole circle of the defenses of his position—to make him aware of the relative strength of each—to give him a scientific insight into the grounds on which his faith rested. Here, at any rate, the appeal to what he had himself known and tasted of the powers of the world to come, might well have found room. For, to use the words of Coleridge, "Is not a true, efficient conviction of a moral truth, is not *the creating of a new heart*, which collects the energies of a man's whole being in the focus of the conscience, the one essential miracle, the same and of

the same evidence to the ignorant and to the learned, which no superior skill can counterfeit, human or demoniacal; is it not emphatically that leading of the Father, without which no man can
come to Christ; is it not that implication of doctrine in the miracle,
and of miracle in the doctrine, which is the bridge of communication between the senses and the soul—that predisposing warmth
which renders the understanding susceptible of the specific impressions from the historic, and from all other outward, seals of testimony?" And even if arguing with one who had never submitted
himself to these blessed powers, and to whose experience therefore
no like appeal could be made, yet even for him there is the outward
utterance of this inward truth, in that which he could not deny,
save as he denied or was ignorant of everything, which would
make him one to be argued with at all—the fact, I mean, of a
Christendom—the standing miracle of Christendom "commensu-
rate and almost synonymous with the civilized world"—the
mighty changes which this religion has wrought in the earth—the
divine fruits which it everywhere has borne—the new creation
which it has been—the way in which it has taken its place in the
world, not as a forcible intruder, but finding all that world's pre-es-
tablished harmonies ready to greet and welcome it, ready to give it
play and room—philosophy, and art, and science practically confessing that only under it could they attain their highest perfection,
that in something they had all been dwarfed and stunted and insufficient before. Little as it wears of the glory which it ought to
have, yet it wears enough to proclaim that its origin was more than
mundane; surely from a Christendom, even such as it shows itself
now, it is fair to argue back to a Christ such as the Church receives
as the only adequate cause. It is an oak which from no other acorn
could have unfolded itself into so goodly a tree.

It is true that in this there is an abandoning of the attempt to
put the proof of Christianity into the same form as a proposition in
an exact science. There is no more the claim made of giving it their
kind of certainty. But this, which may seem at first sight a loss, is
indeed a gain; for the argument for all which as Christians we believe is in very truth not logical and single, but moral and cumula-
tive; and the attempt to substitute a formal proof, where the
deepest necessities of the soul demand a moral, is one of the most
grievous shocks which the moral sense can receive, as it is one, too,
of the most fruitful sources of unbelief. Few who have had books
of evidences put into their hands, constructed upon this principle,

but must remember the shock which they suffered from them—how it took them, it may be, some time to recover the tone of their minds, and how only by falling back upon what they themselves had felt and known of the living power of Christ's words and doctrine in their own hearts, could they deliver themselves from the injurious influences, the seeds of doubt and of misgiving, which these books had now for the first time perhaps sown in their minds. They must remember how they asked themselves, in deep inner trouble of soul: "Are these indeed the grounds, and the only grounds, upon which the deep foundations of my spiritual life repose? Is this all that I have to answer? Are these, and no more, the reasons of the faith that is in me?" And then, if at any moment there arose a suspicion that some link in this chain of outward proof was wanting, or that any would not bear all the weight which was laid upon it—and men will be continually tempted to try the strength of that on which they have trusted all—there was nothing to fall back upon, with which to scatter and put to flight a suspicion such as this. And that such should arise, at least in many minds, were inevitable; for how many points, as we have seen, are there at which a suspicion may intrude. Is a miracle possible? Is a miracle provable? Were the witnesses of these miracles competent? Did they not too lightly admit a supernatural cause, when there were adequate natural ones which they failed to note? These works may have been good for the eyewitnesseses, but what are they for me? And these doubts and questionings might be multiplied without number. Happy is the man, and he only is happy, who, if the outworks of his faith are at any time thus assailed, can betake himself to an impregnable inner citadel, from whence in due time to issue forth and repossess even those exterior defenses, who can fall back on those inner grounds of belief, in which there can be no mistake, that testimony of the Spirit, which is above and better than all.

And as it is thus with him, who entirely desiring to believe, is only unwilling disturbed with doubts and suggestions, which he would give worlds to be rid of forever, so on the other hand the expectation that by arguments thrown apparently into forms of strict reasoning there is any compelling to the faith one who does not wish to believe, is absurd, and an expectation which all experience contradicts. All that he is, and all that he is determined to be, has bribed such a one to an opposite conclusion. Rather than believe that a miracle has taken place, a miracle from the upper world, and connected with doctrines of holiness, to which doctrines he is resolved to yield no obedience, he will take refuge in any the most monstrous supposition of fraud, or ignorance, or folly, or collusion. If no such solution presents itself, he will wait for such, rather than accept the miracle, with its hated adjunct of the truth which it confirms. In what different ways the same miracle of Christ wrought upon different spectators! He raised a man from the dead; here was the same outward fact for all; but how diverse the effects! Some believed, and some went and told the Pharisees (John 11:45, 46). Heavenly voices were heard, and some said it thundered, so dull and inarticulate were those sounds to them, while others knew that they were voices wherein was the witness of God to his own Son (John 12:28–30).

Are then, it may be asked, the miracles to occupy no place at all in the array of proofs for the certainty of the things which we have believed? On the contrary, a most important place. We should greatly miss them if they did not appear in sacred history, if we could not point to them there; for they belong to the very idea of a Redeemer, which would remain most incomplete without them. We could not ourselves, without having that idea infinitely weakened and impoverished, conceive of him as not doing such works; and those to whom we presented him might make answer, "Strange, that one should come to deliver men from the bondage of nature which was crushing them, and yet himself have been subject to its heaviest laws—himself wonderful, and yet his appearance accompanied by no analogous wonders in nature—claiming to be the Life, and yet himself helpless in the encounter with death; however much he promised in word, never realizing any part of his promises in deed, giving nothing in hand, no first fruits of power, no pledges of greater things to come." They would have a right to ask, "Why did he give no signs that he came to connect the visible with the invisible world? Why did he nothing to break the yoke of custom and experience, nothing to show men that the constitution which he pretended to reveal has a true foundation?" And who would not feel that they had right in this, that a Savior who so bore himself during his earthly life, and his actual daily encounter with evil, would have been felt to be no Savior? That he must needs show himself, if he were to meet the wants of men, mighty not only in word but in work? When we object to the use that has been often made of these works, it is only because they have been forcibly severed from the whole complex of Christ's life and doctrine, and presented to the contemplation of men apart from these; it is only because, when on his head who is the Word of God, are "many crowns" (Rev. 29:12), one only has been singled out in proof that he is King of kings, and Lord of lords. The miracles have been spoken of as though they borrowed nothing from the truths which they confirmed, but those truths everything from them; when indeed the true relation is one of mutual interdependence, the miracles proving the doctrines, and the doctrines approving the miracles, and both held together for us in a blessed unity, in the person of him who spoke the words and did the works, and through the impress of highest holiness and of absolute truth and goodness, which that person leaves stamped on our souls—so that it may be more truly said that we believe the miracles for Christ's sake, than Christ for the miracles' sake. Neither when we thus affirm that the miracles prove the doctrine, and the doctrine the miracles, are we arguing in a circle: rather we are receiving the sum total of the impression which this divine revelation is intended to make on us, instead of taking an impression only partial and one-sided.

The Miracles

1.

The Water Made Wine

John 2:1–11

"This beginning of miracles" is as truly an introduction to all other miracles which Christ did, as the parable of the Sower is an introduction to all other parables which he spoke (Mark 4:31). No other miracle would have had so much in it of prophecy, would have served as so fit an inauguration to the whole future work of the Son of God. For that work might be characterized throughout as an ennobling of the common and a transmuting of the mean—a turning of the water of earth into the wine of heaven. Yet not to anticipate remarks which will find their fitter place, when the circumstances of this miracle have been more fully considered, what is this "third day," which St. John gives as the date of this present miracle? It is generally, and, I believe, correctly, answered, the third after the day on which Philip and Nathanael, of whose coming to Christ there is mention immediately before (1:43), had attached themselves to him. He and his newly-won disciples would have passed without difficulty from the banks of Jordan to Cana in two days, and thus might have been easily present at the "marriage," or, better, the marriage festival, upon the third day after that event. But besides the Lord and his disciples, "the mother of Jesus was there" also. It is most likely, indeed there is every reason to suppose, that Joseph was now dead; the last mention of him occurs on the occasion of the Lord's visit as a child to the Temple; he had died, probably, between that time and Christ's open undertaking of his ministry. The disciples called are commonly taken to be the five whom he had so lately gathered, Andrew and Peter, Philip and Nathanael (Bartholemew?), and the fifth, the Evangelist himself. For St. John is generally considered to have been the second of the two scholars of the Baptist mentioned 1:35, 40, of whom Andrew was the other, both from all the circumstances being detailed with so great minuteness, and it being so much in his manner to keep back his own personality under such language as there is used (13:23; 18:15; 19:26, 35). If this was so, he would then be an eyewitness of the miracle which his is relating.

We need not wonder to find the Lord of life at that festival; for he came to sanctify all life—its times of joy, as its times of sorrow; and all experience tells us, that it is times of gladness, such as this was now, which especially need such a sanctifying power, such as presence of the Lord. In times of sorrow, the sense of God's presence comes more naturally out: in these it is in danger to be forgotten. He was there, and by his presence there stuck the key-note to the whole future tenor of his ministry. He should not be as another Baptist, to withdraw himself from the common paths of men, a preacher in the wilderness: but his should be at once a harder and a higher task, to mingle with and purify the common life of men, to witness for and bring out the glory which was hidden in its every relation. And it is not, perhaps without its significance, that this should have been especially *a marriage,* which he "adorned and beautified with his presence and first miracle that he wrought." He foresaw that some hereafter should arise in his Church who would despise marriage, or if not despise, yet fail to give the Christian family all its honor. They should find no countenance from him.

The presence at that feast of himself and his disciples, who were just arrived from a journey, and whose presence might therefore have been in some degree unlooked for, may have increased beyond previous calculation the number of the guests: and so the provision made for their entertainment may have proved insufficient. We gather from verse 5, where the mother of the Lord gives commandment to the servants that she was in a house where it was not unseemly for her to mingle, and in some sort to interfere with the domestic arrangements. It is very possible she may have been akin to one of the parties. *"When they wanted wine,"* she was evidently distressed at their embarrassment, and would willingly have removed it. Yet what exactly she should have expected from her divine Son, when she betook herself to him saying, *"They have no wine,"* is hard to determine. We know that this was his first miracle, the *"beginning of miracles"* (v. 11) so that she could not, from already having witnessed displays of his power and grace, have now been emboldened to look for more in the same kind. Some, indeed, as Maldonatus mentions, and with whom he is inclined to consent, do not take so absolutely the statement which is there made, but with this limitation understood—This was the first of his miracles in which he *showed forth* his glory; other such works he may have perfomed in the smaller circle of his family, and thus have prepared those who laid up such things in their hearts for something of the like kind now. But without evading in this way the plain meaning of the words of the Evangelist, we may well understand how she, who more than any other had kept and pondered in her heart all the tokens and prophetic intimations of the coming glory of her Son, may have believed that in him was a latent power equal to the present need, and which he could put forth at his will, however he had restrained it until now. Others assume that she had no definite purpose in thus speaking, but only that as she had ever found him a wise counselor in the least as well as in greatest things, so she turned to him now. Bengel's explanation is curious, that it was a suggestion to him that they should leave, and thus by their example break up the assembly before the embarrassment of their hosts should appear.

The Romanist expositors have been very anxious to rid our Lord's answer, *"Woman, what have I to do with thee?"* of every shadow of rebuke or blame. Whole essays have been written with this single purpose. Now it is quite true that in the address *"Woman"* there is nothing of the kind—nothing of severity or rebuke, however it may have something of such a sound to an English ear. We find our blessed Lord, even at the moment when probably he was addressing to his mother the last words that he spoke to her on earth—when commending her to the care of the beloved disciple, using the same language, *"Woman,* behold thy son"* (John 19:26). So far from any harshness, the compellation has something solemn in it, and always must have, where the dignity of woman is felt and recognized. But it is otherwise with the words following, *"What have I to do with thee?"* If we compare them with the same or similar expressions elsewhere, the meaning of them will come clearly out, and it is this, "Let me alone; what is there common to thee and me? We stand in this matter on altogether different grounds." All expositors of the early church have allowed, even by the confession of the Romanists themselves, that there is more or less of reproof and repulse in these words; and they themselves are obliged to admit that there is the *appearance* of such; but at the same time they deny the reality. Christ so spoke, they say, to teach, not her, but us, that they were higher respects than those of flesh and blood, even the everlasting interests of God's kingdom, which moved him to the choosing the present moment for the first putting forth of his divine power. This is most true, that it was to teach this; but to teach it first to her, who from her wonderous position as the mother of the Lord, was in chiefest danger of forgetting it. "She had not yet," says Chrysostom, "that opinion of him which she ought, but because she bare him, counted that, after the manner of other mothers, she might in all things command him, whom it was more fitting for her to reverence and worship as her Lord."

Yet whatever amount of rebuke was intended, any harshness which the reply may have in the reading we cannot doubt was mitigated by the manner of its speaking, by the way, too, in which the Lord suffered a near compliance with her request to shine through the apparent refusal. For when she said to the servants, *"Whatsoever he saith unto you, do it,"* it is plain that she saw in his seeming denial a real granting of her desire. Undoubtedly there is something obscure in that command following immediately as it does the words of Christ, *"Mine hour is not yet come."* For these words, and above all, when taken in connection with those that precede them, seem to put off not merely for a brief period—for a few minutes, or for an hour—the manifestation of his glory as the Messiah, but to put it off altogether till some later period of his ministry. Indeed, this *"hour"* is generally, and especially in the language of St. John, the hour of his passion, or of his departure from the world (John 7:30; 8:20; 12:23, 27; 17:1), though in a single instance (John 7:6), it may have, as here, a nearer signification. But it is plain that the Blessed Virgin understood them differently, and, as the sequel showed, rightly. *"Mine hour is not yet come";* not till the wine is wholly exhausted will this time arrive; as yet it was only failing: then will be the time to act, when by its complete failure, manifest to all, the miracle will be above suspicion. Otherwise, in Augustine's words, he might seem rather to *mingle* elements than to *change* them. When all other help fails, then and not till then has Christ's *"hour"* arrived. Luther here notes, and presents to us for an example, the faith of Mary, who from this apparent repulse could yet draw forth an assurance that her petition, whatever may have been the error of pressing it too hastily, or other fault that clung to it, should yet in due time be heard—so that, with entire confidence of this, she said unto the servants, *"Whatsoever he saith unto you, do it,"* evidently believing not merely that he would comply with her request, but in some degree guessing at and even indicating the manner.

Very beautiful is it here to observe the facility with which our Lord yields himself to the supply, not of the absolute wants merely, but of the superfluities, of others. Yet it is not so much the guests whom he has in his eye, as the bridal pair, whose marriage feast, by the unlooked-for shortcoming of the wine, was in danger of being exposed to mockery and scorn. And the gracious Lord has sympathy with *all* needs—with the finer as well as more common needs of our life. For all the grace, and beauty, and courtesy of life are taken account of in Christianity, as well as life's sterner realities; and the spirit of Christ, in himself and in his disciples, does not slight or despise those any more than these. We may contrast this his readiness to aid others, with the strictness with which he refused to come to the help of his own extremest needs. He who made wine out of water, might have made bread out of stones. But he will do nothing at the suggestion of Satan, though all at the suggestion of love.

"There were set there six waterpots of stone, after the manner of the purifying of the Jews, containing two or three firkins apiece." Everything is here narrated, as Chrysostom observes, so as to exclude any possible semblance of collusion. They were water-jars, not wine-vessels, so that none could say that very probably there was a residue or sediment of wine remaining in them, which lent a flavor to water poured on it, and so formed a thinnest kind of wine—even as the same is witnessed against in the praise which the ruler of the feast bestows upon the new supply (v. 10). The fact of these vessels being at hand is no less accounted for: it was not by any premeditated plan, but they were there in accordance with the customs and traditionary observances of the Jews in the matter of washing; for this seems more probable than that this *"purifying"* has reference to any distinctly commanded legal observances. The purifying was such as the Jewish doctors had enjoined and made necessary (Matt. 15:2; Mark 7:2–4; Luke 11:39). The quantity, too, which these vessels contained, was enormous—not such as might have been brought in unobserved; but each of these waterpots contained *"two or three firkins apiece."* And at the beginning they were empty; so that the servants who, in obedience to the commandment, had filled the waterpots with water, and who knew what liquid they had poured

in, were themselves, by this very work which they had done, witnesses of the reality of the miracle. Else it might only have appeared, as in fact it did only appear to the ruler of the feast, that the wine came from some unexpected quarter; *"He knew not whence it was, but the servants which drew the water,"*—that is, not the water now made wine, but who *had drawn* the simpler element, which Christ chose to use as the substratum on which he should afterwards exercise his miraculous powers, *"knew."*

Like most other acts of creation, or more strictly, of becoming, this of the water becoming wine, is withdrawn from sight, and that which is poured into the jars as water is drawn out as wine; but the actual process of the change we labor in vain to conceive. And yet in truth it is in no way stranger, save in the rapidity with which it is effected, than that which is every day going forward among us, but to which use and custom have so dulled our eyes, that commonly we do not marvel at it at all: and because we can call it by its name, suppose that we have discovered its secret. He who does every year prepare the wine in the grape, causing it to drink up and expand with the moisture of earth and heaven, to take this up into itself, and transmute into its own nobler juices, did not gather together all those his slower processes into the act of a single moment, and accomplish in an instant what ordinarily he does not accomplish but in many months. This analogy does not indeed help us to understand what the Lord did now, but yet brings before us that in this he was working in the line of (above, indeed, but not across, or counter to), his more ordinary workings, which we see daily around us, the unnoticed miracles of everyday nature. That which this had of its own peculiar, and taking it out from the order of these, was the power and will by which all the intervening steps of these tardier processes were overleaped, and the result attained at once.

It has been sometimes debated whether *"the ruler of the feast"* was himself one of the guests, who either by general consent or the selection of the host was set over the banquet; or a chief attendant only, charged with ordering the course of the feast, and overlooking the ministrations of the inferior servants. This last is the view taken by Chrysostom and others; but the analogy of Greek and Roman usages seems rather to point him out as himself one of the invited guests, who was invested with this office for the time; and the passage from the Son of Sirach quoted below, shows that a like custom was in use among the Jews. Indeed the freedom of remonstrance which he allows himself with the host seems almost decisive of his position; for such would hardly have found place but from an equal. To him, as having the function of tasting and distributing the wine, the Lord commanded that which he had made to be brought, even in this little matter recognizing and honoring the established order and usages of society, and giving to every man his due. And now *"when the ruler of the feast had tasted the water which was made wine, and knew not whence it was, he called the bridegroom,"* we need not suppose actually summoned him from his place, but he called to him, with something of a festive exclamation, not unsuitable to the season, *"Every man at the beginning doth set forth good wine, and when men have well drunk, then that which is worse: but thou hast kept the good wine until now."*

Many interpreters have been very anxious to rescue the original word, which we have given by *"well drunk,"* from involving aught of excess, as though, did it imply that, we must necessarily conclude that the guests at this marriage festival had already drunken too much, that this was one of the *temulenta* convivia, which St. Cyprian speaks of as too often disgracing a marriage, with all the difficulties, of Christ being present at such an abuse of God's gifts, and stranger still, ministering by his divine power to a yet further excess. But there is no need of such anxious dealing with the word. The ruler of the feast is but alluding to the corrupt customs and fashions too current among men, not to aught which was necessarily going on before his eyes—nay, to something which certainly was not so, for such the Lord would have as little sanctioned by his presence, as he would have helped it forward by a wonder-work of his own. The speaker does no more than refer to a common practice, and in so doing, notices its cause, namely that men's palates after a while are blunted, and their power of discerning between good and bad lost; and that then an inferior wine passes current with them, as it would not have done before. There is no special application to the guests present—except in the minds of them who would mar, if by any means they could, the image of a perfect Holiness, which offends and rebukes them.

Of a piece with this is their miserable objection, who find the miracle incredible, since, if the Lord did not actually minister to an excess already commenced, yet, by the creation of "so large and perilous a quantity of wine" (for the quantity *was* enormous), he would have put temptation in men's way—as though the secret of temperance lay in the scanty supply, and not in the strong self-restraint! In like manner, every gift of God, every large abundance of the vineyard, might be said with equal truth to be a temptation, and so in some sort it is (compare Luke 12:16), a proving of men's temperance and moderation in the midst of abundance. But man is to be perfected, not by being kept *out of* temptation, but rather by being victorious *in* temptation. And for this large giving, it was only that which we should look for. He, a King, gave as a king. No niggard giver in the ordinary bounties of his kingdom of nature, neither was he a niggard giver now, when he brought those his common gifts into the kingdom of his grace, and made them directly to serve him there (cf. Luke 5:6, 7).

But these words, *"Every man at the beginning doth set forth good wine; and when men have well drunk, then that which is worse: but thou hast kept the good wine until now,"* setting forth, as in the letter they do, only a trivial practice of a poor worldly economy, have oftentimes had a higher meaning found for them. It has been excellently noticed how these very words may be used for the setting forth the difference between the manner and order of the world's giving and of Christ's giving. The man, not knowing what he did, gave utterance to a far larger and deeper thought than he meant. The world does indeed give its best and its fairest at the beginning, its *"good wine"* first, but has only baser substitutes at the last. *"When men have well drunk,"* when their spiritual palate is blunted, when they have lost the discernment between moral good and evil, then it puts upon them what it would not have dared to offer at the first—coarser pleasures, viler enjoyments, the swine's husks. The world is for them that worship it, even as that great image which the Babylonian king beheld (Dan. 2:31); its head, indeed, may show as fine gold, but its material grows ever baser, till it finishes in the iron and clay at the last. And so it comes to pass that

> "To be a prodigal's favorite, then, worse lot!
> A miser's pensioner,"

this is the portion of them that have entered on the service of sin and of the world. But it is very otherwise with the guests of Christ, the heavenly bridegroom. He ever reserves for them whom *he* has bidden *"the good wine"* unto the last. In the words of the most eloquent of our divines, "The world presents us with fair language, promising hopes, convenient fortunes, pompous honors, and these are the outside of the bowl; but when it is swallowed, these dissolve in an instant, and there remains bitterness and the malignity of coloquintida. Every sin smiles in the first address, and carries light in the face, and honey in the lip, but when we *'have well drunk,'* then comes *'that which is worse,'* a whip with six strings, fears and terrors of conscience, and shame and displeasure, and a caitiff disposition, and diffidence in the day of death. But when after the manner of purifying of the Christians, we fill our waterpots with water, watering our couch with our tears, and moistening our cheeks with the perpetual distillations of repentance, then Christ turns our water into wine, first penitents and then communicants—first waters of sorrow and then the wine of the chalice . . . for Jesus keeps the best wine to the last, not only because of the direct reservations of the highest joys till the nearer approaches of glory, but also because our relishes are higher after a long fruition than at the first essays, such being the nature of grace, that it increases in relish as it does in fruition, every part of grace being new duty and new reward."

The Evangelist expressly, and, as it would seem, pointedly, excludes from all historic credit the miracles of Christ's infancy, of which so large a crop is to be found in nearly all the apocryphal Gospels. For, of course, he would not say merely that this was the first miracle which Jesus did in Cana, but that this miracle in Cana was the first which he did; it was for him the *"beginning of miracles."* The statement is not unimportant, nor unconnected with one of the main purposes with which the Gospel of St. John was written, which was to repel and remove all unreal notions concerning the person of his Lord—notions which nothing would have helped more to uphold than those merely fantastic and capricious miracles—favorites, therefore, with all manner of Docetic heretics—which are ascribed to his infancy.

But in this work of his he *"manifested forth his glory,"* words that could be used of no lesser than the Son; for all others would have manifested forth the glory of another, but he his own. And this, because the word *"glory"* is to be taken emphatically; it is not merely his excellent greatness, but his divinity: for the glory (‰fiĺ·) is a divine attribute; it is comprehended and involved in the idea of the Logos as the absolute Light: as such he rays forth light from himself, and this effluence is *"his glory"* (John 1:14; Matt. 16:27; Mark 8:38). This "glory" during the time that the Son of God sojourned upon earth, for the most part was hidden; the covering of the flesh concealed it from men's eyes: but in this miracle, this work of his power, St. John would say, it broke through this its fleshly covering, and manifested itself to the spiritual eyes of his disciples; they "beheld his glory, the glory as of the only begotten of the Father." And as a consequence, *"his disciples believed on him."* The work, besides its more immediate purpose, had a further end and aim, the confirming their faith, who already believing in him, were therefore the more capable of receiving increase of faith—of being lifted from faith to faith, from faith in an earthly teacher to faith in a heavenly Lord.

It was said at the outset, that this first miracle of our Lord's had its inner mystical meaning. The first miracle of Moses was the turning of water into blood (Ex. 7:20), and that had its own fitness, for the law was a ministration of death and working wrath; but the first miracle of Christ was a turning of water into wine, and this too was a meet inauguration of the rest, for his was a ministration of life; he came, bringing joy and gladness, the giver of the true wine that maketh glad the hearts of men. There is, too, another prophetic aspect under which this turning of the water into wine has been often contemplated, another, though in truth but a different aspect of the same—that even so should Christ turn the poorer dispensation, the weak and watery elements of the Jewish religion (Heb. 7:18), into richer and nobler, the gladdening wine of a higher faith. The whole Jewish dispensation in its comparative weakness and poverty was aptly symbolized by the water, and only in type and prophecy could it tell of him of the tribe of Judah, who should come "binding his foal into the vine, and his ass's colt into the choice vine"; of whom it is said, "he washed his garments in wine and his clothes in the blood of grapes" (Gen. 49:11; cf. John 15:1); but now by this work of his he gave token that he had indeed come into the midst of his people, that their joy might be full. And apart from all that is local and temporary, this miracle may be taken as the sign and symbol of all which Christ is evermore doing in the world, ennobling all that he touches, making saints out of sinners, angels out of men, and in the end heaven out of earth, a new paradise of God out of the old wilderness of the world. For the prophecy of the world's regeneration, of the day in which his disciples shall drink of the fruit of the vine new in his kingdom, is eminently here—in this humble feast, the rudiments of the great festival which shall be at the open setting up of his kingdom—that marriage festival in which he shall be himself the Bridegroom and his Church the bride—that season when his *"hour"* shall have indeed *"come."*

Ireneus has an interesting passage, in which he puts together this miracle and that of the loaves, and, as I think, contemplates them together as a prophecy of the Eucharist, but certainly sees them as alike witnesses against all Gnostic notions of a creation originally impure. The Lord, he says, might have created with no subjacent material the wine with which he cheered these guests, the bread with which he fed those multitudes; but he rather chose to take his Father's creatures on which to put forth his power, in witness that it was the same God who at the beginning had made the waters and caused the earth to bear its fruits, who did in those last days give by his Son the cup of blessing and the bread of heaven.

2.

The Healing of the Nobleman's Son

John 4:46–54

There is an apparent contradiction in the words that introduce this miracle. It is there said that Jesus "went into Galilee, *for* he himself testified that a prophet hath no honor in his own country," and yet Galilee *was* his own country, and immediately after we are told that the Galileans "received," or gave him honorable welcome. This however is easily got rid of; yet not as Tittmann, and some of the older expositors propose, by making St. John, in fact, to say that the Lord went into Galilee, *though* he had testified that a prophet was unhonored at home; for there is no compelling the words to mean this; nor yet by understanding "his own country" as Judea, and then finding in this saying of his an explanation of his retiring from thence into Galilee. This is Origen's explanation, whom some moderns follow. But the Lord's birth at Bethlehem in Judea being a fact not generally known, the slight esteem in which he was there held, could not have had in this its ground. Rather we must accept "country" as the place where he had been brought up, namely, Nazareth, and then there is here an explanation of his not returning thither (with a direct allusion to the testimony which he himself had borne in its synagogue, "No prophet is accepted in his own country," Luke 4:24); but going in preference to Cana, and other cities of Galilee; "and the Galileans," as St. John, with an emphasis, relates, "received him," though the Nazarenes, the people of his own immediate city, had rejected, and would have killed him.

In treating of this miracle, the first question which occurs is this, namely, whether we have here the same history as that of the servant (_·Ö~) of the centurion related by St. Matthew (8:5), and St. Luke (7:2), and here repeated with only immaterial variations. Ireneus would seem to have looked at them as one and the same history; and Chrysostom and others note such an opinion as held by some in their time, though they themselves oppose it. And this rightly, for there is almost nothing in its favor. Not merely the external circumstances are greatly different; that centurion being a heathen, this nobleman in every probability a Jew; that one pleading for his servant, this for his son; that intercession finding place as the Lord was entering Capernaum, this in Cana; in that the petitioner sending by others, in this himself coming: the sickness there a paralysis, a fever here. But far more than all this, the heart and inner kernel of the two narratives is different. That centurion is an example of a strong faith, this nobleman of a weak faith; that centurion counts that, if Jesus will but speak the word, his servant will be healed, while this nobleman is so earnest that the Lord should come down, because in heart he limits his power, and counts that nothing but his actual presence will avail to heal his sick; the other receives praise, this rebuke, at the lips of Christ. The difference is indeed here so striking, that Augustine draws a comparison, by way of contrast, between the faith of that centurion, and the unbelief of this nobleman.

Against all this, the points of apparent identity are very slight, as the near death of the sufferer, the healing at a distance and by a word, and the returning and finding him healed. It is nothing strange that two miracles should have these circumstances in common.

It has been supposed by some that this nobleman is no other than Chuza, Herod's steward, whose wife was among the holy women that ministered unto the Lord of their substance (Luke 8:3; cf. verse 53). This is not wholly improbable; for it would seem as if only some mighty and marvelous work of this kind would have drawn a steward of Herod's with his family, into the net of the Gospel. But whether this was so or not, he leaving his son exceeding sick at Capernaum, now came and found Jesus, who was just returned from his journey to Jerusalem, in Cana of Galilee, *"and besought him that he would come down and heal his son, for he was at the point of deah."* From the something of severity which comes out in our Lord's first notice of his petition, *"Except ye see signs and wonders, ye will not believe,"* it is evident that this nobleman was one driven to Jesus by the strong constraint of an outward need, a need which no other but he could supply (Is. 26:16), rather than one drawn by the inner necessities and desires of his soul—a man who would not have come but for this; who shared in the carnal temper of the most of his fellow-countrymen (they, by the plural number which our Lord here uses, being, it is most probable, intended to be included in the same condemnation)—one who had (as yet, at least), no organ for perceiving the glory of Christ as it shone out in his person and in his doctrine—whom nothing but miracles, "*signs and wonders,*" would compel to a belief; unlike those Samaritans whom the Lord has just left, and who, without a miracle, had in great numbers "believed because of his word" (John 4:41). But "the Jews require a sign" (1 Cor. 1:22), and this one, in the smallness of his present faith, straightened and limited the power of the Lord, counting it needful that he should "*come down*" if his son was to be healed; being unable to conceive of any other cure, of any word spoken at a distance and yet mighty to save. Not that we are to suppose that the Lord thus speaking meant to cast any slight on the significance of miracles, only they are not to serve for this, namely, to compel the reluctant and unbelieving to the faith, but to confirm the mission of a divine ambassador before them that have already been taken hold of by the power of the truth.

Yet, as Bengel observes, there is a beautiful admixture in this answer, of rebuke and encouragement; an implied promise of a miracle even while the man is blamed, that he needed this, that nothing short of this would induce him to put his trust in the Lord of life. And so the man accepts it; for he does not suffer himself to be repelled by this word of a seeming, and indeed of a real severity; rather he now presses on the more earnestly, "*Sir, come down ere my child die*"—still, it is true, not guessing of any other help save through the Lord's bodily presence; still far off from the faith and humility of that centurion, who said, "Lord, I am not worthy that thou shouldest come under my roof; but speak the word only, and my servant shall be healed"—much less dreaming of a power that could raise the dead; it must be "*ere my child die,*" or the help will be too late. Therefore that gracious Lord, who had always the higher good of those who came in contact with him in his eye, again tries his faith, and in the trying strengthens it, sending him away with a mere word of assurance that it should go well with his child; "*Go thy way, thy son liveth.*" And the nobleman was contented with that assurance; he *"believed the word that Jesus had spoken unto him, and he went his way,"* expecting to find that it should be done according to that word.

There is here again something to be learned by a comparison of the Lord's dealing with this man and with the centurion of the other Gospels. Here being entreated to come, he does not; but sends his healing word. There, being asked to speak that word of healing, he rather proposes himself to come; for here, as Chrysostom, unfolding the motives of his different conduct in the two instances, well brings out, a narrow and poor faith is enlarged and deepened, there a strong faith is crowned and rewarded. By not going he increases this nobleman's faith; by offering to go, he brings out and honors that centurion's humility. Nor shall we fail to observe by the difference of his conduct in the two cases how far was the Lord from being an accepter of persons. He will not come, but only send, to the son of this nobleman (see 2 Kgs. 5:10, 11); he is prompt to visit in his own person the servant of that centurion.

It would seem that now his confidence in Christ's word was so great, that he proceeded leisurely homewards, since it was not till the next day that he reached his house, though the distance between the two cities was not so great that the journey need have occupied many hours. Maldonatus quotes Isaiah 28:16, "He that believeth shall not make haste." It is worthy of note that his inquiry of the servants who met him on his return with news of his child's recovery, was when the child *"began to amend,"* to be a little better. For at the height of his faith, the father had only looked for a slow and gradual amendment, and therefore he used such an expression as this: but his servants answer, that at such an hour, the very hour when Jesus spoke the word, the fever not merely began to subside, there was not merely a turning point in the disease, but it *"left him,"* it suddenly forsook him. *"So the father knew that it was at the same hour in the which Jesus said unto him, Thy son liveth, and himself believed"*—this he did for all the benefits which the Lord had bestowed on him, he accepted another and the crowning benefit, even the cup of salvation; and not he alone, but, as so often happened, and this for the bringing us into the perception of the manner in which each smaller community, as well as the great community of mankind—a nation, or as in this case a family, is united and bound together under its federal head, his conversion drew after it that of all who belonged to him: *"himself believed, and his whole house"* (cf. Acts 16:15, 34; 18:8).

Yet, might it not be asked, Did he not believe before? Was not the healing itself a reward of his faith? Yes, he believed that particular word of the Lord's; but this is the adherence of faith, the entering into the number of Christ's disciples, the giving of himself to him as to the promised Messiah. Or, supposing he already truly believed, there may be indicated here a heightening and augmenting of his faith. For a true faith is yet most capable of this increase; "Lord, increase our faith" (Luke 17:5); and so in him who said, "Lord, I believe, help thou mine unbelief" (Mark 9:24), the true faith was born, though as yet its actings were weak and feeble. So too we read after the last miracle of the water made wine, that "his disciples believed on him" (John 2:11), who yet, being already his disciples, must have believed on him before. Thus in the Old Testament they who suffered themselves to be guided by Moses must have already believed that he was the instrument of God for their deliverance, yet not the less is it said after the great overthrow of Pharoah and his host, that the people "believed the Lord, and his servant Moses" (Ex. 14:31). We have another analogous example, 1 Kings 17:24, where after the mighty work which Elijah did, raising the widow's son, she addresses him thus: "Now *by this* I know thou art a man of God, and that the word of the Lord in thy mouth is truth," while yet she had recognized him as such before (v. 18), now however her faith received a new confirmation; (cf. John 11:15; 13:19); and so we may accept it here.

3.

The First Miraculous Draught of Fishes

Luke 5:1–11

There have been some in all times who have deemed themselves bound to distinguish this narrative from those in St. Matthew (4:18), and St. Mark (1:16–20). Augustine, for example, finds the differences so considerable, that he can only suppose the circumstance narrated by St. Luke to have first happened, our Lord then predicting to Peter that hereafter he should catch men; but not at that time summoning him to enter on the work; that without any sinful drawing back, he and his fellows returned after a while to their usual employments—they only on a somewhat later occasion, that recorded by St. Matthew and St. Mark, hearing the word of command, "Follow me," which then they obeyed, and attached themselves forever to their heavenly Lord.

Now that there are some difficulties, yet such as hardly deserve that name, in the harmonizing of the two accounts, every one will readily admit; but the flying immediately to the resource of supposing an event happened, with slight variations, twice or even three times over, whenever there is any difficulty in bringing the parallel accounts perfectly to agree, seems a very questionable expedient, at least to him who will deal honestly in the matter, and will ask himself whether he would be satisfied with such an explanation in any other history. It is for him a far greater difficulty made than avoided. For the other is nothing so great, indeed in most cases, as here, is none at all. Anyone who knows the various aspects, yet all true, in which the same event will present itself from different points of view to different witnesses, who keeps in mind how very few points in any complex fact or event any narration whatever can seize, least of all a written one, which in its very nature is limited, will little wonder when two or three narrators have in part seized diverse as the culminating points of a narrative, have brought out different moments of an event: he will rather be grateful to that providence of God which thus often sets us not merely in the place of one bystander, but of more; allows us to see the acts of Christ, each part of which is significant, from various points of view; to hear of his discourses, not merely what one heard and carried away, but also that which sunk especially deep into the heart and memory of another.

A work exclusively devoted to the miracles of our Lord has only immediately to do with the narrative of St. Luke, for in that only the miracle appears. That which followed upon the miracle, the effectual calling of our apostles, appears in the parallel narratives as well—he thus by his narrative excellently completing theirs, and explaining to us why the Lord, when he bade these future chiefs of his kingdom to follow him, should have clothed the accompanying promise in that especial shape, "I will make you fishers of men"; words which would anyhow have had their propriety as addressed to fishers whom he found casting their nets, and unconsciously prophesying of their future work, yet winning a peculiar fitness after he has just shown them what successful fishers of the mute creatures of the sea, he could make them, if only they would be obedient to his word: whereupon linking, as was so often his custom, the higher to the lower, and setting forth that higher in the forms of the lower, he bade them exchange their present for a loftier calling; he still contemplating that under the same aspect, as a fishing, though now of men, which at his bidding, and under his direction, they should no less successfully accomplish.

But when we compare John 1:40–42, would it not appear as though of these four, Andrew and Peter at least, and perhaps John himself (v. 35), had been already called? No doubt they had been then, on the banks of Jordan, brought into a transient fellowship with their future Lord; but, as would appear, after that meeting with him mentioned by St. John, had returned to their ordinary occupations, and only at this later period attached themselves finally and fully to him, following him withersoever he went; this miracle most likely being, as indeed seems intimated (v. 8), that which stirred the very depths of their hearts, which gave them such new insights into the glory of Christ's person, as prepared them to yield themselves without reserve unto him. Consistently with this view, the whole transaction bears the stamp of being between those who have not met now for the first time. So far from their betraying no previous familiarity, as some have said, Peter calls Jesus *"Master,"* and his saying *"Nevertheless at thy word I will let down the net,"* implies a previous acquaintance with the Lord, from which he had already received impressions of his power and of the weight of his words. Moreover, that there should thus have been the *two* callings seems quite in the manner of a divine teacher; who would hasten nothing, who was content to leave spiritual processes to advance as do the natural; who could bide his time, and did not expect the full corn in the ear the day after he had sown the seed in the ground. On that former occasion the Lord cast his word in the hearts of Andrew and Peter, and then left it to take root downward and spring upward: and not in vain, for he now returned and found it ready to bear the ripe fruits of faith. Yet it is not that we need therefore presume so gradual a process *in all.* But as some statues are cast at once, others only little by little hewn and polished, according as the material, metal or stone, suits the one or the other process, so are there, to use an expression of Donne's *"fusile* apostles" like St. Paul, whom one and the same word from heaven, as a lightning flash, at once melts and molds; and others by more gradual degrees shaped and polished into the perfect image of what the Lord, the great master-sculptor, would have them to be.

But to enter something more into the miracle itself—our Lord, who had found his future apostles engaged in washing their nets, had been enabled, through Peter's ready compliance with his request, to teach the people, unhindered by the pressure of their multitudes. And having now left speaking, he bade him to put out his boat a little further into the deeper, and therefore the likelier, waters, and to let down his nets for a draught, designing himself, the meanwhile, to take the fisherman in *his* net. For he whose purpose it was by the weak things of the world to confound the strong, who meant to draw emperors to himself by fishermen, and not fishermen by emperors, lest his Church should even seem to stand in the wisdom and power of men, rather than in the wisdom and power of God—he saw in these unlearned fishermen of the Galilean lake the fittest instruments for his work. To this exhortation of his future Lord, Simon Peter replied, that during all the night, in other words, during all the period opportunest for the capture of fish, they had been laboring, and their labor had been utterly without success;

but, with the beginnings of no weak faith already working in him, adds, *"Nevertheless, at thy word I will let down the net."* For these may not be interpreted as the words of one half despairing of the issue: as though he for himself expected nothing, but to satisfy the Master, and to prove to him the fruitlessness of further efforts, would comply with his desire. On the contrary, they are spoken more in the spirit of the Psalmist, when he exclaimed, "Except the Lord build the house, they labor in vain that build it: except the Lord keep the city, the watchman waketh but in vain" (Ps. 127:1). It is as though he would say, "We have done nothing during all the night, and had quite lost hope of doing anything; yet at thy word and bidding we will readily renew our efforts, which we are sure will be no longer in vain." And his act of faith was abundantly re- warded; *"They enclosed a great multitude of fishes,"* so many indeed, that *"their net brake."*

It was not merely that Christ, by his omniscience, knew that now there were fishes in that spot; we may not thus extenuate the miracle; but rather we are to contemplate him as the Lord of nature, who by the secret, yet mighty magic of his will, was able to wield and guide even the unconscious creatures to his aims. Yet since the power that drew the fish to that spot is the same that at all times guides their periodic migrations, which wondrous as it is, we yet cannot call miraculous, there is plainly something that differences this miracle and the other of like kind (John 21:6), with that no less of the stater in the fish's mouth (Matt. 17:27), from Christ's other miracles—in that these three are not comings in of a new and hith- erto unwonted power into the region of nature; but they are coin- cidences, *divinely brought about,* between words of Christ and facts in that world of nature. An immense haul of fishes, or a piece of money in the mouth of one, are themselves no miracles; but the miracle lies in the falling in of these with a word of Christ's, which has beforehand pledged itself that it shall be so. The natural is lifted up into the miraculous by the manner in which it is timed, by the ends which it is made to serve. Christ here appears as the ideal man, the second Adam of the 8th Psalm, "Thou madest him to have dominion over the works of thy hands; thou hast put all things under his feet . . . the fowl of the air, and the fish of the sea, and whatsoever passeth through the paths of the sea" (vv. 6, 8).

When by the assistance of their partners in the other ship, whom they beckoned to their assistance, the fishes were at length hauled in, they were so many as to threaten to sink the ship. And now Peter, while taking others, is himself taken; while drawing the multitudes of fishes into *his* net, he has himself fallen into the net of Christ; one of the first to discover that to be taken in that net is to be taken for life. "Admire," exclaims Chrysostom, "the dispensation of the Lord, how he draws each by the art which is most familiar and natural to him—as the Magians by a star, so the fishermen by fish"—a thought which Donne in a sermon on this text enlarges thus: "The Holy Ghost speaks in such forms and such phrases as may most work upon them to whom he speaks. Of David, that was a shepherd before, God says, he took him to feed his people. To those Magi of the East, who were given to the study of the stars, God gave a star to be their guide to Christ at Bethlehem. To those who followed him to Capernaum for meat, Christ took occasion by that to preach to them of the spiritual food of their souls. To the Samaritan woman whom he found at the well, he preached of the water of life. To these men in our text, accustomed to a joy and gladness when they took great or great store of fish, he presents his comforts agreeably to their taste, they should be fishers still. Christ makes heaven all things to all men, that he might gain all." And Peter, astonished at the strange success of his cast, the same that he ever afterwards appears, as impetuous, yielding as freely to the impulse of the moment, with the beginnings of the same quick spiritual eye which made him the first to see the highest glory of the Savior, even his eternal Sonship, and to confess it, could no longer, in the deep feeling of his own unholiness, endure the nearness of an altogether Holy One, but *"fell down at Jesus' knees, crying, Depart from me, for I am a sinful man, O Lord."* At moments like these all that is merely conventional is swept away, and the deep heart of man speaks out, and the deepest things that are in that heart come forth to the light. And this is the deepest thing that is in man's heart under the law; this sense of the gulf of separation that is between him and God. "Let not God speak with us lest we die"; this was the voice of the people to Moses, as "they removed and stood afar off" (Ex. 20:18, 19). "We shall surely die, because we have seen God" (Judg. 13:22; cf. 6:22, 23; Dan. 10:17; Is. 6:5). Below this is the utterly profane state, in which there is no contrast, no contradiction felt between the holy and the unholy, between God and man. Above it is the state, which is that of grace, in which all the contradiction is felt, the deep gulf perceived which divides between sinful man and a holy God; yet is it felt at the same time that this gulf is bridged over, that it is possible for the two to meet, that in One who is sharer with both they have already been brought together. Into this higher state Christ now invites Peter, not taking him at his word and leaving him as he desired, but bidding him to lay aside his fears, and to accept a function and a work from him. For though his was indeed the presence of God, yet of him with his glory veiled and hidden, so that even sinful men might endure to be near it, and dwelling in that nearness might step by step be prepared for the ultimate seeing of God as he is; which, though it must be death to the mere sinner, yet would be the highest blessedness to him who had been trained and fitted for it by beholding for a while his mitigated spendor in the person of the Incarnate Word, even such a beholding as would more and more have wrought holiness and purity in him.

And hereupon follow the reassuring words, *"Fear not, from henceforth thou shalt catch men,"* from the lips of Jesus; words which were properly the inauguration of Peter and his fellows to the great work whereunto they were about to be sent. For we see continually for them that are called to some signal work in the kingdom of God, an inauguration, not formal, not always the same in its outward accidents; but always the same in this, that in it the earthly grows pale before the heavenly; the man recognizes his nothingness, his vileness, and recognizes it in a way which he never had done before, that so the work in him may be altogether God's and not man's, may not henceforward be spoiled by self intermingling with it. The true parallels to this passage, contemplated as such an inauguration as this, are Exodus 4:10–17; Isaiah 6; Jer. 1:4–10; Judges 6:11–23; Acts 9:3–9; and more remotely Daniel 10, which, with many points of resemblance, is yet unlike in this, that it is not the first sending forth of one to his work in the kingdom of God.

"Henceforth thou shalt catch men," or, in the words of the other Evangelists, "I will make you fishers of men." Christ clothes the promise in forms of that art which was familiar to Peter; the fisherman is to *catch* men, as David, the shepherd, taken from among the sheep-folds, was to *feed* them (Ps. 78:71, 72). There is in these words a double magnifying of Peter's future function as compared with his past; that it is *men* and not poor fishes henceforth which he shall take, and that he shall take them *for life,* and not as he had taken his meaner prey, only for death. For no less than this is involved in the original word by which the catching is expressed, a word which thus supplies with a singular happiness an answer to the malignant sneer of Julian, who observed that the Galilean did indeed

most aptly term his apostles "fishers"; for as the fisherman draws out the fish from waters where they were free and happy, to an element in which they cannot breathe, but must presently perish, so did these. But the expression used singularly excludes such a turn—"Thou shalt take men, and take them *for life,* not for death; those that were wandering at random through the salt-sea waves of the world, among its deep unquiet waters, full of whirlpools and fears, the smaller of them falling a prey to the greater, and all with the weary sense as of a vast prison, thou shalt gather into one, embracing them all within the same folds and recesses of the Gospel net; which if they break not through, not leap over, they shall at length be drawn up to shore, out of the dark gloomy waters into the bright clear light of day, and shall there and then be collected into vessels for eternal life" (Matt. 13:48).

Another point of resemblance is the ignorance on the part of the fisher of what fish he will gather in, whether many or few, or whether any at all will reward his labors. He casts in his net, knowing that the success must be from above; and it is not otherwise with the preaching of the Word. There are yet other peculiar fitnesses in the image drawn from the occupation of the fisher, rather, for instance, than in one borrowed from the nearly allied pursuits of the hunter. The fisher does more often take his prey alive; he draws it *to* him, does not drive it *from* him; and not merely to himself, but draws all which he has taken to one another, even as the Church brings together the divided hearts, the fathers to the children, gathers into one fellowship the scattered tribes of men. Again, the work of the fisher is rather a work of art and skill than of force and violence; so that Tertullian finds in this miracle a commencing fulfillment of Jer. 16:16, "Behold, I will send for many fishers, saith the Lord, and they shall fish them"; though indeed it may very well be a question whether in those words there lies not rather a threat than a promise. It is, however, quite in the spirit of the New Covenant to take a threatening of the Old, and fulfill it, yet so to transform it in the fulfilling that it shall be no longer what it was, a curse, but a blessing. Thus, to fall into the hands of the Lord, would have been in the old time a woe, but it may now be the chiefest blessing; and in this manner his application of the words may at any rate be justified. There is now a captivity which is blessed, blessed because it is deliverance from a freedom which is full of woe—a "being made free from sin and becoming servants to God," that so we may have our "fruit unto holiness, and the end everlasting life" (Rom. 6:20). But the present passage might be brought with a more unquestionable propriety into relation with Ezekiel 47:9, 10, and the prophecy there of the fishers that should stand on Engedi, and the great multitude of fish that should be in the healed waters.

And as the ministers of Christ are fishers, so the faithful are aptly likened to fish. The comparison, which was so great a favorite in the early Church, probably did not derive its first impulse from these words of our Lord; but rather from the fact that it was the waters of baptism through which men were brought into life, and that only by abiding in that element into which they were introduced they continued to draw a true life: so that the two images cannot stand at the same time, excluding as they mutually do one another; for in one the blessedness is to remain in the waters, as in the vivifying element, in the other to be drawn forth from them into the purer and clearer air. In one Christ is the Fish, in the other the chief Fisherman—addressed therefore in that grand Orphic hymn attributed to the Alexandrian Clement, in words which may thus be translated—

> Fisher of mortal men,
> All that the saved are,
> Ever the holy fish,
> From the fierce ocean
> Of the world's sea of sin
> By thy sweet life those enticest away.

And bringing their ships to shore, *"they forsook all, and followed him."* But what was that *"all"* which *"they forsook"* ask some, that they should afterwards seem to make so much of it, saying, "Behold we have forsaken all, and followed thee: what shall we have therefore?" (Matt. 19:27). It was their *all,* and therefore, though it might have been but a few poor boats and nets, it was much. And the forsaking consists not in the more or less that is forsaken, but in the spirit in which it is left. A man may be holden by love to a miserable hovel with as fast bands as to a sumptuous palace; for it is the worldy affection which holds him, and not the world: just as we gather from the warnings scattered through the ascetic books of the middle ages how they who had renounced, it may be, great possessions in the world, would now, if they did not earnestly watch against it, come to cling to their hood, their breviary, the scanty furniture of their bare cell, with the same feelings of poverty as they once exercised in ampler matters, so witnessing that they had no more succeeded in curing themselves of worldly affections, than a man would succeed in curing himself of covetousness by putting out the eye which in times past had been often the inlet of desire. These apostles might have left little, when they left their possessions, but they left much, when they left their desires.

A word or two here in conclusion may find place generally upon the symbolic acts of our Lord, whereof according to his own distinct assurance, we here have one. The desire of the human mind to set forth the truth which it deeply feels in acts rather than by words, or it may be by blended act and word, has a very deep root in our nature, which always strives after the concrete; and it manifests itself not merely in the institution of *fixed* symbolic acts, as the anointing of kings, or the casting earth into a grave; but more strikingly yet, in acts that are the free and momentary products of some creative mind, which has more to utter than it can find words to be the bearers of, or would utter it in a more expressive manner than these permit. This manner of teaching, however frequent in Scripture (1 Kgs. 2:30, 31; 22:11; Acts 13:51), yet belongs not to Scripture only, nor is it even peculiar to the East, although there it is most frequent, and most entirely at home; but everywhere, as men have felt strongly and deeply, and desired to make others feel so, they have had recourse to such a language as this, which has many advantages for bringing home its truth. When Hannibal, for instance, as he was advancing into Italy, set some of his captives to fight, placing before them freedom and presents and rich armor for the victor, and at least escape from present extreme misery for the slain; who does not feel that he realized to his army the blessings which not victory alone, but even the other alternative of death, would give them, in affording release from the intolerable evils of their present state, as words could never have done? Or that Diogenes expressed his contempt for humanity by his noonday lantern more effectually than by all his scornful words he could ever have expressed it? As the Cynic, so too the Hebrew prophets, though in quite another temper, would oftentimes weave their own persons into such parabolic acts, would use themselves as part of their own symbol, and that because nothing short of this would satisfy the earnestness with which the truth of God, whereof they desired to make others partakers, possessed their own souls (Ezek.

12:1–12; Acts 21:11). And thus, too, not this only, but many actions of our Lord's were such an embodied teaching, the incorporation of a doctrine in an act, having a deeper significance than lay upon the surface, and being only entirely intelligible when we recognize in them a significance such as this (Matt. 21:18, 19; John 21:19). Christ being the Word, his deeds who is the Word, are themselves also words for us.

4.

The Stilling of the Tempest

Matthew 8:23–27; Mark 4:35–41; Luke 8:22–25

The three Evangelists who relate this history agree in placing it immediately before the healing of the possessed in the country of the Gadarenes. It was evening, the evening, probably, of that day on which the Lord had spoken all those parables recorded in Matthew 13 (cf. Mark 4:35), when, dismissing the multitude, he would fain pass over to the other side of the lake, and so, for a little while, withdraw from the tumult and the press. With this intention, he was received by the disciples "even as he was in the ship." But before the transit was accomplished, a sudden and violent squall, such as these small inland seas, surrounded with mountain gorges, are notoriously exposed to, descended on the bosom of the lake: and the ship which bore the Savior of the world appeared to be in imminent peril, as, humanly speaking, no doubt it was; for these men, exercised to the sea many of them from their youth, and familiar with all the changes of that lake, would not have been terrified by the mere shadow of danger. But though the danger was so real, and was ever growing more urgent, until "the waves beat into the ship, so that now it was full," their Master, weary, it may be, after the toils of the day, continued sleeping still: he was, with details which St. Mark alone has preserved, "in the hinder part of the ship, asleep upon a pillow"; and was not roused by all the tumult and confusion incident on such a moment. We behold him here as exactly the reverse of Jonah; the prophet asleep in the midst of a like danger through a dead conscience, the Savior out of a pure conscience—Jonah by his presence making the danger, Jesus yielding the pledge and the assurance of deliverance from the danger.

But the disciples understood not this. It was long, probably, before they dared to arouse him; yet at length they did so, and then with exclamations of haste and terror; as is evidenced by the double *"Master, Master,"* of St. Luke. In St. Mark, they awaken him with words almost of rebuke, as if he was unmindful of their safety, *"Master, carest thou not that we perish?"* though no doubt they meant in this *"we"* to include their beloved Lord as well as themselves. Then the Lord arose; from St. Mark it would appear, first blaming their want of faith, and then pacifying the storm; though the other Evangelists make the blame not to have gone before, but to have followed after, the allaying of the winds and waves. Probably it did both: he spoke first to them, quieting with a word the tempest in their bosoms; and then, having allayed the tumult of the outward elements, he again turned to them, and more leisurely blamed them for their lack of faith in him.

Yet it is to be observed that he does not, in St. Matthew, call them *"without* faith," but *"of little faith."* They were not wholly *without* faith; for, believing in the midst of their unbelief, they turned to Christ in their need. They had faith, but it was not quick and lively, it was not at hand as it should have been; *"Where is your faith?"* as in St. Luke he asks; so that it was like a weapon which a soldier has, but yet has mislaid, and cannot lay hold of in the moment of extremest need. The imperfection of their faith consisted not in this, that they appealed unto their Lord for help; for herein was faith, but in the *excess* of their terror, in their counting it possible that the ship which bore their Lord, could ever truly perish.

But especially noticeable are the words with which that Lord, as all three Evangelists relate, quieted the storm. He *"rebuked the winds and the sea";* in the spirit of which words St. Mark relates, further, a more direct address to the furious elements, *"Peace, be still,"* which it would be absurd to suppose a mere oratorical personification. Rather, as Maldonatus truly remarks, there is in these words a distinct recognition of Satan and the powers of evil as the authors of the disharmony in the outward world, a tracing of all these disorders up to their source in a person, a carrying of them back to him as to their ultimate ground. The Lord elsewhere uses the same form of address to a fever, for it is said that he *rebuked* it (Luke 4:39), where the same remarks will hold good.

And in the hour of her wildest uproar, nature yielded obedience unto him, who was come to reassert man's dominion over her, and over the evil powers, which held her in thrall, and had made her, who should have always been his willing handmaid, to be oftentimes the instrument of his harm and ruin. And his *word* was sufficient for this. He needed not, as Moses, to stretch a rod over the deep; he needed not, as his servant had needed, an instrument of power, foreign to himself, with which to do his mighty work; but only at his word *"the wind ceased, and there was a great calm."* And then is added the moral effect which this great wonder exercised on the minds of those that were in the ship with him—it may be, also on those that were in the *"other little ships,"* which St. Mark has noted as sailing in their company: *"The men marveled, saying, What manner of man is this, that even the winds and the sea obey him?"* an exclamation which only can find its answer in another exclamation of the Psalmist, "O Lord God of Hosts, who is like unto thee? Thou rulest the raging of the sea: when the waves thereof arise, thou stillest them" (Ps. 79:8, 9). We see then here one of the moral purposes to which, in the providence of God, who ordered all things for the glory of his Son, this miracle should serve. It should lead his disciples into thoughts ever higher and more awful of that Lord whom they followed, and should more and more bring them to feel that in nearness to him was all safety and deliverance from every danger. The danger which exercised, should strengthen, their faith—who indeed had need of a mighty faith, since God, in St. Chrysostom's words, had chosen them to be the athletes of the universe.

An old expositor has somewhat boldly said, "This power of the Lord's word, this admiration of them that were with him in the ship, holy David had predicted in the Psalm, saying, 'They that go down to the sea in ships, that do business in great waters, these see the works of the Lord, and his wonders in the deep,'" and so forward (Ps. 108:23–30). And as in the spiritual world, the inward is ever shadowed forth by the outward, we may regard this outward fact but as the clothing of an inward truth which in the language of this miracle the Lord declares unto men. He would set himself forth as the true Prince of Peace (Is. 11:6–9), as the speaker of peace to the troubled and storm-stirred heart of man, whether the storms that stir it be its own inner passions, or life's outward clamities and temptations. Thus Augustine, making application of all parts of the miracle: "We are sailing in this life as through a sea, and the wind rises, and storms of temptations are not wanting. Whence is this, save because Jesus is sleeping in thee? If he were not sleeping in thee, thou wouldest have calm within. But what means this, that

Jesus is sleeping in thee, save that thy faith, which is from Jesus, is slumbering in thine heart? What shalt thou do to be delivered? Arouse him and say, Master, we perish. He will awaken; that is, thy faith will return to thee, and abide with thee always. When Christ is awakened, though the tempest beat into, yet it will not fill, thy ship; thy faith will now command the winds and the waves, and the danger will be over."

Nor shall we in any wise do wrong to the literal truth of this or any other of Christ's miracles, by recognizing the character at once symbolic and prophetic, which, no doubt, many of them also bear, and this among the number. As the kernel of the old humanity, Noah and his family, was once contained in the Ark which was tossed upon the waves of the deluge, so the kernel of the new humanity, of the new creation, Christ and his apostles, in this little ship. And the Church of Christ has evermore resembled this tempested bark, in that the waves of the world rage horribly around it, in that it has evermore been delivered out of the perils which seemed ready to overwhelm it, and this because Christ is in it; who being roused by the cry of his servants, rebukes these winds and these waters, before they utterly overwhelm this ship. In the Old Testament Ezekiel gives us a magnificent picture of a worldly kingdom under the image of a stately and gorgeous galley, which he describes with every circumstance that could heighten its glory and its beauty (27:4–9); but that ship with all its outward bravery and magnificence utterly perishes: "thy rowers have brought thee into great waters; the east wind hath broken thee in the midst of the seas," and they that have hoped in it and embarked in it their treasures, wail over its wreck with a bitter wailing (vv. 26–36); this kingdom of God meanwhile, which seems by comparison but as the slight and unhonored fishing boat that every wave would engulf, rides triumphantly over all and comes safely into haven at the last.

5.

The Demoniacs in the Country of the Gadarenes

Matthew 8:28–34; Mark 5:1–20; Luke 8:26–39

Before entering upon this, the most important, and, in many respects, the most difficult of the demoniac cures in the New Testament, it is impossible to avoid making generally a few prefatory remarks on the subject of the demoniacs of Scripture. It is a subject of which the difficulty is very much enhanced by the fact that, as in the case of some of the spiritual gifts, the gift, for instance, of tongues, the thing itself, if it still survives among us, yet does so no longer under the same name, nor yet with the same frequency and intensity as of old. We are obliged to put together, as best we can, the separate notices which have come down to us, and from them seek to frame some scheme, which will answer the demands of the different phenomena; we have not, at least with certainty, the thing itself to examine and to question, before our eyes.

It is, of course, easy enough to cut short the whole inquiry, and to leave no question at all, by saying these demoniacs were persons whom we should call insane—epileptic, maniac, melancholic. This has been often said, and the oftener perhaps, because there is a partial truth in the view that these possessions were bodily maladies. There was no doubt a substratum of disease, which in many cases helped to lay open to the deeper evil, and upon which it was superinduced: and in agreement with this view, we may observe that cases of possession are at once classed with those of various sicknesses, and at the same time distinguished from them, by the Evangelists; who thus at once mark the relation and the difference

99

(Matt. 4:24; 8:16; Mark 1:33). But the scheme which confounds these cases with those of disease, does not, as, I think, every reverent handler of God's word must own, exhaust the matter; it cannot be taken as a satisfying solution; and this for more reasons than one.

And first, our Lord himself uses language which is not reconcilable with such a theory; he everywhere speaks of demoniacs not as persons merely of disordered intellects, but as subjects and thralls of an alien spiritual might; he addresses the evil spirit as distinct from the man; "Hold thy peace, and come out of him" (Mark 1:25). And the poor reply, that he fell into and humored the notions of the afflicted in order to facilitate their cure, is cut off by the fact that in his most confidential discourses with his disciples he uses exactly the same language (Matt. 10:8; and especially 17:21, "This kind goeth not out but by prayer and fasting"). The allegiance we owe to Christ as the King of truth, who came, not to fall in with men's errors, but to deliver men out of their errors, compels us to believe that he would never have used language which would have upheld and confirmed so great an error in the minds of men as the supposition of Satanic influences, which did not in truth exist. For this error, if it was an error, was so little an innocuous one, that might have been safely left to drop naturally away, was, on the contrary, one which reached so far in its consequences, entwined its roots so deeply among the very ground-truths of religion, that it could never have been suffered to remain at the hazard of all the misgrowths which it must needs have occasioned.

And then, moreover, even had not the matters at stake been so important, our idea of Christ's absolute veracity, apart from the value of the truth which he communicated, our idea of him as the *Verax*, no less than the *Verus* and the *Veritas,* will not permit us to suppose that he used the language which he did, well knowing that there was no answerable thing, on which the language was founded. And in this there is no making a conscience about gnats, nor denying that figurative nature of all our words, out of which it results that much which is not literally true, is yet most true, inasmuch as it conveys the truest impression—no requiring men to look into the derivations of their words before they venture to use them. It had been one thing for the Lord to have fallen in with the popular language, and to have spoken of persons under various natural afflictions as "possessed," supposing he had found such a language current, but now no longer, however once it might have been, vividly linked to the idea of possession by spirits of evil. This had been no more than our speaking of certain forms of madness as *lunacy;* not thereby implying that we believe the moon to have, or to have had, any influence upon them; but finding the word, we use it: and this the more readily, since its original derivation is so entirely lost sight of in our common conversation, its first impress so completely worn off, that we do not thereby even seem to countenance an error. But suppose with this same disbelief in lunar influences, we were to begin to speak not merely of lunatics, but of persons on whom the moon was working, to describe the cure of such, as the moon's ceasing to afflict them; or if a physician were solemnly to address the moon, bidding it to abstain from harming his patient, there would be here a passing over into quite a different region; we should be here directly countenancing superstition and delusion; and plainly speaking untruly with our lips; there would be that gulf between our thoughts and our words, in which the essence of a lie consists. Now Christ does everywhere speak in such a language as this. Take, for instance, his words, Luke 11:17–26, and assume him as knowing, all the while he was thus speaking, that the whole Jewish theory of demoniac possessions was utterly baseless, that there was no power of the kind which Satan exercised over the spirits of men, and what should we have here for a king of truth

And then, besides this, the phenomena themselves are such as no theory of the kind avails to explain, and they thus bid us to seek for some more satisfying solution. For that madness was not the constituent element in the demoniac state is clear, since not only we have not the slightest ground for supposing that the Jews would have considered all maniacs, epileptic or melancholic persons, to be under the power of evil spirits; but we have distinct evidence that the same malady they did sometimes attribute to an evil spirit, and sometimes not, thus showing that the malady and possession were not identical in their eyes, and that the assumption of the latter was not a mere popular explanation for the presence of the former. Thus, on two occasions they bring to the Lord those that were dumb (Matt. 9:32; 12:22; on the second occasion it is one dumb and blind); and in each of these cases the dumbness is traced up to an evil spirit. Yet it is plain that they did not consider all dumbness as having this root; for in the history given by St. Mark (7:32), of one deaf and dumb, that was the subject of Christ's healing power, it is the evident intention of the Evangelist to describe one laboring only under a natural defect; there is not the slightest appearance there of a desire to trace the source of his malady to any demoniacal influence. There were no doubt signs which were sufficiently distinct by which the different sources of the same defect were capable of being known: in the case of the demoniac there probably was not the outward hindrance, not the still-fastened string of the tongue; it was not the outward organ, but the inward power of using the organ, which was at fault. This, with an entire apathy, a total disregard of all which was going on about him, may have sufficiently indicated that the cause of his malady lay deeper than on the surface. But, whatever may have been the signs which enabled those about the sufferers to make these distinctions, the fact itself that they did so discriminate between cases of the very same malady, proves decisively that there were not certain diseases which, without more ado, they attributed directly to Satan; but that they did designate by this name of possession, a condition which, while it was very often a condition of disease, was also always a condition of much more than disease.

But what *was* the condition which our Lord and his apostles signalized by this name? In what did it differ, upon the one side, from madness—upon the other, from wickedness? It will be impossible to make any advance toward the answer, without saying something, by way of preface, on the scriptural doctrine concerning the kingdom of evil, and its personal head, and the relation in which he stands to the moral evil of our world. Alike excluding, on the one side, the Manichaean doctrine, which would make evil eternal as good, and so itself a god—and the pantheistic, which would deny any true reality to evil at all, or that it is anything else than good at a lower stage, the unripe and therefore still bitter fruit—the Scripture teaches the absolute subordination of evil to good, and its subsequence of order, in the fact that the evil roots itself in a creature, and one created originally pure, but the good in the Creator. Yet, at the same time, it teaches that the opposition of this evil to the will of God is most real, is that of a will which does truly set itself against his will; that the world is not a chessboard on which God is in fact playing both sides of the game, however some of the pieces may be black and some white; but that the whole end of his government of the world is the subduing of this evil; that is, not abolishing it by main force, which were no true victory, but overcoming it by righteousness and truth. And from this one central will, alienated from the will of God, the Scripture derives all the evil in the universe; all gathers up in a person, in the devil, who has most truly a kingdom, as God has—a kingdom with its subordinate ministers—"the devil and his angels." This world of ours stand not isolated, not rounded and complete in itself, but in living relation with two worlds—a higher, from which all good in it proceeds—and this lower, from which all evil. Thus man's sin is continually traced up to Satan; Peter says to Ananias, "Why hath Satan filled thine heart to lie to the Holy Ghost?" (Acts 5:3); and St. John, of Judas Iscariot, "The devil having now put into his heart, to betray him," (John 13:3; cf. John 8:44; 1 John 3:8), the Scripture not thereby denying that the evil of men is truly *their* evil, but affirming with this, that it has its ground in a yet higher evil. It is their evil, since it is an act of their will which alone gives it leave to enter. But it is also true that it is the existance of another world of evil beyond and without our world, which makes all remissness here of such fatal and disastrous issue.

This being so, the question which presents itself is this, namely, what peculiar form of the working of these dark powers of hell Scripture designates by this title of demoniacal possessions. We have not here merely great sufferers; we have not in the demoniacs as in the case of the victims of ghastly and horrible diseases, *only* specimens of the mighty woe which Satan has brought in upon our race through that sin common unto all; although we have such most truly. Nor yet, on the other hand, have we merely signal sinners, eminent servants of the devil, who with heart and will and waking consciousness are doing his work; for this, whatever their antecedent guilt may have been, and often, I should imagine, it has been great, the demoniacs evidently are not. But what strikes us most in them is the strange blending of the physical and the spiritual; the two regions are not kept separate; there is a breaking up of all the harmony of the lower, no less than of the higher life; the same disorder and disorganization manifests itself in both. This too is worthy of notice, that the demoniac does not, like the wicked, stand only in near relation to the kingdom of Satan as a whole; but his state is even as if out of the dark hosts of the abyss, one, or, it may be, more had singled him out for their immediate prey; as when a lion or a leopard, not hunting merely a herd of flying antelopes, has fastened upon and is drinking out the life-blood of some one.

But how had this come to pass? How had men sunken into this woeful state? Been suffered to be entangled so far in the bands of the devil, or so fallen under the dominion of one or more of his angels? Now we should err, no doubt, and get altogether upon a wrong track, if we were to conceive of the demoniacs as the worst of men, and their possession as the plague and penalty of a wickedness in which they had eminently surpassed their fellows. Rather we must judge the demoniac one of the unhappiest, but not of necessity one of the most guilty, of our kind. On the contrary, the most eminent representatives and organs of Satan, false prophets and antichrists, are never spoken of in this language. We all feel that Judas' possession, when Satan entered into him (John 13:27), was specifically different from that of one of the unhappy persons whom Christ came to deliver. Or, to borrow an illustration from the world of fiction, we should not speak of Iago as δαιμονιζόμενος, however all the deadliest malignity of hell was concentrated in him; much more nearly we should find analogies to this state in some moments of Hamlet's life. The Greek poet will supply us with a yet apter example; it is the noble Orestes, whom the "dogs of hell" torture into madness; the obdurate Clytemnestra is troubled on account of *her* deed with no such spectres of the unseen world. Thus, too, in many cases of actual life, the deep anguish of the sinner in the contemplation of his sin may have helped on this overthrow of his spritual life—anguish which a more hardened sinner would have escaped, but escaped it only by being a worse and more truly devilish man; so that in these cases of possession we are not to see the deliberate giving in to the satanic will, of an utterly lost soul, but the still recoverable wreck of that which oftentimes was once a noble spirit.

And, consistently with this, we find in the demoniac the sense of a misery in which he does not acquiesce, the deep feeling of inward discord, of the true life utterly shattered, of an alien power which has mastered him wholly, and now is cruelly lording over him, and ever drawing further away from him in whom only any created intelligence can find rest and peace. His state is in the truest sense of the word "a possession:" another is ruling in the high places of his soul, and has cast down the rightful lord from his seat; and he knows this; and out of his consciousness of it there goes forth from him a cry for redemption, so soon as ever a glimpse of hope is afforded, an unlooked-for Redeemer draws near. This sense of misery, this yearning after deliverance, was, in fact, what made these demoniacs objects and subjects for Christ's healing power. Without it they would have been as little objects of this as the devils, who are complete and circular in evil, in whom there is nothing for the divine grace to take hold of—so that even in their case, as in every other, faith was the condition of healing. There was in them a spark of higher life, not yet trodden out, which, indeed, so long as they were alone, was but light enough to reveal to them their darkness; and which none but the very Lord of life could have fanned again into a flame. But He, who came to dissolve the works of the devil, as he showed himself lord over purely physical evil, a healer of the diseases of men, and lord also of purely spiritual evil, a deliverer of men from their sins—he showed himself also lord in these complex cases partaking of the nature of either, ruler also in this border land, where these two regions of evil join, and run so strangely and unaccountably one into the other.

Yet while thus "men possessed with devils" is not at all an equivalent expression for eminently wicked men, born of the serpent seed, of the devil's regeneration, and so become children of the devil, seeing that in such there is not cry for redemption, no desire after deliverance, yet should it, I think, always on the other hand be held fast, that lavish sin, and especially indulgence in sensual lusts, superinducing as it would often a weakness in the nervous system, which is the especial band between body and soul, may have laid open these unhappy ones to the fearful incursions of the powers of darkness. They were greatly guilty, though not the guiltiest of men. And this they felt, that by their own act they had given themselves over to this tyranny of the devil, a tyranny from which, as far as their horizon reached, they could see no hope of deliverance—that it was to themselves they owed that this hellish might was no longer *without* them, no longer something against which they could shut the door, which if it was resisted would flee from them; but a power which now they could not resist and which would not flee.

The phenomena which the demoniacs of Scripture, especially those now before us, exhibit, entirely justify this view of the real presence of another will upon the will of the sufferer—not merely influences which had little by little molded and modified his will and brought it into subjection, but a power which he, even at the very moment that it is using him, feels to be the contradiction of his truest being; which yet has forced itself upon him, and from which now he cannot defend himself—but is compelled to speak and act merely as the organ of that devilish might which possesses him, however presently again his personal consciousness may reassert itself for a moment. This, that they have not become indissolubly one, that the serpent and the man have not, as in Dante's awful image, grown together, "each melted into other," but that they still are twain; this is, indeed, the redemptive fact which survives amid the ruin of their moral and spiritual being. Yet does it, for the actual time being, give the appearance, though a deceptive one, of a far entirer wreck of their life, than manifests itself in wicked men, who have given themselves over wholly, without reserve and without reluctancy, to do evil with both hands earnestly. In these last, by the very completeness of their loss, there is a unity, a harmony, if one may dare to use the word; there are no merest incoherencies, no violent contradictions at every instant emerging in their words and in their conduct; they are at one with themselves. But all these incoherencies and self-contradictions we trace in the demoniac; he rushes to the feet of Jesus, as coming to him for aid, and then presently he deprecates his interference. There is not in him one vast contradiction to the true end of his being, consistently worked out, but a thousand lesser contradictions, in the midst of which the true idea of his life, not wholly obscured, does yet sometimes by fitful glimpses reappear. There is on his part an occasional reluctancy against this usurpation by another of his spirit's throne—a protest, which for the present, indeed, but augments the confusion of his life—yet which contains in it the pledge of a possible freedom and order, which may be given back to that life at a future time.

There is one objection to this view of the matter which may still be urged, namely, that if this possession is anything more than insanity in its different forms, how comes it to pass that there are no demoniacs now? That they have wholly disappeared from the world? But the assumption that there are none, is itself one demanding to be proved. It is not hard to perceive why there should be few by comparison; why this form of spiritual evil should have lost greatly both in frequency and malignity, and from both these causes be far more difficult to recognize. For in the first place, if there was anything that marked the period of the Lord's coming in the flesh, and that immediately succeeding, it was the wreck and confusion of men's spiritual life which was then, the sense of utter disharmony, the hopelessness, the despair which must have best every man that thought at all—this, with the tendency to rush with a frantic eagerness into sensual enjoyments as the refuge from despairing thoughts. That whole period was the hour and power of darkness—of a darkness, which then immediately before the dawn of a new day, was the thickest. The world was again a chaos, and the creative words, "Let there be light," though just about to be spoken, as yet were not uttered. It was exactly the crisis for such soul-maladies as these, in which the spiritual and bodily should be thus strangely interlinked, and it is nothing wonderful that they should have abounded at that time; for the predominance of certain spiritual maladies at certain epochs of the world's history which were specially fitted for their generation, with their gradual decline and disappearance in others less congenial to them, is a fact itself admitting no manner of question.

Moreover we cannot doubt that the might of hell has been greatly broken by the coming of the Son of God in the flesh; and with this the grosser manifestations of its power; "I beheld Satan as lightning fall from heaven" (Luke 10:18). We believe that his rage and violence are continually hemmed in and hindered by the preaching of the Word and ministration of the Sacraments. It were another thing even now in a heathen land, especially in one where Satan was not left in undisturbed possession, but wherein the great crisis of the conflict between light and darkness was finding place through the first incoming there of the Gospel of Christ. There we should expect very much to find, whether or not in such great intensity, yet manifestations analogous to these. There is a very interesting communication from Rhenius, the Lutheran missionary, in which he gives this as exactly his experience in India—that among the native Christians, even though many of them walk not as children of light, yet there is not this falling under Satanic influence in soul and body, which he traced frequently in the heathen around him; and he shows by a remarkable example, and one in which he is himself the witness throughout, how the assault in the name of Jesus on the kingdom of darkness, as it brings out all forms of devilish opposition into fiercest activity, so calls out the endeavour to counterwork the truth through men who have been made direct organs of the devilish will.

It may well be a question moreover, if an apostle, or one with apostolic discernment of spirits, were to enter now into one of our madhouses, how many of the sufferers there he might not recognize as thus having more immediately fallen under the tyranny of the powers of darkness. Certainly in many cases of mania and epilepsy there is a condition very analogous to that of the demoniacs, though the sufferer, and commonly the physician, apprehend it differently. Yet this apprehension of theirs is not of the essence of the matter; this will but be in general the reflection of the popular notion of the age about it. Thus no doubt the Jews multiplied quite unnecessarily the numbers of the possessed, counting as they did, among the cases of possession, many lower forms of disharmony in the inner life; so too I should believe it was in the early Church, and many then who had not fallen under this immediate tyranny of the devil, may yet have traced up their sufferings directly to him. Now, however, the popular feeling which the unhappy man brings with him into his forlorn state sets the opposite way, and in agreement with this is the language which he uses. But the case which is now before us is one in which no question can exist, since the great Physician himself treats and declares it as one of a veritable possession.

There is something very striking in the connection in which this miracle stands with that other which went immediately before. Our Lord has just shown himself as the pacifier of the tumults and the discords in the outward world; he has spoken peace to the winds and to the waves, and hushed with a word the elemental war. But there is something wilder and more fearful than the winds and the waves in their fiercest moods—even the spirit of man, when it has broken loose from all restraints and yielded itself to be the organ not of God, but of him who brings uttermost confusion wheresoever his dominion reaches. And Christ will do here a yet mightier work than that which he accomplished there; he will prove himself here also the Prince of Peace, the bringer back of the lost harmony; he will speak, and at his potent word this madder strife, this blinder rage which is in the heart of man, will allay itself; and here also there shall be a great calm.

In seeking to combine the accounts given us of this memorable healing, this difficulty meets us at the outset, namely, that St. Matthew speaks of two demoniacs, while St. Mark and St. Luke speak only of one. Many explanations of this have been offered, as that one was a more notable person in the country than the other; or that one was so much more savage as to cause the other, by most persons, hardly to be taken note of; which is that of Maldonatus. Whatever may have been the cause, it is, I think, evident, that one did fall into the background; and, therefore, following the more detailed account of St. Mark and St. Luke, I shall speak in the main as they do, of the one demoniac who met the Lord as he came out of the ship—not in the least as though the other was not present: but the accounts of St. Mark and St. Luke, where there appears but one, being those which, as the fullest, I desire mainly to follow, it would be full of continual embarrassment to use any other language.

The picture of the miserable man is fearful; and in drawing it, each Evangelist has some touches which are peculiarly his own; but St. Mark's is the most eminently graphic of all, adding as it does many strokes which wonderfully heighten the terribleness of the man's condition, and so also magnify the glory of his cure. The man had his dwelling among the tombs, that is, in unclean places, unclean because of the dead men's bones which were there. To those who did not on this account shun them, these tombs of the Jews would afford ample shelter, being either natural caves, or recesses hewn by art out of the rock, often so large as to be supported with columns, and with cells upon their sides for the reception of the dead. Being, too, without the cities, and oftentimes in remote and solitary places, they would attract those who sought to flee from all fellowship of their kind. This man was possessed of that extraordinary muscular strength which maniacs so often put forth (compare Acts 19:16), and thus all efforts to bind and restrain him (and such had been often repeated), had proved ineffectual (Mark 5:6). St. Matthew alone relates how he had made the way impassible for travelers; St. Luke alone that he was without clothing, although this is involved in St. Mark's account, who tells us that after he was healed he was found *"clothed, and in his right mind,"* sitting at Jesus' feet. Yet with all this, he was not so utterly lost, but that there evermore woke up in him a sense of his misery, and of the terrible bondage under which he had come, although this could express itself only in his cries, and in a blind rage against himself, out of which he wounded and cut himself with stones, recognizing no doubt his own evil will as that which had given entrance to this terrible host of Satanic influences into his inmost being.

From such a one as this did the Lord receive his first greeting on those shores which now, probably for the first time, his feet were treading. This man with his companion starting from the tombs, which were their ordinary dwellingplace, rushed down to encounter, it may have been with hostile violence, the intruders that had dared to set foot on their domain. Or it may have been that they were at once drawn to Christ by the secret instinctive feeling that he was their helper, and driven from him by the sense of the awful gulf that divided them from him, the Holy One of God. At any rate, if it *was* with purposes of violence, ere the man reached him his mind was changed; *"for he had commanded the unclean spirit to come out of the man"* (Luke 8:29), and the unclean spirit had recognized one that had a right to command, with whom force would avail nothing; and, like others on similar occasions, sought by a strong adjuration to avert his coming doom. He *"cried with a loud voice, What have I to do with thee, Jesus, thou Son of the most high God?"* that is, "What have we in common? Why interferest thou with us? Why wilt thou not let us alone? *I adjure thee by God that thou torment me not."* Herein the true devilish spirit speaks out, which counts it a torment not to be suffered to torment others, and an injury done to itself, when it is no more permitted to be injurious to others. In St. Matthew they say, *"Art thou come hither to torment us before the time?"* in which last words, *"before the time,"* is the confession upon their part of a time coming, a time, too, not to be averted, when there shall be an entire victory of the kingdom of light over that of darkness, and when all which belong unto the latter shall be shut up in the abyss (Rev. 20:10); when all power of harming shall be taken away from them, and they shall acquiesce in their inevitable doom. And all Scripture agrees with this, that the judgment of the angels is yet to come (1 Cor. 6:3); they are "reserved in everlasting chains under darkness unto the judgment of the great day" (Jude 6); and what the unclean spirits deprecate here, is the bringing in, by anticipation, of that final doom.

But this is here noticeable, that the first bidding of Christ is not immediately obeyed—that the evil spirits remonstrate, and do not at once quit their hold. No doubt the Lord could have forced them to do so had he willed, but the man might have perished in the process. (Cf. Mark 9:24.) Even that first bidding had brought on a terrible paroxysm. It was then of Christ's own will, of the Physician's, wise and tender as he was strong, to proceed step by step. And, first, he demands of him his name—some say for magnifying the greatness of the deliverance and the Deliverer, by showing, through the answer, the power and strength of the foe that was overcome. But, most probably, the question was directed to the man, and was for the purpose of calming him, by bringing him to recollection, to the consciousness of his personality, of which a man's name is the outward expression—that he was a person who had once been apart from, and was not now inextricably intertwined with those spiritual wickednesses now lording over him. The question might thus have been intended to facilitate his cure. But if so meant, either the evil spirit snatches at the answer and replies for himself, or the unhappy man, instead of recurring to his true name, that which should remind him of what he was before he fell under the dominion of these alien powers, in this reply, *"My name is Legion, for we are many"*—a reply in which truth and error are fearfully blended—declares his sense of the utter ruin of his whole moral and spiritual being. Not on one side only, but on every side, the walls of his spirit have been broken down; and he is laid open to all the incursions of evil, torn asunder in infinite ways, now under one hostile and hated power, now under another. The destruction is complete; they who rule over him are "lords many." He can find no other way to express his state than in an image drawn from the reminiscences of his former life. He had seen the thick and serried ranks of a Roman legion, that fearful instrument of oppression, that sign of terror and fear to the conquered nations, and before which the Jew more especially quailed. Even such, at once one and many, cruel and inexorable and strong, were the powers that were tyrannizing over him. When it is said of Mary Magdalene, that out of her had gone *seven* devils (Luke 8:2), something of the same truth is expressed—that her spiritual life was laid waste, not on one side only, but on many. (Cf. Matt 12:45.)

And then again, with that interchange of persons which was continually going forward, that quick shifting, so to speak, of the polarity, so that at one moment the human consciousness became the positive, at another the negative pole, the unclean spirit, or rather the man, become now his organ, speaks out anew, entreating not to be sent into the abyss (Luke 8:31), or, clothing his petition in the form of a notion which belonged to the man whom he possessed, not to be sent away out of the country (Mark 5:8). The request is in each case the same, for, according to Jewish notions, certain countries being assigned to evil as well as good spirits, and they being unable to overpass their limits, to be sent out of the assigned country, no other being open to them, would amount to the same thing as being sent into the abyss, since that alone would remain for them. This request is in fact a repetition of their prayer that they should not be tormented before the time.

Hereupon follows a circumstance that has ever proved one of the chiefest stumbling-blocks which men have found in the Evangelical history. The devils, if they must leave their more welcome habitation, the heart of man, if indeed the Stronger is come, binding the strong and spoiling his goods, taking his thralls out of his power, yet entreat, in their inextinguishable desire of harming, that they may be allowed to enter into the swine, of which a large herd—St. Mark, with his usual punctuality, notes that they were, *"about two thousand"*—were feeding on the neighboring cliffs. But to the evil all things turn to harm. God's saints and servants appear not to be heard; and the very refusal of their requests is to them a blessing (2 Cor. 12:7). The wicked, Satan (Job 1:11), and his ministers and servants, are sometimes heard, and the very granting of their petitions issues in their greater confusion and loss. So was it now: these evil spirits had their prayer heard; but only to their ruin. They are allowed to enter into the swine; but the destruction of the whole herd follows; and that which they dreaded would seem to have come upon them; no longer finding organs in which or through which to work, they are driven perforce to the abysmal deep, which they most would have shunned.

Now the first difficulty, the destruction of the swine, one of the same order as that of the withering of the fig-tree through Christ's word (Matt. 21:19), is hardly worth noticing. A man is of more value than many swine. And if this granting of the request of the evil spirits helped in any way the cure of the man, caused them to resign their hold on him more easily, mitigated the paroxysm of their going forth (cf. Mark 9:26), this would have been motive enough. Or still more probably, it may have been necessary for the permanent healing of the man that he should have an outward evidence and testimony that the hellish powers which held him in bondage, had quitted him. He wanted his deliverance sealed and realized to him in the open destruction of his enemies; not else would he have been persuaded of the truth of that deliverance, and that Christ had indeed and forever set him free: as the children of Israel, coming out of Egypt, must *see* the dead bodies of their oppressors on the shore, ere they could indeed believe that these never again should bring them back into their old bondage.

In regard, too, of the loss incurred by the owners of those swine, there is no more reason why this should have been laid hold of and made an object of cavil than every murrain that causes cattle to die, or inundation that destroys the fruits of the field, or other natural calamity with which God chastens his children, punishes, or seeks to make contrite the hearts of his enemies. For oftentimes the taking away by God is in a higher sense a giving; it is the taking away of the meaner thing, for the purpose of making receptive of the higher. Thus might it well have been intended here, however the sin of these Gadarenes hindered Christ's gracious design. If these herds belonged to Jewish owners, and we know from Josephus, that there were great multitudes of hellenizing Jews just in these parts, there may have been in this loss a punishment meant for them who from motives of gain showed themselves despisers of Moses' law. Yet a great part of the population of the Decapolis was certainly Gentile; Josephus calls Gadara itself a Greek city.

But again, it seems strange that the unclean spirits ask permission to enter into the swine, yet no sooner have they done so than they defeat their own purpose, destroying that animal life, from which if they be altogether driven, they have already confessed they will be obliged to betake them to the more detested place of their punishment. But it is nowhere said that they *drove* the swine down the steep place into the sea. It is just as easy, and much more natural, to understand that against their will the swine, when they found themselves seized by this new and strange power, rushed themselves in wild and panic fear to their destruction—the first leaping down the cliffs, and the rest blindly following. And be it that the creatures thus rushed themselves to their own destruction, or were impelled by the foul spirits, does there not here in either case come out of the very essence of evil in its truest manifestation, that it is evermore outwitted and defeats itself, being as inevitably scourged in the granting of its request as in their refusal; that it is stupid, blind, self-contradicting, and suicidal; that it can only destroy, and will rather involve itself in the common ruin than not destroy

Moreover in their blind hatred against the Lord they may have been content to bring this additional harm, whatsoever it was, upon themselves, in the hopes that by this act they would bring upon him the ill-will, as was actually the case, of the inhabitants of that region, and so limit and hinder his blessed work among them. And this no doubt they did, for it was fear of further losses, and alienation from Christ on account of that which through his presence had already befallen them, which was the motive for their urging him to leave their country.

But the question offering more real matter for consideration is the *entering in* of the devils into the swine—the working of the spiritual life on the bestial, which seems altogether irreceptive of it, and not to possess the organs through which it could operate. I put aside of course here, as both in themselves merely ridiculous, and irreconcilable with the documents as they lie before us, the solutions of Paulus and his compeers, that the demoniac, in the parting paroxysm of his madness, hunted the creatures over the precipices into the lake, or that while the swineherds were drawn by curiosity to watch the encounter between Christ and the demoniac, or had gone to warn him of the danger of meeting the madman, the untended herd fell a fighting, and so tumbled headlong over the crags.

Whatever difficulty is here, it certainly is not so to be evaded; and their perplexity at any rate claims to be respectfully treated, who find it hard to reconcile this incident with what else they have been taught to hold fast as most precious concerning the specific difference between man and the whole order of spiritual existences on the one side; and the animal creation on the other. This difficulty, however, proceeds on the assumption that that lower world is wholly shut up in itself, and incapable of receiving impressions from that which is above it; while certainly all deeper investigations would lead to an opposite conclusion—not to the breaking down the boundaries between the two worlds, but to the showing in what wonderful ways the lower is subject to the impressions of the higher, both for good and for evil. Nor does this working of the spiritual on the physical life stand isolated in this single passage of Scripture, but we are throughout taught the same lesson. Compare Genesis 3:17 with Romans 8:18.

All three Evangelists record the entreaty of the Gadarenes, so unlike hat which the Samaritans (John 4:40) made to our Lord, *"that he would depart out of their coasts"*—an entreaty which surely had not, as Jerome and others suppose, its roots in their humility, was in no respect a parallel to St. Peter's "Depart from me, for I am a sinful man" (Luke 5:8); but, as already observed, was provoked by the injury which already from his brief presence among them, had ensued to their worldly possessions, as perhaps by the greater losses which yet they feared. This was their trial: it was now to be seen whether the kingdom of heaven was the first thing in their esteem; whether they would hold all else as cheap by comparison;: so that in this aspect the destruction of the swine had in regard of them an ethical aim. It was their trial, for the discovering of what temper they were; and under this trial they failed. It was nothing to them that a man, probably a fellow-citizen, was delivered from that terrible bondage, that they saw him *"sitting at the feet of Jesus,"* receiving instruction from him (Luke 10:39; Acts 22:3), *"clothed and in his right mind."* The breach that was made in their worldly prosperity alone occupied their thoughts: for spiritual blessings that were brought near to them they cared nothing, and *"they were afraid,"* they knew not what next might follow. They only knew that the presence of God's Holy One was intolerable to them while they remained in their sins, and to them, so remaining, could only bring mischiefs, of which they had had the first experience already. And having no desire to be delivered from their sins, they *"besought him to depart from them, for they were taken with great fear."* And *their* prayer also was heard; he did depart; he took them at their word; he let them alone. (Cf. Ex. 10:28, 29.)

But the healed man would fain accompany his healer: and as Christ was stepping into the ship to return, entreated that he might be allowed to bear him company. Was it that he feared, as Theophylact supposes, lest in the absence of his deliverer the powers of hell should regain their dominion over him, and only felt safe in immediate nearness to him? Or merely that out of the depth of his gratitude he desired henceforth to be a follower of him to whom he owed this mighty benefit? But whatever was his motive the Lord had other purposes with him: though he was himself leaving them who were as yet unfitted to welcome him, he would not leave himself without a witness among them. This healed man should be a standing monument of his grace and power—that he would have healed them, and was willing to heal them still, of all the diseases of their souls: *"Go home to thy friends, and tell them how great things the Lord hath done for thee, and hath had compassion on thee."* And the man did so, and not without effect: *"He departed, and began to publish in Decapolis how great things Jesus had done for him; and all men did marvel."*

Yet this command that he should go and declare the wonderful works of God in regard of him, may also have rested on other grounds, may have found its motive in the peculiar idiosyncracy of the man. Only with reference to this state are we able to reconcile the apparently contradictory commands which the Lord gave to those whom he had healed—some bidden to say nothing (Matt. 8:4; Luke 8:56)—this one to publish abroad the mercy which he had received. Where there was danger of all deeper impressions being lost and scattered through a garrulous repetition of the outward circumstances of the healing, there silence was enjoined, that so there might be an inward brooding over the gracious and mighty dealing of the Lord. But where, on the contrary, there was a temperament over-inclined to melancholy, sunken and shut up in itself, and needing to be drawn out from self, and into healthy communion with its fellowmen, as was evidently the case with such a solitary melancholic person as we have here, there the command was, that he should go and tell to others the great things which God had done for him, and in this telling preserve the healthy condition of his own soul.

6.
The Raising of Jairus' Daughter

Matthew 9:18, 19, 23–26: Mark 5:22, 24, 35–43; Luke 8:41, 42, 49–56

The present miracle is connected by St. Mark and St. Luke immediately with our Lord's return from the country on the other side of the lake, which he had left at the urgent entreaty of the inhabitants. In St. Matthew other events, the curing of the paralytic, the calling of Matthew, and some dicourses of the Lord with the Pharisees, are inserted between. Yet of these only the latter (9:10–17), the best harmonists find really to have their place here. The two later Evangelists tells us also the name of the father of the child; St. Matthew, who has his eye only on the main fact, and passes over everything that is not absolutely necessary for that, speaks of him more generally as "a certain ruler"; they again telling us what kind of a ruler, namely that he was one of the prefects of the synagogue. This, we can hardly doubt, was the synagogue of Capernaum, where now Jesus was (Matt. 9:1); he was therefore one who most probably afterwards made a part of that deputation which came to the Lord pleading for the heathen centurion (Luke 7:3); for "the elders of the Jews" there, are identical with the "rulers of the synagogue" here.

But he who appears on that later occasion pleading for another, presents himself now before the Lord, touched by a yet nearer calamity; for he comes saying, *"My daughter is even now dead, but come and lay thine hand upon her, and she shall live."* Thus St. Matthew records his words, but the others with an important variation— *"My little daughter lieth at the point of death"* (Mark 5:23). *"He had one only daughter, about twelve years of age, and she lay a dying"* (Luke 8:42). Thus they speak of her as dying when the father came, which the latter part of the history shows to have been the more exact, St. Matthew as already dead. Yet these differences are not hard to adjust; he left her at the last gasp; he knew not whether to regard her as alive or dead; he knew that life was ebbing so fast when he quitted her side, that she could scarcely be living now; and yet, having no certain notices of her death, he was perplexed whether to speak of her as departed or not, and thus at one moment expressed himself in one language, at the next in another. It is singular enough that a circumstance of this kind, so taken from the life, so testifying of the reality of the things recorded, should have been advanced by some as a contradiction between one Gospel and another.

That Lord, upon whose ear the tidings of woe might never fall in vain, at once *"arose and followed him, and so did his disciples."* The crowd who had been listening to his teaching, followed also, that they might see the end. The miracle of the healing the woman with the issue of blood found place upon the way, but it will naturally be better treated apart, especially as it is entirely separable from this history, though not altogether without its bearing upon it; for the delay, the words to the disciples, the conversation with the woman, must all have been a sore trial to the agonized father, now when every moment was precious, when death was shaking the last few sands in the hour-glass of his daughter's life—a trial in its kind similar to that with which the sisters of Lazarus were tried, when they beheld their beloved brother drawing ever nigher to death, and the Lord tarried notwithstanding. But however great the trial, we detect no signs of impatience on his part, and this no doubt was laid to his account. While the Lord was yet speaking to the woman, there came from the ruler's house certain of his friends or servants. St. Luke mentions but one, probably that one who was especially charged with the message, whom others went along with, even as it is common for men in their thirst for excitement to have a kind of pleasure in being the bearers even of evil tidings. They come *"saying to him, Thy daughter is dead, trouble not the Master."* They who, perhaps, had faith enough to believe that Christ could fan the last expiring spark of life into a flame, yet had not the stronger faith which would have enabled them to believe the harder thing, that he could once more enkindle that spark of life, when it was quenched altogether. Their hope had perished: perhaps the father's would have perished too, and thus there would have been no room for this miracle, since faith, the necessary condition, would have been wanting; but a gracious Lord prevented his rising doubts, for *"as soon as he heard the word that was spoken, he saith to the ruler of the synagogue, Be not afraid, only believe."* Here the emphasis should be placed on the first words—*as soon as* the tidings came, on that very instant the Lord spoke, thus leaving no room or place for a doubt to insinuate into the father's mind, before he had preoccupied him with word of confidence and encouragement.

The Lord took with him but three of his apostles, the same three who were allowed, more than once on later occasions, to be witnesses of things hidden from the rest. This, however, is the first time that we read of any such election within the election, and the fact of such now finding place would mark, especially when we remember the solemn significance of the other seasons of a like selection (Matt. 17:2; 26:37), that this was a new era in the life of the Lord. That which he was about to do was so great and holy that those three only, the flower and the crown of the apostolic band, were its fitting witnesses. The parents were present on grounds altogether different. Those, and these, and none other, accompanied him into the house. There, as everywhere else, he appears as the calmer and pacifier: *"Why make ye this ado and weep? The damsel is not dead, but sleepeth."* Some, and those not unbelievers, nor persons who have learned to regard miracles as so much perilous ware, from which it is always an advantage when the Gospels can be a little lightened—Olshausen, for instance, who is as far as possible from wishing to explain away the wonderful works of our Lord—have yet considered his words, repeated by all the narrators, *"The maid is not dead, but sleepeth,"* to be so explicit and distinct a declaration that death had not absolutely taken place, that in obedience, as they believe, to these words of our Lord's they refuse to number this among the actual raisings from the dead. They will count it only a raising from a death-like swoon; though one it may have been from which the maiden would never have returned but for that life-giving touch and voice. Had this, however, been the case, Christ's word to the father would clearly have been different, when the tidings came that the spirit of the child was actually fled. The consolation must have clothed itself in another language. He might have brought out the side of his omniscience, and bidden him not to fear, for *he* knew that no such evil had befallen him as he imagined. But that *"Be not afraid, only believe,"* points another way; it is an evident summoning him to a trust in the all-might of the gracious helper, who is coming with him to his house.

And as regards the Lord's words, that the maiden was not dead, but slept, he uses exactly the same language concerning Lazarus, "Our friend Lazarus sleepeth" (John 11:11), and when Olshausen replies to this obvious objection, that Christ explains there distinctly that he meant the sleep of death, adding presently, "Lazarus is dead," it is enough to answer that he does not do so till his disciples have misunderstood his words: he would have left those words, but for their mistaking them and supposing he had spoken of natural sleep—"Then said Jesus unto them plainly, Lazarus is dead." But as Lazarus only slept, because Jesus was going that he "might awake him out of sleep," so was she only sleeping, because her awakening was so near. Besides this, to speak of death as a sleep, is an image common, I suppose, to all languages and nations. Thereby the reality of the death is not denied, but only the fact implicitly assumed, that death will be followed by a resurrection, as sleep is by an awakening. Nor is it hard to perceive why the Lord should have spoken in this language here. First, in regard of the father, the words are an establishing of a tottering faith, which the sight of all these signs of mourning, these evidences that all was finished, might easily have overturned altogether. They are a saying over again, *"Be not afraid, only believe."* He, the Lord of life, takes away that word of fear, "She is dead," and puts in its room that milder word which gives promise of an awakening, "She sleepeth." And then in regard of the multitude, according to that holy humility which makes him ever withdraw his miracles as much as possible from observation, he will by this word of a double signification cast a veil over that which he is about to accomplish.

And now, having thus spoken, he expelled from the house the crowd of turbulent mourners, and this for two reasons; and first, their presence was evidently inappropriate and superfluous there; they were mourners for the dead, and she was not dead; or, at least, her death was so soon to give place to returning life, that it did not deserve the name; it was but as a sleep and an awakening, though they, indeed, who heard this assertion of the Lord, so little understood it, that they met it with laughter and with scorn, *"knowing that she was dead,"* that they were mourners for the dead. This would have been reason enough for silencing and putting out those mourners. But in addition to this, the boisterous and turbulent grief of some, the hires lamentations, it may be, of others, gave no promise of the true tone and temper, which became the witnesses of so holy and awful a mystery, a mystery from which even apostles themselves were excluded—not to speak of the profane and scornful spirit with which they had received the Lord's assurance, that the child should presently awake. The scorners were not to witness the holy act—the pearls were for others than for them.

The house was now solitary and still. Two souls, believing and hoping, stand like funeral tapers beside the couch of the dead maiden—the father and the mother. His Church the Lord sees represented in his three most trusted apostles. And now the solemn awakening finds place. He took the child, for such she was, being but twelve years of age (Mark 5:42), *"by the hand, and called, saying, Maid, arise."* St. Mark gives us the very words which the Lord spoke in the very language wherein he uttered them, *"Talitha Cumi,"* no doubt as having something especially solemn in them, as he does the *"Ephphatha"* on another occasion (7:34). And at that word, and at the touch of that hand, *"her spirit came again, and she arose straightway* (Luke 8:55) *and walked"* (Mark 5:42). And then at once to strengthen that life which was come back to her, and to prove that she was indeed no ghost, but had returned to the realities of a mortal existence (Luke 24:41; John 21:5; Acts 10:41), *"he commanded to give her meat";* which precaution was the more necessary, as the parents in that ecstatic moment might easily have forgotten it.

These miracles of raising from the dead, whereof we have been now considering the first, have always been regarded as the mightiest outcomings of the power of Christ; and with justice. They are those, also, at which unbelief is readiest to stumble, standing as they do in a yet more striking contrast than any of the other, to all that experience has known. The line between health and sickness is not definitely fixed; the two conditions melt one into the other, and the transition from this to that is frequent. In like manner storms alternate with calms; the fiercest tempest allays itself at last, and Christ's word did but anticipate and effect in a moment, what the very course of nature must have effected in the end. Even the transmutation from water to wine, and the multiplication of the bread, are not without their analogies, however remote; and thus too is it with most of the other miracles. But between being and the negation of being the opposition is not relative but absolute; between death and life a gulf lies, which nothing that nature lends, helps us even in imagination to bridge over. These considerations sufficiently explain how it should come to pass that these raisings from the dead are signs more spoken against than any other among the mighty works which the Lord accomplished.

The present will be an apt moment for saying something concerning them and the relations of difficulty in which they stand, if not to the other miracles, yet to one another. For they are not exactly the same miracle repeated three times over, but may be contemplated as in an ever ascending scale of difficulty, each a greater outcoming of the power of Christ than the preceding. For as the body of one freshly dead, from which life has but just departed, is very different from a mummy or a skeleton, so is it, though not in so great a degree, different from a corpse, whence for some days the breath of life has fled. There is, so to speak, a fresh trodden way between the body, and the soul which just has forsaken and, according to that Jewish legend which may rest on a very deep truth, lingers for a while and hovers near the tabernacle where it has dwelt so long, and to which it knows itself bound by links, which even now have not been divided forever. Even science itself has arrived at the conjecture, that the last echoes of life ring in the body much longer than is commonly supposed; that for a while it is full of the reminiscences of life. Out of this we may explain how it so frequently comes to pass, that all which marked the death-struggle passes presently away, and the true image of the departed, the image it may be of years long before, reappears in perfect calmness and in almost ideal beauty. Which things being so, we shall at once recognize in the quickening of him that had been four days dead, a yet mightier wonder than in the raising of the young man who was borne out to his burial; since that burial, according to Jewish custom, would have followed death by an interval, at most, of a single day; and again in *that* miracle a mightier outcoming of Christ's power than in the present, wherein life's flame, like some newly-extinguished taper, was still more easily re-enkindled again, being brought in contact with him in whom was the fountain-flame of all life. Mightier also than any of these wonders, will be the wonder of that hour, when all the dead of old, that have lain, some of them for so many thousand years, in the dust of death, shall be summoned from and shall leave their graves at the same quickening voice.

7.

The Woman With an Issue of Blood

Matthew 9:20–22; Mark 5:25–34; Luke 8:43–48

In all three accounts which we have of this miracle, it is intertwined with that other of the raising of Jairus' daughter. As the Prince of life was on his road to the accomplishing that other, he accomplished this, as by the way. It is to St. Mark and Luke that we owe the more detailed accounts, which bring out its distinctive features. St. Matthew relates it more briefly: so that, if we had not the parallel narrations, we should be in danger of missing much of the instruction which is here contained for us.

As the crowd followed Jesus, curious to witness what the issue would be, and whether he would indeed raise the dead or dying daughter of Jairus, which by his consenting to accompany him home he seemed to have undertaken to do—as this crowd pressed upon him, there came one, who, not out of curiosity, nor at all as that unmannered multitude, touched him from behind. This was a woman that had labored long, for no less than twelve years, under a disease from which she found no healing from the physicians, but rather she had suffered many aggravations of her disease, from the painfulness of their attempted remedies, the costliness of which, with the expenses that had attended her long sickness, had brought her to poverty. *"All that she had"* had been ineffectually wasted in seeking for restoration, and withal she *"was nothing bettered, but rather grew worse."* The faith that brought her to touch the hem of the Lord's garment was a most real faith (see v. 22, *"Thy faith hath saved thee"*), yet was it not altogether unmingled with error in regard to the manner in which the healing power of Christ presented

123

itself to her mind as working. It would appear as though she did not conceive of the Lord as healing by the power of his holy will, but rather imagined a certain magical influence and virtue diffused through his person and round about him, with which if she could put herself in relation, she would obtain that which she desired: *"If I may touch but his clothes, I shall be whole."* And it is probable that she touched the *hem* of his garment, not merely as their extremest part, and therefore that which she, timidly drawing near, could most easily reach, but attributing to it a peculiar virtue. For this hem or blue fringe on the borders of the garment was put there by divine command, and was to remind the Jews that they were God's people (Num. 15:37–40; Deut. 22:12). It had thus acquired so peculiar a significance, that those who wished to be esteemed eminently religious were wont to make broad, or to "enlarge the borders of their garments" (Matt. 23:5). But her faith, though thus imperfect in its form, and though it did not bear her like a triumphant flood-tide, over the peculiar difficulties which beset *her*, a woman coming to make known what manner of need was hers, was yet most true in its essence. That faith, therefore, was not disappointed, but was the channel to her of the blessing which she sought; no sooner had she touched the hem of his robe than *"she felt in her body that she was healed of that plague."*

But although the Evangelists fall in so far with the current of her thoughts as to use language that would be appropriate to it, and to say, *"Jesus immediately knowing in himself that virtue had gone out of him,"* yet we cannot for an instant suppose that this healing power went forth without the full consent of his will—that we have here, on his part, an *unconscious* healing, anymore than on another occasion, when we read that "the whole multitude sought to touch him, for there went virtue out of him, and healed them all" (Luke 6:19). For we should lose the ethical, which is ever the most important, element of the miracle, if we could suppose that power went forth from him to heal, without reference, on his part, to the spiritual condition of the person upon whom it went forth. He who with the eye of his spirit saw Nathanael under the fig-tree, who needed not that any should testify, for he knew what was in man, must have known of this woman both her bodily and spiritual state—how sorely as to the one she needed his help, and how as regarded the other she possessed that faith which was the one necessary condition of healing, the one channel of communication between him and any human need.

The only argument which could at all be adduced to favor the notion of an unconscious going forth of his power, would be that drawn from the question which he asked, when he *"turned about him in the press, and said, Who touched my clothes?"* This might be construed as implying that he was ignorant of the person who had done it, and only uncertainly apprehended that something had taken place. If he knew, it might be argued, to what purpose the question? But, as the sequel of the history will abundantly prove, there was a purpose; since if she had been allowed to carry away her blessing in secret as she proposed, it would not have been at all the blessing to her, and to her whole after spiritual life, that it now was, when she was obliged by this repeated question of the Lord, to own that she had come to seek, and had found, health from him. And the other objection is easily dissolved, namely, that it would not have been perfectly consistent with truth to have asked as not knowing, when indeed he knew all the while, who had done that, concerning which he inquired. But a father when he comes among his children, and says, Who committed this fault? Himself conscious, even while he asks, but at the same time willing to bring the culprit to a free confession, and so to put him in a pardonable state, can he be said in any way to violate the laws of the highest truth? The same offence might be found in Elisha's "Whence comest thou, Gehazi?" (2 Kgs. 5:25), when his heart went with him all the way that he had gone; and even in the question of God himself to Adam, "Where art thou?" In each of those cases, as here, there is a moral purpose in the question, an opportunity given even at the latest moment for undoing at least a part of the fault by its unreserved confession, an opportunity which they whose examples have been here adduced, suffered to escape; but which she, who it needs not to say had a fault of infinitely a slighter nature to acknowledge, had ultimately grace given her to use.

But this question itself, *"Who touched me?"* when indeed the whole multitude was rudely pressing upon and crowding round him, has often suggested many profitable reflections. Thus it has been often observed how *she* only *touched* with the touch of faith: the others, though as near or nearer in body, yet lacked that faith which is the connecting link between Christ's power and our need; and thus they crowded upon Christ, but did not touch him in any way that he should take note of. And thus it is ever in the Church; many *press* upon Christ: his in name; near to him and to his Sacraments outwardly; yet not *touching* him, because not drawing near in faith, not looking for and therefore not obtaining life and healing from him, and through these.

When the disciples, and Peter at their head, wonder at the question, and in their reply dare almost to find fault with a question which to them seems so out of place, *"Thou seest the multitude thronging thee, and sayest thou, Who touched me?"* the Lord replies, reaffirming the fact, *"Somebody hath touched me; for I perceive that virtue is gone out of me."* Whereupon the woman, finding that concealment was useless, that the denial, which probably she had made with the rest, for it is said, *"all denied"* (Luke 8:45), would profit her nothing; unable, too, to escape his searching glance, for *"he looked round about to see her"* (Mark 5:32), *"came trembling, and falling down before him, she declared unto him,"* and this *"before all the people, for what cause she had touched him, and how she was healed immediately."* Olshausen brings out here, with much beauty, how in all this the loving and gracious dealings of the Son of man, who always sought to make through the healing of the body a way for the healing of the soul, are to be traced. She had borne away a maimed blessing, hardly a blessing at all, had she been suffered to bear it away in secret and unacknowledged. She desired to remain in concealment out of a shame, which, however natural, was untimely here in this crisis of her spiritual life: and this her loving Savior would not suffer her to do: by a gracious force he drew her from it; yet even here he spared her as far as he could. For not before, but after she is healed, does he require the open confession from her lips. She had found it perhaps altogether too hard, had he demanded it of her before; therefore does he graciously wait till the cure is accomplished, and thus helps her through the narrow way. Altogether spare her this painful passage he could not, for it pertained to her birth into the new life.

And now he dismisses her with words of gracious encouragement, *"Daughter, be of good comfort; thy faith hath made thee whole."* Her faith had made her whole, and Christ's virtue had made her whole. It is as when we say that faith justifies: our faith is not itself the blessing; but it is the organ by which the blessing is received; it is the right hand of the soul, which lays hold upon it. *"Go in peace"*; this is not merely, Go with a blessing, but, Go into the element of peace as the future element in which thy life shall move—*"and be whole of thy plague."*

Theophylact brings out a mystical meaning in this miracle. This woman's complaint represents the ever-flowing fountain of sin; the physicians, the philosophers and wise men of this world, that with all their medicines, their systems and their philosophies, prevailed nothing to stanch that fountain of evil in man's heart. To touch Christ's garment is to believe in his Incarnation, wherein he touched us, enabling us to touch him: whereupon that healing, which in all those other things was vainly sought, follows at once. And if we keep in mind how her uncleanness separated her off as one impure, we shall have here an exact picture of the sinner, drawing nigh to the throne of grace, but out of the sense of his impurity not with boldness, rather with fear and trembling, hardly knowing what there he shall expect; but who is welcomed there, and, all his carnal doubtings and questionings expelled, dismissed with the word of an abiding peace resting upon him.

8.

The Opening the Eyes of Two Blind in the House

Matthew 9:27–31

We have here the first of those healings of the blind whereof so many are recorded (Matt. 12:22; 20:30; 21:14; John 9) or alluded to in the Gospel narrative. Nor is this little history without one or two features distinguishing it from others of a like kind. These two blind men appear to have followed Jesus in the way; it may have been, and Jerome supposes it was, as he was returning from the house of Jairus. Yet one would not lay too much stress on the connection in which St. Matthew sets the miracle, or necessarily conclude that he intended to place it in such immediate relation of time and place with the raising of the ruler's daughter. There was the same trial of the faith of these blind men, although in a more mitigated form, as found place in the case of the Syrophenician woman. Not all at once did they receive the boon which they sought; but the Lord seemed at first rather to withdraw himself from them, suffering them to cry after him, and for a while paying no regard to their cries. It was only after they followed him into the house, and had thus shown that they were in earnest in seeking and expecting a boon from him, that he yielded to them the blessing which they sought. But ere he does this, as he has tried them in deed by the delay of the blessing, he proves them also in word. He will have the confession of their faith from their own lips: "Believe ye that I am able to do this? They said unto him, Yea, Lord." And then, when he found that they had this necessary condition for the receiving any one of his blessings, when he perceived that they had faith to be healed "he touched their eyes." And this time it is by that simple touch that he opens those closed eyes (Matt. 20:34); at other times he uses as the conductors of his power, and as helps to the faith of those who should be healed, some further instruments—the clay mingled with spittle (John 9:6, 7), or the moisture of his mouth alone. We do not, I think, anywhere read of his opening the blind eyes simply by his word, although of course that would have been equally easy to him. The words which accompany the act of healing are remarkable—"According to your faith be it unto you"—remarkable for the insight which they give us into the relation of man's faith and God's gift. The faith, which in itself is nothing, is yet the organ of receiving everything. It places the man in relation with the divine blessing; of no esteem in itself, but only in its relation to its object. It is the bucket let down into the fountain of God's grace, without which the man could not draw up out of that fountain; the purse, which though itself of the coarsest material, does yet enrich its owner by that which it contains.

It is very characteristic, and rests on very deep differences, that of the Romish interpreters almost all, indeed I know not an exception, should excuse, or rather applaud, these men for not adhering strictly to Christ's command, his earnest, almost threatening, injunction to them, that they should let none know what he had done, that the expositors of that Church of will-worship should see in their disobedience the overflowings which could not be restrained of grateful hearts, and not therefore a fault but a merit. Some indeed of the ancients, as Theophylact, go so far as to suppose that the men did not disobey at all in proclaiming the miracle, that Christ never intended them to preserve his precept about silence, but gave it out of humility, being best pleased when it was not observed. But the Reformed, whose first principle is to take God's Word as absolute rule and law, and to worship God not with self-devised services, but after the pattern that he has given them, stand fast to this, that obedience is better than sacrifice, even though that sacrifice may appear in honor of God himself; and see in this publishing of the miracle, after the prohibition given, a blemish in the perfectness of their faith who did it, a fault, though a fault into which they only, who were full of gratitude and thankfulness, could have fallen.

9.

The Healing of the Paralytic

Matthew 9:1–8; Mark 2:1–12; Luke 5:17–26

It was at Capernaum, while the Lord was teaching there, and on an occasion when there were present Pharisees and doctors of the law from many quarters, some of whom had come even as far as from Jerusalem (Luke 5:17), that this healing of the paralytic took place. It might have been a kind of conference, more or less friendly upon the part of these, which had brought together as listeners and spectators the great multitude of whom we read, a multitude so great that the avenues of approach to the house were blocked up"; there was no room to receive them, no not so much as about the door," and thus no opportunity, by any ordinary way, of access to the Lord (Matt. 12:46, 47). And now some who arrived late with their sick, who brought with them a poor paralytic "could not come nigh unto him for the press." Only the two later Evangelists record for us the extraordinary method to which the bearers of the suffering man (St. Mark tells us they were four), were compelled to have recourse, for bringing him before the notice of the great healer of bodies and of souls. They first ascended to the roof: this was not so difficult, because commonly there was a flight of steps on the outside of the house, reaching to the roof, as well as, or sometimes instead of, an internal communication of the same kind. Such are to be seen (I have myself seen them), in those parts of the south of Spain which bear a permanent impress of Eastern habits. Our Lord assumes the existence of such, when he says, "Let him that is on the housetop not come down to take anything out of his house" (Matt. 24:17); he is to take the nearest and shortest way of escaping into the country: but he could only avoid the necessity of descending through the house by the existence of such steps as these. Some will

have it, that, on the present occasion, the bearers having thus
reached the roof, did no more than let down their sick through the
grating or trap-door, which already existed therein (cf. 2 Kgs. 1:2),
or, at most, that they might have widened such an aperture, already existing, to enable them to let down the sick man's bed.
Others, that Jesus was sitting in the open court, round which the
houses in the East are commonly built, and that to this they got access by the roof, and breaking through the breast-work or battle-
ment (Deut. 22:8), made of tiles, which guarded the roof, and
removing the linen awning which was stretched over the court, let
him down in the midst before the Lord. But there seems no sufficient reason for departing from the obvious meaning of the words.
In St. Mark, at least, they are so plain and clear, that we can suppose nothing else than that a part of the actual covering of the roof
was removed, that so the bed on which the palsied man lay might
be let down before the Lord. The whole circumstance will be much
more easily conceived, and present fewer difficulties, when we
keep in mind that it was probably the upper chamber (ὑπερῷον),
where were assembled those that were drawn together to hear the
Lord. This, as the most retired (2 Kgs. 4:10, 70; Acts 9:37), and probably the largest room in the house, extending oftentimes over its
whole area, was much used for such purposes as that which now
drew him and his hearers together (Acts 1:13; 20:8).

The merciful Son of man, condescending to every need of man,
and never taking ill that which witnessed for an earnest faith in
him, even though, as here, it manifested itself in a way so novel—
in one, too, which must have altogether disturbed the quiet of his
teaching, saw with an eye well-pleased their faith. Had we only the
account of St. Matthew, we should hardly understand wherein
their special faith, consisted—why here, more than in many similar
instances, it should have been noted; but the other Evangelists admirably complete that which he would have left obscure. They tell
us how it was a faith which pressed through hindrances, and was
not to be turned aside by difficulties. By *"their faith,"* many, as
Jerome and Ambrose, understand the faith of the bearers only, but
there is no need so to confine the words. To them the praise justly
was due, but no doubt the sick man was approving all which they
did, or it would not have been done: so that Chrysostom, with
greater reason, concludes, that it was alike their faith and his which
the Lord saw and rewarded. And this faith, as in the case of all
whom he healed, was not as yet the reception of any certain doc-

trines, but a deep inward sense of need, and of Christ as the one, who only could meet that need.

Beholding this faith, the Lord addressed him, *"Son, be of good cheer; thy sins be forgiven thee"*—a striking example this of the way in which the Lord gives *before* men ask, and *better* than men ask: for this man had not asked anything, save, indeed, in the dumb asking of that earnest effort to come near to Jesus; and all that he dared to ask even in that, or at least all that his friends and bearers hoped for him, was that his body might be healed. Yet there was no doubt in himself a deep feeling of his sickness in its innermost root, as growing out of sin, perhaps as the penalty of some especial sin whereof he was conscious; and some expression of contrition, some exclamation of a penitent heart, may have been the immediate occasion of these gracious words of forgiveness, as, indeed, the address, *"Son, be of good cheer,"* would seem also to imply that he was one evidently burdened and cast down, and, as the Lord saw, with more than the weight of his bodily sicknesses and sufferings. We shall see in other cases how the forgiveness of sins *follows* the outward healing: for we may certainly presume that such a forgiveness did ensue in cases such as that of the thankful Samaritan, of the impotent man who was first healed, and at a later period bidden to sin no more (John 5:14). But here the remission of sin takes the precedence; the reason no doubt being, that in the suffer's own conviction there was so close a connection between his sin and his plague, that the outer healing would have been scarcely intelligible to him, would have scarcely carried to his mind the sense of a benefit, unless his conscience had been also set free; perhaps he was incapable even of receiving it, till there had been spoken peace to his spirit. James 5:14, 15, supplies an interesting parallel, in the connection which exists there also between the raising of the sick and the forgiving of his sin. The others, alluded to above, who had a much slighter sense of the relations between sin and suffering, were not first forgiven and then healed; but their thankfulness for their bodily healing was used to make them receptive of that better blessing which Christ had in store for them.

The absolving words *"Thy sins be forgiven thee,"* are not to be taken as optative merely, as a desire that it might be so, but as declaratory of a fact. They are the justification of the sinner; and, as declaratory of that which takes place in the purposes of God, so also effectual, shedding abroad the sense of forgiveness and reconciliation in the sinner's heart. For God's justification of a sinner is not merely a word spoken about a man, but a word spoken to him and in him; not an act of God's, *immanent* in himself, but *transitive* upon the sinner. In it there is the love of God, and so the consciousness of that love, shed abroad in his heart on whose behalf the absolving decree has been uttered. The murmurers and cavillers understood rightly that Christ, so speaking, did not merely wish and desire that this man's sins might be forgiven him; and that he did not, as does now the Church, in the name of another and wielding a delegated power, but in his own name, forgive the man his sins. They had also a right insight into the meaning of the forgiveness of sins itself, that it is a divine prerogative; that, as no man can remit a debt save he to whom the debt is due, so no one can forgive sin save he against whom all sin is committed, that is, God; and out of this feeling, true in itself, but most false in their present application of it, they said *"This man blasphemeth."*

It is well worth our while to note, as Olshausen here calls us to do, the deep insight into the relations of God and the creature, which is involved in the Scriptural use of the word blasphemy. Profane antiquity knew nothing like it; with it "to blaspheme" meant only to speak something evil of a person (a use which indeed is not foreign to the Scripture), and then, to speak something of an evil omen. Only the monotheistic religion included in blasphemy not merely outward words of cursing and outrage against the Name of God, but all snatchings on the part of the creature at honors which of right belonged only to the Creator (Matt. 26:65; John 10:36). If he who thus spoke had not been the only-begotten Son of the Father, the sharer in all prerogatives of the Godhead, he would indeed have blasphemed, as they deemed, when he thus spoke. Their sin was not that they accused him, a man, of blasphemy; but that their eyes were so blinded that they could not recognize any glory in him higher than man's; that the light shined in the darkness, and the darkness comprehended it not.

It is not for nothing that it is said that Jesus perceived *"in his Spirit"* that such thoughts were stirring in their hearts (Mark 2:8). These words, *"in his Spirit"* are not superfluous, but his knowing faculty, that whereby he saw through the thoughts and counsels of hearts, and knew what was in man, is here attributed to his divine spirit. And these counsels he revealed to them; and in this way first he gave them to understand that he was more than they esteemed, since thoughts of hearts were open and manifest to him, while yet it is God only who searches hearts (1 Sam. 16:7; 1 Chr. 28:9; 2 Chr.

6:30; Jer. 17:10), it is only the divine Word of whom it can be said, that "he is a discerner of the thoughts and intents of the heart" (Heb. 4:12).

Nor is it merely generally that he lays bare their thoughts of him, as being hard and evil, but he indicates the exact line which those thoughts were taking; for the charge which they made against him in their hearts, was not merely that he took to himself divine attributes, but that, doing so, he at the same time kept on the safe side as regarded detection, taking those wherein, by the very nature of things, it was not possible to prove him a false claimant. They were murmuring, no doubt, within themselves, "These honors are easily snatched; any man may go about the world claiming this power, and saying to men, 'Your sins are forgiven you'; but where is the evidence that this word is allowed and ratified in heaven; that what is thus spoken on earth is sealed in heaven? In the very nature of the power which this man claims, he is secure from detection; for this releasing of a man from the condemnation of his sin is an act wrought in the inner spiritual world, attested by no outer and visible sign; therefore it is easily claimed, since it cannot be disproved." And our Lord's answer, meeting this evil thought in their hearts, is in fact this: "You accuse me that I am claiming a safe power, since, in the very nature of the benefit bestowed, no sign follows, nothing to bear witness whether I have challenged it rightfully or not; but now I will put myself to a more decisive proof. I will speak a word, I will claim a power, which if I claim falsely, I shall be convinced upon the instant to be an impostor and a deceiver. I will say to this sick man, *'Rise up and walk'*; by the effects, as they follow or do not follow, you may judge whether I have a right to say to him, *'Thy sins be forgiven thee.'"*

In our Lord's argument it must be carefully noted that he does not ask, Which is easiest, to forgive sins or to raise a sick man? For it could not be affirmed that that of forgiving was easier than this of healing; but, "Which is easiest, to claim this power or to claim that; *to say*, Thy sins be forgiven thee, or *to say*, Arise and walk? That is easiest, and I will now prove my right to say it, by saying with effect and with an outward consequence setting its seal to my truth, the harder word, Arise and walk. By doing that, which is capable of being put to the proof, I will vindicate my right and power to do that which, in its very nature, is incapable of being proved. By these visible tides of God's grace I will give you to know in what direction the great under currents of his love are setting, and that both are obedient to my word. From this which I will now do openly and before you all, you may conclude that it is no "robbery" (Phil. 2:6), upon my part to claim also the power of forgiving men their sins." Thus, to use a familiar illustration of our Lord's argument, it would be easier for a man, equally ignorant of French and Chinese, to claim to know the last than the first; not that the language itself is easier; but that, in the one case, multitudes could disprove his claim; and, in the other, hardly a scholar or two in the land.

In the words, *"power on earth,"* there lies a tacit opposition to *"power in heaven."* "This power is not exercised, as you deem only by God in heaven; but also by the Son of man upon earth. He has brought it down with him here, so that it, which, as you rightly assert, is only exercised by him who dwelleth in the heavens, has yet, in the person of the Son of man, descended also upon earth. Here also is one who can speak, and it is done." The only thing which at all surprises, is our Lord's claiming this power as the *"Son of man."* It is remarkable, since, at first sight, it might appear that this of forgiving sins being a *divine* attribute, the present was not the natural time for specially naming himself by this name, it being as the Son of God, and not as the Son of man, that he remitted sins. The Alexandrian fathers, in their conflict with the Nestorians, made use of this passage in proof of the entire transference which there was, of all the properties of Christ's divine nature to his human; so that whatever one had, was so far common that it might also be predicated of the other. It is quite true that had not the two natures been indissolubly knit together in a single person, no such language could have been used; yet I should rather suppose that "Son of man" being the standing title whereby the Lord was well-pleased to designate himself, bringing out by it that he was at once one with humanity, and the crown of humanity, he does not so use it that the title is in every instance to be pressed, but at times simply as equivalent to Messiah.

Having said this much to the gainsayers, he turns to the poor man with the words, *"Arise, take up thy bed, and go unto thine house,"* in his person setting his seal to all the prerogatives which he had claimed; so that this miracle is eminently what indeed all are, though it is not equally brought out in all, "a sign," an outward sign of an inward truth, a link between this visible and a higher and invisible world. *"And immediately he arose, took up the bed, and went forth before them all"*; they who before blocked up his path, now making way for him, and allowing free egress from the assembly. Concerning the effects of this miracle on the Pharisees, the narration is silent, and this, probably, because there was nothing good to tell—but of the people, far less hardened against the truth, far more receptive of divine impressions, we are told *"they were all amazed, and glorified God"*; altogether according to the intention of the Savior, praising the author of all good for the revelation of his glory in his Son (Matt. 5:16). There was a true sense upon their part of the significance of this fact, in their thankful exultation that God *"had given such power unto men."* Without supposing that they very accurately explained to themselves, or could have explained to others, their feeling, yet they felt rightly that what was given to one man, to the Man Christ Jesus, was given for the sake of all, and ultimately *to* all—that it was indeed given *"unto men"*—that he possessed these powers as the true Head and Representative of the race, and therefore that these gifts to him were a rightful subject of gladness and thanksgiving for every member of that race.

10

The Cleansing of the Leper

Matthew 8:1–4; Mark 1:40–45; Luke 5:12–16

It is said in one place concerning the apostles' preaching, that the Lord confirmed their word with signs following (Mark 16:20). Here we have a very remarkable example of his doing the same in the case of his own. For, according to the arrangement of the events of the Lord's life which I follow, and according to the connection of the events as it appears in St. Matthew, it is after that most memorable discourse of his upon the Mount, that this and other of his most notable miracles find place. It is as though he would set his seal to all that he has taught—would approve himself to be this prophet having right to hold the language which there he has held, to teach as one having authority. He had scarcely ended, ere the opportunity for this occurred. As he was descending from the mountain, "there came a leper and worshiped him," one, in the language of St. Luke, "full of leprosy," so that it was not a spot here and there, but the disease had spread over his whole body: he was leprous from head to foot. He had ventured, it may be, to linger about the outskirts of the listening crowd, and now was not deterred by the severity of the closing sentences of Christ's discourse, from coming to claim the blessings which at its opening were proclaimed for the suffering and the mourning. Here, however, before proceeding to treat more particularly of this cure, it may be good, once for all, since the cleansing of lepers comes so frequently forward in the Gospel history, to say a few words concerning that dreadful disorder, and the meaning of the uncleanness which was attached to it.

And first, a few words may be needful in regard of a misapprehension, which we find in such writers as Michaelis, and in all indeed who can see in the Levitical ordinances little more for the most part than regulations of police or of a board of health, or at the best, rules for the well ordering of an earthly society; who will not recognize in these ordinances the training of man into a sense of the cleaving taint which is his from his birth, into a sense of impurity and separation from God, and thus into a longing after purity and reunion with him. I allude to the common misapprehension that leprosy was catching from one person to another; and that they who were suffering under it were so carefully secluded from their fellowmen, lest they might communicate the poison of the disease to them; as in like manner that the torn garment, the covered lip, the cry "Unclean, unclean" (Lev. 13:45), were warnings to others that they should keep aloof, lest unawares touching the lepers, or drawing into too great a nearness, they should become partakers of their disease. A miserable emptying this, as we shall see, of the meaning of these ordinances. All those who have examined into the matter the closest are nearly of one consent, that the sickness was incommunicable by ordinary contact from one person to another. A leper might transmit it to his children, or the mother of a leper's children might take it from him, but it was by no ordinary contact transferable from one person to another.

All the notices in the Old Testament, as well as in other Jewish books, confirm this view, that it was in no respect a mere sanitary regulation. Thus, where the law of Moses was not observed, no such exclusion necessarily found place; Naaman the leper commanded the armies of Syria (2 Kgs. 5:1), Gehazi, with his leprosy that never should be cleansed, talked familiarly with the king of apostate Israel (2 Kgs. 8:5). And even where the law of Moses was in force, the stranger and the sojourner were expressly exempted from the ordinances in relation to leprosy; which could not have been, had the disease been contagious, and the motives of the leper's exclusion been not religious but civil, since the danger of the spreading of the disease would have been equal in their case and in that of native Israelites. How, moreover, should the Levitical priests, had the disease been this creeping infection, have themselves escaped the disease, obliged as they were by their very office to submit the leper to such actual handling and closest examination? Lightfoot can only explain this by supposing in their case a perpetual miracle.

But no; the ordinances concerning leprosy had quite a different and a far deeper significance, into which it will be needful a little to enter. It is clear that the same principle which made all that had to do with death, as mourning, a grave, a corpse, the occasions of a ceremonial uncleanness, inasmuch as all these were signs and consequences of sin, might in like manner, and with a perfect consistency, have made every sickness an occasion of uncleanness, each of these being also death beginning, partial death—echoes in the body of that terrible reality, sin in the soul. But instead of this, in a gracious sparing of man, and not pushing the principle to the uttermost, God took but one sickness, one of these visible outcomings of a tainted nature, in which to testify that evil was not from him, that evil could not dwell with him; he took but one, with which to link this teaching, and that it might serve in this region of man's life as the substratum for the training of his people into the recognition of a clinging impurity, which needed Pure and a Purifier to overcome and expel, and which no method short of his taking of our flesh could drive out. And leprosy, which was indeed the sickness of sicknesses, was through these Levitical ordinances selected of God from the whole host of maladies and diseases which had broken in upon man's body; to the end that, bearing his testimony against it, he might bear his testimony against that out of which it and all other sicknesses grew, against sin, as not from him, as grievous in his sight; and the sickness itself also as grievous, not for itself, but because it was a visible manifestation, a direct consequence, of the inner disharmony of man's spirit, a commencement of the death, which through disobedience to God's perfect will, had found entrance into a nature made by God for immortality.

And terrible indeed, as might be expected, was that disease, round which this solemn teaching revolved. Leprosy was indeed nothing short of a living death, a poisoning of the springs, a corrupting of all the humors, of life; a dissolution little by little of the whole body, so that one limb after another actually decayed and fell away. Aaron exactly describes the appearance which the leper presented to the eyes of the beholders, when, pleading for Miriam, he says, "Let her not be as one dead, of whom the flesh is half consumed when he cometh out of his mother's womb" (Num. 12:12). The disease, moreover, was incurable by the art and skill of man; not that the leper might not return to health; for, however rare, such cases are yet contemplated in the Levitical law. But then the leprosy left the man, not in obedience to any outward means of healing which had been applied by men, but purely and merely through the good will and mercy of God. This helplessness of man in the matter, is recognized in the speech of the king of Isreal, who, when Naaman is sent to him that he may heal him, exclaims, "Am I God, to kill and to make alive, that this man doth send unto me to recover a man of his leprosy?" (2 Kgs. 5:7). The leper, thus fearfully bearing about in the body the outward and visible tokens of sin in the soul, was handled throughout as a sinner, as one in whom sin had reached its highest manifestation, that is, as one dead in trespasses and sins. He was himself a dreadful parable of death. It is evident that Moses intended that he should be so contemplated by all the ordinances which he gave concerning him. The leper was to bear about the emblems of death (Lev. 13:45), the rent garments, that is, mourning garments, he mourning for himself as for one dead; the head bare, as they were wont to have it who were in communion with the dead (Num. 6:9; Ezek. 24:17); and the lip covered (Ezek. 24:17).

In the restoration, too, of a leper, exactly the same instruments of cleansing were in use, the cedar wood, the hyssop, and the scarlet, as were used for the cleansing of one defiled through a dead body, or aught pertaining to death, and which were never in use upon any other occasion (Compare Num. 19:6, 13, 18, with Lev. 14:4–7). No doubt when David exclaims, "Purge me *with hyssop, and I shall be clean*" (Ps. 51:7), he in this allusion, looking through the outward to the inward, even to the true blood of sprinkling, contemplates himself as a spiritual leper, as one whose sin had been, while he lived in it, a sin unto death, as one needing therefore absolute and entire restoration from the very furthest degree of separation from God. And being this sign and token of sin, and of sin reaching unto and culminating in death, it naturally brought about with it a total exclusion from the camp or city of God. God is not a God of the dead; he has no fellowship with death, for death is the correlative of sin; but only of the living. But the leper was as one dead, and as such was to be put out of the camp (Lev. 13:46; Num. 5:2–4; 2 Kgs. 7:3), or afterwards out of the city; and we find this law to have been so strictly enforced, that even the sister of Moses might not be exempted from it (Num. 12:14, 15); and kings, Uzziah (2 Chr. 26:21), and Azariah (2 Kgs. 15:5), themselves must submit to it; men being by this exclusion taught that what here took place in a figure, should take place in the reality with everyone who was found in the death of sin: he should be shut out of the true city of God. Thus, taking up and glorifying this and like ordinances of exclusion, St. John exclaims of the New Jerusalem, "There shall nowise enter into it anything that defileth, neither whatsoever worketh abomination, or maketh a lie" (Rev. 21:27).

It need hardly be observed, that in all this it was not in the least implied that he who bore this plague was of necessity a guiltier man than his fellows; though being, as it was, this symbol of sin, it was most often the theocratic punishment, the penalty for sins committed against the theocracy, as in the cases of Miriam, of Gehazi, of Uzziah; and we may compare Deut. 24:8, where the warning, "Take heed of the plague of leprosy," is not that they diligently observe the laws about leprosy, but that they beware lest this plague of leprosy come upon them, lest by their disobedience they incur the theocratic penalty. The Jews themselves termed it "The finger of God," and emphatically, "The stroke." They said that it attacked first a man's house, and if he did not turn, his clothing; and then, if he persisted in sin, himself: a fine symbol, whether the fact was so or not, of the manner in which God's judgments, if men refuse to listen to them, reach ever nearer to the center of their life. So, too, they said that a man's true repentance was the one condition of his leprosy leaving him.

Seeing then that leprosy was this outward and visible sign of the innermost spiritual corruption, this sacrament of death, there could be no fitter form of evil over which the Lord of life should display his power. He will prove himself the conqueror of death in life, as of death completed. This victory of his over this most terrible form of physical evil is fitly brought out as a testimony of his Messiahship: "The lepers are cleansed" (Matt. 11:5). Nor may we doubt that the terribleness of the infliction, the extreme suffering with which it was linked, the horror with which it must have filled the sufferer's mind, as he marked it slow but inevitable progress, to be arrested by no human hand, the ghastly hideousness of its unnatural whiteness (Num. 12:10; Ex. 4:6; 2 Kgs. 5:27), must all have combined to draw out his pity, who was not merely the mighty, but no less the loving, Physician and Healer of the bodies as of the souls of men. The medical details concerning this sickness, and the differences between one kind and another, as between the white leprosy (λεύκη), which among the Jews was the most frequent, and the yet more terrible elephantiasis, thought by many to have been that with which Job was visited, and so named because in it the feet swelled to an elephantine size, would be here out of place. It is time to return to the consideration of this particular act of healing.

The leper with whom we now have to do, came *"and worshiped"* Jesus—an act of profound reverence, as from an inferior to a superior, yet not in itself a recognition of anything specially divine in him to whom it was offered. The words with which he expresses what he would have from the Lord are remarkable as the utterance of a simple and a humble faith, which is willing to abide the issue, whatever that may be, and having declared its desire, to leave the complying with it or not to a higher wisdom and love: *"Lord, if thou wilt, thou canst make me clean."* There is no questioning here of the power; nothing of *his* unbelief who said, "If thou canst do anything, have compassion on us and help us" (Mark 9:22). Whereupon the Lord *"put forth his hand and touched him,"* ratifying and approving his utterance of faith, by making the concession of his request in the very words wherein the request itself had been embodied: *"I will, be thou clean."* This touching of the unclean by Christ is itself remarkable, seeing that such contact had been forbidden in the Law (Lev. 14:46). The adversaries of the Law, the Gnostics of old, said that Christ did this to mark his contempt for its ordinances, and in witness that he did not recognize it as coming from the good Deity. But Tertullian gives the true answer to this. He first shows what was the deeper meaning of forbidding to touch the ceremonially unclean, namely, that we should not defile our souls through being partakers in other men's sins, as St. Paul, with allusion, no doubt, to these ceremonial prohibitions, and giving them their higher spiritual significance, exclaims, "Come out from among them, and be ye separate, and touch not the unclean thing; and I will receive you" (2 Cor. 6:17). And these outer prohibitions held good for all, till the coming in of him who was incontaminable, in whom first the tide of this world's evil was arrested and rolled back. Another would have defiled himself by touching the leper; but he, himself remaining undefiled, cleansed him whom he touched; for in him life overcame death—and health, sickness—and purity, defilement. In him, in its most absolute sense, that word was fulfilled "Unto the pure all things are pure."

Ambrose and many others suppose that the Lord's injunction to the man that he should not divulge his cure, was intended to teach his followers that they too should avoid ostentation in their acts of mercy, lest, as he says, they should be themselves taken with a worse leprosy than any which they healed. But if the motive to this prohibition was external, and had not reference to the inner moral condition of the receiver of the benefit, I should think that our Lord's purpose was more likely this, that his stiller ministry might not be hindered or disturbed by the inopportune flowing to him of multitudes, who should be drawn to him merely by the hope of sharing the same worldly benefits, as we see was the case on this very occasion (Mark 1:45), nor yet by the premature violence of his enemies, roused to a more active and keener hate by the great things which were published of him (John 11:46, 47). But there has been already occasion to observe, that probably a deeper purpose lay at the root of this injunction to silence, as of the opposite command to go and proclaim the great things of God's mercy. The precepts to tell or to conceal were interchangeably given according to the different moral conditions of the different persons whom Christ healed. On the present occasion it seems very probable, according to the suggestion of Grotius and Bengel, that the words, *"See thou tell no man,"* are to be taken with this limitation— "till thou hast shown thyself to the priests; lest if a rumor of these things go before thee, the priests at Jerusalem, out of envy, out of a desire to depreciate my work, may deny either that thou wast before a leper, or else that thou art now truly cleansed." We may find perhaps indications of something of this kind in the words of St. Mark, *"he forthwith sent him away,"* or, put him forth; he would allow no lingering, but required him to hasten on his errand, lest the report of what had been done should outrun him.

Some understand the words, *"for a testimony unto them,"* as meaning "for a testimony even to these gainsayers that I am come, not to destroy the Law, but to fulfill it—to remove nothing, not even a shadow, till I have brought in the substance in its room. These Levitical offerings I still allow and uphold, since that to which they point is not yet fully given." But I cannot doubt that the true meaning of the words is *"for a testimony against them;* for a witness against their unbelief, who are refusing to give credence to me, even while I am attesting myself to be all which I claim to be, by such mighty works as these; works of which they themselves shall have ratified the reality by the acceptance of thy gift, by thy readmission, as one truly cleansed, into the congregation of the people" (John 5:36). For the purpose of his going to the priest was this, that the priest might ascertain the fact, if really his leprosy had left him (Lev. 14:3), and, if so, might accept his gift, and offer it as an atonement for him; and might then, when all was duly accomplished, pronounce him clean and admit him anew into the congregation of Israel.

11.
The Healing of the Centurion's Servant

Matthew 8:5–13; Luke 7:1–10

There has been already occasion to speak of the utter impossibility of this healing being one and the same with that of the nobleman's son recorded by St. John (4:43). But while we may not thus seek to harmonize two narratives which relate to circumstances entirely different, yet there is still matter here remaining on which the harmonist may exercise his skill: there are two independent accounts of this miracle, one given by St. Matthew, the other by St. Luke—and, according to the first Evangelist, the centurion comes in his own person to ask the boon which he desires; according to the third he sends others as intercessors between himself and the Lord, with other differences which flow out of this. There can be no doubt that we are to accept the latter as the more strictly literal account of the circumstance, as it actually came to pass—St. Matthew, who is briefer, telling it as though the centurion had done in his own person what, in fact, he did by the intervention of others—an exchange of persons of which all historical narrations and all the language of our common life is full. (Compare Mark 10:35, with Matthew 20:20, for another example of the same.)

This centurion, probably one of the Roman garrison of Capernaum, was by birth a heathen; but, like him in the Acts (10:1), who bore the same office, was one of the many who were at this time deeply feeling the emptiness of all polytheistic religions, and who had attached themselves by laxer or closer bonds to the congregation of Israel and the worship of Jehovah, finding in Judaism a satisfaction of some of the deepest needs of their souls, and a

147

promise of the satisfaction of all. He was one among the many who are distinguished from the seed of Abraham, yet described as fearing God, or worshiping God, of whom we read so often in the Acts—the proselytes, whom the providence of God had so wonderfully prepared in all the great cities of the Greek and Roman world as a link of communication between Gentile and Jew, in contact with both—holding to the first by their race, and to the last by their religion; and who must have greatly helped to the ultimate fusion of both into one Christian Church.

But with the higher matters which he had learned from his intercourse with the people of the covenant, he had learned no doubt this, that all heathens, all "sinners of the Gentiles," were "without"; that there was a middle wall of partition between them and the children of the stock of Abraham; that they were to worship only as in the outer court, not presuming to draw near to the holy place. And thus he did not himself approach, but sent others to, Jesus, in whom he recognized a being of a higher world, entreating him, by them, *"that he would come and heal his servant,"* a servant who, as St. Luke adds, *"was dear unto him,"* but now *"was sick and ready to die."* The elders of the Jews, whom he employed on this errand, were his willing messengers, and appear zealously to have executed their commission, pleading for him as one whose affection for, and active well-doing towards, the chosen people deserved this return of favor: *"for he loveth our nation, and he hath built us a synagogue."*

But presently even this request which he had made seemed to him too great a boldness. In his true and ever-deepening humility he counted it a presumption to have asked, though by the intervention of others, the presence under his roof of so exalted a personage. It was not merely that he was a heathen, and so might claim no near approach to the King of Israel; but there was, no doubt, besides this and mingling with this, a deep and inward feeling of his own personal unworthiness and unfitness for a close communion with a holy being, which caused him again to send, beseeching the Lord to approach no nearer, but only to speak the word, and he knew that straightway his servant would be healed. And thus, in Augustine's words, "while he counted himself unworthy that Christ should enter into his doors, he was counted worthy that Christ should enter into his heart—a far better boon: for Christ sat down in the houses of men, as of that proud, self-righteous Pharisee, whose hearts were not for this the less empty of his presence. But this centurion received *him* in his heart, whom he did not receive in his house. And, indeed, every little trait of his character, as it comes out in the sacred narrative, combines to show him as one in whom the seed of God's word would find the ready and prepared soil of a good and honest heart. For not to speak of those prime conditions, faith and humility, which in so eminent a degree shone forth in him—the evident affection which he had won from those Jewish elders, the zeal which had stirred him to build a house for the worship of the true God, his earnest care and anxiety about a slave—one so generally excluded from all earnest human sympathies on the part of his master, that even a Cicero thinks it needful to excuse himself for feeling deeply the death of such a one in his household—all these traits of character combine to present him to us as one of those "children of God" that were scattered abroad in the world, and whom Christ was to gather together into the one fellowship of his Church (John 11:52).

The manner is remarkable in which the centurion makes easier to himself his act of faith, by the help of an analogy drawn from the circle of things with which he himself is familiar, by a comparison which he borrows from his own military experience. He knows that Christ's *word* will be sufficient, for, he adds, *"I am a man under authority, having soldiers under me, and I say to this man, Go, and he goeth, and to another, Come, and he cometh, and to my servant, Do this, and he doeth it."* His argument is here from the less to the greater. "I am," he would say, "one occupying only a subordinate place, set *under* authority, a subaltern, with tribunes and commanders over me. Yet, notwithstanding, those that are under me, obey me. My word is potent with them. I have power to send them hither and thither, and they go at my bidding, so that sitting still I can yet have the things accomplished which I would. How much more thou, who art not set, as I am, in a subordinate place, but who art as a prince over the host of heaven, who wilt have angels and spirits to obey thy word and run swiftly at thy command. It needs not then that thou comest to my house; do thou only commission one of these genii of healing, who will execute speedily the errand of grace on which thou shalt send him." His view of Christ's relation to the spiritual kingdom is as original as it is grand; and it is so truly that of the Roman officer: the Lord appears to him as the true Caesar and *Imperator,* the highest over the hierarchy, not of earth, but of heaven (Col. 1:16).

In all this there was so wonderful a union of childlike faith and profound humility, that it is not strange to read that the Lord himself was filled with admiration: *"When Jesus heard it, he marveled, and said to them that followed, Verily, I say unto you, I have not found so great faith, no, not in Israel."* It is notable that St. Matthew alone records these words, which before-hand we should rather have expected to have found recorded by St. Luke. For it is he, the companion of the apostle to the Gentiles, that for the most part loves to bring out the side of our Lord's ministry, on which it looked not merely to the Jewish nation but to the heathen world. In these words, and in those which follow, is a solemn warning, on the Lord's part, to his Jewish hearers of their danger of losing privileges, which now were theirs, but which yet they should see pass over from them into the possession of others. Because of their unbelief, they, the natural branches of the olive tree, should be broken off; and in their room the wild olive should be graffed in: *"Many shall come from the east and from the west, and shall sit down with Abraham, and Isaac, and Jacob in the kingdom of heaven,"* shall be partakers of the heavenly festival, which shall be at the inauguration of the kingdom; and from which they who were first invited should be excluded.

And then to him, or to his messengers, it was said, *"Go thy way, and as thou hast believed, so be it done unto thee. And his servant was healed in the self-same hour"*—not merely was there a remission of the strength of the disease, but it altogether left him. There has sometimes been a difficulty concerning the exact nature of the complaint from which he was thus graciously delivered. In St. Matthew the centurion describes it as palsy, with which however the *"grievously tormented"* does not seem altogether to agree, nor yet St. Luke's words that he was *"ready to die,"* since in itself it is neither accompanied with these violent paroxysms of pain, nor is it in its nature mortal. But paralysis with the contraction of the joints is accompanied with strong pain, and when united, as it much oftener is in the hot climates of the East and of Africa than among us, with tetanus, both causes extreme suffering, and would rapidly bring on dissolution.

12.
The Demoniac in the Synagogue of Capernaum

Mark 1:23–26; Luke 4:33–36

The healing of this demoniac, the second miracle of the kind which the Evangelists record at any length, is very far from offering so much remarkable as some other works of the same kind, yet it is not without its peculiar features. That which it has most remarkable, although that is not without its parallels (see Mark 1:34; Matt. 8:29), is the testimony which the evil spirit bears to Christ, and his refusal to accept that testimony. In either of these circumstances, this history stands parallel to the account which we have in the Acts (16:16–18) of the girl with the spirit of Apollo, who bore witness to Paul and his company, "These men are the servants of the Most Hight God, which show unto us the way of salvation," whereat, in like manner, Paul was "grieved," and would not permit it anymore.

Our Lord was teaching, as was his wont upon a Sabbath, in the synagogue of Capernaum; and the people were already wondering at the authority with which he taught. But he was not only mighty in word, but also mighty in work, and it was ordained by the providence of his Heavenly Father, that the opportunity should here be offered him for making yet deeper the impression on his hearers, for here also confirming the word with signs following. *"There was in their synagogue a man with an unclean spirit"*; and this unclean spirit felt at once that One was nigh, who was stronger than all the kingdom whereunto he belonged: hitherto his goods had been at peace; but now there was come One who should divide the spoil. And with the instinct and consciousness of this danger which so nearly threatened the kingdom of hell, he cried out—not the man himself, but the evil spirit which had usurped dominion over him—"*saying, Let us alone: what have we to do with thee, thou Jesus of Nazareth? Art thou come to destroy us? I know thee who thou art, the Holy One of God.*" Earth has not recognized her king, has not yet seen him through his disguise; but heaven and hell alike bear witness unto him: "the devils also believe and tremble."

Yet here this question arises, what could have been the motive to this testimony, thus borne? It is strange that the evil spirit should thus, without compulsion, proclaim to men *his* presence, who was come to be the destroyer of the kingdom of the devil. Rather we should expect that he would have denied, or sought to obscure, the glory of his Person. It cannot be said that this was an unwilling confession to the truth, forcibly extorted by Christ's superior power, since it displeased him in whose favor it professed to be borne, and was by him silenced at once. It remains either, with Theophylact and Grotius, to take this as the cry of base and abject fear, that with fawning and with flattery would fain avert from itself the doom, which with Christ's presence in the world appears to near—to compare, as Jerome does, this exclamation to that of the fugitive slave, dreaming of nothing but stripes and torments when he encounters his well-known lord, and who would now by any means turn away his anger: or else, and so Christ's immediately stopping of his mouth would seem to argue, this testimony was intended only to do harm, to injure the estimation of him in whose behalf it was borne. It was to bring the truth itself into suspicion and discredit, when it was borne witness to by the spirit of lies: and thus these confessions to Christ may have been intended only to anticipate and to mar his great purpose and plan, even as we see Mark 3:22 following hard on Mark 3:11. Therefore the Lord would not allow this testimony; "*Jesus rebuked him, saying, Hold thy peace, and come out of him*"; not as Michael the archangel, "*The Lord rebuke thee*" (Jude 9), but in his own name and in his own power.

It might seem as though the evil spirit was not altogether and at once obedient to the word of Christ, that it was not altogether a word of power; since he bade him to hold his peace, and yet in the next verse it is said, that "*he cried with a loud voice,*" as he was leaving the man. (Cf. Acts 8:7.) But in truth he was obedient to this command of silence; he did not *speak* anymore, and that was the thing which our Lord meant to forbid: this cry was nothing but an inarticulate cry of rage and pain. Neither is there any contradiction between St. Luke (4:35), who says that the evil spirit *"hurt him not,"* and St. Mark, according to whom, he *"tare"* him: he did not do him any permanent injury; no doubt what evil he could do him he did. Even St. Luke says that he cast him on the ground; with which the phrase of the earlier Evangelist, that he threw him into strong convulsions, in fact consents. We have at Mark 9:26 an analogous case, only with worse symptoms accompanying the going out of the foul spirit; for what the devil cannot keep as his own, he will, if he can, destroy; even as Pharoah never treated the children of Israel worse than just when they were escaping from his grasp. Something similar is evermore finding place; and Satan vexes with temptations and with buffetings none so much as those who are in the act of being delivered from under his dominion forever.

13.

The Healing of Simon's Wife's Mother

Matthew 8:14–17; Mark 1:29–31; Luke 4:38–39

This miracle is by St. Mark and St. Luke linked immediately and in a manner that marks a historic connection with that which has just come under our notice. The sacred historians go on to speak of our Lord, saying, "And he arose out of the synagogue, and went into Simon's house"—in St. Mark, "the house of Simon and Andrew." The stronger personality of Peter causes Andrew, the earlier called, and the leader of his brother to Jesus, probably also the elder brother, here as elsewhere to fall into the background. We may infer that he went on this Sabbath day to eat bread there. (Cf. Luke 14:1.) Being arrived, it was told him of Simon's wife's mother, who "was taken with a great fever, and they besought him for her." Here, again, we have the use of a remarkable phrase; Jesus "rebuked the fever," as at other times he "rebuked" the winds and the waves; and with such effect that it left her, and not in that state of extreme weakness and exhaustion which fever usually leaves behind, when in the ordinary course of things it has abated; it left her not gradually convalescent; but so entire and unwonted was her cure, that "immediately she arose and ministered unto them"—was able to provide for them what was necessary for their entertainment—a pattern, as has been often observed, in this to everyone that has been restored to spiritual health, that he should use this strength in ministering to Christ and to his people.

The fame of this miracle and that which immediately preceded it on the same day, spread so rapidly, that *"when the even was come,"*

155

or as St. Mark has it, *"when the sun did set,"* they brought to him many more that were variously afflicted. There are two explanations of this little circumstance, which all three Evangelists are careful to record, that it was not till the sun was setting or had actually set, that they brought these sick to Jesus—either, as Hammond and Olshausen suggest, that they waited till the heat of the middle day, which these sick and suffering were ill able to bear, was past, and brought them in the cool of the evening; or else to say that this day being the Sabbath (cf. Mark 1:21, 29, 32), they were unwilling to violate the sacred rest of the day, which they counted they would have done by bringing their sick to be healed; and so, ere they would do this, waited till the Sabbath was ended. It did end, as is well known, at sunset. Thus Chrysostom in one place, although in another he sees in it more generally a sign of the faith and eagerness of the people, who even when the day was spent, still came streaming to Christ, and laying their sick at his feet.

The quotation which St. Matthew makes from Isaiah, after he has recorded the numerous healings which Christ upon that day effected, is not without its difficulties; *"that it might be fulfilled which was spoken by Esaias the prophet, saying, Himself took our infirmities and bore our sicknesses."* The difficulty does not lie in the fact that St. Peter (1 Pet. 2:24), quotes the same verse rather as setting forth the Messiah as the bearer of the sins than the healer of the sicknesses of his people. As far as the words go, St. Matthew is nearer to the original, which declares he came under our sicknesses and our sorrows, the penal consequences of our sins. And any apparent difference between the two sacred writers of the New Testament vanishes when we keep in mind the intimate connection which in Scripture ever appears between moral and physical suffering; and not in Scripture only; for many, probably all, languages have a word answering to our "evil," which bears in its double meaning of sin and of calamity, the deepest witness—for no witness is so deep as the involuntary witness of language—to this connection.

But the application of the verse is more embarrassing. Those who have best right to be heard on the matter, deny that *"bore"* can mean "bore away," or that *"took"* can be accepted in the sense of "removed," and affirm that the words must mean a taking *upon himself* the sufferings and sorrows from which he delivered his people. But in what sense did our Lord take upon himself the sicknesses which he healed? Does it not seem rather that he abolished them, and removed them altogether out of the way? It is no doubt a perfectly Scriptural thought, that Christ is the κάθαρμα, the piaculum, who is to draw to himself all the evils of the world, in whom all are to center, that in him all may be abolished and done away— yet he did not *become* this through the healing of diseases, anymore than through any other isolated acts of his life and conversation. He was not more this piacular expiation after he had healed these sicknesses than before. We can understand his being said in his death and in his passion to come himself under the burden of those sufferings and pains from which he released others; but how can this be affirmed of him when he was engaged in works of beneficent activity? Then he was rather chasing away diseases and pains altogether, than himself undertaking them.

An explanation, which has found favor with many, has been suggested by those words which we have already noticed, that his labors were not ended with the day, but protracted far into the evening—so that he removed indeed sicknesses from others, but with painfulness to himself, and with the weariness attendant upon labors unseasonably drawn out, and thus may not unfitly be said to have taken those sicknesses on himself. Olshausen, though in somewhat more spiritual a manner, gives the same explanation. He says, the obscurity of the passage only disappears when we learn to think more *really* of the healing activity of Christ, as an actual outstreaming and outbreathing of the fullness of his inner life. As therefore physical exertion physically wearied him (John 4:6), so did spiritual activity long drawn out spiritually exhaust him, and this exhaustion, as all other forms of suffering, he underwent for our sakes. A statement questionable in its doctrine: moreover, I cannot believe that the Evangelist meant to lay any such stress upon the unusual or prolonged labors of this day, or that he would not as willingly have quoted these words in relating any other cure or cures which the Lord performed. Not this day only, even had it been a day of especial weariness, but every day of his earthly life was a coming under, upon his part, of the evils which he removed from others. For that which is the law of all true helping, namely, that the burden which you would lift, you must yourself stoop to and come under (Gal. 6:2), the grief which you would console, you must yourself feel with—a law which we witness to as often as we use the words "sympathy" and "compassion"—was, of course, eminently true in him upon whom the help of all was laid. Not in this single aspect of his life, namely, that he was a healer of sicknesses, were these words of the prophet fulfilled, but rather in the life itself, which brought him in contact with these sicknesses and these discords of man's inner being, every one of which as a real consequence of sin, and as being at every moment contemplated by him as such, did press with a living pang into the holy soul of the Lord. Not so much the healing of these sicknesses was Christ's bearing of them; but his burden was that there were these sicknesses to heal. He *"bore"* them, inasmuch as he bore the mortal suffering life, in which alone he could bring them to an end, and at length swallow up death in victory.

14.

The Raising of the Widow's Son

Luke 7:11–16

The city whither our Lord was bound, and at the gate of which this great miracle was wrought, is not mentioned elsewhere in Scripture. It lay upon the southern border of Galilee, and on the road to Jerusalem, whither our Lord was probably now going to keep the second passover of his open ministry. That our Lord should meet the funeral at the gate of the city, while it belonged no doubt to the wonder-works of God's grace, while it was one of those marvelous coincidences which, seeming accidental, are yet deep laid in the councils of his wisdom and of his love, is at the same time a natural circumstance, to be explained by the fact that the Jews did not suffer the interring of the dead in towns, but had their burial places without the walls. Probably there was very much in the circumstances of the sad procession which he now met, to arouse the compassion even of them who were not touched with so lively a feeling for human sorrows as was the compassionate Savior of men; and it was this which had brought that "much people" to accompany the bier. Indeed, there could little be added to the words of the Evangelist, whose whole narrative here, apart from its deeper interest, is a master-work for its perfect beauty— there could be little added to it to make the picture of desolation more complete—"There was a dead man carried out, the only son of his mother, and she was widow." The bitterness of the mourning for an only son had passed into a proverb, thus, Jeremiah 6:26, "Make thee mourning as for an only son, most bitter lamentation"; and Zechariah 12:10, "They shall mourn for him as one mourneth for his only son"; Amos 8:10, "I will make it as the mourning of an only son."

"*And when the Lord saw her, he had compassion on her, and said unto her, Weep not.*" How different this "*Weep not,*" from the "Weep not" which often proceeds from the lips of earthly comforters, who,

159

even while they speak the words, give no reason why the mourner should cease from weeping; but he that is come that he may one day make good that word, "God shall wipe away all tears from their eyes, and there shall be no more death, neither sorrow, nor crying, neither shall there be any more pain" (Rev. 21:4), does show now some effectual glimpses of his power, wiping away, though not yet forever, the tears from the weeping eyes of that desolate mother. Yet, as Olshausen has observed, it would be an error to suppose that compassion for the mother was the *determining* motive for this mighty spiritual act on the part of Christ: for, in that case, had the joy of the mother been the only object which he had in view, the young man who was raised would have been used merely as a *means*, which yet no man can ever be. That joy of the mother was indeed the nearest consequence of the act, but not the final cause—*that*, though at present hidden, was, no doubt, the spiritual awakening of the young man for a higher life, through which, indeed, alone the joy of the mother became a true and an abiding joy.

The drawing nigh and touching the bier was meant as an intimation to the bearers that they should arrest their steps, and one which they understood, for immediately *"they that bare him stood still."* Then follows the word of power, and spoken, as ever, in his own name, *"Young man, I say unto thee, Arise"*—I, that am the Resurrection and the Life, quickening "the dead, and calling those things which be not, as though they were." And that word was heard, for *"he that was dead sat up, and began to speak."* Christ rouses from the bier as easily as another would rouse from the bed—different in this even from his own messengers and ministers in the Old Covenant; for they, not without an effort, not without a long and earnest wrestling with God, won back its prey from the jaws of death; and this, because there dwelt not the *fullness* of power in them, who were but as servants in the house of another, not as a son in his own house.

And he delivered him to his mother." (Cf. 1 Kgs. 17:23; 2 Kgs. 4:36.) He who did this, shall once, when he has spoken the great "Arise," which shall awaken not one, but all the dead, deliver all the divided, that have fallen asleep in him, to their beloved for personal recognition and for a special fellowship of joy, amid the universal gladness and communion of love which shall then fill all hearts. We have the promise and pledge of this in the three raisings from the dead which prefigure that coming resurrection. The effects of this miracle on those present were for good; *"There came a fear on all,"* a holy fear, a sense that they were standing in the presence of some great one; *"and they glorified God"*—praised him for his mercy in remembering and visiting his people Israel—*"saying that a great prophet is risen up among us."* They concluded that no ordinary prophet was among them, but a *"great"* one, since none but the very greatest prophets of the olden times, an Elijah or an Elisha, had brought the dead to life. In their other exclamation, *"God hath visited his people,"* lay no less an allusion to the long periods during which they had been without a prophet, so that it might have seemed, and many might have almost feared, that the last of these had arrived.

15.

The Healing of the Impotent Man at Bethesda

John 5:1–16

One who is perhaps the ablest among the commentators of the Romish communion begins his observations on this act of healing with the expression of his hearty wish that the sacred historian had added a single word to his narrative, and told us at what "feast of the Jews" it was wrought. Certainly an infinite amount of learned discussion would so have been saved; for this question has been greatly debated, not merely for its own sake, but because of the important bearing which it has upon the whole chronology of St. John's Gospel, and therefore of our Lord's life; for if we cannot determine the duration of his actual ministry from the helps which are supplied by this Gospel, we shall seek in vain to do it from the others. If it can be proved that this "feast of the Jews" was the feast of the Passover, then St. John makes mention of four distinct Passovers, three besides this present, 2:13; 6:4; and the last; and we shall get to the three years and a half, the half of a week of years, for the length of Christ's ministry, which many, with just reason as it seems, have thought they found intimated and designated beforehand for it in the prophecies of Daniel (9:27). But if this feast be that of Pentecost, or, as in later times many have been inclined to accept it, the feast of Purim, then the view drawn from the prophecy of Daniel, of the duration of Christ's ministry, however likely in itself, will yet derive no proof or confirmation from dates supplied by St. John; nor will it be possible to make out from him, with any certainty, a period of more than between two and three years from our Lord's baptism to his death.

And first with regard to the history of the passage, we have no older view than that of Ireneus. Replying to the Gnostics, who pressed the words of Isaiah, "the acceptable *year* of the Lord," to make them mean literally that our Lord's ministry lasted but a single year, he enumerates the Passovers of our Lord's life, and expressly includes this. Origen however and the Alexandrians, who held with the Gnostics that our Lord's ministry lasted but a single year, resting upon the same phrase, "the *year* of the Lord," did not, as indeed consistently they could not, agree with Ireneus; nor did the Greek Church generally; Chrysostom, Cyril, Theophylact, take it for the feast of Pentecost. At a later period, however, Theodoret, wishing to confirm his view of the half week in Daniel, refers to St. John in proof that the Lord's ministry lasted for three years and a half, implying that for him this feast was a Passover. This, too, was the view of Luther, Calvin, and it derived additional support from Sealiger's adherence to it; and were the question only between it and the feast of Pentecost, the point would have been settled long ago, as now on all sides the latter is given up.

But in modern times another scheme has been started, which at present divides the voices of interpreters, and has not a few in its favor, namely, that this feast is a feast of Purim; that namely which went immediately before the *second* Passover of our Lord's ministry, for such in that case would be the one named John 6:4. But the view of Ireneus that this present *"feast of the Jews"* is itself a Passover, and the second—that other consequently the third—though not unencumbered with difficulties, yet is not, I think, to be exchanged for this newer theory. It is perplexing, as must be admitted, to find another Passover occurring so very soon (6:4). Nor may we press the argument, that St. John making mention of *"the feast"* without further addition, means always the chief feast, the Passover; for the examples adduced do not bear this out; he does indeed use this language, yet always with allusion to some mention of the feast made shortly before. But the argument which mainly prevails with me is this—the Evangelist clearly connects the Lord's coming to Jerusalem with the keeping of this feast; it was to celebrate the feast he came. But there was nothing in the feast of Purim to draw him thither. It was no religious feast at all; but only a popular; of human, not of divine institution. There was no temple service pertaining to it; but men kept it at their own houses. And though naturally it would have been celebrated at Jerusalem with more pomp and circumstance than anywhere besides, yet there was nothing in its feasting and its rioting, its intemperance and excess, which would have made our Lord particularly desirous to sanction it with his presence. As far as Mordecai and Esther and the deliverance wrought in their days stand below Moses and Aaron and Miriam and the glorious redemption from Egypt, so in true worth, in dignity, in religious significance, stood the feast of Purim below the feast of the Passover; however a carnal generation may have been inclined to exaggerate the importance of that, in the past events and actual celebration of which, there was so much to flatter the carnal mind. There is an extreme improbability in the hypothesis that it was this which attracted our Lord to Jerusalem; and these considerations strongly prevail with me to believe that the earlier view is the most accurate, and that this feast which our blessed Lord adorned with his presence and signalized with this great miracle, is *"the feast,"* that feast which is the mother of all the rest, the Passover.

The scene of this miracle was the immediate neighborhood of the pool of Bethesda. It has been common for many centuries to point out the large excavation near the gate now called St. Stephen's gate, as the ancient Bethesda. It is true that its immense depth, seventy-five feet, had perplexed many; yet the incurious ease which has misnamed so much in the Holy Land and in Jerusalem had remained without being seriously challenged, until Robinson, our latest, as in the main our best, authority on all such matters, among the many traditions which he has disturbed, affirms that "there is not the slightest evidence which can identify it with the Bethesda of the New Testament." Nor does the tradition which identifies them ascend higher, as he can discover, than the thirteenth century. He sees in that rather the remains of the ancient fosse which protected on the north side the citadel Antonia; and the true Bethesda he thinks he finds, though on this he speaks not with any certainty, in that which goes now by the name of the Fountain of the Virgin, being the upper fountain of Siloam.

In the porches round *"lay a great multitude of impotent folk, of blind, halt, and withered"*; the words which complete this verse, *"waiting for the moving of the water,"* lie under strong suspicion, as the verse following has undoubtedly no right to a place in the text. That fourth verse the most important Greek and Latin copies are alike without, and most of the early versions. In other manuscripts which retain this verse, the obelus which hints suspicion, or the asterisk which marks rejection, is attached to it; while those in which it appears unquestioned belong mostly, as Griesbach shows, to a later recension of the text. And this fourth verse spreads the suspicion of its own spuriousness over the last clause of the verse preceding, which, though it has not so great a body of evidence against it, has yet, in a less degree, the same marks of suspicion about it. Doubtless whatever here is addition, whether only the fourth verse, or the last clause also of the third, found very early its way into the text; we have it as early as Tertullian—the first witness for its presence. The baptismal angel, a favorite thought with him, was here foreshowed and typified; as, somewhat later, Ambrose saw a prophecy of the descent of the Holy Ghost, consecrating the waters of baptism to the mystical washing away of sin; and Chrysostom and others make frequent use of this verse. At first probably a marginal note, expressing the popular notion of the Jewish Christians concerning the origin of the healing power which from time to time these waters possessed, by degrees it assumed the shape in which now we have it: for there are marks of growth about it, betraying themselves in a great variety of readings—some copies omitting one part, and some another of the verse—all which is generally the sign of a later addition: thus, little by little, it procured admission into the text, probably at Alexandria first, the birthplace of other similar additions. There is nothing in the statement itself which might not have found place in St. John. It rests upon that religious view of nature, which in all nature sees something beyond nature, which does not believe that it has discovered causes, when, in fact, it has only traced the sequence of phenomena, and which in all recognizes a going forth of the immediate power of God, invisible agencies of his, whether personal or otherwise, accomplishing his will.

From among the multitude that are waiting here, Christ singles out one on whom he will show his power—one only, for he came not *now* to be the healer of men's bodies, save only as he could link on to this healing the truer healing of their souls and spirits. One construction of the fifth verse would make the poor cripple, the present object of his healing love, to have been actually waiting at the edge of that pool for the *"thirty and eight years"* which are named; while according to another construction, the thirty-eight years express the age of the man. Neither is right, but rather that which our version gives. The eight and thirty years are the duration, not of his life, but of his malady—while yet it is not implied that he had been expecting his healing from that pool for all that time; though, from his own words, we infer that he had there been waiting for it long. The question, *"Wilt thou be made whole?"* at first might seem superfluous; for who would not be made whole if he might? And the very presence of this man at the place of healing witnessed for his desire. But the question has its purpose. This impotent man probably had waited so long, and so long waited in vain, that hope was dead or well-nigh dead within him, and the question is asked to awaken in him anew a yearning after the benefit, which the Savior, compassionating his hopeless case, was about to impart. His heart may have been withered through his long sufferings and the long neglects of his fellowmen; it was something to persuade him that this stranger pitied him, was interested in his case, would help him if he could. So persuading him to believe in his love, he prepared him to believe also in his might. Our Lord was giving him now the faith, which presently he was about to demand of him.

In the man's answer there is not a direct reply to the question, but an explanation why he yet continued in his infirmity. "Right gladly, Sir," he would say, "only *I have no man, when the water is troubled, to put me into the pool.*" The virtues of the water disappeared so fast, they were so preoccupied, whether from the narrowness of the spot, or from some cause which we know not, by the first comer, that he who through his own infirmity and the lack of all friendly help could never be this first, missed always the blessing; *"While I am coming, another steppeth down before me."* But the long and weary years of baffled expectation are at length ended: *"Jesus saith unto him, Rise, take up thy bed and walk,"* and the man believed that power went forth with that word, and making proof, he found that it was even so: *"immediately the man was made whole, and took up his bed and walked."* It is different with him from that other impotent man (Acts 3:2). He, when he was healed, walked and leaped and praised God (v. 8). His infirmity was no chastisement of an especial sin, for he had been "lame from his mother's womb." But this man shall carry his bed, a present memento of his past sin.

But *"the Jews,"* not here the multitude, but some among the spiritual heads of the nation, whom it is very noticeable that St. John continually characterizes by this name (1:19; 7:1; 9:22; 18:12, 14); find fault with the man for carrying his bed in obedience to Christ's command, their reason being because *"the same day"* on which the miracle was accomplished *"was the Sabbath"*; and the carrying of any burden was one of the expressly prohibited works of that day. Here, indeed they had apparently an Old Testament ground to go upon, and an interpretation of the Mosaic Law from the lips of a prophet, to justify their interference, and the offence which they took. But the man's bearing of his bed was not a work by itself; it was merely the corollary, or indeed the concluding act, of his healing, that by which he should make proof himself, and give testimony to others, of its reality. It was lawful to heal on the Sabbath day; it was lawful then to do that which was immediately involved in and directly followed on the healing. And here lay ultimately the true controversy between Christ and his adversaries, namely, whether it was most lawful to do good on that day, or to leave it undone (Luke 6:9). Starting from the unlawfulness of leaving good undone, he asserted that he was its true keeper, keeping it as God kept it, with the highest beneficent activity, which in his Father's case, as in his own, was identical with deepest rest—and not, as they accused him of being, its breaker. It was because he had himself "done those things" (see v. 16), that the Jews persecuted him, and not for bidding the man to bear his bed, which was a mere accident and consequence involved in what he himself had wrought. This, however, first attracted their notice; whereupon they *"said unto him that was cured, It is the Sabbath day: it is not lawful for thee to carry thy bed."* Already the pharisaical Jews, starting from passages such as Exodus 23:12; 31:13–17; 35:2, 3; Numbers 15:32–36; Nehemiah 13:15–22; had laid down such a multitude of prohibitions, and drawn so infinite a number of hairsplitting distinctions, as we shall have occasion to see, Luke 13:15, 16, that a plain and unlearned man could hardly come to know what was forbidden, and what was permitted. This poor man concerned himself not with these subtle casuistries. He only knew that the man with power to make him whole, the man who had shown compassion to him, had bid him do what he was doing, and he is satisfied with this authority: *"He that made me whole, the same said unto me, Take up thy bed and walk."* Surely a good model of an answer, when the world finds fault and is scandalized with what the Christian is doing, contrary to its works and ways, and to the rules which *it* has laid down!

For this man, the greater offender, they inquire now, as being the juster object of censure and of punishment: *"Then asked they him, What man is that which said unto thee, Take up thy bed and walk?"* The malignity of the questioners, coming out as it does in the very shape in which they put their question, is worthy of note. They do not take up the poor man's words on their most favorable side, and that which plainly would have been the more natural; they do not say, "What man is he that made thee whole?" but, probably, themselves knowing perfectly well, or at least guessing, who his Healer was, yet wishing to undermine any influence which he may have obtained over this simple man—an influence already perceptible in his finding the authority of Jesus sufficient to justify him in his own eyes for transgressing their commandment—they insinuate by the form of the question that the man could not be from God, who gave a command at which they, the interpreters of God's Law, were so greatly aggrieved and offended.

But the man could not point out his benefactor, for he had already withdrawn: "*Jesus had conveyed himself away, a multitude being in that place.*" Many say, as Grotius for instance, because he would avoid ostentation and the applauses of the people: but "*a multitude being in that place*" may be only mentioned to explain the facility with which he withdrew: he mingled with and passed through the crowd, and so was lost from sight in an instant. Were it not that the common people usually took our Lord's part in cases like the present, one might imagine that a menacing crowd under the influence of these chiefs of the Jews had gathered together while this conversation was going forward betwixt the healed cripple and themselves, from the violence of whom the Lord withdrew himself, his hour being not yet come.

Though we cannot of course draw any conclusion from the circumstance, yet it is a sign of good augury that "*Jesus findeth him in the temple,*" rather than anywhere else. It is as though he was there returning thanks for the great mercy which had been so lately vouchsafed him. (Cf. Is. 38:22; Acts 3:8.) And now our Lord, whose purpose it ever was to build upon the healing of the body the better healing of the soul, suffers not this matter to conclude without a word of solemn warning, a word which showed that all the past life of the sufferer lay open and manifest before him; even things done more than thirty-eight years ago, before, that is, his own earthly life had commenced: "*Behold, thou art made whole: sin no more, lest a worse thing come unto thee*"—a worse thing than those thirty and eight years of pain and infirmity—words which give us an awful glimpse of the severity of God's judgments. This infirmity had found him a youth and left him an old man; it had withered up all his manhood, and yet "*a worse thing*" even than this is threatened him, should he sin again.

What the past sin of this sufferer had been, to which the Lord alludes, we know not, but the man himeslf knew very well; his conscience was the interpreter of the warning. This much, however, is plain to us; that Christ did connect the man's suffering with his individual sin; for however he rebuked man's uncharitable way of tracing such a connection, or the scheme of a Theodice, which should in every case affirm a man's personal suffering to be in proportion to his personal guilt, a scheme which all experience refutes, much judgment being deferred and awaiting the great day when all things shall be set on the square; yet he meant not thereby to deny that much, very much of judgment is even now continually proceeding. However unwilling men may be to receive this, bringing as it does God so near, and making retribution so real and so prompt a thing, yet is it true none the less. As some eagle pierced with a shaft feathered from its own wing, so many a sufferer, even in this present time, sees and cannot deny that it was his own sin that fledged the arrow of God's judgment, which has pierced him and brought him down. And lest he should miss the connection, oftentimes he is punished, it may be himself sinned against by his fellowman, in the very kind in which he himself has sinned against others. The deceiver is deceived, as Jacob; the violator of the sanctities of family life is himself wounded in his tenderest and dearest relations, as was David. And many a sinner, who cannot read his own doom, for it is a final and a fatal one, yet declares in that doom to others that there is indeed a coming back upon men of their sins: the grandson of Ahab is himself treacherously slain in the portion of Naboth the Jezreelite (2 Kgs. 9:23); William Rufus perishes, himself the third of his family, in the New Forest, the scene of the sacrilege and the crimes of his race.

But to return; *"The man departed, and told the Jews that it was Jesus which had made him whole."* Whom he did not recognize in the crowd, he has recognized in the temple. This is Augustine's remark, who builds on it many valuable observations upon the inner calm and solitude of spirit in which alone we shall recognize the Lord. Yet while these remarks may stand in themselves, they scarcely find place here. The man probably learned from the bystanders the name of his deliverer, and went and told it—scarcely, as some assume, in treachery, or to augment the envy which was already existing against him, at least there is not a trace of this in the narrative itself—but gratefully proclaiming aloud and to the rulers of his nation the physician who had healed him. He expected, probably, in the simplicity of his heart, that the name of him, whose reputation, if not his person, he had already known, whom so many counted as a prophet, if not as the Messiah himself, would have been sufficient to stop the mouths of the gainsayers. Had it been in a baser spirit that he went, as Chrysostom ingeniously observes, he would not have gone and told them *"that it was Jesus which had made him whole,"* but rather that it was Jesus who had bidden him to carry his bed.

His word, however, profited nothing. The Jews were only provoked the more; for so is it ever with the revelation of the divine: what it does not draw to itself drives *from* itself; what it does not win to obedience it arrays in active hostility. They are now more bitterly incensed against the Lord, not merely because he had encouraged this man to break, but had in that act of healing himself broken, the Sabbath—set at nought, that is, their traditions about it. In his reply he seeks to lift up the cavillers to the true standing point from which to contemplate the Sabbath, and his relation to it as the only-begotten of the Father. He is no more a breaker of the Sabbath than God is, when he upholds with an energy that knows no pause the work of his creation from hour to hour, and from moment to moment: *"My Father worketh hitherto, and I work"*; my work is but the reflex of his work. Abstinence from an outward work belongs not to the idea of a Sabbath, it is only more or less the necessary condition of it for beings so framed and constituted as ever to be in danger of losing the true collection and rest of the spirit in the multiplicity of earthly toil and business. Man indeed must cease from *his* work, if a higher work is to find place in him. He scatters himself in his work, and therefore must collect himself anew, and have seasons for so doing. But with him who is one with the Father it is otherwise. In him the deepest rest is not excluded by the highest activity; nay rather, in God, in the Son as in the Father, they are one and the same.

This defence of what he has done only exasperates his adversaries the more. They have here not a Sabbath-breaker only, but also a blasphemer, one who, as they well perceive, however some later may have refused to see it, is putting himself on an equality with God, is claiming divine attributes for himself; and they now not merely persecute, but seek to slay him. Hereupon follows a discourse than which there is no weightier in Holy Scripture, for the fast fixing of the doctrine concerning the relations of the Father and the Son. Other passages may be as important in regard of the Arian, other again in regard of the Sabellian, declension from the truth;

but this upon both sides plants the pillars of the faith; yet it would lead too far from the purpose of this volume to enter on it here.

The subject, however, would not be complete without some further reference to the types and prophetic symbols which many have traced in this history. It has been needful indeed in part to anticipate this matter. We have seen how, of old, men saw in these beneficent influences of the pool of Bethesda a foreshowing and foreshadowing of future benefits, and specially, as was natural, of the benefit of baptism; and, through familiarity with a miracle of a lower order, a helping of men's faith to the receiving the weightier mystery of a yet higher healing which was to be linked with water. They were well pleased also often to magnify the largeness and freedom of the present benefit, by comparing it with the narrower and more stinted blessings of the old dispensation, blessings which, they say, altogether ceased at the death of Christ, with the coming in, that is, and establishing of the new. The pool with its one healed, and that one at distant intervals—once a year Theophylact and most others assumed, although nothing of the kind is said, and the word of the original may mean oftener or seldomer—was the type of the weaker and more restrained graces of the Old Covenant; when not as yet was there room for all, nor a fountain opened and at all times accessible for the healing of the spiritual sicknesses of the whole race of men, but only of a single people.

Thus Chrysostom, in a magnificent Easter sermon, whose allusions have a peculiar fitness, the season of Easter being that at which the great multitudes of neophytes were baptized. He says: "Among the Jews also there was of old a pool of water. Yet learn whereunto it availed, that thou mayest accurately measure the Jewish poverty and our riches. There went down, it is said, an angel and moved the waters, and who first descended into them after the moving, obtained a cure. The Lord of angels went down into the stream of Jordan, and sanctifying the nature of water, healed the whole world. So that there indeed he who descended after the first was not healed, for to the Jews infirm and carnal this grace was given; but here after the first a second descends, after the second a third and a fourth; and were it a thousand, didst thou cast the whole world into these spiritual fountains, the grace were not worn out, the gift expended, the fountains defiled, the liberality exhausted." And Augustine, ever on the watch to bring out his great truth that the Law was for the revealing of sin, and could not effect its removal, for the making men to know their sickness, not for the healing that sickness, for the dragging them out of the lurking places of an imagined righteousness, not for the providing them of itself with any surer refuge, finds a type, or at least an apt illustration of this, in those five porches, which *showed* their sick, but could not *cure* them, in which they *"lay a great multitude of impotent folk, of blind, halt, and withered."* It needed that the waters should be stirred, before any power went forth for their cure. This motion of the pool was the perturbation of the Jewish people at the coming of the Lord Jesus Christ. Then powers were stirring for their healing, and he who *"went down,"* he who humbly believed in his Incarnation, in his descent as a man among us, who was not offended at his lowly estate, he was healed of whatever disease he had. Such are the most important uses in this kind that have been made of this history.

6.

The Miraculous Feeding
of Five Thousand

Matthew 14:15–21; Mark 6:35–44;

Luke 9:12–17; John 6:5–14

In St. Matthew the Lord's retiring to the desert place where this miracle was performed, connects itself directly with the murder of John the Baptist (v. 13). He, therefore, retired, his hour not being yet come. St. Mark and St. Luke put also this history in connection with the account of the Baptist's death, though they do not give that as the motive of the Lord's withdrawal. St. Mark, indeed, mentions another reason which in part moved him to this, namely, that the disciples, the apostles especially, who were just returned from their mission, might have time at once for bodily and spiritual refection and refreshment, might not be always in a crowd, always ministering to others, never to themselves (6:31). But thither, into the wilderness, the multitude followed him, proceeding, not necessarily "afoot" (Mark 6:33), but "by land," as contra-distinguished from him who went by sea: and this with such expedition, that although their way was much further than his, they "outwent" him, anticipated his coming, so that when he "went forth," not, that is, from the ship, but from his solitude, and for the purpose of graciously receiving those who thus came, he found a great multitude waiting for him. Though this their presence was, in fact, an entire defeating of the very purpose for which he had withdrawn himself thither, yet not the less "he received them, and spoke unto them of the kingdom of God, and healed them that had need of healing" (Luke 9:11). St. John's apparently casual notice of the fact that the

Passover was at hand (6:4), is not so much with the intention of giving a point in the chronology of the Lord's ministry, as to explain whence these great multitudes came, that streamed to Jesus: they were journeying toward Jerusalem to keep the feast.

There is this difference in the manner in which the miracle is introduced by the three Evangelists, and by St. John, that they make the first question concerning the manner of providing for the needs of the assembled crowds to come from the disciples, in the shape of a proposal that the Lord now that the day was beginning to decline, should dismiss them, thus giving them opportunity to purchase provisions in the neighboring villages; while in St. John it is the Lord himself who first suggests the difficulty, saying to Philip, *"Whence shall we buy bread that these may eat?"* (6:5). This difference, however, is capable of an easy explanation. It may well have been that our Lord spoke thus unto Philip at a somewhat earlier period of the afternoon; and then left the difficulty and perplexity to work in the minds of the apostles, preparing them in this way for the coming wonder which he was about to work; bringing them, as was so often his manner, to see that there was no help in the common course of things—and when they had acknowledged this, then, and not before, stepping in with his higher aid.

The Lord put this question to Phillip, not as needing any counsel, not as being himself in any real embarrassment, *"for he himself knew what he would do,"* but "tempting him," as Wiclif's translation has it—which word if we admit, we must yet understand in its milder sense, as indeed our later translators have done, who have given it, *"to prove him"* (Gen. 22:1). It was to prove him, what manner of trust he had in him whom he had himself already acknowledged the Messiah—"him of whom Moses in the Law and the prophets did write" (John 1:45)—and whether, remembering the great things which Moses had done, when he gave the people bread from heaven in the wilderness, and the notable miracle which Elisha, though on a smaller scale than that which now was needed, had performed (2 Kgs. 4:43, 44), he could so lift up his thoughts as to believe that he whom he had recognized as the Christ, greater therefore than Moses or the prophets, would be sufficient to the present need. Cyril sees a reason why Philip, rather than any other apostle, should have been selected to have this question put to him, namely that he had the greatest need of the teaching contained in it; and refers to his later words, "Lord, show us the Father" (John 14:8), in proof of the tardiness of his spiritual apprehension. But whether this was so or not, Philip does not on the present occasion abide the proof. Long as he has been with Jesus, he has not yet seen the Father in the Son (John 14:9), he does not yet know that his Lord is even the same who openeth his hand and filleth all things living with plenteousness, who feedeth and nourisheth all creatures, who has fed and nourished them from the creation of the world, and who therefore can feed these few thousands that are now waiting on his bounty. He has not thought of any other supplies save such as natural means could procure, and at once names a sum, *"two hundred pence,"* as but barely sufficient, which yet he would probably imply was a sum much larger than any which they had in their common purse at the moment.

Having drawn this confession of inability to meet the present need from the lips of Philip, he left it to work—till, somewhat later in the day, *"when it was evening, his disciples came to him"* with the proposal, the only one which suggested itself to them, that he should dismiss the crowds, and let them seek for the refreshment which they required in the neighboring hamlets and villages. But the Lord will now bring them yet nearer to the end which he has in view, and replies, *"They need not depart; give ye them to eat:"* and when they repeat with one mouth what Philip had before affirmed, asking if they shall spend two hundred pence (for them an impossible thing), on the food required (Mark 6:37), he bids them go and see what supplies they have actually at command. With their question we may compare Numbers 11:22, "Shall the flocks and the herds be slain for them to suffice them?" For in either question there is a mitigated infidelity, a doubt whether the hand of the Lord can really reach to supply the present need, though his word, here indeed only implicitly, has undertaken it. In the interval between their going and their return to him, they purchase, or rather secure for purchase, the little stock that is in possession of a single lad among the multitude; and thus is explained that in the three first Evangelists, the disciples speak of the five loaves and two fishes as theirs, that is, standing at their command, in St. John as rather belonging to the lad himself.

With this slender stock of homeliest fare, the Lord undertakes to satisfy all that multitude (Chrysostom quotes aptly here Ps. 78:26: "Shall God prepare a table in the wilderness?") and bids his disciples to make them all recline on the *"green grass,"* at that season of the year a delightful resting-place, and which both by St. Mark and St. John is noted to have abounded in the place. St. Mark adds another graphic touch, how they sat down in companies, which consisted some of fifty, some of a hundred, and how these separate companies showed in their symmetrical arrangement like so many garden plots. In this subordinate circumstance we behold his wisdom, who is the lord and lover of order. Thus, all disorder, all noise and confusion were avoided; there was no danger that the weaker, the women and the children, should be passed over, while the stronger and ruder unduly put themselves forward; thus the apostles were able to pass easily up and down among the multitude, and to minister in orderly succession to the necessities of every part.

The taking of the bread in hand would seem to have been a formal act going before the blessing or giving of thanks for it. This eucharistic act Jesus accomplished as the head of the household, and according to that beautiful saying of the Talmud, "He that enjoys aught without thanksgiving, is as though he robbed God." The words themselves are not given; they were probably those of the ordinary grace before meat in use in Israel. Having blessed the food, he delivered it to the apostles, who in their turn distributed to the different tables, if such they might be called—the marvelous multiplication taking place, as many say, first in the hands of the Savior himself, next in those of the apostles, and lastly in the hands of the eaters; yet at all events so that *"they did all eat and were filled."* Of that multitude we may fitly say, that in them the promise of the Savior, "Seek ye first the kingdom of God, and his righteousness, and all these things shall be added unto you," found a practical fulfillment. They had come taking no thought, for three days at least, of what they should eat or what they should drink, only anxious to hear the word of life, only seeking the kingdom of Heaven; and now the meaner things, according to the word of the promise, were added unto them.

Here too, even more than in the case of the water changed into wine, when we seek to realize to ourselves *the manner* of the miracle, it evermore eludes our grasp. We seek in vain to follow it with our imaginations. For, indeed, how is it possible to realize to ourselves, to bring within forms of understanding, any act of creation, any *becoming*? How is it possible in our thoughts to bridge over the gulf between not-being and being, which yet is bridged over in every creative act? And this being impossible, there is no force in the objection which one has made against the historical truth of this narrative, namely, that "there is no attempt by closer description to make clear in its details the manner and process in which this wonderful bread was formed." But this is the wisdom of the sacred narrator, to leave the description of the indescribable unattempted. His appeal is to the same faith which believes "that the worlds were formed *by the Word of God,* so that things which are seen, were not made of things which do appear" (Heb. 11:3).

An anology has been found to this miracle, and as it were a help to the understanding of it, in that which God does yearly in the cornfield, where a simple grain of corn cast into the earth multiplies itself, and in the end unfolds in numerous ears—and out of this thought many beautiful remarks have been made—as this, that while God's everyday miracles had grown cheap in men's sight by continual repetition, he had therefore reserved something, not more wonderful, but more out of use, to awaken men's minds to a new admiration—or, that as in the case of the water made wine, he did but compress into a single moment all those processes which in ordinary circumstances he, the same Lord of nature, caused more slowly to follow one upon another. But true as in its measure is this last observation, yet it cannot be left out of sight that the analogy does not reach through and through. For that other work in the field is the unfolding of the seed according to the law of its own being: thus, had the Lord taken a few grains of corn and cast them into the ground, and, a moment after, a large harvest had sprung up, this might have been termed such a divinely-hastened process. But with bread it is different, since before that is made there must be new interpositions of man's art, and those of such a nature as that by them the very life, which hitherto unfolded itself, must be crushed and destroyed. A grain of wheat could never by itself, and according to the laws of its natural development, issue in a loaf of bread. And, moreover, the Lord does not start from the simple germ, from the lifeful rudiments, in which all the seeds of a future life might be supposed to be wrapped up, and by him rapidly developed, but with the latest artificial result: one can conceive how the oak is enfolded in the acorn, but not how it could be said to be wrapped up in the piece of timber hewn and shaped from itself. This analogy then even as such is not satisfying; and, foregoing any helps of this kind, we must simply behold in this multiplying of the bread an act of divine omnipotence on his part who was the Word of God—not indeed now, as at the first, of absolute creation out of nothing, since there was a substratum to work on in the original loaves and fishes, but an act of creative accretion; the bread did

grow under his hands, so that from that little stock all the multitude were abundantly supplied: *"they did all eat and were filled."*

Thus He, all whose works were "signs," and had a tongue by
which they spoke to the world, did in this miracle proclaim himself
the true bread of the world, that should assuage the hunger of men,
the inexhausted and inexhaustible source of all life, in whom there
should be enough and to spare for all the spiritual needs of all hun-
gering souls in all ages. For, in Augustine's language, once already
quoted, "He was the Word of God; and all the acts of the Word are
themselves words for us; they are not as pictures, merely to look at
and admire, but as letters which we must seek to read and understand.

When all had eaten and were satisfied, the Lord bade the disciples to gather up the fragments which remained of the loaves, that
nothing might be lost; the existence of these was itself a witness
that there was enough and more than enough for all (2 Kgs. 4:43,
44; Ruth 2:14). St. Mark makes mention that it was so done also
with the fishes. For thus with the Lord of nature, as with nature
herself, the most prodigal bounty goes hand in hand with the
nicest and truest economy, and he who had but now shown himself God, again submits himself to the laws and proprieties of his
earthly condition, so that as in the miracle itself his power, in this
command his humility, shines eminently forth. At this bidding they
collected fragments, which immensely exceeded in bulk and quantity the amount of provision with which they began. They filled
twelve baskets with these. An apt symbol this of that love which
exhausts not itself by loving, but after all its outgoings upon others,
abides itself far richer than it would have done but for these, of the
multiplying which there ever is in a true dispensing. (Compare 2
Kgs. 4:1-7, and Prov. 11:24: "There is that scattereth, and yet in-
creaseth.")

St. John—who is ever careful to note whatsoever hastened and
drew on the final catastrophe, whatsoever actively stirred up the
malignity of Christ's enemies, whereto nothing more contributed
than the expression of the people's favor—he alone tells us of the
effect which this miracle had upon the assembled multitude, how
they recognized Jesus as the expected prophet, as him of whom
Moses had foretold, the prophet like unto himself (Deut. 18:15),
whom God would raise up for them; and that, ever eager for new
things, they would fain have set him at their head, the king and lib-
erator of the nation. It was not merely the power which he here dis-

played that moved them so greatly, but it was because a miracle of this very kind was one looked for from the Messiah. He was to repeat, so to say, the miracles of Moses. As he, the first redeemer, had given bread of wonder to the people in the wilderness, even so should the later Redeemer do the same. Thus too, when the first enthusiasm which this miracle had caused was over, the Jews compare it with that which Moses had done, not any longer to find here a proof that one with like or greater powers, was among them, but invidiously to depress the present by comparison with the past miracle; and by the inferiority which they found in this, to prove that Jesus was not that Messiah who had a right to rebuke and command them. "What sign showest thou, that we may see and believe thee? What dost *thou* work? Our fathers did eat manna in the desert, as it is written, He gave them bread *from heaven* to eat" (John 6:30, 31); while thine, they would say, is but this common bread of earth, with which thou hast once nourished a few thousands.

But although there is a resemblance between that miracle and this, yet the resemblance is more striking between this and another in the Old Testament—that which Elisha wrought, when with the twenty loaves of barley he satisfied a hundred men (2 Kgs. 4:42–44). All the rudiments of this miracle there appear; the two substances, one artificial, one natural, from which the many persons are fed, as here bread and fish, so there bread and fresh ears of corn. As here the disciples are incredulous, so there the servitor asks, "Should I set this before a hundred men?" As here twelve baskets of fragments remain, so there "they did eat and left thereof." Yet were they only the weaker rudiments of this miracle, and this for reasons which more than once have been noted. Chrysostom bids us observe this difference between the servant and the Lord; how the prophets having grace only in measure, so in measure they wrought their miracles; but the Son, working with infinite power, and that not lent him but his own, did all with much superabundance. Analogies to this miracle, but of a remoter kind, are to be found in the multiplying of the widow's cruse of oil and her barrel of meal by Elijah (1 Kgs. 17:16), and in that other miracle of the oil, which, according to the prophet's word, continued to flow so long as there were vessels to contain it (2 Kgs. 4:1–7).

17.
The Walking on the Sea
Matt. 14:22–33; Mark 6:45–52; Luke 6:14–21

T he three Evangelists who narrate this miracle agree in placing it in immediate sequence to the feeding of the five thousand, and on the evening of the same day. The two first relate, that when all was over and the multitude were fed, the Lord "straightway constrained his disciples to get into the ship," a phrase in itself not very easily accounted for, and finding probably its best explanation in the fact which St. John alone relates, that the multitude desired to take Jesus and make him a king (6:15). It is likely that the disciples had notice of this purpose of the multitude—indeed, they could scarcely have avoided knowing it; and this was exactly to their mind, so that they were most unwilling to be parted from their Master in this hour, as they deemed it, of his approaching exaltation. St. Jerome gives the reason more generally, that they were reluctant to be separated even for a season from their beloved Lord. While he was dismissing the assemblage, they were to return, according to St. Mark, to Bethsaida, which does not contradict St. John, when he says they "went over the sea towards Capernaum," since this Bethsaida, not the same which St. Luke has made mention of but just before, and which for distinction was called Bethsaida Julias, but that of which we have already made mention (John 1:44), the city of Philip and Andrew and Peter, lay on the other side of the lake, and in the same direction as, and in the neighborhood of, Capernaum. St. Matthew, and St. Mark with him, would seem to make two evenings to this day—one which had already commenced ere the preparations for the feeding of the multitude had begun (v. 15), the other, now when the disciples had entered into the ship and begun their voyage (v. 23). And this was an ordinary way of speaking among the Jews, the first evening being very much our afternoon (compare Luke 9:12, where the "evening" of Matthew and Mark is described as the day beginning to decline); the second evening being the twilight, or from six o'clock to twilight; on which the absolute darkness followed. It was the first evening, or afternoon, when the preparations for feeding the five thousand commenced; the second, when the disciples had taken ship.

But in the absence of their Lord they were not able to make any effectual progress: *"the wind was contrary,"* and the sea was rough: their sails, of course, could profit them nothing. It was now *"the fourth watch of the night,"* near morning therefore, and yet with all their efforts and the toil of the entire night, they had not accomplished more than *"five and twenty or thirty furlongs,"* scarcely, that is, more than half of their way, the lake being forty or forty-five furlongs in breadth. Probably they were ever finding themselves more unable to proceed, the danger probably was ever heightening— when suddenly they see their Lord *"walking on the sea,"* and already close to their bark.

After they had left him, and when he had likewise *"sent the multitude away, he went up into a mountain apart to pray, and when even was come, he was there alone."* But from thence, with the watchful eye of love, *"he saw them toiling in rowing"* (cf. Ex. 3:7; Ps. 56:8), and now, so soon as they had made proof that without him they could do nothing, he was with them once more. For it had been his purpose in all this, as Chrysostom well brings out, to discipline and lead them up to ever higher things than they had learned before. In the first storm he was present in the ship with them; and thus they must have felt all along, that if it came to the worst they might rouse him, and the very consciousness of his presence must have given them the sense of comparative security. But he will not have them to be clinging only to the sense of his bodily presence—as ivy, needing always an outward support—but as hardy forest trees which can brave a blast—and this time he puts them forth into the danger alone, even as some loving mother-bird thrusts her fledglings from the nest, that they may find their own wings and learn to use them. And by the issue he will awaken in them a confidence in his ever-ready help; for as his walking over the sea must have been altogether unimagined by them, they may have easily despaired of that help reaching them, and yet it does not fail them. When he has tried them to the uttermost, *"in the fourth watch of the night,"* he appears beside them, thus teaching them for all their afterlife, in all coming storms of temptation, that he is near them; that however he may not be seen always by their bodily eyes, however they may seem cut off from his assistance, yet is he indeed a very present help in the needful time of trouble.

Nor can we, I think, fail to recognize the symbolic character which this whole transaction wears. As that bark was upon those stormy seas, such is oftentimes the Church. It seems as though it had not its Lord with it, such little way does it make; so baffled is it and tormented by the opposing storms of the world. But his eye is on it still; he is in the mountain apart praying; ever living, an ascended Savior, to make intercession for his people. And when at length the time of urgent need has arrived, he is suddenly with it, and that in marvelous ways past finding out—and then all that before was laborious is easy, and the toiling rowers are anon at the haven where they would be.

The disciples were terrified at the first apparition of the Lord, *"for they supposed it had been a spirit:"* even as often he is mistaken still, when he comes to his people in some unaccustomed form, by some unwonted way, in the shape of some affliction, in the way of some cross; they too cry out for fear, though indeed he comes charged with blessing. They mistake him for some terrible phantom, till his well-known voice, his *"Fear not, it is I,"* reassures them, and they know with whom they have to do. And yet, if indeed it was he, and if he was indeed coming to the help of his own, that which perplexed them the most, being seemingly a contradiction of any such purpose, was, that when he came nigh to the bark, *"he would have passed them by"* (Mark 6:48). It perplexed *them* for a moment; it has perplexed others lastingly: for it has been said by those who are seeking to discover inner inconsistencies int he Gospels, Why wish to pass them by and to escape them, when he was coming for this very purpose, that he might reassure them and aid them? And when he was no sooner discovered, or at least detained by their cries, than he ascended into the ship where they were? There can be no doubt that this, even as every other dealing of God with his people, is difficult to be understood of them, to whom the standing point of faith is altogether strange. This apparent passing by, on the Lord's part, of his disciples, was that by which their prayer was to be called out, that he would *not* forsake them. Exactly in the same way, walking with his two disciples to Emmaus, after his Resurrection, "he made as though he would have gone further," thus drawing out from them the entreaty that he would abide. And at the root of what a multitude of God's other dealings does something of the same kind lie: so that this is not an insulated circumstance, but one which finds its analogies everywhere in the Scripture, and in the Christian life. What part does Christ sustain here different from that which in the parable of the unjust judge (Luke 18:2), or the churlish friend (Luke 11:5), he makes God to sustain? Or different from that which he himself sustained when he came not to the help of the sisters of Bethany when their need seemed the highest? And are not all such cries of the faithful in the Psalms as this, "Lord why hidest thou thy face?" Confessions that he does so deal with his servants, that by delaying and seeming to pass by, he calls out their faith, and their prayers that he would come to them soon and abide with them always

But now, being as it were detained by that cry, he at once scatters and rebukes their fears: *"Be of good cheer, it is I; be not afraid."* Whereupon follows that characteristic rejoinder of Peter, which, with its consequences, St. Matthew alone records: *"Lord, if it be thou, bid me come unto thee on the water."* That *"if"* must not be interpreted as implying any doubts upon his part whether it was the Lord or not: a Thomas, indeed, may have desired to have him with him in the ship, ere he would fully believe that it was no phantom, but the Lord himself; but the fault of a Peter would not be in this line. Rather do the words mean: *"Since* it is thou, command me to come unto thee."* He feels rightly that Christ's command must go before his coming. And, doubtless, there was in the utterance of this desire the promptness of love, which made him desire to be where his Lord was. (Cf. John 21:7.) It may be, too, that he would fain compensate for that exclamation of terror in which he had joined with the rest, by a heroic act of courage and affiance. Yet, at the same time, was there, as the issue proved, something mingling with all this, which made the whole incident a rehearsal of his greater presumption and greater fall, which should hereafter come to pass. In that "Bid *me*," the fault lay. He would go before the other disciples; he would signalize himself by a mightier testimony of faith than any of the others will dare to render. It is but again, "Although all shall be offended, yet will not I."

We should not fail to observe, and with reverence to admire, the wisdom and love of the Lord's answer. Another, having enough of spiritual insight to detect the fault which lurked in Peter's proposal, might yet by a coarser treatment have marred all, and lost for one in Peter's condition the lesson which it so much imported him to receive; had he, for instance, bid him to remain where he was, at once checking the outbreaks of his fervent spirit, which, when purified from all of earthly which clung to them, were to carry him so far in the work of his Lord, and quite losing for him the instruction which by his partial failure he should win. But with more gracious and discriminating wisdom the great Master of souls; who yet, knowing what the event must prove, pledges not himself for the issue of his coming. Peter had said, *"Bid me,"* but he does not reply, "I bid thee." Peter had said to *"come to thee,"* but he does not reply, "Come *to me,"*—only *"Come"*; that is, "Come, if thou wilt; make the experiment, if thou desirest." In that *"Come,"* an assurance is indeed involved that Peter should not be wholly swallowed up by the waves, but no pledge for the successful issue of the feat; which yet, according to his faithfulness, would have been involved, had his words been the entire echo of his disciple's. This successful issue depended upon Peter himself—whether he should keep the beginning of his confidence firm unto the end. And the Lord, who knew what was in him, knew that he would not—that this was not the pure courage of faith—that what of carnal over-boldness there was in it would infallibly be exchanged, when the stress of the trial came, for fear and unbelief.

And so it proved. Peter for a while did walk—so long as he looked to his Lord and to him only, he also was able to walk upon the unsteady surface of the sea; to tread upon the *waters* which for him also were not *waves*. But when he took counsel of flesh and blood, when he saw something else besides Jesus, when, because *"he saw the wind boisterous, he was afraid,"* then he began to sink— not, that is, his feet only to be wetted, but he began to be submerged; and he who thought to make a show openly of his greater courage before all the other disciples, must not in the presence of them all confess his terror, and reveal the weakness, as he had though to display the strength, of his faith. In this his peril his swimmer's art (John 21:7) profits him nothing; for there is no mingling of nature and grace in this way. He who has entered the wonder-world of grace must not suppose that he may fall out of it at any moment that he will, and betake himself to his old resources of nature; he has forgone these, and must carry out what he has begun, or fail at his peril.

But Peter has to do with one who will not let him greatly fall;

his experience shall be that of the Psalmist: "When I said, My foot slippeth, thy mercy, O Lord, held me up." His *"Lord, save me,"* is answered at once. *"Immediately Jesus stretched forth his hand, and caught him."* And then how gracious the rebuke! "Thou little believing," not, "Thou unbelieving"; and *"Wherefore didst thou doubt?"* not, "Wherefore didst thou *come?"* not checking, as he then would have done, the future impulses of his servant's boldness, but rather encouraging them, showing him how he could do all things through Christ strengthening him, and that his fault lay, not in having undertaken too much, but in having too little believed the strength that would uphold him in his undertaking. And not until by that sustaining hand he has restored confidence to the fearful one, and made him feel that he can indeed tread underfoot those waves of the unquiet sea, does he speak even this word of a gentle rebuke. The courage of the disciple has returned, so that the Master speaks of his doubt as of something which is already past: *"Wherefore didst thou doubt?* Before the doubt arose in thy heart, thou didst walk on these waves, and now that thy faith has returned, thou dost walk on them again; thou seest that it is not impossible, that it lies but in thy faithful will; that all things are possible to him that believeth."

Nor can we look at this episode of the miracle as otherwise than itself also symbolic. Peter is here the image of all the faithful of all ages, in the seasons of their weakness and their fear. So long as they are strong in faith, they are able to tread underfoot all the most turbulent agitations of an unquiet world; but when they lose heart and fear, when instead of "looking unto Jesus," they look at the stormy winds and waters, then these prevail against them, and they begin to sink, and were it not for Christ's sustaining hand, which is stretched out in answer to their cry, they would be wholly overwhelmed and swallowed up.

Those that are watching for contradictions between the parallel narratives of the Evangelists, affirm that here they find such a one, between John on one side, and Matthew and Mark on the other; that according to the two last, the Lord did after this ascend into the ship, which indeed from their accounts is plain, for *"he went up unto them into the ship"*; while St. John says only, as these will have it, that they were *willing* to receive him; but implies by his silence that they did not in fact do so, the ship being rapidly, and as would appear, with miraculous swiftness, brought to the end of its course. The whole question turns on the phrase which we translate, and I have no doubt rightly as regards the circumstance which actually

took place, *"They willingly received him into the ship."* It is quite true
that the words themselves mean no more than this: "They were
willing to receive him into the ship"; but with the implicit understanding that what they were willing to do, they did. They who before were terrified and dreaded his approach, as though he had
been a spirit, were now willing to receive him into the ship with
them, and did so receive him. Chrysostom indeed understands it
otherwise, that he did not ascend into the ship. He supposes St.
John to be relating a different event from that recorded by the other
Evangelists, which is beyond measure improbable.

Neither St. Matthew nor St. Mark mentions the swift and sudden bringing of the ship to *"the land whither they went,"* which
seems implied by the account of St. John, but only that *"the wind
ceased"* so soon as the Lord was *"come into the ship."* St. Mark, however, relates how this and all which they had witnessed called forth
the infinite astonishment of his disciples: *"they were sore amazed in
themselves beyond measure, and wondered"*; and St. Matthew tells us
how the impression was not confined to them alone: but others
who were sailing with them, probably the crew, and it may be some
other passengers in the same vessel, described generally as *"they
that were in the ship"*—these also caught a glimpse, a momentary
one it may have been, of him with whom they had to do, and *"came
and worshiped him, saying, Of a truth thou art the Son of God"* (cf. John
1:49); for they felt more or less clearly that they had to do with one
who stood in wonderful relation with him of whom it is written,
"Thy way is in the sea, and thy path in the great waters, and thy
footsteps are not known" (Ps. 77:19); "Thou didst walk through the
sea with thine horses, through the heap of great waters" (Hab.
3:15); "Which alone spreadeth out the heavens, and treadeth upon
the waves of the sea" (Job 9:8).

It is a docetic view of the person of Christ, which conceives of
his body as permanently exempt from the laws of gravity, and thus
explains the miracle; a hard and mechanical view, which makes the
seat of the miracle to have been in the waters rendered solid under
this feet. For rather was it the will of Christ which bore him triumphantly above those waters; even as it was to have been the will
of Peter, that will indeed made in the highest degree energic by
faith on the Son of God, which should in like manner have enabled
him to walk on the great deep, and though with partial and transient failure, did so enable him. It has been already observed that
the miracle, according to its true idea, is not the violation, nor yet

the suspension of law, but the incoming of a higher law, as of a spiritual in the midst of natural laws, and the momentary asserting for that higher law, the predominance which it was intended to have, and but for man's fall it would always have had, over the lower; and with this a prophecy of the prevalence which it shall one day recover. So was there here the sign of the lordship of man's will, when that will is in absolute harmony with God's will, over external nature. In regard of this very law of gravity, a feeble, and for the most part unconsciously possessed, remnant of his power survives to man in the well-attested fact that his body is lighter when he is awake than sleeping; from whence we conclude that the human consciousness, as an inner center, works as an opposing force to the attraction of the earth and the centripetal force of gravity, however unable now to overbear it.

18.

The Opening the Eyes of One Born Blind

John 9

I t appears upon the whole most probable that this work of power was wrought upon the same day on which the memorable discourse was spoken, beginning at John 7:34, and continuing to the end of the seventh chapter—a discourse of which the history of the woman taken in adultery is only an interruption, and an intercalation which easily betrays itself as such. In this case it will be, that as our Lord was passing through the city from the temple, to escape the sudden outbreak of Jewish anger, he paused to accomplish this miracle—probably in the immediate neighborhood of the temple, which we know was oftentimes the place where beggars, cripples and other such sufferers, took their station (Acts 3:1, 2). There is nothing in the narrative to mark a break; on the contrary, the "passed by" of the final verse of chapter eight seems taken up by the same word in the first verse of this. It is an additional argument in favor of this view, that we know that other discourse to have been spoken on a Sabbath: for it was spoken on the last day of the feast of tabernacles (7:37), which was always such, and this healing took place also on a Sabbath (9:14). Moved by these reasons, the ancient interpreters would not see here any break in the narrative, and with them most of the moderns consent.

It has been objected against this, that on that day he evidently departed alone from the temple; while here his disciples are with him. But it is easy to suppose that they also extricated themselves, though not in the same wonderful manner as he did, from the excited multitude, and joined their Lord without. It has been objected, too, that Christ appears to have wrought this work more leisurely, more without fear of interruption, than well could have been, immediately after the moment when he had been compelled to withdraw from the fury of his enemies. Yet this circumstance should be rather taken as affording a beautiful picture of *his* calmness in the midst of his enemies, who found no time unfit for a work of mercy and love; who even at the moment when he had hardly escaped the stones of the Jews, paused to accomplish this work of grace. There seems, indeed, as we shall see, allusion to something of the kind at verses 4, 5. "There is need," our Lord would say, "that I should work this work now, however out of season it may seem: for this *'night,'* which the hatred of the Jews is bringing on, is near, and then the time for working will be over." (Compare the exactly parallel passage, John 11:7–10.)

The sad history of this man *"blind from his birth,"* may have been already familiar to his disciples, as he was evidently a well-known beggar in Jerusalem, one with whose story many were acquainted (v. 8); or it may have been one of his ways of stirring pity and compassion in the passers by, to announce that his calamity reached back so far, and thus it may have come to the knowledge of the disciples, and proved the occasion of their question. They would fain learn from their Master, who was able to solve every difficulty which rose up in their minds, *"Who did sin, this man or his parents, that he was born blind?"* But what they could have meant by this latter alternative, when they supposed as possible that it was for his *own* sins that the man was *born* blind, has naturally been the source of much perplexity.

Three or four explanations have been offered: the first, that the Jews believed in a transmigration of souls; and that these sins which the disciples assumed as possible causes of his blindness, were those of some anterior life—sins which were being punished and expiated now. This, as is well known, is the Buddhist doctrine; and not an accident, but belonging to the center of their religious convictions; but it cannot be proved that there was any such faith among the Jews. It may have been the dream of a few philosophic Jews, but was never the faith of plain and simple men: so that this explanation may be regarded, as Olshausen declares it, altogether as antiquated, and not worthy even to be considered.

Lightfoot adduces passages to show that the Jews believed a child might sin in its mother's womb, in proof of which they referred to the struggle between Jacob and Esau (Gen. 25:22); and he, and others after him, think that out of this popular belief the question grew.

Tholuck, following an earlier interpreter, supposes that the theory of the apostles was, that God had foreknown some great sin which this man would commit, and so by anticipation had punished him. But as such a dealing on God's part is altogether without analogy in Scripture, so is there not the slightest hint that men had ever fallen on it as an explanation of the suffering in the world—and, indeed, they could not: for while the idea of retribution is one of the deepest in the human heart, this of punishment which runs before the crime which it punishes, is not one in which it would easily find itself.

Crysostom imagines that it was upon their part a *reductio ad absurdum* of the argument which connected sin and suffering together. It could not be this man that brought this penalty on himself—for he was born with it. It could not be the sin of his parents that brought it on him; for we know that each man shall bear his own burden—that the children's teeth are not set on edge because the parents ate sour grapes. But this is very artificial, and with little of likelihood in it. Honest and simple-hearted men, like the apostles, would have been the last to try and escape a truth, to which the deepest things in their own hearts bore witness, by an ingenious dilemma.

For myself, I am rather inclined to think that they did not see, at the moment when they asked the question, the self-contradiction, as far at least as words go, which was involved in one side of the question—in the form at least in which they presented it to their Master; that, while they rightly, and by a most true moral instinct, discerned the links which unite the sin and suffering of the world together, yet in this case they did not see how it must have been the sin and suffering, not of this man as an individual, but of him as making part of a great whole, which were thus connected together: how the fact of this calamity reaching back to his birth excluded the uncharitable suspicion, that wherever there was a more than ordinary sufferer, there was a more than ordinary sinner—leaving only the most true thought, that a great sin must be cleaving to a race of which any member could so suffer.

This, as it is continually affirmed in Scripture, so it cannot be denied in Christ's answer, *"Neither hath this man sinned, nor his parents"*—to which words must be added, "that he should be born blind." The Lord neither denies their sin nor his: all that he does is to turn away his disciples from that most harmful practice of diving down with cruel surmises into the secrets of other men's lives, and, like the friends of Job, guessing for them hidden sins in explanation of their unusual sufferings. This blindness, he would say, is the chastening of no *peculiar* sin on his own part, or on his parents'. Seek, therefore, neither here nor there the cause of his calamity; but see what nobler explanation the evil in the world, and this evil in particular, is capable of receiving. The purpose of the life-long blindness of this man is *"that the works of God should be made manifest in him"*; and that through it and its removal the grace and glory of God might be magnified. We must not, indeed, understand our Lord's declaration as though this man was used merely *as a means*, visited with this blindness to the end that the power of God in Christ might be manifested to others in its removal. The manifestation of the works of God has here a wider reach, and embraces the lasting weal of the man himself; it includes, indeed, the manifestation of those works to the world and *on* the man; but it does not exclude, rather of necessity includes, their manifestation *to* him and *in* him. It entered into the plan of God for the bringing of this man to the light of everlasting life, that he should thus for a while be dark outwardly; that so upon this night, and on the night of his heart at once, a higher light might break, and the Sun of righteousness arise on him, with healing in his wings for all his bodily and all his spiritual infirmities: while again this was part of a larger whole, and fitted in, according to his eternal counsels, to the great scheme for the revelation of the glory and power of the Only-begotten unto the world. (Cf. John 11:4; Rom 5:20; 9:17; 11:25, 32, 33.)

Yet while it was thus, we are not to accept this as the whole explanation of this man's blindness. For it is the pantheistic explanation of evil, that it is not really evil, but only the condition of, and the transition to, a higher good; only appearing, indeed, as evil at all from a low standing point, which does not take in the end from the beginning. But this solution of the world's evil, tempting as it is, so tempting that multitudes are unable to resist its attraction, is yet not the Christian, which ever recognizes the reality of evil, even while that evil, through the boundless resources of the Divine love, magnifies more the glory of God, and ultimately exalts higher the blessedness of the creature. This cannot, then be the whole explanation of the blindness which this man had brought with him into the world; but God, who though not the author, is yet the disposer, of evil—who distributes that which he did not himself bring in, according to the counsels of his wisdom and righteousness and grace, had willed that on this man should be concentrated more than the ordinary penalties of the world's universal sin, that a more than ordinary grace and glory might be revealed in their removing.

The Lord's words that follow, *"I must work the works of him that sent me while it is day; the night cometh, when no man can work: As long as I am in the world, I am the light of the world,"* are, as it were, a girding of himself up to, and a justifying of, his coming work. Whatever perils beset that work, yet it must be accomplished; for his time, *"the day"* of his open activity, of his walking up and down among the people, and doing them good, was drawing to an end. *"The night,"* when he should no longer lighten the world with his presence, or have the opportunity of doing, with his own hands at least, works like these, was approaching. He worked in the day, and was himself the light of the day. The image is borrowed from our common day and our common night, of which the first is the time appointed for labor; the latter, by its darkness, opposes to many kinds of labor, obstacles insurmountable. The difficulty which Olshausen finds in the words, *"when no man can work,"* inasmuch as however Christ was himself withdrawn from the earth, yet his disciples did effectually work, rises solely from his missing the point of the proverbial phrase. Our Lord means not to say "The night cometh in which no *other* man can work, in which no work can be done"; but what he would affirm, in the language of a familiar proverb which has its truth when applied to the heavenly kingdom, is this, No man who has not done *his* work in the day, can do it in the night; for him the time cometh in which he cannot work—and he applies this even to himself. And then, with a prophetic allusion to the miracle which he was going to perform, he would say, "What fitter task for me than this of opening the eyes of the blind? For *as long as I am in the world, I am the light of the world:* what work could become me better than this, which is so apt a symbol of my greater spiritual work, the restoring of the darkened spiritual vision of the race of men?"

Having thus justified and explained his coming work, our Lord proceeds to the cure. *"When he had thus spoken he spat on the ground and made clay of the spittle, and he anointed the eyes of the blind man with the clay."* A medicinal value was attributed in old time to saliva, and we have a similar instance of its use in the case of another blind man (Mark 8:23), and also in the case of one who was suffering not from the same defect, but from a defect in the organs of speech and hearing (Mark 7:33); neither are we altogether without examples of the medicinal use of clay. Yet it would plainly be an entirely erroneous view of the matter, to suppose that *besides* his divine power, the Lord *also* used natural remedies, or that these were more than conductors, not in themselves needful, but which he willingly assumed to be the channels for the conveying of his power; for we observe at other healings of the blind no intervention of such means finding place (Matt. 20:30–34). Probably the reasons which induced the use of these means were ethical; it was perhaps a help for the weak faith of the man to find that something external was done.

There may be again a question what was the exact purport of the command, *"Go wash in the pool of Siloam."* Was the healing itself connected with that washing? Or was the moistened clay the one conductor of the healing power, and the washing merely designed to remove the hindrances which the medium of cure would itself, if suffered to remain, have opposed even to the restored organs of vision? Thus I should understand it. Whatever other motive the command may have had, it at any rate served as a proof, however slight a one, of the man's faith, that he willingly went as he was bidden.

It must further be asked, Did St. John trace something significant and mystical in the etymology of Siloam that he should introduce it here—*"which is by interpretation Sent."* It is scarcely probable that he did not acknowledge some allusion in the name to the present fact, or some prophecy of Christ's great work of healing and washing; for had he not done so, it is little likely that he would have brought in the derivation, which, if it had possessed no religious significance, might have been appropriate enough in a lexicon, but one would scarcely expect to meet in a gospel.

Olshausen dissents from Tholuck, who finds in this *"sent"* a reference to Christ himself, on the ground that upon the present occasion the Lord was not the *"Sent,"* but the sender. Yet might there well be allusion here in the mind of the Evangelist, not to this particular healing, in which it is true he is rather sender than sent, but to the whole work of his ministry, which was a *mission*, which he ever characterizes as a work whereto he was sent of God (John 7:29; 8:42); so that he bears this very title, "the *Apostle* of our profession" (Heb. 3:1). These waters of Siloam, in which the blind man washed and was illuminated, may well have been to the Evangelist the image of the waters of baptism, or indeed of the whole cleansing work of a commissioned Savior for the opening the eyes of the spiritually blind; and the very name which the pool bore may have had in his eyes a fitness, which by this notice he would indicate as more than accidental.

The man was obedient to the word of the Lord; *"He went his way therefore, and washed, and came seeing"*; returned, that is, according to all appearance, to his own house; it does not seem that he came back to the Lord. His friends and neighbors are the first who take note of the thing which has been done; well-disposed persons, as would appear, but altogether under the influence of the Pharisees. They wonder, debate whether it is indeed he whom they had known so long; for the opening of the eyes would have altered the whole countenance; being convinced that it is, they would fain learn how the cure was effected, and see him who had wrought it; and at length as the safest course, they bring the man, with no evil dispositions either toward him or toward Christ, to their spiritual rulers—not, that is, before the great Sanhedrin, for that was not always sitting, but the lesser. The work may have seemed questionable to them, especially as having been wrought on the Sabbath; the mention just at this place of the day on which the healing was accomplished seems inserted as the explanation of their having found it necessary to bring the case before their ecclesiastical rulers, *"the Pharisees,"* as St. John calls them; not that the Sanhedrin exclusively consisted of these (for Caiaphas was a Sadducee, and see also Acts 23:6); but these being the most numerous and influential party there, and the bitterest enemies of the Lord.

Here there was a more formal examination into the circumstances under which the healing had taken place, and the man again told his simple tale: *"He put clay on my eyes, and I washed, and do see."* Some of the Pharisees present seek to rob the miracle of its significance, by bringing out that it was accomplished on the Sabbath—so that, granting its reality, it did not prove anything in favor of him that wrought it; rather was it to be inferred, since he was thus an evident transgressor of God's commandment, that he was in connection with the powers of evil. No lighter charge than that which they made at another time, when they said, "He casteth out devils through the prince of the devils" (Matt. 9:34), was involved in this word of theirs. But there was throughout all these events, which were so fatally fixing the fortunes of the Jewish people, more honest and a better party in the Sanhedrin, of which

Nicodemus and Joseph of Arimathea were the noblest representatives; men like the Poles and Contarinis at another great epoch of the Church; not in number, perhaps less in courage, equal to the stemming of the great tide of hostility which was rising against the truth—a tide which probably in the end drew most even of them into its current (compare John 12:42, 43): only here and there one and another, such as those above-named, extricating themselves from it. These from time to time made their voices to be heard in the cause of right and of truth. Thus, on the present occasion, did they at the first claim that he should not at once be adjudged a sinner and a breaker of God's law, who had done such signs as these. Even their own Rabbis were not altogether at one concerning what was permitted on the Sabbath, and what not: some allowing quite as much as this and more, for only the alleviation of disorders in the eyes. Therefore they might plead that the Spirit of God might well have directed him in this that he did, and they ask, *"How can a man that is a sinner do such miracles?"* Yet the shape which their interference takes, the form of a question in which it clothes itself, is as Chrysostom remarks, that of timid and irresolute men, who dare only to hint their convictions. No wonder that they should be in the end overborne and silenced by their more unscrupulous adversaries, even as now they prove unequal to the obtaining a fair and impartial hearing of the matter.

The interrogation in the verse following, *"What sayest thou of him, that he hath opened thine eyes?"* has been frequently, though erroneously, understood, not as one question, but as two. The mistake is a very old one, for Theodore of Mopsuestia finds fault with them who divide the question here into two clauses, *"What sayest thou of him? That he hath opened thine eyes?"* making the second to have its rise in the doubts which the Pharisees felt or pretended to feel concerning the reality of the miracle. In truth there is but one question, *"What sayest thou of him in that he hath opened thine eyes? What conclusion drawest thou from thence?"* And thus the answer is to the point, *"He said, He is a prophet:"*—not yet the Son of God, not yet the Messiah; of these higher dignities of his benefactor he as yet has no guess, but what he believes him he boldly declares him, *"a prophet,"*—one furnished with powers and a message from above. When they asked this, it was not that they cared in the least for the judgment of the man, but they hoped to mold him and make him an instrument for their own wicked purposes. Chrysostom, indeed, whom Theophylact and Euthymius follow,

makes this *"What sayest thou of him?"* The speech of the better-dis-
posed in the Sanhedrin, who hope that the testimony of the man
himself may go for something; but this is little probably. They
would fain have had him turn against his benefactor, and they
hoped that, seeing what would be welcome to them, he would follow the suggestions which they had thrown out, and attribute the
opening of his eyes to the power of an evil magic. But a rare
courage from above is given to him, and he dares in the face of
these formidable men whom he is making his foes, to avouch his
belief that the work and the doer of the work were of God.

They now summon his parents, hoping to be more successful in
dealing with them. Their desire is to get a lie from them, and that
they should say their son had not been born blind. But neither in
this quarter do they find any help. His parents make answer as persons who refuse to be made accomplices in a fraud, although without any high desire to witness or to suffer for the truth's sake; on
the contrary, there is something of selfishness in the manner in
which they extricate themselves from the difficulty, leaving their
son in it. They avail themselves of the fact that he was of full age,
able therefore judicially to answer for himself, and altogether decline to enter on the question of how his sight had been restored to
him; since they could not have told the truth without saying something that should have been to the honor of Jesus—and so they
would have come under the penalties which the Sanhedrin had
lately declared against any that should *"confess that he was Christ."*
We are not to understand by this that the Sanhedrin had formally
declared him to be an impostor, a false Christ, but only that while
the question of the truth or falsehood of his claims to be the
Messiah was not yet clear—and they, the great religious tribunal of
the nation, had not given their decision—none were to anticipate
that decision; and the penalty of so doing, of a premature confession of him, was, that he who made it should be cast out of the synagogue—that is, should be excommunicated. Now there appear to
have been two, or some say three, kinds of excommunication
among the Jews, greatly differing in degrees and intensity, and our
Lord often alludes to them, not as though they were a slight matter, but as among the sharpest trials which his servants would have
to endure for his name's sake. The mildest was an exclusion for
thirty days from the synagogue, to which period, in case the excommunicated showed no sign of repentance, a similar or a longer
period, according to the will of those that imposed the sentence,

was added: in other ways too it was made keener; it was accompanied with a curse; none might hold communion with him now, not even his family, except in cases of absolute necessity. Did he show himself obstinate still, he was in the end absolutely separated from the fellowship of the people of God, cut off from the congregation—a sentence answering, as many suppose, to the delivering to Satan in the apostolic Church (1 Cor. 5:5; 1 Tim. 1:20).

The man had been removed, while his parents were being examined. The Pharisees now summon him again, and evidently by their address would have him to believe that they had gotten to the root of all, and discovered the whole fraud, so that any longer persisting in it would be idle. They are as men seeking to obtain confession from one they suspect, by assuring him that others have confessed, and so that for him to stand out in denying, will only make matters worse for him in the end. Now we know, they would say, that it is all a collusion; we have indubitable proofs of it; do thou also give glory to God, and acknowledge that it is so. Our *"Give God the praise,"* sets the reader of this passage quite upon a wrong track. The Pharisees do not mean, "Give the glory of your cure to God, and not to this sinful man, who in truth could have contributed nothing to it—attempting," in Hammond's words, "to draw him from that opinion of Christ which he seemed to have, by bidding him to ascribe the praise of his cure wholly to God, and not to look on Christ with any veneration." So indeed Jeremy Taylor, in his sermon, *On the return of prayers;* "The spiteful Pharisees bid him give glory to God, and defy the minister; for God indeed was good, but he wrought that cure by a wicked hand." But this cannot be their meaning; for they did not allow that any cure had taken place at all, on the contrary, professed to believe that it was all a fraud, gotten up between Christ and the man who was before them. The words are rather an adjuration to him that he should speak the truth. Hitherto he has been acting as though he could deceive not merely men but God, but now let him honor God, give glory to him in uttering that which is truth before him, showing so that he believes him to be a God of truth and righteousness and power, whom no lie will escape, and who will be the avenger of all ungodliness of men. And then in proof they add, "We *know that this man is a sinner,* a more than ordinary transgressor, one therefore, to whom least of all would God have given this higher power; your story then cannot be true; we that have the best means for knowing, know this." They will overbear him with the authority of their place and station, and with their confident assertion.

The man whom we recognize throughout as a ready-witted, brave, and genial man, declines altogether to enter on the question whether his Healer was this *"sinner"* or not; yet, as Chrysostom observes, does not in the least admit by his answer the alternative that he was so. This is a matter which he knows not; he will speak, however, the thing which he does know, and will let them draw their own conclusions; and that which he does know is, that he was blind and now he is seeing. They perceive that they can gain nothing in this way, and they require him to tell over again the manner of his cure, hoping either to detect some contradictions in his story, or to find something which they can better lay hold of, and wrest into a charge against Christ; or perhaps utterly perplexed how to escape from their present entanglement, they ask for this repetition to gain time, and in the hope that some light may break upon them presently.

But the man has grown weary of the examinations to which his inquisitors are now submitting him anew, and there is something of defiance in his answer. "To what purpose to tell it all over to you again? *I have told you already, and ye did not hear: wherefore would ye hear it again?"* And then, with an evident irony, *"Will ye also be his disciples?"* It is clear that these words cut them to the quick, though it is not so clear what exactly is the taunt conveyed by them. Is it this? "How idle to tell you over again, when there is that deep-rooted enmity in your hearts against this man, that, though convinced a hundred times, you would yet never acknowledge it, or sit as learners at his feet. Will ye also become his disciples? I trow not." This is the commonest explanation of the words, yet it agrees not perfectly with their reply, which is an earnest repelling the indignity of being, or meaning to be, disciples of his. But according to that common view of the man's words, he could not have accused them of any such intention; on the contrary his charge was, that no evidence, no force of truth, could win them to be such. It seems therefore better to suppose that the man, in this last clause of his answer, affects to misunderstand their purpose in asking a repetition of his story. "Is it then, indeed, that the truth is winning you also to its side, so that you too wish now to find my story true, and yourselves to acknowledge this man for your master?" Then the answer of the Pharisees will exactly agree. Nothing could have

been more stinging to them than the bare supposition of such a discipleship on their part: *"They reviled him and said, Thou art his disciple, but we are Moses' disciples."* They set, as was their wont, Moses
against Christ, and contrast their claims. *"We know that God spoke
unto Moses";* we know that he had a commission and an authority;
but *as for this fellow, we know not whence he is;* all is uncertain about
him; there is no proof that God has given him a commission; we
know not whether he be from above or from beneath."

This confession of their inability to explain this new and wonderful appearance, this acknowledgement that they were at fault,
emboldens the man yet further; they had left a blot, and this plain
yet quick-witted man does not fail to take instant advantage of it.
It is impossible to miss any irony keener yet than the last in his retort: "But this at least is wonderful; here is one who has opened my
eyes, who is evidently so clothed with powers mightier than man's,
as to be able to do this miracle; and you, the spiritual rulers of our
nations, you that should try the spirits, that should be able to tell of
each new appearance whether it be of God or not, here acknowledge your ignorance, and cannot tell of this man whence he is,
whether of earth or of heaven. But I know, for you have yourselves
declared it (see v. 24), *that God heareth not sinners;* but he hath heard
this man—he hath enabled him to do a work without parallel;
therefore I know whence he is; he is of God; for were he not, he
could do none of the things which he has done."

It is interesting here to observe how his faith and insight and
courage had grown during this very examination. He who had said
a little while before, *"Whether he be a sinner or no, I know not"* (v. 25),
avoiding the answer, now says boldly, *"We know that God heareth not
sinners."* Nor need we take exception, as many have done, at his
maxim, *"God heareth not sinners,"* nor bring out, as they have
thought it needful to do, that these words have no Scriptural authority, being words neither of Christ nor of one of his inspired servants, but only of a man not wholly enlightened yet, in whose
mind truth and error were yet mingled together. That the words
have not in themselves any authority is most true; yet they may
well be allowed to stand, and in the intention in which the speaker
used them. For the term "sinner" has a two-fold meaning in
Scripture: sometimes it is applied to all men as they are fallen children of Adam, and each one with the burden of his own sin upon
him. If, taking the word in this sense, it were said, *"God heareth not
sinners,"* this were indeed to say, God heareth not any man; or if by

sinners" were understood those who have been in time past more than ordinary transgressors, and it were said that they will not now be heard, though they truly turn, this were indeed an impeaching of the grace of God. But the Scripture knows another and emphatic use of the term *"sinners,"*—men *in their sins,* and not desiring to be delivered out of them; and in this sense, which is the sense of the speaker here, as of the better among the Pharisees, who a little earlier in the day had said, *"How can a man that is a sinner do such miracles?"* (v. 16, cf. 10:21). It is most true that God does not hear sinners; their prayer is an abomination, and even if they ask, they obtain not their petitions (Is. 1:15; 59:1, 2; Prov. 1:28; 15:8; 28:9; Ps. 50:16; 66:18; 109:7; Job 27:9; 35:13; Jer. 14:12; Mic. 3:4).

But this was what least of all they could endure, that the whole relations between themselves and this man should thus be reversed—that he should thus be their teacher; and while it was now plain that nothing could be done with him, that he could neither be seduced nor terrified from his simple yet bold avowal of the truth, their hatred and scorn break forth without any restraint: *"Thou wast altogether born in sins, and dost thou teach us?"*—*"altogether,"* not imperfect in body only, but, as they now perceive, maimed and deformed in soul also. "Thou that comest forth from thy mother's womb with the note of thy wickedness upon thee, dost thou school us? Dost thou presume to meddle and be a judge in such matters as these? *And they cast him out"*—which does not merely mean, as some explain it (Chrysostom, Maldonatus, Grotius, Tholuck), rudely flung him forth from the hall of judgment, wherever that may have been; but, according to the decree which had gone before, they declared him to have come under those sharp spiritual censures which they had threatened against any that should join themselves unto the Lord. Only so the act would have the importance which (v. 35) is attached to it. No doubt the sign and initial act of this excommunication was the thrusting him forth and separating him as unclean from their own company; and so that other explanation of the passage has its relative truth. Yet this was not all, or nearly all, which was involved in these words, *"They cast him out."* This violent putting of him out of the hall of audience, was only the beginning of the things which he should suffer for Christ's sake.

But in him were to be fulfilled in a very eminent sense those words, "Blessed are ye when men shall hate you, and when they shall separate you from their company, and shall reproach you and cast out your name as evil, for the Son of man's sake" (Luke 6:22).

He is cast out from the meaner fellowship, to be received into the higher—from that which was about to vanish away, to be received into a kingdom not to be moved—from the synagogue to the Church: the Jews cast him out, and Christ received him: "When my father and my mother forsake me, the Lord taketh me up" (Ps. 27:12). He has not been ashamed of Christ, and now Christ reveals himself unto him as he had not done before: no longer as the prophet from God, for to this only his faith had hitherto reached, but as the Son of God himself. Thus, "to him that hath is given," and he ascends from faith to faith. *"Jesus heard that they had cast him out,"* and, himself the Good Shepherd, went in search of this sheep in this favorable hour for bringing him home to the true fold—*"and when he had found him,"* encountered him, it may be, in the temple (cf. John 5:14), *"he said unto him, Dost thou believe on the Son of God?"* The man knows what the title means, that it is equivalent to Messiah, but he knows not anyone who has a right to claim it for his own: such trust, however, has he in his Healer, that whomsoever he will point out to him as such, he will recognize. *"He answered and said unto him, Who is he, Lord, that I might believe on him? And Jesus said unto him, Thou hast both seen him, and it is he that talketh with thee."* These words, "Thou has seen him," do not refer to some anterior seeing—for it does not appear that the man after his eyes were opened at the pool, returned to the Lord, or that he had enjoyed any opportunity of seeing him since. This past then is in some sense a present: "Thou hast seen him already; this seeing is not something yet to do; ever since thou hast been speaking with me thine eyes have beheld him, for it is no other than he himself that talketh with thee."

And now that to which all that went before was but an introduction, has arrived; *"He said, Lord, I believe; and he worshiped him:"* not that even now we need suppose that he knew all that was contained in that title, Son of God—or that in this worshiping him we are to understand the very highest act of adoration as unto God. For the fact of "God manifest in the flesh," is far too great a one for any man to receive at once: the minds, even of apostles, could only dilate little by little to receive it. There were, however, in this man the preparations for that ultimate and crowning faith: the seeds which would unfold into it were safely laid in his heart; and he fell down at the feet of Jesus as of one more than man, with a deep religious reverence and fear and awe. And thus the faith of this poor man was accomplished; step by step he had advanced, following faithfully the light which was given him, undeterred by opposition which would have been fatal to a weaker faith, and must have been so to his, unless the good seed had cast its roots in a soil of more than ordinary depth. But because it was such a soil, therefore, when persecution arose, as it soon did, for the Word's sake, he was *not* offended (Matt. 13:21); but endured, until at length the highest grace was vouchsafed to him, to know the only-begotten Son of God, however yet he may not have seen *all* the glorious treasures that were contained in the knowledge of him.

So wonderful was the whole event, so had it brought out the spiritual blindness of those that ought to have been the seers of the nation, so had it ended in the illumination, spiritual as well as bodily, of one who seemed among the blind, that it called out from the Savior's lips those remarkable words in which he moralized the whole: *"For judgment I am come into this world, that they which see not might see, and that they which see might be made blind:* I am come to reveal every man's innermost state; I, as the highest revelation of God, must bring out men's love and their hatred of what is divine as none other could (John 3:19–21): I am the touchstone; much that seemed true shall at my touch be proved false, to be merely dross; much that for its little sightliness was nothing accounted of, shall prove true metal: many, whom men esteemed to be seeing, such as the spiritual chiefs of this nation, shall be shown to be blind; many, whom men counted altogether unenlightened, shall, when my light touches them, be shown to have powers of spiritual vision undreamed of before." Christ was the King of truth—and therefore, his open setting up of his banner in the world was at once and of necessity a ranging of men in their true ranks, as lovers of truth or lovers of a lie; and he is here saying of himself the same thing which Simeon had said of him before: "Behold, this child is set for the fall and rising again of many in Israel . . . . *that the thoughts of many hearts may be revealed"* (Luke 2:34, 35). He is the stone on which men build, and against which men stumble—and set for either purpose (1 Pet. 2:6–8; cf. 2 Cor. 2:16). These words call out a further contradiction on the part of the Pharisees, and out of this miracle unfolds itself that discourse which reaches down to verse 21 of the ensuing chapter. They had shown what manner of shepherd of the sheep they were in their exclusion of this one from the fold: "with force and with cruelty have ye ruled them" (Ezek. 34:4): our Lord sets over against them himself, the good Shepherd and the true.

The Restoring of the Man with a Withered Hand

Matthew 12:9–13; Mark 3:1–5; Luke 6:6–11

This is not the first of our Lord's Sabbathic cures, which stirs the ill-will of his adversaries, or is used by them as a pretext for accusing him; for we saw the same to occur in the case of the miracle immediately preceding; yet I have reserved for this the considering once for all the position which our Lord himself took in respect of the Jewish Sabbath, and the light in which he regarded it. The present is the most favorable occasion which will occur, since here, and in the discourse which immediately precedes this miracle, and which stands, if not quite in such close historic connection as might at first sight appear on reading it in the Gospel of St. Matthew, yet in closest inner relation to it, our Lord himself enters upon the subject, and delivers the weightiest words which upon this matter fell from his lips. To go back then to that preceding discourse, and the circumstances which gave rise to it—the Pharisees found fault with the disciples for plucking ears of corn and eating them upon the Sabbath; they accused them to their Master as transgressors of the law: "Behold, why do they on the Sabbath day that which is not lawful?" It was not the thing itself, as though it had been an invasion of other men's property, for that was by the law itself expressly permitted; they might not thrust in a sickle to another man's field, but might pluck the ripe ears for the stilling of their present hunger (Deut. 23:25). By restrictions upon an absolute proprietorship, even slight as this, did God assert that he was indeed the true proprietor of all the land, and that the hold-ers held it only of him. It was in the day on which they plucked these ears that their fault consisted.

Our Lord seeks to raise the objectors to a truer standing point from which to contemplate the act of his disciples; and by two examples, and these taken from that very law which they believed they were asserting, would show them how the law, if it is not to work mischievously, must be spiritually handled and understood. These examples are borrowed, the one from the Old Testament history, the other from the service of the temple which was evermore going on before their eyes. The first, the well-known event which occurred during David's flight from Saul (1 Sam. 21:1–6), his claiming and obtaining from the high priest the holy bread, was such as would naturally carry much weight with them whom Christ was seeking to convince, David being counted the great pattern and example of Old Testament holiness; "Will ye affirm that they did wrong—David who in that necessity claimed, or the priest who gave to him, the holy bread?" The second example came yet nearer home to them with whom he was speaking, and was more stringent still, for it was not an exceptional case, but grounded in the very constitution of the Levitical service: "Ye do yourselves practically acknowledge it right that the rest of the Sabbath should give place to a higher interest, to the service of the temple; that, as the lesser, it should be subordinated, and, where needful, offered up to this as the greater: the sacrifices, with all the laborious preparations which they require, do not cease upon the Sabbath; (Num. 28:8, 9); all which is needful for completing them, is upon that day carried through: yet no one accounts the priests to be therefore in any true sense profaners of that holy day; rather would they be so, if they did not do these things."

And then, lest the Pharisees should retort, or in their hearts make exception, that the work referred to was done in the service of the temple, and was therefore permitted, but that here there was no such serving of higher interests, he adds, "But I say unto you, that in this place is one greater than the temple"; one whom therefore, by still better right, his servants might serve and be guiltless. He contemplates his disciples as already the priests of the new Covenant, of which he is himself the living Temple. It was in their needful service and ministration to him, and because that so occupied them as that they had not time regularly to prepare food or to eat, that they were hungered (v. 1), and profaned, as the adversaries accounted it, the Sabbath. But if those who yet ministered in that temple which was but the shadow of the true, were thus privileged—if, as every man's conscience bore witness, they were blameless in all this, and only seemingly transgressed the law, really to keep it, how much more those who ministered about the Temple not made with hands—the true Tabernacle, which the Lord had pitched and not man

The Lord continues: "But if ye had known," if with all your searching into the Scripture, all your busy scrutiny of its letter, you had ever so entered into the spirit of the Law, whereof you profess to be the jealous guardians and faithful interpreters, as to understand "what this meaneth, I will have mercy and not sacrifice, ye would not have condemned the guiltless"; you would not have found fault with them in whom no true fault can be found. The quotation is from Hosea 6:7, and leaves some ambiguity on the mind of an English reader; which would have been avoided by some such translation as this, "I *desire* mercy and not sacrifice," the words themselves containing one of those prophetic glimpses of the Gospel, one of those slights cast upon the Law even during the time when the Law was in force, an example of that "finding fault" with it which the apostle notes (Heb. 8:8), whereby a witness was borne even to them that lived under it, however some may have refused to receive that witness, that it was not the highest thing, but that God had something better and higher in store for his people. The prophet of the Old Covenant is here anticipating the great apostle of the New, and saying with as clear a voice, "Though I speak with the tongues of men and of angels .... and though I bestow all my goods to feed the poor, and though I give my body to be burned, and have not charity, it profiteth me nothing" (1 Cor. 13:1–3). He is declaring, That which God longs for on the part of men is not the outward observance, the sacrifice in the letter, but the inward outpouring of love—that which the "sacrifice" symbolized, the giving up of self in the self-devotion of love (Cf. Heb. 10:5–10). This must underlie every outward sacrifice and service to give it value; and when the question arises between the form and the spirit, so that the one can only be preserved by the loss of the other, then the form must yield to the life, as the meaner to the more precious.

But the application of the words in the present case still remains unsettled. For it may be either, "If you had truly understood what God asks of men, what service from them pleases him best, you would have understood that my disciples were offering that, who in true love and pity for perishing souls had so labored and toiled as to go without their necessary food, and were therefore thus obliged to satisfy the cravings of a present hunger—that their loving transgression was better than many a man's cold and heartless clinging to the letter of the commandment." Or else the words may have more direct reference to the Pharisees themselves: "If you had understood the service wherein God delighted the most, you would have sought to please him by meekness and by mercy—by a charitable judgment of your brethren—by that love out of a pure heart, which to him 'is more than all whole burnt offerings and sacrifices' (Mark 12:33). Ye would not thus have been judges of evil thoughts" (Prov. 17:15). Thus Olshausen, who adds: "This merciful love was just what was wanting in the fault-finding of the Pharisees. It was no true bettering of the disciples which they desired; no pure zeal for the cause of God urged them on. Rather sought they out of envy and an inner bitterness to bring something against the disciples; and, in fact, out of this did, in an apparent zeal for the Lord, persecute the Lord in his disciples. They 'condemned the guiltless'; for the disciples had not out of *ennui*, for mere pastime's sake, plucked the ears, but out of hunger (v. 1). Their own they had forsaken, and they hungered now in their labor for the kingdom of God. Therefore stood they in the same position as David the servant of God, who, in like manner, with them that were with him, hungered in the service of the Lord; as the priests, who in the temple must labor on the Sabbath, and so for the Lord's sake seem to break the law of the Lord. While this was so, "*they* also might without scruple eat of the showbread of the Lord: what was God's that was theirs."

St. Mark has alone preserved for us the weighty words which follow (2:27): "The Sabbath was made for man, and not man for the Sabbath." The end for which the Sabbath was ordained was to bless man; the end for which man was created, was not to observe the Sabbath. A principle is here laid down, which it is clearly impossible to confine to the Sabbath alone. Rather it must extend to the whole circle of outward ordinances. It does in fact say this, The Law was made for man; not man for the Law. Man is the end, and the ordinances of the Law the means; not these the end, and man the means. Man was not made to the end that he might observe these; but these were given, that they might bless man, that they might train and discipline him till he should be ready to serve God from the free impulses of his spirit. And all this being so, "therefore the Son of man is Lord also of the Sabbath." Now to say here is Grotius, that "Son of man" is equivalent to man, and that the meaning of these words is, The Sabbath was made for man, and man therefore can do with it as he will, is evidently an error. For, in the first place, there is no passage in the New Testament in which "Son of man," occurring as it does eighty-eight times, does not mean the Messiah, *the* man in whom the idea of humanity was fully realized; and, again, with all the bold things which St. Paul speaks of man's relations to the Law, he never speaks of him, even after he is risen with Christ, as being its lord. He is not under it; he is released from its rule, so that it is henceforth with him as a friendly companion, not as an imperious schoolmaster. But it is God's Law, and so long as he is still in the flesh, and therefore may continually need its restraints upon his flesh, he never stands above it; rather, at the first moment of his falling away from the liberty of a service in Christ, will come under it anew.

Even the ceremonial law man is not lord of, to loose *himself* from it, as upon the plea of insight into the deeper mysteries which it shadows forth: he must wait a loosing from it at the hands from which it first proceeded, and which first imposed it. Simply as man, Christ himself was "made under the law" (Gal. 4:4). But as Son of man, as the Messiah, who is also Son of God, he has power over all these outward ordinances: he himself first gave them for the training of man, as a preparatory discipline, and when they have done their work, when this preparatory discipline is accomplished, he may remove them; he may say when the shadow shall give place to the substance, when his people so possess the last that they may forego the first. And it was the sign and augury that they had done their work, when he was come, in whom the highest gifts of God to men were given. The very fact that he was trusted with the highest, involved his power over all lower forms of teaching. Christ is "the end of the law"— is every way the end, as that to which it pointed, as that in which it is swallowed up; being himself living law, not therefore in any true sense the destroyer of the law, as the adversaries charged him with being, but its transformer and glorifier, changing it from law into liberty, from shadow to substance, from letter to spirit.

To this our Lord's clearing of his disciples, or rather of himself in his disciples (for the accusation was truly against him), the healing of the man with a withered hand is attached immediately, as we have seen, by St. Matthew, although St. Luke shows us that it did not find place till the following Sabbath. Like another healing, very similar in its circumstances, that of the woman with the spirit of infirmity (Luke 13:11), like that too of the demoniac at Capernaum (Mark 1:2, 3), it was wrought in a synagogue. There, on the ensuing Sabbath, in *"their synagogue,"* the synagogue of those with whom he had thus disputed, he encountered *"a man who had his hand withered."* St. Luke tells us that it was his *"right hand"* which was thus affected. The disease under which this man labored, and which probably extended throughout the whole arm, was one occasioned by a deficient absorption of nutriment in the limb; it was in fact a partial atrophy, showing itself in a gradual wasting of the size of the limb, with a loss of its powers of motion, and ending with its total death. When once thoroughly established, it is incurable by any art of man.

The apparent variation in the different records of this miracle, that in St. Matthew the question proceeds from the Pharisees, in St. Mark and Luke from the Lord, is no real one—the reconciliation of the two accounts is easy. The Pharisees first ask him, *"Is it lawful to heal on the Sabbath day?"* He answers this question, as was his wont (see Matt. 21:24), by another question. That this is such another counter-question comes out most plainly in St. Luke: *"I will ask you one thing. Is it lawful on the Sabbath days to do good or to do evil? To save life or destroy it?"* Our Lord with the same infinite wisdom which we admire in his answer to the question of the lawyer, "Who is my neighbor?" (Luke 10:29), shifts the whole argument and lifts it altogether into a higher region, where at once it is seen on which side is the right and the truth. They had put the alternative of doing or not doing; here there might be a question. But he shows that the alternatives are, doing good or failing to do good, which last he puts as identical with doing evil, the neglecting to save as equivalent with destroying. Here there could be no question: this under no circumstances could be right; it could never be good to sin. Therefore it is not merely allowable, but a duty, to do some things on the Sabbath. "Yea," he says, "and things much less important and earnest than that which I am about to do, you would not leave undone. Which of you would not draw your sheep from the pit into which it has fallen on the Sabbath; and shall I, the true shepherd, not rescue a sheep of my fold, a man, that is far better than a sheep? Your own consciences tell you that that were a true Sabbath work; and how much worthier this! You have asked me, Is it lawful *to heal* on the Sabbath? I answer, It is lawful *to do well* on that day, and therefore to heal" They can answer him nothing further—*"they held their peace."*

"Then," that is, as St. Mark tell us, *"when he had looked round about on them with anger, being grieved for the hardness of their hearts, saith he to the man, Stretch forth thy hand."* The existence of grief and anger together in the same heart is no contradiction: indeed, with him who was at once perfect love and perfect holiness, grief for the sinner must ever have gone hand in hand with anger against the sin; and this anger, which with us is ever in danger of becoming a turbid thing, of passing into anger against the man, who is God's creature, instead of being anger against the sin, which is the devil's corruption of God's creature—with him was perfectly pure: for is not the agitation of the waters, but the sediment at the bottom, which troubles and defiles them, and where no sediment is, no impurity will follow on their agitation. The man obeyed the word, which was a word of power; he stretched forth his hand, *"and it was restored whole like as the other."*

The madness of Christ's enemies rises to the highest pitch; he had not merely broken their traditions, but he had put them to silence and to shame before all the people. Wounded pride, rancorous hate, were mingled with and exasperated their other feelings of evil will to him: *"They were filled with madness"* (Luke 6:11); and in their blind hate they snatch at any weapon whereby they may hope to destroy him. They do not shrink from joining league with the Herodians, the Romanizing party in the land—attached to Herod Antipas, the ruler of Galilee, who was only kept on his throne by Roman influence—if between them they may bring to nothing this new power which seems equally to threaten both. So, on a later occasion (Matt. 22:16), the same parties combine together to ensnare him. For thus it is with the world: it lays aside for the moment its mutual jealousies and enmities, to join in a common conspiracy against the truth. It is no longer a kingdom divided against itself, when the kingdom of light is to be opposed. Herod and Pilate can be friends together, if it be for the destroying of the Christ (Luke 22:12). He meanwhile, aware of their machinations, withdraws himself from their malice to the neighborhood of the sea of Galilee.

20.

The Woman with a Spirit of Infirmity

Luke 13:10–17

We have here another of our Lord's cures which, being accomplished on the Sabbath, awoke the indignation of the chief teachers of the Jewish Church; cures, of which many, though not all, are recorded chiefly for the sake of showing how the Lord dealt with these cavillers; and what he himself contemplated as the true hallowing of that day. This being the main point which the Evangelist has in his eye, everything else falls into the back-ground. We know not where this healing took place; we are merely told that it was "in one of their synagogues." While there was but one temple in the land, and indeed but one for all the Jews in all the world, there were synagogues in every place: and in one of these Christ, as was often his wont, was teaching upon the Sabbath. Among those present there was a woman that was bent double, that had, in the words of St. Luke, "a spirit of infirmity," which showed itself in this permanent and unnatural contraction of her body. Had we only these words, "spirit of infirmity," we might be doubtful whether St. Luke meant to trace up her complaint to any other cause beyond the natural causes, whence flow the weaknesses and sufferings which afflict our race. But our Lord's later words concerning this woman—"whom Satan hath bound"—are more explicit, and leave no doubt of his meaning. Her calamity had a deeper root; she should be classed with those possessed by evil spirits, though the type of her possession was infinitely milder than that of most, as is shown by her permitted presence at the public worship of God. Her sickness, having its first

215

seat in her spirit, had brought her into a moody melancholic state, of which the outward contraction of the muscles of her body, the inability to lift herself, was but the sign and the consequence.

Our Lord did not here wait till his aid was sought, though it may be that her presence in that place was, on her part, a tacit seeking of his help—as, indeed, seems implied in the words of the ruler of the synagogue, bidding the multitude upon other days than the Sabbath to *"come and be healed."* Seeing her, he himself *"called her to him, and laid his hands on her"*—those hands being here the channel by which the streams of his truer life, which was to dissolve those bonds, spiritual and bodily, whereby she was held, should flow into her—saying at the same time (for though recorded, as was necessary, one after another, we are to assume the words and imposition of hands as identical in time), *"Woman, thou are loosed from thine infirmity."* And the effect followed the words and the hands laid on: *"immediately she was made straight, and glorified God."* She glorified, too, no doubt the author of her salvation, and this was what the ruler of the synagogue could not bear (cf. Matt. 21:15, 16)—a *"hypocrite,"* as the Lord calls him—zeal for God being but the cloak which he wore to hide, whether from others only, or, in a sadder hypocrisy, from his own heart also, his true hatred of all that was holy and divine. He was not, in fact, disturbed because the Sabbath was violated, but because Christ was glorified. Therefore drew he down upon himself that sharp rebuke from him, whose sharpest rebuke was uttered only in love, and who would have torn, if that had been possible, from off this man's heart, the veil which was hiding his true self even from his own eyes. Another part of his falseness was, that not daring directly to find fault with the Lord, he seeks obliquely to reach him through the people, who were more under his influence, and whom he feared less. He takes advantage of his position as the interpreter of the Law and the oracles of God, and from "Moses' seat" would fain teach the people that this work done to the glory of God—this restoring of a human body and a human soul—this undoing the heavy burden—this unloosing the chain of Satan—was a servile work, and one, therefore, forbidden on the Sabbath. Blaming them for coming to be healed, he indeed is thinking not of them, but means that rebuke to glance off on him who has put forth on this day his power to help and to save.

Every word of Christ's answer is significant. It is not a defense of his breaking the Sabbath, but a declaration that he has not broken it at all. "You have your relaxations of the Sabbath strictness, required by the very nature and necessities of your earthly condition; you make no difficulty in the matter, where there is danger that loss would ensue, that your possessions would be periled by the leaving some act undone. Your ox and your ass are precious in your sight, and you count it no violation of the day to lead them away to water. Yet is not a human soul more precious still? The loosing this as allowable as the loosing those? Every word in his answer *tells*. "Each one of you, whatever your scheme and theory may be concerning the strictness with which the Sabbath ought to be kept, disciplees of Hillel or disciples of Schammai, you loose your beasts; yet ye will not that I should loose a human spirit—one who is of more value than many oxen and asses—and this you do, though they have not been tied up for more than for some brief space; while, in your thoughts, I may not unloose from the thraldom of Satan this captive of eighteen years. Yours, moreover, is a long process of unfastening and leading away to water—which yet (and rightly), you make no difficulty about; but ye are offended with me who have spoken but a word and released a soul." There lies at the root of this argument, as of so much else in Scripture, a deep assertion of the specific difference between man, the lord of the creation, for whom all things were made, and all the inferior orders of beings that tread the same earth with him, and with whom upon the side of his body he is akin. He is something more than the first in this chain and order of beings: he is specifically different. (Cf. 1 Cor. 9:9. "Doth God take care of oxen?" and Ps. 8:8). And more than merely this: the woman was a *"daughter of Abraham."* Some think here that the Lord means to magnify her claim to this benefit, as being an heir of the faith of Abraham—one, indeed, who, for the saving of her soul in the day of the Lord, had come for some sin under the scourge of Satan and this long and sore affliction of the flesh. Yet it is more probable that he means but this, that she was one of the chosen race, a daughter of Abraham after the flesh—however, after this healing, she may have become something more, a child of the faith of Abraham.

21.

The Healing of the Man with a Dropsy

Luke 14:1–6

Ⓐll which is most remarkable in the circumstances of this miracle has been already anticipated in others, as especially in the two immediately preceding, to which the reader is referred. Our Lord, not even at this late period of his ministry treating the Pharisees as wholly and finally hardened against the truth, but still seeking to win, if it were possible, them also for his kingdom, had accepted the invitation of one of the chief among them "to eat bread" in this house. This was upon the Sabbath, the day which the Jews ordinarily selected for their festal meals: for the idea of the Sabbath among the Jews was not at all that of a day to be austerely kept, but very much the contrary. The practical abuses of it were the turning it into a day of rioting and excess. But the invitation, though accepted in love, yet seems not to have been given in good faith, but in the hope that the nearer and more accurate watching of the Lord's words and ways, which such an opportunity would give, might afford some new matter of accusation against him. Such was, probably, the spring of the apparent courtesy which they showed him now, and so did they reverence the sacred laws of hospitality.

It has been suggested that the man with a dropsy was of design placed where he was, since he would scarcely without permission have found entrance into a private house. But although it is quite conceivable of these malignant adversaries of Christ, that they should have laid such a snare for him as this, yet there is nothing in the narration to give it likelihood here; and the difficulty that, without such design, the man would scarcely have found his way into the house of the Pharisee, rests upon an ignorance of the amost public life of the East, and a forgetting how easily in a moment of high excitement, such as this must have been, the feeble barriers which the conventional rules of society would oppose might be broken through (Luke 7:36, 37). At any rate, if there was such a plot, the man himself was no party to it; for the Lord *"took him, and healed him, and let him go."*

Yet, ere he did this, he justified the work which he would accomplish, as more than once he had justified other similar works of grace and love wrought upon the Sabbath, saying to these interpreters of the Law, *"Is it lawful to heal upon the Sabbath?"* Here, as in so many matters of debate, it only needs for the question to be truly put, to be once rightly stated, and the answer at once is given; all is so clear, that the possibility of its remaining a question any longer has forever vanished. As was the case before, he obtains no answer from them—for they will not approve, and they cannot gainsay. "As on other occasions (Matt. 12:11; Luke 13:15), the Lord brings back those present to their own experience, and lets them feel the keen contradiction in which their blame of Christ's free work of love sets them with themselves, in that, where their worldly interests were at hazard, they did that very thing whereof they made now an occasion against him." We may observe, that as in that other case where the woman was *bound,* he adduces the example of *unbinding* a beast (Luke 13:15)—so in this, where the man was dropsical, suffering, that is, from water, the example he adduces has its equal fitness. "You grudge that I should deliver this man upon this day from the water that is choking him, yet if the same danger from water threatened one of your beasts, *an ass or an ox,* you would make no scruple of extricating it on the Sabbath from the dangers which threatened it; how much then is a man better than a beast?" *"And they could not answer him again to these things";* they were silenced, that is, but not convinced. The truth, which did not win them, did that which alone else it could do, exasperated them the more: and they replied nothing, biding their time. (See Matt. 12:14.)

22.
The Cleansing of the Ten Lepers
Luke 17:11–19

The Jews that dwelt in Galilee very commonly in their necessary journeys to the feasts at Jerusalem took the longer route, which led them across the Jordan, and through the region of Perea, the Gilead of the old Testament, that so they might avoid the vexations and annoyances and even worse outrages which they sometimes met in passing through the unfriendly land of the Samaritans. For these, always unfriendly, would naturally be most unfriendly of all to those that were traveling up to the great feasts of the holy city, and were thus giving witness in act against the will-worship of Mount Gerizim, and the temple of Samaria in which no presence of God dwelt. It is generally understood that now, despite these vexations and the discomforts of that inhospitable route (see Luke 9:51–56; John 4:9), our Lord, with the band of his disciples, on this his last journey to the holy city, took the more direct and shorter way which led him straight from Galilee through the midst of Samaria to Jerusalem. It is certain that the words of the original may bear this meaning, yet none the less I should understand the Evangelist to say that the Lord passed between these two regions, having, that is, one on his right hand, the other on his left, and skirting them both. This explains the mention of Samaria first, which in the ordinary explanation of the words is almost inexplicable. The Lord traveled due eastward toward Jordan, having Galilee on his left hand, and Samaria, which is therefore first named, on his right: and on reaching the river, he either passed over it at Scythopolis, where we know there was a bridge, recrossing the river near Jericho, or kept on the western bank till he reached that city, where presently we find him (18:35).

"And as he entered into a certain village, there met him ten men, that were lepers." Their common misery had drawn them together (2 Kgs. 7:3); nay, had even caused them to forget the fierce national antipathy which reigned between Jew and Samaritan. In this border land too it was more natural then elsewhere that they should find themselves in one company, and thus a Samaritan had found admission into this forlorn assembly. There has been already occasion to speak of the nature and meaning of leprosy in the Law of Moses; that it was the outward symbol of sin in its deepest malignity—of sin therefore as involving entire separation from God; not of spiritual sickness only, but spiritual death, since absolute separation from the one fountain of life must needs be no less. These lepers, in obedience to the commandment, *"stood afar off"*; and out of a deep sense of their misery, yet not without hope that a Healer was at hand, *"lifted up their voices and said, Jesus, Master, have mercy on us!"* They were now in earnest to receive the mercy, however at a later period they were slack in giving thanks for it.

Wonderful is it and most instructive to observe the differences in our Lord's dealing with the different sufferers and mourners that are brought in contact with him; how the Physician, who is all wisdom and all tenderness, varies his treatment for the varying needs of his patients; how he seems to resist a strong faith, that he may make it stronger yet; how he meets a weak faith, lest it should prove altogether too weak in the trial; how one he forgives first, and heals after; and another, whose heart could only be softened by first receiving an earthly benefit, he first heals and then pardons. There is here, too, no doubt a reason why these ten are dismissed as yet uncleansed, and bidden to go show themselves to the priests; while that other, whose healing was before recorded, is first cleansed, and not till afterwards bidden to present himself in the temple. Doubtless there was here a keener trial of their faith. While as yet there were no signs of restoration upon them, they were bidden to do that, which implied they were perfectly cleansed, to take a journey, which would have been ridiculous, a labor in vain, unless Christ's words and promise proved true. In their prompt going was an evident proof that there were in them weak beginnings of faith, though these, in the greater number, came to nothing, and brought no fruit to perfection. For they could not have thought that they were sent to the priests as though these should heal them,

since they must have well known that it was no part of the priests'
functions to cure, but only to declare cured; that these cleansed, not
in the sense of ridding men of their disease; but, when their sickness had disappeared, restoring them with ceremonial washings
and offerings to the fellowship of the congregation. There was also
here a greater temptation to ingratitude. When they first felt and
found their benefit, their benefactor was not immediately before
them, so that it should be an easy thing, a costless effort, to return
thanks to him: but they were, probably, already out of his sight, and
some little way upon their journey; we know not *how* far, for we are
only told, that *"as they went, they were cleansed."*

Some, indeed, suppose that this returning of the Samaritan to
give thanks, did not take place till after he had accomplished all
which was commanded him; that he had been at Jerusalem—that
he had offered his gift—that he had been pronounced clean—and,
this his first duty accomplished, that he returned to render due
thanks to his benefactor; and that so the sacred narrative leaps over
a large space of time and many intermediate events for the purpose
of connecting together the beginning and the end of this history.
But certainly the impression which the narrative leaves is different—that, having advanced some very little way on their commanded journey, so little that no time would have been really lost
by the return, perhaps in the very village itself, they perceived
what had taken place in them—that they were healed; and then
this one returned in the fullness of a grateful heart to give glory to
God, and thanks to his great Healer and Savior; like the Syrian
Naaman, who when delivered from the same disease, came back
with all his company, beseeching the man of God to take a blessing
at his hands (2 Kgs. 5:15); the others meanwhile enduring to carry
away the benefit without one thankful acknowledgment rendered
unto him who was its author and its source, and to whose feet the
slightest labor would have brought them. A sin only too common!
For as Bishop Sanderson says, with allusion to their former crying:
"We open our mouths wide till he open his hand; but after, as if the
filling of our mouths were the stopping of our throats, so are we
speechless and heartless."

It gives a special significance to this miracle, and to its place in
the Gospel of St. Luke, the Gospel for the heathen, that this thankful one should have been no other than a Samaritan, a stranger
therefore by birth to the covenants of promise, while the nine unthankful were of the seed of Abraham. Thus there spoke out in this

circumstance that the Gentiles (for this Samaritan was no better), were not excluded from the kingdom of God, nay, rather might find a place in it before others who by nature and birth were children of the kingdom; that the ingratitude of these might exclude them, while the faith of those might give to them an abundant entrance into all its blessings.

Even the Savior himself, who knew what was in man, who had already had so many proofs of the ingratitude of men, seems to have marveled here: for he asks, *"Were there not ten cleansed? But where are the nine? There are not found that returned to give glory to God, save this stranger."* Him he dismisses with a new and a better blessing; the first had reached but to the healing of his body, and that he had in common with the unthankful nine: but gratitude for a lower mercy obtains for him a higher, a peculiar blessing, which is singularly his, which reaches not merely to the springs of bodily health, but to the very fountains of his spiritual being. These also are healed; that which the others missed, to which their bodily healing should have led them up, he has obtained; for to him and to him only it is said, *"Go thy way; thy faith hath made thee whole."*

It is difficult not to be struck with the aptness of the image which this history supplies, to set forth the condition of the faithful in this world. They are to take Christ's word that they will be cleansed. In Baptism is the pledge and promise and the initial act of it all. And they are to believe this, while they yet feel in themselves the leprous taint of sin—to go forward in faith, being confident that in the use of his Word, and of his Sacraments, slight as they may seem to meet and overcome such mighty mischiefs, they will find that health, which according to the sure word of promise is already theirs; and as they go, believing this word, using these means, they *are* healed. And for them, too, a warning is here—that they forget not the purging of their old sins—nor what those sins were, how hideous, how loathsome; in this way sinning like these nine, who perhaps did not return because they would fain have obliterated the very memory of the fact that they had ever been those lepers. There is a warning here for the spiritually cleansed, that they keep in memory the times of their past anguish of soul— the times when everything seemed defiled to them, and they to everything; when they saw themselves as "unclean, unclean," shut out from all holy fellowship of God and man, and cried out in their anguish, *"Jesus, Master, have mercy on us"*—a warning to them that now they are at peace, they forget not the time of their trouble, but that the remembrance of the absolving cleansing word which was spoken to them then, with each new consciousness of a realized deliverance from the power of sin, bring them to the Savior's feet, giving glory to God by him; lest failing in this, they be worse than even these unthankful nine. For they carried away only temporal mercies unacknowledged; but we should in that case be seeking to carry away spiritual; though that never could truly be, since the spiritual mercy which is not evermore referred to its author, does sooner or later inevitably case from him who would seek on any other condition to retain it.

23.

The Healing of the Daughter of the Syrophenician Woman

Matthew 15:21–28; Mark 7:24–30

It is not probable that our blessed Lord actually overpassed the limits of the Jewish land, now or at any other moment of his earthly ministry; though when it is said that he "departed into the coasts of Tyre and Sidon," this may seem at first to favor such a supposition. St. Mark, however, tells us that he only "went into the borders of Tyre and Sidon," and the true meaning which even St. Matthew's words will abundantly bear, is, that he came into the confines of that heathen land. The general fitness of things, and more especially his own words on this very occasion, "I am not sent but unto the lost sheep of the house of Israel," would make it extremely unlikely that he had now brought his healing presence into a heathen land; and, moreover, when St. Matthew speaks of the "woman of Canaan" as coming out of that district, "of the same coasts," he clearly shows that he has no other intention than to describe the Lord as having drawn close to the skirts of that profane land.

Being there, he *"entered into a house, and would have no man know it:"* but as the ointment bewrayeth itself, so he whose Name is like ointment poured out, *"could not be hid";* and among those attracted by its sweetness, was a woman of that country—*"a woman of Canaan,"* as St. Matthew terms her, *"a Greek, a Syrophenician,"* as St. Mark, meaning by the first term to describe her religion, that it was not Jewish but heathen; by the second, the stock of which she came, which was even that accursed stock which God had once doomed to a total excision, but of which some branches had been spared by those first generations of Israel that should have extirpated them root and branch. Everything, therefore, was against her; yet she was not hindered by that everything from coming and craving the boon that her soul longed after. She had heard of the mighty works which the Savior of Israel had done: for already his fame had gone through all Syria; so that they brought unto him, besides other sick, "those which were possessed with devils, and those which were lunatic, and he healed them" (Matt. 4:24). And she has a boon to ask for her daughter, or rather indeed for herself, for so entirely has she made her daughter's misery her own, that she comes saying, *"Have mercy on me, O Lord, thou Son of David; my daughter is grievously vexed with a devil"*; as on a later occasion the father of the lunatic child, "Have compassion on *us*, and help *us*" (Mark 9:22).

But very different she finds him from that which report had described him to her; for that spoke of him as the merciful Son of man, who would not break the bruised reed, nor quench the smoking flax, who encouraged every weary and afflicted soul to come and find rest with him. He who of himself came to meet the needs of others, withdrew himself from hers; *"He answered her not a word."* In the language of Chrysostom, "The Word was no word; the fountain is sealed; the physician withholds his remedies"; until at last the disciples, wearied out with her long entreaties, and seemingly more merciful than their Lord, themselves come to him, making intercession for her that he would grant to her her petition and send her away. Yet was there in truth the worm of selfishness at the root of this seemingly greater compassion of theirs, and it shows itself when they give their reason why he should dismiss her with the boon she asks: *"For she crieth after us"*; she is making a scene; she is drawing on us unwelcome observation. Theirs is one of those heartless grantings of a request, whereof we all are conscious; when it is granted out of no love to the suppliant, but to leave undisturbed the peace and selfish ease of him from whom at length it is extorted—such as his who said, "Lest by her continual coming she weary me." Here, as so often, under a seeming severity lurks the real love, while selfishness hides itself under the mask of bounty. But these intercessors meet with no better fortune than the suppliant herself; and Christ stops their mouth with words unpromising enough for her suit: *"I am not sent but unto the lost sheep of the house of Israel."* (Cf. Matt. 10:5, 6.)

But in what sense was this true? All prophecy which went before declared that in him, the promised Seed, not one nation only, but all nations of the earth, should be blessed: he himself declared, "Other sheep I have, which are not of this fold; them also I must bring, and they shall hear my voice" (John 10:16). It has happened indeed with others, as with the founders of false religions, that as success increased, the circle of their vision has widened; and they who meant at first but to give a faith to their nation, have aspired at last to give one to the world. But here all must have been known: the world-embracing reach of his faith was contemplated by Christ from the first. In what sense then, and under what limitations, could it be said with truth that he was not sent but unto Israel only? Clearly in his own personal ministry. That, for wise purposes in the counsels of God, was to be confined to his own nation; and every departure from this was, and was clearly marked as, an exception. Here and there, indeed, he gave preludes of the coming mercy; yet before the Gentiles should glorify God for his mercy, Christ was first to be "a minister of the circumcision for the truth of God, to confirm the promises made unto the fathers" (Rom. 15:8, 9). It was only as it were by a rebound from them that the grace was to light upon the heathen world; while yet that issue, which seemed thus accidental, was laid deep in the deepest counsels of God (Acts 13:44–49; Rom. 11). In the form of Christ's reply, as St. Mark gives it, *"Let the children first be filled,"* the refusal does not appear so absolute and final, and a glimpse appears of the manner in which the blessing will pass on to others, when as many of these, of *"the children,"* as will, have accepted it. But there, too, the *present* repulse is absolute: the time is not yet; others intermeddle not with the meal, till the children have had enough.

The woman hears the repulse, which the disciples who had ventured to plead for her, receive; but she is not daunted or disheartened thereby. Hitherto she had been crying after the Lord, and at a distance; but now, instead of being put further still, *"came she and worshiped him, saying, Lord, help me."* And now he breaks the silence which hitherto he has maintained toward her; but it is with an answer more discomfortable than was the silence itself: *"He answered and said, It is not meet to take the children's bread, and to cast it to dogs."* "The children" are, of course, the Jews, "the children of the kingdom" (Mattt. 8:12). He who spoke so sharply *to* them, speaks thus honorably *of* them; nor is there any contradiction in this: for here he is speaking of the position which God has given them in his kingdom; there, of the manner in which they have realized that position. On the other hand, extreme contempt was involved in the title of dog given to anyone, it being remarkable that the nobler characteristics of the animal, which yet were not unknown to antiquity, are never brought out in Scripture (See Deut. 32:18; Job 30:1; 1 Sam. 17:43; 24:15; 2 Sam. 3:8; 9:8; 16:9; 2 Kgs. 8:13; Matt. 7:6; Phil. 3:2; Rev. 22:15).

This at length would have been enough for many; and, even if they had persevered thus far, now at least they would have gone away in anger or despair. But not so this woman; she, like the centurion, and under still more unfavorable circumstances than his, was mighty in faith; and from the very word which seemed to make most against her, with the ready wit of faith, she drew an argument in her own favor. She entangled the Lord, himself most willing thus to be so entangled, in his own speech; she takes the sword out of his own hand, with that sword to overcome him: *"Truth, Lord: yet the dogs eat of the crumbs which fall from their masters' table."* Upon these words Luther, who has dwelt on all the circumstances of this little history with a peculiar love, and seems never weary of extolling the mighty faith of this woman, exclaims, "Was not that a masterstroke? She snares Christ in his own words." And oftentimes he sets this Canaanitish woman before each troubled and fainting heart, that it may learn from her how to wring a Yea from God's Nay; or rather, how to hear the deep-hidden Yea, which many times lies in his seeming Nay. "Like her, thou must give God right in all he says against thee, and yet must not stand off from praying, till thou overcomest as she overcame, till thou hast turned the very charges made against thee into arguments and proofs of thy need—till thou too hast taken Christ in his own words.

Our translation of the woman's answer is not, however, altogether satisfactory. For indeed she consents to Christ's declaration, not immediately to make exception against the conclusion which he draws from it, but to show how *in that very declaration* is involved the granting of her petition. "Saidest thou *dogs?* It is well; I accept the title and the place: for the dogs have a portion of the meal—not the first, not the children's portion, but a portion still—the crumbs which fall from the table. In this very statement of the case thou bringest us heathen, thou bringest *me,* within the circle of the blessings which God, the great householder, is ever dispensing to his family. We also belong to his household, though we occupy but the lowest place in it. According to thine own showing, I am not wholly an alien, and therefore I will abide by this name, and will claim from thee all its consequences." By the *"masters"* she does not mean the Jews, which is Chrysostom's mistake; for thus the whole image would be disturbed; they are *the children:*" but by the *"master,"* she would signify God, using the plural on account of the plural *"dogs,"* which Christ had used before; in the same way as Christ himself says, "Then the *sons* are free" (Matt. 17:29), having spoken plurally before of "the *kings* of the earth," while yet it is only the one Son, the only-begotten of the Father, whom he has in his eye. He, the great Master of the Lord, spreads a table, and all that depend on him, in their place and order are satisfied from it— the children at the table, the dogs beneath the table. There is in her statement something like the Prodigal's petition, "Make me as one of thy hired servants"—a recognition of diverse relations, some closer, some more distant, in which diverse persons stand to God— yet all blessed, who, whether in a nearer or remoter station, are satisfied from his hands.

And now she has conquered. She who before heard only those words of a seeming contempt, now hears words of a most gracious commendation—words of which the like are recorded as spoken but to one other in all the Gospel history; *"Oh woman, great is thy faith!"* He who at first seemed as though he would have denied her the smallest boon, now opens to her the full treasure-house of his grace, and bids her to help herself, to carry away what she will: *"Be it unto thee even as thou wilt."* He had shown to her for awhile, like Joseph to his brethren, the aspect of severity; but, like Joseph, he could not maintain it long—or rather he would not maintain it an instant longer than it was needful, and after that word of hers, that mighty word of an undaunted faith, it was needful no more: in the words of St. Mark, *"For this saying go thy way; the devil is gone out of thy daughter."*

Like the centurion at Capernaum, like the nobleman at Cana, she made proof that his word was potent, whether spoken far off or near. Her child, indeed, was at a distance; but she offered in her faith a channel of communication between it and Christ. With one hand of that faith she had held on to that Lord in whom all healing grace was stored, with the other to her suffering child—thus herself a living conductor by which the power of Christ might run like an electric flash from him to her beloved. *"And when she was come to her house, she found the devil gone out, and her daughter laid upon the bed,"* weak and exhausted as it would appear from the paroxysms of the spirit's going out; or, the circumstance which last is mentioned may indicate only that she was now taking that quiet rest, which hitherto the evil spirit had not allowed. It will answer so to the "clothed and in his right mind" (Luke 8:30), of another who had been tormented in the same way.

But the interesting question remains, *Why* this bitterness was not spared her, why the Lord should have presented himself under so different an aspect to her, and to most other suppliants? Sometimes he anticipated their needs, "Wilt thou be made whole?" (John 5:6), or if not so, he who was waiting to be gracious required not to be twice asked for his blessings. Why was it that in this case, to use the words of an old divine, Christ "stayed long, wrestling with her faith, and shaking and trying whether it were fast-rooted" or not? Doubtless because he knew that it was a faith which would stand the proof, and that she would come victorious from this sore trial; and not only so, but with a stronger, higher, purer faith than if she had borne away her blessing at once. Now she has learned, as then she never could have learned, that men ought always to pray and not to faint; that, with God, to delay a boon is not therefore to deny it. She had learned the lesson which Moses must have learned, when "the Lord met him, and sought to kill him" (Ex. 6:24), she won the strength which Jacob had won before, from his night-long struggle with the Angel. There is, indeed, a remarkable analogy between this history and that last (Gen. 32:24–32). There as here, there is the same persevering struggle on the one side, the same persevering refusal on the other; there, as here, the stronger is at last overcome by the weaker. God himself yields to the might of faith and prayer; for a later prophet, interpreting that mysterious struggle, tells us the weapons which the patriarch wielded: "He wept and made supplication unto him," connecting with this the fact that "he had power over the angel and prevailed" (Hos. 12:3, 4). The two histories, indeed, only stand out in their full resemblance, when we keep in mind that the angel there, the Angel of the covenant, was no other than that Word, who, now incarnate, "blessed" this woman at last, as he had blessed at length Jacob at Peniel—in each case rewarding thus a faith which had said, "I will not let thee go, except thou bless me."

Yet, when we thus speak of man overcoming God, we must never, of course, for an instant lose sight of this, that the power whereby he overcomes the resistance of God, is itself a power supplied *by* God. All that is man's is the faith or the emptiness of self, which enables him to appropriate and make so largely his own the fullness and power of God; so that here also that word comes true,

"Blessed are the poor in spirit, for theirs is the kingdom of heaven." Thus when St. Paul (Col. 1:29) speaks of himself under an image, which rested originally on Jacob's struggle, if there was not a direct allusion to it in the apostle's mind, as *striving* for the Colossians, striving, that is, with God in prayer (see 4:12), he immediately adds, "according to *his* working which worketh in me mightily."

We may observe, in conclusion, that we have three ascending degrees of faith, as it manifests itself in the breaking through of hindrances which would keep from Christ, in the paralytic (Mark 2:4), the blind man at Jericho (Mark 10:48), and this woman of Canaan. The paralytic broke through the outward hindrances, the obstacles of things merely external; blind Bartimaeus through the hindrances opposed by his fellowmen; but this woman, more heroically than all, through apparent hindrances even from Christ himself. These, in their seeming weakness, were the three mighty ones, not of David, but of David's Son, that broke through opposing hosts, until they could draw living water from wells of salvation (2 Sam. 23:16).

24.

The Healing of
One Deaf and Dumb

Mark 7:31–37

St. Matthew tells us in general terms how when the Lord had returned from those coasts of Tyre and Sidon unto the sea of Galilee, "great multitudes came unto him, having with them those that were lame, blind, dumb, maimed, and many others, and cast them down at Jesus' feet, and he healed them" (15:30); but out of this multitude of cures St. Mark selects one to relate more in detail, and this, no doubt, because it was signalized by some circumstances not usual in other like cases of healing. It was that of a man deaf and having an impediment in his speech, one who, if he was not altogether dumb, was yet probably incapable of making any articulate sounds. His case differs, apparently, from that of the dumb man mentioned Matthew 9:32; for while that man's evil is traced up distinctly and directly to a spiritual source, nothing of the kind is intimated here, nor are we, as Theophylact suggests, to presume such. Him his friends now brought to the great Healer, "and they beseech him to put his hand upon him." It is not, however, exactly in this way that he is willing to heal him.

It has been already observed, that there is no doubt a deep meaning in all the variations which mark the different healings of different sick and afflicted, a wisdom of God ordering all the circumstances of each particular cure. Were we acquainted as accurately as he who knew what was in man, with the spiritual condition of each who was brought within the circle of his grace, we should then perfectly understand why one was healed in the crowd, another led out of the city ere the work of restoration was

235

commenced; why for one a word effected a cure, for another a touch, while a third was sent to wash in the pool of Siloam, ere he came seeing; why for these the process of restoration was instantaneous, while again another saw at first "men as trees walking." At all events, we are not for an instant to suppose in these gradually accomplished cures any restraint on the power of the Lord, save such as was willingly imposed by himself—and this, doubtless, in each case having reference to, and being explicable by the moral and spiritual state of the person who was passing under his hands; though our ignorance of this prevents us from at once seeing the manifold wisdom which ordered each of his proceedings, and how it was conducted so as best to make the bodily healing a passage to the spiritual, which the Lord had ever in his eye.

On the present occasion him that he would heal he first *"took aside from the multitude,"* with which notice we may compare Mark 8:23; "He took the blind man by the hand and led him out of the town." But for what reason does he isolate him thus? The Greek Fathers say generally, for the avoiding of all show and ostentation; but it cannot be for this, since of all the miracles which he did we have but two in which any such withdrawal is recorded. Shall we say then that there was show and ostentation in the others? It is not much better to find, with Calvin, the reason in this, that he may pray with greater freedom. He, whose whole life was altogether prayer, needed not solitude for this. But rather his purpose in this was, that apart from the din and tumult and interruptions of the crowd, in solitude and silence, the man might be more recipient of deep and lasting impressions; even as the same Lord does not oftentimes lead a soul apart when he would speak with it, or heal it; sets it in the solitude of a sick chamber, or in loneliness of spirit, or takes away from it earthly companions and friends. He takes it aside, as this deaf and dumb out of the multitude, that in the hush of the world's din it may listen to him; as on a great scale he took his elect people aside into the wilderness, when he would first open their spiritual ear, and speak unto them his law.

The putting his finger into the ears of the man, the spitting and touching the man's tongue therewith, are easily recognized as symbolic actions. Nor is it hard to perceive why he should specially have used these in the case of one afflicted as this man was—almost all other avenues of communication, save by sight and feeling, were of necessity precluded. Christ by these signs would awaken his faith, and stir up in him the lively expectation of a blessing. The fingers are put into the ears as to bore them, to pierce through the obstacles which hindered sounds from reaching them. This was the fountain-evil; he did not speak plainly, because he did not hear; this defect, therefore, is mentioned as being first removed. Then, as it is often through excessive drought that the tongue cleaves to the roof of the mouth, so the Lord gives here, in the second thing which he does, the sign of the removal of this evil, of the unloosing of the tongue. And, at the same time, all the healing virtue he shows to reside in his own body; he looks not for it from any other quarter; he takes nothing from anyone else: but with the moisture of his own mouth upon his finger touched the tongue which he would set free from the bands which held it fast. It is not for its medicinal virtue that use is made of this, but as the suitable symbol of a power residing in and going forth from his body.

St. Mark, abounding as he always does in graphic touches, reproducing before our eyes each scene which he describes, tells us of the Lord, how this doing, *"and looking up to heaven, he sighed."* Nor has he failed to preserve for us the very word which Christ spoke, in the very language in which he uttered it; he *"saith unto him, Ephphatha, that is, Be opened."* The looking up to heaven was a claiming of the divine help, or rather, since the fullness of divine power abode in him permanently, and not by fitful visitation as with others, this was an acknowledgement of his oneness with the Father, and that he did no other things save those which he saw the Father do. (Cf. Matt. 14:19; John 11:41, 42.) Some explain the words *"he sighed,"* or *"he groaned,"* which are the words in the Rhemish version, as the deep voice of prayer in which he was at the moment engaged; but it is more probable to suppose that this poor helpless creature now brought before him, this living proof of the wreck which sin had brought about, of the malice of the devil in deforming the fair features of God's original creation, then wrung that groan from his heart. He that always felt, was yet now in his human soul touched with an especially lively sense of the miseries of the race of man. Compare John 11:33, "He groaned in the spirit and was troubled," a trouble which had in like manner its source in the thought of the desolation which sin and death had wrought. As there the mourning hearts which were before him were but a specimen of the mourners of all times and all places, so was this poor man of all the variously afflicted and suffering children of Adam. In the preservation of the actual Aramaic *"Ephphatha,"* which Christ spoke, as in the *"Talitha cumi"* of Mark 5:14, we rec-

ognize the narrative of an eye and ear witness, from whom the
Evangelist had his account, and in whose soul the words of power,
which were followed with such mighty consequences, which
opened the ears, and loosed the tongue, and raised the dead, had
indelibly impressed themselves.

The words *"He charged them that they should tell no man,"* would
seem to imply that the friends of this afflicted man had perhaps
accompanied Jesus out of the crowd, and having been witnesses of
the cure, were now included with him in the same prohibition
of divulging what had been done. The reasons which induced
the Lord so often to give this charge of silence there has been occasion to enter on elsewhere, and to say something on the amount of
guilt involved in the disobedience to this injunction. The exclamation in which the surprise and admiration of the beholders finds
utterance, *"He hath done all things well,"* reminds us of the words of
the first creation (Gen. 1:31), upon which we are thus not unsuit-
ably thrown back, for Christ's work is in the truest sense "a new
creation." In the concluding remark of St. Matthew, *"They glorified
the God of Israel,"* is involved, that of those present a great number were heathens, which we might easily expect in this half-
hellenized region of Decapolis, and that from their lips was
brought the confession, that the God, who had chosen Israel, was
indeed above all gods.

25.
The Miraculous Feeding of Four Thousand

Matthew 15:32–39; Mark 8:1–9

There is very little, that might be said upon this miracle, which the preceding one of the same nature has not already anticipated. Whether this was wrought nearly in the same locality, namely, in the desert country belonging to Bethsaida, and not rather on the western, as the former on the eastern, side of the lake, has been sometimes debated. Yet it seems most probably that it was wrought nearly on the same spot. For thither the narrative of St. Mark appears to have brought the Lord. Leaving the coasts of Tyre and Sidon after the healing of the daughter of the Syrophenician woman, he is said to have again reached the sea of Galilee, and this through the midst of the coasts of Decapolis (7:31). But all the cities of the Decapolis save one lay beyond Jordan, and on the eastern side of the lake; this notice therefore places him on the same side also. And, again, when immediately after the miracle he took ship and came to the region of Magdala (Matt. 15:39), since Magdala was certainly on the western side, and his taking ship was most probably to cross the lake, and not to coast along its shores, there is here a confirmation of the same view.

With all the points of similarity, there are also some points differencing this second narrative from the first. Here the people had continued with the Lord three days, but on the former occasion nothing of the kind is noted; the provision too is somewhat larger, seven loaves and a few fishes, instead of five loaves and two fishes; as the number fed is somewhat smaller, four thousand now instead of five thousand, as it was then; and the remaining fragments in this case fill but seven baskets, while in the former they had filled twelve. Of course the work, considered as a miraculous putting forth of the power of the Lord, in each case remains exactly the same.

At first it excites some surprise that the apostles, with that other miracle fresh in their memories, should now have been equally at a loss how the multitude should be fed as they were before. Yet this surprise rises out of our ignorance of man's heart, of our own heart, and of the deep root of unbelief which is there. It is evermore thus in times of difficulty and distress. All former deliverances are in danger of being forgotten; the mighty interpositions of God's hand in former passages of men's lives fall out of their memories. Each new difficulty appears insurmountable, as one from which there is no extrication; at each recurring necessity it seems as though the wonders of God's grace are exhausted and have come to an end. God may have divided the Red Sea for Israel, yet no sooner are they on the other side, than because there are no waters to drink, they murmur against Moses, and count that they must perish for thirst (Ex. 17:1–7), crying, "Is the Lord among us or not?" or, to adduce a still nearer parallel, once already the Lord had covered the camp with quails (Ex. 16:13), yet for all this even Moses himself cannot believe that he will provide flesh for all that multitude (Num. 11:21, 22). It is only the man of a full formed faith, a faith such as apostles themselves at this time had not, who argues from the past to the future, and truly derives confidence from God's former dealings of faithfulness and love. (Cf. 1 Sam. 17:34–37; 2 Chr. 16:7, 8.)

And were it not so, even granting that they did remember how their Master had once spread a table in the wilderness, and were persuaded that he could do it again, yet they might very well have doubted whether he would choose a second time to put forth his creative might—whether there was in these present multitudes that spiritual hunger, which was worthy of being met and rewarded by this interposition of divine power; whether these too were seeking the kingdom of heaven, and were so worthy to have all other things, those also which pertain to this lower life, to the supply of their present needs, added unto them.

26.

The Opening the Eyes of One Blind at Bethsaida

Mark 8:22–26

There is little peculiar in this miracle which has not been treated of elsewhere. For Christ's leading the man out of the town, and touching his eyes as he did, see what has been said already on the miracle last treated of but one. The Lord links on his power, as was frequent with him, to forms in use among men; working through these forms something higher than they could have produced, and clothing the supernatural in the forms of the natural. It was not otherwise, when he bade his disciples to anoint the sick with oil—one of the most esteemed helps for healing in the East. Not the oil, but his Word was to heal, yet without the oil the disciples might have found it too hard to believe in the power which they were exerting—those who through their faith were to be healed, in the power which should heal them (Mark 6:13; James 5:14). So the figs for Hezekiah's boil were indeed the very remedy which a physician with only natural appliances at command would have used (Is. 38:22); yet now, hiding itself behind this nature, clothing itself in the forms of this nature, did an effectual work of preternatural healing go forward.

The only circumstance which remains distinctive of this narration is the progressiveness of the cure; which is not itself without analogies in other cures, as in that of the man blind from his birth, who only after he had been to wash in Siloam, "came seeing" (John 9:7); yet the steps of the progress are marked more plainly here than in any other instance. For first *"when he had spit on his eyes, and put his hands upon him, he asked him if he saw aught. And he looked up and said, I see men, as trees, walking"*; certain moving forms about him, but without the power of discerning their shape or magnitude—trees he should have accounted them from their height, but men from their motion. Then the Lord perfects the cure: *"He put his hands again upon his eyes, and made him look up, and he was restored, and saw every man clearly."*

Chrysostom and others find the reasons for this only progressive cure, in the imperfectness of this blind man's faith, whereof they see an evidence in this, that while others in like case cried with their own voices to Jesus for the opening of their eyes, this man was brought to him by others, himself perhaps scarcely expecting a benefit. The gracious Lord, then, who would not reject him, but who could as little cure him so long as there was on his part this desperation of healing, gave a glimpse of the blessing, that he might kindle in him a longing for the fullness of it, that he might show him how he was indeed an opener of the blind eyes. Others again see a testimony here of the freeness of God's grace, which is linked to no single way of manifestation, but works in diverse manners, sometimes accomplishing in a moment what at other times it brings about only little by little.

There has oftentimes been traced in this healing an apt symbol of the manner in which he who is the Light of the world makes the souls that come to him partakers of the illumination of his grace. Not all at once are the old errors and the old confusions put to flight, not all at once do they see clearly: for a while there are many remains of their old blindness, much which for a season still hinders their vision; they see men but as trees walking. Yet in good time Christ finishes the work which he has begun; he lays his hands on them anew, and they see every man clearly.

27.

The Healing of the Lunatic Child

Matthew 17:14–21; Mark 9:14–29; Luke 9:37–42

T he old adversaries of our Lord, the Scribes, had taken advantage of his absence in the Mount of Transfiguration, to win a temporary triumph, or at least something like one, over his disciples, who were themselves weakened by the absence of their Lord; and with him of three, the chiefest among themselves—those, too, in whom, as habitually the nearest to him, we may suppose his power most mightily to have resided. It was here again, as it was once before during the absence of Moses and his servant Joshua, on his mount of a fainter transfiguration. Then, too, in like manner, the enemy had found his advantage, and a while prevailed against the people (Ex. 32).

It would seem that the disciples who were left below had undertaken to cast out an evil spirit of a peculiar malignity, and had proved unequal to the task; *"they could not,"* And now the Scribes were pressing the advantage which they had gained by this miscarriage of the disciples to the uttermost. A great multitude too were gathered round, spectators of the defeat of the servants of Christ; and the strife was at the highest—the Scribes, no doubt, arguing from the impotence of the servants to the impotence of the Master, and they denying the conclusion; when suddenly he concerning whom the strife was, appeared, returning from the holy mount, his face and person yet glistening, as there is reason to suppose, with reminiscences and traces of the glory which had clothed him there, remininscences and traces which had not yet disappeared, nor faded into the light of common day—so that *"all the people, when they beheld him, were greatly amazed."* Yet here the impression which that glory made was other than the impression of the countenance of Moses. When the multitude saw *him* as he came down from *his* mountain, the skin of his face shining, "they were afraid to come nigh him" (Ex. 34:30), for that glory upon his face was a threatening glory, the awful and intolerable brightness of the Law. But the glory of God shining in the face of Christ Jesus, though awful too, was also an attractive glory, full of grace and beauty, drawing men to him, not driving them from him, and thus, indeed, *"all the people, when they beheld him, were greatly amazed,"* such gleams of brightness played around him still; yet did they not therefore flee from him, but rather, as taken with that brightness, they *"running to him, saluted him"* (Compare 2 Cor. 3:18.)

Yet the sight and sounds which greeted him on his return to our sinful world, how different were they from those which he had just left upon the holy mount! There the highest harmonies of heaven; here some of the wildest and harshest discords of earth. There he had been receiving honor and glory from the Father; here his disciples, those to whom his work had been entrusted in his absence, had been procuring for him, as far as in them lay, shame and dishonor. But as when some great captain, suddenly arriving upon a field of battle, where his subordinate lieutenants have well nigh lost the day, and brought all into a hopeless confusion, with his eye measures at once the necessities of the moment, and with no more than his presence causes the tide of victory to turn, and everything to right itself again, so was it now. The Lord arrests the advancing and victorious foe: he addresses himself to the Scribes, and saying, *"What question ye with them?"* Takes the baffled and hard pressed disciples under his own protection, implying by his words, "If you have any question, henceforth it must be with me." But they to whom these words were spoken were slow to accept the challenge; for it was one from among the multitude, the father of the suffering child, which was his only one, who took up the word, and kneeling down before Jesus, declared all his own misery and his son's.

St. Mark paints the whole scene with the hand of a master, and his account of this miracle, compared with those of the other Evangelists, would be alone sufficient to vindicate for him an original character, and to refute the notion of some, that we have in him only an epitomizer, now of one, and now of the other. All the symptoms, as put into the father's mouth, or described by the sacred historians, exactly agree with those of epilepsy—not that we have here only an epileptic; but this was the ground on which the deeper spiritual evils of this child were superinduced. The fits were sudden and lasted remarkably long; the evil spirit *"hardly departeth from him"*—*"a dumb spirit,"* St. Mark calls it, a statement which does not contradict that of St. Luke, *"he suddenly crieth out"*; this dumbness was only in respect of articulate sounds; he could give no utterance to these. Nor was it a natural defect, as where the string of the tongue has remained unloosed (Mark 8:32), or the needful organs for speech are wanting, nor a defect under which he had always labored; but the consequence of this possession. When the spirit took him in its might, then in these paroxysms of his disorder it tare him, till he foamed and gnashed with his teeth: and altogether he pined away like one the very springs of whose life were dried up. And while these accesses of his disorder might come upon him at any moment and in any place, they often exposed the unhappy sufferer to the worst accidents: *"ofttimes he falleth into the fire, and oft into the water."* In St. Mark the father attributes these fits to the direct agency of the evil spirit: *"ofttimes it hath cast him into the fire, and into the waters, to destroy him"*; yet such calamities might equally be looked at as the natural consequences of his unhappy condition.

But when the father told the Lord of the ineffectual efforts which the disciples had made for his relief, *"I spoke to thy disciples that they should cast him out, and they could not,"* he with a sorrowful indignation exclaimed, *"O faithless generation, how long shall I be with you? How long shall I suffer you?"* And here we have two different applications of these words. Some, as for instance Origen, apply them to the disciples, and them alone; they suppose that our Lord speaks thus, grieved and indignant at the weakness of their faith, and that even so brief a separation from him had shorn them of their strength, and left them powerless against the kingdom of darkness; and the after discourse (Matt. 17:20) seems to make for such an application. Others, as Chrysostom, and generally the early interpreters, would pointedly exclude the disciples from the rebuke; and they give it all to the surrounding multitude, and certainly the term *"generation"* seems to point to them, though less personally; than as being specimens and representatives of the whole Jewish people, the father himself coming singularly forward as an example of the unbelieving temper of the whole generation to which he pertained (Mark 9:22), and therefore being an especial sharer in the condemnation. In St. Mark indeed it is primarily addressed to him: *"He answereth him, and saith, O faithless generation"*; yet the language shows that the rebuke is intended to pass on to many more. And indeed the most satisfactory explanation is that which reconciles both these views; the disciples are not exclusively aimed at, nor chiefly, but rather the multitude and the father: they, however, are included in the rebuke; their unfaithfulness and unbelief had brought them, for the time, back to the level with their nation, and they must share with them in a common reproach. *"How long shall I be with you?"* are words not so much of one longing to put off the coil of flesh, as rather of a master, complaining of the slowness and dullness of his scholars. "Have I abode with you all this time, and have you profited so little by my teaching?" Feeling, it may be, at the same time that till their task was learned, he could not leave them, he must abide with them still. We may compare his words to Philip, "Have I been so long time with you, and yet hast thou not known me, Philip?" (John 14:9).

And now he says, *"Bring him unto me."* As the staff in Gehazi's hand could not arouse the dead child, but the prophet himself must come and take the work in hand, before ever a cure can be wrought, so must it be now. Yet the first bringing of the child to Jesus causes another of the fearful paroxysms of his disorder, so that *"he fell on the ground and wallowed, foaming."* The kingdom of Satan in small and in great is ever stirred into a fiercer activity by the coming near of the kingdom of Christ. Satan has great wrath, when his time is short. But as the Lord on occasion of another difficult cure (Mark 5:9) began a conversation with the sufferer himself, seeking thus to inspire him with confidence, to bring back something of calmness to his soul, so does he now with the representative of the sufferer, the father, it being impossible, from his actual condition, to do it with himself: *"How long is it ago since this came unto him?"* But the father, answering indeed the question, that it was *"of a child,"* and for the stirring of more pity, describing again the miserable perils in which these fits involved his child, yet ill content that anything should come before the healing, if a healing were possible, having, too, present before his mind the recent failure which the disciples had made, added, *"If thou, if thou more than these, canst do anything, have compassion on us, and help us."* He says *"us,"* so entirely is his own life knit up with his child's life: as the Canaanitish woman, pleading for her daughter, had cried,

"Have mercy *on me*" (Matt. 15:22). Yet at the same time he reveals by that *"if"* how he had come with no unquestioning faith in the power of the Lord to aid, but was rendering the difficult cure more difficult still by his own doubting and unbelief.

Our Lord's answer is not without its difficulty, especially as it appears in the original, but the sense of it is plainly the following; "That '*if*' of thine, that uncertainty whether this can be done or not, is to be resolved by thee and not by me. There is a condition without which this thy child cannot be healed; but the fulfilling of the condition lies with no other than thyself. The absence of faith on thy part, and not any overmastering power in this malignant spirit, is that which straitens me; if this cure is hard, it is thou that renderest it so. Thou hast said, If *I* can do anything; but the question is, '*If thou canst believe*'; this is the hinge upon which all must turn— and then with a pause, and no merely suspended sense as in our translation, follow those further words, *"All things are possible to him that believeth."* So that faith is here, as in all other cases, set as the condition of healing; on other occasions it is the faith of the person; but here, that being impossible, the father's is accepted instead; even as the Syrophenician mother's in the room of her daughter's (Matt. 15:22). Thus the Lord appears, in Olshausen's words, in some sort a μαιευτὴς πίστεως, helping the birth of faith in that empty soul. And now, though with pain and with sore travail, it has come to the birth, so that the father exclaims, *"Lord, I believe"*; and then, the little spark of faith which is enkindled in his soul revealing to him the abysmal deeps of unbelief which are there, he adds this further, *"Help thou mine unbelief."* For thus it is ever: only in the light of the actual presence of a grace in the soul does any man perceive the strength and prevalence of the opposing corruption. Before he had no measure by which to measure his deficiency. Only he who believes, guesses aught of the unbelief of his heart.

But now, when this condition of healing is no longer wanting on his part, the Lord, meeting and rewarding even the weak beginnings of his faith, accomplishes the cure. We may observe, in Christ's address to the foul spirit, the majestic *"I charge thee"*; no longer one whom thou mayest dare to disobey, against whom thou mayest venture to struggle, but I, the Prince of the kingdom of light, *"charge thee, come out of him."* Nor is this all: he shall not take advantage of his long possession, presently to come back (Matt. 12:45), and reassert his dominion; the cure shall be perfect and lasting. Most unwillingly the evil spirit departs, seeking to destroy that which he can no longer retain; as Fuller, with wit which is in season and out of season, expresses it, "like an outgoing tenant that cares not what mischief he does." So fearful was this last paroxysm, so entirely had it exhausted all the powers of the child, *"that he was as one dead; and many said, He is dead; but Jesus took him by the hand,"* and from that touch of the Lord of life there came into him life anew: even as we often elsewhere find a reviving power to be by the same channel conveyed (Dan. 10:8, 9; Rev. 1:17; Matt. 17:6–8).

Afterwards the disciples asked privately how it came to pass that they were baffled in the attempts which they had made to accomplish the cure, since they were not exceeding their commission (Matt. 10:8), and had on former occasions found the devils subject to them; and the Lord tells them, because of their unbelief, because of their lack of that to which, and to which only, all things are possible. They had made by a languid use of the means for stirring up and strengthening faith; while yet, though their locks were shorn, they would go forth, as before, against their enemies, being certain to be foiled whensoever they encountered, as they did here, an enemy of peculiar malignity; for the phrase *"this kind"* marks that there are orders of evil spirits, that as there is a hierarchy of heaven, so is there an inverted hierarchy of hell. The same is intimated in the mention of the unclean spirit going and taking "seven other spirits, *more wicked than himself*" (Matt. 12:45), and at Eph. 6:12, there is probably a climax, St. Paul mounting up from one degree of spiritual power and malignity to another. *"This kind,"* he says, *"goeth not out but by prayer and fasting."* The faith which shall be effectual against this must be a faith exercised in prayer, that has not relaxed itself by a habitual compliance with the demands of the lower nature, but often girt itself up to an austerer rule, to rigour and self-denial.

But as the secret of all weakness is in unbelief, so of all strength is faith; and this our Lord teaches them when he adds, "For verily I say unto you, If ye have faith as a grain of mustard seed, ye shall say unto this mountain, Remove hence to yonder place, and it shall remove; and nothing shall be impossible unto you." The image reappears with some modifications, Luke 17:6; and St. Paul probably alludes to these words of his Lord, 1 Cor. 13:2. Many explain "faith as a grain of mustard seed" to mean lively faith, with allusion to the keen and biting powers of that grain. But it certainly is not upon this side that the comparison is to be brought out, rather, as Maldonatus rightly remarks, it is the smallest faith, with a tacit contrast between a grain of mustard seed, a very small thing, and a mountain, a very great. The least spiritual power shall be potent for the overthrow of the mightiest powers which are merely of this world.

28.

The Stater in the Fish's Mouth

Matt. 17:24–27

This miracle finds a place only in the Gospel of St. Matthew, and a nearer contemplation of its features will show why we might even beforehand have expected to meet it, if in one only, then in that which is eminently the theocratic Gospel. But its significance has oftentimes been wholly missed, and the entire transaction emptied of its higher meaning, robbed too of all its deeper lessons, by the assumption that this money which was demanded of Peter was a civil impost, a tribute owing, like the penny of a later occasion (Matt. 22:19), to the Roman emperor; and the word "tribute" used in our translation, rather upholds this error, and leads men's thoughts in the wrong direction—and to consider it this civil impost, instead of what it truly was, a theocratic payment, due to the temple and the temple's God. And this error has brought in with it and necessitated another: for, as the only means of maintaining any appearance of an argument in our Lord's words, it has been needful to understand the kingly dignity, the royal birth, on the ground of which Christ here exempts himself from the payment, to be his Davidical descent, and not, as it is indeed, his divine.

It is true that this erroneous interpretation has been maintained by some, I may say by many expositors, ancient and modern, of high authority; yet rather, it would seem in most cases, from not having the true interpretation, which carries conviction with it, before them, than from deliberately preferring the other. Thus Augustine adduces this passage in connection with Rom. 13:1–7, "Let every soul be subject to the higher powers . . . . Render, therefore, to all their dues, tribute to whom tribute is due—and finds in it a motive for a willing obedience on the part of the faithful to the civil power; and Clement of Alexandris draws from it the same lesson. Origen, too, supposes it a civil payment; and Jerome, also, throughout takes this wrong standing point from which to explain this miracle, so too, in modern times, Maldonatus, who is aware of, but distinctly rejects, the correcter interpretation—being here, for once, at one with Calvin, the great object of his polemical hatred. The last, however, upholds this view in a modified form—he supposes that the money claimed was indeed the temple dues, but yet which now had been by the Romans alienated from its original destination, they compelling the Jews to pay it into historically incorrect, that alienation not having taken place till a later time.

The arguments for the other interpretation, both external and internal, are so prevailing, as hardly to leave a residue of doubt upon any mind before which they are fairly brought. For, in the first place, this didrachm was exactly the sum which we find mentioned Ex. 30:11–16, as the ransom of the soul, to be paid by every Israelite above twenty years old, to the service and current expenses of the tabernacle, or, as it afterwards would be, of the temple. It is true that there it seems only to have been ordered to be paid on the occasions, which most probably were rare, of the numbering of the people. But whether from such having been the real intention of the divine Legislator, or from a later custom which arose only after the Babylonian captivity, it had grown into an annual payment. Some have thought they found traces of it earlier— and, indeed, there seem distinct notices of it, 2 KGs. 12:4; 2 Chr. 24:5, 6, 9; and all the circumstances of what is there described as the collection which "Moses the servant of God laid upon Israel in the wilderness," seem to make for the supposition. At Nehemia 10:32, the circumstance that it is a *third* part of a shekel, and not a half, which they agree to pay, makes it more questionable, as they would scarcely have ventured to alter the amount of a divinely instituted payment; yet the fact that it was yearly, and that it was expressly for the service of the house of God, would lead us to think that it can be no other payment which is meant; and they may have found an excuse for the alteration in their present distress. Josephus mentions that it was an annual payment in his time; and Philo, who tells us how conscientiously and ungrudgingly it was paid by the Jews of the Dispersion, as well as by the Jews of Palestine, so that in almost every city there was a sacred treasury for the collection of these dues, some of which came from cities beyond the limits of the

Roman empire; and then at certain times there were sacred messengers selected from among the worthiest to bear the collected money to Jerusalem. It was only after the destruction of that city, that Vespasian caused this capitation tax to be henceforward paid into the imperial treasury, instead of the treasury of the temple, which now no longer existed.

The words of Josephus on this matter are as explicit as can be; these words I will quote, as the only argument produced against this scheme is, that it was *before* the present time, and as early as Pompey, that these monies were diverted from their original destination, and made payable to the Roman treasury. Of Vespasian he says, "He imposed a tribute on the Jews wheresoever they lived, requiring each to pay yearly two drachms to the capitol, as before they were wont to pay them to the temple at Jerusalem." But of Pompey he merely says, that "he made Jerusalem tributary to the Romans," without any mention whatever of his laying hands on this tax, of which we have already seen that abundant evidence exists that it continued long after his time to be rendered to the temple. Not otherwise indeed could Titus, when he was reproaching the Jews with the little provocation which they had for their revolt, have reminded the revolters how the Romans had permitted them to collect their own sacred imposts.

We may observe again that it is not the publicans that are said to come demanding this tribute, which would have been the natural appellation of the collectors, had they been the ordinary tax-gatherers, or this the ordinary tax. And the tone again of the demand, *"Doth not your master pay the didrachm?"* is hardly the question of a rude Roman tax-gatherer, who had detected anyone in the act of evading, as he thought, the tax; but exactly in keeping, when the duty of paying was a moral one, which yet if any declined, there was scarcely at hand any power to compel the payment.

But the most prevailing argument of all, that this was God's money which should be rendered to God, and not Cesar's which was to be rendered to Cesar, is, that there would be no force whatever in the Lord's conclusion, *"Then are the children free,"* as giving *him* this exemption, unless it was from dues owing to God, and not to Cesar, that by the preceding process of argument he was claiming his freedom. As a Son in his own house, he affirmed his exemption from the first. How could he *on this ground* have claimed immunity from the last? On the ground, that is, of being the son of him on whose behalf the tax was claimed. For he was no son of Cesar. He might indeed have asserted his immunity on other grounds, though *that* he would not, since he had come submitting himself during his earthly life to every ordinance of man. But this claim which he does put forward, only hold good on the supposition that the payment is one made to God. They who maintain the contrary interpretation are driven to say that it is his royal Davidical descent, on the score of which he claims this immunity. But neither can this stand: for the argument then would be, that because Jesus is one king's son, therefore he is exempted from the tribute owing to another king, and that other, one of a hostile dynasty—in itself a most insufficient argument, and certainly not that of the sacred text: *"Of whom do the kings of the earth take custom or tribute" Of their own children or of strangers? Peter saith unto him, Of strangers. Jesus saith unto him, Then are the children free."*

We may presume, then, that our Lord and Peter, with others also, it is most probable, of his disciples, were now returning to Capernaum, which was "his city," after one of their usual absences. The Lord passed forward without question, but the collectors detained Peter, who, having lingered a little behind, was now following his Lord. Chrysostom suggests that their question may be a rude and ill-mannered one: "Does your Master count himself exempt from the payment of the ordinary dues? We know his freedom: does he mean to exercise it here?" Yet on the other hand it may have been, as I should suppose it was, the exact contrary. Having seen or heard of the wonderful works which Christ die, they may really have been uncertain in what light to regard him, whether to claim from him the money or not, and in this doubting and inquiring spirit, they may have put the question to Peter. This Theophylact suggests. But after all, we want that which the history has not given, the *tone* in which the question was put, to know whether it was a rude one or the contrary. To their demand Peter, over-hasty, as was so often the case, at once replied that his master would pay the money. No doubt zeal for his master's honor made him so quick to pledge his Lord: he was confident that his piety would make him prompt to every payment sanctioned and sanctified by God's Law.

Yet at the same time there was here on the part of the apostle a failing to recognize the higher dignity of his Lord: it was not in this spirit that he had said a little while before, "Thou art the Christ, the Son of the living God." He understood not, or at least for the time had lost sight of, his Lord's true position and dignity, that he was a Son over his own house, not a servant in another's house—that he was the Head of the theocracy, not one of its subordinate members, so that it was *to* him in his Father that payments were to be made, not *from* him to be received. This last had been out of all reason; for he who was to be a ransom for all other souls, could not properly give a ransom for his own. It was not for him who was "greater than the temple," and himself the true temple (John 2:21), identical with it according to its spiritual significance, and in whom the Shechinah glory dwelt, to pay dues for the support of that other temple built with hands, which was now fast losing its significance, since the true tabernacle was set up, which the Lord had pitched and not man.

It is then for the purpose of bringing back Peter, and with him the other disciples, to the true recognition of himself, from which they had in part fallen, that the Lord puts to him the question which follows; and being engaged, through Peter's hasty imprudence, to the rendering of the didrachm, which now he could scarcely recede from, yet did it in the remarkable way of this present miracle—a miracle which should testify that all things served him, from the greatest to the least, even to the fishes that walked through the paths of the sea—that he was Lord over nature, and having nothing, yet in his Father's care for him, was truly possessed of all things. Here, as so often in the life of our Lord, the depth of his poverty and humiliation is lightened up by a gleam of his glory. And thus, by the manner of the payment, did he re-assert the true dignity of his person, which else by the payment itself might have been obscured and compromised in the eyes of some, but which it was of all importance for the disciples that they should not lose sight of, or forget. The miracle, then, was to supply a real need—slight, indeed, as an outward need, for the money could assuredly have been in some other and more ordinary ways procured; but as an inner need, most real: in this, then, differing in its essence from the apocryphal miracles, which are continually mere sports and freaks of power, having no ethical motive or meaning whatever.

And we may see this purpose of our Lord's coming clearly out from the very first. He did not wait for Peter to inform him what he had done, and to what he had engaged him; but as soon as *"he was come into the house, Jesus prevented,"* or anticipated, his communication, showing that he was acquainted with it already—that he was a discerner of the thoughts of the heart—that it was for him, as though he had been present at that conversation between his disciple and the collectors of the money. Preventing him thus, he said, "*What thinkest thou, Simon?* On what principle has thou been promising this for me? Is not all the analogy of things earthly against it? *Of whom do the kings of the earth,*" (with an emphasis on these last words, for there is a silent contrasting of these with the King of heaven, as at Ps. 2:2) "*take custom or tribute?*" Christ argues here from the less to the greater, from things earthly to things heavenly, not as thought the things earthly could prove the things heavenly; but, since those are the shadows of these, from the shadow concluding the form of the substance. And when Peter confessed that it was not of their own children, but "*of strangers,*" then at once he brought him to the conclusion whither he was leading him, that "*the children,*" or as it would be better, "the sons," were "*free.*"

But this plural, "*the sons,*" and not "the Son," has sometimes been brought against the interpretation, which would make our Lord to have had himself and himself only, as the only-begotten Son of God, in his eye when he thus spoke. Yet it is obvious that while he is making a general statement of the worldly relations from which he borrows his analogy, and by which he is helping the understanding of his disciples, as there might be not merely one but many sons to a worldly king, or as there are many kings of whom he is speaking, so was it natural for him to throw his speech into a plural form; and it is just as natural, when we come to the heavenly order of things which is there shadowed forth, to restrain it to the singular, to the one Son; since to the King of heaven, who is set against the kings of the earth, there is but one, the only-begotten of the Father. And the explanation, namely, that he intends to extend the liberty to his people, to all that in this secondary sense are the sons of God, cannot be admitted: for it is not the fact concerning dues owing to God. Nor even if this discourse had relation to a civil payment, would it be true; however such an interpretation might be welcome to Anabaptists, having found favor also with some of the extreme Romish canonists, as an argument for the exemption of the clergy from payments to the state, although others among themselves truly remark that it must include all the faithful or none. It is not thus, not as one of many, not as the first among many sons, but as the true and only Son of God, he claims this liberty for himself; and "we may observe, by the way, that the reasoning itself is a strong and convincing testimony to the proper

Sonship, and in the capacity of Son to the proper relationship of Jesus Christ to the Father, which those who deny that relationship will not easily evade or impugn." There is in these words the same implicit assertion of Christ's relation to God as a different one from that of other men, which there is throughout the parable of the Wicked Husbandmen, in the distinction which is so markedly drawn between the son and the servants of the householder: and these statements on the matter, which are thus, as it were, bedded deep in Scripture, assumed as the foundation of further super-structures, not lying on the surface, or contained in single isolated expressions, will always carry with them a peculiar weight. It is true that for the unbelieving, for those that are determined not to be convinced, there is always a loop-hole of escape, as from other declarations, so also from these; in the present instance, the plural *"sons"* affords for those who seek it the desired opportunity of eva-sion.

But under this protest Christ will pay the money; *"Lest we should offend them,* lest they should say we despise the temple, or should count that we are come to destroy the law"—lest they who knew not the awful secret of his birth, should imagine that he was using a false liberty; or even lest it might appear unseemly if he went back from that to which his follower had engaged him, he will pay it. Thus will he provide things honest in the sight of men. There was no need, only a becomingness in the payment; in the same way as there was no necessity for his baptism; it was that whereto of his own choice he willingly submitted; nor yet for the circumcision which he received in his flesh; but he took on him the humiliations of the law, that he might deliver from under the law. And here comes out the deeper meaning of the Lord not paying for himself only, but for Peter, the representative of all the faithful—*"for me and for thee"*—he came under the same yoke with men, that they might enter into the same freedom which was his. But, as on other occasions, at his presentation in the temple (Luke 2:22–24), and again at his baptism, there was something more than common which should hinder the misunderstanding of that which was done—at the presentation, in Simeon's song and Anna's thanks-giving; at the baptism, first in John's reluctance to baptize him, and then in the opened heaven and the voice from thence—so also is there here a protest of Christ's immunity from the present pay-ment, first in his own words, *"Then are the children free,"* and next in the novel method by which he supplies the emergent need.

For putting back Peter to his old vocation, he says, *"Go thou to the sea, and cast a hook, and take up the fish that first cometh up; and when thou hast opened his mouth, thou shalt find a piece of money,"* of stater," as it is in the margin. It is remarkable, and a solitary instance of the kind, that the issue of the bidding is not told us: but we are, of course, meant to understand that at his Lord's command Peter resumed his old occupation, went to the neighboring lake, cast in his hook, and in the mouth of the first fish that rose to it, found, according to his Lord's word, the money that was needed. *"That take, and give unto them for me and thee."* He says not "for us," but as elsewhere, "I ascend unto *my* Father and *your* Father; and to *my* God and *your* God" (John 25:17), so does he use the same language here; for while he has made common part with his brethren, yet he has done this by an act of condescension, not by a necessity of nature; and for them it greatly imports that they should not confound the two, but see ever clearly that here is a delivered and a deliverer, a ransomed and a ransomer, however to the natural eye it may seem that there are two who alike are ransomed.

As has been observed on the miraculous draught of fishes, the miracle does not lie only in a foreknowledge on the Lord's part that so it should be in the first fish which came up, for it was not merely that he foreknew the fact; but he himself, by the mysterious potency of his will, which ran through all nature, drew the particular fish to that spot at that moment, and ordained that it should swallow the hook. Compare Jon. 1:17, "The Lord *had prepared* a great fish to swallow up Jonah." Thus we see the sphere of animal life unconsciously obedient to his will; that also is not *out* of God, but moves *in* him, as does every other creature (1 Kgs. 13:24; 20:36; Amos, 9:3).

All attempts to get rid of a miracle, and to make the Evangelist to be telling, and meaning to tell, an ordinary transaction, as the scheme for instance of Paulus, who will have it that the Lord bade Peter go and catch as many fish as would sell for the required sum, and who maintains that this actually lies in the words—all such, it is at once evident, are hopelessly absurd. Yet, on the other hand, it is an idle and unwarranted multiplication of miracles, to assume that the stater was created for the occasion, and it is in fact a stepping out of the region of miracle altogether into that of absolute creation; for in the miracle, as distinguished from the act of pure creation, there is always a nature-basis to which the divine power which works the wonder, more or less closely links itself. That divine power which dwelt in Christ, restored, as in the case of the sick and blind; it multiplied, as the bread in the wilderness; it ennobled, as the water at Cana; it quickened, as Lazarus and others; it brought together, as here, by wonderful coincidences, the already existing; but, as far as we can see, it formed no new limbs; it made no bread, no wine, out of nothing; it created no new men: it did not, as far as our records reach, pass over on any one occasion into the region of absolute creation.

The allegorical interpretations, or rather uses, of this miracle, for they are seldom meant for more, have not in them much to attract, neither that of Clement, with which Theophylact's mainly agrees, that each skillful fisher of men will, like Peter, remove the coin of pride and avarice and luxury, from the mouth of them whom they have drawn up by the hook of the Gospel from the waste waters of the world; nor yet that which St. Ambrose brings forward, wherein the stater plays altogether a different, indeed, an opposite part; nor has Augustine's more to draw forth our assent. The miracle is rich enough already in meaning and in teaching, without our seeking to press it further.

29.

The Raising of Lazarus

John 11:1–54

The fact of this miracle being past over altogether by the first three Evangelists—a miracle so memorable in itself, so weighty too in its consequences, since the final and absolute determination to put the Lord out of the way resulted immediately from it—this must ever remain a mystery: the utmost that can be hoped is to suggest some probably solution of the omission. The following among the explanations which have been offered have found most favor. First, it has been said by some that the three earlier Evangelists, writing in Palestine, and while Lazarus was yet alive or at least while some of his family yet survived, would not willingly draw attention, and it might be, persecution upon them; but that no such causes hindered St. John, who wrote at a much later period, and out of Palestine, from bringing forward this miracle. The omission on their part, and the mention upon his, will then be a parallel to a like omission and mention in regard of the disciple who actually smote off the ear of the high priest's servant. Only St. John mentions that it was Peter who did it (18:18). This is Olshausen's view, and that of Grotius before him, who refers to John 12:10, in proof of the danger that ensued to Lazarus from being this living witness of Christ's power. But how far-fetched a theory is this! At the furthest it would apply only to the Gospel of St. Matthew; that of St. Mark was probably written at Rome, and for the Gentile Christians, certainly not in Palestine; as little was that of St. Luke, which was addressed to his friend Theophilus, whom many intimations in that Gospel would make us conclude to have lived in Italy. Moreover, the existence of that danger, and of those snares against his life, while the miracle and the impression

of the miracle were yet fresh, is no proof of their existence long
years after. The tide of things had swept onward; new objects of
hostility had arisen—not to say that if there was danger, and if the
danger would have been thus augmented, yet Lazarus was now a
Christian, and would not have shrunk from that danger, nor would
those who truly loved him have desired to save him from the post
of honorable peril. For what else would it have been, but to have
shrunk from confessing Christ, for him to have desired that a work
which revealed so much of the glory of the Lord should remain untold lest some persecution or danger might from the telling accrue
to himself

Others again, feeling this explanation to be insufficient, have
observed how the three earlier Evangelists have confined themselves almost entirely to the miracles that the Lord wrought in
Galilee, leaving those wrought in Jerusalem and its neighborhood
nearly untouched, and that so they came to omit this. It is perfectly
true that they did so. But this is not explaining, it is only stating in
other words the fact which has to be explained; and the question
still remains, Why they should have done so? And to this it is difficult to find now the satisfactory answer.

In the house of Martha at Bethany, for St. Luke (10:38) speaks of
her as if alone the mistress of the house, the Lord had often found
a hospitable reception; and not in the house only; he had found too
a place in the hearts of the united and happy family which abode
under that roof; and he loved with a peculiar human affection
"Martha, and her sister, and Lazarus." It was to Bethany, after the
day's task was over in the hostile city, that probably he was often
wont to retire for the night (Mark 11:11–19); its immediate nearness
to the city—it was not more than fifteen furlongs distant—allowing
him to return thither betimes in the morning. And in the circle of
this family, with Mary, who "sat at this feet and heard his word,"
with Martha, who was only divided between this and the desire to
pay as much outward honor as she could to her divine guest, with
Lazarus his friend, we may think of him as often wont to find rest
and refreshment, after a day spent amid the contradiction of sinners, and among the men who daily mistook and wrested his
words.

But now there has fallen a cloud upon this happy household of
love; for not they even whom Christ loves are exempt from their
share of earthly trouble and anguish; rather are they bound over to

it the more surely. Lazarus is sick; and the sisters in their need turn to him, whom, it may be, they have themselves proved to be a helper in every time of trouble, whom at any rate they have beheld to be such in the extremest needs of others. He is at a distance, beyond Jordan, probably at Bethabara, having withdrawn thither from the fury of his adversaries (John 10:39, 40; cf. John 1:28); but the place of his concealment, or retirement rather, is known to the friendly family, and they send a messenger with these tidings, *"Lord, behold, he whom thou lovest is sick."* Very beautiful is it to observe their confidence in him; they take it for granted that this announcement will be sufficient, and say no more; they do not urge him to come; they only tell their need, as being sure that this will be enough; he does not love, and forsake them whom he loves. It is but a day's journey from Bethabara to Bethany, so that they securely count that help will not tarry long.

The words with which the Lord receives the message, and which we are to take as spoken, in the hearing indeed of the apostles, yet primarily *to* the messenger, and for him to bring back to them that sent him, *"This sickness is not unto death,"* are purposely enigmatical, and must greatly have tried the faith of the sisters. For by the time that the messenger returned, it is probable that Lazarus was already dead. Sorely therefore must this confident assurance that the issue of the sickness should not be death, have perplexed them. Could it be that their divine friend had deceived them, or had been himself deceived? Why had he not made the issue certain by himself coming, or, if aught had hindered that, by speaking that word which even at a distance was effectual to heal, that word which he had spoken for others, for those that were well nigh strangers to him, and they had been saved? But as with so many other of the divine promises, which seem to us for the moment to come to nothing and utterly to fail, and this because we so little dream of the resources of the divine love, and are ever limiting them by our knowledge of them, so was it with this word—a perplexing riddle, till the event had made it plain. Even now, in the eyes of him who saw the end from the beginning, that sickness was not unto death; as they too should acknowledge that it was not, when they should find that death was not to be its last issue, but only a moment of transition to a restored, and a higher life than any which yet Lazarus had lived—a higher life, for when Christ declares the meaning of that sickness, that it was *"for the glory of God, that the Son of God might be glorified thereby,"* he certainly includes in this *"glory of God"* the perfecting for Lazarus of his own spiritual being, as we cannot doubt that it *was* perfected through these wondrous events of his existence. This was his hard yet blessed passage into life. That which was the decisive crisis in his spiritual development was also a signal moment in the gradual revelation of the glory of Christ unto the world. The Son of God was first glorified *in* Lazarus, and then on him, and through him to the world (Compare the exact parallel, John 9:2, 3).

It has been sometimes proposed to connect verse 5 with what goes before, so making it to contain an explanation of the message, and of the ready confidence which the sisters show in the Lord's help; or sometimes, as by Olshausen, with the verse following; and then St. John will be bringing out into the strongest contrast the Lord's love to the distressed family at Bethany, and his tarrying notwithstanding for two days where he was, even after the message claiming his help had reached him. The Evangelist will in that case be suggesting to the thoughtful reader all that is involved in this love which waited so long, ere it would step in to save. But I am inclined to think that Maldonatus has caught a truer view of the sequence of thought, when he connects this verse not with the *one*, but with the *two* which follow. He understands St. John to say, Jesus loved Martha and the others; when therefore he heard that Lazarus was sick, he abode indeed two days where he was, but "then after that saith he to his disciples, Let us go into Judea again." To conceive any other reason for his tarrying where he was those two days, than that he might have room to work that great miracle, is highly unnatural. Sometimes it has been assumed that he had in hand some great work for the kingdom of God where he was, some work which would not endure to be left, and which therefore he could not quit for the most pressing calls of private friendship (See 10:41, 42). But he could have healed with his word at a distance as easily as by his actual presence; and this tarrying was rather a part of the severe yet faithful discipline of divine love; he would let the need come to the highest before he interfered. We have frequent instances of the like. He comes in with mighty help, but not till every other help has failed, till even *his* promise has seemed to the weak faith of men to have failed and come utterly to nothing.

But now, when all things are ready for him, he will return to Judea again. The wondering and trembling disciples remonstrate; it was but now that he escaped instant death at the hands of his Jewish foes; it was the necessity of withdrawing from their active

malice which brought him here, and will he now affront that danger anew? In these their remonstrances with their Lord, their entreaties that he should not thus return to the scene of his former
perils, there spoke out indeed truest love to him; but with it were
mingled apprehensions for their own safety, as is revealed in verse
16, where Thomas takes it for granted that to return with him is to
die with him. We must keep this in mind, if we would understand
our Lord's answer to their remonstrance, *"Are there not twelve hours
in the day?"* Or, rather, "Are not the hours of the day twelve?" In
other words, "Is there not a time which is not cut short or abridged
by premature darkness, but consists of twelve full hours, during
any part of which a man may walk and work without stumbling,
being enlightened by the light of this world, by the natural sun in
the heavens? Such an unconcluded day there is now for me, a day
during any part of which I can safely accomplish the work given
me by my Father, whose light I, in like manner, behold. So long as
the day, the time appointed by my Father for my earthly walk, endures, so long as there is any work forme yet to do, I am safe, and
you are safe in my company." The passage which yields the most
helps to fix its meaning, is the very similar one spoken under similar circumstances of danger, John 9:4. And then, at verse 10, leaving all allusion to him and contemplating his disciples alone, he
links another thought to this, and warns them that they never walk
otherwise than as seeing him who is the Light of men—they never
walk as in the night—they undertake no task, they affront no danger, unless looking to him, unless they can say, The Lord is my
Light; for as to do were to involve themselves in sure peril and
temptation. The final words which explain why such a walker in
the night should stumble, *"because there is no light in him,"* are a forsaking of the figure, which would have required something of this
kind, "there is no light *above* him"; but in the light above us, and
not to have it in us: for the having it here is only the reflex and the
consequence of seeing it there (Cf. 1 John 2:8–11).

We are not to suppose that the Lord receives new and later tidings from the house of sickness, announcing that it is now the
house of death, and by this supposition to explain the new communication which he makes to his disciples. But by the inner
power of his Spirit he knows how it has fared with his friend;
Lazarus is dead," or, as Christ first expresses it, speaking in the heavenly tongue, *"sleepeth"*; *"but I go,"* he adds, *"that I may awake him out
of sleep."* Thus simply does he speak of the mighty work which he

is about to accomplish; so does he use concerning it a language which shall rather extenuate than exalt its greatness: it is but as a sleep and an awaking. The disciples, however, misunderstood his words, and thought that he spoke of natural sleep, an indication often of a favorable crisis in a disorder, and which they assume to be such here; *"Lord, if he sleep, he shall do well."* What need then, they would imply, that their beloved Lord should expose himself and them to peril, when his presence was not required, when all was going favorably forward without him? Hereupon the Lord explained to them that he spoke of another sleep, even the sleep of death, from which he was going to awaken Lazarus. The image of death as a sleep is so common, belongs so to the natural symbolism of all nations, that it was no difficulty in the image itself which occasioned the misunderstanding upon their part; but while it was equally possible for them to take his words in a figurative or in a literal sense, they erroneously took them in the latter. They make an exactly similar mistake, though one involving a greater lack of spiritual insight, Matt. 16:5–12., *"Then said Jesus unto them plainly, Lazarus is dead"*; anticipating at the same time a difficulty which might have risen up in their minds, namely, why he was not there to save him. Through his absence there should be a higher revelation of the glory of God than could have been from his earlier presence; one that should lead them, and in them all the Church, to higher stages of faith, to a deeper recognition of himself, as the Lord of life and of death; *"I am glad for your sakes that I was not there, to the intent that you may believe."* He is glad that he was not there, for had he been upon the spot he could not have suffered the distress of those that were so dear to him to reach the highest point, but must have interfered at an earlier moment.

When he proposes to go to him now, it is plain that in the mind of one of the disciples at least the anticipation of death, as the certain consequence of going, is not overcome. In the words of Thomas to his fellow-disciples, when he finds the perilous journey determined on, *"Let us also go, that we may die with him,"* there is a remarkable mixture of faith and unfaithfulness—faith, since he counted it better to die with his Lord, than to live forsaking him—unfaithfulness, since he conceived it possible that so long as his Lord had a work to accomplish, he or those in his company could be overtaken by any peril which should require them to die together. Thomas was, most probably, of a melancholic, desponding character; most true to his master, yet ever inclined to look at things on their darkest side, finding it most hard to raise himself to the standing oint of faith—to believe other and more than what he saw (John 14:5; 20:25)—to anticipate higher and more favorable issues than those which the earthly probabilities of an event promised. Men of all temperaments and all characters were within that first and nearest circle of disciples, that they might be the representatives and helpers of all that hereafter, through one difficulty and another, should attain at last to the full assurance of faith. Very beautifully Chrysostom says of this disciple, that he who now would hardly venture to go *with* Jesus as far as to the neighboring Bethany, afterwards *without* him traveled to the ends of the world, to the furthest India, daring all the perils of remote and hostile nations.

Martha and Mary had not, probably, ventured to send to the Lord for help, till the sickness of their brother had assumed a most alarming character, and he had most likely died upon the same day that the messenger announcing his illness had reached the Lord, else he would scarcely have been four days in his grave when Jesus came. The day of the messenger's arrival on this calculation would be one day; two our Lord abode in Perea after he had dismissed him, and one more he would have consumed in the journey from thence to Bethany—for it was not more than the journey of a single day from the one place to the other. Dying upon that day, he had, according to the custom of the Jews, which made the burial immediately to follow on the death, been buried upon the same day, as a comparison of this verse with verse 39 clearly shows (Cf. Acts 5:6–10).

But before the arrival of him, the true Comforter, other comforters, some formal, all weak, had arrived. It was part of the Jewish ceremonial of grief, which was all most accurately defined, that there should be numerous visits of condolence, a great gathering of friends and acquaintance, not less than ten, as in the case of a marriage company, round those that were mourning for their dead (1 Chr. 7:22); sometimes, and on the part of some, a reality, yet oftentimes also for the mourners a most weary and burdensome form. Job's comforters give witness how little sympathy there sometimes existed with the sufferers. At times, too, it was a bitter mockery, when the authors of the grief professed to be the comforters in it (Gen. 37:35). But now *he* comes, who could indeed comfort the mourners, and wipe away tears from the eyes. Yet he comes not to the house; that had been already occupied by those who were for the most part alien, if not hostile, to him: and not amid the disturbing influences of that uncongenial circle, would he have his first interview with the sorrowing sisters find place. Probably he tarried outside the town, and not very far from the spot where Lazarus was buried, as indeed seems implied by the supposition of the Jews, that when Mary went to meet him, she had gone to the grave (v. 31). Abiding there, he may have suffered the tidings to go before him that he was near at hand.

When it is said that Martha, hearing of his approach, *"went and met him, but Mary sat still in the house,"* we are not in this hastening of the one, and tarrying of the other, to trace, as many have done, the different characteristics of the two sisters, or to find a parallel here with Luke 10:39. For when Mary on that former occasion chose to sit still, it was because it was at the feet of Jesus that she was sitting; this nearness to him, and not the sitting still, was then the attraction. The same motives which kept her, on that other occasion, in stillness there, would now have brought her with the swift impulses of love to the place where Jesus was. And moreover, no sooner did Mary hear that her lord was come than *"she arose quickly and came unto him"* (v. 29), for it is evident that Martha's words, *"The master is come, and calleth for thee"* (v. 28), are the first intimation which Mary receives of the arrival of their heavenly friend. So Chrysostom, who says "It was not that Martha was now more zealous, but Mary had not heard." This much characteristic of the two sisters there may very probably be in the narrative, namely, that Martha, engaged in active employment even in the midst of her grief, may have been more in the way of hearing what was happening in the outer world, while Mary, in her deeper and stiller anguish, was sitting retired in the house, and less within the reach of such rumors.

I know not whether it is an accident of the narration which is fuller at once place than at the other, or whether it belongs to the characteristic touches which escape us at the first glance, but of which Scripture is so full, that nothing should be said of Martha falling at the Lord's feet, while this is noted of her sister (v. 32). Martha too is ready to change words with Christ, but the deeper anguish of Mary finds utterance in that one phrase, the one thought which was uppermost in the heart of either: *"Lord, if thou hadst been here, my brother had not died"*; and then she is silent. For it is the bitterest drop in their whole cup of anguish, that all this might have been otherwise: had this sickness befallen at another moment, when Christ was nearer, had he been able to hasten to their aid so soon as he was summoned, all might have been averted, they might have been rejoicing in a living, instead of mourning over a dead, brother. Yet even now Martha has not altogether renounced every hope, though she ventures only at a distance to allude to this hope which she is cherishing still. *"But I know that even now,"* now, when the grave was closed upon him, *"whatsoever thou wilt ask of God, God will give it thee."* High thoughts and poor thoughts of Christ mingle here together—high thoughts, in that she sees him as one whose effectual fervent prayers will greatly prevail—poor thoughts, in that she thinks of him as *obtaining* by prayer what indeed he *has* by the oneness of his nature with God.

With words which yet are purposely ambiguous, being meant for the trying of her faith, Jesus assures her that the deep, though unuttered, longing of her heart shall indeed be granted—*"Thy brother shall rise again."* But though her heart could take in the desire for so great a boon, it cannot take in its actual granting; it shrinks back half in unbelief from the receiving it. She cannot believe that these words mean more than that he, with all other faithful Israelites, will stand in his lot at the last day; and with a slight movement of impatience at such cold comfort, comfort that so little met the present longings of her heart, which were to have her brother now, she answers, *"I know that he shall rise again in the resurrection at the last day."* In all this there was much of carnal; hers was as yet an earthly love, clinging passionately to the earthly objects of its affection, and needing infinitely to be exalted and purified. Unless the Lord had lifted her into a higher region of life, it would have profited her little that he had granted her heart's desire. What would it have helped her to receive back her brother, if again she were presently to lose him, if once more they were to be parted asunder by is death or her own? This lower boon would only prove a boon at all, if he and she were both made partakers of a higher life in Christ; then indeed death would have no more power over them, then they would truly possess one another, and forever: and to this the wondrously deep and loving words of Christ would lead her. They are no unseasonable preaching of truths remote from her present needs, but the answer to the very deepest need of her soul; they would lead her from a lost brother to a present Savior, a Savior in whom alone that brother could be truly and forever found. *"I am the Resurrection and the Life;* the true

Life, the true Resurrection; the everlasting triumphs over death, they are *in me*—no distant things, as thou spokest of now, to find place at the end of the world; no things separate or separable from me, as thou spokest of lately, when thou desiredst that I should ask of another that which I possess evermore in myself. In me is victory over the grace, in me is life eternal: by faith in me that becomes yours which makes death not to be death, but only the transition to a higher life."

Such, I cannot doubt, is the general meaning and scope of these glorious words, which yet claim to be considered somewhat more nearly and in detail. When we ask ourselves what Christ means by the title *"The Resurrection,"* which he attributes to himself, we perceive that in one aspect it is something more, in another something less, than that other title of *"The Life,"* which he claims. It is more, for it is life in conflict with and overcoming death; it is life being the death of death, meeting it in hits highest manifestation, of physical dissolution and decay, and vanquishing it there. It is less, for so long as that title belongs to him, it implies something still undone, a mortality not yet wholly swallowed up in life, a last enemy not yet wholly destroyed, and put under his feet (1 Cor. 15:25–26). As he is *"the Resurrection"* of the dead, so is he *"the Life"* of the living—absolute life, having life in himself, for so it has been given him of the Father (John 5:26), the one fountain of life, so that all who receive not life from him pass into the state of death, first the death of the spirit, and then, as the completion of their death, the death also of the body.

The words following, *"He that believeth in me, though he were dead, yet shall he live; and whosoever liveth and believeth in me shall never die,"* are not obscure as far as the gathering the sum total of their meaning: yet so to interpret them, as to prevent the two clauses of the sentence from seeming to contain a repetition, and to find progress in them, is not easy. If we compare this passage with John 6:32–59, and observe the repeated stress which is there laid on the raising up at the last day, as the great quickening work of the Son of God (vv. 39, 40, 44, 54), we shall not hesitate to make the declaration *"yet shall he live,"* in the first clause here, to be equivalent to the words, *"I will raise him up at the last day,"* there, and this whole first clause will then be the unfolding of the words, *"I am the Resurrection"*; as such I will rescue every one that believeth on me from death and the grave. In like manner, the second clause answers to, and is the expansion of, the more general declaration, *"I am the life"*—that is, "Whosoever liveth, every one that draweth the breath of life and believeth upon me, shall know the power of an everlasting life, shall never truly die." Here, as so often in our Lord's words, the temporal death is taken no account of, but quite overlooked, and the believer in him is contemplated as already lifted above death, and made partaker of everlasting life (John 6:47).

Having claimed all this for himself, he demands of Martha whether she can receive it: *"Believest thou this*—that it is I who am this Lord of life and of death? Does thy faith in the divine verities of the resurrection and eternal life after death center in me?" Her answer, *"Yea, Lord, I believe that thou art the Christ, the Son of God, which should come into the world,"* is perhaps more direct than at first sight it appears. For one of the offices of Christ the Messiah was, according to the Jewish expectations, to raise the dead; and thus, confessing to him be the Christ, she implicitly confessed him also to be the quickener of the dead. Or she may mean—"I believe all glorious things concerning thee; there is nought which I do not believe concerning thee, since I believe thee to be him in whom every glorious gift for the world is centerd"—speaking like one whose faith, as that of most person at all times must be, was implicit rather than explicit: she did not know all which that name involved, but all which it did involve she was ready to believe.

She says no more; for now she will make her sister partaker of the joyful tidings that he, the long-desired, is come at last. Some good thing too, it may be, she expects from his high and mysterious words, though she knows not precisely what: a ray of comfort has found its way into her heart, and she would fain make her sister a sharer in this. Yet she told her tidings *"secretly"*; fearing, it may be, that some of their visitors from Jerusalem might be of unfriendly disposition towards the Lord; nor was her suspicion unfounded, as the event showed (v. 46). She says to Mary apart, *"The Master is come, and calleth for thee."* This, that he had asked for Mary, we had not learned from the previous account. At once she rises, and they that are round about her take it for granted that she is hastening in a paroxysm of her grief to the tomb, that she may weep there—as it was the custom of Jewish women often to visit the graves of their kindred, and this especially during the first days of their mourning—and they follow; for thus was it ordained of God that this miracle should have many witnesses. Mary falls at the feet of the Lord Jesus, greeting him exactly in the same words as her sister, *"Lord, if thou hadst been here, my brother had not died."* The words thus repeating themselves a second time from her lips, give us a glimpse of all that had passed in that mournful house, since the beloved was laid in earth—how often during that four days' interval the sisters had said one to the other, how different the issues might have been, if the divine friend had been with them. This had been the one thought in the hearts, the one word upon the lips, of either, and therefore was so naturally the first spoken by each, and that altogether independently of the other. This is indeed one of the finer traits of the narrative.

At the spectacle of all this grief, the sister weeping, and even the more indifferent visitors from Jerusalem weeping likewise, the Lord also *"groaned in spirit and was troubled."*

The word which we translate *"groaned,"* does indeed far more express the feelings of indignation and displeasure than of grief, which, save as a measure of that is contained in all displeasure, it means not at all. But at what and with whom Jesus was thus indignant, has been very differently explained. The notion of some of the Greek expositors, that he was indignant with himself at these risings of pity, these human tears—that the word expresses the inward struggle to repress, as something weak and unworthy, these rising utterances of grief, is not to be accepted for an instant. Christianity knows of no such dead Stoicism; it knows of a regulating, but of no such repressing, of the natural affections; on the contrary, it bids us to weep with them that weep; and, in the beautiful words of Leighton, that we "seek not altogether to dry the stream of sorrow, but to bound it, and keep it within its banks." Some, as Theodore of Mopsuestia and Lampe, suppose that he was indignant in spirit at the hostile dispositions which he already traced and detected among the Jews that were present, the unbelief on their part with which he foresaw that great work of his would be received. Others, that his indignation was excited by the unbelief of Martha and Mary and the others, which they manifested in their weeping, whereby they showed clearly that they did not believe that he would raise their dead. But he himself wept presently, and there was nothing in these their natural tears to have roused a feeling of the kind.

Much better is it to take this as the indignation which the Lord of life felt at all which sin had wrought: he beheld death in all its fearfulness, as the wages of sin; and all the world's woes, of which this was but a little sample, rose up before his eye—all the mourners and all the graves were present to him. For that he was about to wipe away the tears of those present, did not truly alter the case. Lazarus did but rise again, to taste a second time the bitterness of death: these mourners he might comfort, but only for a little while; these tears he might stanch, only again hereafter to flow; and how many had flowed and must flow with no such Comforter to wipe them, even for a season, away? Contemplating all this, a mighty indignation at the author of all this woe possessed his heart. And now he will delay no longer, but will do battle with him, and show in a present, though as yet an incomplete, triumph over him, some preludes of his future victory. With this feeling he demands, *"Where have ye laid him? They said unto him, Lord, come and see. Jesus wept:"* himself borne along with, and not seeking to resist, this great tide of sorrow.

Some of the Jews present, moved to good will by this lively sympathy of the Lord with the sorrows of those around him, exclaimed *"Behold how he loved him!"* But others, perhaps invidiously, *"Could not this man, which opened the eyes of the blind, have caused that even this man should not have died?"* He weeps over this calamity now, but could he not have hindered it? He who could open the eyes of the blind (they allude to the case which, through the judicial investigation that followed, had made so great a stir at Jerusalem, John 9), could he not (by his prayer to God), have hindered that this man should have died? There was indeed in this accusation, as there is so often in similar ones, something contradictory: for their very assumption that he possessed such power and favor with God that he could have stayed the stroke of death, rested on the supposition of so high a goodness upon his part, as would have secured that his power should not have been grudgingly restrained in any case, where it would have been suitably exerted. It is characteristic of the exact truth of this narrative (although it has been brought as an argument against it), that they, dwellers in Jerusalem, should refer to this miracle which had lately occurred there (John 9), rather than to the previous raisings from the dead, which might at first sight appear more to the point. But those, occurring at an earlier period, and in the remote Galilee, would not have been present to them with at all the same liveliness as was this miracle, which had been brought out into especial prominence by the contradiction which it had roused, and the futile attempts which had been made to prove it an imposture. Yet a maker up of the narrative from later and insecure traditions would inevitably have fallen upon those miracles of a like kind, as arguments of the power of Jesus to have accomplished this.

Meanwhile they reach the place where the tomb was, though not without another access of that indignant horror, another of those mighty shudderings that shook the frame of the Lord of life—so dreadful did death seem to him who, looking *through* all its natural causes, at which we often stop short, saw it purely as the seal and token of sin, so unnatural its usurpation over a race made for immortality. The tomb, as the whole course of the narrative shows, was without the town (v. 30), and this according to the universal custom of the East (Luke 7:12), which was not to place the dead among the living. It was a cave. Such were commonly the family vaults of the Jews: sometimes natural (Gen. 23:9), sometimes artificial, and hollowed out by man's labor from the rock (Is. 22:16; Matt. 27:60), in a garden (John 19:41), or in some field, the possession of the family (Gen. 23:9, 17–20; 35:18; 2 Kgs. 21:18); with recesses in the sides, wherein the bodies were laid, occasionally with chambers one beyond another. Sometimes the entrance to these tombs was on a level, sometimes there was a descent to them by steps; this last seems most probable on the present occasion, from the stone being said to lie *on* the tomb. The purpose of this stone was mainly to prevent the entrance of beasts of prey, and especially the numerous jackals, which else might have found their way into these receptacles of the dead, and torn the bodies. It was naturally of size and weight enough not easily to be moved away (Mark 16:3). The tomb of our blessed Lord himself, with its "door," seems rather to have had a horizontal entrance.

Among other slighter indications which we have that Mary and Martha were not at all among the poorest of their people, this is one, that they should possess such a family vault as this. The poor had not, and it lay not within their power to purchase in fee, portions of land to set apart for these purposes of family interment. The possession of such was a privilege of the wealthier orders; only such were thus laid in the sepulchres of their fathers. We have another indication of this in the large concourse of mourners, and those of the higher ranks, which assembled from Jerusalem to console the sisters in their bereavement; for even in grief that word is too often true, that "wealth maketh many friends; but the poor is separated from his neighbor" (Prov. 19:4). So, too, in the pound of ointment of spikenard, *"very costly,"* with which Mary anointed the feet of the Savior (John 12:3); and the language of the original at verse 19, however it may mean Martha and Mary, and not those around them, yet means them *as the center of an assemblage.* This was the general view of the early Church concerning their rank in life. Chrysostom assumes the sisters to have been high-born. Yet though this was most probably the case, it is a mistaken emphasis which some lay upon *"the town of Mary and heer sister Martha"* (v. 1), when they conclude from thence that Bethany belonged to them. The Levitical law rendered, and was intended to render, any such concentration of landed property in the hands of only one or two persons immpossible. As regards the phrase itself, by as good right Bethsaida might be said to have belonged to Andrew and Peter, for the language is exactly similar (John 1:45).

What is it that causes St. John to designate Martha (v. 39) as *"the sister of him that was dead,"* when this is plain from the whole preceding narrative? Probably to explain her remonstrance at the taking away of the stone. She, as a sister of the dead, would naturally be more shocked than another at the thought of the exposure of that countenance, upon which corruption had already set its seal— would most shudderingly contemplate that beloved form made a spectacle to strangers, now when it was become an abhorring even to them that had loved it best. Yet the words of her remonstrance are scarcely, as by so many they are interpreted, an experience which she now makes, but rather a conclusion which she draws from the length of time during which the body had already lain in the grave. With the rapid decomposition that goes forward in a hot country, necessitating as it does an almost immediate burial, the four days might well have brought this about, which she fears. At the same time, it gives the miracle almost a *monstrous* character to suppose it was actually the re-animating of a body which had already undergone the process of corruption. Rather he who sees the end from the beginning, and who had intended that Lazarus should live again, had watched over that body in his providence, that it should not hasten to corruption. If the poet could imagine a divine power guarding from all defeature and wrong the body which was thus preserved only for an honorable burial; by how much more may we assume a like preservation for that body which, not in the world of fiction, but of reality, was to become again so soon the tabernacle for the soul of one of Christ's servants. Neither is there anything in Martha's words to render any other view necessary; no conclusion of an opposite kind can be drawn from them; for they are plainly spoken before the stone is moved away from the opening of the tomb.

Yet this much is certain from the words, that she had already let go the faith which at one moment she had conceived, that even yet her brother might live again. Nor is this strange, for such are ever the alternating ebbs and flows of faith. All that she could see in the command to remove the stone, was probably a desire on the Lord's part to look once more on the countenance of him whom he loved; and from this she would turn him, by urging how death and corruption would have already set their seal upon that: so it must needs be, *"for he hath been dead four days."*

The Lord checks and rebukes her unbelief: *"Said I not unto thee, that, if thou wouldest believe, thou shouldest see the glory of God?"* When had he said this, and to what former conversation does he allude? No doubt to that which he held with her when first they met. It is true that these very words do not occur there, but that conversation was on the power of faith, as the means to make our own the fullness of the powers that dwelt in Christ. There is no need, therefore, to suppose that he alludes to something in that prior discourse, unrecorded by the Evangelist. And now Martha acquiesces: she does believe, and no longer opposes the obstacle of her unbelief to what the Lord would do. And now, when they who are the nearest of kin are thus consenting, the stone is removed; and on this follows the thanksgiving prayer of the Lord; *"And Jesus lifted up his eyes, and said, Father, I thank thee that thou has heard me."* Yet in any thanksgiving to God, and thanksgiving on account of being heard, there lay the possibility of a misinterpretation on the part of his disciples, and of the Church afterwards, when these words were handed down to it—as though it would have been possible for the Father not to have heard him—as though he had first obtained this power to call Lazarus from his grave, after supplication—had, like Elisha, by dint of prayer, painfully won back the life which had departed; whereas the power was most truly his own, not indeed in disconnection from the Father, for what he saw the Father do, that only he did; but in this, his oneness with the Father, there lay the uninterrupted power of doing these mighty acts. Therefore does he explain, not any more in that loud voice which should be heard by the whole surrounding multitude, but yet so that his disciples might hear him, what this *"Father, I thank thee"* means, and why it was spoken. *"I knew that thou hearest me always: but because of the people which stand by I said it, that they may believe that thou hast sent me."* For them it was wholesome: they should thus understand that he claimed his power from above, and not from beneath; that there was no magic, no necromancy here. The thanks *to* God were an acknowledgment that the power was *from* God.

Chrysostom supposes that when this thanksgiving prayer was uttered, Lazarus was already re-animated, and, being re-animated, is now bidden to issue from the tomb. But rather, this cry *"with a loud voice,"* this *"Lazarus, come forth,"* is itself the quickening word, at which life returns to the dead. For it is ever to the *voice* of the Son of God that the power of quickening the dead and calling them from their graves is attributed. Thus, John v. 28, 29, "The hour is coming in the which all that are in the graves shall hear his voice, and shall come forth." So, 1 Thess. 4:16, it is the Lord's descending *"with a shout,"* which is followed by the resurrection of the dead in Christ. Nor, probably, is "the last trump" of 1 Cor. 15:52, anything else but this voice of God which shall sound through all the kingdom of death. Many, in their zeal for multiplying miracles, make it a new miracle, a wonder in a wonder, as St. Basil calls it, that Lazarus was able to obey the summons, while yet he was *"bound hand and foot with grave clothes."* But if so, to what end the further word, *"Loose him and let him go?"* Probably he was loosely involved in these grave clothes, which hindering all free action, yet did not hinder motion altogether; or, it may be, that, in accordance with the Egyptian fashion, every limb was wrapped round with these stripes by itself: in the mummies each separate finger has sometimes its own wrapping.

St. John here breaks off the narrative of the miracle itself, leaving us to imagine their joy, who thus beyond all expectation received back their dead from the grave; a joy, which was well nigh theirs alone, among all the mourners of all times,

> Who to the verge have followed that they love,
> And on the insuperable threshhold stand,
> With cherished names its speechless calm reprove,
> And stretch in the abyss their ungrasped hand.

He leaves this, and passes on to show us the historic significance of this miracle in the development of the Lord's earthly history, the permitted link which it formed in the chain of those events, which were to end, according to the determinate decree and counsel of god, in the atoning death of the Son of God upon the cross.

What the purpose was of these Jews that *"went their ways to the Pharisees, and told them what things Jesus had done,"* has been diversly conceived. By some, as by Origen, it has been supposed that they went with a good intention, thinking to tell them that which even they could no longer resist, which would make them also acknowledge that this was the Christ. Yet the place which this intimation occupies in the narrative seems decisively to contradict this meaning. Many, observes St. John, believed on him, *but* some, not of those that believed, but of the Jews, went and told the Pharisees. What else can this mean, save that these were persons who did not believe; who on one or another plea refused to be convinced by this miracle (Luke 16:31), and went to the professed enemies of the Lord to show them what had been done, to irritate them yet more against the doer, to warn them also of the instant need of more earnestly counter-working him who had done, or seemed to do, so great a sign? And it is observable that St. John joins immediately with their report to the Pharisees the increased activity in the hostile machinations of these against the Lord.

And they are indeed now seriously alarmed; they anticipate the effects, which this greatest miracle that Christ did would have upon the people, which we know historically that it actually had (John 12:10, 11, 17–19); and they gather in council together against the Lord and against his Anointed. They stop not to inquire whether the man, *"this man,"* as they contemptuously call him, who, even according to their own confession, is doing many miracles, may not be doing them in the power of God, whether he may not be doing them in the power of God, whether he may not be indeed the promised King of Israel. The question of the truth or falsehood of his claims seems never to enter into their minds, but only how the acknowledgment of these claims will bear on the worldly fortunes of their order, and this they contemplate under somewhat a novel aspect: *"If we let him thus alone, all men will believe on him: and the Romans shall come and take away both our place and nation."*

For at first sight it seems difficult to understand how they necessarily connected together the recognition of Jesus for the Christ, and the collision with the Roman power. It was probably in this way. "The people will acknowledge him for the Messiah; he will set himself at their head, or they by compulsion will place him there, making him their king (John 6:15); then will follow the vain attempt to throw off the foreign yoke, to be crushed presently by the superior power of the Roman legions; and then these will not distinguish the innocent from the guilty, but will make a general sweep, taking away from us wholly whatsoever survivees of our power and independence, our place and our nation." Or without presuming an actual insurrection, they may have supposed that the mere fact of the acknowledging a Messiah would awaken the suspicions of the Romans, would by them be accounted as an act of rebellion, to be visited with these extremest penalties. We see how on a later occasion the Roman governor instantly comes to this point; his first question is, "Art thou the King of the Jews?" (John 18:33). Augustine understand it somewhat differently—that they were already meditating, as no doubt they were, the great revolt of a later time, and felt how all the nerves of it would be cut by the spread of the doctrines of this

Prince of peace: for where should they find instruments for their purpose? All resistance to the Roman power would become impossible; and whensoever these chose, they would come and rob them of all which remained of their national existence. He is, however, I believe, single in maintaining this view, and the other is far the more natural. The question will still remain, whether they who said this, did truly feel the dread which they professed, or whether they only pretended to fear these consequences from the suffering Christ's ministry to remain uninterrupted, on account of a party in the Sanhedrin, for such there was, more or less well affected to Jesus (see John 9:16), and who could only thus, by this plea of the consequences to them and to the whole nation, be won over to the extreme measures now meditated against him. Chrysostom, and most of the Greek expositors, suppose they did but feign this fear, yet I cannot but think that they were sincere in their alarm.

Probably many half measures had been proposed by one member and another of the Sanhedrin for arresting the growing inclination of the people to recognize Jesus as the Christ, and has been debated backward and forward, such as hindering them from hearing him, proclaiming anew, as had been done before, that any should be excomminicated who should confess him to be Christ (John 9:22). But these measures had already been proved to be insufficient; and in that *"Ye know nothing at all"* of Caiaphas, we hear the voice of the bold bad man, silencing, with ill-suppressed contempt, his weak and vacillating colleagues, who could see the common danger which threatened them, and yet shrunk, though from no righteous principle, from applying the effectual remedy. This man, who threatens to imperil the whole nation, and, whether willingly or not, to compromise it with the Roman power, must be taken out of the way: *"It is expedient for us, that one man should die for the people, and that the whole nation perish not."* Caiaphas, who dares thus to come to the point, and to speak the unuttered thought of many in that assembly, was a Sadducee (Acts 5:17), and held the office of the high priesthood for ten successive years, which makes something of a difficulty here; for St. John's description of him as *"being the high priest that same year,"* might appear to imply that he esteemed the high priesthood as a yearly office and elective, whereas it was in truth for life and hereditary.

Now. though it is quite true, that, through the tyranny of the Romans, the high priesthood was as vilely prostituted as, under very similar circumstances, the patriarch's throne at Constantinople is now by the Turks, and shifted so rapidly from one to another, as sometimes to remain with one occupier even for less than this time, yet according to its idea it was for the life of the holder, and, in the present case, it was held by this one man if not for life, yet at least much more than a single year. The expression has sometimes been explained as if St. John would say that Caiaphas was high priest for that year, that ever-memorable year "when vision and prophecy should be sealed," and in which the Son of god should die upon the cross. But it seems easier to suppose that all which St. Jude meant to express was, that Caiaphas was high priest *then'* whether he was also such before or after was nothing to his present purpose. He desires to bring out that he was high priest at the time when these words were uttered, because this gave a weight and significance to the words which else they would not have possessed; and what significance this was, and why his words should have had it, he explains in what follows.

"This spoke he not of himself; but being high priest that year, he prophesied that Jesus should die for that nation." It is clear that the Evangelist sees here an inner connection between the words spoken and the office which the speaker filled, and herein lies the real knot of the passage, which has to be untied: for that a bad man should have uttered words which were so overruled by God as to become prophetic, would be no difficulty. God, the same who used a Balaam to declare how there should come a Star out of Jacob and a Sceptre out of Israel (Num. 24:17), might have used Caiaphas to

foreannounce other truths of his kingdom. Nor is there any difficulty in such *unconscious* prophecies as this evidently is. How
many prophecies of the like kind—most of them, it is true, rather
in act than in word, meet us in the whole history of the crucifixion!
Or what again the robe and the homage, the sceptre and the crown?
And in the typical rehearsals of the great and final catastrophe in
the drama of God's providence, how many Nimrods and Pharaohs,
antichrists that do not quite come to the birth, have prophetic parts
allotted to them, which they play out, unknowing what they do; for
such is the divine irony; so, in a very deep sense of the words,

Ludit in humanis divina potentia rebus.

But the perplexing circumstance is the attributing to Caiaphas, *as
high priest,* these prophetic words, for prophetic the Evangelist pronounces them plainly to be, and all attempts to get rid of this as his
intention, and to destroy the antithesis between *"speaking of himself"* and *"prophesying,"* are idle. There is no need, however, to suppose (and this greatly lightens the difficulty), that he meant to
affirm this to have been a power which always went along with the
hight priesthood; that the high priest, as such, *must* prophesy; but
only that god, the extorter of those unwilling, or even unconscious,
prophecies from wicked men, ordained this further, that he who
was the head of the theocratic people, for such, till another high
priest had sanctified himself, and his moral character was nothing
to the point, Caiaphas truly was—that the man who according to
the idea of the Levitical constitution was to utter lively oracles,
wearing upon his breastplate, while the priesthood stood in its first
perfection, the oracular stones, the Urim and the Thummim, which
he might consult on all great affairs that concerned the well-being
of the nation—that this man, because he bore this office, should be
the organ of the memorable prophecy concerning Christ and the
meaning and end of his death in regard of that nation.

We are not to take these words which follow, *"and not for that
nation only, but that also he should gather together in one the children of
god that were scattered abroad,"* as part of the meaning which is le-
gitimately involved in the words of Caiaphas, but as St. John's addition to his words, added to prevent a limitation of the benefits of
the death of Christ which might seem to lie in them—a misinterpretation which, now that the words had been made more than
man's words, it was worthwhile to exclude. Caiaphas indeed

prophesied that Jesus should die for that nation, and (St. John himself adds), not for it only, but also for the gathering into one of *all* the children of God which were scattered abroad in the whole world. The best parallel to this verse is 1 John 2:2, "He is the propitiation for our sins; not for ours only, but also for the sins of the whole world." Not the Law, as the Jews supposed, but the atoning death of Christ was that which should bind together all men into one fellowship: "I, if I be lifted up from the earth, will draw all men unto me." The law was rather a wall of separation; it was only that death which could knit together. We may compare Eph. 2:13–22, as the great commentary of St. Paul on these words of St. John. The term *"children of God"* is probably applied here by anticipation— those that, through obeying his call when it reached them, should become hereafter his children. Exactly in the same way, and in a parallel passage, Christ says, "Other sheep I have, which are not of this fold" (John 10:16), others that should be his sheep. There is perhaps a subordinate sense in which they might be termed the children of God already—they were the nobler natures, although now run wild, among the heathen—the "sons of peace" that should receive the message of peace (Luke 10:6); in a sense, "of the truth," even while they were sharing much of the falsehood round them, so "of the truth" that, when the King of truth came and lifted up his banner in the world, they gladly ranged themselves under it (John 18:37; cf. Luke 8:15: John 3:19–21).

It had now come to a solemn decree on the part of the Sanhedrin, that Jesus should be put to death, and from that day forth there were continual counsels among them how his death might be brought about: but he, whose hour was not yet come, withdrew himself awhile from their malice to the neighborhood of the desert country lying northward of Jerusalem, there to abide, till the approach of the Passover should bring him back to the city, to supply at length the true Paschal Lamb.

In the ancient Church there was ever found, besides the literal, an allegorical interpretation of this and the two other miracles of the like kind. As Christ raises those that are naturally dead, so also does he quicken them that are spiritually dead; and the history of this miracle, as it abounds the most in details, so was it the most fruitful field on which the allegorists exercised their skill. Here they found the whole process of the sinner's restoration from the death of sin to a perfect spiritual life shadowed forth; and these allegories are often rich in manifold adaptations of the history, as beautiful as they are ingenious, to that which it is made to set out. Nor was this all; for these three raisings from the dead were often contemplated not apart, not as each portraying exactly the same truth, but in their connection with one another; as setting forth one and the same truth under different and successive aspects. It was observed how we have the record of three persons that were restored to life—one, the daughter of Jairus, being raised from the bed; another, the son of the widow, from the bier; and lastly, Lazarus, from the grave. And it is even thus, men said, that Christ raises to newness of life sinners of all degrees; not only those who have just fallen away from truth and holiness, like the maiden who had just expired, and in whom, as with a taper just extinguished, it was by comparison easy to kindle a vital flame anew—but he raises also them who, like the young man borne out to his burial, have been some little while dead in their trespasses. Nor has he even yet exhausted his power; for he quickens them also who, like Lazarus, have lain long festering in their sins, as in the corruption of the grave, who were not merely dead, but buried—with the stone of evil customs and evil habits laid to the entrance of their tomb, and seeming to forbid all egress thence: even this he rolls away, and bids them to come forth, loosing the bands of their sins; so that anon we see them sitting down with the Lord at his table, there where there is not the foul odor of the grave, but where the whole house is full of the sweet fragrance of the ointment of Christ (John 12:1–3).

30.

The Opening the Eyes of Two Blind Men Near Jericho

Matt. 20:20–34; Mark 10:46–52; Luke 18:35–43

This is one of the events in the life of our Lord which has put the ingenuity of Scripture harmonists to the stretch. The apparent discrepancies which it is their task to reconcile are these. St. Matthew makes our Lord to have restored sight to two blind men, and this as he was going out of Jericho. St. Luke appears at first sight to contradict both these facts, for he makes the cure to have taken place at his coming nigh to the city, and the healed to have been but one; while St. Mark seems to stand between them, holding in part to one of his fellow Evangelists, in part to the other. He with St. Luke names but one whose eyes were opened, but consents with St. Matthew in placing the miracle, not at the entering into, but the going out from, Jericho, so that the narratives curiously cross and interlace one another. To escape all difficulties of this kind there is of course the ready expedient always at hand, that the sacred historians are recording different events, and that therefore there is nothing to reconcile, although oftentimes this is an escape from difficulties of one kind, which only really involves in far greater embarrassments of another. Thus, accepting this solution, we must believe that twice, or even thrice, in the immediate neighborhood of Jericho, our Lord was besought in almost the same words by blind beggars on the wayside for mercy—that on every occasion there was a multitude accompanying him, who sought to silence the vociferations of the claimants, but did only cause them to cry the more—that in each case Jesus stood still and demanded what they wanted—that in each case they made the same reply in very nearly the same words—and a great deal more. All this is so unnatural, so improbable, so unlike anything of actual life, so unlike the infinite variety which the Gospel incidents present, that any solution seems preferable to this.

There are three apparently discordant accounts, none of them entirely agreeing with any other: but they can at once be reduced to two by that rule, which in all reconciliations of parallel histories must be held fast, namely, that the silence of one narrator is not to be assumed as the contradiction of the statement of another; thus St. Mark and St. Luke, making especial mention of one blind man, do not contradict St. Matthew, who mentions two. There remains only the difficulty that by one Evangelist the healing is placed at the Lord's entering into the city, by the others at his going out. This is not, I think, sufficient to justify a duplication of the fact. Nor have I any doubt that Bengel, with his usual happy tact, has selected the right reconciliation of the difficulty; namely, that one cried to him as he drew near to the city, but that he did not cure him then, but on the morrow at his going out of the city cured him together with the other, to whom in the meanwhile he had joined himself—the Evangelist relating by prolepsis, as is so common with all historians, the whole of the event where he first introduces it, rather than, by cutting it in two halves, preserve indeed a more painful accuracy, yet lose the total effect which the whole narrative related at a breath would possess.

The cry with which these blind men sought to attract the pity of Christ was on their part a recognition of his dignity as the Messiah; for this name, *"Son of David,"* was the popular designation of the Messiah. There was therefore upon their part a double confession of faith, first that he could heal them, and secondly, not merely as a prophet from God, but as *the* Prophet, as the one who should come, according to the words of Isaiah, to give sight to the blind. In the case of the man blind from his birth (John 9), we have the same confessions, but following, and not preceding, the cure, and with intervals between; so that first he acknowledges him as a prophet (v. 17), and only later as the Messiah (v. 38).

And here the explanation has been sometimes found of the rebukes which they met from the multitude, who would fain have had them to hold their peace. These, it has been said, desired to hinder their crying, because they grudged to hear given unto Jesus this title of honor, which they were not themselves prepared to accord him. This passage will then be very much a parallel to Luke

19:39; only that there the Pharisees would have Christ himself to rebuke those that were glorifying him and giving him honor, while
here the multitude take the rebuking into their own hands. Yet I
hardly think the explanation good. It was quite in the spirit of the
envious malignant Pharisees to be vexed with those Messianic
salutations, "Blessed be the King, that cometh in the name of the
Lord"; but these well-meaning multitudes, rude and for the most
part spiritually undeveloped as no doubt they were, were yet exempt from those spiritual malignities. We never trace aught of this
kind in them, but rather in the main a sympathy with the Lord; it
was not they who said that his miracles were wrought in the power
of Beelzebub; but they glorified God because of them. And here,
too, I cannot doubt but that it was out of an intention of honoring
Christ, that they sought to silence what appeared to them these ill-
timed and unmannerly clamors. It may be that he was teaching as
he went, and they would not have him interrupted.

But their endevours to suppress the crying of these blind men
profited nothing: on the contrary, *they cried the more, saying, Have
mercy on us, thou Son of David.*" Many admirable homiletic applications of this portion of the history have been made. Here, it has
been often said, is the history of many a soul: when a man is first
in earnest about his salvation, and begins to cry that his eyes may
be opened, that he may walk in his light who is the Light of men,
when he begins to despise the world and to be careless about
riches, he will find infinite hindrances, and these not from professed enemies of the Gospel of Christ, but from such as seem, like
this multitude, to be with Jesus and on his side. Even they will try
to stop his mouth, and to hinder an earnest crying to him. And
then, with a stroke from the life, Augustine makes further application in the same direction of the words which follow in St. Mark,
who, speaking as but of one that cried, sayd, *"And Jesus stood still,
and commanded him to be called. And they called the blind man, saying
unto him, Be of good comfort, rise; he calleth thee!"* For, he observes,
this too repeats itself often in the spiritual history of men's lives. If
a man will only despise these obstacles from a world which calls itself Christian, and overcome them; if despite of all he will go on,
until Christ is evidently and plainly with him, then they who began
by reprehending, will finish by applauding: they who at first said,
He is mad, will end with saying He is a saint.

At this cry of theirs *"Jesus stood still,"* arrested, as ever, by the
cry of need, *"and called them"*; or, in the words of St. Mark (10:49),

who throughout tells but of the one, *"commanded him to be called. And he, casting away his garment,"* to the end that he might obey with the greater expedition, and that he might be hindered by nothing, *"rose and came to Jesus"*—in this ridding himself of all which would have been in his way, used often as an example for every soul which Jesus has called, that it should in like manner lay aside every weight and whatever would hinder it from coming speedily to him (Matt. 13:44, 46; Phil. 3:7). The Lord's question, *"What wilt thou that I should do unto thee?"* is, in part, an expression of his readiness to aid, a comment in act upon his own words, spoken but a little while before, "The Son of man came not to be ministered unto, but to minister" (Matt. 20:28); in part uttered for the calling out into yet livelier exercise the faith and expectation of the petitioner (Matt. 9:28). The man, whose cry has been hitherto a vague general cry for mercy, now singles out the blessing which he craves, declares the channel in which he desires that this mercy may run, and makes answer, *"Lord, that I might receive my sight."* Only St. Matthew mentions the touching of the eyes which were to be restored to vision, and only St. Luke the word of power, the *"Receive thy sight,"* by which the cure was effected. The man, who had hitherto been tied to one place, now used aright his restored eyesight; for he used it to follow Jesus in the way, and this with the free outbreaks of a thankful heart, himself *"glorifying God,"* and being the occasion that others glorified his name as well (Acts 3:8–10).

31.
The Withering of the Fruitless Fig-Tree

Matt. 21:17–22; Mark 11:12–14, 20–24

This miracle was wrought upon the Monday of the week of Passion. On the Sunday of Palms our blessed Lord had made his triumphal entry into Jerusalem, and in the evening—since even now his hour, though close at hand, was not altogether come—he retired from the snares and perils of the city to the safer Bethany, to the house probably of those sisters whom he had so lately enriched with a restored brother, and there passed the night. On the morning of Monday, as he was returning from Bethany to his ministry in the city very early, indeed before sunrise, the word against the fig-tree was spoken. That same evening he with his disciples went back to Bethany to lodge there, but probably at so late an hour that the darkness prevented these from marking the effects which had followed upon that word. It was not till the morning of Tuesday that "they saw the fig-tree dried up from the roots." Such is the exact order of the circumstances, in the telling of which St. Mark shows himself a more accurate observer of times than the first Evangelist—not, indeed, that this gives him any superiority: our advantage is that we have both narrations— St. Matthew's, who was concerned for the inner idea, and hurried on to that, omitting circumstances which came between, that he might present the whole event as one, at a single glance, in a single picture, without the historical perspective—of which he at no time takes so much note, his gifts and his aim being different—and also St. Mark's who was concerned likewise for the picturesque setting forth of the truth in its external details, as it was linked with times and with places, as it gradually unfolded itself before the eyes of men.

But while such differences as these are easily set at one, and they who enhance them into difficulties are the true Pharisees of history, straining at gnats and swallowing camels, there are other and undoubted difficulties in this narrative, and those not unworthy of consideration. And this first, that our Lord, knowing as by his divine power he must, that there were no fruit upon that tree, should yet have gone to seek them there, should have made to his disciples as though he had expected to find them. It might be anxiously asked in what way this was consistent with the perfectness of sincerity and truth. Slight as would have been the deceit, yet, if it was such, it would trouble the clearness of our image of him, whom we conceive of as the absolute Lord of truth. It is again perplexing, that he should have treated the tree as a moral agent, punishing it as though unfruitfulness was any guilt upon its part. This would be in itself perplexing, but becomes infinitely more so by the notice which St. Mark inserts, and which indeed our acquaintance with the order of the natural year would, without this notice, have suggested, that it was not then the time of figs: so that at the time when they could not seasonably be expected, he sought, and was displeased at failing to find them. For, whatever the under-meaning might have been in treating the tree as a moral agent, and granting that to have been entirely justified, yet does it seem again entirely lost and obscured, when it was thus put out of the power of the tree to be otherwise than it was, namely, without fruit? For the symbol must needs be carried through: if by a figure we attribute guilt to the tree for not having fruit, we must be consistent, and show that it might have had such—that there was no just and sufficient excuse why it should have been without this.

Upon the first point, that the Lord went to the tree, appearing to expect that he should find fruit upon it, and yet knowing that he should find none, deceiving thereby those who were with him, who no doubt believed that what he professed to look for, he expected to find, it is sufficient to observe that a similar charge might be made against all figurative teaching, whether by word or by deed: for in all such there is a worshiping of truth in the spirit and not in the letter; often a forsaking it in the letter, for the better honoring and establishing of it in the spirit. A parable is told *as* true, and though the facts are feigned, yet *is* true, because of the deeper truth which sustains the outward fabric of the story; it is true, be-

cause it is the shrine of truth, and because the truth which it en-
shrines looks through and through it. Even so a symbolic action is
done *as real*, as meaning something; and yet, although not meaning
the thing which it professes to mean, is no deception, since it means
something infinitely higher and deeper, of which the lower action
is a type, and in which that lower is lost and swallowed up; trans-
figured and transformed by the higher, whereof it is made the vehicle. What was it, for instance, here, if Christ meant not really to
look for fruit on that tree, being aware that it had none? Yet he did
mean to show how it would fare with a man or with a nation, when
God came looking from it for the fruits of righteousness, and found
nothing but the abundant leaves of a boastful yet empty profession.

As regards the second objection, that he should have put forth
his anger on a tree, the real objection lying at the root of this in
many minds oftentimes is, that he should have put forth his anger
at all; that God should ever show himself as a punishing God; that
there should be any such thing as the wrath of the Lamb, as the giving account of advantages, as a dreadful day. But seeing that such
things are, how needful that men should not forget it: yet they
might have forgot it, as far as the teaching of the miracles went, but
for this one—all the others being miracles of help and of healing.
And even the severity of this, with what mercy was it tempered!
He did not, like Moses and Elijah, make the assertion of God's holiness and his hatred of evil at the cost of many lives, but only at the
cost of a single unfeeling tree. His miracles of mercy were unnum-
bered, and on men; his miracle of judgment was but one, and on a
tree.

But then, say some, it was unjust to deal thus with a tree at all,
since that, being incapable of good or of evil, was as little a fit object of blame as of praise, of punishment as reward. But this very
objection does, in truth, imply that it was *not* unjust, that the tree
was a *thing*, which might therefore lawfully be used merely as a
means for ends lying beyond itself. Many is the prince of creation,
and all things else are to serve him, and then rightly fulfill their
subordinate uses when they do serve him—in their life or in their
death—yielding unto him fruit, or warning him in a figure what
shall be the curse and penalty of unfruitfulness. Christ did not attribute moral responsibilities to the tree, when he smote it because
of its unfruitfulness, but he did attribute to it a fitness for representing moral qualities. All our language concerning trees, a *good*

tree, a *bad* tree, a tree which *ought* to bear, is exactly the same continual transfer to them of moral qualities, and a witness for the natural fitness of the Lord's language—the language indeed of an act, rather than of words. By his word, however (Luke 13:6–9), he had already in some sort prepared his disciples for understanding and interpreting his act; and the not unfrequent use of this very symbol in the Old Testament, as at Hos. 9:10; Joel 1:7, must have likewise helped them to this.

But allowing all this, do not the words of St. Mark, *"for the time of figs was not yet,"* acquit the tree even of this figurative guilt? Does not the fact thus mentioned defeat the symbol, and put it, so to speak, in contradiction with itself? Does it not perplex us as regards our Lord's conduct, that he should have looked for figs, when they could not have been there—that he should have been as though indignant, when he did not find them? The simplest, and as it appears to me, the entirely satisfying explanation of this difficulty is the following. At that early period of the year, March or April, neither leaves nor fruit were naturally to be looked for on a fig tree (the passages often quoted to the contrary not making out, as I think, their point), nor in ordinary circumstances would anyone have sought them there. But that tree, by putting forth leaves, made pretension to be something more than others, to have fruit upon it, seeing that in the fig-tree the fruit appears before the leaves. This tree, so to speak, vaunted itself to be in advance of all the other trees, challenged the passer-by that he should come and refresh himself with its fruit. Yet when the Lord accepted its challenge, and drew near, it proved to be but *as* the others, without fruit as they; for indeed, as the Evangelist observes, the time of figs had not yet arrived—its fault, if one may use the word, lying in its pretension, in its making a show to run before the rest, when it did not so indeed. It was condemned, not so much for having no fruit, as for this, that not the foliage which, being there, did, according to the natural order of the tree's development, give pledge and promise that fruit should be found on it, if sought.

And this will then exactly answer to the sin of Israel, which under this tree was symbolized—that sin being not so much that they were without fruit, as that they boasted of so much. Their true fruit, the true fruit of any people before the Incarnation, would have been to own that they had no fruit, that without Christ, without the incarnate Son of God, they could do nothing; to have presented themselves before God, bare and naked and empty altogether. But this was exactly what Israel refused to do. Other nations might have nothing to boast of, but they by their own showing had much. And yet on closer inspection, the reality of righteousness was as much wanting on their part as anywhere besides.

And how should it have been otherswise? *"For the time of figs was not yet"*—the time for the bare stock and stem of humanity to array itself in bud and blossom, with leaf and fruit, had not come, till its engrafting on the nobler stock of the true Man. All which anticipated this, which would say that it could *be* anything or do anything otherwise than in him and by him, was deceitful and premature. The other trees had nothing, but they did not pretend to have anything; this tree had nothing, but it gave out that it had much. So was it severally with Gentile and with Jew. The Gentiles were bare of all fruits of righteousness, but they owned it; the Jews were bare, but they vaunted that they were full. The Gentiles were sinners, but they hypocrites and pretenders to boot, and by so much further from the kingdom of God, and more nigh unto a curse. Their guilt was not that they had not the perfect fruits of faith, for it was not the season for such; the time of these was not yet; but that, not having, they so boastfully gave out that they had—not that they were not healed, but that, being unhealed, they counted themselves whole. The Law would have done its work, the very work for which God ordained it, if it had stripped them of these boastful leaves, or rather had prevented them from ever putting them forth.

Here then, according to this explanation, there is no difficulty either in the Lord's going to the tree at that unseasonable time—he would not have gone, but for those deceitful leaves which announced that fruit was there—nor in the (symbolical) punishment of the unfruitful tree at this season of the year, when according to the natural order it could not have had any. It was punished not for being without fruit, but for proclaiming by the voice of those leaves that it had such—not for being barren, but for being false. And this was the guilt of Israel, a guilt so much deeper than the guilt of the nations. The attentive study of the epistle to the Romans supplies the true key to the right understanding of this miracle; such passages especially as 2:3, 17–27; 10:3, 4, 21; 11:7, 10. Nor should that remarkable parallel, Ezek. 17:24: "And all the trees of the field shall know that I the Lord . . . have dried up the green tree and made the dry tree to flourish," be left out of account. And then the sentence,

"No man eat fruit of thee hereafter forever," will be just the reversal of the blessing that in them all nations of the earth should be blessed— the symbolic counterstroke to the ratification of the Levitical priesthood, through the putting forth, by Aaron's rod, of bud and blossom and fruit in a night. Henceforth the Jewish synagogue is stricken with a perpetual barrenness; it once was everything, but now it is nothing, to the world; it stands apart, like a thing forbid; what little it has, it communicates to none; the curse has come upon it, that no man henceforward shall eat fruit of it forever.

And yet this *"forever,"* has its merciful limitation, when we come to transfer the curse from the tree to that of which the tree was as a living parable; a limitation which the word itself favors and allows; which lies hidden in it, to be revealed in due time. None shall eat fruit of that tree to the end of the present aeon, not until these "times of the Gentiles" are fulfilled. A day indeed will come when Israel, which now says, "I am a dry tree," shall consent to that word of its true Lord, which of old it denied, "From *me* is thy fruit found," and shall be arrayed with the richest foliage and fruit of all the trees of the field. The Lord, in his great discourse upon the last things (Matt. 24), implies this, when he gives this commencing conversion of the Jews under the image of the re-clothing of the bare and withered fig-tree with leaf and bud, as the sign of the breaking of the new aeon, which he does, saying, "Now learn a parable of the fig-tree. When his branch is yet tender, and putteth forth leaves, ye know that summer is nigh: so likewise ye, when ye shall see all these things, know that it is near, even at the doors." (vv. 32, 33.)

It would appear form St. Matthew that some beginnings of the threatened withering began to show themselves, almost as soon as the word of the Lord was spoken; a shuddering fear may have run through all the leaves of the tree, which was thus stricken at its heart. But it was not till the next morning, as the disciples returned, that they took note of the utter perishing of the tree, which had followed upon that word spoken, so that it was *"dried up from the roots,"* and called their Lord's attention to the same: *"Master, behold the fig tree which thou cursedst, is withered away."* The Lord will not let the occasion go by without its further lesson. What he had done, they might do the same and more. Faith in God would place them in relation with the same power which he wielded, so that they might do mightier things even than this at which they marveled so much.

32.

The Healing of Malchus' Ear

Luke 22:49–51

The cutting off the ear of the servant of the high priest by one of the disciples, who would fain have fought for his Master that he should not be delivered to the Jews, is related by all four evangelists (Matt. 26:51; Mark 14:47; Luke 22:50; John 18:18); but the miracle belongs only to St. Luke, for he only tells how the Lord made good the wrong which his disciple had inflicted. And we may trace, perhaps, in this Evangelist a double interest which might have specially moved him to the including in his gospel this work of grace. As a physician, this cure, the only one of its kind which we know of our Lord's performing, the only miraculous healing of a wound inflicted by external violence, would attract his special attention. And then, besides, there was nothing nearer to St. Luke's heart, or that cohered more intimately with the purpose of his Gospel, than the portraying of the Lord on the side of his gentleness, his mercy, and benignity; all which so gloriously shone out in this gracious work in favor of one who was in arms against his life.

The Evangelist, no doubt, knew very well, but has not thought good to tell us, who it was that struck this blow—whether the deed might still have brought him into trouble, though that appears an exceedingly improbable explanation, or from some other cause. St. Matthew and St. Mark equally preserve silence on this head, and are content with generally designating him, Matthew as *"one of them who were with Jesus,"* Mark as *"one of them which stood by."* And it is only from St. John that we learn, what perhaps otherwise we might have guessed, but could not certainly have known, that it was St. Peter, who in this way sought to deliver his imperilled

Lord. He also alone gives us the name of the high priest's servant who was smitten; *"the servant's name was Malchus."* The last may easily have been unknown to the other Evangelists, though it very naturally came within the circle of St. John's knowledge, who had, in some way that is not explained to us, acquaintance with the high priest (John 18:15), and with the constitution of his household; so accurate an acquaintance, as that he was aware even of so slight a circumstance as that one of those, who later in the night provoked Peter to his denial of Christ, was kinsman of him whose ear Peter had cut off (v. 26).

The whole circumstance is singularly characteristic; the *word*-bearer for the rest of the apostles proves, when occasion requires, the *sword*-bearer also—not indeed in this altogether of a different temper from the others, but showing himself prompter and more forward in action than them all. While they are saying, *"Lord, shall we smite with the sword?"* Perplexed between the natural instinct of defence and love of their perilled Lord, on the one side, and his precepts on the other, that they should not resist the evil—he waits not for the answer, but impelled by the natural courage of his heart, and taking no heed of the odds against him, aims a blow at one, probably the foremost of the band—the first that was daring to lay profane hands on the sacred person of his Lord. This was *"a servant of the high priest's,"* one therefore who, according to the proverb, "like master like man," may very probably have been especially forward in this bad work—himself a Caiaphas of a meaner stamp. Peter was not likely to strike with any other but a right good will, and no doubt the blow was intended to cleave down the aggressor, though by God's good providence the stroke was turned aside, and grazing the head at which it was aimed, but still coming down with sheer descent, cut off the ear—the *"right ear,"* as St. Luke and St. John tell us—of the assailant who thus hardly escaped with his life.

The words with which our Lord rebuked the untimely zeal of his disciples are differently given by different Evangelists, or rather they have each given a different portion, each one enough to indicate the spirit in which all was spoken. In St. Matthew they are related most at length. That moment, indeed, of uttermost confusion seems to have been no fitting one for a discourse so long as that which he records, not to speak of further words recorded by the others; nor is it at first easy to see how he could have found opportunity for them. But if we suppose that he gave this monition to his disciples, while the healing of Malchus was going forward, and while all were attentive to and wondering at that, the difficulty will disappear—not to say that his captors, who may have feared resistance or attempts at rescue on the part of his servants, now that they found his words to be words prohibiting aught of the kind, may have been most willing to suffer him to speak unhindered.

Our Lord, when he joins together the taking the sword and perishing with the sword, refers, no doubt, to the primal law, "Whoso sheddeth man's blood, by man shall his blood be shed" (Gen. 9:6), as again there is probable allusion to these words of his, Rev. 13:10. But the application of the words, *"All they that take the sword shall perish with the sword,"* has been sometimes erroneously made, as though Christ, to quiet Peter, were saying, "There is no need for thee to assume the task of the punishing these violent men: they have taken the sword, and by the just judgment of God they will perish by the sword." But the warning against taking the sword connects itself so closely with the command, *"Put up again thy sword into his place,"* and the meaning of the verse following (Matt. 25:53) is so plainly, "Thinkest thou that I need help so poor as thine, when, instead of you, twelve weak trembling men, inexpert in war, I might even now pray to my Father, and he would give me on the moment twelve legions of mighty angels on my behalf?" That all the ingenuity which Grotius and others use, and it is much, to recommend the other meaning, cannot persuade to a receiving it.

The passage supplies a fine parallel to 2 Kgs. 7:17; a greater than Elisha is here, and by this word would open the spiritual eye of his troubled disciple, and show him the mount of God, full of chariots and horses of fire, armies of heaven which are encamping round him, and whom a beck from him would bring forth, to the utter discomfiture of his enemies. Possibly our blessed Lord, even as he thus spoke, was conscious of the temptation to claim this help from God—the same temptation as constituted the essence of *the* Temptation; but it is one no sooner offered him, than he rejects it at once: for how then should that eternal purpose, that will of God, of which Scripture was the outward expression, *"that thus it must be,"* how should this be fulfilled? (Cf. Zech. 13:7.)

In St. John the same entire sublrdination of his will to the will of the Father, which must hinder him from claiming this unseasonable help, finds its utterance under another image; that of a cup which he needs must drink: *"The cup which my Father hath given me, shall I not drink it?"* The image is frequent in Scripture, resting on the thought of some potion which, however bitter, must yet be drained, since such is the will of him who has put it into the hands. Besides Matt. 2:22, 23; 26:39, where the cup is the cup of holy suffering, there is often, especially in the Old Testament, mention of the cup of God's anger (Is. 51:17, 22; Ps. 11:6; 75:8; Jer. 25:15, 17; 49:12; Lam. 4:21; Rev. 14:10; 16:19); in every case the cup having this in common, that it is one from which flesh and blood shrinks back, which a man would fain put away from his lips if he might, though a moral necessity in the first place, and a physical in the second, will not suffer him to do so.

And the words that follow, *"Suffer ye thus far,"* are to be accepted as addressed still to the disciples: "Hold now; thus far ye have gone in resistance, but let it be no further; no more of this." The other explanation, which makes them to have been spoken by the Lord to those into whose hands he had come, that they should bear with him till he had accomplished the cure, has nothing to recommend it. Having thus checked the too forward zeal of his disciples, and now carrying out into act his own precept, "Love your enemies . . . . do good to them that hate you," he touched the ear of the wounded man, *"and healed him."* Peter and the rest meanwhile, after this brief flash of carnal courage, forsook their divine Master, and, leaving him in the hands of his enemies, fled—the wonder of the crowd at that gracious work of the Lord, or the tumult with the darkness or the night, or these both together, favoring their escape.

33.
The Second Miraculous Draught of Fishes

John 21:1–23

It almost seemed as though St. John's Gospel had found its solemn completion in the words (vv. 30, 31), with which the preceding chapter ended; so that this chapter appears, and probably is, in the exactest sense of the word, a postscript—something which the beloved apostle, after he had made an end, thought it important not to leave untold; which he may have added, perhaps, at the request of his disciples, who had often heard delightedly the narrative from his own lips, and desired that before his departure he should set it down, that the Church might be enriched with it forever.

It was upon the sea of Galilee that this appearance of Christ to his disciples, with the miracle which accompanied it, took place. Doubtless there is a significance to be found in the words, *"Jesus showed,"* or manifested, *"himself,"* as Chrysostom long ago observed—no other than this, that his body after the resurrection was only visible by a distinct act of his will. From that time the disciples did not, as before, *see* Jesus, but Jesus *appeared unto* or *was seen by them.* It is not for nothing that the language is changed, or that in language of this kind all his appearances after the resurrection are related. (Luke 24:34; Acts 13:31; 1 Cor. 15:5, 6, 7, 8.) It is the same with angels and all heavenly manifestations: men do not *see* them, as though it lay in their will to do so or not; such language would be inappropriate: but the *appear* to men (Judg. 6:12; 13:3, 10, 21; Matt. 17:3; Luke 1:11; 22:43; Acts 2:3; 7:2; 16:9; 26:16); are only visible to those for whose sakes they are vouchsafed, and to whom they are willing to show themselves. Those to whom this manifestation was vouchsafed were Simon Peter and Thomas and Nathanael, James and John, and two other disciples that are not named. It makes something for the current opinion that the Nathanael of St. John, is the Bartholomew of the other Evangelists, thus to find him named not after, but in the midst of, some of the very chiefest apostles. Who were the two unnamed disciples cannot, of course, be known. They too were not improbably apostles, disciples in the most eminent sense of the word; Lightfoot supposes that they were Andrew and Philip.

Peter's declaration that he will go to fish, is not, as has been strangely supposed, a declaration that he has lost his hope in Jesus as the Messiah, renounced his apostleship, and therefore returns to his old occupations, there being no nobler work for him in store. But it was quite in the wise manner of the Jewish teachers, to have a manual trade that they might fall back on in the time of need, and thus not be dependent on their scholars for support; what good service Paul's skill in making tents did him is well known; probably also they found it healthful to their own minds, to have some outward occupation for which to exchange at times their spiritual employments. The words themselves, *"I go a-fishing,"* are not merely a declaration of his intention, but a summons to his friends to accompany him, if they are so minded; whereupon they declare their readiness; *"We also go with thee."* During all the night, though that is ever accounted the opportunest time for fishing, they caught nothing. When at early dawn the risen Lord stood upon the shore, they did not at first recognize him. Nor even when he addressed them as *"Children,"* did they know that it was he—the mighty change which had past upon him at his resurrection had so left him at once the same and yet another. (Cf. John 20:14, 15.) When they acknowledged in reply to his question, *"Have ye any meat?"* The ill success which had attended their labors of the night, he bade them cast in their net on the right side of the ship, promising that it should not be in vain. And they, though taking it even now but for the counsel of a kind and, it might be, a skillful stranger, were obedient to his word: *"They cast therefore, and now they were not able to draw it for the multitude of fishes."*

As before, the Lord had made himself known in his higher character through a marvelous success of the like kind, so does he now; yet it is not Peter on the present occasion, but John, that first recognizes in whose presence they are. Thereupon he *"saith unto*

Peter, It is the Lord." Both the apostles come wonderfully out in their proper characters: he of the eagle eye first detects the presence of the Beloved, and then Peter, the foremost ever in act, as John is profoundest in speculation, unable to wait till the ship should be brought to land, throws himself into the sea that he may find himself the sooner at the feet of his Lord. He was before *"naked,"*stripped, that is, for labor, wearing only the tunic, or garment close to the skin, and having put off his upper and superfluous garments: for the word *"naked"* means no more, and is continually used in this sense; but now he girded himself with his fisher's coat, as counting it unseemly to appear without it in the presence of his Lord. Some have supposed that he walked on the sea; but we have no warrant to multiply miracles, and the words, *"cast himself into the sea,"* do not look like this. Rather, he swam and waded to the shore. The distance was not more than about *"two hundred cubits,"* that is, about one hundred yards. The other disciples followed more slowly, for they were encumbered with the net and its weight of fishes, which they drew with them to land. There they find a fire kindled, with fish laid on it, and bread. They are bidden to bring also of their fish, and to unite them for the meal with those already preparing. Peter, again the foremost, drew up the net, which was fastened, no doubt, to the ship, on the beach. The very number of the fish it contained, *"a hundred and fifty and three,"* is mentioned, with also the remarkable circumstance, that although they were so many and so large—*"great fishes"*—yet, differently from that former occasion (Luke v. 6), the net was not broken by their weight, or by their efforts to escape.

Now we can scarcely believe that all this happened, or that it was all recorded in its minuteness and its details, without some meaning more than lies upon the surface; indeed, the whole is told with an emphasis which will hardly allow us to rest content with such a supposition. Rather here, as we have seen so often before, Christ is speaking to us by his acts. Nor can I doubt that Augustine has rightly attributed in more places than one a symbolical meaning to this miracle; and that, whether or not we may consent to ever detail of his interpretation, yet in the outline and main features he had given the true one. He brings this miraculous draught of fishes in comparison with the other which fell out before the resurrection, and sees in that first, the figure of the Church as it now is, and as it now gathers its members from the world; in this the figure of the Church as it shall be after the resurrection, with the great incoming, the great sea-harvest of souls, which then shall find place. Then on that first occasion the apostles were not particularly bidden to cast the net to the right hand or to the left; for, had he said to the right, it would have implied that none should be taken but the good—if to the left, that only the bad; while yet in the present mixed condition of the Church, both bad and good are inclosed in the nets; but now he says, *"Cast the net on the right side of the ship,"* implying that now all who should be taken should be good. Then the nets were broken with the multitude of fishes, so that all were not secured which once were within them—and what are the schisms and divisions of the present condition of the Church, but rents and holes through which numbers, that impatiently bear to be restrained in the net, break away from it? But now, in the end of time, *"for all there were so many, yet was not the net broken."* Then the fish were brought into the ship, which yet was itself still on the unquiet sea, even as it is thus that men in the present time who are taken for Christ, are brought into the Church, still itself exposed to the world's tempests: but now the nets are drawn up to land, to the safe and quiet shore of eternity. Then the ships were well nigh sunken with their burden, for so is it with the ship of the Church—encumbered with evil livers till it well nigh makes shipwreck altogether: but nothing of a like kind is mentioned here. There it is merely mentioned that a great multitude were enclosed, but here is a definite number, even as the number of the elect is fixed and preordained; and there, no doubt, small and great fishes, for nothing to the contrary is said; but here they are all *"great,"* for so shall they all be that belong to that kingdom, being equal to the angels.

That which follows is obscure, and without the key which the symbolical explanation supplies, would be obscurer yet. What is the meaning of this meal which they found ready prepared for them on the shore, with the Lord's invitation that they should come and share it? It could not be needful for him with his risen body, and as little for them, whose dwellings were near at hand. But we must continue to see an under-meaning, and a rich and deep one, in all this. As that large capture of fish was to them the pledge and promise of a labor that should not be in vain, so the meal, when the labor was done, a meal of the Lord's own preparing, and *upon the shore*, was the symbol of the great festival in heaven with which, after their earthly toil was over, he would refresh his servants, when he should cause them to sit down with Abraham, and Isaac, and Jacob in the kingdom. And as they were bidden to bring of their fish to that meal, so should the souls which they had taken for life be their crown and rejoicing in that day, should help and contribute to their gladness then.

When the Evangelist tells us that at this meal *"none of the disciples durst ask him, Who art thou? Knowing that it was the Lord"*; this again is difficult; for if they knew, where was even the temptation to make this inquiry? And yet it seems on the surface of the narration that they *were* tempted to ask such a question, and were only hindered by the solemn fear and awe which was shed on them by his presence. But the right meaning of the words, no doubt, is that none of them dared to show so much of unbelief and uncertainty as would have been involved in the question *"Who art thou?"* There was shed over them such a mysterious awe, such a sense of the presence of their beloved Master, witnessing for itself in the inmost depths of their spirits, that, unusual and unlike as was his outward appearance to that whereunto their eyes were accustomed, yet none of them durst ask for a clearer evidence that it was he, even though it would have been a satisfaction to them to hear from his own lips that it was indeed himself and no other.

The most interesting conversation which follows hangs too closely upon this miracle to be omitted; in fact, as appears almost universally the case with St. John, the miracle is not recorded so much for its own sake, as for the sake of that which grows out of it. Here, after the Lord has opened the eyes of his apostles to the greatness of their future work, and given to them in type a prophetic glimpse both of their successful labor and their abundant reward, he now declare to them the one condition both of accomplishing this work, and inheriting this reward. Love to Christ, and the unreserved yielding up of self to God—these were the sole conditions, and all which follows is to teach this: so that the two portions of the chapter are intimately connected, and together form a complete whole. When the meal was ended, *"Jesus said unto Simon Peter, Simon, son of Jonas, lovest thou me more than these?"* With an evident allusion to Peter's boasting speech, "Though all men shall be offended because of thee, yet will I never be offended (Matt. 26:33), as is proved by Peter's answer, wherein appealing to the Lord, the Searcher of hearts, he affirms that indeed he loves him, but does not now cast any slight by comparison on the love of his fellow-disciples. The main object of the Lord in his rejoinder, *Feed my sheep,"* *"Feed my lambs,"* is not to say, "Show then thy love in act," but rather, "I restore to thee thy apostolic function; this grace is thine, that thou shalt yet be a chief shepherd of my flock." It implies, therefore, the fullest forgiveness of the past, since none but the forgiven could rightly declare the forgiveness of God. The question, *"Lovest thou me?"* Is thrice repeated, that by three solemn affirmations the apostle may efface his three denials of his Lord. At last, upon the third repetition of the question, Peter was saddened, as though the Lord doubted his word; and with yet more emphasis than before, appeals to his Savior in his all-knowing and all-searching character, whether it was not true that indeed he loved him: *"Lord, thou knowest all things, thou knowest that I love thee."*

There does not seem anything in the distinction which some have made between the two commands, *"Feed my lambs"* and *"Feed my sheep,"* as though the first were the more imperfect Christians, the little children in Christ; the other the more advanced, the grown men. And still more groundless and trifling is the interpretation made in the interests of Rome, as though the *"lambs"* are the laity, and the *"sheep"* the clergy; and that here to Peter, and in him to the Roman pontiffs, was given dominion over both. The commission should at least have run, Feed my sheep, Feed my shepherds, if any conclusions of the kind were to be drawn from it, though an infinite deal would even then have remained to be proved.

But *"Feed my sheep,"* is not all. This life of labor is to be crowned with a death of painfulness; such is the way, with its narrow and strait gate, which even for a Peter is the only one which will lead to eternal life. The Lord would show him beforehand what great things he must suffer for his sake. For this is often his manner with his elect servants, with an Ezekiel (3:25), with a Paul (Acts 21:11), and now with a Peter. *"When thou wast young, thou girdedst thyself, and walkedst wither thou wouldest, but when thou shalt be old, thou shalt stretch forth thy hands, and another shall gird thee, and carry thee wither thou wouldest not."* There cannot, I think, be a doubt that there is allusion here to the crucifixion of Peter, since St. John himself declared that Jesus spoke thus, *"signifying by what death he should glorify God"*; and no tolerable ground exists for calling in question the tradition of the Church, that such was the manner of the apostle's martyrdom. Doubtless it is here *obscurely* initimated; but this is of the very nature of prophecy, and there is quite enough in the description to show that the Lord had this and no other manner of death in his eye. The stretched forth hands are the hands extended upon either side on the transverse bar of the cross. The girding by another is the binding to the cross, for the sufferer was attached to the instrument of punishment not only with nails, but also was bound thereto with cords. It cannot be meant by the bearing *"whither thou wouldest not,"* that there should be any reluctancy on the part of Peter to glorify God by his death, except indeed the reluctancy which there always is in the flesh to suffering and pain; which yet in this case, as in the Lord's (compare Matt. 26:39), should be overruled by the higher willingness to do and to suffer the perfect will of God. In this sense, as it was a violent death—a death which others chose for him—a death from which flesh and blood would naturally shrink, it was "whither he would not"; though, in a higher sense, as it was the way to a nearer vision of God, it was that at which he had all his life been aiming; and then he was borne wither most he would; and the exulting words of another apostle, at the near approach of his martyrdom (2 Tim. 4:6–8), would have suited his lips just as well.

Nor may we exclude the symbolical meaning, which we have found in the earlier parts of the chapter, from this part also. The "girding himself" is to be taken as the sign and figure of promptness and an outward activity (Ex. 12:11; Luke 12:35; 1 Pet. 1:13; Eph. 6:14); and, in fact, our Lord is saying to Peter, "When thou wert young, thou actedst for me, thou wentest wither thou wouldest, thou wert free to work for me, and to choose thy field of work; but when thou art old, thou shalt learn another lesson, a higher and a harder; thou shalt suffer for me; thou shalt no more choose thy work, but others shall choose it for thee, and that work shall be the work of passion rather than of action." Such is the history of the Christian life, not in Peter's case only, but this is the very course and order of it in almost all of God's servants; it is begun in action, it is perfected in suffering. In the last, lessons are learned which the first could never teach; graces exercised, which but for this, would not at all, or would only have very weakly, existed.

Thus it was, for instance, with a John Baptist. He begins with Jerusalem and all Judea flowing to him to listen to his preaching; he ends with lying long, a seemingly forgotten captive, in the dungeon of Machaerus. So was it with a St. Chrysostom. The chief cities of the world wait upon him with reverence and homage while he is young, and he goes wither he would; but when he is old, he is borne wither he would not, up and down, a sick and suffering exile. Thus should it be also with this great apostle. It was only in this manner that whatever of self-will and self-choosing survived in him still, should be broken and abolished, that he should be brought into an entire emptiness of self, a perfect submission to the will of God.

And then the Lord, as he has shown him the end, will also show him the way; for *"when he had spoken this, he saith unto him, Follow me."* Now these words do more than merely signify, in a general way, "Be thou an imitator of me. Such an explanation would show that we had altogether failed in realizing to ourselves this solemn scene, as it was on this day enacted on the shore of Gennesaret. That scene was quite as much in deed as in word; and here, at the very moment that the Lord spoke the words, it would seem that he took some paces along the rough and rocky shore, bidding Peter to do the same; thus setting forth to him in a figure his future life, which should be a following of his divine Master in the rude and rugged way of Christian action. That all this was not so much spoken as done, is clear from that which follows, which only is explicable so. Peter, *"turning about"*—looking, that is, behind him—*"seeth the disciple whom Jesus loved"*—words not introduced idly, and as little so the allusion to his familiarity at the paschal supper, but to explain the boldness of John in following unbidden; him he seeth *"following"* and inquires, *"Lord, what shall this man do?"* He would know what shall be his lot, and what the issue of his earthly conversation: shall he, too, follow by the same rugged path.

It is not very easy to determine the spirit out of which this question proceeded. Augustine thinks it is that of one who was concerned that his friend should seem to be left out, and not summoned to the honor of the same close following of his Lord. Others, however, have oftentimes taken this question in quite a different sense; that it is a question put more in the temper of Martha, when she said to the Lord, concerning her sister Mary, "Lord, dost thou not care that my sister hath left me to serve alone?" (Luke 10:40), being not pleased that Mary should remain quietly sitting at Jesus' feet, while she was engaged in active service for him. Certainly the rebuke which here, as there, the question calls out, implies that the source out of which it proceeded, whether this or another, was not altogether pure. Peter, understanding well what that *"Follow me,"* addressed to himself, meant, may have felt a moment's jealousy at that easier portion which seemed allotted to his fellow apostle.

This was most likely the thought, and then the rebuke exactly meets it. Peter had perceived what the leaving John, and bidding *him* to follow, implied. John was to *"tarry,"* doing a still work in the Church; the rougher paths were not for his treading, but rather he was to be perfected by another discipline; not borne away from the earth in the fire-chariot of a painful martyrdom, but, tarrying long, he should crown a peaceful and honored old age by a natural death. It was not, indeed, that he, or any other saint, should escape his share of worldly tribulation, or that the way for him, or for any, should be other than a straight way. Yet do we see daily how the sufferings of different members of the kingdom are allotted in very different proportions; with some, they are comparatively few and far between, while for others, their whole life seems a constant falling from one trial to another. And our Lord's answer to Peter's speech is in fact this: "Hast thou a right to complain, if it be thus? What is it to thee how I apportion the lots of my other servants? Nay, if I were to will that he should never see death—that he should altogether escape that narrow and painful passage into life, and tarry till my coming again, what would that be to thee? Do thou thine allotted task; *follow thou me."*

St. John mentions by the way how these words of his Lord were misunderstood by some, who had from thence assumed that he was never to die, but to continue among the living until the time of Christ's return; an interpretation which he anxiously disclaims, showing that the words conveyed no such meaning, and that only through an inaccurate report of them, or a laying upon them of a meaning far greater than they themselves would justify, could they be made to convey any such impression: *"Jesus said not unto him, He shall not die, but, If I will that he tarry till I come, what is that to thee?"* Yet this explicit declaration that no such meaning lay in the words, was not sufficient to extinguish altogether such a belief or superstition in the Church. We find many traces of it at many times; even his death and burial, which men were compelled to acknowledge, were not sufficient to abolish it. For his death, men said, was not really death, but only the appearance of death, and he yet breathed in his grave; so that even an Augustine was unable wholly to resist the reports which had reached him, that the earth yet heaved over the apostle's grave, and the dust was lightly stirred by the regular pulses of his breath. The fable of his still living Augustine at one rejects, but is more patient with this report than one would have looked for, counting it possible that a permanent miracle might there be finding place.

Introductory Essay

I.

On the Definition
of the Parable

Writers who have had occasion to define a parable have found it no easy task to give such a satisfying definition as should omit none of its distinctive marks, and at the same time include nothing superfluous and merely accidental. Rather than attempt to add another to the many definitions already given, I will seek to note briefly what seems to me to difference it from the fable, the allegory, and such other forms of composition as are most nearly allied to, and most closely border upon it. In the process of thus distinguishing it from those forms of composition with which it is most likely to be confounded, and of justifying the distinction, something will have been said for the distinction, something will have been said for the bringing out of its essential properties more clearly than in any other way I could hope to do this.

1. There are some who have identified the parable with the Aesopic *fable*, or drawn a slight and hardly perceptible line of distinction between the two: as for instance Lessing and Storr, who affirm that the fable relates an event as having actually taken place at a certain time, while the parable only assumes it as possible. But not to say that examples altogether fail to bear them out in this assertion, the difference is much more real, and far more deeply-seated, than this. The parable is constructed to set forth a truth spiritual and heavenly: this the fable, with all its value, is not. It is essentially of the earth, and never lifts itself above the earth. It never has a higher aim than to inculcate maxims of prudential morality, industry, caution, foresight, and the like: and these it will sometimes recommend even at the expense of the higher self-forgetting virtues. The fable just reaches that pitch of morality which

the world will understand and approve. But is has no place in the Scripture, and in the nature of things could have none, for the purpose of Scripture excludes it; that purpose being the awakening of man to a consciousness of a divine original, the education of the reason, and of all which is spiritual in man, and not, except incidentally, the sharpening of the understanding. For the purposes of the fable, which are the recommendation and enforcement of the prudential virtues, the regulation of that in man which is instinct in beasts, *in* itself a laudable discipline, but *by* itself leaving him only a subtler beast of the field—for these purposes, examples and illustrations taken from the world beneath him are admirably suited. That world is therefore the haunt and the main region, though by no means the exclusive one, of the fable. Even when men are introduced, it is on the side by which they are connected with that lower world; while on the other hand, in the parable, the world of animals, though not wholly excluded, finds only admission in so far as it is related to man. The relation of beasts to one another not being spiritual, can supply no analogies, can be in no wise helpful for declaring the truths of the kingdom of God. But all man's relations to man are spiritual; many of his relations to the world beneath him are so as well. His lordship over the animals, for instance, rests on his higher spiritual nature, is a dominion given to him from above (Gen. 1:28; 22:19; 9:2; Ps. 8:6–8); will serve, therefore, as in the instance of the shepherd and sheep (John 10), and elsewhere, to image forth deeper truths of the relation of God to man.

It belongs to this, the loftier standing-point of the parable, that it should be deeply earnest, allowing itself therefore in no jesting nor raillery at the weaknesses, the follies, or the crimes of men. Severe and indignant it may be, but it never jests at the calamities of men, however well deserved, and its indignation is that of holy love: while in this raillery and in these bitter mockings the fabulist not unfrequently indulges; he rubs biting salt into the wounds of men's souls—it may be, perhaps generally is, with a desire to heal those hurts, yet still in a very different spirit from that in which the affectionate Savior of men poured oil and wine into the bleeding wounds of humanity.

There is another point of different between the parable and the fable. While it cannot be affirmed that the fabulist is regardless of truth, since it is neither his intention to deceive, when he attributes language and discourse of reason to trees and birds and beasts, nor is anyone deceived by him; yet the severer reverence for truth, which is habitual to the higher moral teacher, will not allow him to indulge even in this sporting with the truth, this temporary suspension of its laws, though upon agreement, or at least with tacit understanding. In his mind, the creation of God, as it came from the Creator's hands, is too perfect, has too much of reverence owing to it, to be represented otherwise than as it really is. The great Teacher by parables, therefore, allowed Himself in no transgression of the established laws of nature—in nothing marvelous or anomalous; He presents to us no speaking trees nor reasoning beasts, and we should be at once conscious of an unfitness in his so doing.

2. The parable differs from the *mythus*, inasmuch as in the mythus the truth, and that which is only the vehicle of the truth, are wholly blended together: and the consciousness of any distinction between them, that it is possible to separate the one from the other, belongs only to a later and more reflective age than that in which the mythus itself had birth, or those in which it was heartily believed. The mythic narrative presents itself not merely as the vehicle of the truth, but as itself being the truth: while in the parable, there is a perfect consciousness in all minds, of the distinctness between form and essence, shell and kernel, the precious vessel and yet more precious wine which it contains. There is also the mythus of another class, the artificial product of a later self-conscious age, of which many inimitable specimens are to be found in Plato, devised with the distinct intention of embodying some important spiritual truth, of giving an outward subsistence to an idea. But these, while they have many points of resemblance with the parable, yet claim no credence for themselves either as actual or possible (in this differing from the parable), but only for the truth which they embody and declare. The same is the case when upon some old legend or myth that has long been current, there is thrust some spiritual significance, clearly by an after-thought; in which case it perishes in the letter that it may live in the spirit; all outward subsistence is denied to it, for the sake of asserting the idea which it is made to contain. To such a process, as is well known, the later Platonists submitted the old mythology of Greece. For instance, Narcissus falling in love with his own image in the water-brook, and pining there, was the symbol of man casting himself forth into the world of shows and appearances, and expecting to find the good that would answer to his nature there, but indeed finding only disappointment and death. It was their meaning hereby to vindicate that mythology from charges of absurdity or immorality,

to put amoral life into it, whereby it should maintain its ground against the new life of Christianity; though, indeed, they were only thus hastening the destruction of whatever lingering faith in it there might yet survive in the minds of men.

3. The parable is also clearly distinguishable from the *proverb*. though it is true that, in a certain degree, the words are used interchangeably in the New Testament, and as equivalent the one to the other. Thus, 'Physician, heal thyself' (Luke 4:23), is termed a parable, being more strictly a proverb; the same may be affirmed of Luke 5:36; which is a proverb or proverbial expression, rather than a parable, which name it bears: compare 1 Sam. 24:13; 2 Chr. 7:20; Ps. 44:14; Wisd. v. 3. On the other hand, those are called 'proverbs' in St. John, which, if not strictly parables, yet claim much closer affinity to the parable than to the proverb, being in fact allegories: thus Christ's setting forth of his relations to his people under those of a shepherd to his sheep, is termed a 'proverb,' though our Translators, holding fast to the sense rather than to the letter, have rendered it a 'parable' (John 10:6: cf. 16:25, 29). It is easy to account for this interchange of the words. Partly it arose from one word in Hebrew signifying both parable and proverb; which circumstance must have had considerable influence upon writers accustomed to think in that language, and is itself to be explained from the parable and proverb being alike enigmatical and somewhat obscure forms of speech, 'dark sayings,' uttering a part of their meaning, and leaving the rest to be inferred. This is evident of the parable, and is not in fact less true of the proverb. For though such proverbs as have become the heritage of an entire people, and have obtained universal currency, may be, or rather may have become, plain enough; yet in themselves proverbs are very often enigmatical, claiming a quickness in detecting latent affinities, and not seldom a knowledge which shall enable to catch more or less remote allusions, for their right comprehension. And yet further to explain how the terms should be often indifferently used—the proverb, though not necessarily, is yet very commonly, parabolical, that is, it rests upon some comparison either expressed or implied, as for example, 2 Pet. 2:22. Or again, the proverb is often a concentrated parable; for instance, that one above quoted, 'If the blind lead the blind, both shall fall into the ditch,' might evidently be extended with ease into a parable; and not merely might many proverbs thus be beaten out into fables, but they are not unfrequently allusions to or summings up in a single phrase of some fable already well known.

4. It remains to consider wherein the parable differs from the *allegory*. This it does in form rather than in essence; in the allegory an interpenetration of the thing signifying and the thing signified finding place, the qualities and properties of the first being transferred to the last, and the two thus blended together, instead of being kept quite distinct, and placed side by side, as is the case in the parable. Thus, John 15:1–8, 'I am the true Vine, &c.,' is throughout an allegory, as there are two allegories scarcely kept apart from one another, John 10:1–16; the first, in which the Lord sets Himself forth as the Door, the second as the good Shepherd, of the sheep. So, 'Behold the Lamb of God,' is an allegorical—'He is brought as a lamb to the slaughter,' a parabolical expression. The allegory needs not, as the parable, an interpretation to be brought to it from without, since it contains its interpretation within itself; and, as the allegory proceeds, the interpretation proceeds hand in hand with it, or at all events never falls far behind. And thus the allegory stands to the metaphor, as the more elaborate and long drawn out composition of the same kind, in the same relation that the parable does to the isolated comparison or simile. And as many proverbs are concise parables, so also many are brief allegories. For instance, the following, which is an Eastern proverb—'This world is a carcass, and they who gather round it are dogs,'—does in fact interpret itself as it goes along, and needs not, therefore, that an interpretation be brought to it from without; while it is otherwise with the proverb spoken by our Lord, 'Wheresoever the carcass is, there will the eagles be gathered together';—this gives no help to its own interpretation from within, and is a saying, of which the darkness and difficulty have been abundantly witnessed by the many and diverging interpretations which it has received.

To sum up all, then, the parable differs from the fable, moving as it does in a spiritual world, and never transgressing the actual order of things natural—from the mythus, there being in the latter an unconscious blending of the deeper meaning with the outward symbol, while the two remain separate and separable in the parable—from the proverb, inasmuch as it is more fully carried out, and not accidentally and occasionally, but necessarily figurative—from the allegory, comparing as it does one thing *with* another, but, at the same time, maintaining their distinctness as an inner and an outer, and not transferring, as does the allegory, the properties and qualities and relations of one *to* the other.

II.

On Teaching by Parables

owever our Lord may on one or more occasions have made use of this manner of teaching by parables, with the intention of withdrawing from certain of his hearers the knowledge of truths, which they were unworthy or unfit to receive; so that, in Fuller's words, the parables on such occasions were 'not unlike the pillar of cloud and fire, which gave light to the Israelites, but was a cloud of darkness to the Egyptians; yet we may assume as certain that his general aim was not different from that of others who have used this method of teaching, and who have desired thereby to make clearer, either to illustrate or to prove the truths which they had in hand—I say either to illustrate or to prove; for the parable or other analogy to spiritual truth appropriated from the world of nature or man, is not merely illustration, but also in some sort proof. It is not merely that these analogies assist to make the truth intelligible, or, if intelligible before, present it more vividly to the mind, which is all that some will allow them. Their power lies deeper than this, in the harmony unconsciously felt by all men, and which all deeper minds have delighted to trace, between the natural and spiritual worlds, so that analogies from the first are felt to be something more than illustrations, happily but yet arbitrarily chosen. They are arguments, and may be alleged as witnesses; the world of nature being throughout a witness for the world of spirit, proceeding from the same hand, growing out of the same root, and being constituted for that very end. All lovers of truth readily acknowledge these mysterious harmonies, and the force of arguments derived from them. To them the things on earth are copies of the things in heaven. They know that the earthly tabernacle is made after the pattern of things seen in the Mount (Ex. 25:40; 1 Chr. 28:11, 12); and the question suggested by the angel in Milton is often forced upon their meditations—

317

What if earth
Be but the shadow of heaven, and things therein
Each to other like, more than on earth is thought

For it is an entire misunderstanding of the matter to regard these as happily, but arbitrarily, chosen illustrations, skillfully selected out of the great stock and storehouse of unappropriated images; from whence the same skill might have selected others as good, or nearly as good. Rather they belong to one another, the type and the thing typified, by an inward necessity; they were linked together long before by the law of a secret affinity. It is not a happy accident which has yielded so wondrous an analogy as that of husband and wife, to set forth the mystery of Christ's relation to his Church (Eph. 5:23–32). There is far more in it than this: the earthly relation is indeed but a lower form of the heavenly, on which it rests, and of which it is the utterance. When Christ spoke to Nicodemus of a new birth (John 3), it was not merely because birth into this natural world was the most suitable figure that could be found to express that spiritual act which, without any power of our own, is accomplished upon us when we are brought into God's kingdom; but all the circumstances of this natural birth had been preordained to bear the burden of so great a mystery. The Lord is King, not borrowing this title from the kings of the earth, but having lent his own title to them—and not the name only, but having so ordered, that all true rule and government upon earth, with its righteous laws, its stable ordinances, its punishment and its grace, its majesty and its terror, should tell of Him, and of his kingdom which ruleth over all—so that 'kingdom of God' is not a figurative expression, but most literal: it is rather the earthly kingdoms and the earthly kings that are figures and shadows of the true. And as with the world of man and human relations, so also is it with the world of nature. The untended soil which yields thorns and briers as its natural harvest is a permanent type and enduring parable of man's heart, which has been submitted to the same curse, and without a watchful spiritual husbandry will assuredly put forth *its* briers and *its* thorns. The weeds that *will* mingle during the time of growth with the corn, and yet are separated from it at the last, tell ever one and the same tale of the present admixture, and future sundering, of the righteous and the wicked. The decaying of the slight unsightly seed in the earth, and the rising up, out of that decay and death, of the graceful stalk and the fruitful ear, contain evermore the prophecy of the final resurrection; even as this is itself in its kind a resurrection—the same process at a lower stage—the same power putting itself forth upon meaner things (1 Cor. 15:35–38). Of all such correspondences, as drawn out in Scripture, we ought not to say that they are finely chosen similitudes, but rather rightly appropriated types.

Doubtless it will be always possible for those who shrink from contemplating a higher world-order than that imperfect one around them—and this, because the thought of such would rebuke their own imperfection and littleness—who shrink too from a witness for God so near them as even that imperfect order would render, to deny this conclusion. It will be possible for them to reply that it is not as we affirm; but that our talk of heavenly things is only a transferring of earthly images and relations to them—that earth is not a shadow of heaven, but heaven, such at least as we conceive it, a dream of earth; that the names Father and Son for instance (and this is Arianism) are only *improperly* used, and in a secondary sense, when applied to Divine Persons, and then are terms so encumbered with difficulties and contradictions that they had better not be used at all; that we do not find and recognize heavenly things in their earthly counterparts, but only dexterously adapt them. This denial will be always possible, and has a deeper root than that it can be met with argument; yet the lover of a truth which shall be loftier than himself will not be moved from his faith that however man may be the measure of all things here, yet God is the measure of man—that the same Lord who sits upon his throne in heaven, does with the skirts of his train fill his temple upon earth—that these characters of nature which everywhere meet the eye are not a common but a sacred writing—that they are hieroglyphics of God: and he counts this his blessedness, that having these round about him, he is therefore never without admonishment and teaching.

For such is in truth the condition of man. Around him is a sensuous world, yet one which need not bring him into bondage to his senses, being so framed as, if he will use it aright, continually to lift him above itself—a visible world to make known the invisible things of God, a ladder leading him up to the contemplation of heavenly truth. And this truth he shall encounter and make his own, not in fleeing from his fellows and their works and ways, but in the mart, on the wayside, in the field—not by stripping himself bare of all relations, but rather recognizing these as instruments

through which he is to be educated into the knowledge of higher
mysteries; and therefore dealing with them in reverence, seeking
by faithfulness to them in their lower forms to enter into their yet
deeper significance—entertaining them, though they seem but
common guests, and finding that he has unawares entertained
angels. And thus, besides his revelation in worlds, God has another
and an elder, and one, indeed, without which it is inconceivable
how that other could be made, for from this it appropriates all
its signs of communication. This entire moral and visible world
from first to last, with its kings and its subjects, its parents and its
children, its sun and its moon, its sowing and its harvest, its light
and its darkness, its sleeping and its waking, its birth and its death,
is from beginning to end a mighty parable, a great teaching of
supersensuous truth, a help at once to our faith and to our understanding.

It is true that men are ever in danger of losing 'the key of
knowledge,' which should open to them the portals of this palace:
and then, instead of a prince in a world of wonder that is serving
him, man moves in the midst of this world, alternately its taskmas-
ter and its drudge. Such we see him to become at the two poles of
savage and falsely cultivated life—his inner eye darkened, so that
he sees nothing, his inner ear heavy, so that there come no voices
from nature unto him: and indeed in all, save only in the one Man,
there is more or less of the dulled ear, and the filmed eye. There is
none to whom nature tells out all that she has to tell, and as constantly as she would be willing to tell it. Now the whole of
Scripture, with its ever-recurring use of figurative language, is a
reawakening of man to the mystery of nature, a giving back to him
of the key of knowledge, of the true *signatura rerum:* and this comes
out, as we might expect, in its highest form, but by no means exclusively, in those which by pre-eminence we call the parables.
They have this point of likeness with the miracles, that those, too,
were a calling of heed to powers that were daily working, but
which, by their continual and orderly repetition, which ought to
have kindled the more admiration, had become *wonder*–works no
more, had lost the power of exciting admiration or even attention,
until men had need to be startled anew to the contemplation of the
energies which were ever working among them. In like manner the
parables are a calling of attention to the spiritual facts which underlie all processes of nature, all institutions of human society, and
which, though unseen, are the true ground and support of all.

Christ moved in the midst of what seemed to the eye of sense an old and worn-out world, and it evidently became new at his touch; for it told to man *now* the inmost secrets of his being, answered with strange and marvelous correspondences to another world within him, helped to the birth great thoughts of his heart, which before were helplessly struggling to be born—these two worlds, without him and within, each throwing a light and a glory on the other. For on this rests the possibility of a real teaching by parables, such as, resting upon a substantial ground, shall not be a mere building on the air, or painting upon a cloud—on this, namely, that the world around us is a *divine* world, that it is God's world, the world of the same God who is leading us into spiritual truth; that the ghastly dream of Gnostic and Manichaean, who would set a great gulf between the worlds of nature and of grace, ascribing this to a good, but that to an imperfect or an evil power, is a lie, and that, being originally God's world, it is therefore a sharer in his redemption.

And yet this redeemed world, like man, is in part redeemed only in hope (Rom. 8:20); being in no present possession, but only in the assured certainty, of a complete deliverance. For this, too, we must not forget, that nature, in its present state, like man himself, contains but a prophecy of its coming glory; it 'groaneth and travaileth'; it cannot tell out all its secrets; it has a presentiment of something, which it is not yet, but hereafter shall be. It, too, is suffering under our curse: yet thus in its very imperfection wonderfully serving us, since thus it has apter signs and symbols to declare to us our disease and our misery, and the processes of their healing and removing; it has symbols not merely of God's grace and power, but also of man's sins and wretchedness. It has its sores and its wounds, its storms and its wildernesses, its lion and its adder, by these interpreting to us death and all that leads to death, no less than, by its more beneficent workings, life and all that tends to the restoring and maintaining of life.

But while thus it has this gracious adaptation to our needs, not the less does it, this fallen estate, come short of its full purpose and meaning: it fails in part to witness for divine order, *tanta^ stat proedita culpa^*—as one, whose eye was mainly directed to this its disorder and deficiency, exclaimed. It does not give always a clear witness, nor speak out in distinct accents, of God's truth and love. Of these it is oftentimes an inadequate expression—yea, sometimes seems not to declare them at all, but rather in volcano and in earthquake, in ravenous beasts and in poisonous herbs, to tell of strife, and discord, and disharmony, and all the woeful consequences of the Fall. But one day it will be otherwise; one day it will be translucent with the divine idea which it embodies, and which even now, despite these dark spots, shines through it so wondrously. For no doubt the end and consummation will be, not the abolition of this nature, but the glorifying of it; that which is now nature *(natura)*, always, as the word expresses, striving and struggling to the birth, will then be indeed born. The new creation will be as the glorious child born out of the world-long throes and anguish of the old. It will be as the snake casting its wrinkled and winter skin; not the world, but *'the fashion* of the world,' passing away, when it puts off its soiled work-day garments, and puts on its holiday apparel for the great Sabbath which shall arrive at last. Then, when it too shall have been delivered from its bondage of corruption, all that it now has of dim and contradictory and perplexing shall disappear. This nature, too, shall be a mirror in which God will perfectly glass Himself, for it shall tell of nothing but the marvels of his wisdom and power of love.

But at present, while this natural world, through its share in man's fall, has won in fitness for the expression of the sadder side of man's condition, the imperfection and evil that cling to him and beset him, it has in some measure lost in fitness for the expressing of the higher. It possesses the best, yet, oftentimes inadequate, helps for this. These human relationships, and this whole constitution of things earthly, share in the shortcoming that cleaves to all which is of the earth. Obnoxious to change, tainted with sin, shut in within brief limits by decay and death, they are often weak and temporary, where they have to set forth things strong and eternal. A sinful element is evidently mingled with them, while they yet appear as symbols of what is entirely pure and heavenly. They break down under the weight that is laid upon them. The father chastens after his own pleasure, instead of wholly for the child's profit; in this unlike that heavenly Father, whose character he is to declare. The seed which should set forth the word of God, that Word which liveth and abideth forever, itself decays and perishes at last. Festivals, so frequently the image of the pure joy of the kingdom, of the crowning communion of the faithful with their Lord and with one another, will often, when here celebrated, be mixed up with much that is carnal, and they come to their close in a few hours. There is something exactly analogous to all this in the typical or parabolical personages of Scripture—the men that are to set forth the Divine Man. Through their sins, through their infirmities—yea, through the necessary limitations of their earthly condition, they are unable to carry the correspondences completely out. Sooner or later they break down; and very often even the part which they do sustain, they sustain it not for long. Thus few would deny the typical character of Solomon. His kingdom of peace, the splendor of his court, his wisdom, the temple which he reared, all point to a Greater whom he foreshadowed and foreshowed. Yet this gorgeous forecasting of the coming glory is vouchsafed to us only for an instant; we catch a glimpse of it and no more. Even before his reign is done, all is beginning to dislimn again, to lose the distinctness of its outline, the brightness of its coloring. His wisdom is darkened, the perfect peace of his land has disappeared (1 Kgs. 11:14, 23, 26); and the gloom on every side encroaching warns us that this is but a fleeting image, not the very substance, of the true kingdom of peace.

Again, there are men who only in some single point of their history are brought into typical relation with Christ; such was Jonah, the type of the Resurrection; others, again, whose lives at one moment and another seem suddenly to stand out as symbolic, but who then sink back so far that we hesitate whether we may dare to consider them as such at all, and with whom the attempt to carry out the resemblance into greater detail would involve in infinite embarrassment. Samson will at once suggest himself as one of these. Doubtless something more was meant than is contained in the letter, when he out of the eater brought forth meat, and out of the strong, sweetness (Judg. 14:14); or when he wrought a mightier deliverance for Israel through his death than he had wrought in his life (Judg. 16:30). Yet we hesitate how far we may proceed. And so it is in every case, for somewhere or other every man is a liar; he is false, that is, to the divine idea, which he was meant to embody, and fails to bring it out in all its fullness and perfection. So that of the truths of God in the language of men (this language of course including man's acts as well as his words), of these sons of heaven married to the daughters of earth, it may truly be said, 'we have this treasure in earthen vessels.' And we must expect that somewhere or other the earthen vessel will appear, that the imperfection which cleaves to our forms of utterance, to men's words and to their works, will make itself felt either in the misapprehensions of those to whom the language is addressed (as at John 3:4), or by the language itself, though the best that human speech could supply, by the men themselves, though the noblest, it may be, of their age and nation—yet failing to set forth the divine truth in all its fullness and completeness.

No doubt it was a feeling, working more or less consciously, of the dangers and drawbacks that attend all our means of communication—a desire, also, to see eye to eye, or as St. Paul terms it, face to face (1 Cor. 13:12), which caused the Mystics to press with such earnestness and frequency, that we should seek to abstract ourselves from all images of things; that to raise ourselves to the contemplation of pure and naked truth is the height of spiritual attainment, towards which we should continually be struggling. But in requiring this as a test and proof of spiritual progress—in setting it as the mark toward which men should strive, they were not merely laying unnecessary burdens on men's backs, but actually leading astray. For whether one shall separate in his own consciousness the form from the essence—whether the images which he uses shall be to him more or less conscious symbols—does not depend on his greater or less advance in spiritual knowledge, but on causes which may or may not accompany religious growth, and mainly on this one—whether he has been accustomed to think upon his thoughts, to reflect upon the wonderful instrument which in language he is using. One who possesses the truth only as it is incorporated in the symbol, may have a far stronger hold upon it, may be influenced by it far more mightily, may far more really be nourished by it than another, who, according to the mystic view, would be in a higher and more advanced state. It is true, indeed, that for them who have not merely to live upon the truth themselves, but to guard it for others—not only to drink themselves of the streams of divine knowledge, but to see that the waters of its well-heads be not troubled for their brethren—for them it is well that they should be conscious, and the more conscious the better, of the marvelous thing which language is—of the power and mystery, of the truth and falsehood, of words; and as a part of this acquaintance, that the truth, and that which is the vehicle of the truth, should for them be separable; but then it should be even for them as soul and body, not as kernel and husk. This last comparison has been often used, but may easily be pushed into an error. It has been said that, as when the seed is cast into the ground, after a time the kernel disengages itself from the outer coating, and alone remains and fructifies, while the husk decays and perishes, so in the seed of God's word, deposited in man's heart, the sensible form must fall off, that the inner germ, releasing itself, may germinate. But the image, urged thus far, does not aptly set forth the truth, it will lead in the end to a perilous slighting of the written word, under pretense of having the inner life. The outer covering is not to fall off and perish, but to become glorified, being pierced and penetrated by the spirit that is within. Man is body and soul, and, being so, the truth has for him need of a body and soul likewise; it is well that he should know what is body, and what is soul, but not that he should seek to kill the body, that he may get at the soul.

Thus it was provided for us by a wisdom higher than our own, and all our attempts to disengage ourselves wholly from sensuous images must always in the end prove unsuccessful. It will be only a changing of our images, and that for the worse; a giving up of living realities which truly stir the heart, and a getting of dead metaphysical abstractions in their room. The aim of the teacher who would find his way to the hearts and understandings of his hearers, will never be to keep down the parabolical element in his teaching, but rather to make as large use of it as he can. To do this effectually will demand a fresh effort of his own; for while all language is, and must be figurative, yet long familiar use is continually wearing out the freshness and sharpness of the stamp—(who, for example, that speaks of *insulting*, retains the lively image of a leaping on the prostrate body of a foe?); so that language is ever needing to be recalled, minted and issued anew, cast into novel forms, as was done by Him of whom it is said, that without a parable spoke He nothing; He gave no doctrine in an abstract former, no skeletons of truth, but all clothed, as it were, with flesh and blood. He did, as He declared his Apostles must do, if they would be scribes instructed unto the kingdom, and able to instruct others (Matt. 13:52); He brought forth out of his treasure things new and old: by the help of the old He made intelligible the new; by the aid of the familiar He introduced that which was strange; from the known He passed more easily to the unknown. And in his own manner of teaching He has given us the secret of all effectual teaching, of all speaking which shall leave, as was said of the eloquence of Pericles, strings in the minds and memories of the hearers. There is a natural delight in this manner of teaching, appealing, as it does, not to the understanding only, but to the feelings, to the imagination; calling the whole man, with all his powers and faculties, into pleasurable activity: and things thus learned with delight are those longest remembered.

Had our Lord spoken naked spiritual truth, how many of his words, partly from his hearers' lack of interest in them, partly from their lack of insight, would have passed away from their hearts and memories, and left no trace behind them. But being imparted to them in this form, under some lively image, in some short and perhaps seemingly paradoxical sentence, or in some brief but interesting narrative, they aroused attention, excited inquiry, and even if the truth did not at the moment, by the help of the illustration used, find an entrance into the mind, yet the words must thus often have fixed themselves in their memories and remained by them. And here the comparison of the seed is appropriate, of which the shell should guard the life of the inner germ, till that should be ready to unfold itself, till there should be a soil prepared for it, in which it could take root and find nourishment suitable to its needs. His words, laid up in the memory, were to many that heard Him like the money of another country, unavailable for present use—the value of which they only dimly knew, but which yet was ready in their hand, when they reached that land, and were naturalized in it. When the Spirit came, and brought all things to their remembrance, then He filled all the outlines of truth which they before possessed with its substance, quickened all its forms with the power and spirit of life. Not perhaps at once, but gradually, the meaning of what they had heard unfolded themselves to them. Small to the small, they grew with their growth, And thus must it ever be with all true knowledge, which is not the communication of information, the transfer of a dead sum or capital of facts or theories from one mind to another, but the opening of living fountains within the heart, the scattering of sparks which shall kindle where they fall, the planting of seeds of truth, which shall take root in the new soil where they are cast, and striking their roots downward, and sending their branches upward, shall grow up into goodly trees.

Nor must we forget, when we are estimating the amount of the parabolic element in Scripture, how much besides the spoken, there is there of acted, parable. In addition to those parables which, by a more especial right, we separate off, and call by that name, every type is a *real* parable. The whole Levitical constitution, with its outer court, its Holy, its Holiest of all, its High priest, its sacrifices, and all its ordinances, is such, and is declared to be such, in the Epistle to the Hebrews (9:9). The wanderings of the children of Israel have ever been regarded as a parable of the spiritual life. In like manner we have parabolic persons, who teach us not merely by what in their own characters they did, but as they represented One higher and greater; men whose actions and whose sufferings obtain a new significance, inasmuch as they were in these drawing lines, though often quite unaware of it themselves, which Another and a greater should hereafter fill up; as Abraham when cast out the bondwoman and her son (Gal. 4:30), Jonah in the whale's belly, David in his hour of peril or of agony (Ps. 22). And in narrower circles, without touching on the central fact and Person in the kingdom of God, how often has He chosen that his servants should teach by an acted parable rather than by any other means, and this because no other treaching was fitted to make so deep and so lasting and impression. Jeremiah breaks in pieces a potter's vessel, that he may foretell the complete destruction of his people (19:1–11); he wears a yoke, himself a prophecy and a prophecy and a parable of their approaching bondage (27:2; 28:10); he redeems a field, in pledge of a redemption in store for all the land (32:6–15); and these examples might be infinitely multiplied. And as God will have his servants by these signs to teach others, He continually teaches *them* by the same. It is not his word only that comes to his prophets, but the great truths of his kingdom pass before their eyes incorporated in symbols, addressing themselves first to the spiritual eye, and only through that to the spiritual ear. They are eminently *Seers*. Ezekiel, Daniel, and Zechariah will at once suggest themselves, as those of whom, more than, perhaps, any others, this was true. And in the New Testament we have a great example of the same teaching in St. Peter's vision (Acts 10:9–16), and in all the visions of the Apocalypse. Nay, we might venture to affirm that so it was with the highest and greatest truth of all, that which includes all others—the manifestation of God in the flesh. This, inasmuch as it was a making intelligible of the otherwise unintelligible; a making visible of the invisible; a teaching, not by doctrine, but by the embodied doctrine of a divine life, was the highest and most glorious of all parables.

It would be an interesting study to trace the distinctive character of the several Gospels in the parables which they severally record; or, when the parables are common to more than one, in the especial circumstances which they bring prominently out. Here, indeed, only St. Matthew and St. Luke will come into comparison, St. John having allegories, as of the Good Shepherd, the True Vine, but no parables; while St. Mark has only when parable peculiarly his own (4:26), and in his record of those which he shares with the other two, presents no very distinctive features. We may say generally of the parables of judgment—St. Luke's, of mercy; those are statelier, these tenderer. St. Matthew's are frequently introduced as containing mysteries of the kingdom of God, language which nowhere occurs in St. Luke. In St. Matthew's God evermore appears as the King who, sitting on his throne, scattereth away all evil with his eyes, and has in readiness to avenge all disobedience of men; many of them concluding with distinct judgment acts of a greater or a lesser severity (13:42, 49: 18:34; 20:14; 21:41; 22:7, 13; 25:12, 30). Such judgment acts are not wanting in the parables of St. Luke, but less frequently occur; while mercy supplies to them their ground-tone, as it does to the whole Gospel whereunto they belong. They are of the tree which was spared at the gardener's intercession (13:6); of the Samaritan who poured oil and wine into the traveler's wounds (10:30); of the father who welcomed back his penitent son (15:11); nay, even the parable of Dives and Lazarus is a parable of mercy, for it is the declaration of what the issues of *not* showing mercy will be.

Nowhere do the characteristic differences of the two Evangelists come out more strikingly than where they record parables, whose features in many respects resemble one another. Thus compare St. Matthew's parable of the Marriage of the King's Son (22:1) with St. Luke's of the Great Supper (14:16). These are not, as I hope by and by to show, two different versions or reports of the same parable, but separate parables, akin to, but yet distinct from, one another. As nothing is so ductile as fine gold, so was it with the find gold of the Savior's doctrine; which yielded itself easily to be fashioned and shaped into new forms, as need might require; the Evangelists severally giving prominence to that aspect of the parable which corresponded most to their own spiritual predispositions, which consented best with the special purpose of their Gospel. The parable in St. Matthew is of a king, and a king's son, for whom a marriage-festival is made. All is here of the theocracy; roots itself in the hopes which the Old Testament cherishes, in the promises with which it abounds. And then, how characteristic of this Evangelist is the double doom—first, of the open foe, and then of the false friend? In St. Luke all is different, and all characteristic.

No longer a king, but simply a certain man, makes a supper; the two judgment acts fall into the background; one indeed disappears altogether; while far more is made of the grace and goodness of the giver of the feast, which lead him again and again to send forth his servant that he may gather in the meanest, the most despised, the most outcast, to his table. These are but slight hints on a matter which each student of the parables may profitably follow out for himself.

III.

On the Interpretation
of Parables

The parables, fair in their outward form, are yet fairer within, 'apples of gold in network of silver'; each one of them like a casket, itself of exquisite workmanship, but in which jewels yet richer than itself are laid up; or as fruit, which, however lovely to look upon, is yet in its inner sweetness more delectable still. To find, then, the golden key for this casket, at whose touch it shall reveal its treasures; so to open this fruit, that nothing of its hidden kernel shall be missed or lost, has naturally been regarded ever as a matter of high concern. In this, the interpretation of the parable, a subject to which we have now arrived, there is one question of more importance than any other—one so constantly presenting itself anew, that it will naturally claim to be the first and most fully considered. It is this, How much of them is to be taken as significant? And to this question answers the most different have been returned. There are those who lay themselves out for the tracing a general correspondence between the sign and the thing signified, and this having done refuse to advance any further; while others aim at running out the interpretation into the minutest details; with those who occupy every intermediate stage between these extremes. Some have gone far in saying, This is merely drapery and ornament, and not the vehicle of essential truth; this was introduced either to give liveliness and a general air of verisimilitude to the narrative, or as actually necessary to make the story, the vehicle of the truth, a consistent whole, without which consistency the hearer would have been perplexed or offended; or else to hold together and connect the different parts—just as in the most splendid house there must be passages, not for their own sake, but to lead from one room to another. They have used often the illustration of the knife, which is not all edge; of the harp, which is not all strings; urging that much in the knife, which does not cut, the handle for example, is yet of prime necessity—much, in the musical instrument, which is never intended to give sound, must yet not be wanting: or, to use another comparison, that many circumstances 'in Christ's parables are like the feathers which wing our arrows, which, though they pierce not like the head, but seem slight things and or a different matter from the rest, are yet requisite to make the shaft to pierce, and do both convey it to and penetrate the mark. To this school Chrysostom belongs. He continually warns against pressing too anxiously all the circumstances of a parable, and often cuts his own interpretation somewhat short in language like this, 'Be not over-busy about the rest.' It is the same with the interpreters who habitually follow him, Theophylact and others, though not always faithful to their own principles. So also with Origen, who illustrates his meaning by a comparison of much beauty: 'For as the likenesses which are given in pictures and statues are not perfect resemblances of those things for whose sake they are made—but for instance the image which is painted in wax on a plain surface of wood, contains a resemblance of the superficies and colors, but does not also preserve the depressions and prominences, but only a representation of them—while a statue, again, seeks to preserve the likeness which consists in prominences and depressions, but not as well that which is in colors—but should the statue be of wax, it seeks to retain both, I mean the colors, and also the depressions and prominences, but is not an image of those things which are within—in the same manner, of the parables which are contained in the Gospels so account, that the kingdom of heaven, when it is likened to anything, is not likened to it according to all the things which are contained in that with which the comparison is instituted, but according to certain qualities which the matter in hand requires.' Exactly thus Tilloston has said that the parable and its interpretation are not to be contemplated as two planes, touching one another at every point, but oftentimes rather as a plane and a globe, which, though brought into contact, yet touch each other only at one.

On the other hand, Augustine, though himself sometimes laying down the same canon, frequently extends the interpretation through all the branches and minutest fibres of the narrative; and

Origen no less, despite the passage which I have just quoted. And in modern times, the followers of Cocceius have been particularly earnest in affirming all parts of a parable to be significant. There is a noble passage in the writings of Edward Irving, in which he describes the long and laborious care which he took to master the literal meaning of every word in the parables, being confident of the riches of inward truth which every one of those words contained; he goes on to say: 'Of all which my feeling and progress in studying the parables of our Lord, I have found no similitude worthy to convey the impression, save that of sailing through between the Pillars of Hercules into the Mediterranean Sea, where you have to pass between armed rocks, in a strait, and under a current—all requiring careful and skillful seamanship—but, being passed, opening into such a large, expansive, and serene ocean of truth, so engirdled round with rich and fertile lands, so inlaid with beautiful and verdant islands, and full of rich colonies and populous cities, that unspeakable is the delight and the reward it yieldeth to the voyager. He and others have protested against that shallow spirit which is ever ready to empty Scripture of its deeper significance, to exclaim, 'This means nothing; this circumstance is not to be pressed'; which, satisfying itself with sayings like these, fails to draw out from the word of God all the rich treasures contained in it for us, or to recognize the manifold wisdom with which its type is often constructed to correspond with the antitype. They bid us to observe that of those who start with the principle of setting aside so much as non-essential, scarcely any two, when it comes to the application of their principle, are agreed concerning what actually is to be set aside; what one rejects another retains, and the contrary: and further, that the more this scheme is carried out, the more the peculiar beauty of the parable disappears, and the interest of it is lost. For example, when Calvin will not allow the oil in the vessels of the wise Virgins (Matt. 25:4) to mean anything, nor the vessels themselves, nor the lamps; or when Storr, who, perhaps more than nay other, would leave the parables bare trunks, stripped of all their foliage and branches, of everything that made for beauty and ornament, denies that the Prodigal leaving his father's house has any direct reference to man's departure from the presence of his heavenly Father, it is at once evident of how much not merely of pleasure, but of instruction, they would deprive us. It is urged, too, in opposition to this interpretation of the parables merely in the gross, that when our Lord Himself interpreted the two first which He delivered, namely, that of the Sower and of the Tares, He most probably intended to furnish us with a rule for the interpretation of all. These explanations, therefore, are most important, not merely for their own sakes, but as supplying principles and canons of interpretation to be applied throughout. Now, in these the moral application descends to some of the minutest details: thus, the birds which snatch away the seed sown, are explained as Satan who takes the good word out of the heart (Matt. 13:19), the thorns which choke the good seed correspond to the cares and pleasures of life (Matt. 13:22), with much more of the same kind.

On a review of the whole controversy it may safely be said, that there have been exaggerations upon both sides. The advocates of interpretation in the gross and not in detail have been too easily satisfied with their favorite maxim, 'Every comparison must halt somethwere'; since one may fairly demand, 'Where is the necessity?' There is no force in the reply, that unless it did so, it would not be an illustration of the thing, but the thing itself. Such is not the fact. Two lines do not cease to be two, nor become one and the same, because they run parallel through their whole course. Doubtless in the opposite extreme of interpretation there lies the danger of an ingenious trifling with the word of God; a danger, too, lest the interpreter's delight in the exercise of this ingenuity, with the admiration of it on the part of others, may not put somewhat out of sight that the sanctification of the heart through the truth is the main purpose of all Scripture: even as we shall presently note the manner in which heretics, through this pressing of all parts of a parable to the uttermost, have been able to extort from it almost any meaning that they pleased.

After all has been urged on the one side and on the other, it must be confessed that no absolute rule can be laid down beforehand to guide the expositor how far he shall proceed. Much must be left to good sense, to spiritual tact, to that reverence for the word of God, which will show itself sometimes in refusing curiosities of interpretation, no less than at other times in demanding a distinct spiritual meaning for the words which are before it. The nearest approach, perhaps, to a canon of interpretation on the matter is that which Tholuck lays down—'It must be allowed,' he says, 'that a similitude is perfect in proportion as it is on all sides rich in applications; and hence, in treating the parables of Christ, the expositor must proceed on the presumption that there is import in every sin-

gle point, and only desist from seeking it when either it does not result without forcing, or when we can clearly show that this or that
circumstance was merely added for the sake of giving intuitiveness
to the narrative. We should not assume anything to be non-essential, except when by holding it fast as essential, the unity of the
whole is marred and troubled.' For, to follow up these words of
his—in the same manner as a statue is the more perfect in the measure that the life, the idea that was in the sculptor's mind, breathes
out of and looks through every feature and limb, so much the
greater being the triumph of spirit, penetrating through and glorifying the matter which it has assumed; so the more translucent a
parable is in all parts with the divine truth which it embodies, the
more the garment with which that is arrayed, is a garment of light,
pierced through, as was once the rainment of Christ, with the
brightness within—illuminating it in all its recesses and corners,
and leaving no dark place in it—by so much the more beautiful and
perfect it must be esteemed.

It will much help us in this determining of what is essential
and what not, if, before we attempt to explain the particular parts,
we obtain a firm grasp of the central truth which the parable
would set forth, and distinguish it in the mind as sharply and accurately as we can from all cognate truths which border upon it;
for only seen from that middle point will the different parts appear in their true light. 'One may compare,' says a late writer on
the parables, 'the entire parable with a circle, of which the middle
point is the spiritual truth or doctrine, and of which the radii are
the several circumstances of the narration; so long as one has not
placed oneself in the center, neither the circle itself appears in its
perfect shape, nor will the beautiful unity with which the radii
converge to a single point be perceived, but this is all observed as
soon as the eye looks forth from the center. Even so in the parable;
if we have recognized its middle point, its main doctrine, in full
light, then will the proportion and right signification of all particular circumstances be clear unto us, and we shall lay stress upon
them only so far as the main truth is thereby more vividly set
forth.'

There is another rule which it is important to observe, one so
simple and obvious, that were it not continually neglected, one
would be content to leave it to the common sense of every interpreter. It is this, that as, in the explanation of the fable, the introduction (προμύθιον) and application (ἐπιμύθιον) claim to be most

carefully attended to, so here what some have entitled the pro-parabola and epi-parabola, though the other terms would have done sufficiently well; which are invariably the finger-posts pointing to the direction in which we are to look for the meaning—the key to the whole matter. The neglect of these often involves in the most untenable explanations; for instance, how many interpretations which have been elaborately worked out of the Laborers in the Vineyard, could never have been so much as once proposed, if heed had been paid to the context, or the necessity been acknowledged of bringing the interpretation into harmony with the saying which introduces and winds up the parable. These helps to interpretation, though rarely or never lacking, are yet given in no fixed or formal manner; sometimes they are supplied by the Lord Himself (Matt. 22:14; 25:13); sometimes by the inspired narrators of his words (Luke 15:1, 2; 18:1); sometimes, as the prologue, they precede the parable (Luke 18:9; 19:11); sometimes, as the epilogue, they follow (Matt. 25:13; Luke 16:9). Occasionally a parable is furnished with these helps to a right understanding both at the opening and the close; as is that of the Unmerciful Servant (Matt. 18:23), which is suggested by the question which Peter ask (v. 21), and wound up by the application which the Lord Himself makes (v. 35). So again the parable at Matt. 20:1–15 begins and finishes with the same amount of help for its right understanding.

Again, we may observe that a correct interpretation, besides being thus in accordance with its context, must be so without any very violent means being necessary to bring it into such agreement; even as, generally, the interpretation must be easy—if not always easy to discover, yet, being discovered, easy. For it is here as with the laws of nature; the proleptic mind of genius may be needful to discover the law, but, once discovered, it throws back light on itself, and commends itself unto all. And there is this other point of similarity also; it is a proof that we have found the law, when it explains all the phenomena, and not merely some; if, sooner or later, they all marshal themselves in order under it; so it is good evidence that we have discovered the right interpretation of a parable, if it leave none of the main circumstances unexplained. A false interpretation will inevitably betray itself, since it will 'invariably paralyze and render nugatory some important member of an entire account.' If we have the right key in our hand, not merely some of the wards, but all, will have their parts corresponding; they key too will turn without grating or over-much forcing; and if we have the right interpretation, it will scarcely need to be defended and made plausible with great appliance of learning, to be propped up by remote allusions to Rabbinical or profane literature, by illustrations drawn from the recesses of antiquity.

Once more: the parables may not be made primary sources and seats of doctrine. Doctrines otherwise and already established may be illustrated, or indeed further confirmed by them; but it is not allowable to constitute doctrine first by their aid. They may be the outer ornamental fringe, but not the main texture, of the proof. For from the literal to the figurative, from the clearer to the more obscure, has been ever recognized as the order of Scripture interpretation. This rule, however, has been often forgotten, and controversialists, looking round for arguments with which to sustain some weak position, for which they can find no other support in Scripture, often invent for themselves supports in these. Thus Bellarmine presses the parable of the Good Samaritan, and the circumstance that in that the thieves are said *first* to have stripped the traveler, and *afterwards* to have inflicted wounds on him (Luke 10:30), as proving certain views upon which the Romish Church sets a high value, on the order of man's fall, the succession in which, first losing heavenly gifts, the robe of a divine righteousness, he afterwards, and as a consequence, endured actual hurts in his soul. And in the same way Faustus Socinus argues from the parable of the Unmerciful Servant, that as the king pardoned his servant merely on his petition (Matt. 18:32), and not on the score of any satisfaction made, or any mediator intervening, we may from this conclude, that in the same way, and without requiring sacrifice or intercessor, God will pardon sinners simply on the ground of their prayers.

But by much the worst offenders against this rule were the Gnostics and Manichaaeans in old time, and especially the former. Their whole scheme was one, which however it may have been a result of the Gospel, inasmuch as that set the religious speculation of the world vigorously at work, was yet of independent growth; and they only came to the Scripture to find a varnish, an outer Christian coloring, for a system essentially antichristian—they came, not to learn its language, but to see if they could not compel it to speak theirs; with no desire to draw *out of* Scripture its meaning, but only to thrust *into* Scripture their own. When they fell thus to picking and choosing what in it they might best turn to their ends, the parables naturally invited them almost more than any other portions of Scripture. In the literal portions of Scripture they could no color for their scheme; their only refuge therefore was in the figurative, in those which might receive more interpretations than one; such, perhaps, they might bend or compel to their purposes. Accordingly, we find them claiming continually the parables for their own; with no joy, indeed, in their simplicity, or practical depth, or ethical beauty; for they seem to have had no sense or feeling of these; but delighted to superinduce upon them their own capricious and extravagant fancies. Ireneus is continually compelled to rescue the parables from the extreme abuse to which these submitted them; for, indeed, they not merely warped and drew them a little aside, but made them tell wholly a different tale from that which they were intended to tell. Against these Gnostics he lays down that cannon, namely, that the parables cannot be in any case the primary, much less the exclusive, foundations of any doctrine, but must be themselves interpreted according to the analogy of faith; since, if every subtle solution of one of these might raise itself at once to the dignity and authority of a Christian doctrine, the rule of faith would be nowhere. So to build, as he shows, were to build not on the rock, but on the sand.

Tertullian has the same conflict to maintain. The whole scheme of the Gnostics, as he observes, was a great floating cloud-palace, the figment of their own brain, with no counterpart in the world of spiritual realities. They could therefore mold it as they would; and thus they found no difficulty in forcing the parables to seem to be upon their side, shaping, as they had no scruple in doing, their doctrine according to the leadings and suggestions of these, till they brought the two into apparent agreement with one another. There was nothing to hinder them here; their creed was not a fixed body of divine truth, which they could neither add to nor diminish; which was given them from above, and in which they could only acquiesce: but an invention of their own, which they could therefore fashion, modify, and alter as best suited the purpose they had in hand. We, as Tertullian often urges, are kept within limits in the exposition of the parables, accepting, as we do, the other Scriptures as the rule of truth, as the rule, therefore, of their interpretation. It is otherwise with these heretics; their doctrine is their own; they can first dexterously adapt it to the parables, and then bring forward the conformity between the two as a testimony of its truth.

As it was with the Gnostics of the early Church, exactly so, was it with the sects which, in a later day, were their spiritual successors, the Cathari and Bogomili. They, too, found in the parables no teaching about sin and grace and redemption, no truths of the kingdom, but fitted to the parables the speculations about the creation, the origin of evil, the fall of angels, which were uppermost in their own minds; which they had not drawn from Scripture; but which having themselves framed, they afterwards turned to Scripture, endeavoring to find there that which they could compel to fall into their scheme. Thus, the apostasy of Satan and his drawing after him a part of the host of heaven, they found set forth by the parable of the Unjust Steward. Satan was the chief steward over God's house, who being deposed form his place of highest trust, drew after him the other angels, with the suggestion of lighter tasks and relief from the burden of their imposed duties.

But to come to more modern times. Though not testifying to evils at all so grave in the devisers of the scheme, nor leading altogether out of the region of Christian truth, yet sufficiently injurious to the sober interpretation of the parables is such a theory concerning them as that entertained, and in actual exposition carried out, by Coceius and his followers of what we may call the historico-prophetical school. By the parables, they say, and so far they have right, are declared the mysteries of the kingdom of God. But then, ascribing to those words, 'kingdom of God,' a far too narrow sense, they are resolved to find in every one of the parables a part of the history of that kingdom's progressive development in the world to the latest time. They will not allow any to be merely ethical, but affirm all to be historico-prophetical. Thus, to let one of them speak for himself, in the remarkable words of Krummacher: 'The parables of Jesus have not primarily a moral, but a politico-religious, or theocratic purpose. To use a comparison, we may consider the kingdom of God carried forward under his guidance, a the action, gradually unfolding itself, of an Epos, of which the first germ lay prepared long beforehand in the Jewish economy of the Old Testament, but which through Him began to unfold itself, and will continue to do so to the end of time. The name and superscription of the Epos is, THE KINGDOM OF GOD. The parables belong essentially to the Gospel of the kingdom, not merely as containing its doctrine, but its progressive development. They connect themselves with certain fixed period of that development, and, as soon as these periods are completed, lose themselves in the very completion; that is, considered as independent portions of the Epos, remaining for us only in the image and external letter.' He must mean, of course, in the same manner and degree as all other fulfilled prophecy; in the light of such accomplished prophecy, he would say, they must henceforth be regarded.

Boyle gives some, though a very moderate, countenance to the same opinion: 'Some, if not most, do, like those oysters that, besides the meat they afford us, contain pearls, not only include excellent moralities, but comprise important prophecies'; and, having adduced the Mustardseed and the Wicked Husbandmen as plainly containing such prophecies, he goes on, "I despair not to see unheeded prophecies disclosed in others of them. Vitringa's *Elucidation of the Parablese* is a practical application of this scheme of interpretation, and one which will scarcely win many supporters for it. Thus, the servant owing the ten thousand talents (Matt. 18:23), is the Pope or line of Popes, placed in highest trust in the Church, but who, misusing the powers committed to them, were warned by the invasion of Goths, Lombards, and other barbarians, of judgment at the door, and indeed seemed given into their hands for doom; but being mercifully delivered from this fear of imminent destruction by the Frankish kings, so far from repenting and amending, on the contrary now more than ever oppressed and maltreated the true servants of God, and who therefore should be delivered over to an irreversible doom. He gives a yet more marvelous explanation of the Merchant seeking goodly pearls, this pearl of price being the Church of Geneva and the doctrine of Calvin, opposed to all the abortive pearls, that is, to all the other Reformed Churches. Other examples may be found in Cocceius—an interpretation, for instance, of the Ten Virgins, after this same fashion. Deyling has an interesting essay on this school of interpreters, and passes a severe, though not undeserved, condemnation on them. Prophetical, no doubt, many of the parables are; for they declare how the new element of life, which the Lord was bringing into the world, would work—the future influences and results of his doctrine—that the little mustardseed would grow to a great tree—that the leaven would continue working till it had leavened the whole lump. But they declare not so much the *facts* as the *laws* of the kingdom. Historico-prophetical are only a few; as that of the Wicked Husbandmen, which Boyle adduced, in which there is a clear prophecy of the death of Christ; as that of the

Marriage of the King's Son, in which there is an equally clear announcement of the destruction of Jerusalem, and the transfer of the kingdom of God from the Jews to the Gentiles. But this subject will again present itself, when we consider, in their relation to one another, the seven parables in the thirteenth chapter of St. Matthew.

IV.

On Other Parables Besides Those in the Scriptures

The most perfect specimens of this form of composition, and those by which the relative value of all other in the like kind is to be measured, must be sought in that Book which is the most perfect of all books; yet they do not belong exclusively to it. The parable, as St. Jerome has noted, is among the favorite vehicles for conveying moral truth throughout all the East. Our Lord took possession of it, honored it by thus making it his own, by using it as the vehicle for the highest truth of all. But there were parables before the parables which issued from his lips. It belongs to our subject to say something concerning those, which, though they did not give the pattern to, yet preceded his—concerning those also which were formed more or less immediately on the suggestion and in imitation of his, on the Jewish, that is, and the Christian.

The Jewish parables will occupy us first. Some, indeed, have denied that this method of teaching by parables was current among the Jews before our Savior's time. They have feared, it would seem lest it should detract from his glory to suppose that He had availed Himself of a manner of teaching in use already. Yet surely the anxiety to cut off the Lord's teaching from all living connection with his age and country is very idle; and the suspicion with which parallels from the uninspired Jewish writings have been regarded is altogether misplaced. It is the same anxiety which would cut off the Mosaic legislation and institutions altogether from Egypt; which cannot with honesty be done, and which there is no object in attempting. For if Christianity be indeed the world-religion, it must gather into one all dispersed rays of light; it must appropriate to itself all elements of truth which are anywhere scattered abroad; not thus adopting what is alien, but rather claiming what is its own. Our blessed Lord so spoke, as that his doctrine, in its outward garb, should commend itself to his countrymen. There were inner obstacles enough to their receiving of it; the more need therefore that outwardly it should be attractive. Thus, He appealed to proverbs in common use among them. He quoted the traditionary speeches of their elder Rabbis, to refute, to enlarge, or to correct them. When He found the theological terms of their schools capable of bearing the burden of the new truth which He laid upon them, He willingly used them; and in using, did not deny their old meaning; while at the same time, making all things new, He glorified and transformed it into something infinitely higher, breathed into them the spirit of a new life. 'Thy kingdom come' formed already a part of the Jewish liturgy, yet not the less was it a new prayer on the lips of all who had realized in any measure the idea of the kingdom, and what the coming of that kingdom meant, as *He* first had enabled them to realize it. So 'Peace be unto you' was an ordinary salutation among the Jews, yet having how much deeper a significance, and one how entirely new upon his lips, who *is* our Peace, and who, first causing us to enter ourselves into the peace of God, enabled us truly to wish peace, and to speak peace, to our brethren. So, too, a proselyte was in the Jewish schools entitled "a new creature,' and his passing over to Judaism was "a new birth'; yet these terms expressed little more than a change in his outward relations: it remained for Christ to appropriate them to the higher mysteries of the kingdom of heaven. Nor less is it certain that the illustrating of doctrines by the help of parables, or briefer comparisons, was common among the Jewish teachers; of them it might almost be said as of Him, that without a parable they spoke nothing. The very formulas with which their parables were introduced remind us of those we meet in the Gospels; for instance, the question, 'Whereunto shall I liken it?' is of continual recurrence. But what then? It was not in the newness of the forms, but in the newness of the spirit, that the transcendent glory and excellency of Christ's teaching consisted.

As some may desire to see what these Jewish parables are like, I will quote, not, as is often done, the worst but the best which I have had the fortune to meet. The following is occasioned by a question which has arisen—namely, Why the good so often die young? God, it is answered, foresees that if they lived they would fall into sin. 'To what is this like? It is like a king who, walking in his garden, saw some roses which were yet buds, breathing an ineffable sweetness. He thought, "If these shed such sweetness while yet they are buds, what will they do when they are fully blown?" After a while, the king entered the garden anew, thinking to find the roses now blown, and to delight himself with their fragrance; but arriving at the place, he found them pale and withered, and yielding no smell. He exclaimed with regret, "Had I gathered them while yet tender and young, and while they gave forth their sweetness, I might have delighted myself with them, but now I have no pleasure in them." The next year the king walked in his garden, and finding rosebuds scattering fragrance, he commanded his servants, "Gather them, that I may enjoy them before they wither, as last year they did." The next is ingenious enough, though a notable specimen of Jewish self-righteousness; 'A man had three friends: being summoned to appear before the king, he was terrified, and looked for an advocate: the first, whom he had counted the best, altogether refused to go with him; another replied that he would accompany him to the door of the palace, but could not speak for him; the third, whom he had held in least esteem, appeared with him before the king, and pleaded for him so well as to procure his deliverance. So every man has three friends, when summoned by death before God, his Judge: the first, whom he prized, his money, will not go with him a step; the second, his friends and kinsmen, accompany him to the tomb, but no further, nor can they deliver him in the judgment; while the third, whom he had in least esteem, the Law and good works, appears with him before the king, and delivers him from condemnation.' But this is in a nobler strain; it is suggested by those words, 'In thy light shall we see light.' 'As a man traveling by night kindled his torch, which, when it was extinguished, he again lit, and again, but at length exclaimed, "How long shall I weary myself in my way? Better to wait till the sun arise, and when the sun is shining I will pursue my journey,"—so the Israelites were oppressed in Egypt, but delivered by Moses and Aaron. Again, they were subdued by the Babylonians, when Channaniah, Misael, and Azariah delivered them. Again, they were subdued by the Grecians, when Mattathias and his sons helped them. At length the Romans overcame them, when they cried to God, "We are weary with the continual alteration of oppression and deliverance; we ask no further that mortal man may shine upon us but God, who is holy and blessed forever."' There is a fine one of the fox, which, seeing the fish in great trouble, daring hither and thither, while the stream was being drawn with nets, proposed to them to leap on dry land. This is put in a Rabbi's mouth, who, when the Graeco-Syrian kings were threatening with death all who observed the law, was counseled by his friends to abandon it. He would say, 'We, like the fish in the stream, are indeed in danger now; but yet, while we continue in obedience to God, we are in our proper element, and in one way or another may trust to live; but if, to escape one way or another may trust to live; but if, to escape the danger, we forsake that, then we inevitably perish.' Again, one of much tenderness explains why a proselyte is dearer to the Lord than even a Levite. Such proselyte is compared to a wild goat, which, brought up in a desert, joins itself freely to the flock, and which is cherished by the shepherd with especial love; since, that his flock which from its youth he had put forth in the morning and brought back at evening, should love him, was nothing strange; but that the goat, brought up in deserts and mountains, should attach itself to him, demanded an especial return of affection. There are besides these a multitude of briefer ones, *similitudes* rather than *parables*. Thus there is one, urging collection of spirit in prayer, to this effect: 'If a man brought a request to an earthly monarch, but, instead of making it, were to turn aside and talk with his neighbor, might not the king be justly displeased? In another, the death common to all, and the doom after death so different to each, is likened to a king's retinue entering a city at a single gate, but afterward lodged within it very differently, according to their several dignity. There is a singular one, to explain why God has not told which command should have the greatest reward for its keeping. In another it is shown how body and soul are partners in sin, and so will justly be partners in punishment.

These, among the Jewish parables, with two or three more, which, bearing some resemblance to Evangelical parables, will be noted in their due places, are the most memorable which I have met. The resemblance, it must be owned, even where the strongest, lies on the surface merely, and is nothing so extraordinary as is often given out. To some, indeed, the similarity has appeared so great, that it needed in one way or another to be accounted for. These have supposed that our Lord adopted such parables as would in any way fit his purpose, remodeling them and improving as they passed under his hands. Others have thought that the Jewish parables are of later origin in those in the

Gospels, and that the Rabbis, while they searched the Christian books for the purpose of ridiculing, or gainsaying them, enriched themselves with their spoils, borrowing materials which they afterwards turned to account, concealing carefully the quarter from whence these were derived. Lightfoot has a collection of such sayings under the title: *Wit stolen by the Jews out of the Gospel*; but neither here, nor in the parallels elsewhere adduced, is the resemblance so striking as to carry any conviction of the necessity, or even the probability, of a common origin. The hatred and scorn with which the Jews regarded all foreign literature, and most of all the sacred books of the Christians, make this last supposition extremely improbably.

The resemblance is such as could hardly have been avoided, when the same external life, and the same outward nature, were used as the common storehouse, from whence images, illustrations, and examples were derived alike by all. It may be well at once to consider one, and one of the best, among these Talmudical parables, which pretend to any similarity with our Lord's It has been sometimes likened to that later part of the Marriage of the King's Son, which relates to the wedding garment. 'The Rabbis have delivered what follows, on Eccl. 12:7, where it is written, "The spirit shall return unto God who gave it." He gave it to thee unspotted, see that thou restore it unspotted to Him again. It is like a mortal king, who distributed royal vestments to his servants. Then those that were wise folded them carefully up, and laid them by in the wardrobe; but those that were foolish went their way, and, clothed in these garments, engaged in their ordinary work. After a while, the king required his garments again: the wise returned them white as they had received them; but the foolish, soiled and stained. Then the king was well pleased with the wise, and said, "Let the vestments be laid up in the wardrobe, and let these depart in peace"; but he was angry with the foolish, and said, "Let the vestments be given to be washed, and those servants be cast into prison"—so will the Lord do with the bodies of the righteous, as it is written, Is. 57:2; with their souls, 1 Sam. 25:29; but with the bodies of the wicked, Is. 48:22; 57:21; and with their souls, 1 Sam. 25:29.' But, with the exception of a king appearing in each, and the praise and condemnation turning on a garment, what resemblance is there here? In fact, if we penetrate a little below the surface, there is more real similarity between this parable and that of the Talents, as in each case there is the restoration of a deposit, and a dealing with the servants according to their conduct in respect of that deposit. But then, how remote a likeness! How capricious everything here! The distributing of garments which were not to be worn, and afterwards reclaiming them—what resemblance has this to anything in actual life? How different from the probability that a nobleman, going into a distant country, should distribute his goods to his servants, and returning, demand from them an account.

This much in regard of the Jewish parables. Among the Fathers of the Christian Church there are not many who have deliberately constructed parables for the setting forth of spiritual mysteries. Two or three such we meet in the *Shepherd* of Hermas. The whole of its third book is indeed parabolical, as it sets forth spiritual truth under sensuous images, only it does this chiefly in visions, that is, in parables for the eye rather than for the ear. There are, however, parables in the strictest sense of the word; this, for example, which is an improved form of the rabbinical parable last quoted: 'Restore to the Lord the spirit entire as then hast received it: for if thou gavest to a fuller a garment which was entire, and desiredst so to receive it again, but the fuller restored it to thee rent, wouldest thou receive it? Wouldest thou not say in anger, "I delivered to thee my garment entire, wherefore hast thou torn it and made it useless? It is now, on account of the rent which thou hast made in it, of no more service to me." If thou then grievest for thy garment, and complainest because thou receivest it not entire again, how, thinkest thou, will the Lord deal with thee, who gave thee a perfect spirit, but which spirit thou hast marred, so that it can be of no more service to its Lord? For it became useless when it was corrupted by thee.' There are several parables, formally brought forward as such, in the writings of Ephraem Syrus, but such of these as I am acquainted with could scarcely be tamer than they are. Origen has what may be termed a parable, and a very striking one, by which he seeks to illustrate the peculiar character and method of St. Paul's teaching; its riches, its depths, its obscurities, its vast truths, only partially shown by him, and therefore only partially seen by us. The great characteristics of the Apostle's teaching have not often been so happily seized. Eadmer, a disciple of Anselm, has gathered up a basket of fragments from his sermons and his table-talk. Among these are so many of his similitudes and illustrations as to give a name to the whole collection. There are not a few complete parables here, though none perhaps of that beauty which the works coming directly from his hand might lead us to expect. In the works of St. Francis of Assisi there are two parables, but of little or not value. For better are those interspersed through the Greek religious romance of the seventh or eight century, *Barlaam and Josaphat*, ascribed to John of Damascus, and often printed with his works. They have been justly admired, yet more than one of them is certainly not original, being easily traced up to earlier sources. A very interesting one will be found in the note below. Those which are entitled parables in the writings of St. Bernard, and, whether they be his or no, having much of beauty and instruction in them, are rather allegories than parables, and so do not claim here to be considered.

But if parables, which are professedly such, occur rarely in the works of the early Church writers, the parabolical element is, notwithstanding, very predominant in their teaching, especially in their homilies, which are popular in the truest sense of the word. What boundless stores, for instance, of happy illustration, which might with the greatest ease be thrown into the forms of parables, are laid up in the writings of St. Augustine. One is only perplexed, amid the endless variety, what instances to select: but we may take this one as an example. He is speaking of the Son of God and the sinner as in the same world, and appearing under the same conditions of humanity: 'But,' he proceeds, 'how vast a distance there is between the prisoner in his dungeon, and the visitor that has come to see him! They are both within the walls of the dungeon: those who did not know might suppose them under equal restraint, but one is the compassionate visitor, who can use his freedom when he will, the other is fast bound there for his offenses. So great is the difference between Christ, the compassionate visitor of man, and man himself, the criminal in bondage for his offenses.' Or, rebuking them that date in their ignorance to find fault with the arrangements of Providence: 'If you entered the workshop of a blacksmith, you would not dare to find the skill of the workman, but the consideration of a man, what would you say? "It is not without cause the bellows are placed here; the artificer knew, though I do not know, the reason." You would not venture to find fault with the blacksmith in his shop, and do you dare to find fault with God in the world?' Chrysostom, too, is rich in similitudes, which need nothing to be parables, except that they should be presented for such; as for instance, when speaking of the redemption of the creature, which shall accompany the manifestation of the sons of God, he says, 'To what is the creation like? It is like a nurse that has brought up a royal child, and when he ascends his paternal throne, she too rejoices with him, and is partaker of the benefit.' But the field here opening before me is too wide to enter on. It is of the parables of our Lord, and of those only, that I propose to speak.

The Parables

1.
The Sower

Matt. 13:3–8, and 18:23; Mark 4:4–8, and 14–21;

Luke 8:5–8, and 11–15

On the relation in which the seven prables recorded in the thirteenth chapter of St. Matthew, of which this of the Sower is the first, stand to one another, there will be need to say something. But this will best follow after they have all received their separate treatment; and till then, therefore, I shall defer it.

It is the evident intention of the Evangelist to present these parables as the first which the Lord spoke, this of the Sower introducing a manner of teaching which He had not hitherto employed. As much is indicated in the question of the disciples, 'Why speakest Thou unto them in parables?' (v. 10), and in our Lord's answer (vv. 11–17), in which He justifies his use of this method of teaching, and declares his purpose in adopting it; it is involved no less in his treatment of this parable as the fundamental one, on the right understanding of which will depend their comprehension of all which are to follow: *'Know ye not this parable? And how then will ye know all parables/"* (Mark 4:13). And as this was the first occasion on which He brought forth these new things out of his treasure (see verse 22), so was it the occasion on which He brought them forth with the largest hand. We have nowhere else in the Gospels so rich a group of parables assembled together, so many and so costly pearls strung upon a single thread.

It will not be lost labor to set before ourselves at the outset as vividly as we can, what the aspects of that outward nature were, with which our Lord and the multitudes were surrounded, as He uttered, and they listened to, these divine words. *'Jesus went out*

from the house,' probably at Capernaum, which was the city where
He commonly dwelt after his open ministry began (Matt. 4:13), 'his
own city' (Matt. 9:1), 'which is upon the seacoast,' and, going out,
He *'sat by the sea-side,'* that is, by the lake of Genesaret, the scene of
so many incidents in his ministry. This lake, called in the Old
Testament 'the sea of Chinnereth' (Num. 34:11; Josh. 12:3; 13:27),
from a town of that name which stood near its shore (Josh. 19:35),
'the water of Gennesar' (1 Macc. 11:67), now Bahr Tabaria, goes by
many names in the Gospels. It is simply 'the sea' (Matt. 4:15; Mark
4:1), invariably in St. Luke, either 'the lake' (8:22), or 'the lake of
Genesaret' (v. 1); sometimes, but this only in St. John, 'the sea of
Tiberias,' from the great heathen city of Tiberias on its shores (6:1;
21:1); being indeed no more than an inland sheet of water, of moderate extent, some sixteen miles in length, and not more than six in
breadth. But it might well claim regard for its beauty, if not for its
extent. The Jewish writers would have it that it was beloved of God
above all the waters of Canaan; and indeed, almost all ancient authors who have mentioned it speak in glowing terms of the beauty
and rich fertility of its banks. Hence, as some say, its name of
Genesaret, or 'the garden of riches,' but the derivation is insecure.
And even now, when the land is crushed under the rod of Turkish
misrule, many traces of its former beauty remain, many evidences
of the fertility which its shores will again assume in the day which
assuredly cannot be very far off, when that rod shall be lightened
from them. It is true that the olive-gardens and vineyards, which
once crowned the high and romantic hills bounding it on the east
and the west, have disappeared; but the citron, the orange, and the
date-tree are still found there in rich abundance; and in the higher
regions the products of a more temperate zone meet together with
these; while, lower down, its banks are still covered with aromatic
shrubs, and its waters, as of old, are still sweet and wholesome to
drink, and always cool, clear, and transparent to the very bottom,
and as gently breaking on the fine white sand with which its shores
are strewn as they did when the feet of the Son of God trod those
sands, or walked upon those waters. On the edge of this beautiful
lake the multitude were assembled; the place was convenient, for,
'whilst the lake is almost completely surrounded by mountains,
those mountains never come down into the water; but always leave
a beach of greater or lesser extent along the water's edge.' Their
numbers were such, that probably, as on another day (Luke 5:1),
they pressed upon the Lord, so that He found it convenient to enter

into a ship; and putting off a little from the shore, He taught them from it, speaking *'many things unto them in parables.'*

First in order is the parable of the Sower; common to the three synoptic Gospels; being with that of the Wicked Husbandmen the only two which they all possess alike. It rests, as so many others, on one of the common familiar doings of daily life. Christ, lifting up his eyes, may have seen at no great distance a husbandman scattering his seed in the furrows, may have taken in, indeed, the whole scenery of the parable. As it belongs to the essentially popular nature of the Gospels, that parables should be found in them rather than in the Epistles, where indeed they never appear, so it belongs to the popular character of the parable, that it should thus rest upon the familiar doings of common life, the matters which occupy

'the talk
Man holds with week-day man in the hourly walk
Of the world's business';

while the Lord, using these to set forth eternal and spiritual truths, at the same time ennobles them, showing them continually to reveal and set forth the deepest mysteries of his kingdom. *'A sower went forth to sow'*—what a dignity and significance have these few words, used as the Lord uses them here, given in all after-times to the toils of the husbandman in the furrow.

The comparison of the relations between the teacher and the taught to those between the sower and the soil, the truth communicated being the seed sown, rests on analogies between the worlds of nature and of spirit so true and so profound, that we must not wonder to find it of frequent recurrence; and this, not merely in Scripture (1 Pet. 1:23; 1 John 3:9), but in the writings of all wiser heathens who have realized at all what teaching means, and what sort of influence the spirit of one man may exercise on the spirits of his fellows. While all words, even of men, which are better than mere breath, are as seeds, able to take root in their minds and hearts who hear them, have germs in them which only unfold by degrees; how eminently must this be true of the words of God, and of these uttered by Him who was Himself the seminal Word which He communicated. Best right of all to the title of seed has that word, which exercising no partial operation on their hearts who receive it, wholly transforms and renews them—that word of living and expanding truth by which men are born anew into the kingdom of God, and which in its effects 'endureth forever' (1 Pet. 1:23, 25). I cannot doubt that the Lord intended to set Himself forth as the chief sower of the seed (not, of course, to the exclusion of the Apostles and their successors), that here, as in the next parable, *'he that soweth the good seed'* is the Son of man; and this, even though He nowhere, in as many words, announces Himself as such. His entrance into the world was a going forth to sow; the word of the kingdom, which word He first proclaimed, was his seed; the hearts of men his soil; while others were only able to sow, because He had sown first, they did but carry on the work which He had auspicated and begun.

"*And when he sowed, some seeds fell by the way side* [*and it was trodden down* (Luke 8:5)], *and the fowls came, and devoured them up.'* Some, that is, fell on the hard footpath or road, where the glebe was not broken, and so could not sink down in the earth, but lay exposed on the surface to the feet of passers-by, till at length it fell an easy prey to the birds, such as in the East are described as following in large flocks the husbandman, to gather up, if they can, the seed-corn which he has scattered. We may indeed see the same nearer home. This parable is one of the very few, whereof we possess an authentic interpretation from the Lord's own lips; and these words He thus explains: *'When anyone heareth the word of the kingdom, and understandeth it not, then cometh the Wicked One, and catcheth away that which was sown in his heart.'* In. St. Luke, Satan appears yet more distinctly as the adversary and hinderer of the kingdom of God (of whom as such there will be fitter opportunity of speaking in the following parable), the reason why he snatches the word away being added—*'lest they should believe and be saved.'* How natural it would have been to interpret *'the fowls'* impersonally, as signifying, in a general way, worldly influences hostile to the truth. How almost inevitably, if left to ourselves, we should have so done. Not so, however, the Lord. He beholds the kingdom of evil as it counterworks the kingdom of God gathered up in a personal head, *'the Wicked One.'*

The words which St. Matthew alone records, *'and understandeth it not,'* do much for helping us to comprehend what this first condition of mind and heart is, in which the word of God fails to produce even a passing effect. The man *'understandeth it not'*; he does not recognize himself as standing in any relation to the word which he hears, or to the kingdom of grace which that word proclaims.

All that speaks of man's connection with a higher invisible world, all that speaks of sin, of redemption, of holiness, is unintelligible to him, and without significance. But how has he arrived at this state? He has brought himself to it; he has exposed his heart as a common road to every evil influence of the world, till it has become hard as a pavement, till he has laid waste the very soil in which the word of God should have taken root: he has not submitted it to the ploughshare of the law, which would have broken it up; which, if he had suffered it to do its appointed work, would have gone before, preparing that soil to receive the seed of the Gospel. But what renders his case the more hopeless, and takes away even a possibility of the word germinating there, is, that besides the evil condition of the soil, there is also *one* watching to take advantage of that evil condition, to use every weapon that man puts into his hands, against man's salvation; and he, lest by possibility such a hearer *'should believe and be saved,'* sends his ministers in the shape of evil thoughts, worldly desires, carnal lusts; and so, as St. Mark records it, *'cometh immediately and taketh away the word that was sown in their hearts.' 'This is he which received seed by the way side.'*

There was other seed, which promised at the first to have, but in the end had not truly any, better success. *'Some fell upon stony places, where they had not much earth; and forthwith they sprung up, because they had no deepness of earth. And when the sun was up, they were scorched; and because they had not root, they withered away.'* The *'stony places'* here are to be explained by the *'rock'* of St. Luke, and it is important that the words in St. Matthew, or rather in our Version (for *'rocky* places'—as, indeed, the Rhemish Version has it—would have made all clear), do not lead us astray. A soil, mingled with stones is not meant; these, however numerous or large, would not certainly hinder the roots from striking deeply downward; for those roots, with an instinct of their own, would feel and find their way, penetrating between the interstices of the stones, till they reached the moisture below. But what is meant is ground such as to a great extent is that of Palestine, where a thin superficial coating of mold covers the surface of a rock; this stretching below it, would present a barrier beyond which it would be wholly impossible that the roots could penetrate, to draw up supplies of nourishment from beneath. While the seed had fallen on shallow earth, therefore the plant the sooner appeared above the surface; and while the rock below hindered it from striking deeply downward, it put forth its energies the more luxuriantly in the stalk. It sprang up without delay, but rooted in no deep soil; and because therefore *'it lacked moisture,'* it was unable to resist the scorching heat of the sun, and being smitten by that, withered and died.

We recur again to the Lord's interpretation of his own words: *'But he that received the seed into stony places, the same is he that heareth the word, and anon with joy receiveth it.'* Though the issue proves the same in this case as in the last, the promise is very different. So far from the heart of this class of hearers appearing irreceptive of the truth, the good news of the kingdom is received at once, and with gladness. The joy itself is most appropriate. How should not he be glad, whom the glad tidings have reached (Acts 8:8; 16:34; Gal. 5:22; 1 Pet. 1:6)? But alas! In this case the joy thus suddenly conceived is not, as the sequel too surely proves, a joy springing up from the contemplation of the greatness of the benefit, even after all the counterbalancing costs, and hazards, and sacrifices, have been taken into account, but a joy which springs from an overlooking and leaving out of calculation those costs and hazards. It is this which fatally differences the joy of this class of hearers from that of the finder of the treasure (Matt. 13:44), who 'for joy thereof' went and *sold all that he had,* that he might purchase the field which contained the treasure—that is, was willing to deny himself all things, and to suffer all things, that he might win Christ. We have rather here a state of mind not stubbornly repelling the truth, but woefully lacking in all deeper earnestness; such as that of the multitudes that went with Jesus, unconscious what his discipleship involved—to whom He turned and told, in plainest and most startling words, what the conditions of that discipleship were (Luke 14:25–33; Josh. 24:19). This is exactly what the hearer now described has not done; whatever was fair and beautiful in Christianity as it first presents itself, had attracted him—its sweet and comfortable promises, the moral loveliness of its doctrines; but not its answer to the deepest needs of the human heart; as neither, when he received the word with gladness, had he contemplated the having to endure hardness in his warfare with sin and Satan and the world; and this will explain all which follows: *'Yet hath he not root in himself, but dureth for a while; for when tribulation or persecution ariseth because of the word, by and by he is offended.'* It is not here as in the last case, that Satan needs merely to come and take the word out of the heart without further trouble. That word has found some place there, and it needs that he bring some hostile influences to bear against it. What he brings in the present case are outward or inward trials, these being compared to the burning heat of the sun. It is true that the light and warmth of the sun are more often used to set forth the genial and comfortable workings of God's grace (Mal. 4:2; Matt. 5:45; Is. 60:19, 20); but not always, for see Ps. 121:6; Is. 49:10; Rev. 7:16. As that heat, had the plant been rooted deeply enough, would have furthered its growth, and hastened its ripening, fitting it for the sickle and the barn—so these tribulations would have furthered the growth in grace of the true Christian, and ripened him for heaven. But as the heat scorches the blade which has no deepness of earth, and has sprung up on a shallow ground, so the troubles and afflictions which would have strengthened a true faith, cause a faith which was merely temporary to fail. When these afflictions for the truth's sake arrive, '*he is offended*,' as though some strange thing had happened to him: for then are the times of sifting, and of winnowing; and then, too, every one that has no root, or as St. Matthew describes it, '*no root in himself*,' no inward root, falls away.

The having of such an inward root here would answer to having a foundation on the rock, to having oil in the vessels, elsewhere (Matt. 7:25; 25:4). It is not an unfrequent image in Scripture (Eph. 3:17; Col. 2:7; Jer. 17:8; Hos. 9:16; Job 19:28); and has a peculiar fitness and beauty, for as the roots of a tree are out of sight, while yet from them it derives its firmness and stability, so upon the hidden life of the Christian, that life which is out of the sight of other men, his firmness and stability depend; and as it is through the hidden roots that the nourishment is drawn up to the stem and branches, and the leaf continues green, and the tree does not cease from bearing fruit, even so in that life which 'is hid with Christ in God' lie the sources of the Christian's strength and of his spiritual prosperity. Such a '*root in himself*' had Peter, who, when many were offended and drew back, exclaimed, 'To whom shall we go? Thou has the words of eternal life' (John 6:68). So, again, when the Hebrew Christians took joyfully the spoiling of their goods, knowing in themselves that they had 'in heaven a better and an enduring substance' (Heb. 10:34), this knowledge, this faith concerning their unseen inheritance, was the root which enabled them joyfully to take that loss, and not to draw back unto perdition, as so many had done. Compare 2 Cor. 4:17, 18, where faith in the unseen eternal things is the root, which, as St. Paul declares, enables him to count the present affliction light, and to endure to the end (cf. Heb. 11:26).

Demas, on the other hand, lacked that root. It might at first sight
seem as if he would be more correctly ranged under the third class
of hearers; since he forsook Paul, 'having loved this present world'
(2 Tim. 4:10). But when we examine more closely Paul's condition
at Rome at the moment when Demas forsook him, we find it one of
extreme outward trial and danger. It would seem then more probable that the immediate cause of his going back, was the tribulation
which came for the word's sake.

But there is other seed, of which the fortunes are still to be told.
'And some fell among thorns'; as fields were often divided by hedges
of thorn (Ex. 22:6; Mic. 7:4), this might easily come to pass (Jer. 4:3;
Job 5:5); *'and the thorns sprung up, and choked them,'* or as Wiclif has,
'strangled it,' so that, as St. Mark adds, *'it yielded no fruit,'* This seed
fell not so much among thorns that were full grown, as in ground
where the roots of these had not been diligently extirpated, in
ground which had not been thoroughly purged and cleansed; otherwise it could not be said that *'the thorns sprang up with it'* (luke
8:7). They grew together; only the thorns over-topped the good
seed, shut them out from the air and light, drew away from their
roots the moisture and richness of earth by which they should have
been nourished. No wonder that they pined and dwindled in the
shade, grew dwarfed and stunted, for the best of the soil did not
feed them—forming, indeed, a blade, but unable to form a full corn
in the ear, or to bring any fruit to perfection. It is not here, as in the
first case, that there was no soil, or none deserving the name; nor
yet, as in the second case, that there was a poor or shallow soil.
Here there was no lack of soil—it might be good soil; but what
lacked was a careful husbandry, a diligent eradication of the mischievous growths, which, unless rooted up, would oppress and
strangle whatever sprang up in their midst.

This section of the parable the Lord thus explains: *'He also that
received seed among the thorns is he that heareth the word; and the care of
this world, and the deceitfulness of riches [and the lusts of other things entering in* (Mark 4:19)] *choke the word, and he becometh unfruitful,'* or as
St. Luke gives it, *'they bring no fruit to perfection.'* It is not here, as in
the first case, that the word of God is totally ineffectual, nor yet, as
in the second case, that after a temporary obedience to the truth,
there is an evident falling away from it, such as the withering of the
stalk indicates: the profession of a spiritual life is retained, the
'name to live' still remains; but the power of godliness is by degrees eaten out and has departed. And to what disastrous influ-

ences are these mournful effects attributed? To two things, the care of this world and its pleasures; these are the thorns and briers that strangle the life of the soul. It may sound strange at first hearing that two causes apparently so diverse should yet be linked together, and have the same hurtful operation ascribed to them. But the Lord, in fact, here presents to us this earthly life on its two sides, under its two aspects. There is, first, its oppressive crushing side, the poor man's toil how to live at all, to keep the wolf from the door, the struggle for a daily subsistence, *'the care of this life,'* which, if not met in faith, hinders the thriving of the spiritual word in the heart. But life has a flattering as well as a threatening side, its pleasures no less than its cares; and as those who have heard and received with gladness the word of the kingdom are still in danger of being crushed by the cares of life, so, no less, of being deceived by its flatteries and its allurements. The old man is not dead in them; it may seem dead for a while, so long as the first joy on account of the treasure found endures; but, unless mortified in earnest, will presently revive in all its strength anew. Unless the soil of the heart be diligently watched, the thorns and briers, of which it seemed a thorough clearance had been made, will again grow up apace, and choke the good seed. While that which God promises is felt to be good, but also what the world promises is felt to be good also, and a good of the same kind, instead of a good merely and altogether subordinate to the other, an attempt will be made to combine the service of the two, to serve God and mammon. But the attempt will be in vain: they who make it will bring no fruit to perfection, will fail to bring forth those perfect fruits of the Spirit which it was the purpose of the word of God to produce in them.

But it is not all the seed which thus sooner or later perishes. The spiritual husbandman is to sow in hope, knowing that with the blessing of the Lord he will not always sow in vain, that a part will prosper. *'But other fell into good ground, and brought forth fruit, some a hundredfold, some sixtyfold, some thirtyfold.'* St. Luke says simply, *'and bare fruit a hundredfold,'* leaving out the two lesser proportions of return; which St. Mark gives, but reverses the order of the three, beginning from the lowest return, and ascending to the highest. The return of a hundred for one is not unheard of in the East, though always mentioned as something extraordinary; thus it is said of Isaac, that he sowed, 'and received in the same year a hundredfold, and the Lord blessed him' (Gen. 26:120; and other examples of the same kind are not wanting.

We learn that *'he that received seed into the good ground, is he that heareth the word, and understandeth it; which also beareth fruit, and bringeth forth, some a hundredfold, some sixty, some thirty,'* or, with the important variation of St. Luke, *"That on the good ground are they, which in an honest and good heart, having heard the word, keep it, and bring forth fruit with patience'*—important, because in these words comes distinctly forward a difficulty, which equally existed in every record of the parable, but might in the others have been overlooked and evaded; while yet on its right solution a successful interpretation must altogether depend. What is this *'honest and good heart?'* How can any heart be called *'good'* before the Word and the Spirit have made it so? And yet here the seed *finds* a good soil, does not *make* it. The same question elsewhere recurs, as when Christ declares, 'He that is of God heareth God's words' (John 8:47); and again, 'Every one that is of the truth heareth my voice' (John 18:37). For who in this sinful world can be called 'of the truth?' Is it not the universal doctrine of Scripture that men *become* 'of the truth' through hearing Christ's words, not that they hear his words because they are 'of the truth'; that the heart is good, through receiving the word; not that it receives the word, because it is good? This is certainly the scriptural doctrine, and he teaches *preposterously*, to use the word in its most proper sense, who teaches otherwise. At the same time those passages in St. John, and the words before us, with much else in Scripture, bear witness to the fact that there are conditions of heart which yield readier entrance to the truth than others—'being of the truth'—'being of God'—'doing the truth'— 'having the soil of *an honest and good heart'*—all pointing in this direction. Inasmuch as these all express a condition *anterior* to hearing God's word—to coming to the light—to bringing forth fruit—they cannot indicate a state of mind and heart in which the truth, in the highest sense of that word, is positive and realized, but only one in which there is a preparedness to receive and to retain it. There is none good but One (Matt. 19:17); and yet the Scripture speaks often of *good* men: even so no heart is absolutely a good soil; yet relatively it may be affirmed of some, that their hearts are a soil fitter for receiving the seed of everlasting life than those of others. Thus the 'son of peace' will alone receive the message of peace (Luke 10:6; Matt. 10:13; cf. Acts 13:48), while yet only the reception of that message will make him truly and in the highest sense a 'son of peace.' He was before, indeed, a *latent* son of peace, but it is the Gospel which first makes actual that which hitherto was only potential. And thus the preaching of the word may be likened to the scattering of sparks, which, where they find tinder, fasten there, and kindle into a flame; where they do not find it, expire; or that word of the truth may be regarded as a loadstone thrust in among the world's rubbish, attracting to itself all particles of true metal, which but for it *would* never, as they *could* never, have extricated themselves from the surrounding mass, however they testify their affinity to the loadstone, now that it is brought in contact with them.

Exactly thus among those to whom the word of the Gospel came, there were two divisions of men, and the same will always subsist in the world. There were, first, the false-hearted, who called evil good and good evil, who loved their darkness, and hated the light that would make that darkness manifest (John 3:20; Eph. 5:13), who, when that light of the Lord shone round about them, only drew further back into their own darkness; self-excusers and self-justifiers; such as were for the most part the Scribes and the Pharisees with whom He came in contact. But there were also others, sinners as well, often, as regards actual transgression of positive law, much greater sinners than those first, but who yet acknowledged their evil—had no wish to alter the everlasting relations between right and wrong—who, when the light appeared, did not refuse to be drawn to it, even though they knew that it would condemn their darkness, that it would require an entire renewing of their hearts and remodeling of their lives: such were the Matthews and the Zacchaeuses, and sinful women not a few, with all who confessed their deeds, justifying not themselves but God. Not that I would prefer to instance these as examples of the '*good and honest heart,*' except in so far as it is needful to guard against a Pelagian abuse of the phrase, and to show how the Lord's language here does not condemn even great and grievous sinners to an incapacity for receiving the word of life. Nathanael would be a yet more perfect specimen of the class referred to—the 'Israelite indeed, in whom was no guile' (John 1:47), in other words, the man with the soil of '*an honest and good heart,*' fitted for receiving and nourishing the word of everlasting life, and for bringing forth fruity with patience; one of a simple, truthful, earnest nature; who had been faithful to the light which he had, diligent in the performance of the duties which he knew, who had not been resisting God's preparation in him for imparting to him at the last his best gift, even the knowledge of his Son; who with all this, knowing himself a sinner, did not affirm that he was righteous. For we must keep ever in mind that the good soil as much comes from God as the seed which is to find there its home. The law and the preaching of repentance, God's secret and preventing grace, run before the preaching of the word of the kingdom; and thus when that word comes, it finds men with a less or a greater readiness to receive it for what indeed it is, a word of eternal life.

When the different measures of prosperity are given, the seed bringing forth 'some a hundredfold, some sixtyfold, some thirtyfold,' it seem difficult to determine whether these indicate different degrees of fidelity in those that receive the truth, according to which they bring forth fruit unto God more or less abundantly; or rather different spheres of action, more or less wide, which they are appointed to occupy—as in another parable to one servant were given five talents commited to him, though these talents were many more in one case than in the other (Luke 19:16–19): probably the former. The words which St. Luke records (v. 18), 'Take heed therefore how ye hear: for whosoever hath, to him shall be given; and whosoever hat not from him shall be taken even that which he seemeth to have' (cf. Mark 4:33), are very important for the avoiding of a misunderstanding, which else might easily have arisen here. The disciples might have been in danger of supposing that these four conditions of heart, in which the word found its hearers, were permanent, immutable, and fixed forevermore; and therefore that in one heart the word must flourish, in another that it could never germinate at all, in others that it could only prosper for a little while. There is no such immoral fatalism in Scripture. It left to the Gnostics to range men in two classes, one capable of a higher life, and the other incapable. All it declares to be capable; even as it summons all to be partakers of the same; and the warning, 'Take heed how ye hear,' testifies as much, for it tells us that in each case, according as the word is heard and received, will its success be— that, while it is indeed true that all which has gone before in a man's life will greatly influence the manner of his reception of that word, for every event will have tended wither to the improving or the deteriorating of the soil of his heart, and will therefore render it more or less probably that the seeds of God's word will prosper there, yet it lies on every man now to take heed how he hears, and through this taking heed to insure, with God's blessing, that it shall bring forth in him fruit that shall remain (James 1:21).

For while it is true, and the thought is a very awful one, that there is such a thing as laying waste the very soil in which the seed of eternal life should have taken root—that every act of sin, of un- faithfulness to the light within us, is, as it were, a treading of the ground into more hardness, so that the seed shall not sink in it—or a wasting of the soil, so that the seed shall find no nutriment there—or a fitting of it to a kindlier nourishing of thorns and briers than of good seed—yet on the other hand, even for those who have brought themselves into these evil conditions, a recovery is still, through the grace of God, possible: the hard soil may again become soft—the shallow soil may become rich and deep—and the soil beset with thorns open and clear. For the heavenly seed in this dif- fers from the earthly, that the latter, as it finds, so it must use its soil, for it cannot alter its nature. But the heavenly seed, if acted upon by the soil where it is cast, also reacts more mightily upon it, soft- ening it where it was hard (Jer. 23:29), deepening it where it was shallow, cutting up and extirpating the roots of evil where it was encumbered with these; and, wherever it is allowed free course, transforming and ennobling each of these inferior soils, till it has become that which man's heart was at the beginning and before the Fall; good ground, fit to afford nourishment to that divine word, the seed of everlasting life (1 Pet. 1:23–25).

2.
The Tares

Matthew 13:24–30, and 36–43

Another parable put He forth unto them, saying, The king-dom of heaven is likened unto a man which sowed good seed in his field: but while men slept, his enemy came and sowed tares among the wheat, and went his way.' Our Lord did not imagine here a form of malice without example, but adduced one which may have been familiar enough to his hearers, one so easy of execution, involving so little risk, and yet effecting so great and lasting a mischief, that it is not strange, where cowardice and mal-ice met, that they should have often displayed themselves in this shape. We meet traces of it in many quarters. In Roman law the possibility of this form of injury is contemplated; and a modern writer, illustrating Scripture from the manners and habits of the East, with which he had become familiar through a sojourn there, affirms the same to be now practised in India. 'See,' he says, 'that lurking villain watching for the time when his neighbor shall plough his field: he carefully marks the period when the work has been finished, and goes in the night following, and casts in what the natives call pandinellu, i.e. pig-paddy; this being of rapid growth, springs up before the good seed, and scatters itself before the other can be reaped, so that the poor owner of the field will be for years before he can get rid of the troublesome weed. But there is another noisome plant which these wretches cast into the ground of those they hate, called perum-pirandi, which is more destructive to vegetation than any other plant. Has a man purchased a field out of the hands of another, the offended person says, "I will plant the perum-pirandi in his grounds."'

Of this parable also we have an authentic interpretation from the lips which uttered it. And this is well: for on the interpretation of it very much has turned before now. References or allusions to it occur at every turn of the controversy which the Church maintained with the Donatists; and its whole exposition will need to be carried out with an eye to questions which may seem out of date, but which, in one shape or another, continually reappear, and demand to receive their solution. There can be no question who is the Sower of the good seed here. *'He that sowed the good seed is the Son of man.'* This title, by which our Lord most often designates Himself, is only in a single instance given to Him by another (Acts 7:56), and then can hardly indicate more than that the glorified Savior appeared, wearing still a human shape, to the eyes of Stephen. To the Jews this name, though drawn from the Old Testament, from the great apocalyptic vision of Daniel (7:13), was so strange, that when they heard it, they asked, 'Who is this Son of man?' (John 12:34); not 'Son of man,' but 'Son of David,' being the popular name for the expected Messiah (Matt. 9:27; 12:23; 15:22; 20:31, &c.). He claimed by this title a true participation in our human nature; this, and much more than this. He was 'Son of man,' as alone realizing all which in the idea of man was contained—as the second Adam, the head and representative of the race—the one true and perfect flower which had ever unfolded itself out of the root and stalk of humanity. Claiming this title for his own, He witnessed against opposite poles of error concerning his person—the Ebionite, to which the exclusive use of the title 'Son of David' might have led, and the Gnostic, which denied the reality of the human nature that He bore.

But if Christ is the Sower in this, exactly in the same sense as in the preceding, parable, the seed here receives an interpretation different from that which it there obtained. There 'the seed is the word of God' (Luke 8:11), or 'the word of the kingdom'; here *'the good seed are the children of the kingdom.'* And yet there is no real disagreement; only a *progress* from that parable to this. In that, the word of God is the instrument by which men are born anew and become children of the kingdom (James 1:88; 1 Pet. 1:23); in this that word has done its work; has been received into hearts; is incorporated with living men; is so vitally united with them who through it have been made children of the kingdom, that the two cannot any more be contemplated asunder (cf. Jer. 31:27; Hos. 2:23; Zech. 10:9).

The next words, *'The field is the world,'* at once bring us into the heart of that controversy referred to already. Over these few words, simple as they may seem, there has perhaps been more of fighting than over any single phrase in the Scripture, if we except the consecrating words at the Holy Eucharist. Apart from mere personal questions affecting the regularity of certain ordinations, the grounds on which the Donatists of Africa justified their separation from the Church Catholic were these: The idea of the Church, they said, is that of a perfectly holy body; holiness is not merely *one* of its essential predicates, but *the* essential, its exclusive note. They did not deny that hypocrites might possibly lie concealed in its bosom; but where the evidently ungodly are suffered to remain in communion with it, not separated off by the exercise of godly discipline, there it forfeits the character of the true Church, and the faithful must come out from it, if they would not, by contact with these unholy, themselves be defiled. Such was the position, in support of which they urged Is. 52:1, and all such Scriptures as spoke of the Church's future freedom from all evil. These were meant, they said, to apply to it in its present condition; and consequently, where they failed to apply, *there* could not be the Church.

On this, as on so many other points, the Church owes to Augustine, not the forming of her doctrine, for that she can owe to no man, but the bringing out into her own clear consciousness that which hitherto she had implicitly possessed, yet had not wrought out into a perfect clearness even for herself. He replied, not gainsaying the truth which the Donatists proclaimed, that holiness is an essential note of the Church; but only refusing to accept their definition of that holiness, and showing that in the Church which they had forsaken this note was to be found, and combined with other as essential ones—catholicity, for instance, to which *they* could make no claim. The Church Catholic, he replied, despite all appearances to the contrary, *is* a holy body, for they only are its members who are in true and living fellowship with Christ, and therefore partakers of his sanctifying Spirit. All others, however they may have the outward marks of belonging to it, are *in* it, but not *of* it: they *press* upon Christ, as the thronging multitude; they do not *touch* Him, as did that believing woman, on whom alone his virtue went forth (Luke 8:45). There are certain outward conditions without which one cannot belong to his Church, but with which one does not of necessity do so. And they who are thus in it, but not of it, whether hypocrites lying hid, or open offenders who from their numbers may not without worse inconveniences ensuing be

expelled, do not defile the true members, so long as these neither
share in their spirit, nor communicate with their evil deeds. They
are like the unclean animals in the same ark as the clean (Gen. 7:2),
goats in the same pastures with the sheep (Matt. 25:32), bad fish in
the same net with the good (Matt. 13:47), chaff on the same barn-
floor as the grain (Matt. 3:13), vessels to dishonor in the same great
house with the vessels to honor (2 Tim. 2:20), or, as here, tares
growing in the same field with the wheat, endured for a while, but
in the end to be separated from it, and forever.

The Donatists would have fain made the Church, in its visible
form and historic manifestation, identical and coextensive with the
true Church which the Lord knoweth and not man. Augustine also
affirmed the *identity* of the church now existing with the final and
glorious Church; but denied that the two were coextensive. For
now the Church is clogged with certain accretions, which shall
hereafter be shown *not* to belong, and never to have belonged, to it.
He did not affirm, as his opponents charged him, two Churches,
but two conditions of one Church; the present, in which evil is endured in it; the future, in which it shall be free from all evil—not
two bodies of Christ; but one body, in which now are wicked men,
but only as evil humors in the natural body, which in the day of
perfect health will be expelled and rejected altogether, as never
having more than accidentally belonged to it; and he laid especial
stress upon this fact, that the Lord Himself had not contemplated
his Church, in its present state, as perfectly free from evil. At this
point of the controversy the present parable and that of the Draw-
net came in. From these he concluded that, as tares are mingled
with wheat, and bad fish with good, so the wicked shall be with the
righteous, and shall remain so mingled to the end of the present
age; and this not merely as a historic fact; but that all attempts to
have it otherwise are, in this parable at least, expressly forbidden
(v. 29). The Donatists were acting as the servants would have done,
if, in face of the householder's distinct prohibition, they had gone
and sought forcibly to root out the tares.

The Donatists were put to hard shifts to escape these conclusions. They did, however, make answer thus: 'By *"the world"* (v. 38);
the parable, therefore, does not whether ungodly men should be
endured *in the world* (Which we all allow), but whether they should
be suffered *in the Church.*' It must, however, be evident to every one
not warped by a previous dogmatic interest, that the parable is, as
the Lord announces, concerning 'the kingdom of heaven,' or the

Church. It required no special teaching to acquaint the disciples that *in the world* there would ever be a mixture of good and bad; while they could have so little expected the same in the Church, that it behoved to warn them before hand, both that they might not be offended, counting the promises of God to have failed, and also that they might know how to behave themselves, when that mystery of iniquity, now foretold, should begin manifestly to work. Nor need the term *'world'* here used perplex us in the least. No narrower term would have sufficed for Him, in whose prophetic eye the word of the Gospel was contemplated as going forth into all lands, as seed scattered in every part of the great outfield of the nations.

It was *'while men slept'* that the enemy sowed his tares among the wheat. Many have found this statement significant, have understood it to suggest negligence and lack of watchfulness on the part of the rulers in the Church, whereby ungodly men creep into it unawares, introducing errors in doctrine and in practice (Acts 20:29, 30; Jude 4: 2 Pet. 2:1, 2, 19); even as the sleeping of the wise virgins no less than the foolish has been sometimes urged in the same sense (Matt. 25:5). There is, alas! Always more or less of this negligence; yet I cannot think that it was meant to be noted here; and as little there. If any should have watched, it is *'the servants'*; but they first appear at a later period in the story; nor is any want of due vigilance laid to their charge. The men therefore who slept are not, as I take it, those who should or could have done otherwise, but the phrase is equivalent to 'at night,' and must not be further urged (Job 33:15; Mark 4:27). This enemy seized his opportunity, when all eyes were closed in sleep, and wrought the secret mischief upon which he was intent, and having wrought it undetected, withdrew.

'The enemy that sowed them is the devil.' We behold Satan here, not as he works beyond the limits of the Church, deceiving the world, but in his far deeper malignity, as he at once mimics and counterworks the work of Christ: in the words of Chrysostom, 'after the prophets, the false prophets; after the Apostles, the false apostles; after Christ, Antichrist.' Most worthy of notice is the plainness with which the doctrine concerning Satan and his agency, his active hostility to the blessedness of man, of which there is so little in the Old Testament, comes out in the New; as in the parable of the Sower, and again in this. As the lights become brighter, the shadows become deeper. Not till the mightier power

of good had been revealed, were men suffered to know how mighty was the power of evil; and even now it is only to the innermost circle of disciples that the explanation concerning Satan is given. Nor is it less observable that Satan is spoken of as *his* enemy, the enemy of the Son of man; for here, as so often, the great conflict is set forth as rather between Satan and the Son of man, than between Satan and God. It was essential to the scheme of redemption, that the victory over evil should be a *moral* triumph, not one obtained by a mere putting forth of superior strength. For this end it was most important that man, who lost the battle should also win it (1 Cor. 15:21); and therefore as by and through man the kingdom of darkness was to be overthrown, so the enmity of the Serpent was specially directed against the seed of the woman, the Son of man. In the title 'the wicked one,' which he bears, the article is emphatic, and points him out as the absolutely evil, the very *ground* of whose being is evil. For as God is light, and in Him is no darkness at all (1 John 1:5; James 1:17), so Satan is darkness, and in him is no light at all; 'there is *no* truth in him' (John 8:44). Man is in a middle position; he detains the truth in unrighteousness (Rom 1:18); light and darkness in him are struggling; but, whichever may predominate, the other is there, kept down indeed, but still with the possibility of manifesting itself. And thus a redemption is possible for man, for his will is only *perverted*; but Satan's is *inverted*. He has said what no man could ever fully say, or, at least, act on to the full: 'Evil, be thou my good'; and therefore, so far as we can see, a redemption and restoration are impossible for him.

The mischief done, the enemy *'went his way'*; and thus the work did not evidently and at once appear to be his. How often, in the Church, the beginnings of evil have been scarcely discernible; and that which bore the worst fruit in the end, has shown at first like a higher form of good. St. Paul, indeed, could detect a mystery of iniquity as yet in its obscure beginnings, could detect the *punctum saliens* out of which it would unfold itself; but to many, evil would not appear as evil till it had grown to more ungodliness. *'But when the blade was sprung up, and brought forth fruit, then appeared the tares also'*; appeared, that is, for what they were, showed themselves in their true nature. Many have noted the remarkable similarity which exists between the wheat and this *lolium* or tare, as long as they are yet in the blade. Being only distinguishable when the ear is formed, they fulfill literally the Lord's words, *'by their fruits* ye shall know them.' Augustine, upon this that only when the blade began to ripen and bring forth fruit, the tares showed themselves as such indeed, most truly remarks, that it is the opposition of good which first makes evil to appear; 'None appear evil in the Church, except to him who is good'; and again, 'When any shall have begun to be a spiritual man, judging all things, then errors begin to appear to him'; and elsewhere, drawing from the depths of his Christian experience: 'It is a great labor of the good, to bear the contrary manners of the wicked; by which he who is not offended has profited little; for the righteous, in proportion as he recedes from his own wickedness, is grieved at that of others.' As there must be light with which to contrast the darkness, height wherewith to measure depth, so there must be holiness to be grieved at unholiness; only the new man in us is grieved at the old either in ourselves or in others.

'So the servants of the housholder came, and said unto him, Stir, didst not thou sow good seed in thy field? From whence then hath it tares?' These servants are not, as Theophylact suggests, the angels (the are 'the reapers'; vv. 30, 41); but rather men, zealous for the Lord's honor, but not knowing what spirit they are of, any more than James and John, who would fain have called fire from heaven on the inhospitable Samaritan village (Luke 9:54). The question which they ask, 'Didst not thou sow good seed in thy field?' expresses well the perpexity, the surprise, the inward questionings which must often be felt, which in the first ages, before long custom had too much reconciled to the mournful fact, must have been felt very strongly by all who were zealous for God, at the woeful and unlooked-for spectacle which the visible Church presented. Where was the 'glorious Church, not having spot or wrinkle, or any such thing/' Well, indeed, might the faithful have questioned their own spirits, have poured out their hearts in prayer, of which the burden should have been exactly this, 'Didst not Thou sow good seed in thy field? From whence then hath it tares?—didst not Thou constitute thy Church to be a pure and holy communion?—is not the doctrine such as should only produce fruits of righteousness?—whence then is it that even within the holy precincts themselves there should be so many who themselves openly sin and cause others to sin? In the householder's reply, 'Any enemy hath done this,' the mischief is traced up to its source; and that not the imperfection, ignorance, weakness, which cling to everything human, and which would prevent even a Divine idea from being more than very imperfectly realized by men; but the distinct counterworking of the great spiritual enemy; *'the tares are the children of the Wicked One; the enemy that sowed them is the devil.'*

In the question which follows, *'Wilt thou then that we go and gather them up?'* The temptation to use violent means for the suppression of error, a temptation which the Church itself has sometimes failed to resist, finds its voice and utterance. But they who thus speak are unfit to be trusted in this matter. They have often no better than a Jehu's 'zeal for the Lord' (2 Kgs. 10:16); it is but an Elias-zeal at the best (Luke 9:54). And therefore *'he said, Nay.'* By this prohibition are forbidden all such measures for the excision of heretics, as shall leave them no room for after repentance or amendment; indeed the prohibition is so clear, so express, that whenever we meet in Church history with ought which looks like a carrying out of this proposal, we may be tolerably sure that it is not wheat making war on tares, but tares seeking to root out wheat. The reason of the prohibition is given: *'Lest while ye gather up the tares, ye root up also the wheat with them.'* This might be, either by rooting up what were not tares, but hereafter should become wheat—*'children of the kingdom'*; or through the servants' error, who, with the best intentions, should fail to distinguish between these and those, and involve good and bad in a common doom; or who perhaps, leaving tares, might pluck up wheat. It is only the Lord Himself, the Searcher of hearts, who with absolute certainty 'knoweth them that are his.' The later Roman Catholic expositors, and as many as in the middle ages wrote in the interest of Rome, in these words, *'lest ye root up also the wheat with them,'* find a loophole whereby they may escape the prohibition itself. Thus Aquinas will have it to be only then binding, when this danger exists of plucking up the wheat together with the tares. To which Maldonatus adds, that in each particular case the householder is to judge whether there be such danger or not; and the Pope being now the representative of the householder, to him the question should be put, *'Wilt thou that we go and gather up the tares,'* and he concludes his exposition with an exhortation to all Catholic princes, that they imitate the zeal of these servants, and rather, like them, need to have their eagerness restrained, than require, as did so many, to be stimulated to the task of rooting out heresies and heretics.

At the same time this *'Nay'* does not imply that the tares shall never be plucked up, but only that this is not the time, and they not the doers; for the householder adds, *'Let both grow together until the harvest.'* Pregnant words, which tell us that evil is not, as so many dream, gradually to wane and disappear before good, the world to find itself in the Church, but each to unfold itself more fully, out of its own root, after its own kind: till at last they stand face to face, each in its highest manifestation, in the persons of Christ and of Antichrist; on the one hand, an incarnate God, on the other, the man in whom the fullness of all Satanic power will dwell bodily. Both are to grow 'until the harvest,' till they are ripe, one for destruction, and the other for full salvation.

And they are to grow 'together'; the visible Church is to have its intermixture of good and bad until the end of time; and, by consequence, the fact of bad being found mingled with good will in nowise justify a separation from it, or an attempt to set up a little Church of our own. Where men will attempt this, besides the guilt of transgressing a plain command, it is not difficult to see what darkness it must bring upon them, into what a snare of pride it must cast them. For while, even in the best of men, there is the same intermixture of good and evil as in the visible Church, such a course will infallibly lead a man to a willful shutting of his eyes alike to the evil in himself, and in that little schismatical body which he will then call the Church, since only so the attempt will even seem to be attended with success. Thus Augustine often appeals to the fact that the Donatists had not succeeded—they would not themselves dare to assert that they had succeeded—in forming what should even externally appear a pure communion: and since by their own acknowledgment there might be, and probably were, hypocrites and undetected ungodly livers among them, this of itself rendered all such passages as Is. 52:1, as inapplicable to them as to the Catholic Church in its present condition: while yet, on the strength of this freedom from evil gratuitously assumed by them, they displayed a spirit of intolerable pride and presumptuous uncharitableness towards the Church from which they had separated. And the same sins cleave more or less to all schismatical bodies, which, under plea of a purer communion, have divided from the Church Catholic: the smallest of these, from its very smallness persuading itself that it is the most select and purest, being generally the guiltiest here. None will deny that the temptation to this lies very close to us all. Every young Christian, in the time of his first zeal, is tempted to be somewhat of a Donatist in spirit. It would argue little love or holy earnestness in him, if he had not this longing to see the Church of his savior a glorious Church without spot or wrinkle. But he must learn that the desire, righteous and holy as in itself it is, yet is not to find its fulfillment in this present evil time; that, on the contrary, the suffering from false brethren is one of the pressures upon him, which shall wring out from him a more earnest prayer that the kingdom of God may appear. He must learn that all self-willed and impatient attempts, such as have been repeated again and again, to anticipate that perfect communion of saints, are works of the flesh; that, however, fairly they may promise, no blessing will rest upon them, nor will they for long even *appear* to be crowned with success.

Some in modern times, fearing lest arguments should be drawn from this parable to the prejudice of attempts to revive stricter discipline in the Church, have sought to escape the dangers which they feared, by urging that in our Lord's explanation no notice is taken of the proposal made by the servants (v. 28), nor yet of the householder's reply to that proposal (v. 29). They conclude from this that they parable is not to teach us what the conduct of the servants of a heavenly Lord *ought* to be, but merely prophetic of what generally it *will* be—that this proposal of the servants is merely brought in to afford an opportunity for the master's reply, and that of this reply the latter is the only significant portion. But, assuredly, when Christ asserts that it is his purpose to make a complete and solemn separation at the end, He implicitly forbids—not the exercise in the mean time of a godly discipline, not, where that has become necessary, absolute exclusion from where that has become necessary, absolute exclusion from Church-fellowship—but any attempts to anticipate the final irrevocable separation, of which He has reserved the execution to Himself. '*In the time of harvest I will say to the reapers, Gather ye together first the tares, and bind them in bundles to burn them: but gather the wheat into my barn.*' Not now, but '*in the time of harvest,*' shall this separation find place; and even then, not they, but '*the reapers,*' shall carry it through. This '*time of harvest,*' as the Lord presently explains, is '*the end of the world,*' and '*the reapers are the angels*'; who are here, as everywhere else, set forth as accompanying their Lord and ours at his coming again to judgment (Matt. 16:27; 24:31; 2 Thess. 1:7; Rev. 19:140, and fulfilling his will both in respect of those who have served (Matt. 24:31) and those who have served Him not (Matt. 13:49; 22:13).

"*As therefore the tares are gathered and burned in the fire, so shall it be in the end of this world. The Son of man shall send forth his angels, and they shall gather out of his kingdom all things that offend, and them which do iniquity*'; in the words of Zephaniah, 'the stumbling-blocks with the wicked' (1:3). The setting forth of the terrible doom of ungodly men under the image of the burning with fire of thorns, briers, weeds, offal, chaff, barren branches, dead trees, is frequent in Scripture; thus see 2 Sam. 23:6, 7; Matt. 3:10, 12; 7:19; John 15:6; Heb. 6:8; 10:26, 27; Is. 5:24; 9:18, 19; 10:16, 17; 33:11, 12; 66:24; 2 Esd. 16:77, 78. But dare we speak of it as an image merely? The fire reappears in the interpretation of the parable; the angels *shall cast them,* those, namely, *which do iniquity,* *into a furnace of fire.* Fearful words indeed! And the image, if it be an image, at all events borrowed from the most dreadful and painful form of death in use among men. Something we read of it in Scripture. Judah would have fain made his daughter-in-law (Gen. 38:24), and David, alas! Did make the children of Ammon (2 Sam. 12:31 taste the dreadfulness of it. It was in use among the Chaldeans (Jer. 29:22; Dan. 3:6); and in the Jewish tradition, which is probably of great antiquity, Nimrod cast Abraham into a furnace of fire for refusing to worship his false gods. It was one of the forms of cruel death with which Antiochus Epiphanes sought to overcome the heroic constancy of the Jewish confessors in the time of the Maccabees (2 Macc. 7; Dan. 11:33; 1 Cor. 13:3); while the 'tunica molesta' with which Nero clothed the early Christian martyrs, when he desired to turn from himself upon them the odium of the burning of Rome, is well known. In modern times, Chardin makes mention of penal furnaces in Persia; while the fires of the Inquisition cast their baleful light over whole centuries of the Church's history. Whatever the *furnace of fire* may mean here, or 'the lake of fire' (Rev. 19:20; 21:10), 'the fire that is not quenched' (Mark 9:44), the 'everlasting fire' (Matt. 25:41; cf. Luke 16:24; Mal. 4:1), elsewhere, this at all events is certain; that they point to some doom so intolerable that the Son of God came down from heaven and tasted all the bitterness of death, that He might deliver us from ever knowing the secrets of anguish, which, unless God be mocking men with empty threats, are shut up in these terrible words: *There shall be wailing and gnashing of teeth* (cf. Matt. 22:13; Luke 13:28). All which has just gone before makes very unlikely their explanation of the *gnashing of teeth,* who take it as a chattering from excessive cold; who, in fact, imagine here a kind of Dantean hell, with alternations of heat and cold, alike unendurable. We take these rather as the utterances generally of rage and impatience (Acts 7:54), under the sense of intolerable pain and unutterable loss.

Then, after it has been thus done with the wicked, *shall the righteous shine forth as the sun in the kingdom of their Father.'* As *fire* was the element of the dark and cruel kingdom of hell, so is *light* of the pure heavenly kingdom. '*Then,*' when the dark hindering element has been removed, shall this element of light, which was before struggling with and obstructed by it, come forth in its full brightness (see Co. 3:4; Rom. 8:18; Prov. 4:18; 25:4, 5). A glory shall be revealed *in* the saints; not merely brought *to* them, and added from without; but rather a glory which they before had, but which did not before evidently appear, shall burst forth and show itself openly, as once in the days of his flesh, at the moment of his Transfiguration, did the hidden glory of their Lord (Matt. 17:2). That shall be the day of 'the manifestation of the sons of God'; they '*shall shine forth as the sun*' when the clouds are rolled away (Dan. 12:3); they shall evidently appear, and be acknowledged by all, as 'the children of light,' of that god who is 'the Father of Lights' (James 1:17); who is Light, and in whom is no darkness at all (1 John 1:5). And then, but not till then, shall be accomplished those glorious proophecies so often repeated in the Old Testament; 'Henceforth there shall no more come into thee the uncircumcised and the unclean' (Is. 52:1); 'In that day there shall be no more the Canaanite in the house of the Lord of Hosts' (Zech. 14:21); 'Thy people also shall be all righteous' (Is. 9:21; cf. Is. 35:8; Joel 3:17; Ezek. 37:21–27; Zeph. 3:13).

3.
The Mustard-Seed

Matthew 13:31, 32; Mark 4:30–32; Luke 13:18, 19

The four parables which follow group themselves into two pairs. Those of the Mustard-seed and the Leaven constitute the first pair, and might seem at first sight, merely repetitions of the same truth; but in this, as in every other case, upon nearer inspection essential differences reveal themselves. They have indeed this much in common, that they both describe the small and slight beginnings, the gradual progress, and the final marvelous increase of the Church—or how, to use another image, the stone cut out without hands should become a great mountain, and fill the whole earth (Dan. 2:34, 35; cf. Ezek. 47:1–5. But each also has much which is its own. That other has to do with the kingdom of God which 'cometh not with observation'; this with that same kingdom as it displays itself openly, and cannot be hid. That declares the intensive, this the extensive, development of the Gospel. That sets forth the power and action of the truth on the world brought in contact with it; this is the power of the truth to develop itself from within; as the tree which, shut up within the seed, will unfold itself according to the law of its own being.

Chrysostom traces finely the connection between this parable and those which have just gone before. From that of the Sower the disciples may have gathered that of the seed which they should sow three parts would perish, and only a fourth part prosper; while that of the Tares had opened to them the prospect of further hindrances which would beset even that portion which had taken root downward, and sprung upward; now then, lest they should be tempted quite to lose heart and to despair, these two parables are spoken for their encouragement. 'My kingdom,' the Lord would say, 'shall survive these losses, and surmount these hindrances, until, small as its first beginnings may appear, it shall, like a mighty tree, fill the earth with its branches—like potent leaven, diffuse its influence through all the world.' The growth of a mighty kingdom is not here for the first time likened to that of a tree. Many of our Lord's hearers must have been familiar with such a comparison from the Scriptures of the Old Testament. The upcoming of a worldly kingdom had been set forth under this image (Dan. 4:10–12; Ezek. 31:3–9), that also of the kingdom of God (Ezek. 17:22–24; Ps. 80:8).

By why, it may be asked, among all trees is a *mustard*-tree chosen here? Many nobler plants, as the vine, or taller trees, as the cedar (1 Kgs. 4:33; Ezek. 17:3), might have been named. Doubtless this is chosen, not with reference to greatness which it obtains in the end, for in this many surpass it, but to the proportion between the smallness of the seed and the greatness of the tree which unfolds itself therefrom. For this is the point to which the Lord calls especial attention—not the greatness of the mustard-tree in itself, but its greatness as compared with the seed from whence it springs; for what He would fain teach his disciples was not that his kingdom should be glorious, but that it should be glorious despite its weak and slight and despised beginnings. And the comparison had in other ways its fitness too. The mustard-seed, minute and trivial as it might seem, was not without its significance and acknowledged worth in antiquity. It ranked among the nobler Pythagorean symbols; was esteemed to possess medicinal virtues against the bites of venomous creatures and against poisons, and used as a remedy in many diseases. Nor can I, with a modern interpreter, account very ridiculous the suggestion that the Savior chose this seed on account of further qualities possessed by it, which gave it a peculiar aptness to illustrate the truth which He had in hand. Its heat, its fiery vigor, the fact that only through being bruised it gives out its best virtues, and all this under so insignificant an appearance and in so small a compass, may well have moved Him to select this seed by which to set forth the destinies of that word of the kingdom, that doctrine of a crucified Redeemer, which, to the Greeks foolishness, and to the Jews a stumbling-block, should prove to them that believed 'the power of God unto salvation.'

But not Christ's doctrine merely, nor yet even the Church which He planted upon earth, is this grain of mustard-seed in its central meaning. He is Himself at once the mustard-seed and the Man that sowed it. He is the mustard-seed, for the Church was originally enclosed in Him, and unfolded itself from Him, having as much oneness of life with Him as the tree with the seed in which its rudiments were all enclosed, and out of which it grew; and the Sower, in that by a free act of his own, He gave *Himself* to that death whereby He became the Author of life unto many; as Himself has said, 'Except a corn of wheat fall into the ground and die, it abideth alone; but if it die, it bringeth forth much fruit' (John 12:24). And the field in which He sowed this seed was the world—'*his field,*' or, as St. Luke expresses it (13:19), '*his* garden'; for the world was made by Him, and coming to it, 'He came unto his own.'

This seed, when cast into the ground, is '*the least of all seeds*'— words which have often perplexed interpreters, many seeds, as of poppy or rue, being smaller. Yet difficulties of this kind are not worth making; it is sufficient to know that 'small as a grain of mustard-seed' was a proverbial expression among the Jews for something exceedingly minute (see Luke 17:6). The Lord, in his popular teaching, adhered to the popular language. And as the mustard-seed, so was his kingdom. What, to the eye of flesh, could be less magnificent, what could have less of promise, than the commencements of that kingdom in his own person? Growing up in a distant and despised province, till his thirtieth year He did not emerge from the bosom of his family; then taught for two or three years in the neighboring towns and villages, and occasionally at Jerusalem; made a few converts, chiefly among the poor and unlearned, and at length, falling into the hands of his enemies, with no attempt at resistance on his own part or that of his followers, died a malefactor's death upon the cross. Such, and so slight, was the commencement of the universal kingdom of God; for herein that kingdom differs from the great schemes of this world; these last have a proud beginning, a shameful and miserable end—towers as of Babel, which at first threaten to be as high as heaven, but end a deserted misshapen heap of slime and bricks; while the works of God, and most of all his chief work, his Church, have a slight and unobserved beginning, with gradual increase, and a glorious consummation. So is it with his kingdom in the world, a kingdom which cam not with observation; so is it with his kingdom in any single heart: there too the word of Christ falls like a slight mustard-seed, seeming to promise little, but effecting, if allowed to grow, mighty and marvelous results. For that seed which was the smallest of all seeds, '*when it is grown, it is the greatest among herbs, and becometh a tree, so that the birds of the air come and lodge in the branches thereof.*' There is no exaggeration here. In hot countries, as in Judaea, the mustard-tree attains a size of which we do not so much as dream in our colder latitudes, sometimes such as will allow a man to climb up into hits branches (this, however, was counted worth recording), or to ride on horseback under them, as a traveler in Chili mentions that he has done. Maldonatus assures us, that in Spain he has seen large ovens heated with its branches; often, too, he has noted when the seed was ripening, immense flocks of birds congregating upon the boughs, which yet were strong enough to sustain the weight without being broken. All this was probably familiar to our Lord's hearers as well, and presented a lively image to their minds. They, too, had behed the birds of the air coming and lodging in the branches of the mustard-tree, and finding at once their food and their shelter there.

There is prophecy too in these words. As in that grand announcement of the kingdom of God (Ezek. 17:22–24) which has so many points of contact and resemblance with this parable, it is said of the tender twig which the Lord shall plant, 'it shall bring forth boughs, and bear fruit, and be a goodly cedar, and under it shall dwell all fowls of every wing; in the shadow of the branches thereof shall they dwell'; and as these last words announce there the refuge and defense which men shall find in the Church of god (cf. Ezek. 31:6, 12), so must they have the same meaning here. Christ's kingdom shall attract multitudes by the shelter and protection which it offers; shelter, as it has often proved, from worldly oppression, shelter from the great power of the devil. Itself a tree of life whose leaves are for medicine and whose fruit for food (Ezek. 47:12; Rev. 22:2), all who need the healing of their soul's hurts, all who need the satisfying of their soul's hunger, shall betake themselves to it; and all who do so shall be enabled to set their seal to the words of the Son of Sirach (14:20, 26, 27), 'Blessed is the man that doth meditate good things in Wisdom. . . . He shall set his children under her shelter, and shall lodge under her branches, by her he shall be covered from heat, and in her glory shall he dwell.'

4.
The Leaven

Matthew 13:33; Luke 13:20, 21

Another parable spoke He unto them: The kingdom of heaven is like unto leaven, which a woman took, and hid in three measures of meal, till the whole was leavened.' This parable relates also to the marvelous increase of the kingdom of God; but, while the last set forth its outward visible manifestation, this declares its hidden working, its mysterious influence on the world which on all sides it touches. The mustard-seed does not for some while attract observation; nor until it has grown to some height, do the birds of the air light upon its branches; but the leaven has been actively working from the first moment that it was hidden in the lump. Here, indeed, we are met at the outset by Gurtler, Teelman, and some little bands of modern separatists, who altogether deny that the parable has anything to do with the glorious developments of the kingdom of God. They take it rather as a prophecy of the heresies and corruptions which should mingle with and adulterate the pure doctrine of the Gospel—of the workings, in fact, of the future mystery of iniquity. The woman that hides the leaven in the meal is for them the apostate Church; which, with its ministers, they observe, is often represented under this image (Prov. 9:13; Rev. 17:1; Zech. 5:7–11). The argument on which they mainly rely in support of this interpretation is, of course, the fact that leaven is oftenest employed in the Scripture as the symbol of something evil (1 Cor. 5:7; Luke 12:1; Gal. 5:9). This is undoubtedly true. As such it was forbidden in the offerings under the Law (Ex. 13:3; Lev. 2:11; Amos 4:5), though not without an exception (Lev. 23:17). The strict command to the children of Israel, that they should carefully put away every particle of leaven out of their houses during the Passover week, rests on this view of it as evil; they were thus reminded that if they would rightly keep the feast, they must seek to cleanse their hearts from all workings of malice and wickedness. But conceding all upon which they rest their argument, it would still be impossible to accept their interpretation as the true. The parable, as the Lord declares, is of 'the kingdom of heaven'; it would in that case be a parable of another kingdom altogether. Announcing that there was one who should leaven through and through with a leaven of falsehood and corruption the entire kingdom of heaven, He would have announced that the gates of hell should prevail against it; He would have written failure upon his whole future work; there would, in that case, have remained no re-active energy, by which it could ever have been unleavened again.

But the admitted fact that leaven is, in Scripture, most commonly the type of what is false and corrupting, need not drive us to any interpretation which should be encumbered with embarrassments like these. It was not, therefore, the less free to use it in a good sense. In those other passages, the puffing up, disturbing, souring properties of leaven were the prominent points of comparison; in the present, its warmth, its penetrative energy, the way in which a little of it lends a savour and virtue to much wherewith it is brought in contact. The figurative language of Scripture is not so stereotyped, that one figure must always stand for one and the same thing. The devil is 'a roaring *lion*, seeking whom he may devour' (1 Pet. 5:8); yet this does not hinder the same title from being applied to Christ, '*the Lion* of the tribe of Judah' (Rev. 5:5); only there the subtlety and fierceness of the animal formed the point of comparison, here the nobility and kingliness and conquering strength. The silliness of the dove is in one place the oint of comparison (Hos. 7:11), its simplicity at another (Matt. 10:16). St. Cyril then could scarcely have had this parable in his mind, when he said: 'Leaven, in the inspired writings, is *always* taken as the type of naughtiness and sin.' Ignatius shows rather by his own application of the image, how it may be freely used, now in a good, now in a bad sense; for, warning against judaizing practices, he writes: 'Lay aside the evil leaven which has grown old and maketh sour, and be transmuted into the new leaven, which is Christ Jesus.' Nor is it to be forgotten that if, on one side, the operation of leaven upon meal presents an analogy to something evil in the spiritual world, it does also on the other to something good; its effects on bread being to render it more tasteful, lighter, more nourishing, and generally more wholesome.

We need not then hesitate to take the parable in its obvious sense—that it prophesies the diffusion, and not the corruptions, of the Gospel. By the leaven we are to understand the word of the kingdom, which Word, in its highest sense, Christ Himself was. As the mustard-seed, out of which a mighty tree should unfold itself, was *'the least of all seeds,'* so too the leaven is something apparently of slight account, but at the same time mighty in operation; in this fitly setting forth Him, of whom it was said, 'He hath no form nor comeliness, and when we shall see Him, there is no beauty that we should desire Him'; but then presently again, 'By his knowledge shall my righteous Servant justify many . . . and He shall divide the spoil with the strong' (Is. 53:2, 11, 12); and who, when He had communicated of his life and spirit to his Apostles, enabled them too, in their turn, poor and mean and unlearned as they were, to become 'the salt of the earth,' the leaven of the world. For, in Chrysostom's words, 'that which is once leavened becomes leaven to the rest; since as the spark when it takes hold of wood, makes that which is already kindled to transmit the flame, and so seizes still upon more, thus it is also with the preaching of the word.'

It is part of the natural machinery of the parable, the act of kneading being proper to women (Gen. 18:6; 1 Sam. 28:24), that it should be *'a woman'* who hides the leaven in the three measures of meal? Or shall we look for something more in it than this? A comparison with Luke 15:8 (*the woman* who loses, and then seeks and finds, her piece of money) may suggest that the divine Wisdom (Prov. 9:1–3), the Holy Spirit, which is the sanctifying power in humanity (and it is of that sanctifying that the word is here), may be intended. But if it be asked, Why represented as a woman? To this it may be replied, that the organ of the Spirit's working is the Church, which evidently would be most fitly represented under this image. In and through the Church the Spirit's work proceeds: only as the Spirit dwells in the Church (Rev. 22:17), is that able to mingle a nobler element in the mass of humanity, to leaven the world. So again, why should *'three'* measures of meal be mentioned? It might be enough to answer, because it was just so much as would be often kneaded at one time (Gen. 18:6; Judg. 6:19; 1 Sam. 1:24). Yet the *'three'* may intend something more, may prophesy of the spread of the Gospel through the three parts then known of the world; or, as Augustine will have it, of the ultimate leavening of the whole human race, derived from the three sons of Noah; which amounts to much the same thing. And those who, like Jerome and Ambrose, find in it a pledge of the sanctification of spirit, soul, and body (1 Thess. 5:23), are not upon a different track, if, as has not been ill suggested, Shem, Japheth, and Ham, do indeed answer to these three elements, spirit, soul, and body, which together make up the man—the one or other element having, as is plainly the case, predominance in the descendants severally of the three.

But the leaven which is thus mingled with the lump, which acts on and coalesces with it, is at the same time different from it; for the woman *took* it from elsewhere to mingle it therein: and even such is the Gospel, a kingdom not of this world (John 18:36), not the unfolding of any powers which already existed therein, a kingdom not rising, as the secular kingdoms, 'out of the earth' (Dan. 7:17), but a new power brought into the world from above,; not a philosophy, but a Revelation. The Gospel of Christ was a new and quickening power cast into the midst of an old and dying world, a center of life round which all the moral energies which still survived, and all which itself should awaken, might form and gather—by the help of which the world might constitute itself anew. This leaven is not merely mingled with, but *hidden* in the mass which it renewed. For the true renovation, that which God effects, is ever thus from the inward to the outward; it begins in the inner spiritual world, though it does not end there: for it fails not to bring about, in good time, a mighty change also in the outward and visible world. This was wonderfully exemplified in the early history of Christianity. The leaven was effectually hidden. How striking is the entire ignorance which heathen writers betray of all that was going forward a little below the surface of society—the manner in which they overlooked the mighty change which was preparing; and this, not merely at the first, when the mustard-tree might well escape notice, but, with slight exceptions, even up to the very moment when the open triumph of Christianity was at hand. Working from the center to the circumference, by degrees it made itself felt, till at length the whole Roman world was, more or less, leavened by it. Nor must we forget, that the mere external conversion of that whole world gives us a very inadequate measure of the work which had to be done: besides this, there was the eradication of the innumerable heathen practices and customs and feelings which had enwoven and entwined their fibres round the very heart of society; a work which lagged very far behind the other, and which, in fact, was never thoroughly accomplished till the whole structure of Graeco-Roman society had gone to pieces, and the new Teutonic framework had been erected in its room.

But while much has thus been effected, while the leavening of the mass has never ceased to go forward, yet the promise of the parable has hitherto been realized only in a very imperfect measure; nor can we consider these words, '*till the whole is leavened,*' as less than a prophecy of a final complete triumph of the Gospel— that it will diffuse itself through all nations, and purify and ennoble all life. We may also fairly see in these words a pledge and assurance that the word of life, received into any single heart, shall not there cease its effectual working, till it has brought the whole man into obedience to it, sanctifying him wholly, so that he shall be altogether a new creation in Christ Jesus. It shall claim every region of man's being as its own, and make its presence felt through all. In fact the parable does nothing less than set forth to us the mystery of regeneration, both in its first act, which can be but once, as the leaven is but once hidden: and also in the consequent renewal by the Holy spirit, which, as the further working of the leaven, so mixed thoroughly with the whole, that although it appeareth not in any part of it visibly, yet every part hath a tincture from it.' We may fitly conclude, in the words of St. Ambrose: 'May the Holy Church, which is figured under the type of this woman in the Gospel, whose meal are we, hide the Lord Jesus in the innermost places of our hearts, till the warmth of the Divine wisdom penetrate into the most secret recesses of our souls.'

5.
The Hid Treasure

Matthew 13:44

The kingdom of God is not merely a general, it is also an individual and personal, thing. It is not merely a tree overshadowing the earth, or leaven leavening the world, but each man must have it for himself, and make it his own by a distinct act of his own will. He cannot be a Christian without knowing it. He may indeed come under the shadow of this great tree, and partake of many blessings of its shelter: he may dwell in a Christendom which has been leavened with the leaven of the truth, and so in a degree himself share in the universal leavening. But more than this is needed, and more than this in every elect soul will find place. There will be a personal appropriation of the benefit; and we have the history of this in these two parables which follow. They were spoken, not to the multitude, not to those 'without,' but in the house (v. 36), and to the inner circle of disciples; who are addressed as having lighted on the hid treasure, having found the pearl of price; and are now warned of the surpassing worth of these, and that, for their sakes, all which would hinder from making them securely their own, must be joyfully renounced.

The second parable repeats what the first has said, but repeats it with a difference; they are each the complement of the other: so that under one or other, as finders either of the pearl or of the hid treasure, may be ranged all who become partakers of the blessings of the Gospel of Christ. Of these there are some who feel that there must be some absolute good for man, in the possession of which he shall be blessed and find the satisfaction of all his longings; who are therefore seeking everywhere and inquiring for this good. Such are likened to the merchant that has distinctly set before himself the purpose of seeking and obtaining goodly pearls. They are the fewer in number, but all likely to prove the noblest servants of the truth. There are others, who do not discover that there is an aim and a purpose for man's life, or that there is a truth for him at all, until the truth as it is in Jesus is revealed to them. Such are compared to the finder of the hid treasure, who stumbled upon it unawares, neither expecting nor looking for it. While the others felt that there was a good, and were looking for it, the discovery of the good itself for the first time reveals to these that there is such at all; whose joy, therefore, as greater—being the joy at the discovery of an unlooked-for treasure—is expressed; that of the others, not. Thus Hammond, bringing out this distinction, paraphrases the two parables thus: 'The Gospel being by some not looked after, is yet sometimes met with by them, and becomes matter of infinite joy and desire to them: and so is likened fitly to a treasure, which a man finding casually in a field, hid again, or concealed it, and then, designing to get into his possession, accounts no price he can pay too dear for it. Others there are which have followed the study of wisdom, and thirsted after some instruction: and then the Gospel of Christ comes as a rich prize doth to a merchant, who is in pursuit of rich merchandise, and meeting with a jewel for his turn, lays out all his estate upon it.'

The cases of Jew and Gentile will respectively exemplify the contrast between the Pearl and the Hid Treasure; though in the case of the Jews, or the larger number of them, the illustration cannot be carried through, as they, though seeking pearls, having a zeal for righteousness, yet, when the pearl of great price was offered to them, were not willing to 'sell all,' to renounce their peculiar privileges, their self-righteousness, and all else which they held dear, that they might buy that pearl. The Gentiles, on the contrary, came upon the treasure unawares. Christ was found of them that sought Him not, and the blessings of his truth revealed to them who before had not divined that there were such blessings for man (Rom. 9:30). Or, again, we might instance Nathanael as an example of the more receptive nature, of one who has the truth found for him; or a still more striking example—the Samaritan woman (John 4), who, when she came on that memorable day to draw water from the well, anticipated anything rather than lighting on the hid treasure. Yet in this character there cannot be a total absence of a seeking for the truth; only it is a desire that has hitherto slumbered in the soul, and displays itself rather as a love of the truth when revealed, and at once a joyful and submissive acquiescence to it, than in any active previous quest. In both, there must be the same willingness to embrace it when known, and to hold it fast, at whatever costs and hazards. On the other hand, we have, perhaps, no such record of a noble nature, seeking for the pearl of price, and not resting till he had found it, as that which Augustine gives of himself in his *Confessions;* though others are not wanting, such as Justin Martyr's account of his own conversion, given in his first dialogue with Trypho, in which he tells how he had traveled through the whole circle of Greek philosophy, seeking everywhere for that which would satisfy the deepest needs of his soul, and ever seeking in vain, till he found it at length in the Gospel of Christ. We derive a further confirmation of this view of the parables, and that it is not a mere fancy, from the forms which they severally assume. In this the treasure is the prominent circumstance; *'The kingdom of heaven is like unto a merchantman';* so that the person seeking is in that parable at the center of the spiritual picture, the thing found, in this. This is scarcely accidental.

The circumstance which supplies the groundwork of this first parable, namely, the finding of a concealed treasure, is of much more frequent occurrence in an insecure state of society, such as in almost all ages has prevailed in the East, than happily it can be with us. A writer on Oriental literature and customs mentions that in the East, on account of the frequent changes of dynasties, and the revolutions which accompany them, many rich men divide their goods into three parts: one they employ in commerce, or for their necessary support; one they turn into jewels, which, should it prove needful to fly, could be easily carried with them; a third part they bury. But as they trust no one with the place where the treasure is buried, so is the same, should they not return to the spot before their death, as good as lost to the living (Jer. 41:8), until, by chance, a lucky peasant digging in his field, lights upon it. And thus, when we read in Eastern tales, how a man has found a buried treasure, and, in a moment, risen from poverty to great riches, this is, in fact, no strange or rare occurrence, but a natural consequence of the customs of these people. Modern book of travels bear witness to the universal belief in the existence of such hid treasures; so that the traveler often finds much difficulty in obtaining information about antiquities, is sometimes seriously inconvenienced, or even endangered, in his researches among ancient ruins, by the jealousy of the neighboring inhabitants, who fear lest he is coming to carry away concealed hoards of wealth from among them, of which, by some means or other, he has got notice. And so also the skill of an Eastern magician in great part consists in being able to detect the places where these secreted treasures will successfully be looked for. Often, too, a man abandoning the regular pursuits of industry will devote himself to treasure-seeking, in the hope of growing, through some happy chance, rich of a sudden (Job 3:21; Prov. 2:4). The contrast, however, between this parable and the following, noticed already, will not allow us to assume the finder here to have been in search of the treasure, he rather stumbles upon it, strikes it with plough or spade, unawares, and thinking of no such thing: probably while engaged as a hireling in cultivating the field of another.

Some draw a distinction between 'the field' and 'the treasure.' The first is the Holy Scriptures; the second, the hidden mystery of the knowledge of Christ contained in them, which when a man has partly perceived—discovered, that is, and got a glimpse of the treasure—he is willing to renounce all meaner aims and objects; that, having leisure to search more and more into those Scriptures, to make them his own, he may enrich himself forever with the knowledge of Christ which therein is contained. Yet to me 'the field' rather represents the outer visible Church, as contradistinguished from the inward spiritual, with which 'the treasure' will then agree. As the man who before looked on the field with careless eyes, prized it but as another field, now sees in it a new worth, resolves that nothing shall separate him from it, so he who recognizes the Church, not as a human institute, but a divine, as a dispenser, not of earthly gifts, but of heavenly—who has learned that God is in the midst of it—sees now that is something different from, and something more than, all earthly societies, with which hitherto he has confounded it: and henceforth it is precious in his sight, even to its outermost skirts, for the sake of that inward glory which is revealed to his eyes. And he sees, too, that blessedness is unalterably linked to communion with it. As the man cannot have the treasure and leave the field, but both or neither must be his, so he cannot have Christ except in his Church and in the ordinances of his Church; none but the golden pipes of the sanctuary are used for the conveyance of the golden oil (Zech. 4:12); he cannot have Christ in his heart, and, at the same time, separate his fortunes from those of Christ's struggling, suffering, warring Church. The treasure and the field go together; both, or neither, must be his.

This treasure *'when a man hath found, he hideth'*; having laid it open in discovering, he covers it up again, while he goes and effects the purchase of the field. This cannot mean that he who has discovered the treasures of wisdom and knowledge hidden in Christ Jesus, will desire to keep his knowledge to himself; since rather he will feel himself, as he never did before, a debtor to all men, to make all partakers of the benefit. He will go to his brother man, like Andrew to Peter, and saying to him, 'We have found the Messias' (John 1:41), will seek to bring him to Jesus. If he hid the treasure, this hiding will be, not lest another should find, but lest he himself should lose it. In the first moments that the truth is revealed to a soul, there may well be a tremulous fear lest the blessing found should, by some means or other, escape again. The anxiety that it may not do so, the jealous precautions for this end taken, would seem to be the truth signified by this re-concealment of the found treasure.

But having thus secured it for the moment, the finder, *'for joy thereof, goeth and selleth all that he hath, and buyeth that field.'* The joy is expressly mentioned here, being that in the strength whereof the finder of the spiritual treasure is enabled to part with everything besides. No compulsion, no command is necessary; *'for joy thereof'* or *'in his joy,'* for both are possible renderings, he cannot do otherwise; all other things have now no glory, 'by reason of the glory which excelleth.' Augustine excellently illustrates from his own experience this part of the parable. Describing the crisis of his own conversion, and how easy he found it, through this joy, to give up all which he had long dreaded to be obliged to renounce, which had so long held him fast bound in the chains of evil custom; and which if he renounced, it had seemed to him as though life itself would not be worth living, he exclaims: 'How sweet did it at once become to me, to want the sweetnesses of those toys! And what I feared to be parted from was now a joy to part with. For Thou didst cast them forth from me, Thou true and highest sweetness. Thou castedst them forth, and, for them, enteredst in Thyself, sweeter than all pleasure.' The parting with those sinful delights which had hitherto held him bound, was, in Augustine's case, the selling of all that he had, that he might buy the field. Compare Phil. 3:4–11, where St. Paul declares how he too sold all that he had, renounced his trust in his own righteousness, in his spiritual and fleshly privileges, that he might 'win Christ, and be found in Him,' In each of these illustrious instances, the man parted with the dearest thing that he had, so to make the treasure his own: though, in each case, the thing parted with how different! So, too, whenever any man renounces what is closest to him, rather than that that should hinder his embracing and making his own all the blessings of Christ— when the lover of money renounces his covetousness—and the indolent man, his ease—and the lover of pleasure, his pleasure—and the wise man, his confidence in the wisdom of this world, then each is selling what he has, that he may buy the field which contains the treasure. Yet this selling of all is no arbitrary condition, imposed from without, but rather a delightful constraint, acknowledged within: even as a man would willingly fling down pebbles and mosses with which he had been filling his hands, if pearls and precious stones were offered him in their stead; or as the dead leaves of themselves fall off from the tree, when propelled by the new buds and blossoms which are forcing their way from behind.

A difficulty has been sometimes found in the circumstance of the finder of the treasure purchasing the field, at the same time withholding, as plainly he does, from the owner the knowledge of a fact which enhanced its value so much; and which had the other known, either he would not have parted with it at all, or only at a much higher price. They argue that it is against the decorum of the divine teaching and of the Divine Teacher, that an action, morally questionable at least, if not absolutely unrighteous, should be used even for the outward setting forth of a spiritual actions which is commended as worthy of imitation; that there is a certain approbation of the action conveyed even in the use of it for such ends; in fact, they find the same difficulty here as in the parables of the Unjust Steward and the Unjust Judge. Olshausen, so far from evading the difficulty, or seeking to rescue the present parable from lying under the same difficulty as undoubtedly cleaves to one of those, himself urges the likeness which exists between the two, and affirms that, in both, *prudence* (klugheit) in respect of divine things is commended; so that they are parables of the same class, and in this aspect, at least, containing the same moral. But to the objection thus urged it seems enough to reply, that not every part of his conduct who found the treasure is proposed for imitation, but only his earnestness in securing the treasure found, his fixed purpose to make it at all costs and all hazards his own, and (which, I suppose, is Olshausen's meaning) his prudence, without any affirmation that the actual manner in which that prudence was exercised was praiseworthy or not.

6.
The Pearl of Great Price
Matthew 13:45, 46

Almost all which it would have needed to say upon this parable, had it stood alone, has been anticipated in the sister parable, had it stood alone, has just gone before. The relations in which the two stand to one another have been already noticed. We have not here, as there, merely a finder, but also a seeker, of true wisdom— 'Again the kingdom of heaven is like unto a merchant-man seeking goodly pearls.' To find them has been the object of his labors: 'the search is therefore determinate, discriminative, unremitting.' He has set this purpose distinctly before him, and to it is bending all his energies; as one assured that man was not made in vain, that there must be a center of peace for him, a good which will satisfy all the cravings of his soul, and who is determined not to rest till he has found that good. As yet he may not know that it is but one, for at the outset he is seeking many goodly pearls; but perhaps imagines that it is to be made up and combined from many quarters: but this also will be revealed to him in due time.

It makes much for the beauty of the parable, and the fitness of the image used to set forth the surpassing value of the kingdom of God, that we keep in mind the esteem in which pearls were held in antiquity, sums almost incredible having been given for single pearls, when perfect of their kind. There were many defects which materially diminished their value, as for instance, if they had a yellow or dusky tinge, or were not absolutely round or smooth. The skill and wariness which the pearl-merchant therefore needed, if he would not have a meaner thing imposed on him in place of the best, will not be without its answer in the spiritual world. There are many pearls of an inferior quality, but this merchant is seeking *'goodly'* pearls; as he whom the merchant represents, has set before himself, not low and poor, but noble and worthy, aims; and this even in times anterior to that in which he finds the pearl of price. He is not one living for sensual objects. He had not made pleasure, or gain, or the high places of the world, the end and scope of his toils. But he has been, it may be, a philanthropist, a seeker of wisdom, a worshiper of the beautiful in nature or in art; one who has hoped to find his soul's satisfaction in some one of these things. *'Who, when he had found one pearl of great price, went and sold all that he had, and bought it.'* This *'pearl of great price,'* what is it? Many answers have been given, which yet, diverging as they may seem from one another, grow all out of one and the same root; all ultimately resolve themselves into one. Whether we say the pearl is the kingdom of God within a man—or the knowledge of Christ—or Christ Himself—we do but in different ways express one and the same thing.

The merchant, having found this excellent pearl, *'went and sold all that he had, and bought it.'* What this selling implies, has been already seen; and to understand what the buying means, and what it does not mean, we may compare Is. 55:1; Matt. 25:9, 10; Rev. 3:18; and Prov. 23:23, 'Buy the truth, and sell it not'; obtain the truth at any price, and let no price tempt you to part with it. Chrysostom calls our attention here to the *one* pearl which the merchant finds, and the *many* which he had been seeking. The same contrast is marked elsewhere; Martha is troubled about *many* things; Mary has found that but *one* thing is needful (Luke 10:41, 42). There is but one such pearl (though every seeker may obtain that one), since the truth is one, even as God is one; and the truth possessed restores that unity to the heart of man, which sin had destroyed. The heart which had been as a mirror shattered into a thousand fragments, and every fragment reflecting some different object, is now reunited again, and the whole with more or less clearness reflects, as it was at the first intended to do, the one image of God. It is God alone in whom any intelligent creature can find its center and true repose: only when man has found *Him*, does the great *Eureka* burst forth from his lips; in Augustine's beautiful and often-quoted words, 'Lord, Thou hast made us *for* Thee, and our heart is disquieted till it resteth *in* Thee.'

Before leaving this parable, it may be worthwhile to mention an interpretation which strangely reverses the whole matter. According to this, the merchant seeking goodly pearls is Christ Himself. The Church of the elect is the pearl of price: which that He might purchase and make his own, He parted with all that He had, emptying Himself of his divine glory, and taking the form of a servant. Or yet more ingeniously, the pearl, as in the common explanation, is the kingdom of heaven; but Christ the merchant, who to secure that kingdom to us and make it ours, though He was so rich, gladly made himself poor, buying that pearl and that treasure—not indeed for Himself, but for us.

7.
The Draw-Net
Matthew 13:47–50

This parable might at first sight seem merely to say over again what the Tares had said already. Maldonatus, ascribing absolute identity of purpose to the two, conceives the parables of this chapter not to be set down in the order wherein the Lord spoke them, but this to have immediately followed upon that. Here, however, he is clearly mistaken; there is this fundamental difference between them, that the central truth of that is the present intermixture, of this, the future separation, of the good and the bad; of that, that men are not to effect the separation; of this, that the separation will one day, by God, be effected. The order in which we have the parables is that in which they were spoken; that other relating to the progressive development, this to the final consummation, of the Church. Olshausen draws a further distinction between the two; in that, the kingdom of God is represented rather in its idea, coextensive, as it shall ultimately be, with the whole world; in this, in its present imperfect form, as a less contained in a greater, though tending to spread over and embrace that greater; the Church gathering in its members from the world, as the net its fish from the sea.

With all this, the parables resemble one another so nearly, that much which has been already said, in considering the other, will apply to this. The same use has been made of both; there is the same continual appeal to both in the Donatist controversy; both convey the same lesson, namely, that He who founded a Church upon earth did not contemplate that Church as a communion free from all intermixture of evil; but that as there was a Ham in the ark, and a Judas among the twelve, so there should be a Babylon even within the bosom of the spiritual Israel; Esau should contend with Jacob even in the Church's womb, till, like another Rebekah, she should often be compelled to exclaim, 'Why am I thus/" (Gen. 25:22). They convey, too, the same further lesson, that all this will in nowise justify self-willed departure from the fellowship of the Church, and impatient leaping over, or breaking through, the nets, as here it has often been called. The separation of a more unerring hand than man's is patiently to be waited for, which shall not fail to arrive when the mystery of the present dispensation has been accomplished.

This parable, the last in this grand series, commences thus: *'Again, the kingdom of heaven is like unto a net, that was cast into the sea, and gathered of every kind.'* If we ask to what manner of net the kingdom of heaven is likened here, the heading of the chapter in our Bibles calls it a *'draw-net,'* and the word of the original leaves no doubt upon the subject. The sagene, seine, or sean, for the word has been naturalized in English, is a net of immense length, suffering nothing to escape from it. This its all-embracing nature is no accidental or unimportant feature, but makes the parable prophetic of the wide reach and effectual operation of the Gospel. The kingdom of heaven should henceforward be a net, not cast into a single stream as hitherto, but into the broad sea of the whole world, and gathering *'of every kind,'* out of every kindred and tongue and people and nation; or, as some understand it, men good and bad; that as the servants, in another parable, 'gathered together all, as many as they found, both bad and good' (Matt. 22:10); so here they collect of all kinds within the folds of their net; men of every diversity of moral character having the Gospel preached to them, and finding themselves within the confines of the visible Church.

But as all use not aright the advantages which fellowship with Christ in his Church affords, an ultimate separation is necessary. Our Lord proceeds to describe it—*'which, when it was full, they drew to shore, and sat down, and gathered the good into vessels, but cast the bad away.'* Whether these *'bad'* are dead putrid fish, such as a net will sometimes include, or fish worthless and good for nothing, 'that which was sick and unwholesome at the season,' or such as from their kind, their smallness, or some other cause, are profitable for nothing, and therefore flung carelessly aside to rot upon the beach, or to become food for the birds of prey (Ezek. 29:4, 5; 32:3, 4), has been often a question; and it is not easy, as it is not very important, to decide. The interpretation, which is not affected by a determination in one of these senses or in another, is obvious. '*So shall it be at the end of the world.*' When all nations have been gathered into the external fellowship of the Church, when the religion of Christ has become the religion of the world, then the severing of the precious from the vile, of the just from the unjust, shall begin, But who are they that shall effect it? To whom shall this awful task be confided? Here I must entirely dissent from those, Vitringa, for example, and Olshausen, who urge that they who first carry out the net, and they who discriminate between its contents, being, in the parable, the same; therefore, since the former are evidently the Apostles and their successors, now become, according to the Lord's promise, 'fishers of men' (Matt. 4:19; Luke 5:10; Ezek. 47:10; Jer. 26:16); the latter must be in like manner, not the angelic ministers of God's judgments, but the same *messengers* of the Covenant, and as such, '*angels*' (v. 49); to whom, being equipped with divine power, the task of judging and sundering should be committed. No doubt the Church, in her progressive development, is always thus judging and separating (1 Cor. 5:4, 5; 2 Thess. 3:6; 2 John 10; Matt. 18:17; Jude 22, 23) putting away one and another from her communion, as they openly declare themselves unworthy of it. But she does not count that she has thus cleansed herself, or that a perfect cleansing can be effected by the exercise of any power which now she possesses. There must be a final judgment and sundering, not any more from within, but from without and from above; and of this decisive crisis we find everywhere else in Scripture the angels of heaven distinctly named as the instruments (Matt. 13:41; 24:31; 25:31; Rev. 14:18, 19). It is contrary then to the analogy of faith so to interpret the words before us as to withdraw this office from them. It is indeed true that in that familiar occurrence of our workday world which supplies the groundwork of the parable, the same who carry out the net would also bring it to shore; as they too would inspect its contents, selecting the good, and casting the worthless away. But it is a pushing of this, which in fact is the weak side of the comparison, too far, to require that the same should hold good in the spiritual thing signified. In the nearly allied parable of the Tares, there was no improbability in supposing those who watched the growth of the crop to be different from those who should finally gather it in; and, accordingly, such a difference is marked: those are the 'servants' these are the 'reapers'; just as in every other parable of judgment there is a marked distinction between the present ministers of the kingdom, and the future executors of doom; in the Marriage of the King's Son between the 'servants' and 'those that stand by' (Luke 19:24). That the agents in the one work and in the other are not the same could not here be so easily marked; but it is slightly, yet sufficiently, indicated in another way. The fishers are not once mentioned by name. The imperfection of the human illustration to set forth the divine truth is kept in good part out of sight, by the whole circumstance being told, as nearly as may be, impersonally. And when the Lord Himself interprets the parable, He passes over, without a word, the beginning; thus still further drawing away attention from a feature of it, upon which to dwell might have needlessly perplexed his hearers; and explains only the latter part, where the point and stress of it lay. Assuming, then, as we may and must, the angels of heaven to be here, as everywhere else, the takers and the leavers, we may recognize and emphasis in the *'coming forth'* attributed to them. Ever since the first constitution of the Church they have been hidden—for ages withdrawn from men's sight. But then, at that grand epoch, the winding up of the present age, they shall again *'come forth'* from before the throne and presence of God, and walk up and down among men, the visible ministers of his judgments.

The deliberate character of that judgment-act which they shall accomplish, the fact that it shall be no hasty work confusedly huddled over, is intimated in the *sitting down* of the fishers for the sorting and separating of the good from the bad. From some image like that which our parable supplies, the 'taking' and 'leaving' of Matt. 24:41, 42, must be derived. There too the *taking* is probably for blessedness, the selecting of the precious; the *leaving* for destruction, the rejecting of the vile. Some reverse the meaning, yet hardly with justice; for what is the *'left'* but the refused, and the *refused* but the *refuse*? We dare not lay any stress upon the order here, that the good are *first 'gathered into vessels,'* even though it is also the order of Matt. 25:34, 41, seeing that it is exactly reversed in the cognate parable of the Tares, where with a certain emphasis it is said, 'Gather ye together *first* the tares' (v. 30). Of these *'vessels,'* Christ gives no interpretation; nor indeed is any needed. They are the 'barn' of verse 30; the 'many mansions' of John 14:2; the 'everlasting habitations' of Luke 16:9; the 'city which hath foundations' for which Abraham looked, of Heb. 11:10, 12, 22; the 'New Jerusalem that cometh down out of heaven' of Rev. 3:12. This tasks accomplished, those who drew the net to shore *'cast the bad away.'* These words hardly prepare us for the fearful meaning which in the interpretation they receive—'*and shall cast them,*' that is, the wicked, '*into the furnace of fire; there shall be wailing and gnashing of teeth.*' No wonder that Chrysostom should characterize this as 'a terrible parable'; that Gregory the Great should style it one 'rather to be feared than expounded.' But on this '*furnace of fire*' something has been said already (p. 104). Thus, and thus only, when God Himself takes in hand to cleanse his Church, shall that entire freedom from all evil which belongs to the idea of the Church be at length brought about (Rev. 22:15).

Comparing once more this parable with that of the Tares, we find that, notwithstanding seeming resemblances, the lessons which they teach are very different. The lesson of that it is needless to repeat; but of this it clearly is, that we be not content with being included within the Gospel-net, since 'they are not all Israel who are of Israel'; that in the 'great house' of the Church 'there are not only vessels of gold and silver, but of wood and of earth, and some to honor, and some to dishonor'; that each of us therefore seek to be 'a vessel unto honor, sanctified and meet for the master's use' (2 Tim. 2:20, 21); since despite of all the confusions of the visible Church, 'the Lord knoweth them that are his,' and will one day bring these confusions to an end, separating the precious from the vile, the gold from the dross, the true kernel of humanity from the husk in which for a while it was enveloped.

I conclude with a few remarks on the relation of these parable to one another. The mystical number seven has tempted not a few interpreters to seek some hidden mystery here; and when the seven petitions of the Lord's Prayer, and the names of the seven first deacons (Acts 6:5), have been turned into prophecy of seven successive conditions of the church, not to speak of the seven apocalyptic Epistles (Rev. 2:3), it was scarcely to be expected that these seven parables should escape being made prophetic of the same. They have, in fact, so often been dealth with as prophecy, that a late ingenious writer needed not to apologize for an attempt in this kind, as though he were suggesting something altogether novel and unheard of before. 'It is,' he says, 'my persuasion that the parables in this chapter are not to be considered disjointedly, but to be taken together as a connected series, indicating, progressively , the several stages of advancement through which the mystical kingdom of Christ, upon earth, was to proceed, from its commencement to its consummation . . . . It will be understood, then, that each parable has a period peculiarly its own, in which the state of things, so signified, predominates; but when another state of things commences, the former does not cease. It only becomes less prominent; operative as really as ever, but in a way subsidiary to that which now takes the lead. It will follow that each succeeding stage implies a virtual combination of all that has gone before, and of course the grand concluding scene will contain the sublimated spirit and extracted essence of the whole.' Bengel has anticipated all this. He refers the first parable to the times of Christ and his immediate Apostles, when was the original sowing of the word of eternal life. The second, that of the Tares, belongs to the age immediately following, when watchfulness against false doctrine began to diminish, and heresies to creep in. The third, that of the Mustard-seed, to the time of Constantine, when the Church, instead of even seeming to need support, evidently gave it, and the great ones of the earth sought its shadow and protection. The fourth, that of the Leaven, sets forth the diffusion of true religion through the whole world. The fifth, of the Hid Treasure, refers to the more hidden state of the Church, signified in the Apocalypse (12:6) by the woman flying into the wilderness. The sixth, that of the Pearl, to the glorious time when the kingdom shall be esteemed above all things, Satan being bound. The seventh, of the Draw-net, describes the ultimate confusion, separation, and judgment.

In rejecting this notion of an historico-prophetical character, as belonging to these parables, for which certainly there is no warrant whatever, we must not at the same time refuse to acknowledge that the mystical number seven has here, as almost everywhere else in Scripture, its purpose and meaning, that the parables possess a most significant unity of their own, being knit to one another by very real bonds, succeeding one another in a logical order, and together constituting a complete and harmonious whole. But it is the ideas and laws, not the actual facts, of the Church's history which they declare. Thus in the Sower are set forth the causes of the failures and success which the word of the Gospel meets, when it is preached in the world. In the Tares, the obstacles to the internal development of Christ's kingdom, even after a Church has been hedged in and fenced round from the world, are traced up to their true author, with a warning against methods in which men might be tempted to remove those obstacles. The Mustard-seed and the Leaven announce, the first, the outward, and the second, the inward, might of that kingdom; and therefore implicitly prophesy of its development in spite of all these obstacles, and its triumph over them. As these two are objective and general, so the two which follow, the Hid Treasure and the Pearl, are subjective and individual; declaring the relation of the kingdom to every man, its supreme worth, and how those who have discovered that worth will be willing to renounce all things for its sake. They have besides mutual relations already touched on, and in the same way as the Mustard-seed and the Leaven, complete one another. Finally this of the Draw-net declares how that entire separation from evil, which it is right to long for, but wrong by self-willed efforts prematurely to anticipate, shall in God's own time come to pass; looking forward to which, each should give diligence so to use the privileges and means of grace which the communion of the Church affords him, that he may be among the 'taken' and not the 'left,' when the great 'Fisher of men' shall separate forever between the precious and the vile.

8.

The Unmerciful Servant

Matthew 18:21–35

Aquestion of Peter's gives occasion to this parable, that question growing out of some words of Christ, in which He had declared to the members of his future kingdom how they should bear themselves towards an offending brother. Peter would willingly know more on this matter, and brings to the Lord his question: 'Lord, how oft shall my brother sin against me, and I forgive him? Till seven times?' Chrysostom observes the Peter, thus instancing seven as the number of times of forgiveness, accounted probably that his charity was taking a large stretch, these seven being four times oftener than the Jewish masters enjoined; grounding as they did the duty of forgiving three times and not more, upon Amox 1:3; 2:6; and on Job 33:29, 30. He extended their three to seven, no doubt, out of a just sense that the spirit of the new law of love which Christ has brought into the world—a law larger, freer, more long-suffering than the old—demanded this. There was then in Peter's mind a consciousness of this new law of love—though an obscure one; else he would not have deemed it possible that love could ever be overcome by hate, good by evil. But there was, at the same time a fundamental error in the question itself; for in proposing a limit beyond which forgiveness should not extend, it was evidently assumed, that a man in forgiving, gave up a right which he might, under certain circumstances, exercise. In this parable the Lord will make clear that when God calls on a member of his kingdom to forgive, He does not call on him to renounce a right, but that he has now no right to exercise in the matter; for having himself sought and accepted forgiveness, he has implicitly pledged himself to show it; and it is difficult to imagine how any amount of

407

didactic instruction could have brought home this truth with at all the force and conviction of the parable which follows.

'Jesus saith unto him, I say not unto thee, Until seven times; but, Until seventy times seven. Therefore,'—to the end that Peter may understand the larger demands made on him by the new law of love—*'is the kingdom of heaven likened unto a certain king, which would take account of his servants.'* This is the first of the parables in which God appears as King. *We* are the servants with whom He takes account. This account, as is plain, is not the *final* reckoning, not therefore identical with the reckoning of Matt. 25:19; 2 Cor. 5:10; Rev. 20:11, 12; but rather such as that of Luke 16:2. To this He brings us by the preaching of the law—by the setting of our sins before our face—by awakening and alarming our conscience that was asleep before—by bringing us into adversities (2 Chr. 33:11–13)—by casting us into sore sicknesses (Job 33:19–30), into perils of death; so that there is not a step between us and it (2 Kgs. 20:4); He takes account with us, when He makes us feel that we could not answer Him one thing in a thousand, that our trespasses are more than the hairs of our heads; when by one means or another He brings our careless carnal security to an end (Ps. 1:21; Acts 16:30). Thus David was summoned before God by the word of Nathan the prophet (2 Sam. 12); thus the Ninevites by the preaching of Jonah (Jon. 3:4); thus the Jews by John the Baptist (Luke 3:3–14).

'And when he had begun to reckon, one was brought unto him, which owed him ten thousand talents.' The sum is great, whatever talents we assume; if Hebrew talents, it will be enormous indeed; yet thus only the fitter to express the immensity of every man's transgression in thought, word, and deed, against God. Over against the Ten Commandments which he should have kept, are the ten thousand talents—for the number is not accidental—setting forth the debts (see Matt. 6:12) which he has incurred. So far as the letter of the parable reaches, we may account for the vastness of the debt by supposing the defaulter to have been one of the chief officers of the king, a farmer or administrator of the royal revenues. Or, seeing that in the despotisms of the East, where a nobility does not exist, and all, from the highest to the lowest, stand in an absolutely servile relation to the monarch, this name of *'servant'* need not hinder us from regarding him as one, to whom some chief post of honor and dignity in the kingdom had been committed—a satrap who should have remitted the revenues of his province to the royal treasury. The king had not far to go, he had only *'begun to reckon'*

when he lighted on this one; perhaps the first whose accounts were examined; there may have been others with yet larger debts behind. This one *'was brought unto him,'* for he never would have come of himself; more probably would have made that *'ten thousand'* into twenty; for the secure sinner goes on, heaping up wrath against the day of wrath, writing himself an ever deeper debtor in the books of God.

'But forasmuch as he had not to pay, his lord commanded him to be sold, and his wife, and children, and all that he had, and payment to be made.' The sale of the debtor's wife and children rested upon the assumption that they were a part of his poverty. Such was the theory and practice of the Roman law. That it was allowed under the Mosaic law to sell an insolvent debtor, is implicitly stated, Lev. 25:39; and from verse 41 we infer that his family came into bondage with him; no less is implied at Ex. 22:3; 2 Kgs. 4:1; Neh. 5:5; Is. 50:1; 58:6; Jer. 34:8–11; Amos 2:6; 8:6. The later Jewish doctors disallowed this practice, except where a thief should be sold to make good the wrong which he had done; and in our Lord's time a custom so harsh had probably quite disappeared from among the Jews. Certainly the imprisonment of a debtor, twice occurring in this parable (vv. 30, 34), formed no part of the Jewish law; and, where the creditor possessed the power of selling him into bondage, was totally superfluous. *'The tormentors'* also (v. 34) have a foreign appearance, and dispose us to look for the scene of the parable among the Oriental monarchies, and not in the Jewish commonwealth, where a more merciful legislation tempered the rights of the rich and the strong. For the spiritual significance, this of having nothing to pay expresses the utter bankruptcy of every child of Adam as he stands in the presence of a holy God, and is tried by the strictness of his holy law (Rom. 3:23; Job 42:5, 6). The dreadful command that he shall be sold and all that he has (cf. Ps. 44:12), is the expression of God's right and power altogether to alienate from Himself, reject, and deliver over into bondage, all those who have thus come short of his glory (Ps. 44:12); that by a terrible but righteous sentence these, unless this sentence be reversed, shall be punished by everlasting destruction from the presence of the Lord and the glory of his power.

'The servant therefore,' hearing the dreadful doom pronounced against him, betakes himself to supplication, the one resource that is left him; he *'fell down, and worshiped him.'* The formal act of worship, or adoration, consisted in prostration on the ground, with the

embracing and kissing of the feet and knees. Origen bids us here to note a nice observance of proprieties in the slighter details of the parable. This servant *'worshiped'*—which, as between equals, would have been out of place—he only *'besought'* him. His *'Lord, have patience with me, and I will pay thee all,'* is characteristic of the anguish of the moment, out of which he is ready to promise impossible things, even mountains of gold, if only he may be delivered from his present fear. When words corresponding to these find utterance from a sinner's lips in the first conviction of his sin, they testify that he has not yet attained to a full insight into his relations with God; but has still much to learn; and this chiefly, that no future obedience can make up for past disobedience; since that future obedience God claims for his own, and as nothing more than his due. It could not, therefore, even were there no fault or flaw in it, and there will be many, make compensation for the defects of the past; and in this *'I wil pay thee all,'* we must detect the voice of self-righteousness, imagining that, if only time were allowed, it could make all past shortcomings good. This goes far to explain the later conduct of this suppliant. It is clear that he whom this servant represents, had never come to a true recognition of the immensity of his debt. Little, in the subjective measure of his own estimate, has been forgiven him, and therefore he loves little, or not at all (Luke 7:47). It is true that by his demeanor and his cry he did recognize his indebtedness, else would there have been no setting of him free; and he *might* have gone one, and, had he only been true to his own mercies, he would have gone on, to an ever fuller recognition of the grace shown him: but as it was, in a little while he lost sight of it altogether, and showed too plainly that he had 'forgotten that he was purged from his old sins' (2 Pet. 1:9).

However, at the earnestness of his present prayer, *'the lord of that servant was moved with compassion, and loosed him, and forgave him the debt.'* The severity of God only endures till the sinner is brought to acknowledge his guilt- like Joseph's harshness with his brethren, it is love in disguise; and having done its work, having brought him to own that he is verily guilty, it reappears as grace again; that very reckoning, which at first threatened him with irremediable ruin, being, if he will use it aright, the chiefest mercy of all; bringing indeed his debt to a head, but only bringing it to his head, that it may be forever abolished (Ps. 103:12: Jer. 50:20; Mic. 7:19). That, however, must be first done. There can be no forgiving in the dark. God will forgive; but He will have the sinner to know what and how much he is forgiven; there must be first a 'come now, and let us reason together,' before the scarlet can be made white as snow (Is. 1:18). The sinner must know his sins for what they are, a mountain of transgression, before ever they can be cast into the deep sea of God's mercy. He must first have the sentence of death in himself, ere the words of life will have any abiding worth for him.

Such abiding worth they have not for the servant who, crying for mercy, has obtained it (Wisd. 12:18, 19). *'The same servant went out,'* that is, from his master's presence, *'and found,'* on the instant, as it would seem, and while the memory of his lord's goodness should have been fresh upon him, *'one of his fellow-servants, which owed him a hundred pence.'* May we press this *'went out,'* and say that we go out from the presence of our God, when we fail to keep an ever-lively sense of the greatness of our sin, and the greatness of his forgiveness? So more than one interpreter; yet I cannot see more in this than what the outward conditions of the parable require. He is said to go out, because in the actual presence of his lord he could not have ventured on the outrage which follows. The term *'fellow-servant'* here does not imply equality of rank between these two, or that they filled similar offices; but only that they stood both in the relation of servants to a common lord. And this sum is so small, *'and hundred peace,'* as the other had been so large, *'ten thousand talents,'* to signify how little any man can offend against his brother, compared with that which every man has offended against God; so that, in Chrysostom's words, these offenses to those are as a drop of water to the boundless ocean.

The whole demeanor of this unrelenting creditor toward *his* debtor is graphically described: *'He laid hands on him, and took him by the throat, saying, Pay me that thou owest.'* Some press the word in the original, and find therein an aggravation of this servant's cruelty, as though he was not even sure whether the debt were owing or not. There is no warrant for this. That the debt was owing is plain; he found, we are told, *'one of his fellow-servants, which owed him a hundred pence.'* Any different assumption would mar the proprieties of the story, would turn the edge of the parable, and we should have here a vulgar extortioner and wrong-doer. But such a one the law would have sufficiently condemned; there would have been no need to speak for this a parable of the kingdom of heaven. The lessons which it teaches are different; lessons which they need to learn who are not under the law, but under grace; and this chiefly—that it is not always *right*, but often the most opposite to right, to press our *rights,* that in the kingdom of grace the *summum jus* may be the *summa injria.* This man would fain have been measured to by god in one measure, while he measure to his fellows in another. He would fain be forgiven, while yet he did not forgive. But this may not be. A man must make his choice. It is free to him to dwell in the kingdom of grace: but then, receiving grace, he must show grace; finding love, he must exercise love. If, on the contrary, he pushes his rights as far as they will go, if the law of severest justice is the law of his dealings with his fellowmen, he must look for the same as the law of God's dealings with him, and in the measure wherein he has meted, that it shall be measured to him again.

It was in vain that *'his fellow-servant fell down at his feet, and besought him, saying, Have patience with me, and I will pay thee all';* unconsciously using exactly the same words of entreaty which he, in the agony of his distress, had used, and, using, had found mercy. *'He would not; but went and cast him into prison, till he should pay the debt';* dragging, as we may suppose, his debtor with him till he could consign him to the safe custody of the jailer; refusing, in Chrysostom's words, 'to recognize the port in which he had himself so lately escaped shipwreck'; and all unconscious that he was condemning himself, and revoking his own mercy. But such is man, so harsh and hard, when he walks otherwise than in a constant sense of forgiveness received from God. Ignorance or forgetfulness of his own guilt makes him harsh, unforgiving, and cruel to others; or at best, he is only hindered from being such by those weak defenses of natural character which may at any moment be broken down. The man who knows not his own guilt, is ever ready to exclaim, as David in the time of his worst sin, 'The man that hath done this thing shall surely die' (2 Sam. 12:5); to be as extreme in judging others, as he is remiss and indulgent in judging himself; while, on the other hand, it is to them 'who are spiritual' that St. Paul commits the restoring of a brother 'overtaken in a fault' (Ga. 6:1); and when he urges on Titus the duty of showing meekness unto all men, he finds the motive here—'for we ourselves also were sometimes foolish, disobedient, deceived, serving diverse lusts and pleasures' (Tit. 3:3). It is just in man to be merciful (Matt. 1:19), to be *humane* is *human*. None but the altogether Righteous may press his utmost rights; whether He will do so or not is determined by altogether different considerations, but He has not that to hold his hand, which every *man* has, even the sense of his own proper guilt (John 8:7–9).

"So when his fellow-servants saw what was done, they were very sorry, and came and told unto their lord all that was done.' It is not in heaven only that indignation is felt when men thus measure to others in so different a measure from that which has been measured to them. There are on earth also those who have learned what is the meaning of the mercy which the sinner finds, and what the obligations which it imposes on him; and who mourn in their prayer when this is greatly forgotten by others round them. The servants were *'sorry';* their lord, as we read presently, was *'wroth'* (v. 34); to them grief, to him anger, is ascribed. The distinction is not accidental, nor without its grounds. In man, the sense of his own guilt, the deep consciousness that whatever sin he sees come to ripeness in another, exists in its germ and seed in his own heart, with the knowledge that all flesh is one, and that the sin of one calls for humiliation from all, will rightly make sorrow the predominant feeling in his heart, when the spectacle of moral evil is brought before his eyes (Ps. 119:136, 158; Rom. 9:2; 2 Pet. 1:7); but in God the pure hatred of sin, which is, indeed, his love of holiness at its opposite pole, finds place. At the same time the sorrow which is here ascribed to the servants is not, as Bengel has well observed, without its own admixture of indignation. As the servants of the king here, so the servants of a heavenly King complain to Him, mourn over all the oppressions that are wrought in their sight: the things which they cannot set right themselves, the wrongs which they are weak to redress, they can at least bring to Him; and they do not bring them in vain. *'Then his lord, after that he had called him, said unto him, O thou wicked servant'*—this, which he had not called him on account of his debt, he now calls him on account of his ingratitude and cruelty—*'I forgave thee all that debt, because thou desiredst me: shouldest not thou also have had compassion on thy fellow-servant, even as I had pit on thee?* The guilt which he is charged with is, not that, *needing mercy,* he refused to show it, but that, *having received mercy,* he remains unmerciful still (cf. 1 John 4:11). A most important difference! They, therefore, who like him are hardhearted and cruel, do not thereby bear witness that they have received no mercy: on the contrary, the stress of their offense is, that having received an infinite mercy, they remain unmerciful yet. The objective fact, that Christ has put away the sin of the world, and that we have been baptized into the remission of sins, stands firm, whether we allow it to exercise a purifying, sanctifying, humanizing influence on our hearts or not. Our faith apprehends, indeed, the benefit, but has not

created it, any more than our opening of our eyes upon the sun, has first set the sun in the heavens.

'*And his lord was wroth, and delivered him to the tormentors, till he should pay all that was due unto him*'—according to that word, 'He shall have judgment without mercy, that hath showed no mercy' (James 2:13). The king had dealt with him before as a creditor with a debtor, now as a judge with a criminal. '*The tormentors*' are those who, as the word implies, shall make the life of the prisoner bitter to him; wring out from him the confession of any concealed hoards which he may still possess; even as there are '*tormentors*' in that world of woe, whereof this prison is a figure—fellow-sinners and evil angels—instruments of the just yet terrible judgments of God. But here it is strange that the king delivers the offender to prison and to punishment not for the evil which he had just wrought, but for that old debt which had seemed unconditionally remitted to him. When Hammond says, that the king 'revoked his *designed* mercy,' and would transfer this view of the transaction to the relation between God and sinners, this is one of those evasions of a difficulty by help of an ambiguous expression, or a word ingeniously thrust in, which are too frequent even in good interpreters of Scripture. It was not merely a *designed* mercy; the king had not merely *purposed* to forgive him, but, as is distinctly declared, '*forgave him the debt.*' It has been ingeniously suggested that the debt for which he is now cast into prison, is the debt of mercy and love, which, according to that pregnant word of St. Paul's, 'Owe no man anything, but to love one another,' he owed, but had so signally failed to pay. Few, however, would be satisfied with this. As little are the cases of Adonijah and Shimei (1 Kgs. 2) altogether in point. They, no doubt, on occasion of their later offenses, were punished far more severely than they would have been, but for their former faults; yet for all this it is not the former offenses which are revived that they may be punished, but the later offense which calls down its own punishment; and moreover, parallels drawn from questionable acts of imperfect men, go but a little way in establishing the righteousness of god.

The question which seems involved in all this, Do sins, once forgiven, return on the sinner through his after offenses? Is one frequently and fully discussed by the Schoolmen; and of course the parable takes always a prominent place in such discussions. But it may be worth considering, whether difficulties upon this point do not arise mainly from too dead and formal a way of contemplating

the forgiveness of sins; from our suffering the earthly circumstances of the remission of a debt to embarrass the heavenly truth,
instead of regarding them as helps, but weak and often failing
ones, for the setting forth of that truth. One cannot conceive of remission of sins apart from living communion with Christ; being
baptized into Him, we are baptized into the forgiveness of sins;
and the abiding in Christ and the forgiveness of sins go ever henceforward hand in hand, are inseparable one from the other. But if we
cease to abide in Him, we then fall back into that state which is of
itself a state of condemnation and death, and one on which the
wrath of God is resting. If then, setting aside the contemplation of
a man's sins as a formal debt, which must either be forgiven to him
or not forgiven, we contemplate the life out of Christ as a state or
condition of wrath, and the life in Christ as one of grace, the one a
walking in darkness, and the other a walking in the light, we can
better understand how a man's sins should return upon him; that
is, he sinning anew falls back into the darkness out of which he had
been delivered, and, no doubt, all that he has done of evil in former
times adds to the thickness of that darkness, causes the wrath of
God to abide more terribly on that state in which he now is, and
therefore upon him (John 5:14). Nor may we leave out of sight that
all forgiveness, short of that crowning and last act, which will find
place on the day of judgment, and will be followed by a blessed
impossibility of sinning any more, is conditional—in the very nature of things so conditional, that the condition must in every case
be assumed, whether stated or no, that condition being that the forgiven man continue in faith and obedience, in that state of grace
into which he has been brought; which he who by this unmerciful
servant is figured to us here, had evidently failed to do. He that
will partake of the final salvation must abide in Christ, else he will
be 'cast forth as a branch and withered' (John 15:6). This is the condition, not arbitrarily imposed from without, but belonging to the
very essence of the salvation itself; just as if one were drawn from
the raging sea, and set upon the safe shore, the condition of his
continued safety would be that he remained there, and did not
again cast himself into the raging waters. In this point of view 1
John 1:7 will supply an interesting parallel: 'If we walk in the light,
as He is in the light, we have fellowship one with another, and the
blood of Jesus Chris his Son cleanseth us from all sin.' He whom
this servant represents does not abide in the light of love, but falls
back into the old darkness; he has, therefore, no fellowship with his

brother, and the cleansing power of the blood of Jesus Christ ceases from him.

It is familiar to many that the theologians of Rome have drawn an argument for purgatory from the words, *'till he should pay all that was due,'* and no less from the parallel expression, Matt. 5:26; as though they marked a limit beyond which the punishment should not extend. But the phrase is proverbial, and all which it signifies is, that the offender shall now taste of the extreme rigor of the law; shall have justice without mercy; and always *paying,* shall yet never have *paid off,* his debt. For since the sinner could never acquit the slightest portion of the debt in which he is indebted to God, the putting that as a condition of his liberation, which it is impossible could ever be fulfilled, may be the strongest possible way of expressing the everlasting duration of his punishment. When the Phocaeans, abandoning their city, swore that they would not return till the mass of iron which they plunged into the sea appeared once more upon the surface, this was the most emphatic form they could devise of declaring that they would *never* return; such an emphatic declaration is the present.

The Lord concludes with a word of earnest warning: *'So likewise shall my heavenly Father do also unto you, if ye from your hearts forgive not every one his brother their trespasses.'* *'So'*—with the same rigor; such treasures of wrath, as well as such treasures of grace, are with Him: He who could so greatly forgive, can also so greatly punish. *'My heavenly Father'*—not thereby implying that in such case He would not be *theirs,* since they, thus acting, would have denied the relationship; for our Lord says often *'My Father'* (as verse 19), when no such reason can be assigned. On the declaration itself we may observe that the Christian stands in a middle point, between a mercy received and a mercy which he yet needs to receive. Sometimes the first is urged upon him as an argument for showing mercy—'forgiving one another, as Christ forgave you' (Col. 3:13: Eph. 4:32); sometimes the last, 'Blessed are the merciful, for they shall obtain mercy (Matt. 5:7); 'With the merciful Thou wilt show Thyself merciful' (Ps. 18:25); 'Forgive, and ye shall be forgiven' (Luke 6:37); while sometimes the other and more menacing side of the same truth is urged, as in this present parable, and in words recorded by St. Mark, 'But if ye do not forgive, neither will your Father which is in heaven forgive your trespasses' (11:26; cf. James 2:13); and in the same way by the Son of Sirach (28:3, 4), 'One man beareth hatred against another, and doth he seek pardon from the

Lord? He showeth no mercy to a man who is like himself, and doth he ask forgiveness of his own sins?' And thus, while he must ever look back on a mercy received as the source and motive of the mercy which he shows, he looks forward as well to the mercy which he yet needs, and which he is assured that the merciful, according to what Bengel beautifully calls the *benigna talio* of the kingdom of God, shall obtain, as a new provocation to its abundant exercise. Tholuck has some good remarks upon this point: 'From the circumstance that mercy is here [Matt. 5:7] promised as the recompense of anterior mercy on our part, it might indeed be inferred that under "merciful" we are to imagine such as have not yet in any degree partaken of mercy; but this conclusion would only be just on the assumption that the divine compassion consisted in an isolated act, of which man could be the object only once for all in his life. Seeing, however, that it is an act which extends over the whole life of the individual, and reaches its culminating point in eternity, it behoves us to consider the compassion of God for man, and man for his brethren, as reciprocally calling forth and affording a basis for one another.' And a difficulty which Origen suggests, finds its explanation here. He asks, *where in time* are we to place the transactions shadowed forth in this parable? There are reasons on the one hand why they should be placed at the end of this present dispensation; since at what other time does God take account with his servants for condemnation or acquittal? While yet, if placed there, what further opportunity would the forgiven servant have for displaying the harshness and cruelty which he actually does display towards his fellow-servant? The difficulty disappears, when we no longer contemplate forgiveness as an isolated act, which must take place at some definite moment, and then is past and irrevocable; but contemplate it as ever going forward, as running parallel with and extending over the entire life of the redeemed, which, as it is a life of continual sin and shortcoming, so has need to be a life of continual forgiveness.

9.

The Laborers in the Vineyard

Matthew 20:1–16

This parable stands in closest connection with the words which went immediately before—that is, with the four last verses of the preceding chapter, and can only be rightly understood by their help; which being so, the actual division of chapters is here peculiarly unfortunate; often causing, as it does, the parable to be explained with no reference to the context, and with no attempt to trace the circumstances out of which it sprung. And yet on a right tracing of this connection, and the showing how it grew out of, and was in fact an answer to, Peter's question, 'What shall we have?' The success of the exposition will mainly depend. It is a parable which stands only second to that of the Unjust Steward in the number and wide divergence from one another of the explanations that have been proposed for it, and only second to that, if indeed second, in the difficulties which it presents. These Chrysostom states clearly and strongly; though few will be wholly satisfied with his solution of them. There is, first, the difficulty of bringing it into harmony with the saying by which it is introduced and concluded, and which it is plainly intended to illustrate; and secondly, there is the moral difficulty, the same which the elder brother in the paraable of the Prodigal Son presents to us—namely, how can one who is himself a member of the kingdom of God 'be held,' as Chrysostom terms it, 'by that lowest of all passions, envy, and an evil dyd,' grudging in his heart the favors shown to other members of that kingdom? Or, if it be denied that the murmurers of this parable are members of that kingdom, how this denial is reconcilable with their having labored all day long in the vineyard, and ultimately carrying away their own reward? And lastly, it is not easy, but most hard, to determine what is the drift and scope of the parable, its leading intention and purpose.

Of its many interpreters there are, first, those who see in the equal penny to all, the key to the whole matter, and for whom its lesson is this—the equality of rewards in the kingdom of God. This was Luther's explanation in his earlier works, though he afterwards saw reason to withdraw it. But however this may appear to agree with the parable, it evidently agrees not at all with the saying which sums it up, and contains its moral: *'Many that are first shall be last, and the last shall be first'*; for such an equality would be no reversing of the order of the first and last, but a setting of all upon a level.

Others affirm that the parable is meant to set forth this truth—that God does not regard the length of time during which men are occupied in his work, but the fidelity and strenuous exertion with which they accomplish that work. Of this explanation there will presently be occasion to speak more at large; it will be enough not to observe that if all had turned on the fact that the last-hired laborers had worked more strenuously than the first, it is impossible that this circumstance should have been omitted.

Calvin's explanation is this, a little modified, and in fact amounts to the same thing. There is a warning here that we be not over-confident, because we may have begun well; lest (though this is not his illustration), like the here in the fable, waxing careless and remiss, we let others pass us by; and so, from the first, fall into the hindmost rank: that no one begin to boast, or consider the battle won, till he put off his armour (1 Kgs. 20:11). But to him also it may be replied that the parable affords no warrant for the assumption that the laborers first engaged and slackened their exertions during the latter part of the day.

There are others who find in the successive hours at which the different bands of laborers were hired, the leading feature of the parable. And these interpreters may be again subdivided, according as they regard these hours as successive ages in the world's history, or successive periods in the lives of individual men. There are, first, those who, as Ireneus, Origen, and Hilary, see here a history of the different summonses to a work of righteousness which God has made to men from the beginning of the world—to Adam—to Noah—to Abraham—to Moses—and lastly to the Apostles, bidding them, each in his time and order, to go work in his vineyard. Of these laborers, all the earlier lived during weaker and more imperfect dispensations, and underwent, therefore, a harder toil, as having less abundant gifts of the spirit, less clear knowledge of the grace of God in Christ, to sustain them, than the later called, the members of the Christian Church. Their heavier toil, therefore, might aptly be set forth by a longer period of work, and that at the more oppressive time of the day (cf. Acts 15:10); while the Apostles, and the other faithful called into God's vineyard at the eleventh hour ('the last time,' or 'the last *hour*,' as St. John ([1 Ep. 2:18] terms it), and partakers of the larger freer grace now given in Christ, had little by comparison to endure. But of these interpreters, it may be fairly asked, *When* could that murmuring have taken place, even supposing God's servants of one age *could* thus grudge because of the larger grace bestowed upon others? This could not have been in their lifetime; for before the things were even revealed which God had prepared for his people that came after, they were in their graves. It is still less conceivable as finding place in the day of judgment, or in the kingdom of love made perfect. Unless, then, we quite explain away the murmuring, accepting Chrysostom's ingenious solution of it, that it is only brought in to enhance the greatness of the things freely given in the last days, things so glorious, that those earlier and more scantly endowed might be tempted to murmur, comparing themselves with their more richly furnished successors—this explanation seems untenable; as, were it worthwhile, much more might be urged against it.

The other subdivision of this group of interpreters see in the different hours at which the laborers are hired, different periods in men's lives, at which they enter on the Lord's work; affirming that its purpose is to encourage those who have entered late on his service, now to labor heartily, not allowing the consciousness of past negligences to make slack their hands; since they too, if only they will labor with their might for the time, long or short, which remains, shall receive with the others a full reward. This is, in the main, Chrysostom's view: but with a free admission that, under certain limitations, such encouragement may be drawn from the parable, it is another thing to say that this is the admonishment which it is especially meant to convey. In what living connection would the parable then stand with what went before, with Peter's question, or with the temper out of which that question grew, and which this teaching of the Lord was intended to meet and to correct

But nearer to the truth than all these explanations is that which finds here a warning and a prophecy of the causes which would lead to the rejection of the Jews, the first called into the vineyard of the Lord—these causes being mainly their proud appreciation of themselves and of their own work; their displeasure at seeing the Gentiles, aliens so long, put on the same footing, admitted to equal privileges, with themselves in the kingdom of God: and an agreement or covenant being made with the first hired, and none with those subsequently engaged, has been urged as confirming this view. No interpretation of the parable can be true which excludes this application of it. It *was* notably fulfilled in the Jews; while yet this fulfillment of it was only one out of many; for our Lord's words are so rich in meaning, so touch the central heart of things that they are continually finding their fulfillment. Had this, however been his primary meaning, we should expect to hear of but two bands of laborers, the first hired and the last: all who come between would only serve to confuse and perplex. The solution sometimes given of this objection—that the successive hirings represent successive summonses to the Jews; first, under Moses and Aaron; secondly, under David and the kings; thirdly under the Maccabaean chiefs and priests; and lastly, in the time of Christ and his Apostles; or that these are severally Jews, Samaritans, and proselytes of greater and less strictness—seems devised merely to escape from an embarrassment, and only witnesses for its existence without removing it.

Better then to say that the parable is directed against a wrong temper and spirit of mind, which, indeed, was notable manifested in the Jews, but one against which all men in possession of spiritual privileges, have need to be, men in possession of spiritual privileges, have need to be, and herein are, warned: this warning being primarily addressed not to them, but to the Apostles, as the foremost workers in the Christian Church, the earliest called to labor in the Lord's vineyard—'the first,' both in time, and in toil and pains. They had seen the rich young man (19:22) go sorrowful away, unable to abide the proof by which the Lord had mercifully revealed to him how strong the bands by which the world was holding him still. They (for Peter here, as so often, is spokesman for all), would fain know what *their* reward should be, who had done this very thing from which he had shrunk, and forsaken all for the Gospel's sake (v. 27). The Lord answers them first and fully, that they and as many as should do the same for his sake, should reap an abundant reward (vv. 28, 29). But for all this the question itself, 'What shall we have?' was not a right one; it put their relation to their Lord on a wrong footing; there was a tendency in it to bring their obedience to a calculation of so much work, so much reward. There lurked too a certain self-complacency in it. That spirit of self-exalting comparison of ourselves with others, which is so likely to be stirring, when we behold any signal failure on their part, was obscurely at work in them; so obscurely that they may have been hardly conscious of it themselves; but He who knew what was in man, saw with a glance into the depths of Peter's heart, and having replied to the direct question, 'What shall we have?' went on to crush the evil in the bud, and before it should unfold itself further. 'Not of works, lest any man should boast,' this was the truth which they were in danger of missing, and which He would now by the parable enforce; and if nothing of works, but all of grace for all, then no glorying of over another, no grudging of one against another, no claim as of right upon the part of any. In that question of theirs there spoke out something of the spirit of the hireling, and it is against this spirit that the parable is directed, which might justly be entitled, *One the nature of rewards in the kingdom of God*—the whole finding a most instructive commentary in Rom. 4:1–4, which supplies not a *verbal*, but more deeply interesting, a *real* parallel to the parable before us.

So far as it is addressed to Peter, and in him to all true believers, it is rather a warning against what *might* be, if they were not careful to watch against it, than a prophecy of what *would* be. For we cannot conceive of him who dwells in love as allowing himself in envious and grudging thoughts against any of his brethren, because, though they have entered later on the service of God, or been engaged in a lighter labor, they will yet be sharers with him of the same heavenly reward; or refusing to welcome them gladly to all the blessings and privileges of the communion of Christ. Least of all can we imagine him so to forget that he also is saved by grace, as to allow such hateful feelings to come to a head, taking form and shape, which they do in the parable; or as justifying these to himself and to God, like the spokesman among the murmurers here. We cannot conceive this even here in our present imperfect state, much less in the perfected kingdom hereafter; for love 'rejoices in the truth,' and the very fact of one so grudging against another would prove that he himself did not dwell in love, and therefore was under sentence of exclusion from that kingdom. It is then a warning to the Apostles, and through them to all believers, of what might be, not a prophecy of what shall be for any who share in the final reward. They are taught that, however long continued their work, abundant their labors, yet without this charity to their brethren, this humility before God, they are nothing—that pride and a self-complacent estimation of their work, like the fly in the precious ointment, would spoil the work, however great it might be, since that work stands only in humility; and from first they would fall to last. There is then this difference between the parabolic framework, and the truth of which it is the exponent, that while the householder could not with equity altogether deprive the first laborers of their hire, notwithstanding their pride and discontent, who consequently receive their wages, and are only punished by a severe rebuke, yet the lesson taught to Peter, and through him to us all, is, that the first may be altogether last; that those who seem chiefest in labor, yet, if they forget withal that the reward is of grace and not of works, and begin to boast and exalt themselves above their fellow-laborers, may *altogether* lost the things which they have wrought; while those who seem last, may yet, by keeping their humility, be acknowledged first and foremost in the day of God. With these preliminary remarks, which the difficulties of the parable have made it necessary to draw out at length, we may now proceed to consider its details.

'*The kingdom of heaven is like unto a man that is a householder, which went out early in the morning to hire laborers into his vineyard:*' in other words, The manner of God's dealings with those whom He calls to the privileges of working in his Church is like to that of a householder, who should to out early in the morning to hire laborers. Here as ever in the kingdom of heaven in it God who seeks his laborers, and not they who seek Him: 'You have not chosen Me, but I have chosen you (John 15:16; Mark 3:13; Luke 5:10; John 1:43; 1 Tim. 1:12). Every summons to a work in the heavenly vineyard is from the Lord. The original impulse is always his: all which is man's in the matter is, that he do not resist the summons, which it is his melancholy prerogative that he is able to do. It is 'a call,' according to the instructive Scriptural expression: but as in the natural world a call implies no force, may obeyed or may be disregarded, so also is it in the spiritual.

"*And when he had agreed with the laborers for a penny a day, he sent them into his vineyard.*' The different footing upon which the different bands of laborers went to their work,would scarcely have been so expressly noted, if not signification were to be found therein. An agreement was made by these first-hired laborers before they entered on their labor, the same which Peter would have made, 'What shall we have?'—while those subsequently engaged went in a simpler spirit, relying on the householder's assurance that whatever was right, they should receive. We have here already hints of that wrong spirit on the part of some, which presently comes to a head (vv. 11, 12); on the part of others, we have the true spirit of humble waiting upon the Lord, in full confidence that He will give far more than his servants can desire or deserve, that God is not unrighteous to forget any labor of love which is wrought for Him.

At the third, at the sixth, and at the ninth hour—or at nine in the morning, at midday, and at three in the afternoon—the householder again went into the marketplace, and those whom he found waiting there, sent into his vineyard; incidents which call for no remark, as first and last are the only ones on whom the parable ultimately turns. *"And about the eleventh hour he went out, and found others standing idle, and saith unto them, Why stand ye here all the day idle.' 'They say unto him, Because no man hat hired us.'* There lay a certain amount of rebuke in the question, which this answer shall clear away; for it belongs to the idea of the parable, that the explanation which they offer should be accepted as perfectly satisfactory. It is not then in a Christian land, where men grow up under sacramental obligations, with the pure word of God sounding in their ears, that this answer could be given; or at least, only in such woeful instances as that which, alas! Our own land at the present affords, where in the bosom of the Church multitudes have been allowed to grow up ignorant of the blessings which her communion affords, and the responsibilities which this lays upon them; and even in *their* mouths there would only be a partial truth in this, *'No man hath hired us'*; since even they cannot be *altogether* ignorant of their Christian vocation. Only when the kingdom of God is first set up in a land, enters as a new and hitherto unknown power, could any with fully truth reply, *'No man hath hired us:*—if we have been living in disobedience to God, it has been because we were ignorant of Him; if we were serving Satan, it was because we knew no other master and no better service.'

While then the excuse which these laborers plead, appertains not to them who, growing up within the church, have despised to the last, or nearly to the last, God's repeated biddings to go work in his vineyard; while the unscriptural corollary cannot be appended to the parable, that it matters little at what time of men's lives they enter heartily upon his service, how long they despise his vows which have been upon them from the beginning; yet one would not therefore deny that there is such a thing even in the Christian Church as men being called—or to speak more correctly, since they were called long before—as men obeying the call and entering the Lord's vineyard, at the third, or sixth, or ninth, or even the eleventh hour. Only their case will be parallel not to that of any of these laborers—in regard of being able to make the same excuse as they did, but rather to that of the son, who, bidden to go work in his father's vineyard, at first refused, but afterwards repented and went (Matt. 21:28); and one of these, instead of clearing himself as respects the past, which these laborers do, will humble himself most deeply, while he considers all his neglected opportunities and the long-continued despite which he has done to the Spirit of grace. Yet while thus none can plead, 'No man hath hired us,' in a land where the Christian Church has long been established, and the knowledge of Christ more or less brought home unto all, the parable is not therefore without it application in such, since there also there will be many entering into the Lord's vineyard at different periods, even to a late one, of their lives; and who, truly repenting their past unprofitableness, and not attempting to excuse it, may find their work, be it brief or long, graciously accepted now, and may share hereafter in the full rewards of the kingdom. For in truth time belongs not to the kingdom of God. Not "How much has thou done?' but "What art thou now?' Will be the great question of the last day. Of course we must never forget that all which men have *done* will greatly affect what they *are;* yet still the parable is a protest against the whole *quantitative* appreciation of men's works (the Romanist), as distinct from the *qualitative,* against all which would make the works the end, and man the means, instead of the man the end, and the works the means—against that scheme which, however unconsciously, lies at the root of so many of the confusions in our theology at this day. Against all these the words of the householder, 'Go ye also into the vineyard, and whatsoever is right, that shall ye receive,' are a living protest.

'So when even was come, the lord of the vineyard saith unto his steward, Call the laborers, and give them their hire, beginning from the last unto the first.' This householder will fulfill strictly the precept of the law; the hired laborer shall not have his payment deferred till tomorrow: 'At his day thou shalt give him his hire, neither shall the sun go down upon it; for he is poor, and setteth his heart upon it' (Deut. 24:15; cf. Lev. 19:13; Job 7:2; Mal. 3:5; James 5:4; Tob. 4:14).

Christ is the 'steward,' or overseer rather, set over all God's house (Heb. 3:6; John 5:27; Matt. 11:27). The whole economy of salvation has been put into his hands, and as part of this the distribution of rewards (Rev. 2:7, 10, 17, 28, &c). The last hired, those who came in without any agreement made, the laborers of the eleventh hour, are the first to be paid 'They received every man a penny.' Here is encouragement—not to delay entering on God's service till late in our lives; for everywhere in Scripture there waits a marked blessing on early piety—but encouragement for those who have so done to work for the time which remains heartily and with their might. Misgivings concerning the acceptance of their work do not make men work the more strenuously; on the contrary, go far to cut the nerves of all exertion. There is much here to dispel such misgivings in those who would be most likely to feel them: let them labor in hope; they too shall be sharers in a full salvation.

It may be securely inferred that all between the last and the first hired received the penny as well; though it is the first hired alone who remonstrate, as those in whose case the injustice, for so it seemed to them, appeared the most fragrant. To assume, with Chrysostom, Maldonatus, Hammond, Waterland, and Olshausen, that these first hired had been doing their work negligently by comparison, while the last hired, such for instance as a Paul, whom Origen, quoting 1 Cor. 15:15, suggests, had done it with their might, and had in fact accomplished as much in their hour as the others in their day, is to assume that of which there is no slightest trace in the narrative. And more than this, such an assumption effectually turns the edge of the parable, defeats its whole purpose and intention; for what does it teach, if it does not teach us this, namely that men may do and suffer much, infinitely more than others, and yet be rejected, while those others are received—that first may be last, and last first? It is nothing strange that a rationalist like Kuinoel should adopt this explanation; for the whole matter is thus taken out of a higher spiritual world, and brought down to the commonest region of sense; since if one man accomplishes as much in a single hour as another in twelve, there is nothing wonderful in his receiving an equal reward. Every difficulty disappears—except indeed this, how the Lord should have cared to utter a parable for the justifying of so very ordinary a transaction; or, doing this, should have omitted that one thing which constituted the justification. But indeed this interpretation exactly brings us back to the level, from which to raise us the parable was spoken;

we have a Jewish, instead of an Evangelical, parable; and affirmation that the reward is not of grace, but of debt—the very error which it was meant to rebuke and to reprove.

When the first hired received the same sum as the others and no more, *'they murmured against the goodman of the house, saying, These last have wrought but one hour, and thou has made them equal unto us, which have borne the burden, and heat of the day.'* These other, they would say, have been laboring not merely for a far shorter time; but when they entered on their tasks it was already the cool of the evening, when toil is no longer so oppressive, while we have borne the scorching heat of the middle noon. But here the perplexing dilemma meets us, Either these are of the number of God's faithful people—how then can they murmur against Him, and grudge against their fellow-servants? Or they are not of that number—what then can we understand of their having labored the whole day through in his vineyard, and actually carrying away at last the penny, the reward of eternal life? It is an unnatural way of escaping the difficulty, to understand *'Take that which is thine,'* as meaning, 'Take the damnation which belongs to thee, the just punishment of thy pride and discontent; or as Basil the Great has it, 'Take the earthly reward, the "hundredfold" promised in this present time, but lose the "everlasting life," which thou shouldst have had in addition' (Matt. 19:29). Theophylact and others seek to mitigate as much as possible the guilt of their murmuring, and see in it no more than the expression of that surprise and admiration which will escape from some, at the unexpected position that others, of perhaps small account here, will occupy in the future kingdom of glory. But the expression of their discontent is too strong, and the rebuke that it calls out too severe, to admit of an extenuation such as this. Better to say that no analogy will be found for this murmuring in the future world of glory—and only where there is a large admixture of the old corruption, in the present world of grace. There is here rather a teaching by contraries; as thus, 'Since you cannot conceive such a spirit as that here held up before you, and which you feel to be so sinful and hateful, finding room in the perfected kingdom of God, check betimes its beginnings, check all inclinations to look grudgingly at your brethren, who, having lingered and loitered long, have yet found a place beside yourselves in the kingdom of grace, and are sharers in the same spiritual privileges; or to look down upon and despise those who occupy a less important field of labor, who are called in the providence of God to endure and suffer less than yourselves: repress all inclinations to pride yourselves on your own doings, as those they gave you a claim of right upon God, instead of accepting all of his undeserved mercy, and confessing that you as well as others must be saved entirely by grace.'

On the fact that the murmurers actually receive their penny, a Roman Catholic expositor ingeniously remarks that the denarius or penny was of different kinds; there was the double, the treble, the fourfold; that of brass, of silver, and of gold. The Jew (for he applies to the parable to Jew and Gentile) received what was his, his penny of the meaner metal, his earthly reward, and with that went his way; but the Gentile the golden penny, the spiritual reward, grace and glory, admission into the perfected kingdom of God. Ingenious as this is, no one will accept it as a fair explanation of the difficulty; and yet it may suggest valuable considerations. The penny *is* very different to the different receivers; *objectively* the same, *subjectively* it is very different; it is in fact to every one exactly what he will make it. What the Lord said to Abraham, He says to each and to all, 'I am the exceeding great reward'; and He has no other reward to impart to any save only this, namely Himself. To 'see Him as He is,' this is his one reward, the penny which is common to all. But they whom these murmuring laborers represent had been laboring for something else besides the knowledge and enjoyment of God, with an eye to some other reward, to something on account of which they could glory in themselves, and glory over others. It was not merely to have *much* which they desired, but to have *more* than others; not to grow together with the whole body of Christ, but to get before and beyond their brethren; and therefore the penny, because common to all, did not seem enough, while in fact it was to each what he would make it. For if the vision of God shall constitute the blessedness of the coming world, then they whose spiritual eye is most enlightened, will drink in most of his glory; then, since only like can know like, all advances which are here made in humility, in holiness, in love, are a polishing of the mirror that it may reflect more distinctly the divine image, a purging of the eye that it may see more clearly the divine glory, an enlarging of the vessel that it may receive more amply of the divine fullness; just as, on the other hand, all pride, all self-righteousness, all sin of every kind, whether it stop short with impairing, or end by altogether destroying, the capacities for receiving from God, is in its degree a staining of the mirror, a darkening of the eye, a narrowing of the vessel. In the present case, where pride and envy and self-esteem had found place, darkening the eye of the heart, the reward as a consequence seemed no reward; it did not appear enough; instead of being exactly what each was willing, or rather had prepared himself, to make it.

'But he answered one of them,' the loudest and foremost as we may suppose in the utterance of his discontent, *'and said, Friend, I do thee no wrong; didst not thou agree with me for a penny?'* 'Friend' is commonly a word of address, as it would be among ourselves, from a superior to an inferior, and in Scripture is a word of an evil omen, seeing that, besides the present passage, it is the compellation used to the guest who wanted a wedding garment, and to Judas when he came to betray his Master (Matt. 22:12; 26:50). *'I do thee no wrong'*; he justifies his manner of dealing with them, as well as his sovereign right in his own things. They had put their claim on the footing of right, and on that footing they are answered. *'Take that thine is, and go thy way. I will give unto this last even as unto thee. Is it not lawful for me to do what I will with mine own?'* (with which compare Rom. 9:20–24; Is. 29:16; 45:9); *'Is thine eye evil, because I am good?* so long as I am just to thee, may I not be good and liberal to others?' The solution of the difficulty that these complainers should get their reward and carry it away with them, has been already suggested, namely that, according to the human relations to which the parables must adapt itself, it would not have been consistent with equity to make them forfeit their own hire, notwithstanding the bad feeling which they displayed. Yet we may say their reward vanished in their hands; and the sentences which follow sufficiently indicate that with God an absolute forfeiture might follow, nay, must necessarily follow, where this grudging, unloving, proud spirit has come to its full head; as much is affirmed in the words which immediately follow, *'So the last shall be first, and the first last.'* Many expositors have been sorely troubled how to bring these words into agreement with the parable; for in it *'first'* and *'last'* are all set upon the same footing: while here it is rather a reversing of places which is asserted; those who seemed highest, it is declared shall be set the lowest, and the lowest highest: when too we compare Luke 13:30, where the words recur, there can be no doubt that a total rejection of the *'first,'* the unbelieving Jews, accompanied with the receiving of the *'last,'* the Gentiles, into covenant, is declared. Origen, whom Maldonatus follows, finds an explanation in the fact that the *'last'* hired are the *'first'* in order of

payment; but this is so infinitesimally small an advantage, if one at all, that the explanation cannot be admitted. Moreover, the fact of the last hired being the first paid is evidently introduced for convenience-sake; if the first hired had been first paid, and, as would naturally follow, had then gone their way, they would not have seen that the others obtained the same penny as themselves, and so would have had no temptation to express their discontent. Neander so entirely despairs of reconciling the parable with the words which introduce and finish it, that he proposes a desperate remedy, and one under the frequent application of which we should lose all confidence in the trustworthiness of the Evangelical records. He thinks the sentences and the parable to have been spoken on different occasions, and only by accident to have been here brought into connection; and asserts that one must wholly pervert this weighty parable, to bring it through forced artifices into harmony with words which are alien to it. But if what has been observed above be correct, the saying is not merely in its place here, but is absolutely necessary to complete the moral, to express that which the parable did not, and, according to the order of human affairs, could not express—namely, the *entire* forfeiture which would follow on the indulgence of such a temper as that displayed by the murmurers here.

There is more difficulty in the closing words, *'for many be called, but few chosen.'* They are not hard in themselves, but only in the position which they occupy. The connection is easy and the application obvious, when they occur as the moral of the Marriage of the King's Son (Matt. 22:14); but here they have much perplexed those who will not admit entire rejection from the heavenly kingdom of those whom the murmuring laborers represent. Some explain, 'Many are called, but few have the peculiar favor shown to them, that, though their labor is so much less, their reward should be equal'; thus Olshausen, who makes the *'called'* and the *'chosen'* alike partakers of final salvation, but assumes that by these terms are signified lower and higher standings of men in the kingdom of heaven (cf. Rev. 17:14). These last hired had, in his view, labored more abundantly, but this their more abundant labor was to be referred to a divine election, so that the name *'chosen'* or elect well becomes them to whom such especial grace was given. But this assumption of larger labor upon their part mars and defeats the whole parable, and cannot for a moment be admitted. Others understand by the *'called'* some not expressly mentioned, who had refused altogether to work; in comparison with whom the *'chosen,'* those who at any hour had accepted the invitation, were so few, that the Lord could not bear that any of these should be shut out from his full reward. But the simplest interpretation seems to be: Many are called to work in God's vineyard, but few retain that humility, that entire submission to the righteousness of God, that utter abnegation of any claim as of right on their own part, which will allow them in the end to be partakers of his reward.

10.

The Two Sons

Matthew 21:28–32

O ur Lord had put back with another question (vv. 24, 25) the question (v. 230 with which his adversaries had hoped either to silence Him, if He should decline to answer; or to obtain matter of accusation against Him, if He should give the answer which they expected: and now, becoming Himself the assailant, He commences that series of parables, in which, as in a glass held up before them, they might see themselves, the impurity of their hearts, their neglect of the charge laid upon them, their ingratitude for the privileges vouchsafed them, the aggravated guilt of that outrage against Himself which they were already meditating in their hearts. Yet even these, wearing as they do so severe and threatening an aspect, are not words of defiance, but of earnest tenderest love, spoken with the intention of turning them, if this were yet possible, from their purpose, of winning them also for the kingdom of God. The first, that of the Two Sons, goes not so deeply into the heart of the matter as the two that follow, and is rather retrospective, while those other are prophetic as well.

"*But what think ye?*" We have the same introduction to a longer discourse, 17:25—'*A certain man had two sons.*' Here, as at Luke 15:11, are described, under the figure of two sons of one father, two great moral divisions of men, under one or other of which might be ranged almost all with whom our blessed Lord in his teaching and preaching came in contact. Of one of these classes the Pharisees were specimens and representatives, though this class as well as the other will exist at all times. In this are included all who have sought a righteousness through the law, and by help of it have been preserved in the main from gross and open outbreakings of evil. In

433

the second class, of which the publicans and harlots stand as representatives, are contained all who have thrown off the yoke, openly and boldly transgressed the laws of God, done evil as 'with both hands earnestly.' Now the condition of those first is of course far preferable; that righteousness of the law better than this open unrighteousness—provided always that it be ready to give place to the righteousness of faith, when that appears; provided that it knows and feels its own incompleteness; which will ever be the case, where the attempt to keep the law has been truly and honestly made; the law will then have done its proper work, and have proved 'a schoolmaster to Christ.' But if this righteousness is satisfied with itself—and this will be, where evasions have been sought out to escape the strictness of the requirements of the law; if, cold and loveless and proud, it imagines that it wants nothing, and so refuses to submit itself to the righteousness of faith, then far better that the sinner should have had his eyes open to perceive his misery and guilt, even though this had been by means of manifest and grievous transgressions, than that he should remain in this ignorance of his true state, of all which is lacking to him still—just as it would be better that disease, *if in the frame*, should take a definite shape, so that it might be felt and acknowledged to be disease, and then met and overcome, than that it should be secretly lurking in, and pervading, the whole system; its very existence being denied by him the springs of whose life it was sapping. From this point of view St. Paul speaks, Rom. 7:7–9; and this same lesson, that there is no such fault as counting we have no fault, is taught us throughout all Scripture. It is taught us in the bearing of the elder son towards his father and returning brother in the parable of the Prodigal Son (Luke 15:28–30); and again in the demeanor of the Pharisee who had invited Jesus to his house toward Him and toward the woman 'which was a sinner' (Luke 7:36–50); and in that of another Pharisee, whose very prayers this spirit and temper made to be nothing worth (Luke 18:10; cf. 29–32).

   '*And he came to the first, and said, Son, go working today in my vineyard.*' This command, which we may compare with that of Matt. 20:1–7, was the general summons made both by the natural law in the conscience, and also by the revealed law which came by Moses, that men should bring forth fruit unto God. This call the publicans and harlots, and all open sinners, manifestly neglected and despised. The son first bidden to go to the work '*answered and said, I will not.*' The rudeness of the answer, the absence of any attempt to excuse his disobedience, are both characteristic. The representative of careless, reckless sinners, he has dismissed even the hypocrisies with which others cloke their disobedience; cares not to say, like those invited guests, 'I pray thee have me excused'; but flatly refuses to go. *'But afterward he repented and went.'* There came over him a better mind, even as we know that such under the preaching of the Baptist and afterwards of the Lord Himself came over many who before had stood out against God.

'And he came to the second, and said likewise; and he answered and said, I go, sir.' The Scribes and Pharisees, as professing zeal for the law, set themselves in the way as though they would fulfill the command. But they said, and did not (Matt. 23:2); the prophet Isaiah had long since described them truly (Matt. 14:8; cf. Is. 29:13), 'This people draweth nigh unto Me with their mouth, and honoreth Me with their lips, but their heart is far from Me.' So was it here. When the marked time arrived, when the Baptist came to them *'in the way of righteousness,'* and summoned to an earnest repentance on the part of all, when it was needful to take decisively one side or the other, then when many hitherto openly profane were baptized, confessing their sins (Matt. 3:5, 6), *'repented and went:'* the real unrighteousness of the Pharisees, before concealed under show of zeal for the law, was clearly displayed: professing willingness to go, they *'went not.,'*

to the Lord's question, *'Whether of them twain did the will of his father?'* His adversaries cannot plead inability to reply, as they had pleaded to a former question (v. 27); they have no choice but to answer, though their answer condemns themselves. *'They say unto Him, The first:'* not, of course, that he did it absolutely well, but by comparison with the other. Then follows the application to themselves of the acknowledgment reluctantly wring from them: *'Verily, I say unto you, That the publicans and harlots go into the kingdom of God before you'* (cf. Luke 7:29, 37–50). In these words, *'go before you,'* or 'take the lead of you,' there is a gracious intimation that for them too the door of hope was open still, that as yet no irreversible doom excluded them from that kingdom: the others indeed had preceded them; but they might still follow, if they would. And why are they thus proving the last to enter into the kingdom, if indeed they shall enter it at all? *'For John came unto you in the way of righteousness, and ye believed him not.'* An emphasis has been sometimes laid on the words, *'in the way of righteousness,'* as though they were brought in to aggravate the sin of the Pharisees, as though the Lord would say,

'The Baptist came, a pattern of that very righetousness of the law, in which you profess to exercise yourselves. He did not come, calling to the new life of the Gospel, of which I am the pattern, and which you might have misunderstood; he did not come, seeking to put new wine into the old bottles, but himself fulfilling that very form and pattern of righteousness which you professed to have set before yourselves; became an earnest ascetic (Matt. 9:11–14); separating himself from sinners; while yet you were so little hearty about *any* form of goodness, that for all this he obtained no more acceptance with you than I have done. You found fault with him for the strictness of his life, as you find fault with Me for the condescension of mine (Matt. 1:16–19). And this unbelief of yours was not merely for a time; but afterward, when God had set his seal to his mission, when *the publicans and the harlots believed him,* even then ye could not be provoked to jealousy: *ye, when ye had seen it, repented not afterward, that ye might believe him.*'

In many copies, and some not unimportant ones, it is the son that is first spoken to, who promises to go, and afterwards disobeys; and the second who, refusing first, afterwards changes his mind, and enters on the work. Probably the order was thus reversed by transcribers, who thought that the application of the parable must be to the successive callings of Jews and Gentiles, and that therefore the order of their calling should be preserved. The parable, however, does not primarily apply to the Jew and Gentile, but rather to the two bodies within the bosom of the Jewish Church. It is not said, *'the Gentiles,'* but *'the publicans and the harlots, go into the kingdom of heaven before you';* while yet that former statement, if the parable had admitted (and if it had admitted, it must have required it), would have been a far stronger way of provoking them to jealousy (Acts 22:21, 22; Rom. 10:19–21). The application of the parable to Gentile and Jew need not indeed be excluded, since the whole Jewish nation stood morally to the Gentile world in the same relation which the more self-righteous among themselves did to notorious transgressors. But not till the next parable do Jew and Gentile, in their relations to one another, and in their several relations to the kingdom of God, come distinctly and primarily forward.

11.

The Wicked Husbandmen

Matthew 21:33–45; Mark 12:1–12; Luke 20:9–19

The Lord's adversaries had by this time so manifestly gotten the worse, that, for this day at least, they would willingly have brought the controversy which they had so imprudently provoked (see verse 23) to a close. But no; He will not let them go: He has begun and will finish: 'Hear another parable'; as though He would say, 'I have still another word for you of warning and rebuke,' and to that He now summons them to listen. Uttered in the presence at once of the Pharisees and of the multitude, to St. Matthew it seemed rather addressed to the former, while St. Luke records it as spoken to the people (20:9); but there is no real difference here. The opening words, 'There was a certain householder, which planted a vineyard,' and still more those which immediately follow, suggest, and were intended to suggest, a reference to Is. 5:1–7. He who came not to destroy, but to fulfill, takes up the prophet's words, connects his own appearing with all which had gone before in the history of the nation, presents it as the crown and consummation of all God's dealings through a thousand years with his people. Nor is it to that passage in Isaiah alone that the Lord links on his teaching here. The image of the kingdom of God as a vine-stock, or as a vineyard, runs through the whole Old Testament (Deut. 32:32; Ps. 80:8–16; Is. 37:1–7; Jer. 2:21; Ezek. 15:1–6; 19:10; Hos. 10:1); and has many fitnesses to recommend it. The vine, the lowest, is at the same time the noblest of plants. Our lord appropriates it, among earthly symbols, to Himself; He is the mystical Vine (John 15:10; had been in prophecy compared to it long before (Gen. 49:11). It is a tree which spreads and diffuses itself, cast out its tendrils and branches on every side; so that of that

Vine which the Lord brought out of Egypt the Psalmist could say, 'it filled the land' (80:9). Nor may we, while drawing out these points of similitude, omit the fact that there was no property so valuable, nor which yielded returns so large, as a vineyard (Cant. 8:11, 12); yet only yielding these in answer to the most unceasing diligence and toil.

In Isaiah, the vineyard and the Jewish Church are one; 'The vineyard of the Lord of Hosts is the house of Israel, and the men of Judah his pleasant plant.' It is therefore described, not as transferred to others, but as laid waste (vv. 5, 6). Here, where the vineyard is not laid waste, but transferred to more faithful husbandmen, and the judgment lights not on it, but on those who so guiltily sought to seize it for their own, we must regard it rather as the kingdom of God in its idea, which idea Jew and Gentile have been successively placed in the condition to realize; a failure in this involving for both alike a forfeiture of the tenure. Inasmuch, indeed, as Israel according to the flesh was the first called to realize the heavenly kingdom, it may be said that for a time the vineyard *was* the Jewish Church; but this arrangement was accidental and temporary, not necessary and permanent, as the sequel abundantly proved. It was the fatal mistake of the Jews, witnessed against in vain by the prophets of old (Jer. 7:4), by the Baptist (Matt. 3:9), and now and often by the Lord Jesus Himself (Matt. 8:12; Luke 13:29), that they and the kingdom were so identified, that it could never be parted from them.

The householder is more than possessor of this vineyard: he has himself *'planted'* it (Ex. 15:17; Ps. 44:2). This planting dates back to the times of Moses and Joshua, to the founding of the divine polity in the land of Canaan; and is described, Deut. 32:12–14; cf. Ezek. 16:9–14; Neh. 9:23–25. But this was not all. Having planted, he also *'hedged it round about, and digged a wine-press in it, and built a tower.'* This hedge might be either a stone wall (Prov. 24:31; Num. 22:24; Is. 5:5), or a fence of thorns or other quickset; this last, if formed, as is common in the East, of the prickly wild aloe, or of some other briars with which Judaea abounds, would more effectually exclude the enemies of the vineyard, the fox (Cant. 2:15; Neh. 4:3), and the wild boar (Ps. 88:13, than any wall of stone. The vineyard of Isaiah v. 5 is furnished with both. That it should possess a *'wine-press'* would be a matter of course. Not less needful would be the *'tower'*; by which we understand not so much the kiosk, or ornamental building, serving mainly for delight, as a place of shelter for the watchmen who should guard the fruits of the vineyard, and a receptacle for the fruits themselves.

The question, which to an interpreter of the parables must so often recur, presents itself here. Shall we attach any special signification to these several details? Do they thus belong to the very substance of the parable, or are they drapery only, and, if expressing anything, yet only in a general way the care of the heavenly householder for his Church, that provision of all things necessary for life and godliness which He made for his people? Many in this as in similar cases will allow nothing more than this last. But, whatever may be said of the wine-press and the tower, it is difficult, with Eph. 2:14 before us, where the law is described as 'the middle wall of partition' between the Jew and Gentile, to refuse to the hedging round of the vineyard a spiritual significance. By their circumscription through the law, the Jews became a people dwelling alone, and not reckoned among the nations (Num. 23:9); that law being at once a hedge of separation and of defense, 'a wall of fire' (Zech. 2:5; cf. Ps. 125:2; Is. 27:3), which, preserving them distinct from the idolatrous nations round them and from their abominations, gave them the pledge and assurance of the continued protection of God. Add to this that not inwardly only, but outwardly as well, Judaea, through its geographical position, was hedged round; by the bounty of nature on every side circumscribed and defended; being guarded on the east by the river Jordan and the two lakes, on the south by the desert and mountainous country of on the south by the desert and mountainous country of Idumaea, on the west by the sea, and by Anti-Libanus on the north: for so, observes Vitringa, had God in his counsels determined, who willed that Israel should dwell alone. It is not so easy to point out distinct spiritual benefits shadowed forth by the wine-press and the tower. Many attempts to discover such have been made; but they all have something fanciful and arbitrary about them; and, though often ingenious, yet fail to command an unreserved assent.

The householder, who might now say, 'What could have been done more to my vineyard, that I have not done?' 'let it out to husbandmen' (Cant. 8:11); 'and went into a far country'; and as St. Luke adds, 'for a long while.' What the terms of his agreement with the husbandmen were, we are not expressly told, but, as the sequel clearly implies, having made a covenant with them to receive a fixed proportion of the fruits in their season. Since, as is evident, the *'husbandmen'* must be distinguished from the vineyard they were set to cultivate and keep, we must understand by them the spiritual chiefs of the nation, to whom God, in the very constitution of the Jewish polity, had given authority to sit in Moses' chair, and from it to teach the people (Mal. 2:7; Ezek. 34:2; Matt. 23:2, 3). By the vineyard itself will then naturally be signified the great body of the nation, who, instructed and taught by these, should have brought forth fruits of righteousness unto God. In the miracles which went along with the deliverance from Egypt, the giving of the law from Sinai, and the planting in Canaan, God openly dealt with his people, made, as we know, an express covenant with them; but this done, withdrew for a while, not speaking any more to them face to face (Deut. 34:10–12), but waiting in patience to see what the law would effect, and what manner of works they, under the teaching of their appointed guides, would bring forth.

'*And when the time of the fruit drew near, he sent his servants to the husbandmen, that they might receive the fruits of its,*' his share of the produce, whatever that may have been (Cant. 8:12). There was, of course, no time when God did not demand obedience, gratitude, love from his people; all times therefore are in one sense '*times of the fruit*' (Isai. 5:7). But he conditions of the parable demand this language; and moreover, in the history of souls and of nations, there are seasons which even more than all other are '*times of fruit*'; when God requires such with more than usual earnestness, when it will fare very ill with a soul or nation, if these be not found. But the '*servants*' who should receive these fruits, how, it may be asked, should these be distinguished from the '*husbandmen*'? Exactly in this, that the '*servants,*' that is, the prophets and other more eminent ministers and messengers of God, *were sent*; being raised up at critical epochs, each with his own direct mission and message; the '*husbandmen,*' on the other hand, are the more permanent ecclesiastical authorities, whose authority lay in the very constitution of the theocracy itself. On this receiving of the fruits Olshausen says well, 'These fruits which are demanded, are in nowise to be explained as particular works, nor yet as a condition of honesty and uprightness, but much rather as the repentance and the inward longing after true inward righteousness, which the law was unable to bring about. It is by no means implied that the law had not an influence in producing uprightness: it cuts off the grosser manifestations of sin, and reveals its hidden abomination; so that a righteousnes according to the law can even under the law come forth as fruit;

while yet, to be sufficing, this must have a sense of the need of a redemption for its basis (Rom. 3:20). The servants therefore here appear as those who seek for these spiritual needs, that they may link to them the promises concerning a coming Redeemer: but the unfaithful husbandmen who had abused their own position denied and slew these messenger of grace. This *'time of the fruit'* would not, according to the Levitical law, have arrived till the fifth year after the planting of the vineyard. For three years the fruit was to be uncircumcised, and therefore ungathered; in the fourth, it was 'holy to praise the Lord withal'; and only in the fifth could those who tended the vineyard either themselves enjoy the fruit or render of the same to others (Lev. 19:23–25). During this long period the husbandmen may have managed to forget that they were tenants at all, and not possessors in fee; and this may help to explain what follows.

'And the husbandmen took his servants, and beat one, and killed another, and stoned another. Again, he sent other servants more than the first, and they did unto them likewise.' The two later Evangelists record the wickedness of these wicked husbandmen more in detail than the first, St. Luke tracing very distinctly their advance under the sense of impunity from bad to worse. When the first servant came, they *'beat him, and sent him away empty.'* The next they *'entreated shamefully';* or according to St. Mark, who defies the very nature of the outrage, *'at him they cast stones, and wounded him in the head, and sent him away shamefully handled.'* One might almost gather from these last words that in their wanton insolence they devised devices of scorn and wrong, not expressly named, against this servant; such, perhaps, as Hanun did, when he 'took David's servants' and shaved off the one half of their beards, and cut off their garments in the middle, and sent them away' (2 Sam. 10:4). The third they wounded, and cast out of the vineyard with violence; flung him forth, it might be, with hardly any life in him. In the two earlier Evangelists the outrage reaches even to the killing of some of the subordinate messengers; while in St. Luke this extremity of outrage is reserved for the son. The latter thus presents the series of crimes on an ever-ascending scale; but the former are truer to historical fact, seeing that not a few of the prophets were not merely maltreated, but actually put to death. Thus, if we may trust Jewish tradition, Jeremiah was stoned by the exiles in Egypt, Isaish sawn asunder by king Manasseh. For an abundant historical justification of this description, and as showing that the past ingratitude of the

people is not painted here in colors too dark, see Jer. 20:1, 2; 37:15; 38:6; 1 Kgs. 18:13; 19:14; 22:24–27; 2 Kgs. 6:31; 21:16; 2 Chr. 24:19; 22; 36:16, 16: and also Acts 7:52; 1 Thess. 2:15; the whole passage finding its best commentary in the words of the Epistle to the Hebrews: 'And others had trial of cruel mockings and scourgings yea, moreover of bonds and imprisonment: they were stoned, they were sawn asunder, were tempted, were slain with the sword . . . of whom the world was not worthy' (11:37, 38).

The patience of the householder under these extraordinary provocations is wonderful, sending as he does messenger after messenger to win back these wicked men to a sense of their duty, instead of resuming at once possession of his vineyard, and inflicting summary vengeance upon them. It needs to be thus magnified, seeing that it represents to us the infinite patience and long-suffering of God: 'Howbeit I sent unto you all my servants the prophets, rising early and sending them, saying Oh, do not this abominable thing that I hate' (Jer. 44:4). 'Nevertheless, they were disobedient, and rebelled against thee, and cast thy law behind their backs, and slew thy prophets who testified against them, to turn them to thee, and they wrought great provocations' (Neh. 9:26). This whole confession of the Levites is in itself an admirable commentary on this parable.

'But last of all he sent unto them his son,' or in the still more affecting words of St. Mark,' 'Having yet therefore one son, his well-beloved, he sent him also last unto them, saying, They will reverence my son' (cf. Heb. 1:1, 2). When the householder expresses his conviction, that however those evil men may have outraged and defied his inferior messengers, they will reverence his son, we need not embarrass ourselves, as some have done, with the fact that He whom the householder represents must have fully known from the beginning what treatment his Son would obtain from those to whom He sent Him. Not that there is not a difficulty, but it is the same which meets us everywhere, that of the reconciliation of man's freedom with God's foreknowledge. That they are reconcilable we know, and that we cannot reconcile them we know; and this is all which can be said upon the matter. The description of this the last of the ambassadors as the son of the householder, as his only one, 'his well-beloved,' all marks as strongly as possible the difference of rank between Christ and the prophets, the superior dignity of his person who only was a Son in the highest sense of the word (Heb. 3:5, 6); and some, doubtless, of those who heard, quite understood what He meant, and the honor which He thus claimed as peculiarly his own, however unable to turn his words against Himself, and to accuse Him of making Himself, as indeed He did, the Son of God (John 5:18). In this sending of his own Son by the heavenly Father, is the last and crowning effort of divine mercy. If it fail, on the one side all the resources even of heavenly love will have been exhausted; while on the other, those whose sin has caused it to fail will have filled up the measure of their guilt.

'But when the husbandmen saw the son, they said among themselves, This is the heir; come, let us kill him, and let us seize on his inheritance.' Compare John 11:47–53, and the counsels of Joseph's brethren against him: 'When they saw him afar off, even before he came near unto them, they conspired against him to slay him, and they said one to another, Behold, this dreamer cometh. Come now therefore, and let us slay him . . . and we shall see what will become of his dreams' (Gen. 37:19, 20). As they, thinking to disappoint the purpose of God concerning their younger brother, help to bring it to pass, so the Jewish rulers were the instruments to fulfill that same purpose concerning Christ, which they meant forever to defeat (Acts 3:18; 4:27, 28). *'This is the heir'*; the word is not used here in its laxer sense as a synonym for lord, like *heres* for *dominus*; but more accurately, he for whom the inheritance is meant, who is not in present possession, but to whom it will in due course rightfully arrive, not, as in earthly relations, by the death, but by the free appointment, of the actual possessor. Christ is 'heir of all things' (Heb. 1:2), not as He is the Son of God, for the church has always detected Arian tendencies lurking in that interpretation, but as He is the Son of man (Eph. 1:20–23; Phil. 2:9–11). So Theodoret: 'The Lord Christ is heir of all things, not as God, but as man; for as God He is maker of all.'

It is the heart which speaks in God's hearing (Ps. 53:1); the thought of men's heart is their true speech, and is therefore here regarded as the utterance of their lips. We cannot, indeed, imagine the Pharisees, even in their most secret counsels, ever trusting one another so far, or daring to look their own wickedness so directly in the face, as *to say*, in as many words, 'This is the Messiah, therefore let us slay Him.' But they desired that the inheritance might be theirs. What God had willed should only be transient and temporary, enduring till the times of reformation, they would fain have seen permanent—and this, because they had prerogatives and privileges under that imperfect condition of things, which would cease when that what was perfect had come; or rather which, not ceasing, would yet be transformed into other and higher privileges, for which they had no care. The great Master-builder was about to take down the scaffolding provisionally reared, but which had now served its end; and this his purpose they, the under-builders, were setting themselves to oppose, and were determined, at whatever cost, to resist to the uttermost. What God had founded, they would fain possess without God and against God; and imagined that they could do so; for indeed is not all self-righteousness an attempt to kill the heir, and to seize on the divine inheritance, a seeking to comprehend and take down into self that light, which is only light so longas it is recognized as something above self, and whereof man is permitted to be a partaker; but which he neither himself originated, nor yet can ever possess in fee, or as his own, or otherwise then as continually receiving from on high; a light too, which, by the very success of the attempt to take it into his own possession, is as inevitably lost and extinguished as would be a ray of our natural light if we succeeded in cutting it off from its luminous source

'*And they caught him, and cast him out of the vineyard, and slew him.*' All three Evangelists describe the son as thus '*cast out of the vineyard,*' reminding us of Him who 'suffered without the gate' (Heb. 13:12, 13; John 19:17); cut off in the intention of those who put Him to death from the people of God, and from all share in their blessings. Thus when Naboth perished on charges of blasphemy against God and the king, that is, for theocratic sins, 'they carried him forth out of the city, and stoned him with stones, that he died' (1 Kgs. 21:13; cf. Acts 7:58; 21:30). In St. Mark the husbandmen slay the son first, and only afterwards cast out the body (12:8; cf. Jer. 22:19). They deny it the common rites of sepulture; fling it forth, as much as to say, *that* is their answer to the householder's demands. The Lord so little doubts the extremities to which the hatred of his enemies will proceed, that in the parable He holds up to them the crime which they were meditating in their hearts, and which a few days should bring to the birth, as one already accomplished; not indeed thus binding them to this sin, of it, and, if this were possible, terrifying them from its actual consummation.

If, however, this might not be, and if, like the husbandmen in the parable, they were resolved to consummate their crime, what should be their doom? This too they may see reflected in the mirror which He holds up before their eyes. '*When the lord, therefore, of the vineyard cometh, what will he do unto those husbandmen?'* It is very instructive to note the way in which successive generations, which during so many centuries had been filling up the measure of the iniquity of Israel, are contemplated throught but as one body of husbandmen; God's word being everywhere opposed to that shallow nominalism which would make 'nation' no more than a convenient form of language to express a certain aggregation of individuals. God will deal with nations as living organisms, and as having a moral unity of their own, and this continuing unbroken from age to age. Were it otherwise, all confession of our fathers' sins would be a mockery, and such words as our Lord's at Matt. 23:32–35, without any meaning at all. Neither is there any injustice in this law of God's government with which He encounters our selfish, self-isolating tendencies; for while there is thus a life of the whole, there is also a life for every part; and thus it is always possible for each individual even of that generation which, having filled up the last drop of the measure, is being chastised for all its own and its fathers' iniquities, by personal faith and repentance to withdraw himself from the general doom; not indeed always possible for him to escape his share in the outward calamity (though often there will be a Pella when Jerusalem is destroyed an Ark when a world perishes, but always from that which is the woe of the woe, from the wrath of God, of which the outward calamity is but the form and expression (Jer. 39:11; Ezek. 11:16).

The necessity of preserving the due probabilities of the narrative makes it impossible that the son himself should execute the final vengeance on these wicked husbandmen. He is slain, and cannot, like Him whom he shadows forth rise again to exact the penalties of their guilt. This *'the lord of the vineyard,'* now for the first time so called, must do: neither is there anything here inconsistent with the general teaching of Scripture, for it is the Father, revealing Himself in the Son, who both gave the law at Sinai, and who also, when the time had arrived, visited and judged the apostate Church of Israel.

Perhaps the Pharisees, to whom Christ addressed the question, making the same appeal to them which Isaiah had made to their fathers (v. 3), and extorting their condemnation from their own lips, had hitherto missed the scope of the parable, and before they were aware, pronounced sentence against themselves: *'He will miserably destroy those wicked men, and will let out his vineyard unto other husbandmen, which shall render him the fruits in their seasons'*; or it may be that, perceiving well enough, they had yet hitherto pretended not to perceive his drift, and so drew from Him words more explicit still; such as it was useless any longer to affect to misunderstand: *'Therefore say I unto you, The kingdom of God shall be taken from you, and given to a nation bringing forth the fruits thereof.'* For then at length Christ and his adversaries stood face to face, as did once before aprophet and a wicked king of Israel, when the prophet, having obtained in his disguise a sentence from the lips of the king against himself, removed the ashes from his face, and the king 'discerned him that he was of the prophets,' and understood that he had unconsciously pronounced his own doom (1 Kgs. 20:41). The *'God forbid,'* which the *'people'* uttered (Luke 20;16), the Pharisees had too much wariness and self-command to allow any such exclamation to escape from their lips—shows plainly that the aim of the parable had not escaped *them*, that they saw the drift of it betimes. The exclamation itself was either an expression of fear, desiring that such evil might be averted; or else of unbelief, 'That shall never be; we are God's people, and shall remain such to the end:' and this more probably than that, from the spirit and temper of those who utter it (Ezek. 33:24; Matt. 3:9; Rom. 2:17).

But this truth, so strange and unwelcome to his hearers, rests not on his word alone. The same was long ago foreannounced in those Scriptures to which is adversaries professed to cling, and from which they condemned Him: *'did ye never read in the Scriptures, The stone which the builders rejected, the same is become the head of the corner?'* The quotation is from Ps. 118:22, 23, a psalm which the Jews acknowledged as applying to the King Messiah (Matt. 19:38), and of which there is a like application at Acts 4:11; 1 Pet. 2:7; with an allusion somewhat more remote, at Eph. 2:20. The passage quoted forms an exact parallel with this parable; all which the Lord threatens here, being implicitly threatened there. *'The builders'* there correspond to *'the husbandmen'* here; as those were appointed of God to carry up the spiritual temple, so these to cultivate the spiritual vineyard; the rejection of the chief corner-stone corresponds to the denying and murdering of the heir. There is another motive for abandoning the image of the vineyard; I mean its inadequacy to set forth one important moment of the truth, which yet must by no means be passed over; namely this, that the malice of men should not defeat the purpose of God, that the Son should yet be the heir; and that not merely vengeance should be taken, but that He should take it. Now all this is distinctly involved in the

Lord's concluding words: *'Whosoever shall fall on this stone shall be broken; but on whomsoever it shall fall, it will grind him to powder.'* The rejected stone, having become the head of the corner, is itself the instrument of their punishment who have set it at nought. *They* fall on the stone who are offended at Christ in his low estate (Is. 8:14; 53:2; Luke 2:34; 4:22–29; John 4:44); of this sin his hearers were already guilty. There was a worse sin which they were on the point of committing, which He warns them would be followed by a more tremendous punishment; they on whom the stone falls are those who set themselves in self-conscious opposition against the Lord; who, knowing who He is, do yet to the end oppose themselves to Him and to his kingdom; and these shall not merely fall and be broken; for one might recover himself, though with some present harm, from such a fall as this; but on them the stone shall fall as from heaven, and shall grind them to powder—in the words of Daniel (2:350, 'like the chaff of the summer threshing-floors'— crushing and destroying them forever.

All three Evangelists note the exasperation of the Chief Priests and Pharisees, when they perceived, as all did at last, though some sooner than others, that the parable was spoken against *them* (cf. Jer. 18:18). They no longer kept any terms with the Lord, and, only that *'they feared the multitude,'* would have laid violent hands on Him at once. Yet not even so does He give them up; but having, in this parable, set forth their relation to God as a relation of *duty,* shown them that a *charge* was laid upon them, with the guilt the incurred in neglecting to fulfill it, so in that which follows, He sets forth to them the same in a yet more inviting light, as a relation of *privilege.* He presents to them their work not any more as a burden laid upon them, but as a grace imparted to them—which, therefore, they incurred an equal guilt, or indeed a greater, in counting light of or despising. If this is a more legal, that is a more evangelical, parable.

12.
The Marriage of the King's Son

Matthew 22:1–14

This is sometimes called the parable of the Wedding Garment. The name is a faulty one, being drawn from that which is but an episode in it after all, and the title given above, the same which it bears in our Bible, quite as effectually distinguishes it from the Great Supper of St. Luke (14:16). Such distinction indeed it is needful to maintain, for the two must not be confounded, as merely different recensions of the same discourse. Both indeed rest on the image of a festival to which many are bidden, some refusing the invitation and some accepting; but this is not sufficient to identify them with one another. They were spoken on different occasions—that at a meal, this in the temple. They belong to very different epochs of our Lord's ministry, that to a much earlier period than this. When that was spoken the Pharisees had not openly broken with the Lord; it was indeed in the house of a Pharisee, wither He had gone to eat bread, that the parable was uttered (Luke 14:1). But when this was spoken, their enmity had reached the highest pitch; they had formally resolved by any means to remove Him out of the way (John 11:47–53). Then there was hope that the chiefs of the nation might yet be won over to the obedience of the truth; now they are fixed in their rejection of the counsel of God, and in their hatred of his Christ. In agreement with all this, the parable as last spoken, or as we have it here, is far severer than when first uttered, than St. Luke as recorded it. In that the guests, while they decline the invitation, are yet at pains to make civil excuses for so doing; in this they put it from them with a defiant and absolute No—so hating the message that some among them maltreat and kill the bearers of it; even as we cannot doubt that, had it consisted with decorum,

449

and if the parable would have borne it, the king's son himself, as the last ambassador of his grace, would have been the victim of their outrage, as is the householder's son in the parable preceding. It is there a private man whose bidding is contemptuously set aside, it is here a king. It is there an ordinary entertainment, here the celebration of the marriage of his son. In the higher dignity of the person inviting, in the greater solemnity of the occasion, there are manifest aggravation of the guilt of the despisers. And as the offense is thus heavier, as those were but discourteous guests, while these are rebels, so is the doom more dreadful. In St. Luke's parable they are merely shut out from the festival; in this, their city is burned, and they themselves destroyed; the utmost which in fact is threatened there being that God, turning from one portion of the Jewish people—from the priests and the Pharisees—would offer the privileges which they despised to another portion of the same nation, the people that knew not the law, the publicans and harlots, with only slightest intimation (v. 23) of a call of the Gentiles; while here the forfeiture of the kingdom by the whole Jewish people, who with fewest exceptions had shown themselves unworthy of it, is announced.

A late objector, taking no account of these altered conditions, which justify and explain the different forms in which the parable appears, asserts that St. Luke is here the only accurate reporter of Christ's words, St. Matthew mixing up with them some foreign elements—reminiscenses, for instance, of the maltreatment and murder of the servants, drawn from the parable preceding; and also blending into the same whole fragments of another parable, that, namely, of the Wedding Garment, which, when uttered, was totally distinct. For the first assertion his only plausible argument is, that while it is quite intelligible that husbandmen should maltreat servants of their lord, who came demanding rent from them; it is inconceivable, and therefore could find no place in a parable, of which perfect likelihood is the first condition, that invited guests, however unwilling to keep their engagement, should abuse and even kill the servants sent to remind them that the festival, to which they were engaged, was actually ready. This, it is true, *can* with difficulty be conceived, so long as we suppose no other motive but unwillingness to keep their engagement at work in them. But may not a deep alienation from their lord, with a readiness to resist and rebel against him, existing long before, have found their utterance here? The presence of these his ambassadors, an outrage against whom would constitute an outrage against himself, may have afforded the desired opportunity for displaying a hostility which, though latent, had long been entertained. If there be something monstrous in their conduct, it is only the fitter to declare the monstrous fact, that men should maltreat, and slay the messengers of God's grace, the ambassadors of Christ, who come to them with glad tidings of good things—should be ready at once to rend *them*, and to trample their pearls underfoot.

His other assertion, that the episode of the wedding garment cannot have originally pertained to the parable, rests partly on the old objection, that the guest could not with any justice be punished for wanting that which, as the course of the story goes, he had no opportunity of obtaining—on which something will presently be said—and partly upon this, that an entirely new and alien element is here introduced into the parable; marring its unity; awkwardly appended to, not intimately cohering with, it. But it is no so. Most needful was it that a parable, inviting sinners of every degree to a fellowship in the blessings of the Gospel, should also remind them that, for the lasting enjoyment of these, they must put off their former conversation; that if, as regarded the past, they were freely called, still for the present and time to come they were called unto holiness—in Theophylact's words, 'that the entrance, indeed, to the marriage-feast is without scrutiny, for by grace alone we are called, as well bad as good; but the life of those that have entered, hereafter shall not be without scrutiny; that the King will make a very strict examination of those who, having entered into the faith, shall be found in filthy garments.'

Thus much on the relation in which this parable stands to the similar one in St. Luke. When we compare it with that which it immediatley follows, we see a marked advance. The Lord revealing Himself in ever clearer light as they central figure of the kingdom, gives here a far plainer intimation than there of the dignity of his person, they nobility of his descent. There He was indeed the son, the only and beloved one, of the householder; but here his race is royal, and He appears as Himself at once the King, and the King's Son (Ps. 42:1). It is thus declared that the sphere in which this parable moves is that of the kingdom; which, announced and prepared before, was only actually present with the advent of the King. In that other, a parable of the Old-Testament history, the Son Himself appears rather as the last and greatest in the line of its prophets and teachers, crowning and completing the old, than as inaugurating the new. In that, a parable of the law, God appears *demanding* some-thing *from* men; in this, a parable of grace, He appears more as *giving* something *to* them. There, He is displeased that his demands are not complied with; here, that his goodness is not accepted. There He requires; here He imparts. And thus, as we so often find, the two mutually complete one another, this taking up the matter where the other left it.

'*And Jesus answered, and spoke unto them again by parables.*' That HE spoke is plain, but that He '*answered*' seems to require some ex-planation, seeing that no question had been addressed to Him. It is sufficient to observe that he '*answers*,' on whom an occasion, or it may be a necessity, speaking has been imposed. So is it here. This new parable is the Lords' answer to the endeavor of the Chief Priests and Pharisees to lay hands upon Him. '*The kingdom of heaven is like unto a certain king, which made a marriage for his son.*' The two favorite images under which the prophets of the Old Covenant set forth the blessings of the New, and of all near communion with God, that of a festival (Is. 25:6; 65:13; Cant. 5:1), and of a marriage (Is. 61:10; 62:5; Hos. 2:19; Matt. 9:15; John 3:29; Eph. 5:32; 2 Cor. 11:9), meet and interpenetrate one another in the marriage festival here. There results indeed this inconvenience, a consequence of the inadequacy of things earthly to set forth things heavenly, that the members of the Church are at once the guests invited to the feast, and, in their collective capacity, constitute the bride at whose es-pousals the feast is given. But as we advance in the parable the cir-cumstances of the marriage altogether fall out of sight; the bearing of the several invited guests is that to which our whole attention is directed. This, like the last, has its groundwork and rudiments in the Old Testament (Ex. 24:11; Zeph. 1:7, 8; Prov. 9:1–6); and it en-tered quite into the circle of Jewish expectation that the setting up of the kingdom of the Messiah should be ushered in by a glorious festival: our Lord Himself elsewhere making use of the same image for the setting forth of the same truths (Luke 22:18, 30). The mar-riage indeed of which He there speaks, and at Rev. 19:7, will not be celebrated till the end of the present age, while it is here as already present. We put the two statements in harmony with one another, when we keep in mind how distinct the espousals and the actual marriage were held in the East, and regard his first coming as the time of his espousals, while only at his second He leads home his bride.

"*And sent forth is servants to call them that were bidden to the wed-*

ding' (cf. Prov. 9:3–5). In the corresponding parable of St. Luke, the giver of the feast, a private man, 'bade many.' Here we may assume a still more numerous company, from the higher rank and dignity of the author of the feast, and the greater solemnity of the occasion (cf. Esth. 1:3–9). This summoning of thse already bidden was, and, as modern travelers attest, is still, quite in accordance with Eastern manners. Thus Esther invites Haman to a banquet on the morrow (Esth. v. 8); and when the time has actually arrived, the chamberlain comes to usher him to the banquet (6:14). There is therefore no slightest reason why we should make *'them that were bidden'* to mean them that were now *to be* bidden; such an interpretation not merely violating all laws of grammar, but the higher purposes with which the parable was spoken; for our Lord, assuming that the guests had been invited long ago, does thus remind his hearers that what He brought, if in one sense new, was in another a fulfillment of the old; that He claimed to be heard, not as one suddenly starting up, unconnected with ought which had gone before, but as himself 'the end of the law,' to which it had been ever tending, the birth with which the whole Jewish dispensation had been pregnant, and which alone should give a meaning to it all. In his words, *'them that were bidden,'* is involved the fact that there was nothing abrupt in the coming of his kingdom, that its rudiments had a long while before been laid, that all to which his adversaries clung as precious in their past history was prophetic of blessings now actually present to them in Him. The original invitation, which had now come to maturity, reached back to the foundation of the Jewish commonwealth, was taken up and repeated by each succeeding prophet, as he prophesied of the crowning grace that should one day be brought to Israel (Luke 10:24; 1 Pet. 1:12), and summoned the people to hold themselves in a spiritual readiness to welcome their Lord and their King.

Yet the actual calling pertained not to these, the prophets of the older dispensation. They spoke of good things, but of good things to come. Not till the days of John the Baptist was the kingdom indeed present, was there any manifestation of the King's Son, any actual summoning of the guests, bidden long before, to come to the marriage (Luke 3:4–6). By the first band of servants I should understand John the Baptist (Matt. 3:2), the Twelve in that first mission which they accomplished during the lifetime of the Lord (Matt. 10)—and the Seventy (Luke 10). His own share in summoning the guests, inviting them, that is, unto Himself (Matt. 4:17;

Mark 1:14, 15), his 'Come unto Me,' naturally in the parable falls out of sight. It would have disturbed its proprieties had the king's son been himself a bearer of the invitation. A condescension so infinite would have seemed unnatural; for it is only the Son of the *heavenly* King who has ever stooped so far. He indeed was content, even while the marriage was made for Himself, to be as one of those sent forth to call the guests thereunto. It is not implied that on this first occasion the servants had any positive ill-usage to endure. They found indeed a general indifference to the message, and alienation from the messengers; but nothing worse. In agreement with this we have no record of any displays of active enmity against the Apostles or disciples during the lifetime of the Lord, nor at the first against the Lord Himself. It was simply, *'they would not come.'*

'Again he sent forth other servants, saying, Tell them which are bidden, Behold, I have prepared my dinner; my oxen and my fatlings are killed'—a token this of the immediate nearness of the feast—*'and all things are ready; come unto the marriage.'* The king graciously assumes that these guests deferred their coming through some misunderstanding, unaware perhaps that all the preparations were completed; and instead of threatening and punishing, only bids the servants whom he now sends to press the message with greater instancy and distinctness than before. Something of this same gracious overlooking of the past breathes through the language of St. Peter in all his discourses after Pentecost, 'And now, brethren, I wot that through ignorance ye did it' (Acts 3:17), a willingness to regard the sin which hitherto the people had committed in the mildest possible light. This second summons I take to represent the invitation to the Jewish people, as it was renewed to them at the second epoch of the kingdom, that is, after the Resurrection and Ascension. It is true that of these events, as of the crucifixion no more, nothing is hinted in the parable, where indeed they could have found no room. It need not perplex us that this second company is spoken of as *'other servants,'* while, in fact, many of them were the same; for, in the first place, there *were* many now associated with these, as Paul, perhaps too as Stephen and barnabas, who not till after Pentecost were added to the Church. Those, too, who *were* the same, yet went forth as other men, full of the Holy Ghost, and with a message still more gracious than at the first; not preaching any more a kingdom of God at hand, but one already come—'Jesus and the resurrection'; declaring, which the servants had not been empowered to do on their first mission, that all things were now ready, that 'the fullness of time' had arrived, and that all obstacles to an entrance into the kingdom, which the sin of men had reared up, the grace of God had removed (Acts 2:38, 39; 3:19–26; 4:12, 17, 30); that in that very blood which they had impiously shed, there was forgiveness of all sins, and free access to God.

If the king's servants had found dull and deaf ears on their first mission, they find a more marked averseness from themselves and from their message on the second. The guests, when they heard the reiterated invitation, *'made light of it, and went their ways, one to his farm, another to his merchandise.'* The question presents itself, Can we trace a distinction between the serveral guests? Did the divine utterer of the parable intend a distinction? Perhaps, if we regard the first as one who went *to his estate* (and the word of the original will perfectly bear out this meaning), a distinction will appear. The first is the landed proprietor, the second the merchant. The first would *enjoy* what he already possesses, the second would *acquire* what as yet is his only in anticipation. The first represents the rich (1 Tim. 6:17); the second those that desire to be rich (1 Tim. 6:9). This will agree with Luke 14:18, 19; where the guest who must try his five yoke of oxen, belongs to the second. The temptations which beset the *having* and the getting, though nearly allied, are not always and altogether the same; there is quite difference enough between them to account for the mention of them both. One of the guests, being urged to come, turned to that which by his own toil, or the toil of others who went before him, he had already won—another to that which he was in the process of winning. We have here those whoa re full, and those who are striving to be full; and on both the woe pronounced at Luke 6:25 has come. This apparent fullness proves a real emptiness; keeping men away from Him who would have indeed filled and satisfied their souls.

But these are not the worst. *'The remnant took his servants, and entreated them spitefully, and slew them.'* The oppositions to the truth are not merely *natural*, they are also *devilish*. Of those who reject the Gospel of the grace of God, there are some who do not so much actively hate it, as that they love the world better than they love it. We have just heard of these. But there are others in whom it rouses a fierce opposition, whose pride it wounds, whose self-righteousness it offends; who, where they dare, will visit on the bringers of the message the hate which they bear to itself. Three forms of outrage are enumerated here: and how full a commentary on these prophetic words do the Acts of the Apostles, and much else in the later Scriptures, supply. Those who should have received with all honors these ambassadors of the Great King *'took,'* or laid violent hands on, them (Acts 4:3; 5:18; 8:3); they *'entreated them spitefully'* (Acts 5:40; 14:5, 19; 16:23; 17:5; 21:30; 23:2; 1 Thess. 2:15); they *'slew them'* (Acts 7:58; 12:2; cf. Matt. 23:34; John 16:2).

'But when the king heard thereof, he was wroth.' The insult was to him, and was intended for him; as in every case where an ambassador is outraged, it is his master whom the blow was intended to reach (2 Sam. 10). As such it is punished; for the king *'sent forth his armies,'* that is, as some say, God sent forth his avenging angels, the armies in heaven (Rev. 19:14), the legions at his bidding there (Matt. 26:53; 1 Kgs. 22:19; 2 Sam. 24:16): or, it may be, the hosts of Rome (Dan. 9:26), which were equally *'his armies,'* since even ungodly men are men of God's hand, by whom He punishes his own people that have sinned, or executes vengeance on others more wicked than themselves (thus Is. 10:5, 'O Assyrian, the rod of *mine* anger'; cf. 13:5; Ezek. 16:41; 29:18–20; Jer. 22:7; 25:9, 'Nebuchadnezzar, *my servant'*). The two explanations do in fact flow into one; for when God's judgments are abroad, the earthly and visible ministers of those judgments and the unseen armies of heaven are evermore leagued together. The natural eye sees only those, the spiritual eye beholds the other behind them. It is ever at such moments as it was with Israel of old (1 Chr. 21:16). The multitude, to whom the purged spiritual eye was wanting, beheld only the outward calamity, the wasting pestilence; but 'David lifted up his eyes and saw the angel of the Lord stand between the earth and the heaven, having a drawn sword in his handstretched out over Jerusalem.' *'And destroyed those murderers, and burned up their city'*; the city, that is, of those murderers; no longer 'the city of the great King,' who will not own it for his any more. Compare our Lord's word a little later: *'Your* house is left unto you desolate (23:38); *your* house, and not mine; however it may still bear my name'; and see Ex. 32:7. This city is of course Jerusalem, the central point of the Jewish theocracy (Matt. 23:34, 35; Luke 13:33, 34; Acts 7:39; 12:2, 3); burned once already (2 Kgs. 25:9; Jer. 39:8; 52:13); as was the constant doom of a taken city (Num. 31:10; Josh. 6:24; 8:19; 11:11; Judg. 1:8; 18:27; 20:40; Is. 1:7; Amos 1:7; and often); and now threatened with a repetition of the same terrible fate.

'Then saith he to his servants, The wedding is ready; but they which were bidden were not worthy.' The Scripture does not refuse to recog-

nize a worthiness in men (Matt. 10:10, 11; Luke 20:35; 21:36; 2 Thess. 1:5, 11; Rev. 3:4); nor is it any paradox to say that this worthiness largely consists in a sense of unworthiness; the unworthiness, on the other hand, of those whom the bidden represent consisting in the absence of any such divine hunger in their hearts after a righteousness which they had not, as would have brought them, eager guests, to the marriage supper of the Lamb. *'Go ye therefore into the highways, and as many as ye shall find, bid to the marriage.'* Compare Matt. 8:11, 12, which contains, so to speak, this parable in the germ. There, as here, that truth long ago foreannounced by Psalmist (Ps. 18:43, 44) and by prophet (Is. 56:1), but not the less strange and unwelcome to Jewish ears (see Acts 22:21, 22), the calling of the Gentiles, and that by occasion of the disobedience of the Jews, the diminishing of these which should be the riches of those (Rom. 11), is plainly declared.

'So those servants went out into the highways, and gathered together all as many as they found, both bad and good.' In the spirit of this command, 'Philip went down to the city of Samaria, and preached Christ unto them' there (Acts 8:5); Peter baptized Cornelius and his company (Acts 10:48); and Paul proclaimed to the men of Athens how God now commanded *'all men everywhere* to repent' (Acts 17:30). When it is said they gathered in *'bad'* as well as *'good'*—in which statement there is a passing over from the figure to the reality, since moral qualities would scarcely be predicated of the guests as such—this is not to prepare and account for one presently being found without a wedding garment. *'Bad'* here is not equivalent to *'not having a wedding garment'* there; on the contrary, many were *'bad'* when invited (1 Cor. 6:9–11), who, accepting the invitation, passed into the number of the *'good:'* for the beautiful words of Augustine on Christ's love to his Church may find here their application, 'He loved her foul, that He might make her fair.' Neither may *'bad and good,'* least of all the latter, be pressed too far: for in strictest speech none are *'good'* till they have been joined to Him, who only is the Good (Matt. 19:17), and made sharers in his Spirit. At the same time there are varieties of moral life, even anterior to obedience to the Gospel call. There are *'good,'* such as Nathanael, as Cornelius, as those Gentiles that were a law to themselves (Rom. 2:14; cf. Luke 8:15); and *'bad,* in whom the sin common to all has wrought more mightily than in others (Ps. 58:3–5); the sickness of which the whole body of humanity is sick, concentrating itself in some of the members more than in others. The kingdom of heaven

is as a draw-net, which brings within its ample folds of the best and of the worst, of those who have been before honestly striving after a righteousness according to the law (Rom. 2:14, 15), and of those who have been utterly 'dead in trespasses and sins.' *'And the wedding was furnished with guests.'*

At this point the other and earlier spoken parable concludes (Luke 14:16); but what constitutes the whole in it is only as the first act in this present; and another judgment act is still in reserve. The judgment of the avowed foe has found place; that of the false friend has still to follow. Hitherto the parable has set forth to us their guilt and their punishment who openly reject the Gospel of the grace of God; as the great body of the Jewish people with their chiefs and rulers were doing. It is now for others, and contains an earnest warning for is now for others, and contains an earnest warning for them who have found a place in his kingdom. Besides the separation between those who come and those who refuse to come, it shall be also proved who among the actual comers are walking worthy of their vocation, and who not; and as it is thus or thus, there shall be a second sifting and separation. But as in the parable of the Tares it was not the office of the servants to discern between the tares and the wheat (Matt. 13:29, 30), as little is it their office here to separate decisively between worthy partakers of the heavenly banquet and unworthy intruders; and, indeed, how should it be, seeing that the garment which distinguishes those from these is worn, not on the body, but on the heart? This office is for another, for One to whom all hearts are open and manifest, who only can carry it through with no liability to error (Heb. 4:13). Of Him, 'whose fan is in his hand, and who will throughly purge his floor,' we now hear.

'And when the king came in to see the guests, he saw there a man which had not on a wedding garment.' It pertained to the dignity of the king, that he should not appear till all were assembled, nor, indeed, till all had occupied their places; for that the guests were arranged, and as we, though with a certain incorrectness, should say, seated, is implied in the word which describes them now. At a glance he detected one, a spot in that feast (Jude 12), who, apparelled as he was, should not have presumed to take his place at a royal festival, or enter a royal presence. Him he addresses, as yet with a gentle compellation, for possibly he can explain away his apparent contempt; and he shall have the opportunity of doing so, if he can: *'Friend, how camest thou in hither, not having a wedding garment?'* But

explanation to offer he had none; *'he was speechless.'* Why could he not answer that it was unreasonable to expect of him, brought in of a sudden and without warning from the highways, to be furnished with such? That he was too poor to provide, or that no time had been allowed him to go home and fetch, such a garment? Some, willing to get rid of any semblance of harshness in the after con- duct of the king, and fearing lest such might redound on Him whom the king represents, maintain that no such excuse would have served, or would really have touched the oint which the king's question raised. They remind us that in the East, when kings or great personages made an entertainment, they were wont to pre- sent costly dresses to the guests; that such a custom is here tacitly assumed; and therefore that this guest could only appear at the wedding not having such a garment, because he had rejected it when offered to him; in the same act pouring contempt on the gift and on the giver, and declaring plainly that he counted his ordi- nary work-day apparel, with any soil and stain which it might have gathered, sufficiently good in which to appear in the presence of the king.

Many, however, deny that any certain traces of such a custom can anywhere be found, that what alone resembles such a usage is the modern custom of clothing with a caftan those admitted into the presence of the Sultan. It must be owned that Judg. 14:13, often adduced in proof, proves nothing; and perhaps no distinct evi- dence of any such practice is forthcoming. Still we know enough of the undoubted customs of the East to make it extremely likely that presents of dresses were often distributed among the guests at a marriage festival, especially at one like the present, celebrated with great pomp and magnificence; and if this were the case, our Lord's hearers, to whom those customs were familiar, would naturally have supplied the omission in the parable, and taken for granted such a gift going before; most of all, when they found one so se- verely punished for a want which in any other case he could scarcely have avoided. We know, in the first place, that it was and is part of the magnificence of Oriental princes and potentates to have vast stores of costly dresses laid up, a large portion of their wealth being often invested in these (Job 27:16; Is. 3:6; James 5:2; 2 Kgs. 10:22). We know, moreover, that costly dresses were often given as marks of peculiar favor (Gen. 41:42; 45:22; 1 Sam. 18:4; 2 Kgs. 5:5, 22; 10:22; Dan. 5:7; Esth. 6:8; 8:15; 1 Macc. 10:20); being then, as now, the most customary gift; that marriage festivals (Esth.

2:180, and other seasons of festal rejoicing (2 Sam. 6:19), were naturally those at which gifts were distributed with the largest hand. Gifts of costly raiment it would certainly be expected should be worn at once; so proclaiming the magnificence of the giver, and adding to the splendor of the time—not to say that a slighting of the gift is in the very nature of things a slighting of the giver.

But this rejection of the gift, if such may be safely assumed, involved a further affront—namely, the appearing of this guest at a high festival in unsuitable, probably in mean and sordid, apparel. Even with us there are occasions when this would be felt as a serious lack of respect; much more in those Eastern lands where outward symbols possess so much more significance than with us. It is evident, too, that the more honorable the person, and the more solemn the occasion, the more flagrant the offense; here the person is a king, and the occasion the marriage of his son. And thus, however others may have been forward to say many things in this guest's behalf—as that he could not help appearing as he did, or that his fault, after all, was a trival one—*he* did not count that he had anything to say for himself; *'he was speechless,'* or literally, his mouth was stopped, he was gagged, with no plea to allege for his contemptuous behavior. He stood self-condemned, at once convinced and convicted, and his judgment did not tarry; but of that presently.

When we seek to give a spiritual signification to this part of the parable, there are many questions, and some most important, which demand an answer. And first, When does the great King come in *'to see,'* or to scrutinize, *'the guests?'* In one sense He is doing so evermore; as often as by any judgment-act hypocrites are revealed, or self-deceivers laid bare to themselves or to others—at every time of trial, which is also in its very nature a time of separation, a time when the thoughts of many hearts are laid bare. But while this is true, while we must not relegate to a day of final judgment all in this kind which, indeed, is continually going forward, it is not the less true that for that day the complete separation is reserved; and then all that has been partially fulfilling in one and another will be altogether fulfilled in all.

But the guest himself *'which had not on a wedding garment'*—does he represent one or many? Some, unwilling to let go the singleness of this guest, and fain to hold it fast in the interpretation of the parable, have suggested that Judas Iscariot may be immediately intended. Assuredly a mistake, except in so far as words calculated for every hypocrite and deceiver were eminently calculated for him. Others of the historico-prophetical school, as Vitringa and Cocceius, see in him the man of sin, by whom they understand the Pope. It is little likely, however, that any single person is intended, but rather that many are included in this one; the *'few'* presently said to be *'chosen,'* as compared with the *'many called,'* implying that a great sifting has found place. Why this *'many'* cast out should be represented as a single person has been explained in different ways. Townson instances it as an example of what he happily calls 'the lenity of supposition,' which marks our Lord's parables; just as in another *one* servant only is brought forward as failing to turn his lord's money to account (Matt. 25:18; Luke 19:20). Gerhard ingeniously suggests, that 'if many had been thrust out from the marriage, the nuptial festivities might appear to have been disturbed.' But more valuable is another suggestion which he offers, namely, that the matter is thus brought home to the conscience of every man: 'so diligent and exact will be the future scrutiny, that not so much as one in all that great multitude of men shall on the last day escape the piercing eyes of the Judge. Nor is there any difficulty in thus contemplating the whole multitude of evil-doers as a single person. For as the faithful are one, being gathered under their one head, which is Christ, so the congregation of the wicked are one, being gathered also under their one head, which is Satan. The mystical Babylon is one city no less than the mystical Jerusalem. There is a *kingdom* of darkness (Matt. 12:25, 26), as well as a kingdom of God.

What the wedding garment itself is, and what he lacked, who had it not, has been abundantly disputed. Was it faith? Or was it charity? Or was it both? That it was something indispensable is self-evident, and theologians of the Roman Church, eager to draw an argument form hence that charity is the one indispensable grace, have urged that it must have been charity, and not faith, which this unworthy guest was without; for faith, as they argue, he must have had, seeing that without that he would not have been present at the feast at all. But, arguing thus, they take advantage of the double meaning of the word faith, and play off its use as a bare assent to, or intellectual belief in, the truth, against St. Paul's far deeper use—and this with injustice, since only in the latter sense would any attribute this guest's exclusion to his wanting faith. Were it needful so to limit the meaning of the wedding garment that it must signify *either* faith or charity, far better to restrain it to the former. Such would be the deeper and truer interpretation, since the flower is wrapped up in the root, but not the root in the flower, and so charity in faith, but not faith in charity. There is, however, no need so to determine for one of these interpretations, as to exclude the other. The foremost teachers of the early Church put themselves in no contradiction with one another, when some of them asserted that what the intruder lacked was charity, and others faith; nor with themselves, when they gave now the one interpretation, and now the other. For what this guest wanted was *righteousness*, both in its root of faith and its flower of charity. He had not, according to the pregnant image of St. Paul, here peculiarly appropriate, *'put on* Christ'—in which putting on of Christ, both faith and charity are included—faith as the investing power, charity or holiness as the invested robe. By faith we recognize a righteousness out of and above us, and which yet is akin to us, and wherewith our spirits can be clothed; which righteousness is in Christ, who is therefore the Lord our Righteousness. And this righteousness by the apporpriative and assimilative power of faith we also make our own; we are clothed upon with it, so that it becomes, in that singularly expressive term, our *habit*—the righteousness imputed has become also a righteousness infused, and is in us charity or holiness, or more accurately still, constitutes the complex of all Christian graces as they abide in the man, and show themselves in his life.

Setting aside then all narrower interpretations, not as erroneious, but as insufficient, we may affirm of the wedding garment that it is righteousness in its largest sense, the whole adornment of the new and spiritual man; including the faith without which it is impossible to please God (Heb. 11:6), and the holiness without which no man shall see Him (Heb. 12:14, or shall, like this guest, only see Him to perish at his presence. It is at once the faith which is the root of all graces, the mother of all virtues, and likewise those graces and virtues themselves. Whether we contemplate this guest as a self-righteous person, trusting in a righteousness of his own, instead of a righteousness of Christ's, imputed and imparted—or see in him a more ordinary sinner, who with the Christian profession and privileges is yet walking after the flesh and not after the spirit—in either case the image holds good; he is rejecting something, even the true robe of his spirit, bestowed on him when he was made a member of Christ; and which if he has since let go, he may yet, on the strength of that gift, freely at any moment reclaim; he is a despiser, counting himself good enough merely as he is in himself, in the flesh and not in the spirit (John 3:6), to appear in the presence of God (Prov. 16:2). But a time arrives when every man will discover that he needs another covering, another array for his soul; that this is a garment narrower than he can wrap himself withal. It is woe to him, if, like the guest of this parable, he only discovers this, when it is too late to provide himself with such; and then suddenly stands confessed to himself and to others in all his moral nakedness and shame. As it was the king's word which struck the intruder speechless, so will it be the light of God shining round and shining in upon the sinner, which will one day reveal to him all the hidden things of his heart, all that evil whereof he has hitherto willfully chosen to be ignorant, but now can remain ignorant no longer. He then, like the unworthy guest, will be *'speechless.'* However forward he may have been in other times to justify himself, as there are now a thousand cloaks for sins (Gen. 3:12, 13; James 1:13; 1 Sam. 15:21, in that day his mouth will be stopped; he will not even pretend to offer any plea why judgment should not proceed against him at once.

'Then said the king to the servants'—to the 'ministering attendants' rather, for they differ both in name and office from the *'servants'* that brought in the guests, being no other than the angels, who 'shall gather out of the kingdom all things that offend, and all that do iniquity' (Matt. 13:41, 49; Luke 19:24)—*'Blind him hand and foot'*; which work of the heavenly *lictors* is by some understood to express that upon the sinner the night is come, in which no man can work, that for him all opportunities of repentance and amendment are gone by. I take it rather to express the impotence to which in a moment every proud fighter against God will be reduced. The hands by whose aid resistance, the feet by whose help escape, might have been meditated, are alike deprived of all power and motion (Acts 21:11; 2 Sam. 3:34). This agrees better with that *'take him away,'* which follows, being the sinner's exclusion from the Church now glorious and triumphant in heaven (Matt. 13:48; 2 Thess. 1:9). Nor is the penalty merely privative; it is not only this loss of good, but also the presence of evil. They who carry out the judgment shall *'cast him into outer darkness.'* The phrase occurs only in St. Matthew, but there thrrice; 8:12; 25:30; and here. The image is suggested by the parable itself. Within the king's palace is feasting and light and joy; without is desolation and darkness and cold. Not otherwise does the *'outer darkness'* lie wholly beyond and external

to God's kingdom of light and joy; for as light is the element of that kingdom, so whatever is outside of that kingdom is darkness—even that exterior or *'outer darkness'* into which all fall back, who, refusing to walk in the light of God's truth, fail to attain in the end to the light of everlasting life (cf. Wisd. 17:21; 18:1). *'There shall be weeping and gnashing of teeth'*; something on these words has been said already; see p. 105. With all this it is interesting to compare Zeph. 1:7, 8: 'The Lord hath prepared a sacrifice, He hath bid his guests. And it shall come to pass in the day of the Lord's sacrifice, that I will punish the princes and the king's children, and all such as are *clothed with strange apparel.'*

Christ moralizes the whole parable, as He had already done that of the Laborers in the Vineyard (Matt. 20:16, with those solemn words, *'For many are called, but few are chosen'* (cf. 1 Cor. 9:24). To these *'called'* and not *'chosen'* belong others besides this unworthy guests; for the words are intended to include those who did not so much as seem (which he had done) to embrace the invitation, and who expiated their contumacy in the destruction of themselves and their city. And how many of the severer dealings of God with those who, within the Covenant, yet despise the mercies of that Covenant, do these words sum up. They are evermore finding their fulfillment. They were fulfilled on how large a scale in the history of that entire generation which went out of Egypt; these were all *'called'* to a kingdom, yet were not in the end *'chosen,'* since with most of them God was not well pleased, and they died in the wilderness (Num. 14:22–30; 1 Cor. 10:1–10; Heb. 3:7–9; Jude 5). They were fulfilled on a smaller scale in those twelve, to whom it was given the first to see the promised land; two only drew strength and encouragement from that sight, and they only were *'chosen'* to inherit it (Num. 14:23, 24). They found their fulfillment in the thirty and two thousand of Gideon's army; these all were *'called,'* but only three hundred were found worthy, and in the end *'chosen'* to be helpers in and sharers of his victory—such a sifting and winnowing had there previously been (Judg. 7). They were fulfilled too in a type and figure, when of all the maidens brought together to the palace of the Persian king, Esther alone was *'chosen'* by him, and found lasting favor in his sight (Esth. 2).

13.

The Ten Virgins

Matthew 25:1–13

'T hen'—in that great day of decision, wherein the Lord shall have shown Himself "a swift witness against the hypocrite and unbeliever (Matt, 24:51), He shall in other ways also bring the faith of his servants to the final test, and, as they endure or fail under this, shall receive or reject them forever. 'Then shall the kingdom of heaven be likened unto ten virgins, which took their lamps, and went forth to meet the bridegroom' The circumstances of a marriage among the Jews, so far as they furnish the groundwork of this parable, are well known, and have been abundantly illustrated by writers on Jewish antiquities. Use also may be here made of notices gathered by modern travelers in the East; the lapse of centuries having changed little or nothing in that stationary world. That the virgins should be ten in number is not accidental; exactly so many formed, according to Jewish notions, a company; which fewer would have failed to do. These 'took their lamps,' marriages in the East being celebrated of old, as they are now, invariably at night; hence the constant mention of lamps and torches as borne by the friends and attendants: cf. 2 Esdr. 10:2; and Jer. 25:10; Rev. 18:23; in both which passages 'the light of a candle,' and 'the voice of the bridegroom and the bride,' stand close to one another. Thus furnished, they 'went forth to meet the bridegroom.' The order of the bridal procession appears to have been as follows: the bridegroom, accompanied by his friends, 'the children of the bride-chamber' (Matt. 9:15), 'the friends of the bridegroom' (John 3:29; see Judg. 14:11), went to the house of the bride, and led her with pomp and gladness (1 Macc. 9:37–39) to his own home, or, where that was too narrow to receive the guests, to some larger apartment provided for the occasion. She was accompanied from her father's house by her youthful friends and companions (Ps. 45:15), while other of these, the 'virgins' of the parable, joined the procession at some convenient point, and entered with the rest of the bridal company into the hall of feasting (Cant. 3:11). Some take rather differently the circumstances which furnish the machinery of the parable. They suppose these virgins to meet the bridegroom, not as he returns with, but as he goes to fetch, the bride; accompanying him first to her home, and only then to his own. But such was not the manner either with the Jews or the Greeks; while the spiritual significance of the parable is seriously disturbed thereby. The virgins, we may confidently affirm, 'went forth to meet the bridegroom and the bride'—however the last words, found in some earlier Versions, have no right to a place in the text.

But these 'virgins,' why are they so called, and whom do they represent? There are two mistakes to which the pressing too far the title which they bear has given rise. There is first theirs who argue, All are virgins; all, therefore, belong at the inmost center of their life unto Christ. Some, it is true, are found unready at the decisive moment, and therefore suffer loss (1 Cor. 3:13), even a long deferring of their blessedness. Yet the honorable name bestowed alike upon all gives assurance that all are saved in the end, none finally shut out from the kingdom of glory. They who make this milder estimate of the guilt of the foolish virgins, and of the character of their doom, usually connect with this the doctrine of the thousand years' reign of Christ upon earth and a first resurrection; from the blessedness of which these should be shut out for this unreadiness of theirs, whether at the hour of their death, or of the second coming of their Lord. Their imperfections, and the much in them remaining unmortified and unpurified still, will need the long and painful purging of this exclusion, and of the fearful persecutions to which all thus excluded shall be exposed: but the root of the matter being in them, they do not forfeit everything, nor finally fall short of the heavenly joy. But the premises from which these conclusions are drawn appear to me nothing worth. There would be something in the fact that unwise as well as wise are here by the Lord styled 'virgins,' if others sometimes undertook the office of welcoming the bridegroom, and He, notwithstanding, had chosen to give the appellation of virgins to these. But seeing that to such the office in the usual order of things appertained, *their* arguments who, like Von Meyer, Olshausen, Stier, press to such conclusions as

I have just stated the title of virgins which the foolish bear, appear to me to possess no force at all.

Into the second error Chrysostom, with others, has fallen; who, accepting the title of virgins in the literal, while everything else is accepted in a figurative, sense, limit the application of the parable to those who had made a profession of outward virginity; instead of seeing that the virginity here is the profession of a pure faith, the absence of spiritual fornication, of apostasy from the one God (Rev. 14:4; 2 Cor. 11:2). This all the virgins have; and in the number of these must be included all who profess to be waiting for the Son of God from heaven, to love his appearing; all who with their lips join in the confession, 'I believe in Jesus Christ our Lord, who shall come again to judge both the quick and the dead,' and who do not in their lives openly deny this hope; all are included, who would desire to include themselves in the number of his believing people. The whole company of the virgins have this in common, that they confess to the same Lord, and to the same hope in Him—as is involved in the fact of all alike taking their lamps, and going forth to meet the bridegroom.

That which constitutes a distinction among them first appears in the words that follow. When it is added *'And five of them were wise, and five were foolish,'* the numbers make nothing to the case; only the division is essential. They are not divided into good and bad, but, as the hearers elsewhere (Matt. 7:25–27), into *'wise'* and *'foolish'*; for, as a certain degree of good-will toward the truth is assumed there on the part of the *'foolish,'* as evidenced in their willingness to hear, and in the super-structure, however weak, which they raise, so on the part of these in their going forth even with the intention of meeting the bridegroom. They are severally described, the wise 2 Pet. 1:5–8, and the foolish 2 Pet. 1:9. We are next informed wherein consisted the foolishness of these, and the wisdom of those: *'They that were foolish took their lamps, and took no oil with them; but the wise took oil in their vessels with their lamps.'* Here is the turning-point of the parable. On a right apprehending of what the having, or the not having, a reserved supply of oil may mean everything must depend. Again we meet with a controversy between Roman Catholics and the early Reformers, and one differing in little from that to which 'the wedding garment' gave occasion (see p. 24). The Reformers asserted that what the foolish virgins lacked was the living principle of faith; that what they had were the outer circumstances of a Christian profession; these were their lamps shining before men; but they wanted the inner spirit of life, the oil which they should have had, if their lamps were to be found burning in the day of Christ's appearing. The Roman Catholic reversed the whole; for him what they had was faith, but faith which, not having works, was 'dead, being alone' (James 2:17); they were not careful to maintain good works, to nourish the lamp of faith, which they carried before men, with deeds of light done for and in the sight of God; they did not by well-doing stir up the grace of God that was in them, and so the unused grace was taken from them; their lamps burned dim, and at last were wholly extinguished, and they had not wherewith to revive them anew.

Here again it is only necessary to call attention to the different senses in which the two contending parties employ the word *faith*—the Roman Catholics as the outward profession of the truth—the Reformers as the root and living principle of Christian life. Except for these diverse uses of the same term, the two interpretations would not be opposed to , or exclude, one another—would indeed admit of a fair reconciliation. For we may equally contemplate the foolish virgins, unprovided with oil, as those going through a round of external duties, without life, without love, without any striving after inward conformity to the law of god, whose religion is all husk and no kernel; or, again, as those who, confessing Christ with their lips, and holding fast the form of the truth, are for all this remiss in the work of the Lord, in acts of charity, of humility, and self-denial; and who therefore, by that law which decrees that from him who hath not shall be taken even that which he hath, gradually lose that grace which they had, and discover that they have lost it altogether, at the decisive moment when they need to have it in largest measure. It is clear that whatever is merely outward in the Christian profession is the lamp; whatever is inward and spiritual is the oil reserved in the vessels. When we contemplate with St. James (2:14) the faith as the body, and the works as witnessing for an informing vivifying soul, then the faith is the lamp, the works the oil in the vessels; but when, on the other hand, we contemplate with St. Paul the works as only having a value from the living principle of faith out of which they spring, then the works are the lamp, and the faith the oil which must feed it. Yet in either case, before we have exhausted all the meaning of the oil, we must get beyond both the works and the faith to something higher than either, the informing Spirit of God which prompts the works and quickens the faith, of which Spirit oil is ever in Scripture the standing symbol (Ex. 30:22–33; Zech. 4:2, 12; Acts 10:38; Heb. 1:9; 1 John 2:20, 27).

But under whatever aspect we regard the relation between the oil in the lamps and in the vessels, the purpose of the parable is, as we cannot doubt (see ver. 13), to impress upon all members of the Church their need of vigilance. Regarded in the one view, it is a warning that they be careful to maintain good works, that they be not satisfied, as some, with saying, 'Lord, Lord,' while they do not the things that He says. Regarded under the other aspect, is it a warning that they be watchful over their inward state—over their affections—over all which, withdrawn from the eyes of man, is seen only of God—that they seek to have a constant supply of the Spirit of Christ Jesus in their innermost hearts, to approve themselves before God, as well as to show fairly and unblamably before the world. In either case, we must remember, and it adds much to the solemnity of the lesson, that by the foolish virgins are meant—not hypocrites, not self-conscious dissemblers, much less openly profane and ungodly—but the negligent in prayer, the slothful in work, and all those whose scheme of a Christian life is laid out rather to satisfy the eyes of men than to please Him who seeth in secret. Nor is it that they are wholly without oil; they have some, but not enough; their lamps, when they first go forth, are burning, otherwise they could not speak of them as on the point of expiring just as the bridegroom is approaching. In fact, the having no oil provided in the vessels is exactly parallel to having no deepness of earth (Matt. 13:5); the seed springs up till the sun scorches it; the lamps burn on till their oil is exhausted through the length of the bridegroom's delay. In each case something more is implied than a mere external profession, conscious to itself that it is nothing besides; it is not that there was no faith, but only that *fides temporaria* which could not endure temptation, nor survive delay. *They,* on the other hand, are like the wise virgins, who recognize the possibility that the Bridegroom may tarry long, that the Church may not very soon, perhaps not in their days, enter into its glory; who, therefore, foresee that they may have a long life before them of patience and self-denial, before they shall come to the kingdom, or the kingdom to them; and who therefore rightly judge that it is not a few warm excited feelings which will carry them triumphantly through all this, and enable to endure unto the end, for such are but as a fire among straw, quickly blazing up, and as quickly extinguished. They understand that principles as well as feelings must be engaged in the work, that their first good impulses will carry them but a very little way, unless revived, strengthened, and purified, by a continual supply of the Spirit of God. If the bridegroom were to come at once, it might be another thing; but their wisdom is that, since it may very well fare otherwise, they make provision against such a contingency.

'While the bridegroom tarried, they all slumbered and slept.' We may number this among the many hints that the time of the Lord's return might possibly be delayed very far beyond the expectation of his first disciples. It was a hint, and no more. Had more been granted, had He said plainly that many centuries should elapse before his return, then the earlier ages of the Church would have been placed at a manifest disadvantage, being deprived of that powerful motive to holiness and diligence which each generation finds in the possibility of his return in their time. It is not that He desires each succeeding generation to believe that in their day He will certainly return; for He does not desire our faith and our practice to be founded on a mistake, as then the faith and practice of all generations but the last would be. But it is a necessary element of the doctrine concerning the second coming of Christ, that it should be *possible* at any time, that none should regard it improbable in theirs. The love, the earnest longing of those first Christians made them to assume that coming to be close at hand. In the strength and joy of this faith they lived and suffered; and when they died, the kingdom was indeed come unto them. As a further reason why the Church should not have been acquainted from the first with the precise moment of her Lord's return, it may be added, that it is in itself, no doubt, undetermined. Prophecy is no fatalism, and it has been always open to every age by faith and prayer to hasten that coming, so that St. Peter can speak of the faithful not merely as looking for, but also as *hasting*, the coming of the day of God (2 Pet. 3:12); with which we may compare Acts 3:19, 'Repent ye . . . *that* the times of refreshing may come'; these 'times of refreshing' being identical with 'the times of restitution of all things' (v. 21), the glorious setting up of the kingdoms the same truth, that the quicker or tardier approach of that day is conditional, being elsewhere declared in clearest terms (2 Pet. 3:9). We too have learned to pray that it may please God 'to accomplish the number of his elect, and to *hasten* his kingdom.' But while the matter was left by the wisdom of God in this uncertainty, it imported much that after the expectations of the first ages of the Church had failed, those who examined the Scriptures should see plainly there that no pledge had thus been broken, that no prophecy had failed, that what had actually come to pass was contemplated from the first.

The steps by which the virgins fell into deep sleep are marked; first they nodded the head or slumbered, and next they slept profoundly. Some have understood by this sleeping *of all,* a certain unreadiness that will have overtaken the whole Church, a too great acquiescence in the present time and in the present things even among the faithful themselves—though with this difference, that *their* unreadiness will be remediable, and easily removed; this removal being actually signified by the trimming and replenishing of their lamps; while that of others will be capable of no such remedy. Augustine proposes this interpretation, but only to reject it; for he asks, Why were those wise admitted, unless for the very reason that their love had *not* grown cold? But there is, he goes on to say, a sleep common to all, the sleep of death, which is indicated here. We may fitly prefer this, which is the explanation of nearly all the ancient interpreters, to that which understands by this sleeping the negligences and omissions of even the best Christians. Our Lord would scarcely have given, as it were, this allowance for a certain measure of negligence, seeing that with all the most earnest provocations to diligence, there will ever be too much of this. Least of all would He so do in a parable, whose very aim and moral is, that we be always ready, that we be *not* taken unprepared.

And yet by this slumbering and sleeping more may not after all be meant than that all, having taken such measures as they counted needful to enable them to meet the bridegroom as they would wish, securely awaited his approach. For, indeed, the fitnesses of the parable, which demand to be observed, required such a circumstance as this. Had the foolish virgins been in a condition to mark the lapse of time, and the gradual waning of their lamps, they, knowing that they had not wherewith to replenish them, would naturally have bestirred themselves, and that in time to procure a new supply. The fact that they fell asleep, and were only awakened by the cry of the approaching bridal company, gives— and nothing else would give—a natural explanation of their utter and irremediable destitution of oil at the moment when it most needed that they should have it in abundance. So too if the wise virgins had not slept as well, had they been represented as watching while the others were sleeping, it would have been a failure of love upon their parts, not to rouse their companions, and warn them of the lapse of time and the increasing dimness with which their lamps were burning, while help was still within reach.

So fared it with all, until 'at midnight there was a cry made, Behold, the bridegroom cometh: go ye out to meet him.' The cry which at this midnight hour startles the sleepers is either that of the retinue running before, or of the jubilant multitude, who, even till that late hour, had waited for the passing of the procession through the streets, and now welcomed it with these acclamations. Its spiritual signification has been variously given. Most have understood by it the descent of the Lord 'with a shout, with the voice of the Archangel and the trump of God' (1 Thess. 4:16), when He, the heavenly Bridegroom, shall at length draw nigh, accompanied by the angels, the friends of the bridegroom, and leading home his bride, the triumphant Church, and looking to be met and greeted by the members of his Church yet militant on earth, themselves a part of that mystical bride, that so He may bring her to the glorious mansion, the house of everlasting joy and gladness which He has prepared for her. Some, however, understand this cry as proceeding from watchers in the Church, such as shall not be altogether lacking in the last times (Is. 62:6); by whom the signs of the times shall have been observed, and who shall proclaim the near advent of the Lord. And this cry is 'at midnight.'It was a belief current among the later Jews, that the Messiah would come suddenly at midnight, as their forefathers had gone out from Egypt, and obtained their former deliverance, at that very hour (Ex. 12:29); from which belief Jerome supposes the apostolic tradition of not dismissing the people on Easter eve till the middle night was past, to have been derived. But it is idle to suppose that midnight is here named for any other reason than because it is a time when deep sleep falls upon men, when therefore such an event as the passage of a bridal company through the streets would be expected the least; and because thus the unlooked-for character of that day of the Lord, which 'cometh as a thief in the night' (1 Thess. v. 2), would be in the liveliest manner set out.

The parable will obtain a wider application if we keep in memory that, while there is one crowning advent of the Lord at the last, He comes no less in all the signal crises of his Church, at each new manifestation of his Spirit; and at each of these too there is a separation among those who are called by his name, into wise and foolish, as they are spiritually alive or dead. Thus at Pentecost, when by his Spirit He returned to his Church, He came: the prudent in

Israel went in with Him to the feast, the foolish tarried without. Thus too He came at the Reformation: those that had oil went in; those that had empty lamps, the form of godliness without the power, tarried without. Each of these was an example of that which shall be more signally fulfilled at the end.

'*Then all those virgins arose, and trimmed their lamps*'; and in this act of trimming, the foolish discovered to their dismay that theirs were going out, and that they had not wherewith to feed the expiring flame. In a higher sense, every one at the last prepares to give an account of his works, inquires into the foundations of his faith, seriously searches whether his life has been one which will have praise not merely of men, for that he now feels will avail nothing, but also of God. Many put off this proving of the grounds of their hope to the last moment, nay, some manage to defer it, with all its miserable discoveries, beyond the grave, even till the day of judgment—but further it cannot be deferred. When the day of Christ comes, it will be impossible for any to remain ignorant any longer of their true state, for that day will be a revelation of the hidden things of men, of things hitherto hidden even from themselves; a flood of light will then pour into all the darkest corners of all hearts, and show every man to himself exactly as he is; so that self-deception will be possible no longer (Prov. 16:2; 21:2; Rom. 2:16).

The foolish virgins turn in their extremity of need to their wiser companions, saying, '*Give us of your oil, for our lamps are gone out*'; or rather, as it is more correctly in the margin, '*are going out.*' Had their lamps already '*gone out,*' they would have needed not merely to trim and feed them, but must have further asked permission to kindle them anew, of which we hear nothing. The request, with the refusal which it meets—like the discourse between Abraham and Dives (Luke 16:24–31)—can be only the outer clothing of the truth, but of truth how momentous! No other than this, that we shall look in vain from men for that grace which God only can supply, that we shall be miserably disappointed, if we think thus to borrow in an easy lazy way that which must be *bought*—won, that is, by earnest prayer and diligent endeavour. And the answer of the wise, "*not so; lest there be not enough for us and you,*' has its lesson also. It tells us that every man must live by his own faith. There is that which one can communicate to another, and make himself the richer; as one who imparts a light to another has not therefore less light, but walks henceforth in the light of two torches instead of one: but there is also that which, being divine, is in its very nature incommunicable from man to man, which can be obtained only from above, which each must obtain for himself. One can indeed point out to another where he is to dig for the precious ore, but after all is said, each one must bring it up to himself, and by labor of his own.

In the reason which the wise virgins give for declining to comply with the other's request, *'lest there be not enough for us and you,'* there lies a witness against works of supererogation, however Roman Catholic expositors may resist the drawing of any such conclusion from it. 'The righteous shall scarcely be saved' (1 Pet. 4:18). The wise do not imagine that they have anything over, which, as not needing for themselves, they may transfer to others; happy if their own lamps are burning so brightly that they may be themselves allowed to make part of the bridal company, and to enter with them that enter into the joy of the festal chamber. To their unhappy companions they give the only counsel that, under the circumstances, is possible, *'But go ye rather to them that sell, and buy for yourselves.'* They bid them turn to the dispensers of heavenly grace, to those whom God has appointed in the Church as channels of his gifts; or, as some would explain it, to the prophets and Apostles, that they might learn of them how to revive the work of God in their souls, if yet there should be time. Some take the words as ironical; but how much more consistent with their character whom the wise virgins represent, to see in them a counsel of love, of that love which 'hopeth all things,' an exhortation to their fellows that they trust not in man, but betake themselves to the source from which effectual grace can alone be obtained, that they seek even at this last to revive the work of grace in their hearts.

What the wise had ventured to hope for themselves is granted. While the others are absent, vainly seeking to repair the negligence of the past, *'the bridegroom came, and they that were ready,'* they whose lamps were burning, having been fed anew from their vessels, *'went in with him to the marriage; and the door was shut'*; shut as much for the security and the joy without interruption of those within, as for the exclusion of those without (Gen. 7:16; Rev. 3:12). 'What door?' exclaims the author of an ancient homily on this parable: 'that which now is open to those coming from the east and from the west, that they may sit down with Abraham, and Isaac, and Jacob, in the kingdom of heaven—that Door which saith, Him that cometh to Me I will in nowise cast out. Behold how it is now open, which shall then be closed forevermoremore. Murderers come, and they are admitted—publicans and harlots come, and they are received—unclean and adulterers and robbers, and whosoever is of this kind, come, and the open door doth not deny itself to them; for Christ, the Door, is infinite to pardon, reaching beyond every degree and every amount of wickedness. But then what saith He? *"The door is shut."* No one's penitence—no one's prayer—no one's groaning shall any more be admitted. That door is shut, which received Aaron after his idolatry—which admitted David after his adultery, after his homicide—which not only did not repel Peter after his threefold denial, but delivered its keys to be guarded by him' (Luke 16:26).

'*Afterward came also the other virgins, saying, Lord, Lord, open to us';*—not that we are to suppose that they have now obtained oil; but, having sought it in vain, they return entreating that the want of it on their part may be overlooked; as those suing for mercy, when now the time of judgment has arrived (Prov. 1:28). In the title '*Lord,*' by which they address the bridegroom, they claim to stand in a near and intimate relation to him; as in the '*Lord, lord,*' twice repeated, is an evidence—not, as some say, of their vain confidence—but of the earnestness with which they now seek admission (Gen. 22:11; Ex. 3:4; 1 Sam. 3:10; Matt. 27:46; Luke 8:24; 10:41; 13:25, 34; 22:31; Acts 9:4); of the misgiving which already possesses them, lest the shut door should refuse to open any more. Even so it proves. All which they hear from within is the sentence of their exclusion: '*He answered and said, Verily, I say unto you, I know you not*' (cf. Matt. 7:23); he does not *know* them, that is, in that sense in which the Good Shepherd *knows* his sheep, and is known of them (John 10:14). Other parallel passages in which exactly the same emphasis is laid on the word are these: Ps. 37:18; 144:3; Nah. 1:7; Amos 3:2; Hos. 13:5; Matt. 25:12; 2 Tim. 2:19. Such knowledge is of necessity reciprocal, so that Augustine's remark, seeming a slight, is indeed a very profound one, that this, '*I have you not,*' is nothing else than, 'Ye know not Me.'

The exclusion of the foolish virgins from the marriage feast, if this interpretation be correct, is not temporary; but, so far as our horizon reaches, final. Many regard it in a different light, as who would not gladly do? And the views of some of these have been touched on already; but to me the sterner and severer interpretation alone approves itself as the true (Is. 65:13). On this exclusion of theirs Bengel observes, that there are four classes, which among them will include the whole company of the saved and of the lost.

There are those to whom 'an entrance is ministered *abundantly* into the kingdom,' entering as with sails set into the haven of their rest; those secondly, that are just saved, like shipwrecked mariners who hardly reach the shore: and on the other side, there are those who travel plainly on the broad way to destruction, whose sins go before them to judgment; while lastly, there are such as, though they might have seemed not 'far off from the kingdom of God,' yet fall short of it after all. Of this last class were these foolish virgins; and their fate, who were so near a crown and a kingdom, and yet missed them notwithstanding, he observes with truth, must always appear the most miserable of all. Lest that may be our lot, the Lord says to us—for what He said to his hearers then, He says unto all, to his Church and to every member of it in every age—*'Watch therefore; for ye know neither the day nor the hour'*; and while we know not, the only sure way to be ready upon *that* day, is that we be ready upon *every* day: unreadiness upon that day being unreadiness forever; and this doom of the foolish virgins proclaiming that the work, which should have been the business of a life, cannot be huddled up and accomplished in a moment (Luke 12:40; 21:34–36; 1 Thess. v. 6; 2 Pet. 3:10; Rev. 3:3).

A few words on the relation in which this parable stands to that of the Marriage of the King's Son, and to explain the fact that in that the unworthy guest actually obtains admission to the marriage supper (Matt. 22:11), and is only from thence cast out, while in this the foolish virgins are not so much as admitted to the feast. It would be easy to say, that this is an accidental difference growing out of the different structure of the two parables; but by such answers everything distinctive in the parables may be explained away; and we treat them with more reverence, when we look for some deeper-lying reason. May it not be that the marriage festivities there are different from the present? In Gerhard's words, 'Those are celebrated during this life in the Church militant, these at the last day in the Church triumphant. To those even they are admitted who are not adorned with the wedding garment, but to these only they to whom it is granted that they should be arrayed in the fine linen which is the righteousness of saints (Rev. 19:8); to those men are called by the trumpet of the Gospel, to these by the trumpet of the archangel. To those who enters can again go out from them, or be cast out, nor is cast out from them any more: wherefore it is said, *"The door was shut."*

14.
The Talents

Matthew 25:14–30

While the virgins were represented as waiting for their Lord, we have here the servants working for Him. There the inward spiritual life of the faithful was described, here their external activity. There, by the fate of the foolish virgins, we were warned against negligences and decays in the inner life; here, by the doom of the slothful servant, against indolence in our outward vocation and work. That parable enforced the need of keeping the heart with all diligence; this of putting all diligence also into our outward service, if we would give our account with joy and not with sorrow. Very fitly, therefore, that precedes, and this follows, since the maintenance of the life of God in the heart is the sole condition of a profitable outward activity for the kingdom of God. There is another light in which we may consider the virgins and the servants, and the distinction between them; namely, that those represent the more contemplative, these the more active laboring members of the Church. It is true that every member should partake of both, of contemplation and action, so that even when thus regarded, both parables will retain their application to all, but at the same time one element of the Christian life may predominate in one member, the other in another. Each must endeavor in his own case to adjust these, to give fuller development to the one or to the other, according to the gifts which he finds in himself, and the needs which he beholds in others around him.

St. Mark has a briefer recension of this parable (13:34–36), but with important variations, and reminiscences of the Ten Virgins ('lest coming suddenly He find you sleeping,' ver. 36); and blending into one of the two parables which with a stricter accuracy St.

Matthew keeps apart. St. Luke too has preserved for us a parable, that of the Pounds (19:12), having many points of contact with this, yet assuredly not identical with it. That was spoken when Jesus was now drawing near to Jerusalem, but had not yet made his triumphal entry—this, while He was seated on the Mount of Olives, the third day after his entry into the city. That was addressed to the multitude as well as to his disciples; this to the innermost circle of trusted followers who should carry forward the work which *He* had commenced on the earth. The scope of that, which is the more complex parable, is two-fold, and may be thus defined. The multitude, and perhaps many that were following the Lord with true hearts, supposed that He was now about to take his kingdom and to reign (John 6:15; Acts 1:6). He would make them to understand that any open assumption of his kingdom is yet far distant; that He must go away, and only after a long period return; and that not till then should opposition to his kingdom cease. Meanwhile (and here the two parables run parallel with one another), those who owned allegiance to Him were not indolently to wait the time of his return, but earnestly to set forward his kingdom, each according to the ability given him, confident that He would reward every man's work; in St. Luke's parable this further circumstance appearing, that He at his return would utterly destroy those who had sent after Him messages of hate and defiance. The scope of *his* parable then is twofold. It is addressed, in part, to that giddy light-minded multitude, who were now following Jesus, expecting that He would suffer Himself to be made such a king as they desired; and who, when He refused the royalty which they would have forced upon Him, might, perhaps, turn against Him, and join in the cry, 'Crucify Him.' These are warned that they be not offended though the manifestation of the King and the kingdom should be deferred for long; warned above all that they be not found in the ranks of his foes, whose dreadful doom might tarry long, but would arrive at last. To the disciples also that parable conveys a warning, namely, that the long interval between his going away and his coming again in glory must be no period of sluggish inactivity, but one for the showing of all good fidelity to an absent Lord: which fidelity would by Him be abundantly rewarded, even as sloth and a neglect of his interests would meet also their due recompense of reward.

A recent assailant of the historical accuracy of the record which in the four Gospels we have of our Lord's words and works fancies that he detects in that parable of St. Luke, just as in St. Matthew's record of the Marriage of the King's Son (Matt. 22:1, see p. 220), a blending together, through loose and floating tradition, of heterogeneous materials—that in fact we have there what should have been two parables, but these joined in one; and this so awkwardly, that the points of juncture are plainly discernible. He urges that 'servants' (v. 13) and 'citizens' (v. 14) stand in no relation to one another, that with slightest alterations, verses 12, 14, 15, 27 would form a complete whole, and might be entitled the parable of the Rebellious Citizens; the remaining verses constituting the parable of the Pounds, which would then be free from all admixture of foreign elements. But let it only be kept in mind, that there were two groups of hearers in different moral conditions and needing different admonishments to whom the Lord addressed the parable of St. Luke, and it will at once be perceived how He divided to all, to his own disciples and to the multitude, according to their several necessities. In St. Luke the parable is more complex, as having a more complex purpose to fulfill. In St. Matthew it is simpler; for it is addressed to the disciples alone, and the parts intended for the multitude would have been superfluous here, and accordingly are not introduced.

I reserve then the parable of the Pounds to be dealt with in its own place; for the present we have to do with this of the Talents alone. *'The kingdom of heaven is as a man traveling into a far country, who called his own servants, and delivered unto them his goods.'* It will be expedient to keep in mind here the relation of masters and *slaves* in antiquity; and not to confound this with that between masters and *servants,* as now existing among us. The master of a household going away does not leave with his servants—it would be foreign to all the relations between them—moneys wherewith to trade in his absence; nor, if he did, could he punish them on his return for neglect of his interests, as the slothful servant is punished here. But slaves in antiquity were often artisans, as was lately the case with serfs in Russia and slaves in America; paying some fixed yearly tax to their master: or money was committed to them wherewith to trade on his account, or with which to enlarge their business, bringing in to him a share of their profits. Some such arrangement as this we may here assume. The *'man traveling into a far country'* is the Lord Jesus Himself; who, as He had come from the Father, was about to return to the Father; and who, that his servants might be furnished in his absence, was about to entrust them, and all their successors whose representatives they were, with many excellent gifts. The day of Pentecost was the time when the *'goods,'* that is, spiritual powers and capacities, were by Him most manifestly and most largely communicated to his servants, that they might profit withal (John 16:7–10; Eph. 4:8–12). Yet not for the first time then. Much the Lord had imparted during his sojourn with them upon earth (John 15:3), much before his Ascension (John 20:22); and from that day forth He has been evermore delivering his goods to each successive generation of his servants (1 Cor. 12:4–11). This being so, the parable is good for all times and for all persons. As primarily addressed to the Apostles, the *'goods'* are those spiritual gifts which they needed; yet since all are called in their measure to edify one another, and are entrusted with gifts, more or fewer, for which they must render an account, the application of the parable stops not with them, but passes on to all. Nor, because it relates first to *spiritual* gifts, has it therefore no relation to other means and opportunities of serving God, as wealth, reputation, abilities, learning; which, though not in themselves spiritual, are yet given to men that they may be turned to spiritual ends—are capable of being consecrated to his service; for the use or abuse of which the possessors will have therefore to render an account. Our wide use of the word talent in English, growing as it does altogether out of this parable, is a remarkable evidence of the extent to which this conviction has wrought itself into the thoughts and language of them.

But different men receive these gifts in very different proportions: *'Unto one he gave five talents, to another two, and to another one.'* Not that the talents, as Theophylact explains it, were to each 'according to the measure of his faith and purity,' for the faith which purifies is itself on of the chiefest of these gifts; but he gave *'to every man according to his several ability,'* inasmuch as the natural is the ground upon which the spiritual is superinduced, and grace does not dissolve the groundwork of the individual character, nor abolish all its peculiarities, nor bring all that are subject to it to a common standard (see 1 Cor. 12:4–31; Eph. 4:16). The natural gifts are as the vessel, which may be large or may be small, and which receives according to its capacity (Rom. 12:6); but which in each case is, or may be, *filled.* We should not therefore think of him who had received the two talents as incompletely furnished in comparison with him who had received five, any more than a small circle is imperfect as compared with a large. Unfitted he might be for so wide a sphere of labor, but altogether as perfectly equipped for that to which he was destined; for 'there are diversities of gifts, but the same Spirit:' and as the body is not all eye, nor all ear, nor are all in an army captains or commanders, so neither in the Church are all furnished to be leaders and governors. Yet while we speak of natural capacity being as the vessel for receiving the wine of the Spirit, we must not leave out of account, that comparative unfaithfulness, stopping very short of that which would cause the gift to be quite withdrawn, will narrow the vessel; even as fidelity has the tendency to dilate it; so that one with far interior natural gifts will often bring in a more abundant return than another with superior powers, who yet does bring in something. Certain broad cases are mentioned in the parable; but they do not exclude other combinations of the talents committed and the talents gained. There may be cases where he of the two, or even of the one talent, as that of James Davies, the Welsh schoolmaster, will have gained five; there will be other where he of the five will have added to them but two.

Having thus committed the talents to his servants, and divided unto each according to his several powers, the lord *straightway took his journey.'* In the things earthly the householder's distribution of the gifts naturally and of necessity *precedes* his departure; in the heavenly it is not altogether so; the Ascension, or departure, goes before Pentecost, the chief day of the distribution of gifts; yet the *'straightway'* still remains in force; the interval between them was the smallest, one following hard upon the other, however the order was reversed.

We are next told what the servants did with the talents thus committed to them; how they spent that time, so full of temptations to sloth and indolence, during which their lord was away. *'Then he that had received the five talents went and traded with the same, and made them other five talents. And likewise he that had received two, he also gained other two.'* There is this variation between the present parable and St. Luke's, that here the faithful servants multiply their unequal sums in the same proportions; while there they multiply their equal sums in different proportions; all had alike received a pound, but one gained with that pound ten pounds and another five (Luke 19:16, 18). Two most important truths are thus brought out, as could scarcely have been done if only one parable had been spoken; first by St. Matthew this, that according as we have received will it be required from us; and then by St. Luke this other, that as men differ in fidelity, in zeal, in labor, so will they differ in the amount of their spiritual gains. But while two are thus faithful in the things committed to them, it is otherwise with the third: *'He that had received one went and digged in the earth, and hid his lord's money.'* How apt an image this, for the failing to use divinely imparted gifts, since 'wisdom that is hid, and treasure that is hoarded up, what profit is in them both? Better is he that hideth his folly than a man that hideth his wisdom' (Ecclus. 20:30, 31). In St. Luke he hides his pound *'in a napkin'*; but that would have been scarcely possible with so large a sum as a talent, which is therefore more fitly said to have been concealed *'in the earth.'*

'After a long time the lord of those servants cometh, and reckoneth with them.' In this *'after a long time'* Christ gave another hint (see ver. 5) that his return might not follow so soon on his departure as his disciples were disposed to take for granted. When, however, He does come, it shall be to take account of every man's work. This reconing is not identical with that of the rich man with the unjust steward (Luke 16:2), nor yet of the king with the unmerciful servant (Matt. 18:23, 24), for both of those are in this present life, while this is at the close of all. *'And so he that had received five talents came and brought other five talents, saying, Lord, thou deliveredst unto me five talents; behold, I have gained besides them five talents more.'* In the joyful coming forward of the two faithful servants, we have an example of 'boldness in the day of judgment.' They had something to show, as Paul was confident he should have, when to his beloved Thessalonian converts he said, 'What is our hope, or joy, or crown of rejoicing? Are not even ye in the presence of our Lord Jesus Christ at his coming?' (1 Thess. 2:19; 2 Cor. 1:14; Phil. 4:1). The faithful servant says here, *'Behold, I have gained'*; in St. Luke, *'Thy pound hat gained'*; thus between them they make up the speech of St. Paul, 'I—yet not I, but the grace of God that was with me. And even this, *'I have gained,'* is introduced by that other word, *'thou deliveredst unto me'*;—it is his lord's money which has so multiplied in his hands. In this parable, as has been observed, the gain is according to the talents, five for five, and two for two. Consistently with this, the commendation of the servants is expressed in exactly the same language, even as the reward to each is precisely the same. Each hears the same *'Well done'*; to each it is said, *'Enter thou into the joy of thy lord'*; each, that is, is invited to a fellowship in his lord's joy. The image on which this language rests is that of a festival, with which the master celebrates his return, in the joy of which each of the servants, so soon as he has rendered his account, and shown that he has been true to his master's interests in his absence, is bidden freely to share. Under certain circumstances a master's invitation of his slave to sit down with him at table did itself constitute the act of manumission; henceforth he was free. Perhaps there may be here allusion to something of the kind—the incorporation in an act of what once He had spoken in words, 'Henceforth I call you not servants . . . . but I have called you friends' (John 15:15; Luke 12:37; Rev. 3:20). It need hardly be observed that since all, when they have done all, are to say of themselves' We are unprofitable servants' (Luke 17:10), in this *'Well done'* there utters itself the indulgence, the ἐπιείκεια, of the Gospel, and not the rigor of the law.

'Then he which had received the one talent came and said, Lord, I knew thee that thou art a hard man, reaping where thou has not sown, and gathering where thou has not strawed; and I was afraid, and went and hid thy talent in the earth: lo, there thou hast that is thine." We can well understand why he should linger to the last, his heart secretly misgiving him, whatever face he may attempt to put on the matter. It is true that he had not wasted his master's goods like the unjust steward (Luke 16:1), nor spent all his portion in riotous living like the prodigal (Luke 15:13), nor was he ten thousand talents in debt like the unmerciful servant (Matt. 18:24); and it is an entire mistake to confound his guilt with theirs, from which it should be kept wholly distinct; for so the very persons whose consciences the parable was meant to reach escape its force. When we weave the meshes of the spiritual net so large, all but the biggest offenders contrive to slip through; and the parable is not for gross sinners, who by their whole lives evidently deny that they count Christ to be their Lord and Master at all; who squander their talent, or refuse to acknowledge that they have ever received one. The law and their own hearts tell *them* plainly enough of their sin and danger. But the warning here is for those who *hide* their talent, who, being equipped of God for a sphere of activity in his kingdom, do yet choose, in Lord Bacon's words, 'a goodness solitary and particular, rather than generative and seminal.' Such might only too easily deceive themselves, the temptations being so many to a shrinking form the labor and pains involved in a diligent laying out of this talent. There is a show of humility in the excuses which would palliate this sloth: as for instance, 'The care of my own soul is sufficient to occupy me wholly; the responsibilities of any spiritual work are so awful, that I dare not undertake them; while I am employed about the souls of others, I may perhaps be losing my own.'

How often we read in the early Church of some who on please like these declined charges to which they were called, and, when they should have been the salt of the earth, thought rather to keep their own saltness by withdrawing from all those active ministries in which they might have served their brethren in love.

Very instructive also is the fact that it is the recipient of the one talent who is the defaulter here. Nothing in the scheme of the parable hindered the attribution of this guilt to him of the five talents, or to him of the ten; for there are only too many of those whom God has gifted the most richly, who altogether fail to turn to his glory the marvelous powers with which He has endowed them. Yet no, it is neither of these; but the servant of the one talent; that so henceforward none may excuse his sloth on a plea like this, 'So little is committed to my charge, that it cannot matter how I administer that little. It is so little that I can do for God, what signifies that little whether it be done or left undone?' Christ will teach us here that it is not the more or the less which has been entrusted, but the fidelity with which this has been administered, which differences now in character, and will difference at the last in doom, one servant from another.

What the root was out of which the sin of this servant grew, he himself declares: *'Lord, I knew thee that thou art a hard man'*—for this is no excuse framed for the occasion; but a true expression of the aspect in which this servant did really contemplate his lord. The churl accounted him churlish, esteemed him such a one as himself. He did not believe in his lord's forgiving love, and in his gracious acceptance of that work, with all its shortcomings, which was done for him out of a true heart, and with a sincere desire to please him. This was his willful and guilty ignorance concerning the true character of the master whom he was called to serve. But to know the name or, in other words, the true character of God is to trust in Him; and this knowledge will save from any pusillanimous or slothful shrinking from work for Him. They, indeed, who undertake this are only too well aware that they shall commit manifold mistakes in their service, which they might have avoided, if they had declined that service altogether; that they will be guilty of many shortcomings, fall into many faults in the handling of holy things, which they might escape if they held aloof from these altogether. But shall those competently furnished and evidently called be therefore justified or excused in so doing? Would they not, so acting, come under the condemnation of this servant? Testify that they deemed of God, as *he* deemed of his master, that He was a hard Lord—extreme to mark what was amiss—making no allowances—never accepting the will for the deed, but ever on the watch to take advantage of the least failure or mistake on the part of his servants

But this is not all. Proceeding still upon the plan of turning the tables on his lord, and anticipating the accusation which shall be made against himself, by first accusing him—in a speech half cowering and half defiant, a wonderful picture of the sinner's bearing towards God, he scruples not to ascribe to him the character of a harsh unreasonable despot, who requires the bricks, but refuses the straw (Ex. v. 7), who would reap what others have sown, and gather with the rake, where others have winnowed with the fan, thus unrighteously entering on the fruits of other men's toil. He declares himself thus as much mistaken in the nature of the work, as in the character of the master for whom that work should have been done. In the darkness of his heart he regards the work as something outward, to be done *for* God, not to be wrought *in* Him, or rather, which He would work in and through his servants; as though God called to a labor, and gave no ability for the labor, imposed a task, and put no joy nor consolation into the hearts of them that fulfilled it. No wonder, therefore, that he should go on to say, *'I was afraid and went and hid thy talent in the earth';* justifying the caution and timidity which he had shown, explaining why he would attempt nothing, and venture upon nothing. He feared to trade on that talent, lest in the necessary risks of business, seeking to gain other he might lose that one, and so enrage his master against himself; even as men might profess to fear to lay themselves out for the winning of other souls, lest, so doing, they might endanger their own. *'Lo, there thou has that is thine.'* As it is not denied that he does give back the talent to his lord, how, it may be asked, could this be? How, that is, can God's gifts be hidden, and yet restored to Him entire; since the suffering them to lie idle is in fact one form of wasting them? In reality, they could not be so restored. It is only that men imagine they can be thus given back, when they take for granted that keeping the negative precepts is all that God requires, that this done they will restore to Him his own.

The lord of the parable is at no pains to dispute or deny the character which this recreant servant has drawn of him, but answers him on his own grounds, making his own mouth to condemn him (Job 15:6; 2 Sam. 1:16): *'Thou wicked and slothful ser-*

vant'—*'wicked,'* in that he defended himself by calumniating his lord, and *'slothful,'* as all which he had left undone declared—*'thou knewest that I reap where I sowed not, and gather where I have not strawed; thou oughtest therefore to have put my money to the exchangers (or 'to the bankers'), and then at my coming I should have received mine own with usury.'* Be it so, grant that I am all which thou sayest, severe, exacting, harsh; and yet thou oughtest to have done me justice still; and this with little or no peril to thyself thou mightest have done; and obtained for me, if not the larger gains possible through some bolder course, yet some small and certain returns for my moneys.' It is hard to find any distinct spiritual signification for this putting the money to the exchangers—confidently to determine whether it has such, or is only introduced to add vivacity to the narrative; as the natural exclamation of an offended master. Olshausen ingeniously explains it: 'Those timid natures which are not suited to independent labor in the kingdom of God, are here counselled at least to attach themselves to other stronger characters, under whose leading they may lay out their gifts for the service of the Church.' Perhaps, without pressing the words quite so much in detail, we should not err in saying that they mean generally, "if thou wouldest not do and dare for me in great ventures of faith, yet at all events in humbler paths, in safer and less perilous, thou mightest have shown fidelity, and have preserved me from loss.'

His doom, who had neither on a large scale, nor yet on a small, set forward his master's interests, is now pronounced. It has two sides; it is first, the forfeiture of the neglected talent; and secondly, the casting of him who possessed that talent, but would not use it, into *'the outer darkness.'* And first, he forfeits what he had, and sees it transferred to another: *"Take therefore the talent from him'*—(we have here an important limitation of Rom. 11:29), *'and give it unto him which hath ten talents.'* This deprivation, in part the directly *penal*, is in part the *natural*, consequence of his sloth. For there is this analogy between things natural and spiritual, that as a limb, never called into exercise, loses its strength by degrees, its muscles and sinews disappearing, even so the powers which God gives us, unexercised, fade and fail from us: *'From him that hath not shall be taken away even that which he hath.'* And, on the other hand, as the limb is not wasted by strenuous exertion, but rather nerved and strengthened more, so fares it with the gifts of God; they are multiplied by being laid out; a truth we recognize in our proverb,

'Drawn wells are seldom dry'; and thus, *'Unto every one that hath shall be given, and he shall have abundance.'* Nor is it merely that the one receives more than before he had, and the other loses what he had. This is not all, but *that very gift* which the one forfeits the other obtains; one is enriched with a talent withdrawn from the other; one takes the crown which another has let go (Rev. 3:11); even as we see continually one by the ordinance of God stepping into the place and the opportunities which another has neglected, despised, or misused, and so has lost (Gen. 25:34; 27:36; 49:4, 8; 1 Sam. 16:1, 13; 1 Kgs. 2:35; Is. 22:15–25; Acts 1:25, 26; Rom 11:11). Neither let us forget that this taking away of the unused talent, which will find its consummation at the day of judgment, is in this present time continually going forward. And herein is mercy, that this is not done all at once, but little by little; so that, till all is withdrawn, all may be recovered. At each successive step in the withdrawal, there is still some warning to hold fast what is left, 'to strengthen the things which remain, that are ready to die.' True it is that at each successive stage of this decline the effort required for this is greater, the strength for it less. But to complain of this, is to complain that sin is sin, and brings a curse with it; and it still remains possible till the last spark is extinguished, to fan that spark again into a flame: the sense of increasing darkness and death being that which may arouse to a consciousness of danger, and to the need of an earnest revival of God's work in the soul. But this servant never awoke to the sense of his danger till all was irrevocably lost. And now the sentence of the forfeiture of his unused talent is pronounced—the forfeiture itself had in some sort taken place already. Nor is this all. It is further said to those that stand by (see Luke 19:24), *'And cast ye the unprofitable servant into outer darkness: there shall be weeping and gnashing of teeth'* (Matt. 13:42; 22:13). Olshausen would fain distinguish between the *'outer darkness'* of this passage and of Matt. 22:13, and 'the furnace of fire' of Matt. 13:42, that while the latter is the expression of total and final loss, the former, though punitive, is also remedial. But not to urge other objections against a scheme which has no scriptural warrant, namely, that for those who have been brought within the sphere of the Gospel, the present dispensation is not decisive, the words which in each case follow, *'There shall be weeping and gnashing of teeth,'* set the two dooms on the same awful level, however one may have a more dreadful sound than the other.

A comparison of the causes which led to this servant's exclusion, and those which led to this servant's exclusion, and those which led to that of the foolish virgins, is full of warning and instruction for all. Those virgins erred through a vain *over*–confidence, this servant through an *under*–confidence, that was equally vain and sinful. They were overbold, he was not bold enough. Thus two wrong aspects under which we might be tempted to regard God's service, two rocks upon opposite sides on which faith is in danger of making shipwreck, are laid down for us, as in a chart, that we may avoid them both. Those virgins counted it too easy a thing to serve the Lord; this servant counted it too hard. They esteemed it but as the going forth to a festival which should presently begin: he as a hard, dreary, insupportable work for a thankless master. In them we behold the perils which beset the *sanguine*, in him the *melancholic*, complexion. *They* represent a class needing such warnings as this: 'Strait is the gate, and narrow is the way, that leadeth unto life, and few there be that find it' (Matt. 7:14); 'Work out your own salvation with fear and trembling' (Phil. 2:12); 'If any man will come after Me, let him deny himself' (Matt. 16:24). *He* is representative of a class which should need to be reminded: 'Ye have not received the spirit of bondage again to fear' (Rom. 8:15); 'Ye are not come unto the mount that might be touched, and that burned with fire, nor unto blackness, and darkness, and tempest . . . but ye are come unto Mount Sion, and unto the city of the living God . . . and to Jesus, they Mediator of the new covenant, and to the blood of sprinkling, that speaketh better things than that of Abel' (Heb. 12:18, 22, 24).

15.

The Seed Growing Secretly

Mark 4:26–29

This parable, the only one peculiar to St. Mark, declares, like that of the Leaven, whose place it occupies, the secret invisible energy of the divine word—that this has a life of its own, and will unfold itself according to the law of its own being; while, besides all which it has in common with that parable, it teaches further, that this divine word has that in it which will allow it to be confidently left to this inherent energy which it possesses.

'So is the kingdom of God, as if a man should cast seed into the ground; and should sleep, and rise night and day, and the seed should spring and grow up, he knoweth now how.' It is better to deal with the main difficulty in the parable at once—not so much to wait till it arises, as rather to go to seek it. It is this. Whom shall we understand by the man casting seed in the ground? Is it the Son of man Himself? Or is it those who, in subordination to Him, declare the Gospel of the kingdom? Embarrassments attend either explanation. If we say that the Lord is Himself the sower here, how then shall we explain ver. 27? It cannot be affirmed of Him that He *'knoweth not how'* the seed which He Himself has sown springs and grows; since it is only by the continual presence of his Spirit in the hearts of his people that it grows at all; while certainly it is a poor evasion of this difficulty to say with Erasmus, that, *'he knoweth not how,'* ought rather to be *'it'*—that is, the seed itself—*'knoweth not how.'* For who would think of denying this? Neither can He fitly be compared to a sower who, having scattered his seed, goes his way, and occupies himself in other tasks, knowing that it lies beyond the range of his power to do more for the seed; which must live, if it live at all, by its own life; and that his activity will not being again,

489

till the time of the harvest has come round. This is no fit description of Him, who is not merely 'the author and finisher of our faith,' but conducts it through all intermediate stages, and without whose blessing and active cooperation it could make no growth or progress at all. Shall we, to escape these embarrassments, take the sower here to represent the inferior ministers and messengers of the truth; the purpose of the parable being to teach such, that the word which they bear has a life which is quite independent of him who may have been the instrument of its first communication; even as child, once born, has a life no longer dependent on theirs from whom it was originally derived? But on this explanation attends another and not slighter difficulty; for at ver. 29 it is said, *'when the fruit is brought forth, immediately he'* (the same clearly who sowed the seed) *'putteth in the sickle, because the harvest is come.'* Of whom can it be affirmed, save of the Son of man, 'the lord of the harvest,' that *'he putteth in the sickle'*—that he gathers the saints, when they are ripe for glory—when the work of faith has been accomplished in their hearts—into everlasting habitations? The perplexity then is this—If we say that Christ intends Himself by the central figure of the parable, then a part is assigned to Him falling short of that which to Him rightly appertains; while if, on the other hand, we take Him to intend those who, in subordination to Himself, are bearers of his word, then higher prerogatives are ascribed than belong rightly to any other than Him.

I can see no perfectly satisfactory way of escape from this perplexity. Some seek to escape the embarrassments which beset the first explanation, and urge that the sleeping, and the rising night and day, with the leaving the seed meanwhile to its own inherent powers of growth, are accidental features not to be pressed, and belonging to the drapery, not to the essential framework, of the parable. Yet this is only an evasion, for clearly in the sower absenting himself after he has committed the seed to the ground, and leaving it to grow without him, the moral of the whole must lie; and to omit this in the interpretation is to leave all without purpose or point.

But without pleading this, I take, as do these interpreters, the sower to represent first, though not exclusively, the Lord Himself. It remains to see how far the acknowledged difficulties are capable of removal or mitigation. This sleeping, and rising night and day, express, as by nearly all is allowed, not the after carefulness with which the sower follows up his sowing, but the absence upon his part of any such after carefulness; as indeed any other explanation runs counter to the whole drift of the parable. He does not think it necessary to keep a continual watch, having once entrusted the seed to the ground, but sleeps securely by night, and by day rises and goes about his ordinary business, leaving with full confidence the seed to itself; which meanwhile *'should spring and grow up, he knoweth not how.'* These words present no difficulty—on the contrary, are full of most important instruction—so long as we apply them to those who under Christ are sowers of the seed of eternal life. They are here implicitly bidden to have faith in the word which they preach; for it is the seed of God. When it has found place in a heart, they are not to be tormented with anxiety concerning the final issue, as though they were to keep it alive, and that it could only live through them; for this of maintaining its life is God's part and not theirs, and He undertakes to fulfill it (1 Pet. 1:23–25). They are instructed also to rest satisfied that it should grow and spring up without their knowing the exact steps of this growth. Let them not be searching at its roots to see how they have stricken into the soil, nor seek prematurely to anticipate the shooting of the blade, or the forming of the corn in the ear; for the mystery of the life of God in any and in every heart is unsearchable; all attempts to determine that its course shall be exactly this way, or that way, can only work mischief. It has a law, indeed, of orderly development, *'first the blade, then the ear, after that the full corn in the ear;* words which suggest a comparison with 1 John 2:12–14, where in like manner the Apostle distributes the faithful according to their progress in the spiritual life, into 'little children,' 'young men,' and 'fathers'; but this law is hidden; and the works of God in nature, where He never *exactly* repeats Himself, are not more manifold than are his works in grace. Therefore let the messengers of the Gospel be content that the divine word should grow in a mysterious manner, and one whereof the processes are hidden from themselves; and, the seed once sown and having taken root, let them commit what remains to God, being satisfied that this seed is incorruptible, and that He will bring his own work to perfection. Of course it can be never meant that they are not to follow up the work which has been through their instrumentality commenced; for as, when it is said, *'the earth bringeth forth fruit of herself,'* this excludes not the rain, and sun, and other favorable influences, so neither, when we affirm that the seed of God implanted in any heart has a life of its own, does this imply that it will not require the nourishment suitable for it—nay, rather it is involved that it will require it.

A dead thing would want nothing of the kind; but because it is living, it needs whereon it may feed. Still it is a different thing to impart life, and to import the sustenance of life: this latter the Church has still to do for her children; but then it is in faith that they have a life of their own once given and continually maintained from on high, by which they can assimilate to themselves this spiritual food provided for them, and grow thereby (Eph. 4:16). It may excite surprise that instead of the words last quoted, *'the earth bringeth forth fruit of herself,'* we do not rather read, 'the seed groweth and springeth up of itself'; for that, stricktly speaking, is the point which the Lord is now urging: and if the earth signifies here, as it must, the heart of man, it is not in it, but in the word which it receives, that the living power resides. But his purpose, in using this language, is pointedly to exclude the agency of the sower, at least a continuous agency on his part of the same kind as he exercises at the first, and this done, He is not careful for more.

It still remains to consider in what sense this leaving of the seed to itself can be attributed to Christ. It is true. Olshausen observes, that the inner spiritual life of men is in no stage of its development without the care and watchful oversight of Him who was its first author: yet there are two moments which, more than any other, are peculiarly his own; one, when the divine life is by Him first implanted in a soul; this is the seed-time; the other, when that soul is ripe for his kingdom, and He gathers it to Himself; this is the harvest. Between these lies an interval, in which his work is going forward, not indeed without the daily supplies of his Spirit, and the daily ordering of his providence, but without any putting to of his hand so distinct and immediate as at those two cardinal moments. And the difficulty will be slighter, when we make application of all this—as undoubtedly we ought—to the growth and progress of the universal Church, and not to that of any single soul alone. The Lord at his first coming in the flesh sowed the word of the kingdom in the world, planted a Church; which having done He withdrew Himself; the heavens received Him till the time of the consummation of all things. Often and often since the cry has ascended in his ears, 'Oh, that Thou wouldest rend the heavens, that Thou wouldest come down! Often it has seemed as though his Church were at the last gasp, its enemies about to prevail against and extinguish it forever, unless He appeared for its deliverance. But for tall this He has not come forth; He has left it to surmount its obstacles, not without his mighty help, for He is with it always, yet with his visible interference. He has left the divine seed, the plant which He has planted, to grow on by night and by day, through storm and through sunshine, increasing secretly with the increase of God; and this shall continue, till it has borne and brought to maturity all its appointed fruit. And only then, when the harvest of the world is ripe, when the number of his elect is accomplished, will He again the second time appear, fulfilling that glorious vision beheld by the seer in the Apocalypse: 'And I looked, and behold a white cloud, and upon the cloud one sat, like unto the Son of man, having on his head a golden crown, and in his hand a sharp sickle. And another angel came out of the temple, crying with a loud voice to Him that sat on the cloud, Thrust in thy sickle and reap: for the time is come for Thee to reap; for the harvest of the earth is ripe. And He that sat on the cloud thrust in his sickle on the earth, and the earth was reaped' (Rev. 14:14–16).

16.
The Two Debtors

Luke 7:41–43

It may be taken as lifted up above all doubt that the two earlier Evangelists and the last, in their several records of the anointing of Christ by a woman, refer to one and the same event (Matt. 26:7; Mark 14:3; John 12:3). The question whether St. Luke refers to the same, and the woman in his Gospel, 'which was a sinner,' be Mary the sister of Lazarus, as then must follow, is more difficult, and has been variously answered from earliest times in the Church. The main arguments for the identity not merely of three, but of all four relations are, first, the name Simon, as that of the giver of the feast on one occasion (Luke 7:40), and most probably so on the other, for he certainly is the master of the house where it was given (Matt. 26:6); secondly, the unlikelihood that the Lord should have been twice honored in so very unusual a manner; and thirdly, the further unlikelihood that there should have been twice on the part of some present a misinterpretation of the homage offered, and an offense taken.

To all this it may be fairly replied, that the name Simon was much too common among the Jews for any stress to be laid upon its recurrence. Then, too, the anointing of the feet with odors or with ointments, though less usual than the anointing of the head, yet was not without precedent; the only remarkable coincidence here being, that Mary the sister of Lazarus, and the woman *'which was a sinner,'* should have each wiped the feet of the Lord with the hairs of the head (Luke 7:38; John 12:3). Now if this had been any merely fantastic honor paid to the Lord, which to offer would scarcely have suggested itself to more persons than one, we might well wonder to find it on two independent occasions repeated. But

regard it as an expression of homage, such as would naturally rise
out of the deepest and truest feelings of the human heart, and then
its repetition is nowise wonderful. And such it is; in the hair is the
glory of the woman (1 Cor. 11:15), long beautiful tresses having
evermore been held as her chiefest adornment; while if they in the
human person are highest in place and in honor, the feet are lowest in both. What then was this service, but the incorporation in an
outward act, of the inward truth, that the highest and chiefest of
man's honor and glory and beauty are lower and meaner than the
lowest that pertains to God; that they only find their true place,
when doing service to Him? And what wonder that He, who
stirred as none else might ever do, feelings of intensest love and
profoundest reverence in a multitude of hearts, should twice have
been the object of this honor? An honor, we may observe, with
some differences in the motives which on the one occasion and the
other called it forth. In one case, in that of Mary the sister of
Lazarus, the immediately impelling motive was intense gratitude.
She had found the words of Christ words of eternal life to herself,
and He had crowned his gifts by restoring to her a beloved brother
from the grave. The pound of ointment 'very costly' was her thank-
offering; and as less of shame was mingled in her feelings, she
anointed both her Lord's feet and also his head. But what brought
this woman with the alabaster box of ointment to Jesus, was an
earnest yearning after the forgiveness of her sins; and she, in her
deep abasement of soul before Him, preseumed not approach Him
nearer than to anoint his feet only, standing the while behind Him.
Kissing them with those lips, with which she had so often enticed
the simple (Prov. 5:3; 7:13), and wiping with the hairs of her head,
which had been so often nets with which she had entangled souls
(1 Pet. 3:3), she realized, as in an outward act, the bidding of St.
Paul, 'As ye have yielded your members servants to uncleanness
and to iniquity unto iniquity, even so now yield your members servants to righteousness unto holiness' (Rom. 6:19). And the precious
unguent, once poured upon her own person, to enhance the unholy seduction of her charms (Judith 10:3), this she now devotes to
the service of her Lord! Just as the women of Israel gave the look-
ing-glasses of their vanity to be made into the laver of brass for the
tabernacle (Ex. 38:8). And to the third argument it may be answered, that though the two incidents have this in common, that in
both the act was misinterpreted and some offended, yet beyond
this there is no similarity. In the one instance, the Pharisee, the

giver of the feast, is offended; in the other, some of the disciples, and mainly Judas: the Pharisee is offended with the Lord, Judas not so much with Him as with the woman; the Pharisee, because the Lord's conduct seems inconsistent with his reputation for holiness, but Judas from a meaner and baser motive of covetousness. To all which we may add, that there is nothing to make probable, that Mary of the happy family circle in Bethany, to whom the Lord bears such honorable testimony (Luke 10:42), had ever been aforetime one to whom the title of *'sinner,'* as it is here meant, could belong; and, as one has ingeniously urged, with the risen Lazarus sitting at the table (John 12:2), even this Pharisee would hardly have jumped so rapidly to his conclusion that his guest was no prophet of God after all.

These arguments appear to convincing, that one is surprised to discover how much opinion has fluctuated from the first, on the relation of these histories one to another—the Greek fathers generally keeping them apart, while they are identified by the Latin. This last opinion, however, finally prevailed, and was almost universal from the time of Gregory the Great, who threw all his weight into this scale, until the times of the Reformation. Then, when the Scriptures were again subjected to a more critical examination, the other interpretation gradually became prevalent anew, and had for some while been recognized almost without a dessentient voice, till Schleiermacher not very long ago, and still more lately Hengstenberg have maintained, and both with extraordinary acuteness, that the anointing happened but once. But to enter further on this debate would be alien to the present purpose: and the passage containing the parable of the Two Debtors will be considered without any reference to the histories in the other Gospels, with which, as I am convinced, it has certain accidental coincidence, but this is all.

Our Lord had been invited by one of the Pharisees, and this was not the only occasion, for see Luke 11:37, that He would eat with him; He was as prompt to accept the invitation of a Pharisee as of a chief publican, for they equally needed Him; *'and He went into the Pharisee's house, and sat down to meat.'* That a woman, and one not better reputed than this woman was, should have pressed into the guest-chamber, uninvited by the master of the house or by the Lord, and should have there been permitted to offer to Him the homage which she did, may seem strange—yet does not require the supposition of something untold to explain it, as that she was related to Simon (Hengstenberg thinks she was his sister-in-law, Simon being for him the husband of Martha), or lived in the same house—suppositions altogether foreign to the narrative, not to say in contradiction to it. A little acquaintance with the manners of the East, where meals are so often almost public, where ranks are not separated by such rigid barriers as with us, will make us understand how easily all which is recorded here might have taken place, not to say that, even had there been obstacles, and such as would have seemed insuperable to another, or to herself in another state of mind, these would easily have been put aside, or broken through, by an earnestness such as now possessed her; it being the very nature of such an earnestness to break through and despise these barriers, nor ever to ask itself whether, in the world's judgment, it be 'in season,' or 'out of season.'

In the thoughts which passed through the heart of the Pharisee—displeased that the Lord did not repel the suppliant, but graciously accepted her homage—the true spirit of a Pharisee betrays itself, unable to raise himself above a ceremonial defilement, or to understand of holiness as standing in ought save the purifying of the flesh; who would have said to that woman, had she dared to approach *him,* 'Stand by thyself, for I am holier than thou!' In the conclusion to which he arrives, *'This man, if He were a prophet, would have known who and what manner of woman this is,'* we trace the prevailing belief, that discerning of spirits was one of the notes of a true prophet, above all of the greatest prophet of all, the Messiah—a belief founded on Is. 11:3, 4 (see 1 Kgs. 14:6; 2 Kgs. 1:3; 5:26); nor can it be doubted that such a power of searching hearts is in the New Testament and with a certain emphasis claimed continually for the Lord into this dilemma—Either He does not know the true character of this woman, in which case He lacks that discernment of spirits which pertains to a true prophet; or, if He knows, and yet endures her touch, and is willing to accept homage at such hands, He lacks that holiness which is no less the note of a prophet of God; such therefore in either case He cannot be. As these thoughts passed through his mind, he may have already repented of the superfluous honor he had shown to one, whose pretensions to a mission from God he had in this summary way convinced himself were unfounded.

The Lord shows that He is indeed a discerner of the thoughts of hearts, by reading at once what is passing in *his.* Laying his finger without more ado on the tainted spot which was there, He says,

'*Simon, I have somewhat to say unto thee.*' The other cannot refuse to hear, nor has he so entirely renounced all faith in the higher character of his guest, but that he still addresses Him with an appellation of respect: '*Master, say on.*' With this leave to speak asked and obtained, the parable is uttered: '*There was a certain creditor which had two debtors: the one owed five hundred pence, and the other fifty.*' In the words themselves there is no difficulty, but in their application one or two will presently claim to be considered. God, it needs not to say, is the creditor, men the debtors (Matt. 18:240, and sins the debts (Matt. 6:12). The sums named, '*give hundred pence,*' and '*fifty,*' vary indeed, but not at all in the same proportion as those in the parable of the Unmerciful Servant (Matt. 18:24, 28). There one owes ten thousand talents, and another a hundred pence—an enormous difference, even as the difference is enormous between the sins which a man commits against God, and those which his fellowman may commit against him; here the difference is immeasurably less, the sums varying only in the proportion of ten to one, for no such incalculable difference exists between the sins which one man and another commits against God.

'*And when they had nothing to pay, he frankly forgave them both. Tell Me therefore, which of them will love him most? Simon answered and said, I suppose that he, to whom he forgave most. And He said unto him, Thou has rightly judged.*' Our difficulties meet us in the transfer of what is here said, from the natural world to the spiritual. Are we to conclude, as at first might appear, that there is any advantage in having multiplied transgressions; in owing five hundred pence rather than fifty; that the wider one has wandered from God, the closer, if he be brought back at all, he will cleave to Him afterwards? The more sin, the more love? Would it not then follow, 'Let us do evil, that good may come'—let us sin much now, that hereafter we may love much, avoiding that lukewarmness of affections which will be their condition that have sinned but little? And must we not then conclude, that for a man to have been preserved from gross offenses in the time before he was awakened to a deeper religious earnestness—or, better still, to have grown out of his baptismal root—this, instead of being a matter of everlasting thanksgiving, would interpose an effectual barrier to any very near and high communion of love with his Savior? And to understand the passage thus, would it not involve a moral contradiction—that the more a man has emptied himself of good—the more he has laid waste all nobler affections and powers—the deeper his heart has

sunk in selfishness and sensuality (for sin is all this), the more capable he will be of the highest and purest love

But the whole matter is clear, if we contemplate the debt, not as
an *objective*, but a *subjective* debt—not as so many outward transgressions and outbreaks of evil, but as so much conscience of sin;
which we know is nowise in proportion to a man's actual and positive violations of God's law. Often they who have least of what the
world can call sin, or rather crime (for the world knows nothing of
sin), have the strongest sense of the exceeding sinfulness of sin, are
most conscious of it as a root of bitterness within them, and therefore, as they have most groaned under the evil, are the most thankful for the gift of a Redeemer. But *'he to whom little is forgiven'* is not
necessarily one who has sinned little, but one who lacks any strong
conviction of the malignity of sin, and of his own share in the universal corruption; who therefore, while he may have no serious objection to God's plan of salvation, nay, a cold respect, as had this
Pharisee, for Christ, yet esteems that he could have done as well, or
nearly as well, without Him. He loves little, or scarcely at all, because he has little sense of a deliverance wrought for him; because
he never knew what it was to lie under the curse of a broken law,
and then by that merciful Savior to be set free, and brought into the
liberty of the children of God.

Simon himself was an example of one who thus loved little,
who having little sense of sin, but slightly felt his need of a
Redeemer, and therefore loved that Redeemer but little; and he had
betrayed this lack of love in small yet significant matters. Counting
the invitation itself a sufficient honor done to his guest, he had
withheld from Him courtesies almost universal in the East; had
neither given Him water for the feet (Gen. 18:4; Judg. 19:21; 1 Tim.
5:10), nor offered Him the kiss of peace (Gen. 33:4; Ex. 18:7), nor
anointed his head with oil, as was ever the custom at festivals (Ps.
23:5; 141:5; Matt. 6:17). But while *he* had fallen thus short of the customary courtesies, that woman had far exceed them. He had not
poured water on the Savior's feet, she had washed them, not with
water, but with her tears—the blood of her heart, as Augustine calls
them; and then wiped them with the hairs of her head; he had not
given the single kiss of salvation on the cheek, she had multiplied
kisses, and those upon the feet; he had not anointed the head of
Jesus with ordinary oil, but she with precious ointment had
anointed even his feet.

'Wherefore I say unto thee, Her sins, which are many, are forgiven; for

she loved much: but to whom little is forgiven, the same loveth little.' There is an embarrassment, by all acknowledged, on the face of these words; first, how to bring them into agreement with the parable, for in that the debtor is said to love much, because forgiven much, and not to be forgiven much, because he loved much; and again, and how to bring them into agreement with the general tenor of Scripture, which ever teaches that we love God, because He first loved us—that faith is the one previous condition of forgiveness, and not love, which is not a condition at all, but a consequence. Some have felt these difficulties so strongly, that in their fear lest the Romanists should draw any advantage for their *fides formata* from the passage—which indeed they are willing enough to do—they have affirmed that the word designating the cause stands for that designating the consequence—that *'her sins are forgiven, for she loved much,'* means *'her sins are forgiven, therefore she loved much.'* But, in the first place, she did not as yet know her sins to be forgiven—the absolving words are only spoken in the next verse—and moreover, this escape from a doctrinal embarrassment, by violence done to the plain words of the text, will at once be rejected by all, who believe that in the interpretation of Scripture, as of any other book, grammar, and the laws of human speech, should first be respected; that the doctrine can and will take care of itself, and will never in the end be found in contradiction with itself. And as regards advantage which Roman Catholic conversialists would fain draw from the passage, such, whatever the explanation, there can be none. The parable stands in the heart of the narrative, an insuperable barrier against such. He who owed the larger debt is not forgiven it as freely as the other is his smaller debt, *because* of the greater love which he before felt towards the creditor; but, on the contrary, the sense of a larger debt remitted makes him afterwards love him that remitted it more. Moreover, were it meant that her sins were forgiven, because—in their sense who would make charity justify, and not faith—she loved much, the other clause in the sentence would necessarily be, *'but he who loveth little, to the same little is forgiven.'*

But the words, *'for she loved much,'* may best be explained by considering what the strong sorrow for sin, and the earnest desire after forgiveness, such as this woman displayed, mean, and from whence they arise. Surely from a deep sense in the sinner's heart, that by his sins he has separated himself from that God who is Love, while yet he cannot do without his love—from a feeling that the heart must be again permitted to love Him, again assured of his love towards it, else it will utterly wither and die. Sin unforgiven is felt to be the great hindrance to this; and the desire after forgiveness—if it be not a mere selfish desire after personal safety, in which case it can be nothing before God—is the desire for the removal of this hindrance, that so the heart may be free to love and to know itself beloved again. This desire then is itself love at its negative pole; not as yet made positive, for the absolving word of grace can alone make it this. It is the flower of love desiring to bud and bloom, but not daring and unable to put forth its petals in the chilling atmosphere of God's anger; but which will do this at once, when to the stern winter of his wrath the genial spring of his love succeeds. In this sense that woman *'loved much.'* All that she did attested the intense yearning of her heart after a reconciliation with a God of love, from whom she had separated herself by her sins. All her tears and her services witnessed how much she desired to be permitted to love Him and to know herself beloved of Him; and on account of this her love, which, in fact, was faith (see ver. 50, *'Thy faith hath saved thee'),* she obtained forgiveness of her sins. This acknowledgment that a life apart from God is not life but death, with the conviction that in God there is fullness of grace and blessing, and that He is willing to impart of this fullness to all who bring the vessels of empty hearts to be filled by Him; this, call it faith or intiatory love, is what alone makes man receptive of any divine gift; and this the Pharisee, in the self-sufficiency of his legal righteousness, had scarcely at all, he therefore deriving little or not profit from that nearness to Christ into which by God's good providence he was brought. But that woman had it in large measure; she therefore bore away the choicest and best blessing which the Son of God had to bestow, to her those words of joy were spoken, *'Thy sins are forgiven'* (cf. Luke 5:20). Many were offended; *'they that sat at meat with Him began to say within themselves, Who is this, that forgiveth sins also?'* Offended as others before at a similar bestowal of pardon had been (Matt. 9:2, 3; Mark 2:7), yet not venturing openly to utter their displesuere; He meanwhile, not disconcerted by these murmers of theirs, but implicitly reasserting his claim to forgive sins, followed up one word of grace and power by another, *'Thy faith hath saved thee* (cf. Mark 10:52; Matt 9:29); *go in peace';* and thus in her it was fulfilled, that 'where sin abounded, grace did much more abound.'

17.
The Good Samaritan
Luke 10:30–37

We need not ascribe to the lawyer who 'stood up' and proposed to our Lord the question out of which this parable presently grew, any malicious intention; least of all that deep malignity which moved some other questioners, who were in fact laying snares for his life (John 8:6; Matt. 22:16). The question itself, 'What shall I do to inherit eternal life?' Was not an ensnaring one: of another who put the same we are assured that Jesus loved him (Mark 10:21); it was not, like that of the tribute-money, one which it might be hoped would compromise the answerer, whatever reply He made. Neither was the spirit which dictated the question captious or mocking. So much we gather from the earnestness of the Lord's reply; who was not wont to answer mere cavillers or despisers so. It is true that this scribe or lawyer (Matt. 22:35, compared with Mark 12:28, shows the identity of the two) put his question to Christ, 'tempting Him.' But exactly the same is affirmed of another lawyer (Matt. 22:35); who could have tempted with no ill intention, seeing that Christ bears testimony to him, 'Thou art not far from the kingdom of God' (Mark 12:34). For indeed 'to tempt' means properly no more than to make trial of; and whether the tempting be honorable or the contrary, is determined by the motive out of which it springs. Thus God 'tempts' man, putting him to wholesome proof, revealing to him secrets of his own heart, to which else even he himself might have remained a stranger to the end (James 1:12); He 'tempts' man, to bring out his good and to strengthen it (Gen. 22:1; Heb. 11:17); to show him his evil, that he, made aware of this, may strive against and overcome it—to humble him, and to do him good in his latter end (Deut. 8:3,

16). Only he who bears the Tempter's name (Matt. 4:3), a name which he has earned too well (Gen. 3:1–5), 'tempts' with the single purpose of irritating, calling out, and multiplying man's evil. If the intention of this lawyer is not that high and holy one, as little is it this malignant and devilish. Rather we may suppose that the fame of this young Galilean teacher has reached his ears; and he will now make proof of his skill, measure his depths; and counts that he cannot do this more effectually than by proposing to Him the question of questions, 'What shall I do to inherit eternal life?'

Our Lord answers question with question: *'What is written in the law? How readest thou?'* As much as to say, 'What need of inquiring further? Is not the answer to thy question contained in that very law of which thou professest thyself a searcher and expounder?' The lawyer shows himself not altogether unworthy of the name he bears; for in answer to this appeal he quotes rightly Deut. 6:5, in connection with Lev. 19:18, as containing the quintessence of the law. That he should thus lay his finger at once on 'the great commandment,' by the Lord Himself accepted as such (Matt. 22:36), showed no little spiritual discernment. His words are right words, however he may be ignorant of their full import, of all which they involve; and the Lord declares as much: *'Thou hast answered right; this do, and thou shalt live.'* Let this which he knows express itself in his life, and all will be well. His conscience is touched at last; he feels himself put on his defense, and it is, as the Evangelist declares, out of a desire to clear himself that his next question proceeds: *'But he, willing to justify himself, said unto Jesus, And who is my neighbor?'* He may not have been large and free in the exercise of love towards his fellowmen; but then how few had claims upon him, and how difficult it was to determine which were these. *'Who is my neighbor?'* The very question, like Peter's 'How oft shall my brother sin against me, and I forgive him' (Matt. 18:21)? Was not merely one which might receive a wrong answer, but did itself involve a wrong condition of mind, out of which alone it could have proceeded. He who enquired, *'Who is my neighbor?'* Who wished the entire extent of his obligation to others to be declared to him beforehand, showed in this how little he understood of that love, whose essence is that it owns no limit except its own inability to proceed further, receives a law from itself alone, being a debt which they who are ever paying, are best contented still to owe (Rom. 13:8).

What he needed who could propose such a question as this, was, that his eye should be taken off from those, the more or fewer, towards whom, as he conceived, love should be shown, and turned backward upon him who should show the love; and this which he needed the Lord in his infinite wisdom and grace provided for him in the parable which follows. Without further preface He begins: '*A certain man went down from Jerusalem to Jericho.*' We are not expressly told that this '*certain man*' was a Jew; but I cannot doubt that we were intended to regard the traveler between Jerusalem and Jericho as such; though here and there an expositor denies this, and will see in him a heathen, much to the weakening of the lesson which the parable is meant to convey. He '*went*' or '*was going down,*' not merely because Jerusalem stood considerably higher than Jericho—the latter lying nearly six hundred feet below the level of the Mediterranean sea, so that the language has its fitness in this respect—but because the going to Jerusalem, as to the metropolis, was always regarded as a going *up* (Acts 18:22). The distance between the two cities was about a hundred and fifty stadia—the road lying through a desolate and rocky region, 'the wilderness that goeth up from Jericho' (Deut. 34:3; Josh. 16:1). The plain of Jericho, an oasis in the wilderness, was of rare fertility and beauty, the Tempe of Judaea, well watered, and abounding in palms ('the city of palm'trees,' Deut. 34:3; Judg. 1:16; 2 Chr. 28:15), in roses, in balsam, in honey, and in all the choicest productions of Palestine. The squalid village of Riha marks now the spot where once this glorious city stood. On his way he '*fell among thieves,*' or rather '*among robbers*'—but at the time when our Translation was made, there was no strongly-marked distinction between the words—violent and bloody men, who '*stripped him of his raiment, and wounded him, and departed, leaving him half dead.*' The mention of stripping first and wounding afterwards may seem to reverse the natural order in the succession of events; but is indeed exactly what would happen. The murderous banditti will not injure the raiment which shall be a part, probably an important part, of the spoil by gashes, or stain it with the blood of their victim. The incident is drawn from the life. Josephus more than once mentions the extent to which Palestine in those later days was infested with banditti; and from St. Jerome we learn that the road leading from one of these cities to the other, was at one place called the Red or the Bloody Way, from the blood which had been there shed; that in his own time there was in this wilderness a fort with a Roman garrison, for the protection of travelers. Nor has the danger now ceased; Arabs of the wilderness, having their lurking places in the deep caves of the rocks, now as of old infest the road, making it unsafe even for the vast host of pilgrims to descend to the Jordan without the protection of a Turkish guard.

As the poor traveler lay bleeding in the road, *'by chance there came down a certain priest that way'*; *'by coincidence,'* we might say, by that wonderful falling-in of one event with another, which often seems chance to us, being indeed the mysterious weaving-in, by a higher hand, of the threads of different men's lives into one common wool. That hand brings the negative pole of one man's need into relation with the positive of another man's power to help, one man's emptiness into relation with another's fullness. Many of our summonses to acts of love are of this kind, and they are those, perhaps, which we are most in danger of missing, through a failing to see in them this ordering of God. At all events he who *'came down that way'* missed *his* opportunity—a priest, perhaps one of those residing at Jericho, which was a great station of the priests and other functionaries of the temple, and now on his way to Jerusalem, there to execute his office 'in the order of his course' (Luke 1:8); or who, having accomplished his turn of service, was now returning home. But whether thus or not, he was one who had never learned what that meant, 'I will have mercy, and not sacrifice'; who, whatever duties he might have been careful in fulfilling, had 'omitted the weightier matters of the law, judgment, mercy, and faith'; for *'when he saw him, he passed by on the other side. And likewise a Levite,'* but with aggravation in his cruelty; for he, *'when he was at the place, came and looked on him,'* and having seen the miserable condition of the wounded man, claiming as it did instant help—for the life that remained was fast ebbing through his open gashes—he too *'passed by on the other side.'* Tacitus, while he paints in darkest colors the unsocial character of the Jews, must yet admit this much to their honor, that, however unfriendly to all others, they were prompt to show pity among themselves; but even this redeeming grace is wanting here; they on whose part it is wanting being the express guardians and interpreters of a law so careful in urging the duties of humanity, that it twice said, 'Thou shalt not see thy brother's ass, or his ox, fall down by the way, and hide thyself from them; thou shalt surely help him to lift them up again' (Deut. 22:4; Ex. 23:5). Here not a brother's ox or his ass, but a brother himself, was lying in his blood, and they hid themselves from him (Is. 58:7).

No doubt they did, in some way or other, justify their neglect to their own consciences; made excuses to themselves: as that where one outrage had happened, there was danger of another—that the robbers could not be far distant, and might return at any moment—or that the sufferer was beyond all human help—or that one found near him might himself be accused as his murderer. The priest, we may imagine, said he could not tarry; the service of the temple must not wait, must not be left incomplete during his absence; and why should he? Was not the Levite close behind, to whom such ministries of help would more naturally appertain, and by whom his lack of service, service which the circumstances of the case rendered it impossible that he should render, would inevitably be supplied? And then the Levite in his turn may have thought with himself, that there could be no obligation on him to undertake a perilous office, from which the priest had just shrunk; duty it could not be, else that other would never have omitted it. For him to thrust himself upon it now would be a kind of affront to his superior, an implicit charging of him with inhumanity and hardness of heart. And so, falling back on these or similar pleas, they left their fellow-countryman to perish.

'*But a certain Samaritan, as he journeyed, came where he was.*' This man was exposed to exactly the same dangers as those who went before him; moreover it was no fellow-countryman who demanded his help; one rather of an alien and hostile race; but he neither took counsel of selfish fears, nor steeled his heart against all pity with the thought that the wounded and bleeding man was a Jew, whom he as a Samaritan was bound to detest; but when he saw him, '*he had compassion on him.*' This, as the best thing which he gave or had to give, is mentioned first; the rest will follow. While the priest and Levite, boasting themselves the ministers of the God of all pity and compassion, neglected the commonest duties of humanity, it was left to the excommunicated Samaritan, whose very name was a bye-word of contempt among the Jews, and synonymous with heretic (John 8:48), to show what love was; and this toward one of an alien stock; one of a people who would have no dealings with his people, who anathematized them; as, no doubt, all the influences which had surrounded him from his youth would have led him, as far as he yielded to them, to repay insult with insult, and hate with hate. For if the Jew called the Samaritan a Cuthite—a proselyte of the lions (2 Kgs. 17:24, 25, 30)—an idolater worshiping the image of a dove—if he cursed him publicly in his synagogue—prayed that he might have no portion in the resurrection of life, and by refusing under any conditions to admit him as a proselyte, did his best to secure the fulfillment of this prayer—proclaimed that his testimony was naught and might not be received—that he who entertained a Samaritan in his house was laying up judgments for his children—that to eat a morsel of his food was as the eating of swine's flesh—and would rather suffer any need than be beholden to him for the smallest office of charity—if he set it as an object of desire that he might never so much as *see* a Cuthite; the Samaritan was not behindhand in cursing, and as little in active demonstrations of enmity and ill-will. We have proofs of this in the Gospels (John 4:9; Luke 9:53), and from other sources more examples of their spite may be gathered.

For example, the Jews being in the habit of communicating the exact time of the Easter moon to those of the Babylonian Captivity, by fires kindled first on the Mount of Olives, and then taken up from mountain top to mountain top, a line of fiery telegraphs which reached at length along the mountain ridge of Auranitis to the banks of the Euphrates, the Samaritans would give the signal on the night preceding the right one, so to perplex and mislead. And Josephus mentions that they sometimes proceeded much further than merely to refuse hospitality to the Jews who were going up to the feasts of Jerusalem; they fell upon and murdered many of them; and once, most horrible profanation of all (see 2 Kgs. 23:13, 14; Matt. 23:27; Luke 11:44; Num. 19:16; Ezek. 39:150, a Samaritan entering Jerusalem secretly, polluted the whole temple by scattering in it human bones.

But the heart of this Samaritan was not hardened; though so many influences must have been at work to steel it against the distresses of a Jew; though he must have known that any Jew who was faithful to the precepts of the Jewish schools would not merely have left, but have made it a point of conscience to leave, him in his blood, would have counted that he was doing a righteous act therein. All the details of his tender care toward the poor stranger, of whom he knew nothing, save that he belonged to a nation the most bitterly hostile to his own, are given with a touching minuteness. He *'bound up his wounds,'* no doubt with strips torn from his own garments, *'pouring in oil and wine,'* wine to cleanse them, and oil to assuage their smart and to bring gently their sides together (Is. 1:6), these two being costly and highly esteemed remedies in all the East. No little time must have been thus consumed, and this when there was every motive for haste. Having thus ministered to the wounded man's most urgent needs, and revived in him the dying spark of life, he *'set him on his own beast'* (cf. 2 Chr. 28:150, himself pacing on foot; *'and brought him to an inn,'* we may suppose that at Bachurim. Neither did he then commit him to the care of strangers, so long as he could himself tend him; but there, as one who counted nothing done, while anything remained which he could do, *'took care of him,'* tended him as his state required. Nor even so did he account that he had paid the whole debt of love, but with considerate foresight provided for the further wants of the sufferer: *'And on the morrow, when he departed, he took out two pence, and gave them to the host, and said unto him, Take care of him; and whatsoever thou spendest more, when I come again, I will repay thee.'* The sum may not seem large, though considerably larger than it sounds; but we may assume that he was journeying on some needful business to Jerusalem, and that a day or two would bring him back.

Beautiful as is this parable when thus taken simply in the letter, bidding us to 'put on bowels of mercies,' to shrink from no offices of love, even though they should be painful and perilous; yet how much fairer still, how much more mightily provoking to love and good works, when, with most of the Fathers, and with many of the Reformers, we trace in it a deeper meaning still, and see the work of Christ, of the merciful Son of man Himself, portrayed to us here. None can refuse to acknowledge the facility with which all the circumstances of the parable yield themselves to this interpretation. It has been indeed objected, that it leaves the parable beside the mark, and nothing to the matter immediately in hand. But this is not so. For what is that matter? To magnify the law of love, to show who fulfills it, and who not. But if Christ Himself, He who accounted Himself every man's brother, fulfilled it the best, showed how we ought to love and whom; and if his example, or rather faith in his love towards us, is alone effectual in kindling our love to one another, He might well propose Himself and his act in succouring the perishing humanity, as the everlasting pattern of self-forgetting love, and place it in strongest contrast with the carelessness and selfish neglect of the present leaders of the theocracy. Such a meaning as this, lurking behind, though one day to pierce through, the literal, and to add to the parable a yet more endearing charm, would be of course latent at the first uttering. He to whom it was then spoken, took al in the obvious meaning; nor is the parable less effectual in commending man's love to his fellow, because it further shadows forth the Son of man's crowning act of love to the whole race of mankind.

Regarding it in this mystical sense, the traveler will be the personified human Nature, or Adam as the representative and head of
our race. He has forsaken Jerusalem, the heavenly City, the city of
the vision of peace, and is going down to Jericho, the profane city,
the city under a curse (Josh. 6:26; 1 Kgs. 16:34). But no sooner has
he thus left the holy City and the presence of his God, and turned
his desires toward the world, than he falls into the hands of him
who is at once a robber and a murderer (John 8:44), and is by him
and his evil angels stripped of the robe of his original righteousness, grievously wounded, left covered with almost mortal strokes,
every sinful passion and desire a gash from which the life-blood of
his soul is streaming. But for all this he is not absolutely dead; for
as the utmost cares of the Samaritan would have been spent in vain
upon the poor traveler, had the spark of life been wholly extinct, so
a restoration for man would have been impossible, had there been
nothing to restore, no spark of divine life, which by a heavenly
breath might be fanned into flame; no truth in him, which might be
extricated from the unrighteousness in which it was detained.
When the angels fell, by a free self-determining act of their own
will, with no solicitation from without, their loss was not in part,
but altogether. With man it is otherwise. He is *'half dead'*; he has the
sense of something lost, and at times a longing for its recovery. His
case is desperate, were there none to restore him but himself; but
not desperate in the hands of an almighty and all-merciful
Physician.

He, and He only, can restore to man what he has lost, can bind
up the bleeding hurts of his soul, can say to him in his blood, Live
(Ezek. 16:6). The Law could not do it. 'If there had been a law
which could have given life, verily righteousness should have been
by the law' (Gal. 3:21). That was but like Elisha's staff, which might
be laid on the face of the dead child, but life did not return to it the
more (2 Kgs. 4:31); Elisha himself must come ere the child revive.
Or as Theophylact here expresses it: 'The law came and stood over
him where he lay, but then, overcome by the greatness of his
wounds, and unable to heal them, departed.' Nor could the sacrifices do better; they could not 'make the comers thereunto perfect,'
nor 'take away sins,' nor 'purge the conscience.' Priest and Levite
were alike powerless to help: so that, in the eloquent words of a
scholar of St. Bernard's, 'Many passed us by, and there was none to
save. That great patriarch Abraham passed us by, for he justified
not others, but was himself justified in the faith of One to come.

Moses passed us by, for he was not the giver of grace, but of the law, and of that law which leads none to perfection; for righteousness is not by the law. Aaron passed us by, the priest passed us by, and by those sacrifices which he continually offered was unable to purge the conscience from dead works to serve the living God. Patriarch and prophet and priest passed us by, helpless both in will and deed, for they themselves also lay wounded in that wounded man. Only that true Samaritan beholding was moved with compassion, as He is all compassion, and poured oil into the wounds, that is, Himself into the hearts, purifying all hearts by faith. Therefore the faith of the Church passes by all, till it attain to Him who alone would not pass *it* by' (Rom. 8:3).

Were it absolutely needful to attach a precise meaning to the 'oil' and the 'wine,' we might say with Chrysostom, that the former is the anointing of the Holy Spirit, the latter the blood of passion. On the *binding up* of the wounds it may be observed that the Sacraments have been often called the *ligaments* for the wounds of the soul; and the hurts of the spirit are often contemplated as bound up, no less than those of the body; and God as He who binds them up. The Samaritan setting the wounded man on his own beast, himself therefore pacing on foot by his side, reminds us of Him, who, though He was rich, yet for our sakes became poor, that we through his poverty might be rich—and who came not to be ministered unto, but to minister. Neither is it far-fetched to regard the 'inn' as the figure of the Church, the place of spiritual refection, in which the healing of souls is ever going forward—called therefore by some a hospital—whither the merciful Son of man brings all whom He has rescued from the hand of Satan, and where He, the good physician, cares for them until they shall have been restored to perfect health (Mal. 4:2; Hos. 14:4; Ps. 103:3; Matt. 13:15; Rev. 22:2; and typically, Num. 21:9).

And if, like the Samaritan, He cannot tarry, cannot always be in body present with those whose cure He has begun, if it is expedient that He should go away, yet He makes for them a rich provision of grace till the time of his return. It would be entering into curious minutiae, such as tend to bring discredit on this scheme of interpretation, to affirm decidedly of the 'two pence,' that they mean either the two Sacraments, or the two Testaments, or the Word and the Sacraments, or unreservedly to accede to any one of the ingenious explanations which have been offered for them. Better to say that they include all gifts and graces, sacraments, powers of healing, of remission of sins (or other powers which the Lord has left with his Church, that it may keep house for Him till his return. As the Samaritan *'took out two pence, and gave them to the host, and said unto him, Take care of him'*, even so He said to Peter, and in him to all the Apostles, 'Feed my sheep,' 'Feed my lambs' (John 21:15–17; cf. 20:22, 23). To them, and in them to all their successors, He has committed a dispensation of the Gospel, that as stewards of the mysteries of God, they may dispense these for the health and salvation of his people. And as it was promised to the hose, *'Whatsoever thou spendest more, when I come again, I will repay thee,'* so has the Lord engaged that no labor shall be in vain in Him, that what is done to the least of his brethren shall be accounted as done to Himself, that they who 'feed the flock of God, not for filthy lucre, but of a ready mind,' 'when the chief Shepherd shall appear, shall receive a crown of glory that fadeth not away' (1 Pet. 5:2, 4).

Let us reverently admire as it deserves to be admired, the divine wisdom with which, having brought this parable to an end, Christ reverses the question of the lawyer, and asks, *'Which now of these three, thinkest thou, was neighbor unto him that fell among the thieves?'* The lawyer had asked, 'Who is the neighbor to whom it is my duty to show love?' But the Lord, answering question with question, demands, 'Who is a neighbor, he who shows love, or he who shows it not?' For it was this which he desired to teach, that love has its own measure in itself; like the sun, which does not inquire upon what it shall shine, or whom it shall warm, but shines and warms by the very law of its own being, so that nothing is hidden form its light and heat. The lawyer had said, 'Designate my neighbor to me; tell me what marks a man to be such? Is it one faith, one blood, the obligation of mutual benefits, or what else, that I may know to whom I owe this debt?' The Lord rebukes the question, holding up to him a man, and this man a despised Samaritan, who so far from seeking limits to his love, freely and largely exercised it towards one whose only claim upon him consisted in his needs; who assuredly had none of the marks of a neighbor, in the lawyer's sense of the word. The parable is a reply, not to the question, for to that it is no reply, but to the spirit out of which the question proceeded. 'You inquire, Who is my neighbor? Behold a man who asked quite another question, "To whom can I be a neighbor?" And then be yourself the judge, whether you or he have most of the mind of God; which is most truly the door of his will, the imitator of his perfections.'

To the Lord's questions, *'Which now of these three, thinkest thou, was neighbor unto him that fell among the thieves?'* the lawyer circuitously replies, *'He that showed mercy on him'*—let us hope from no grudging reluctance to give the honor directly and by name to a Samaritan; although it certainly has something of this appearance. But let that have been as it might, *'Go,'* said the Lord to him, *'and do thou likewise'* (Luke 6:36; Col. 3:12; 1 Pet. 3:8). These last words will hardly allow us to agree with those who in later times have maintained that this parable and the discourse that led to it are, in fact a lesson on justification by faith—that the Lord sent the questioner to the law, to the end that, being by that convinced of sin and of his own shortcomings, he might discover his need of a Savior. The intention seems rather to make the lawyer aware of the mighty gulf which lay between his knowing and his doing—how little his actual exercise of love kept pace with his intellectual acknowledgment of the debt of love due from him to his fellowmen: on which subject no doubt he had secret misgivings himself, when he asked, *'Who is my neighbor?'* It is true, indeed, that this our sense of how short our practice falls of our knowledge, must bring us to the conviction that we cannot live by the keeping of the law, that by the deeds of the law no flesh shall be justified, so that here also we shall get at last to faith as it which alone can justify; but this is a remoter consequence, and not the immediate teaching, of the parable.

18.
The Friend at Midnight

Luke 11:5–8

The connection between this parable and the words that go before is easy to be traced. As the Lord 'was praying in a certain place, when He ceased, one of his disciples said unto Him, Lord, teach us to pray, as John also taught his disciples.' In reply to this prayer of theirs He graciously gives them that perfect form of words, which, coming immediately from Him, has ever borne his name; but having done this, He now instructs them further in what spirit, with what instancy and perseverance, they ought to pray. There is the same argument as in the parable of the Unjust Judge (Luke 18:2–8), from the less to the greater, or more accurately, from the worse to the better—but with this difference, that here the tardy selfishness of man is set against the prompt liberality of God, while there it is the unrighteousness of man which is tacitly contrasted with the righteousness of God. The conclusion is, if churlish man can be won by mere importunity to give, and unjust man to do right, how much more certainly shall the bountiful Lord bestow, and the righteous Lord do justice. Perhaps there is this further distinction, that here it is prayer for the needs of others, in which we are bidden to be instant; while there it is rather prayer for the supply of our own. In neither case may we urge the illustration so far, as to conceive of prayer as an overcoming of God's reluctance, when it is, in fact, a laying hold of his highest willingness. For though there is an aspect under which God may present Himself to us, similar to that of the Unjust Judge and of the churlish Friend, yet always with this essential difference—that his is a seeming unwillingness to grant, theirs is a real. Under such an aspect of seeming unwillingness to hear did the merciful Son of man present

Himself to the Syro-Phoenician woman (Matt. 15:21). But why? Not because He was reluctant to give, but because He knew that her faith would carry her triumphantly over all obstacles in her path; that through such resistance as He opposed to that faith for a while, it would be called out, strengthened, purified, as, had this trial been spare it, it could never otherwise have been. In like manner the great Angel of the Covenant contended with Jacob, wrestled with him all the night; yet allowing Himself at the last to be over-come by him, left a blessing behind Him; and Jacob henceforth was Israel; being permanently lifted up through that conflict into a higher condition, as was expressed by that nobler name which henceforth he bore, 'for as a Prince hast thou power with God and with men, and hast prevailed' (Gen. 32:38).

The parable of the Friend at Midnight rests on a familiar incident of common life; and, spoken to humble men, may easily have come within the range of their own experience: *'Which of you shall have a friend, and shall go unto him at midnight, and say unto him, Friend, lend me three loaves; for a friend of mine in his journey is come to me, and I have nothing to set before him?'* These words have yielded ample scope for allegorical and mystical interpretations, and some of no little beauty; though we cannot regard them as more than graceful adaptations for pious uses of the Lord's words. For example, the guest arriving at midnight has been explained as the spirit of man, which, weary of its wanderings in the world, of a sudden desires heavenly sustenance; begins to hunger and thirst after righteousness. But the host, or man himself, in so far as he is 'sensual, not having the Spirit,' has nothing to set before this unlooked-for guest, and in this his spiritual emptiness is here taught to appeal to God, extorting in earnest prayer from Him that which is bread indeed, and heavenly food for the soul. Another interesting adaptation in the same kind we owe to Augustine. He is urging on his hearers the duty of being able to give a reason for their faith, and one not merely defensive, but such as shall win an dpersuade others; and this, since it may well happen that one from the heathen world, or a heretic, or even a nominal Catholic, weary of his wanderings in error, and longing to know something of the Christian faith, though lacking confidence or opportunity to go to the bishop or catechists, may come to them, claiming instruction in righteousness at their lips. How greatly it behoved in such a case that they have something to set before him; or having nothing, they are taught in this parable to whom they should seek for the supply of their own needs and the needs of their friend, that they go to God, beseeching Him to teach *them,*that so they may be competent to teach others. Vitringa's explanation is a modification of this. For him the guest is the heathen world; the host who receives him are the servants and disciples of Jesus; who in this parable are instructed that they can nourish with bread of life those coming to them, only as they themselves have obtained the same from God; which therefore they must solicit with all perseverance and instancy of supplication. Where such a mystical interpretation has found room, it will naturally follow that in the *'three loaves'* which the suppliant asks for, some special significance will be looked for. In them various scriptural triads have been traced; as that the host, craving these, craves the knowledge of the Holy Trinity, of God in his three persons; or the three choicest gifts and graces of the Spirit, faith, hope, and charity; with more of the same kind.

'And he from within shall answer and say, Trouble me not; the door is now shut'; the house is made up for the night, barred and bolted; *'and my children'* or, as many take it, *'my servants are with me in bed; I cannot rise and give thee'* (cf. Cant. 5:3). In the parable allegorically interpreted these last words find their spiritual equivalent, and are understood to mean, 'All, who by earlier application have obtained right to be called my children, have secured their admission into my kingdom, and are now resting with Me there; it is too late to apply, when the time of admission is past.'

'I say unto you, Though he will not rise, and give him, because he is his friend, yet because of his importunity he will rise and give him as many as he needeth.' The strength of the word which the Lord uses here has been a little reduced by our Translators. It is not his *'importunity'* which so much prevails as his *'shamelessness'*; so that we may suppose many askings, each more urgent than the last; although only that one is recorded which at length extorts the gift. Yet it is a *'shamelessness'* mitigated by the fact, that not for himself, but for another, and that he may not fail in the sacred duties of hospitality, he thus pertinaciously urges his request; even as the same may be affirmed of Abraham, who offers us another example of successful *'importunity,'* rising almost to *shamelessness* in asking; he too is pleading not for himself, but for the city where his kinsman dwelt (Gen. 18:23–33). With no other arms than those which his *'importunity'* supplies, the suppliant here triumphs in the end; he obtains, not merely the *'three loaves'* which he asked, but *'as many as he needeth'*; like that woman already referred to, from whom the

Savior at first seemed to have shut up all his compassion, but to whom He threw open at the last the ample treasure-house of his grace, bidding her to help herself. Nor is it merely that he thus at last gives all which the other desires; but he who refused at first so much as to send one of his household, himself now rises, and supplies all the wants of his friend; for so 'the kingdom of heaven suffereth violence, and the violent take it by force.' On the return of prayers not being always immediately Augustine has many excellent observations, not a few in connection with this parable—as this: 'When sometimes God gives tardily, He commends his gifts, He does not deny them'—'Things long desired, are more sweet when obtained; those quickly given, soon lose their value'—and again: 'God withholds his gifts for a time, that thou mayest learn to desire great things greatly.' Faith, patience, humility, are all called into exercise by these temporary denials. It is then seen who will pray always and not faint; and who will be daunted by the first ill-success; like the leopard, which, failing to attain its prey at the first spring, turns sullenly back, and cannot be induced to repeat the attempt.

A few concluding words give the moral of all which has been spoken: '*And I say unto you, Ask, and it shall be given you; seek, and ye shall find; knock, and it shall be opened unto you.*' More is here than merely three repetitions of the same command; since to '*seek*' is more than to '*ask*,' and to '*knock*' than to '*seek.*' In this ascending scale of earnestness, an exhortation is implicitly contained not merely to prayer, but to increasing urgency in prayer, even till the suppliant carry away the boon which he requires, and which God is only waiting for the arrival of the proper moment to bestow.

19.

The Rich Fool

Luke 12:16–21

In the midst of one of our Lord's discourses an interruption occurs. One among his hearers is so slightly interested in his
teaching, but has so much at heart the redressing of a wrong,
which he has, or believes that he has, sustained in his worldly interests, that, unable to wait for a more convenient season, he breaks
in with that request, at all events untimely, which gave occasion for
this parable, 'Master, speak to my brother, that he divide the inheritance with me.' From this confident appeal, made in the presence
of so many, it is likely that his brother did withhold from him a
share of the patrimony which was justly his. The contrary is often
taken for granted—that he had no right, and knew that he had no
right, to what he is here claiming, but hoped to win from the Lord's
unacquaintance with the matter a decision in his favor. There is
much in the parable which found its motive in this request, to lead
us to the opposite conclusion. That contains a warning, not against
unrighteousness, but against 'covetousness' (v. 15); which may display itself quite as much in the spirit wherewith we hold or reclaim
our own, as in the undue snatching at that of another. It was the extreme inopportuneness of the time he chose for urging his claim,
which showed him one in whom the worldly prevailed to the danger of making him totally irreceptive of the spiritual, and drew this
warning word from the lips of the Lord. That he should have desired Christ as an umpire or arbitrator, for this was all he claimed
(see Acts 7:27, 35; Ex. 2:14); and this was all which the Lord, without publicly recognized authority, could have been, in itself was
nothing sinful. St. Paul himself recommended the settling of differences among brethren by means of such an appeal (1 Cor. 6:1–6);

519

and how serious a burden this arbitration afterwards became for the bishops of the Church is sufficiently known.

But although no fault could be found with the request itself, Christ absolutely refused to accede to it; declined here, as ever, to interfere in affairs of civil life. It was indeed most certain that the truth He brought, received into the hearts of men, would modify and change the whole framework of society, that his word and his life were the seed out of which Christian States, with laws, affecting property as everything else, in due time would unfold themselves; but his work was from the inward to the outward. His adversaries more than once sought to thrust upon Him the exercise, or to entangle Him in the assumption, of a criminal jurisdiction, as in the case of the woman taken into adultery (supposing John 8:3–11 to be authentic); or else in a jurisdiction civil and political, as in the matter of the Roman tribute (Matt. 22:17). But on each such occasion He carefully avoided the snare laid for Him, the rock on which so many religious reformers, as eminently Savonarola, have made shipwreck; keeping Himself within the limits of that moral and spiritual world, from which alone an effectual renovation of the outer life of man could proceed. The language in which He puts back this claimant of his interference, *'Man, who made Me a judge or a divider over you?'* contains an allusion, which it is impossible to miss, to Ex. 2:14. Almost repeating the words there spoken, He declares plainly that He will not fall into the error of Moses, nor thrust Himself into matters which lie outside of the present range of his mission. But though refusing this man what he sought, He gives to him something much better than he sought, a warning counsel; and not to him only, but to that whole multitude present: *'Take heed, and beware of covetousness,'* or better, *'of all covetousness; for a man's life consisteth not in the abundance of the things which he possesseth.'*

Fully to understand these words we must understand what *'man's life'* is, which thus does not stand in the abundance of earthly goods; of which therefore this petitioner would not have had more, if instead of half, he had secured the whole of the disputed inheritance. While we have but one word for *'life,'* the Greek possesses two—one to express the life *which we live,* another to express that life *by which we live;* and it is of this latter which Christ is speaking here. A man may have his living, his $\beta io\varsigma$, the sustenance of his lower life, out of his earthly goods; nay more, they may themselves be called by this very name (Mark 12:44; Luke 8:43; 15:12; 21:4; 1 John 3:17); but his life itself, his ζωή, he cannot draw from them. The breath of his nostrils is of God; not all his worldly possessions, be they ever so large, will retain his spirit an instant if that breath be withdrawn. And if this be true of life, merely as the animating principle of man's earthly existence, how much less can life, as identical with peace, joy, blessedness here, and with immortality hereafter, consist in these things which are at once outside of a man's earthly existence, how much less can life, as identical with peace, joy, blessedness here, and with immortality hereafter, consist in these things which are at once outside of a man and beneath him? They may overlay, hinder, strangle this life; they were threatening to do this in one who evidently cared so much more for a patch of earth than for the kingdom of heaven; but they cannot produce it. This life is *from* God, as it is *to* God. In this double meaning of '*life*' lies the key to this passage, all whose force they fail to educe who accept '*life*' either exclusively in the lower, or exclusively in a higher, sense.

And this solemn truth, that a man's life consists not in his goods; that his lower life may come to an abruptest end, and that losing hold of this, he may have lost hold of all, this Christ proceeds to illustrate by the parable which follows. '*The ground of a certain rich man brought forth plentifully.*' We have no spoiler here, no extortioner, no remover of his neighbor's landmark. His riches are fairly gotten; the earth empties its abundance into his lap; his wealth has come to him in ways than which none can be conceived more innocent, namely, through the blessing of God on toils which He has Himself commanded. But here, as so often, the Giver is forgotten in the gift, and that which should have brought nearer to Him only separates further from Him. The wise king had said long before, 'The prosperity of fools shall destroy them' (Prov. 1:32): this man sets his seal to this word, his prosperity ensnaring him in a deeper worldliness, drawing out the selfish propensities of his heart into stronger action; for indeed out of how profound a heartknowledge that warning word of the Psalmist proceeds, "if riches increase, set not thy heart upon them.' It might beforehand be assumed that the danger of setting the heart on riches would be the greatest when they were escaping from our grasp, perishing under our hand. Experience teaches another lesson, that earthly losses are remedies for covetousness, while increase in worldly goods rouses and provokes it; serving, not as water to quench, but as fuel to feed, the fire: 'He that loveth silver shall not be satisfied with silver, nor he that loveth abundance with increase' (Ecc. 5:10).

'And he thought within himself, saying, What shall I do, because I have no room where to bestow my fruits?' some find in these words the anxious deliberations of one brought into sore straits by that very abundance for which others were envying him; not knowing which way to turn, and as painfully perplexed through his riches as another through his poverty. Better to say, that the curtain is here drawn back, and we are admitted into the inner council-chamber of a worldling's heart, glorying in his abundance, and realizing to the very letter the making 'provision for the flesh, to fulfill the lusts thereof.' To his first words, *'I have no room where to bestow my fruits,'* it has been answered well, 'Thou *hast* barns—the bosoms of the needy—the houses of the widows—the mouths of orphans and of infants.' Had he listened to the admonition of the Son of Sirach, 'Shut up alms in thy storehouses' (39:19), he would not have found his barns too narrow. To one about to bestow his fruits amiss, and so in danger of losing them, Augustine addresses this affectionate admonition: 'God desires not that thou shouldst lose thy riches, but that thou shouldst change their place; He had given thee a counsel, which do thou understand. Suppose a friend should enter thy house, and should find that thou hadst lodged thy fruits on a damp floor, and he, knowing by chance the tendency of those fruits to spoil, whereof thou wert ignorant, should give thee counsel of this sort, saying, "Brother, thou losest the things which with great labor thou hast gathered: thou has placed them in a damp place; in a few days they will corrupt"—"And what, brother, shall I do?" "Raise them to a higher room"; thou wouldest listen to thy brother suggesting that thou shouldst raise thy fruits from a lower to a higher floor; and thou wilt not listen to Christ advising that thou raise thy treasure from earth to heaven, where that will not indeed be restored to thee which thou layest up; for He bids thee lay up earth, that thou mayest receive heaven, lay up perishable things, that thou mayest receive eternal.'

This would have been *his* wisdom, to provide thus for himself 'bags which wax not old, a treasure in the heavens which faileth not' (v. 33). But he determines otherwise; he has another scheme altogether: *'This will I do: I will pull down my barns, and build greater; and there will I bestow all my fruits and my goods. And I will say to my soul, Soul, thou hast much goods laid up for many years; take thine ease, eat, drink, and be merry.'* Having now at last a citadel and strong tower, to which he may flee and be safe, he will rest from his labors, and henceforth, to put heathen language into the mouth of this truly heathen man, not defraud his genius anymore. There is again an irony as melancholy as profound in making him address this speech, not to his body, but to his *soul;*—for that soul, though capable of being thus dragged down to a basest service of the flesh, embodied and imbruted, was also capable of being quickened by the divine Spirit, of knowing and loving and glorifying God. And then, though the wise king had said, 'Boast not thyself of tomorrow' (Prov. 27:1), he boasts himself of *'many years'* (cf. Ecclus. 5:1); expects, like Job, to multiply his days as the sand, and to die in his nest (Job 29:18). Some words in the Apocrypha (Ecclus. 11:18, 19) constitute a remarkable parallel: 'There is that waxeth rich by his weariness and pinching, and this is the portion of his reward: whereas he saith, I have found rest, and now will eat continually of my goods; and yet he knoweth not what time shall come upon him, and that he must leave those things to others, and die.' Such a man is here. We have heard what he was saying to himself; it is now permitted us to hear what God at the same instant was saying to him: *'Thou fool, this night thy soul shall be required of thee.'* 'Thou fool,'—this title is opposed to the opinion of his own foresight which he entertained,—*'this night,'* to the *'many years'* which he promised to himself,—and that *'soul'* which he purposed to nourish and make fat, it is declared shall be inexorably *'required'* of him, and painfully rendered up. But how, it is sometimes asked, did God speak to him? Was it by a sudden presentiment of approaching death, by some strong alarm of conscience, by some mortal sickness at this instant falling upon him, or by what other means? In none of these or like ways, as I understand the words. It fared not with him as with the Babylonian king, to whom, while the word of pride was yet in his mouth, there came a voice from heaven, announcing that the kingdom was departed from him (Dan. 4:31); nor yet as it fared with Herod, stricken in the hour of his profane apotheosis (Acts 12:23). Not thus, but more awfully still, while those secure deliberations were going on in his thoughts, this sentence was being determined in the counsels of God; for so does the Lord in heaven deride the counsels of sinners, knowing how soon He will bring them to nothing. Not *as yet* was there any sign or token importing the nearness of the divine judgment; but at the very moment when the decree was going forth that his thread of life should so soon be cut in twain, he was promising himself the long spaces of an uninterrupted security.

Nor is it merely, as our Translation has it, that his soul *'shall be required,'*—it *'is required,'*—of him; the doom is so fearfully near that the present can alone express its nearness. In another point our Version may be bettered. Why not render, *'This night do they require thy soul of thee'* (cf. Job 27:20), leaving who *'they'* are that shall thus require it in the fearful obscurity of the original? Violent men, it may be; but more probably the avenging angels are intended, the ministers of judgment (cf. Job 33:22: 'Yea, his soul draweth near unto the grave, and his life *to the destroyers')*; so that we have here the reverse of that 'carried by the angels into Abraham's bosom,' of Luke 16:22. The force of this *'required'* (cf. Wisd. 15:8: 'His life which was lent him *shall be demanded'*), is well brought out by Theophylact: 'For like pitiless exactors of tribute, terrible angels shall require thy soul from thee unwilling, and through love of life resisting. For from the righteous his soul is not *required,* but he commits it to God and the Father of spirits, pleased and rejoicing, nor finds it hard to lay it down, for the body lies upon it as a light burden. But the sinner who has enfleshed his soul, and embodied it, and made it earthy, has prepared to render its divulsion from the body most hard: wherefore it is said *to be required* of him, as a disobedient debtor that is delivered to pitiless exactors'; cf. Job 27:8: 'What is the hope of the hypocrite, though he hath gained, when God *taketh away* his soul?' God 'taketh it away'; for he is not as a ship, which has long been waiting in harbor, and when the signal is given, lifts joyfully its anchors, and makes sail for the haven of eternity; but like one by fierce winds dragged from its moorings, and driven furiously to perish on the rocks. The mere worldling is violently separated from the world, the only sphere of delight which he knows, as the fabled mandrake is torn from the earth, shrieking and with bleeding roots.—*'Then whose shall those things be, which thou hast provided?'* 'He heapeth up riches, and knoweth not who shall gather them' (Ps. 39:6). Solomon long before had noted, among the vanities that cling to wealth, the uncertainty upon whom at the death of the gatherer it would devolve, as of the uses to which he would turn it: 'Yea, I hated all my labor which I had taken under the sun, because I should leave it unto the man that shall be after me: and who knoweth whether he shall be a wise man or a fool?' (Eccl. 2:18, 19, 21, 26; cf. Ps. 49:6–20; Jer. 17:11; Job 27:16, 17).

'*So is he that layeth up treasure for himself, and is not rich toward God.*' Self and God are here contemplated as the two poles between which the soul is placed, for one or other of which it must determine, and then constitute that one the end and object of all its aims and efforts. If for the first, then the man '*layeth up treasure for himself,*' and what the issue of this is, we have seen; the man and his treasure come to nothing together. He has linked himself to the perishable in is inmost being, and he must perish with it. The very enriching of himself outwardly, being made the purpose of his existence, is an impoverishing of himself inwardly, that is, '*toward God*' and in those which are the true riches: for there is a continual draining off to worldly objects, of those affections which should have found their only satisfying object in God; where his treasure is, there his heart is also. Now the Scripture ever considers the heart as that which constitutes a man truly rich or truly poor. He that has no love to God, no large spiritual affections, no sympathies with his brethren, is 'wretched, and miserable, and poor, and blind, and naked,' and shall one day discover that he is so, however now he may be saying, 'I am rich, and increased with goods, and have need of nothing' (Rev. 3:17). He is poor toward God; he has nothing with God; he has laid up in store no good foundation against the time to come. On the other hand, he only is truly rich, who is '*rich toward God,*' who is rich in God; who has made the eternal and unchangeable the first object of his desires and his efforts. He in God possesses all things, though in this world he may have nothing; and for him to die will not be to quit, but to go to, his riches.

Christ, having thus warned his hearers against covetousness, and knowing how often it springs from distrust in the fatherly providence of God (Heb. 13:5), proceeds to teach them where they may find the best antidote to this and to all over-anxious thoughts for the future, namely, in the assurance of his tender watchfulness and care over them (vv. 22–30); the connection being thus as close as it is beautiful between this parable and the instructions which immediately follow. In the mention of the ravens, which are fed, though they neither sow nor reap, have neither storehouse nor barn (v. 24), there is, perhaps, a distinct reminiscence of it, and allusion to it.

20.

The Barren Fig-Tree

Luke 13:6–9

The eagerness of men to be the first narrators of evil tidings, an eagerness which must spring from a certain secret pleasure in these, although one most often unacknowledged even to themselves, may have moved some to hasten to the Lord with tidings of a new outrage which Pilate had committed. These bearers of this report understood rightly that He was speaking, in the words which conclude the last chapter (vv. 58, 59), of the terrible judgments which men draw down upon their own heads through their sins: but, as is the manner of most, they made application of them only to others. Of the outrage itself,—which, however, agrees well with the quarrel between Herod and Pilate (Luke 23:12), and may have been either its cause or its consequence,—there is no notice elsewhere; for we cannot allow that the scattering or slaying by Pilate of some fanatical Samaritan insurgents, recorded by Josephus, and here adduced by some earlier commentators, is the event referred to. But we know that a revolt, or at the least a tumult, was always dreaded at the great festivals, and various precautions taken against it; a very small spark serving to kindle into a blaze the smoldering elements of Jewish resistance to the hated Roman dominion, and to provoke measures of severest retaliation on the part of the Roman authorities. Among the numberless atrocities which ensued, it is nothing strange that this, which must have been but as a drop of water in a great ocean, should remain unrecorded. Some outbreak of that troublesome insurrectionary spirit for which the Galileans were noted, may have been the motive or excuse for this massacre; which yet cannot have been perpetrated in Galilee, where, as subjects of Herod (Luke 23:7, 22), these men would not have been exposed to Pilate's cruelty, but at Jerusalem, which also was the only place where sacrifices were offered (Lev. 17:8, 9; Deut. 12:26, 17; John 4:20). The language in which their slaughter is reported is significant; they were men 'whose blood Pilate had mingled with their sacrifices'; thus blood was mingled with blood, their own with that of the slain beasts which they offered; the narrators possibly urging this as evidence of the peculiar anger of God against those who so perished. If men might be safe anywhere, or at any time, it would be at the altar of God, and in the act of offering sacrifices to Him. But here, they would infer (just as Job's friends inferred some mighty guilt upon his part from the mighty calamities which overwhelmed him), there must have been some hidden enormous guilt, which turned the very sacrifices of these men into sin,—not a propitiation of God, but a provocation,—so that they themselves became peculiar expiations, their blood mingling with, and itself becoming part of, the sacrifices which they offered.

But whether the tellers intended this or not, the Lord at once rebuked the cruel judgments which they certainly had formed concerning those that perished: '*Suppose ye that these Galileans were sinners above all the Galileans, because they suffered such things?*' He does not deny that they were sinners, justly obnoxious to this or any other severest visitation from God, but only that the blood-bath in which they perished marked them out as sinners *above all* their fellow-countrymen; and then He leads his hearers, as was his wont (see Luke 13:23; John 21:22), to take their eyes off from others, and to fix them upon themselves: '*I tell you, Nay; but, except ye repent, ye shall all likewise perish.*' This is the meaning for ourselves of the calamities which befall others; they are loud and earnest calls to repentance. Instead of exalting ourselves above and against the sufferers, as though we were more righteous than they, and therefore exempt from like tribulations, we shall rather acknowledge that whatever befalls another, might justly have befallen ourselves. When, too, we have learned to recognize in ourselves the bitter root of sin, we shall be prompt to confess that whatever deadly fruit it bears in another, it might have borne the same or worse, under like temptations, in ourselves. But when this is felt, it will be no longer possible to triumph over the doom of any sinner. The thoughts of one, thus taught to know himself, will fall back on his own life and on his own heart. He will see in the chastisement which has overtaken another, the image of that which might justly have overtaken himself; and a message of warning to be laid to his own heart. For he will not deny, as neither does Christ here deny, the intimate connection between suffering and sin; but it is the sin of the whole race which is linked with the suffering of the whole race; and not of necessity the sin of the individual with his particular share and portion in this the world's woe. So far from denying this connection, the more the Christian conscience is unfolded in him, the more close will this connection appear. At every new instance of moral and physical evil which he encounters in a world which has departed from God, he will anew justify God as the author of all good, even when He asserts Himself negatively as such, in the misery of man as he is a sinful creature separated from his God, no less than positively, in the blessedness of man as he is redeemed and reunited with God.

Our blessed Lord, more fully to illustrate the truth which He has in hand, Himself brings forward another instance of a swift destruction overtaking many persons at once: *'Or those eighteen, upon whom the tower in Siloam fell, and slew them, think ye that they were sinners above all men'*—or literally, *'debtors above all men'* (Matt. 5:25; 6:12; 18:24; Luke 7:41)—*'that dwelt in Jerusalem?'* As little in this case were cruel judgments to find place. But while none might attribute a preeminence in guilt to those who were crushed by that falling tower, yet here also, in sudden and strange catastrophes like this, all were to recognize a call to repentance; partly as these should remind all of the uncertainty of life, how soon therefore their own day of grace might end; but chiefly as awakening in them a sense and consciousness of sin. For all discords of outward nature, of fire and flood, of earthquake and storm, all fearful accidents, like that of the falling tower, are parts of that subjection of the whole creation to vanity, consequent on the sin of man (Rom. 8:20, 21); all speak to sinners in the same warning language, *'Except ye repent, ye shall all likewise perish.'* The near resemblance between these two calamities just instanced, and the doom which actually did overtake the rebellious Jews, the nation which refused to obey this bidding and to repent, can scarcely be accidental, and demands that we shall give to that *'likewise'* of the Lord all its force. It was indeed *'likewise'* that they perished; for the very same forms of violent death overtook them. As the tower in Siloam fell and crushed eighteen of the dwellers in Jerusalem, exactly so multitudes of its inhabitants in that last siege and assault were crushed beneath the ruins of their temple and city; numbers also were pierced through

by the Roman missiles,—or more miserably yet, by the swords of
their own frantic factions,—in the courts of the temple, in the very
act of preparing their sacrifices, so that literally their blood, like
that of these Galileans, was *'mingled with their sacrifices,'* one blood
with another.

Those two calamities then are adduced as slight foretastes of
the doom reserved for the whole people of the Jews. If they would
lay to heart the warning, and bring forth fruit meet for repentance,
that doom might even now be averted: but if not, then these beginnings of sorrow should usher in at length the overwhelming
calamity which would leave no room for repentance. In the meanwhile, in the fact that hitherto the strokes descended upon them for
warning, and not the stroke for excision, they should see proof of
the long-suffering of God, not willing that any should perish: and
to use Olshausen's words,—'the discourse of Jesus, severe and full
of rebuke, is closed by a parable, in which the merciful Son of man
again brings the side of grace prominently forward. He appears as
the Intercessor for men before the righteousness of the heavenly
Father, as He who obtains for them space for repentance. This idea
of the deferring of the judgment of God, so to leave men opportunity to turn, runs through all Scripture; before the deluge, a period
of a hundred and twenty years was fixed (Gen. 6:3); Abraham
prayed for Sodom (Gen. 18:24); the destruction of Jerusalem did
not follow till forty years after the Ascension of the Lord; and the
coming again of Christ is put off through the patience of God (2
Pet. 3:9).'

We have then a parable here concerning the long-suffering and
the severity of God. *'He spoke also this parable, A certain man had a fig-
tree planted in his vineyard.'* 'The peculiarity of the image—that of a
fig-tree in a *vineyard*,—however unlike to the European notion of a
mass of unbroken vine-clad hills, is natural in Palestine, where,
whether in cornfields or vineyards, fig-trees, thorn-trees, apple-
trees are allowed to grow freely wherever they can get soil to support them.' The vineyard here must be the world, and not, as in the
parable of the Wicked Husbandmen, the kingdom of God: in the
midst of the world the Jewish people were set that they should bear
much fruit, that they should bring much glory to God (Deut. 4:6).
But the parable, though directly addressed to them, is also of universal application; for as Israel was the representative of all and
each who in after times should be elected out of the world to the
privileges of a nearer knowledge of God, therefore a warning is

here for the Gentile Church, and for each particular soul. Compare Matt. 3:2; John 15:2.

'*And he came and sought fruit thereon, and found none.*' There is a wonderful fitness in the simple image running through all Scripture, which compares men to trees, and their work to fruit,—the fruit of a tree, just as the works of a man, being the organic utterance and outcoming of the inner life, not something arbitrarily attached or fastened on from without (Ps. 1:3; Jer. 17:8; John 15:2, 4, 5; Rom. 7:4). The three kinds of works whereof Scripture speaks may all be illustrated from this image: first, *good* works, when the tree, having been made good, bears fruit after its own kind; then *dead* works, such as have a fair outward appearance, but are not the genuine outgrowth of the renewed man,—fruit, as it were, fastened on externally, alms given that they may be gloried in, prayers made that they may be seen; and lastly, *wicked* works, when the corrupt tree bears fruit manifestly after its own kind. Here it is, of course, those good fruits, of which none are found; both the other kinds of fruit the Jewish fig-tree only too abundantly bore.

What is here parabolically related was on another occasion typically done in a kind of *sermo realis* by the Savior: when in the last days of his ministry, 'seeing a fig-tree afar off, having leaves, He came, if haply He might find anything thereon' (Mark 11:13). But He then, as the master of the vineyard now, '*found none.*' Long since the prophets had upbraided their people, that having been ordained to bring forth much fruit to the glory of God, they had fallen short of the purpose for which they were set in the world; bringing forth either bitter fruit or none (Is. 5:2, 7; Jer. 15; and, if our Version is to stand, Hos. 10:1); and now the greatest of the prophets implicitly repeats the charge.

'*Then said he unto the dresser of his vineyard, Behold, these three years I come seeking fruit on this fig-tree, and find none.*' By these '*three years*' Augustine understands the times of the natural law,—of the written law,—and now, at last, of grace. Theophylact: 'Christ came thrice, by Moses, by the prophets, and thirdly in his own person; He comes, when application of the parable is made to the individual,—in childhood, in manhood, in old age.' Olshausen finds allusion to the three year of the Lord's open ministry; but Grotius had already observed against this, and with reason, that if the '*three years*' are chronological, the '*one year more,*' presently granted, must be chronological also; whereas not *one*, but *forty* years of grace were allowed to the Jews, before the Romans came and took away their name and place.—'*Cut it down*' (see Is. 5:5, 6; Matt. 7:19; Luke 19:41–44); '*why [also] cumbereth it the ground?* which '*also,*' helping to explain the sentence passed upon the tree, our Translators have missed. Why should the tree remain, when, besides being itself barren, it '*also*' injured the soil in which it stood; for that '*Why cumbereth it the ground?*' implies something more than that it occupied the room which might have been filled by another and a fruit-bearing tree. The barren tree *mischiefed* the land, 'troubled' it, as Bishop Andrewes renders the word, spreading injurious shade, and drawing off to itself the fatness and fertility which should have gone to trees rendering a return. It was thus with the Jewish Church, which not merely did not itself bring forth fruits of righteousness, but through it the name of God was blasphemed among the Gentiles (Rom. 2:24); the Jews hindering in many ways the spread of the knowledge of God among other nations, through the mischievous influences of their pride and hypocrisy (Matt. 23:13, 15); what was thus true of a Church being not less true of each separate sinner; who is not merely himself unprofitable to God, but by his evil example, by his corrupt maxims, is an obstacle and a stumbling-block to others in the way of godliness.—On that '*Cut it down*' St. Basil bids us note the love which breathes even in the threatenings of God. 'This,' he says, 'is peculiar to the clemency of God toward men, that He does not bring in punishments silently or secretly; but by his threatenings first proclaims them to be at hand, thus inviting sinners to repentance.' That proverb which so finely expresses the noiseless approach of the divine judgments, 'The gods have feet of wool' (**Di** laneos habent pedes), true for others, is *not* true for those who have a listening ear. Before the hewing down begins, the ax is laid at the root of the tree (Matt. 3:10); laid there that it may be ready at hand for immediate use; but laid there also, that, if possible, this sign and prophecy of doom may avert the actual fulfillment of the doom (2 Chr. 33:10).

The vine-dresser, who pleads for the tree, and would fain avert its doom, '*Lord, let it alone this year also, till I shall dig about it, and dung it,*' is the Son Himself, the Intercessor for men (Job 33:23; Zech. 1:12; Heb. 7:25); not indeed as though the Father and the Son had different minds concerning sinners, the counsels of the Father being wrath, and of the Son mercy; for righteousness and love are not qualities in Him who *is* Righteousness and who *is* Love; they cannot, therefore, be set one against the other, since they *are* his essential being. But in our anxiety to escape this error, we must not fall into the opposite, letting go the reality of God's wrath against sin,—the reality of the sacrifice of Christ, not merely on the side with which it looks towards men, but also on that which looks towards God; this sacrifice being indeed a propitiation of God, and not merely an assurance of God's love towards sinners. How these two truths shall be reconciled, and those two errors shunned, is shown in those words: 'the Lamb slain from the foundation of the world' (Rev. 13:8); 'foreordained before the foundation of the world' (1 Pet. 1:20). The sacrifice, though of necessity outwardly brought to pass in time, found place in the purpose of Him who offered, and of Him who accepted it, before all time, or rather, out of time; so that we can never conceive of man as not contemplated by God in Christ. There was no change in God's mind concerning the sinner, because He who beholds the end from the beginning, had beheld him from the first as reconciled and reconstituted in his Son (Rom. 16:25, 26). From this point of view we may regard the high-priestly intercession of Christ as having been effectual even before He passed into the heavens, there to appear before God for us; for to that intercession all the long-suffering of God toward sinners is to be referred; the *praetermission* of sins through the forbearance of God (Rom. 3:25) under the Old Covenant, to be followed by a *remission* of them when the designed sacrifice had been actually accomplished:—'the earth and all the inhabitants thereof are dissolved; I bear up the pillars of it' (Ps. 75:3). Some of the Fathers see here an allusion as well to the intercessory work, which the Church, in its healthy members, is ever carrying forward on behalf of its sick, or that of the Church for the world. No doubt such intercession has a real worth before God (Gen. 18:23–33; 20:7; Ex. 32:11; Job 42:8; 1 Sam. 12:19, 23; 2 Kgs. 19:4, 20; Jer. 15:1; 1 Tim. 2:1–4; James 5:14–18; 1 John 5:16); nor need such be absolutely excluded here; yet, this must first and chiefly be referred to that one Intercessor, on whose intercession that of all others must ultimately rest. It is plain, too, that *He* must be meant, for He only to whom all judgment is committed could have received the command, '*Cut it down*'; to men it could in no case have been given (Matt. 13:29, 30).

This great Intercessor pleads for men, yet not that they may always continue unpunished in their sins, but only that their sentence may for a while be suspended; so to prove whether they will turn and repent; even as the vine-dresser here begs for the barren tree, not that it may be suffered always to stand (for, on the contrary, he allows its doom, should it abide unfruitful, as righteous and good), but asking for it one year of grace; *'If it bear fruit, well; and if not, then after that thou shalt cut it down.'* During this year he *'will dig about it, and dung it'*; will hollow out the earth from around the stem, filling up the space about the roots with manure; as one may now see done to the orange-trees in south Italy. By these appliances is signified that multiplication of the means of grace which is so often granted to men and nations in the last period of their probation, and just before those means are withdrawn from them forever. Thus, before the flood, they had Noah, a 'preacher of righteousness,'—before the great catastrophes of the Jewish people some of their most eminent prophets, as Jeremiah before the taking of Jerusalem by the Chaldeans,—and before its final doom they enjoyed the ministry of Christ and of his Apostles. This last is intended here; that richer supply of grace, that freer outpouring of the Spirit, which should follow on the death, resurrection, and ascension of the Lord. So Theophylact: 'Though they were not made better by the law and the prophets, nor yielded fruit or repentance, yet will I water them by my doctrines and passion; it may be they will then yield fruits of obedience.' No doubt if the history of men's separate lives were written as large as that of nations and Churches, and we could thus read one as plainly as the other, we should oftener perceive that what is true of the one is also true of the other: we should mark critical moments in men's lives to which all the future is linked, on which altogether it turns,—times of gracious visitation, which above all it behooved them to know, and not suffer to escape unimproved. Such a time of visitation to the Jewish people was the Lord's and his Apostles' ministry (Luke 19:42); then was the last digging about and manuring of the tree which had continued barren so long. But it abode in barrenness; its day of grace came therefore to an end; and, as here is threatened, it was inexorably cut down. In the parable, indeed, our Lord does not positively affirm that the tree will remain unfruitful to the last, but suggests the other as a possible alternative: *'If it bear fruit, well'*; for thus the door of repentance is left open still; the free will of man is recognized and respected, and none are left to suppose that they are shut up, except by their own evil will, in unbelief and hardness of heart, that any but themselves can make inevitable their doom.

21.
The Great Supper

Luke 14:15–24

Ishall not repeat the arguments which persuade me that this parable, and that recorded at Matt. 22:1–14, spoken upon different occasions, and with (partially) different aims, should be kept wholly distinct the one from the other. On the present occasion the Lord had been invited to eat bread with one of the chief Pharisees (v. 1). The meal must have been a costly and a ceremonious one. It included probably friends and kinsmen and rich neighbors of his host (v. 12); among whom there were silent contests for precedence (v. 7). But among these guests, hostile as no doubt for the most part they were to the young Galilean teacher, there was one who could not forebear expressing his sympathy with some words which fell from the Lord's lips (v. 15). But there was not the less a certain latent self-satisfaction in this utterance of his. If one reads that utterance aright, above all in connection with the parable which follows, and which we are expressly told was addressed to him, he was untroubled with any misgiving as to his own place among those who should 'eat bread in the kingdom of God.' And yet it was quite possible that when the decisive moment arrived, he might miss the blessedness, of which he spoke in such edifying language; well contented with things here, might refuse to be lifted up into that higher world to which he was bidden. To him, as he was quite unconscious of any such danger, and in him to us all, this parable was vouchsafed.

'*A certain man made a great supper, and bade many*'—'*a supper*,' it has been often explained, because, as such takes place at evening, so in the evening of time, in the 'last hour' (1 John 2:18; 1 Cor. 10:11), Christ came and invited men to the fullness of Gospel blessings. But this is pressing too far a word of fluctuating use; which, even if it does in later Greek signify predominantly a supper, was not upon this account selected here, but as expressing the principal meal in the day. Men's relish for things heavenly is so little, their desire so faint, that God graciously presents these things to them under such inviting and alluring images as this, that so they may be stirred up to a more earnest longing after them. The *'many'* whom the rich man bade are the Jews; yet not so much the entire nation, as those who might be presumed the most favorably disposed for the embracing of the truth; the most religious among the people; and thus, as guardians of the faith, the priests and elders, the Scribes and Pharisees, in opposition to the publicans and sinners, and the more despised portions of the nation; whose turn only arrives when these others have made light of the invitation.

'And sent his servant at supper-time to say to them that were bidden, Come; for all things are now ready.' Some will have it that the guests, in needing thus to be reminded that the hour of the festival had arrived, showed already how lightly they esteemed the invitation. But this is a mistake, such having been, as is noted elsewhere, the usual custom; and their contempt of the honor vouchsafed them, with their breach of promise,—for we must presume they had pledged themselves to come,—is first displayed in their excuses for not appearing at the festival. There was, beyond doubt, in the world's history a time when, more than at any other, it might be said, *'All things are now ready'*; a fullness of time, at the arrival of which, and not till then, the kingdom of heaven was set up, and men invited, the Jew first, and afterwards the Gentile, to enter into that kingdom (Gal. 4:1–4). Some, and I am disposed to think the larger number of, interpreters see in the servant who reminded the guests that the feast was ready, and bade them to enter into the enjoyment of good things, not now far off but near, the Evangelists and Apostles; but this interpretation, which I also adopted once, does not, I must own, now please me so well as the other, which sees in him not any series or company of the servants of the Heavenly King, but one and one only; that One being no less than the great Apostle and High Priest of our profession Himself, who, being in the form of God, yet took upon Him the form of a servant, and as such, according to the prophecies of Him which went before, above all in the later Isaiah, accomplished his Father's will upon earth. In the parable of the Barren Fig-tree the Son assumes

exactly the same subordinate position and functions (Luke 13:7, 8) as would thus be ascribed to Him here.

'*And they all with one consent began to make excuse.*' Whether there is any essential difference between the excuses or 'offcomes,' as they would be called in one of our northern dialects, which the first guest urges, and the second, whether these represent hindrances different in their nature and character, by which different men are kept back from Christ, or whether both would alike teach us the same general lesson, that the love of the world robs men of all desire and relish for heavenly things, it is not easy to determine. Probably there is a difference. Perhaps the first, who pleaded, '*I have bought a piece of ground, and I must needs go and see it,*' represents those who are elate of heart through already acquired possessions. He is going to see his estate, not exactly in the spirit of Ahab when he visited the vineyard made his own by wrong (1 Kgs. 21:15, 16); for there lies no guilt in the thing itself which he is doing; and indeed it adds greatly for the solemnity of the warning here conveyed, that no one of the guests is kept away by an occupation in itself sinful; while yet all become sinful, because the first place, instead of a place merely subordinate, is allotted to them. But he is going to see his possession that he may glory in it, as Nebuchadnezzar gloried as he walked in his palace and said, 'Is not this great Babylon that I have built. . . .by the might of my power, and for the honor of my majesty?' (Dan. 4:30). While he then represents those whom 'the lust of the eye and the pride of life' detain from Christ; with the second guest it is rather the care of this life, not the pride of having, but the anxiety of getting, which so fills his soul that there is no room for higher thoughts or desires. He has made an important purchase, and cannot put off for a single day the trial of how it is likely to turn out; '*I have bought five yoke of oxen, and I go to prove them.*' The number need not perplex us; Elijah finds Elisha plowing with *twelve* yoke of oxen (1 Kgs. 19:19). Both of these offer fair words, '*I pray thee have me excused,*' even while they evade the invitation.

If in these two it is the pride and the business, in the last it is the pleasure, of the world which keeps him from Christ. 'See you not that I have a feast of my own? why trouble me then with yours? *I have married a wife, and therefore I cannot come.*' According to the Levitical law, this would have been reason sufficient why he should not go to battle (Deut. 24:5); but it is none why he should not come to the feast (1 Cor. 7:29). He, however, counts it more than sufficient. The other guests, conscious of the insufficiency of the excuses which they pleaded, gave at least courteous denials, would have the servant carry back fair words to the master of the feast; but this one has a reason perfectly valid why he should not attend, and, except in so far as his 'I will not' clothes itself in the form of 'I cannot,' does not trouble himself to send any apology for his absence. One may trace here the same ascending scale of contumacy in the bearing of the guests, although not so strongly marked, as in the other parable (Matt. 22:5, 6), where some make light of the message, others evil entreat and kill the messengers. The first of these guests would be very glad to come, if only it were possible, if there were not a constraining necessity which unfortunately keeps him away. It is a needs be, so at least he describes it, so he would have it represented to the maker of the feast. The second alleges no such constraining necessity, but is simply going upon sufficient reason on another errand; yet he too prays to be excused. The third has engagements of his own, and declares outright, 'I cannot come.' It is beautifully remarked by Bengel that there is another buying of a field (Matt. 13:44), another setting of the hand to the plow (Luke 9:62), the participation in another wedding (2 Cor. 11:2), which would not have hindered the accepting of this invitation, since rather they would one and all have been identical with it.

In what remarkable connection do their excuses stand to the declaration of the Savior which presently follows: 'If any man come to Me, and hate not his father, and mother, and wife, and children, and brethren, and sisters, yea, and his own life also, he cannot be my disciple'; and how apt a commentary the words of St. Paul supply, 'This I say, brethren, the time is short; it remaineth that both they that have wives be as though they had none, and they that weep as though they wept not, and they that rejoice as though they rejoiced not, and they that buy as though they possessed not, and they that use this world as not abusing it' (1 Cor. 7:29–31); since it was not the having,—for they had nothing which it was not lawful for men to have,—but the unduly loving these things, which proved their hindrance, and ultimately excluded them from the feast.

'So that servant came, and showed his lord these things'; declared the ill success which he has met,—reported to him the excuses which all had made,—even as hitherto in all likelihood not so much as one among the spiritual chiefs of the Jewish nation had attached himself openly and without reserve to Christ (John 7:48). *'Then the master of the house, being angry, said to his servant, Go out quickly into the streets and lanes of the city, and bring in hither the poor, and the maimed, and the halt, and the blind.'* The anger of God, and we have this anger expressly declared in two other of the parables (Matt. 18:34; 22:7), is the anger of despised love; yet not for this the less terrible. This second class of invited must still be sought *within the city;* we have not therefore yet arrived at the calling of the Gentiles. There lies a distinct reminiscence here of the precept given just before to him at whose table the Lord was sitting; 'Call thou the poor, the maimed, the lame, the blind' (v. 13). The great Giver of the heavenly feasts fulfills his own command. *He* bids to *his* table the spiritually sick, the spiritually needy; while the rich in their own virtues, in their own merits, at once exclude themselves, and are excluded by Him (Luke 6:24, 25; Rev. 3:17). The people who knew not the law, the despised and the outcast, these should enter into the kingdom of God, before the wise, the prudent,—before those who said they saw, who thanked God they were not as other men, who had need of nothing.

'And the servant said, Lord, it is done as thou hast commanded, and yet there is room.' Whereupon, since grace will endure a vacuum as little as nature, he receives a new commission: *'God out into the highways and hedges, and compel them to come in, that my house may be filled.'* If those *'in the streets and lanes of the city'* were the more abject among the Jews, the meaner, the more ignorant, the more deeply sunken in sin; then those without the city,—which we must take as the symbol of the theocracy—in the country round about, wandering in the highways, and camping as gypsies now-a-days, under the hedges, will be the yet more despised and morally abject Gentiles, the *pagans,* in all senses of that word. It will thus appear that the parable, hitherto historic, becomes prophetic here; for it declares how God had a larger purpose of grace than could be satisfied by the coming in of a part and remnant of the Jewish people,—that He had prepared a feast, at which more should sit down than they,—founded a Church with room in it for Gentile as for Jew,—those too being 'fellow-citizens with the saints, and of the household of God.' It is not that this is explicitly declared, for the time was not yet for the unfolding of this mystery; but it is here wrapped up, and biding its time.

'Compel them to come in,' has always been a favorite text with the persecutor and inquisitor; with all who, doing violence to the

rights of conscience, would fain find in Scripture a warrant or a pretext for this. It must be owned, too, that others to whom one would very unwillingly apply such names have appealed to these words as justifying that forcible separation of men from their errors, that effort at the saving of men against their will, from which, where the power is present, it is often so difficult to abstain. Thus Augustine, writing to Count Boniface, and urging that a certain constraint on the part of the civil power might be fitly used for the bringing back of the Donatists to the unity of the Church, appeals to this parable in proof. And in what he thus urges Calvin finds nothing amiss, but the contrary rather. And yet it is strange how there ever could have been drawn from these words arguments for any compulsion but a moral one. For first, dealing with the parable in the letter, to suppose any other compulsion save that of strong persuasion is idle; for how can we imagine this single servant,—he is but one throughout,—driving before him, from the country into the city, a flock of unwilling guests, and these gathered from the rude and lawless class unto whom he is now sent? But indeed this *'Compel them to come in,'* is spoken with quite a different intention. The giver of the feast does not anticipate on their parts any reluctance to accept his invitation, nor any indifference toward it, which should need to be forcibly overcome. What rather he expects is that these houseless dwellers in the highways and by the hedges will hold themselves so unworthy of the invitation as hardly to be persuaded that it was intended for them; will not be induced without a certain constraint to enter the rich man's dwelling, and share in his magnificent entertainment. And when we pass on to the spiritual thing signified, since faith cannot be forced, what can this compelling mean, save that strong earnest exhortation, which the ambassadors of Christ will address to their fellows, when themselves deeply convinced of the tremendous issues which are for every man linked with the acceptance or rejection of the message which they bear? They will *'compel,'* but only as the angels; who, when Lot lingered, laid hold upon his hand and brought him forth, and set him forcibly beyond the limits of the doomed city (Gen. 19:16); or the ambassadors of Christ will, in another way, *'compel,'* for they will speak as delivering his message who has a right to be heard by his creatures,—who not merely entreats, but commands, all men everywhere to repent and believe the Gospel. Anselm observes, that God compels men to come in, when He drives them by strong calamities to seek and find refuge with Him and in his

Church; or, as Luther has it, they are compelled to come in, when the law is broadly preached, terrifying their consciences, and driving them to Christ, as their only refuge and hope.

The parable closes with the householder's indignant declaration, *'For I say unto you, That none of those men which were bidden shall taste of my supper.'* The plural *'you'* is perplexing here, only one servant having been named throughout. It cannot be that Christ is now speaking in his own person to the Pharisees round Him, for the words are plainly not his, but the householder's still. Is it that this one servant is considered as the representative of many? or shall we suppose those whom the householder thus addresses to be the guests already assembled? Exclusion, total and final, from the feast, to which, when they saw others entering, they also might desire to be admitted, this shall be the penalty of their contempt. There is such a bitter cry, the repentance as of Esau, when it is plainly seen that the birthright has been transferred to another; but it does not bring back the blessing (Heb. 12:17). That is forfeited forever; and no after earnestness will avail anything to reverse the doom (Prov. 1:28; Matt. 25:11, 12; John 8:21).

Comparing this parable and that of the Marriage of the King's Son, we may note with how fine a skill all the minor circumstances are arranged to be in consistent keeping in each. There the principal person, being a king, has armies at his command, whole bands of servants to execute his behests. The refusal to accept *his* invitation was there, according to Eastern notions of submission, nothing less than rebellion; and, being accompanied with outrages done to his servants, called out that terrible retribution. Here, as the offense is in every way lighter, so also is the penalty; that is, in the outward circumstances which supply the framework of the parable, being no more than exclusion from a festival; though indeed not lighter, when taken in its spiritual signification; for it is nothing less than exclusion from the kingdom of God, 'everlasting destruction from the presence of the Lord and the glory of his power.'

22.
The Lost Sheep
Matthew 18:12–14; Luke 15:3–7

The words with which the three parables of the fifteenth chapter of St. Luke are introduced, 'Then drew near unto Him all the publicans and sinners for to hear Him,' must not be here understood as marking some single and definite moment of time. The Evangelist is describing rather what at this period was the prevailing feature of Christ's ministry (cf. Mark 2:15; Luke 7:37), namely that, as by a secret attraction, it drew the outcasts of the nation to Him and to the hearing of his word. Of these 'publicans and sinners,' the first were men infamous among their countrymen by their very occupation; the second, such as, till awakened by Him to repentance and amendment of life, had been notorious transgressors of God's holy law (Luke 7:39). These He did not repel, as fearing pollution from their touch; but received them graciously, taught them freely, and lived in familiar intercourse with them. At this the Scribes and Pharisees murmured and took offense. They could better have understood a John Baptist, fleeing to the wilderness, separating himself from sinners in the whole outward manner of his life, as well as inwardly in his spirit. And this outward separation from sinners, which was the Old Testament form of righteousness, may have been needful for those who would preserve their purity in those times of the law, and until He came, who brought powers of good to bear upon the world's evil far mightier than ever had been brought before. Hitherto it may have been the wisdom of those who knew themselves predisposed to the infection to flee from the infected; but He was the physician who boldly sought out these, that his health might overcome their disease, his righteousness their sin. But this seeking out and not shunning sinners was just what the Scribes and Pharisees could not understand. They had neither love to hope the recovery of such, nor medicines to effect that recovery; nor yet antidotes to preserve themselves, while making the attempt.

An earlier expression of their discontent had called out those significant words, 'They that are whole need not a physician, but they that are sick; I came not to call the righteous, but sinners to repentance' (Luke 5:31, 32); and now their later murmurings furnish the motive of the three parables which follow. In all of these Christ would shame the murmurers, holding up to them the angels of God, and God Himself, rejoicing at the conversion of a sinner; and contrasting this liberal joy of heaven with the narrow discontents and envious repinings of earth. Heaven and the holy inhabitants of heaven welcomed the penitent; only his fellow sinners kept him proudly aloof, as though there had been defilement for them in his touch; as though they were wronged, if he were freely forgiven.

But this is not all. Not merely was there joy in heaven over the penitent sinner, but *more* joy over one such than over ninety-nine such as themselves. The good that might be in them He does not deny. Many among them, no doubt, had a zeal for God, were following after righteousness such as they knew it, a righteousness according to the law. But if now that a higher righteousness was revealed,—a righteousness by faith, the new life of the Gospel,—they obstinately refuse to participate in it, then such as would receive this life from Him, however widely in times past they might have departed from God, should now be brought infinitely nearer to Him than themselves; as the one sheep was brought home to the house, while the ninety and nine abode in the wilderness; as for the prodigal a fatted calf was slain, while the elder brother had never received so much as a kid (v. 29). Nay, they are bidden at last to beware lest the spirit which they are allowing should exclude them altogether from that new kingdom of righteousness, and peace, and joy in the Holy Ghost, into which they, no less than the publicans and sinners, were invited freely to enter.

Of the three parables in this chapter, the two earlier set forth to us mainly the *seeking* love of God; while the third describes rather the rise and growth, responsive to that love, of repentance in the heart of man. The same truth is thus presented successively under different aspects,—God's seeking love being set forth first, since all first motions towards good are from Him; yet is it the same truth in all; for it is the confluence of these two streams, of this drawing and seeking love from without, and of the faith by this awakened from within, of the objective grace and the subjective faith, out of which repentance springs. And thus the parables together constitute a perfect and harmonious whole. The first two speak nothing of a changed heart and mind toward God; nor, indeed, would the images of a wandering sheep and a lost piece of money give room for this; the last speaks only of this change, and nothing of the antecedent working of the spirit of God in the heart, the goings forth of his power and love, which yet must have found the wanderer, before he could ever have found himself, or found his God. These parables are thus a trilogy, which again is divided into two and one; St. Luke himself distinctly marking the break and the new beginning which at v. 11 finds place.

There are other inner harmonies and relations between them. Thus there is a seeming anti-climax in the numbers,—one in a hundred,—one in ten,—one in two; which is a real climax, as the sense of the value of the lost would increase with the larger proportion which it bore to the whole. And other human feelings and interests are involved in the successive narratives, which enhance in each successive case the anxiety for the recovery of that which is in danger of perishing. The possessor of a hundred sheep is in some sort a rich man, therefore not likely to feel their diminution by one at all so deeply as the woman who, having but ten small pieces of money, should lose one of these; while the intensity of her feeling would fall very short of the affection of a father, who, having but two sons, should behold one out of these two go astray. Thus we find ourselves moving in ever narrower, and so ever intenser, circles of hope and fear and love, drawing in each successive parable nearer to the innermost center and heart of the truth.

So also in each successive case we may see shadowed forth on man's part a deeper guilt, and thus on God's part a mightier grace. In the first parable the guilt implied is the smallest. The sinner is set forth under the image of a silly wandering sheep. It is only one side of the truth, but yet a most real one, that sin is oftentimes an ignorance; nay in a greater or a less degree it is always such (Luke 23:34; Acts 3:17; 1 Tim. 1:13); the sinner knows not what he does, and if in one aspect he deserves wrath, in another he challenges pity. He is a sheep that has gone astray, oftentimes ere it knew what it was doing, ere it had so much as learned that it *had* a shepherd, or belonged to a fold. But there are others, set forth under the lost piece of money, who knowing themselves to be God's with his image

stamped on their souls, even the image of the Great King, do yet
throw themselves away, renounce their high birth, and willfully
lose themselves in the world. *Their* sin is greater; but a sin worse
even than theirs is behind,—the sin of the prodigal. To have tasted
something of the love of God, to have known Him, not as our King
who has stamped us with his image, but as our Father, of whose
family we are; and to have despised that love, and forsaken that
house—this is the crowning guilt; and yet the grace of God is sufficient to forgive even this sin, and to bring back this wanderer to
Him.

With so much of introduction, we may proceed to consider
these parables one by one; and first this of the Lost Sheep. 'What
man of you, having a hundred sheep, if he lose one of them, doth
not leave the ninety and nine in the wilderness, and go after that
which is lost, until he find it?' It might at first sight appear as
though the shepherd were caring for the one sheep strayed at the
hazard of all the others, leaving as he does them, the 'ninety and
nine in the wilderness.' But 'the wilderness' here is no sandy or
rocky desert, the haunt of wild beasts or of wandering robber
hordes; rather wide extended grassy plains, steppes or savannahs,
called 'desert' because without habitations of men, but exactly the
fittest place for the pasture of sheep. Thus we read in St. John (6:10)
that 'there was much grass' in a place which by St. Matthew is
called 'desert' (14:15; cf. Ezek. 34:25); and we commonly attach to
'desert' or 'wilderness' in Scripture, images of far more uniform
sterility and desolation than the reality would warrant. Parts, it is
true, of the larger deserts of Palestine or Arabia are as desolate as
can be imagined, though as much from rock as from sandy levels;
yet on the whole they offer far more variety of scenery, much wider
extents of fertile or at least grassy land, than is commonly assumed.
We must understand then that the residue of the flock are left in
their ordinary and safe pasturage, while the shepherd goes in
search of the one which has strayed. There is a peculiar fitness in
this image as addressed to the spiritual rulers of the Jewish people.
They too were shepherds; continually charged, rebuked, warned,
under this very title (Ezek. 34; Zech. 11:16); under-shepherds of
Him who sets forth his own watchful tenderness for his people by
the same image (Is. 40:11; Jer. 31:10; Ezek. 34:12; 37:24; Zech. 13:7;
cf. Ps. 23:1; 80:1);—yet not only were they no seekers of the lost, no
bringers back of the strayed, no binders-up of the broken, but they
murmured against Him, 'the Shepherd of Israel,' the 'great

Shepherd of the sheep,' because He did in his own person what they, his deputies, so long had neglected to do, making good Himself all these omissions of theirs.

In the order of things natural, a sheep which could wander away from, could also wander back to, the fold. But it is not so with a sheep of God's pasture. Such can lose, but it cannot find itself again. There is in sin a *centrifugal* tendency, and the wanderings of this wanderer could be only further and further away. If, therefore, it shall be found at all, this can only be by its Shepherd's going to seek it; else, being once lost, it is lost forever. The Incarnation of the Son of God was a girding of Himself for such a task as this; his whole life in the days of his flesh a following of the strayed. And He was not weary with the greatness of the way; He shrank not when the thorns wounded his flesh and tore his feet; He followed us into the deep of our misery, came under the uttermost of our malediction; for He had gone forth to seek his own, *'till He had found it.'* And, *'when he hath found it,'* how tenderly does the shepherd of the parable handle that sheep which has cost him all this toil; he does not smite, nor even harshly *drive* it back to the fold; nay, does not deliver it to an underling to carry; but *'layeth it on his [own] shoulders,'*—a delicate touch, which our Translation has let go,—and bears it home (cf. Deut. 32:10). We recognize in this an image of the sustaining grace of Christ, which does not cease, till his rescued are made partakers of final salvation. But when some make much of the weariness which this load must have caused to the shepherd, seeing here an allusion to his sufferings, 'who bare our sins in his own body' (1 Pet. 2:24), upon whom was laid 'the iniquity of us all,' this is a missing of the true significance. That *'until he find it'* has exhausted the whole story of the painfulness of his way who came in search of his lost creature; and this is now the story of his triumphant return to heaven with the trophy that He had won, the spoil which He, a mightier David, had delivered from the lion and the bear (1 Sam. 17:34, 35).

And as the man when he reaches home *'calleth together his friends and neighbors, saying unto them, Rejoice with me, for I have found my sheep which was lost'*—makes them sharers in his joy, as they had been sharers in his anxiety, even so shall joy be in heaven when one wanderer is brought back to the heavenly fold; for heaven and redeemed earth constitute but one kingdom, being bound together by that love which is 'the bond of perfectness.' *'I say unto you, that likewise joy shall be in heaven over one sinner that re-*

penteth, more than over ninety and nine just persons, which need no re-pentance.' Let us not in this *'I say unto you,'* miss a slight yet majestic intimation of the dignity of his person; 'I who know—I who, when I tell you of heavenly things, tell you of mine own (John 1:51; 3:11), announce to you this.' The joy, we may observe, is still in the future; *'joy shall be in heaven';* and this consistently with the tacit assumption of the Good Shepherd's part as his own; for not yet had He risen and ascended, leading 'captivity captive,' bringing with Him his rescued and redeemed.

Were this all, there would be nothing to perplex; but it is not merely joy over one penitent, but joy over this one *'more than over ninety and nine just persons, which need no repentance.'* Now we can easily understand how, *among men,* there should be more joy for a small part which has been in jeopardy, than for the continued secure possession of a much larger portion. It is as when the mother concentrates for the moment all her affection on her sick child, seeming to a bystander to love none but that only; and actually rejoicing at the recovery of that one more than at the uninterrupted health of all the others. Or, to use Augustine's beautiful words, 'What then takes place in the soul, when it is more delighted at finding or recovering the things it loves, than if it had ever had them? Yea, and other things witness hereunto, and all things are full of witness, crying out, "So it is." The conquering commander triumpheth; yet had he not conquered, unless he had fought, and the more peril there was in the battle, so much the more joy is there in the triumph. The storm tosses the sailors, threatens shipwreck; all wax pale at approaching death; sky and sea are calmed, and they are exceeding joyed, as having been exceeding afraid. A friend is sick, and his pulse threatens danger; all who long for his recovery are sick in mind with him. He is restored, though as yet he walks not with his former strength, yet there is such joy as was not when before he walked sound and strong.' Yet whence arises the disproportionate joy? Clearly from the temporary uncertainty which existed about the result. But no such uncertainty could find place with Him, who knows the end from the beginning; whose joy needs not to be enhanced by a fear going before. As little with Him need the earnest love for the periled one, as in the case of the mother and her children, throw into the background, even for the moment, the love and care for the others; so that the analogies and illustrations drawn from this world of ours supply no adequate solution of the difficulty.

And further, how can it be affirmed of any that they *'need no repentance,'* since *'all* like sheep have gone astray'; and all therefore have need to try back their ways? The explanations commonly given do not quite satisfy. We may indeed get rid both of this difficulty and the other, by seeing here an example of the Lord's severe yet loving irony. These *'ninety and nine, which need no repentance,'* would then be,—like those whole who need not, or count that they need not, a physician (Matt. 9:12),—self-righteous persons; as such displeasing to God; whose present moral condition as it causes *no* joy in heaven, it can be nothing strange that a sinner's conversion should occasion more gladness there than the continuance of these in their evil. But the whole structure of the parables refutes this. The ninety and nine sheep have *not* wandered, the nine pieces of money have *not* been lost, the elder brother has *not* left his father's house. These difficulties will only disappear when we regard these *'righteous'* as such indeed, but their righteousness as merely legal, of the old dispensation, so that the least in the kingdom of heaven is greater than they. The law had partially accomplished its work in them, restraining from grosser transgressions; and thus they needed not, like the publicans and sinners, repentance from these; but it had not accomplished all, it had not been 'a schoolmaster to Christ,' bringing them to see their sinfulness, and consequent need of a Savior. The publicans and sinners, though by another path, had come to Him; and He here pronounces that there was more real cause of joy over one of these, now entering into the inner sanctuary of faith, than over ninety and nine of those other, who lingered at the legal vestibule, refusing to go further in.

23.

The Lost Piece of Money

Luke 15:8–10

The preceding parable has anticipated much that might have been said upon this; yet it would be against all analogy of other twin parables, to assume that the two did no more than say the same thing twice over. In the Pearl and the Hid Treasure, in the Leaven and the Mustard-seed, the second may seem at first sight only a repetition of the first; while yet on closer inspection important differences will reveal themselves; and so is it here and elsewhere; thus compare Matt. 9:16, 17, and Luke 14:28–32. If the shepherd in the last parable was Christ, the woman in this may be the Church. Or should we understand by her that Divine Wisdom, so often magnified in Proverbs as seeking the salvation of men, and here set forth as a person and not an attribute (cf. Matt. 11:19), this will be no different view. The two explanations flow into one, if only we contemplate the Church as the organ by which the Holy Spirit seeks for the lost; and which, being quickened by the Divine Spirit, is stirred up to active ministries of love for the seeking of souls (Rev. 22:17). That the Church should be personified as a woman is natural; and the thought of the Holy Ghost as a mother has at different times been near to the minds of men.

'Either what woman having ten pieces of silver, if she lose one piece, doth not light a candle, and sweep the house, and seek diligently till she find it?' In this piece of money expositors, both ancient and modern, have delighted to trace a resemblance to the human soul, originally stamped with the image and superscription of the great King ('God created man in his own image,' Gen. 1:27), and still retaining traces of the mint from which it proceeded; however by sin that image has been nearly effaced, and the superscription become well

551

nigh illegible. One clings with pleasure to so instructive a suggestion; but it must not be forgotten that the Greek drachma; but it
must not be forgotten that the Greek drachma, the coin here
named, had not, like the Latin denarius (Matt. 22:20), the emperor's image and superscription upon it, but some device, as of an
owl, a tortoise, or a head of Minerva. As the woman seeks anxiously her piece of silver, even so the Lord, through the ministrations of his Church, gives diligence to recover the lost sinner, to
brink back the money of God to his treasury, from which originally
it issued. The allusion often found in the lighting of the candle to
the mystery of the Incarnation,—the divine glory which the Savior
has within, shining through the fleshly covering which only in part
concealed it,—must of course give way, if we interpret the parable
as is here proposed. Rather it must be explained by the help of such
hints as Matt. 5:14, 15; Phil. 2:15, 16; Eph. 4:13, supply. The *'candle'*
is the Word of God; which candle the Church holds forth, as it has
and exercises a ministry of this Word. It is by the light of this candle that sinners are found, that they find themselves, that the
Church finds them. With this to aid her, she *'sweeps the house'*;
which sweeping is not effected without dust. What a deranging of
the house for a time! how does the dust which had been suffered to
settle down and to accumulate, begin to rise and fly about; how unwelcome all which is going forward to any, who have no interest in
what is doing, whose only interest is that nothing should trouble
their selfish ease. The charge against the Gospel is still the same,
that it turns the world upside down (Acts 17:6). And in a sense so
it does; for only let its message be proclaimed in earnest, and how
much of latent aversion to the truth reveals itself now as open enmity; how much of torpid estrangement from God is changed into
active hostility; what indignation is there against the troublers of
Israel, the witness in sackcloth who torment the dwellers upon
earth (Rev. 11:10). She meanwhile who bears the candle of the Lord,
amid all this uproar and outcry is diligently looking for and finding her own again.

   In the preceding parable the shepherd sought his strayed sheep
in the wilderness; but *in the house* this piece of money is lost, and in
the house therefore it is sought and found. This is scarcely accidental. In that other there was the returning of the Son to the heavenly places, but in this there is the hint of a visible Church which
has been founded upon earth, and to which sinners are restored.
And there are other slighter variations, intelligible at once when we

see there the more personal and immediate ministry of Christ, and here the secondary ministry of his Church. The shepherd says, '*I have found my sheep*'; but the woman, '*I have found the piece of money*'; not '*my piece of money*,' for it is in no sense *hers*, as the sheep was *his*. He says, '*which was lost*'; but she, '*which I had lost*,' acknowledging a fault of her own as having contributed to the loss; for a sheep strays of itself, but a piece of money could only be missing by a certain negligence on their part who should have kept it.

This woman, if we are right in our interpretation, is the Church, the bride, that is, of the Good Shepherd. What a wonder that in the hour of her joy she does and speaks, almost as He has done and spoken before? And first, '*she calleth her friends and neighbors together*';—they are *female* friends and neighbors, although this nicety in the keeping of the parts (Ruth 4:14, 17) escapes us in English— that these may be sharers in her joy. Yet this need not prevent us from understanding by them the angels,—we have the Lord's warrant for this,—whose place, it will be observed, is not 'in heaven' in this parable, as it was in the preceding; for this is the rejoicing together of the redeemed and elect creation *upon earth* at the repentance of a sinner. Among the angels who walk up and down the earth, who are present in the assemblies of the faithful (1 Cor. 11:10), joying to behold their order, but most of all rejoicing when a sinner is converted, there shall be joy, when the Church of the redeemed, quickened by the Holy Spirit, summons them to join with it in consenting hymns of thanksgiving to God for the recovery of a lost soul. For indeed if the 'sons of God' shouted for joy and sang together at the first creation (Job 38:7), by how much better right when 'a new creation' had found place, in the birth of a soul into the light of everlasting life (Eph. 3:10; 1 Pet. 1:12); for according to that exquisite word of St. Bernard, the tears of penitents are the wine of angels.

24.

The Prodigal Son

Luke 15:11–32

We proceed to consider a parable which, if it be permitted to compare things divine with each other, might be fitly called the pearl and crown of all the parables of Scripture; as again, it is the most elaborate, if we may use a word having a certain unfitness when applied to the spontaneous and the free, but which yet the fullness of all the minor details suggests;—a parable too, containing within itself such a circle of blessed truths as abundantly to justify the title, Evangelium in Evangelio, which it has sometimes borne. Of its relation to the two other in the same chapter there has been occasion to speak already. To the parable itself, therefore, we may address ourselves without further preface.

'*A certain man had two sons.*' Interpreters separate off into two groups at the very outset of their interpretation. There are who see in these two sons the Jew and the Gentile; and therefore in the younger son's departure from his father's house, the history of the great apostasy of the Gentile world; in his return the reception of the same into the privileges of the New Covenant;—as in the elder son a figure of the narrow-hearted self-extolling Jews repining that 'sinners of the Gentiles' should be admitted to the same privileges with themselves, and sullenly refusing blessings which they must possess in common with these. Others, on the contrary, recognize in the two sons not Gentile and Jew, at least not primarily these, but penitent sinners and proud sinners, wheresoever such may be met; and have naturally found the first example of the one in the publicans, of the other in the Pharisees, seeing that the Lord spoke the parable to justify to these his gracious reception of those.

These latter interpreters with good right object to the other interpretation, that it is alien to the scope of the parable; that, so explained, the parable fails to meet the necessity which called it out, or to teach, except by remote inference, the truth which Christ plainly intended to teach by it. He would fain put the Pharisees to a wholesome shame, who were offended with Him for consorting so freely and so graciously with fallen members of the Jewish Church. If indeed *'the publicans and sinners'* whom He so freely admitted to hear Him had been Gentiles and not Jews, the other interpretation might have some claim to stand. A setting forth of the gracious reception by his heavenly Father of the whole Gentile world when it turned to Him, would in that case have been a proper justification of his own receiving of those who might be properly regarded as the first-fruits of the heathen. Some have very eagerly asserted that the *'publicans and sinners' were* heathen; Tertullian, for example, who is in great dread lest, if they be acknowledged as members, though fallen ones, of the Jewish Church, an argument should be drawn from this for receiving back into communion those who, within the Church, and after their baptism, have greatly sinned. He does not scruple to assert that the publicans were always heathen; and this in the face of our Lord's declaration that Zaccheus, a chief publican, was 'a son of Abraham' (Luke 19:9), of the fact that Matthew the Apostle had sat as a publican at the receipt of custom (Luke 5:27), that publicans came to the baptism of John (Luke 7:29). Set by their fellow-countrymen on a level with the heathen, counted traitors by them to the dearest interests of the nation, and till the words of Christ awoke them to a nobler life, many of them, perhaps, deserving all, or nearly all, the scorn which they found, the publicans were yet beyond all question Jews; which being so, we confidently conclude that we have not here the mystery of the calling of the Gentiles into the covenant; whereof during his earthly life the Lord gave only slightest hints; but a truth as precious, namely, that, *within the covenant*, He was come to call and to receive sinners to repentance. For all this the interpretation, which must thus be disallowed as the primary, need not be excluded altogether. Wherever there are penitent sinners and proud sinners, there the parable is finding its fulfillment; and thus in a very real sense the Gentile world *was* the prodigal younger son, and the Jewish synagogue the self-righteous elder. Nor have they by any means exhausted the parable. It stands good also for us. In the Christian Church too prodigals and elder brothers still exist; and as thousands and ten thousands of those have from it taken heart to return to a heavenly Father's house, so will thousands more to the end of time; whom no perverse, narrow-hearted, 'elder-brotherly' interpretation will succeed in robbing of the strong consolation which it affords.

'*And the younger of them said to his father, Father, give me the portion of goods that falleth to me*'; his 'bairndole,' as they would call it in Yorkshire. It is not without a meaning that of the two sons it is the younger who thus enacts the part of the prodigal. 'Childhood and youth are vanity'; cf. Prov. 7:7. This claiming by the prodigal of his share in a technical, and almost legal, form, as a right and not as a favor, is a delicate touch, characteristic of the entire alienation from all home-affections which has already found place in his heart. Such a right the Lord *may* intend to assume that he had; and, no doubt, a custom of the kind existed among some nations of the East, for example, among the Hindus; but no satisfactory proof has been adduced that it ever prevailed among the Jews. But we *need not* conceive of him as asking his portion otherwise than as a favor: 'That portion which will hereafter fall to me, which thou designest for me at last, I would fain receive it now.' A younger brother's portion, according to the Jewish laws of inheritance, would be the half of that which the elder brother should receive (Deut. 21:17; 2 Kgs. 2:9). Contemplated spiritually this request is the expression of man's desire to be independent of God, to become a god to himself (Gen. 3:5), and to lay out his life at his own will and for his own pleasure. Growing weary of living upon God's fullness, he desires to be, and believes that he can be, a fountain of blessedness to himself; that, laying out his life for himself, he will lay it out better than God would have laid it out for him. This sin of pride is the sin of sins; in which all subsequent sins are included; they are all but the unfolding of this one. Over against the prodigal's demand, '*Give me my portion of goods,*' is the children's cry, 'Give us day by day our daily bread'; they therein declaring that they wait upon God, and would fain be nourished from day to day by his hand.

'*And he divided unto them his living.*' The father does not refuse his request. It would have profited nothing to retain *him* at home against his will, who was already in heart estranged from that home: better that he should discover by bitter experience the folly of his request. Such, too, is the dealing of God; He has constituted man a spiritual being, a being with a will; and when *his* service no longer appears a perfect freedom, and man promises himself something better elsewhere, he is allowed to make the trial (Rom. 1:24, 26, 28). He shall discover, and, if need be, by most painful proof, that the only true freedom is a freedom in God; that to depart from Him is not to throw off the yoke, but to exchange a light yoke for a heavy one, and one gracious master for a thousand tyrannous lords.

'*And not many days after the younger son gathered all together.*' Having obtained his portion, a certain interval of time elapses before he actually forsakes his father's house. It is a fine and delicate touch, the apostasy of the heart, as St. Bernard here well observes, often running before the apostasy of the life. The sinner is indeed pleasing himself; but the divergence of his will and God's does not *immediately* appear. This, however, cannot be for long. As the young man in the parable, after a shorter or longer pause, '*gathered all together,*' turned what had fallen to his share into ready money or jewels or other valuables, and then '*took his journey into a far country,*' so '*after not many days*' he too will *openly* depart from God, who in will and affections has departed from Him already. Gathering all together, collecting all his energies and powers, with the deliberate resolve of obtaining, through their help, all the gratification he can out of the world, and now manifestly preferring the creature to the Creator, he will take '*his journey into a far country,*' even into that land where God is not.

And now it must be well with him at last; he has gotten what he desired; no other is lord over him. Henceforth he is his own master;—but only to find the truth of that line which the poet wrote, and to which so many, the poet himself included, have set their seal:

Lord of himself; that heritage of woe!

Nor shall he wait long before he makes proof of this. For in that far land the Prodigal,—fitly so called by the Church, though he nowhere bears this name in the sacred narrative,—'*wasted his substance with riotous living*' (Prov. 29:3); so quickly has his *gathering* issued in a *scattering*, so little was it a *gathering* that deserved the name. For a while the supplies he brought with him may have lasted; and so long he may have congratulated himself, and counted that he had done wisely and well in asserting his own liberty. But anon, '*when he had spent all, there arose a mighty famine in that land; and he began himself to be in want,*' the famine reached even to him. What a picture of the downward progress of a soul that has estranged itself from the one source of happiness and joy. It is not at the first moment that the wretchedness of this is discovered. The world has its attractions, and the flesh its pleasures; the affections are not all at once laid waste, nor the sources of natural delight drawn dry in an instant. But to this spiritual bankruptcy the sinner is more or less rapidly hastening; and the time inevitably arrives when he comes to an end of all the satisfaction which the creature can give him; and he too finds out that there is *'a mighty famine'* in the land where he has chosen to dwell,—a famine of truth and love, and of all whereby the spirit of man indeed lives; that it is an evil thing and bitter to have forsaken the fountain of living waters, and hewn out for himself broken cisterns, which hold no water (Jer. 2:13; 17:5, 6, 13). There need no outward distresses, though often these will not be wanting, to bring on a sense of this famine. A man's worldly possessions may stand in their fullness, may go on abounding more and more; all his external helps to felicity may remain in their strength; while yet in the true riches he may have run through all, and may be beginning *'to be in want.'* The famine of which Christ here speaks presides often at the sumptuous tables of rich men; it finds its way into the palaces of kings. In these palaces, at those tables, the immortal soul may be famishing, yea, ready to *'perish with hunger.'*

It was observed just now that we had a right to trace, as a secondary meaning in this parable, the history of the apostasy of the Gentile world from the knowledge and service of the true God. Regard it in that sense, and then this wasting of goods will be exactly described at Rom. 1:19–23; what remains in that chapter corresponding to the prodigal's joining himself to a citizen of the far country, and seeking to fill his belly with the swine's husks. The great famine of the heathen world was at its height when the Son of God came in the flesh: therein consisted in part 'the fullness of time,' the fitness of that time, above all other, for his appearing. The glory of that old world was fast fading and perishing. All child-like faith in the old religions had departed; 'creeds outworn,' they could no longer nourish, ever so little, the spirit of man. The Greek philosophy had completed its possible circle, but it had found no sufficient answer to the doubts and questionings which tormented humanity. 'What is truth?' this was the question which all asked; some in mockery, some in despair; some without the desire, and all without the expectation, of obtaining an answer.

When the prodigal *'began to be in want,'* there was here a summons to return to the home which he had forsaken. But his proud heart is not yet subdued, his confidence in his own resources, though shaken, not altogether overthrown. God's first judgments do not always tame; but, like Ephraim, the stricken sinner exclaims, 'The bricks are fallen down, but we will build with hewn stone; the sycamores are cut down, but we will change them into cedars' (Is. 9:10; 57:10; cf. Jer. 5:3; Amos 4:6–10; Rev. 16:10, 11). In such a spirit as this *'he went and joined himself to a citizen of that country,'*—'fastened' or 'pinned himself upon' him, as Hammond expresses it, hoping to repair his broken fortunes by his help (Jer. 2:36; Hos. 5:13; 1 Sam. 2:5). 'That citizen,' says St. Bernard, 'I cannot understand as other than one of the malignant spirits, who, sinning with an irremediable obstinacy, and having passed into a permanent disposition of malice and wickedness, are no longer guests and strangers, but citizens and abiders in the land of sin.' But may not this term bring out the deep distinction between the prodigal and the lord to whom he addicted himself for a while? With all his guilt, *he* was not *'a citizen,'* but a stranger, in that *'far land.'* He did not feel himself at home, nor naturalize himself there. The other was well to do; the famine had not touched him; herein how far more miserable, though he knew it not, than he who *'began to be in want.'* There is hope for him who feels himself a miserable alien in the land of sin: but what hope for one who has made himself *'a citizen'* there, who is troubled with no heavenly homesickness, no divine hypochondria, no remembrance of a Father's house which he had forsaken? For the present indeed there is set forth to us here a deeper depth in the sinner's downward course, a fall within a fall,—a more entire and self-conscious yielding of himself in heart and will to the service of evil. He sells himself to the world; the poor deceitful show of being its master has disappeared; he is evidently its slave. A hint is here of that awful mystery in the downward progress of souls, by which he who begins with using the world as a servant to minister to his pleasures, must submit in the end to a reversing of the relations between them, so that the world uses him as its drudge, and sin as its slave. He becomes cheap in the esteem of that very world, in whose service he has forfeited all. Its good wine, which it offered him at the first, it offers him no longer, but, now that he has well drunk, that which is worse (John 2:10). It rejects him, as the sea after a while rejects the carcasses which itself has swallowed up. There is a hint of something like this, Ezek. 23:22.

Bankrupt now in all, it is little help which he finds in the new master on whom he has thrust himself; and who, if he must needs engage one who so crouches to him for a morsel of bread, will yet dismiss him out of sight. *'He sent him into his fields to feed swine,'* put him to an employment than which in the eyes of a Jew, there could be none viler nor more degrading. And now *'he would fain have filled his belly with the husks that the swine did eat; and no man gave unto him.'* Was it that he looked with a longing eye upon these swine's husks, and that even these were denied him? So commonly; for myself I should rather understand that in his unscrupulous hunger he was glad to *'fill his belly'* with these husks, *and did so,*—no man giving him any nobler sustenance (Prov. 13:25). A homely phrase has here been chosen of design; all that these could do for him was just this, to *'fill his belly,'* not to satisfy his hunger; a profound moral truth lying in the words, even this, that God and He only can satisfy the longings of an immortal soul; that none other can fill the heart which was made for Him.

The whole description is wonderful, and in nothing more than the intimate connection in which his punishment stands to his sin. 'He who would not, as a son, be treated liberally by his father, is compelled to be the servant and bondslave of a foreign master; he who would not be ruled by God, is compelled to serve the devil; he who would not abide in his father's royal palace, is sent to the field among hinds; he who would not dwell among brethren and princes, is obliged to be the servant and companion of brutes; he who would not feed on the bread of angels, petitions in his hunger for the husks of the swine.' In his feeding of swine, what a picture have we of man, 'serving diverse lusts and pleasures,' in whom the divine is for the time totally obscured, and the bestial merely predominant; and in his fruitless attempt to fill his belly with the husks, of the sinner seeking through the unlimited gratification of his appetites to appease the fierce hunger of his soul. But in vain, for still 'he enlarges his desire as hell, and is as death, and cannot be satisfied.' One might as well hope to quench a fire by adding fuel to it, as to slake desire by gratifying it (Ezek. 16:28, 29). And the crowning misery is, that the power of sinful gratifications to stay that hunger even for the moment is ever diminishing,—the pleasure which is even hoped for from them still growing fainter, and yet the goad behind urging to seek that pleasure, still becoming fiercer;—the sense of the horrible nature of the bondage ever increasing, with the power of throwing off that bondage ever growing less. All the monstrous luxuries and frantic wickednesses of imperial Rome show like the last despairing effort of man to fill his belly with the husks. In this light we may behold the incredibly sumptuous feast, the golden palaces, the enormous shows and spectacles, and all the pomp and pride of life pushed to the uttermost, the sins of nature, and the sins below nature; while yet from amidst all these the voice of man's misery only made itself the louder heard. The experiment carried out on this largest scale only made the failure more signal, only proved the more plainly that from the food of beasts there could not be drawn the nourishment of men.

It might here be urged, that the picture traced in the parable is an exaggeration alike of the wickedness and of the woe even of those who have forsaken God; that, in the corruptest times not all, and in more moral epochs only a few, even of these fall so low in misery and guilt; that their fall in a thousand ways is mercifully broken. This is quite true; yet all might thus fall; by the first departure from God, all this guilt and all this misery are rendered possible; they are legitimate results; which only do not always follow, because God, in his infinite mercy, does not always follow, because God, in his infinite mercy, does not always suffer sin to put forth *all* the bitter fruits which in it as in a bitter root are contained. In the present case, it *is* allowed to put forth its bitterest and its worst; we have one who has debased himself even unto hell; and the parable would have been faulty but for this; it would not have been a parable for *all* sinners; it would have failed to show that there is no extent of departure from God which precludes a return.

Hitherto we have followed the wanderer step by step in a career which is carrying him ever farther and farther from his God. But now the crisis has arrived, the περιπέτεια of this 'Soul's Tragedy'; and a more grateful task remains—to trace the steps of his return, from the first beginnings of repentance to his full re-investiture in all the rights and privileges of a son. For though he has forsaken his God, he has not been forsaken by Him—not in that far land, nor even among the swine's husks; all the misery which has fallen on him being indeed an expression of God's anger against the sin, but at the same time of his love to the sinner. God hedges up his way with thorns, that he may not find his paths (Hos. 2:6); makes his sin bitter to him, that he may abhor it; pursuing his fugitives, and summoning them back to Himself in that only language which now they will understand. He allows the world to make its bondage hard to them, that they may know the difference between his service and 'the service of the kingdoms of the countries'; and cry to Him, by reason of the bitter bondage (2 Chr. 12:8; 33:11–13). On how many, alas! this severe but loving discipline is wasted. They, perhaps, change their yoke, but they do not break it. They betake them to some other citizen of that far country, who promises them a little better fare, or treatment a little less contemptuous. Or, it may be, they learn to dress their husks, that these shall look like human food, and then deny that they are the fodder of swine. Or, glorying in their shame, and wallowing in the same sty with the beasts they feed, they proclaim that there was never meant to be any difference between men and beasts, that the food of one is the food also of the other. But this is not so with all. It was not so with him whose story we are following here. Under that discipline of love *'he came to himself'*—words of deepest significance, saying as they do that to come to one's self, and to come to God, are one and the same thing; that when we truly find ourselves we find Him; or rather having found Him, find also ourselves; for it is not man in union with God, who is raised above the true condition of humanity; but man separated from God, who has fallen out of, and below that condition.

He remembers now his father's house, and all the abundance there: *'How many hired servants of my father's have bread enough and to spare, and I perish with hunger!'* There is a touch of truest nature here; for the sinner never so feels the discord which he has introduced into his innermost being, as when he compares himself with the creation, animate and inanimate, around him and beneath him. He sees the happy animals, undisturbed with his longings, unable to stain themselves with his sin; he beholds suns and stars traveling in their appointed paths, and all nature fulfilling the purposes for which it was ordained; every where else peace and harmony; he only

> a jarring and a dissonant thing
> Amid this general dance and minstrelsy.

Many too of his fellowmen he sees, who, with no very lofty views about living to the glory of God, with no very lively affections towards Him, do yet find their satisfaction in the discharge of their daily duties; who, though they do his work more in the spirit of servants than of sons, rather looking to their hire than out of the free impulses of love, are not without their reward. It is true, they may fall very short of the highest joy which some of his children know; yet, on the other hand, they are far from the misery and destitution into which he has sunk. *'Hired servants'* of his Father, they yet *'have bread enough and to spare,'* while he, a son, and having once had a son's portion and place, must *'perish with hunger.'*

We may picture the forlorn prodigal to ourselves as having sat long while upon the ground, for the earth presents itself as the natural throne of the utterly desolate (Job 2:8, 13; Is. 3:26; 47:1; Lam. 2:10; Ezek. 26:16), and revolving there into what a depth of wretchedness he has fallen. But now he gathers up anew his prostrate energies, as a better hope wakens in his bosom. Why should he tarry longer among the swine? *'I will arise and go to my father.'* The words were urged by the Pelagians of old in proof that man could turn to God in his own strength, and needed no drawing from above, no grace at once preventing and following; just as the (self-styled) Unitarians of modern times have found in the circumstances of the prodigal's return an argument that man's repentance is of itself sufficient to reconcile him with God, and this without a Mediator or a sacrifice. Following in the same line a German Rationalist at the beginning of this century exclaims: 'All the dogmatic dreams of the upholders of an atonement by blood vanish, like oppressive nightmares, before this single parable.' The assertions are utterly without warrant, such conclusions being sufficiently guarded against by innumerable clearest declarations; as by John 6:44; Heb. 10:19–22, neither have we any right to expect that every passage in Scripture, least of all, that parables, which exist under necessary limitations in their power of setting forth the truth, shall contain the whole circle of Christian doctrine. He who will know the truth of God, must consider not what one Scripture says, but what all; and the silence of one passage must not be pleaded against the plain statements of innumerable other.

'And will say unto him, Father.' That relation his obedience has not constituted, and so his disobedience could not disannul. This was the ground of his confidence, even that a son once is a son ever. The adoption of sonship in baptism, and the gifts and calling of God, are on his part without repentance or recall. They may and will perish, who choose to remain in guilty ignorance to the last that these things have been freely given them of God; but having been once given, they may claim and challenge them for their own whensoever they will; nothing which has passed can have extin-

guished their right to do this. *'I have sinned against heaven, and before thee';* compare for this double confession Ex. 10:16—when we give these words their higher application, the two acknowledgments run into one, *'I have sinned against Thee, my Father in heaven';*—*'and,'* as he goes on to say, *'am no more worthy to be called thy son.'* He shows his repentance to have been divinely wrought, a work of the Holy Spirit, in that he acknowledges his sin in its root, as a transgression of the divine law, as wrought against God. Thus did David: 'Against Thee, Thee only have I sinned' (Ps. 51:4); while yet his offenses had been against the second table. For we may *injure* ourselves by our evil, we may *wrong* our neighbor; but, strictly speaking, we can *sin* only against God; and the recognition of our evil at first and chiefly an offense against Him, is of the essence of all true repentance, and distinguishes it broadly from remorse and all other kinds of sorrow which may follow on evil deeds. This willingness to confess is ever noted in Scripture as the sign of a true repentance begun; even as the sinner's refusal to humble himself in confession before God is the sure note of a continued obduracy (2 Sam. 12:13; Ezra 9:6; Job 9:20; 31:33; 33:27; Ps. 32:5; 38:18; Prov. 28:13; Jer. 2:35; 3:13; 16:10; Hos. 14:2; 1 John 1:9, 10). In Augustine's words, 'He shows himself worthy, in that he confesses himself unworthy'; while a scholar of St. Bernard's here exclaims: 'Keep, O happy sinner, keep watchfully and carefully this they most just feeling of humility and devotion; by which thou mayest ever esteem the same of thyself in humility, of the Lord in goodness. Than it there is nothing greater in the gifts of the Holy Spirit, nothing more precious in the treasures of God, nothing more holy among all graces, nothing more wholesome among all sacraments. Keep, I say, if thou wilt thyself be kept, the humility of that speech and feeling, with which thou confessest to thy Father, and sayest, *"Father, I am no more worthy to be called thy son."* For humility is of all graces the chiefest, even while it does not know itself to be a grace at all. From it they begin, by it they advance, in it they are consummated, through it they are preserved.' Thus far all has been well; but the words that follow, *'Make me as one of thy hired servants,'*—are these, it may be asked, the voice of returning spiritual health, so that we should desire to meet the temper which they imply in every *normal* repentance, or not? For the present we would only call attention to the fact that at a later period he lets them fall (v. 21), and shall then have something more to say on this question.

There is no tarrying now; he makes haste and prolongs not the time; and what he has determined to do, at once he does. *'He arose, and came to his father.'* He had believed in his father's love; he shall find that love far larger and freer than all which he had ventured to believe. *'But when he was yet a great way off, his father saw him.'* We must not suppose it was an accident that his father was the first to see him. He doubtless for many a day, hoping all things, had watched and waited for his return; and now with the quick glance of love detected in the far distance him whom he had thus watched and waited for so long. *'And had compassion, and ran, and fell on his neck* (Gen. 33:4; 45:14, 15; 46:29; Acts 20:37), *and kissed him.'* The evidences of the father's love are described with a touching minuteness; he does not wait till the poor returning wanderer has come all the way, but himself hastens to meet him; neither does he wear at first an aspect of severity, only after a season to be relaxed or laid aside, but at once welcomes him with the kiss, which is more than a token of affection, being the significant, and in the East well understood, pledge of reconciliation and peace (Gen. 33:4; 2 Sam. 14:33; Ps. 2:12); even as the osculum pacis of the Middle Ages. It is thus the Lord draws nigh unto them that draw nigh unto Him (James 4:8); He listens to the first faint sighings of their hearts after Him, for it was He who awoke those sighings there (Ps. 10:17). And though they may be *'yet a great way off,'* with far too slight an insight into the evil of their sin, or into the holiness of God, He meets them, notwithstanding, with the evidences of his favor towards them. Neither does He compel them first to go through a dreary apprenticeship of servile fear at a distance from Him; but at once embraces them in the arms of his love, giving them at this first moment strong consolations—perhaps stronger and more abounding than afterwards, when more settled in their Christian course, they will always receive. And this, because they need such now, to assure them that they are accepted, despite of all the loathsomeness of their sin; to convince them of that which it is often so hard for penitents to believe, which tasks all their faith, that God has indeed put away their transgressions, and is pacified toward them.

But the prodigal, though thus graciously received, with his sin not once mentioned against him, does not the less make the confession which he had meditated when the purpose of returning was first conceived in his heart: *'Father, I have sinned against heaven, and in thy sight, and am no more worthy to be called thy son.'* And this is well; for, though God may forgive, man is not therefore to forget.

Let us note too that it is *after*, and not *before*, the kiss of reconciliation, that this confession is made; for the more the sinner knows
and tastes of the love of God, the more he grieves to have outraged
that love. It is under the genial rays of this kindly love that the
heart, before bound up as by a deadly frost, thaws and melts and
loosens, and the waters of repentance flow freely forth. The knowledge of God's love in Christ is the cruse of salt, which alone can
turn the bitter and barren-making streams of remorse into the healing waters of repentance (2 Kgs. 2:19–22). And thus the truest and
best repentance follows, and does not precede, the sense of forgiveness; and thus too repentance will be a lifelong thing, for every
new insight into that forgiving love will be as a new reason why
the sinner should mourn to have sinned against it. It is a mistake to
affirm that men, those, I mean, in whom a real spiritual work is
going forward, will lay aside their repentance, so soon as they are
convinced of the forgiveness of their sins; and that therefore,—
since repentance, earnest, long-continued, self-mortifying repentance, is a good thing,—the longer men can be kept in suspense
about their forgiveness the better, as thus a deeper foundation of
repentance will be laid. This is a preposterous view of the relation
in which repentance and forgiveness stand to each other; their true
relation being opened to us in such passages as Ezek. 36:31, where
the Lord says, *'Then'* (and for what that *'then'* means, see vv. 24–30;
after I have cleansed you, given you a new heart, heaped my richest blessings upon you, *then*, under the sense of these) 'shall ye remember your own evil ways, and your doings that were not good,
and shall loathe yourselves in your own sight for your iniquities
and your abominations.' See Ezek. 16:60–63, where the Lord
avouches that He has established his covenant with Judah for this
very end—'that thou mayest remember, and be confounded, and
never open thy mouth anymore because of thy shame, *when I am
pacified toward thee for all that thou hast done.'* The younger son, albeit
with the clearest evidence that his father is pacified toward him,
does not the less confess his shame. He does not indeed utter all
that he had once intended; he does not say, *'Make me as one of thy
hired servants:'* though some authorities have brought these words
from v. 19, where they have right, to this verse, where they have
none; for this purpose of shrinking back from his father's love, and
from the free grace which would restore to him all, was the one
troubled element of his repentance; and in his dropping of these
words, in his willingness to be blessed by his father to the utter-

most, there is evidence that the grace already received has not been received in vain. Bengel thinks it possible that his father cut him short, left him no opportunity to say what he intended, but suggests also the truer explanation. This being so, that scholar of St. Bernard's, whose excellent words on the precious grace of humility I quoted just now, is at fault here, exhorting as he does the returning penitent still to persist in taking the place of a servant, even after his father has bidden to resume the position of a son. This is that false humility, of which we meet so much, and which often is so mightily extolled, in monkery, but of which we meet nothing in Scripture. It is the truest humility, when bidden to go up higher, to go. It was true humility in Peter to suffer the Lord to wash his feet; as it would have been false humility, as well as disobedience, to have resisted longer than he did (John 13:6–10). It is true humility in the prodigal, at his father's bidding, to accept at once the position of a son.

'But the father said to his servants, Bring forth'—or more correctly, 'Bring forth quickly—the best robe, and put it on him; and put a ring on his hand, and shoes on his feet. He will restore to him a place and a name in his house, as in these words he plainly declares, all these being ornaments, not of the slave, but of the free; all, therefore, speaking of restoration to his former dignity and honor. Or, if we cannot suppose the Roman customs which accompanied the lifting up of a slave to a freeman's rank, to have been familiarly known in Palestine, or alluded to here, yet since the giving of the robe and ring was ever accounted in the East among the highest tokens of favor and honor (Gen. 41:42; 1 Macc. 6:15), these commands would testify to the same.

Few even of those interpreters usually most averse to the tracing of a spiritual meaning in the minuter details of a parable, have been able to resist the temptation here. It has been debated whether 'the best robe,' as in our Translation, or 'the former robe,' that which he wore of old when he walked a son in his father's house, the robe kept for him long, and now restored, will best express the intention of the original. The difference is not important (though our Translation is clearly right)—nor yet whether we say that by the giving of this robe is signified the imputation of the righteousness of Christ, or the restoration of sanctity to the soul. If we see in it his rehabilitation in his baptismal privileges, then both will be included. They who shall 'bring forth the best robe' have been generally interpreted as the ministers of reconciliation; and if we may imagine them as first removing from him the tattered garments, the poor swineherd's rags, which were hanging about him, then Zechariah 3:4 will supply an interesting parallel. Those who stand before the Lord there, will correspond to the servants here; and what they do for the High Priest there, removing his filthy garments from him, and clothing him with a change of raiment, and setting a fair miter on his head, the same will the servants do here for the son; with the difference only that instead of the miter, the appropriate adornment there of the High Priest, the ring and the shoes are here mentioned; and the symbolic act has in each case the same signification; which there is plainly declared, 'Behold, I have caused thine iniquity to pass from thee.' That passage brought to bear on this leaves it most probable that, by this clothing him with the best robe, is especially signified that act of God which, considered on its negative side, is a release from condemnation, a causing of the sinner's iniquity to pass from him,—on its positive side, is an imputation to him of the merits and righteousness of Christ (Is. 61:10).

This explanation for other reasons is preferable, since we have the gift of restoration of the Spirit indicated in the ring with which the returning wanderer is also adorned. In the East, as with us, the ring was often a seal (Esth. 3:10, 12; Jer. 22:24). Here is a point of connection between the giving of the ring and such Scriptures as Eph. 1:13, 14; 2 Cor. 1:22, in which *a sealing* by God's Spirit is spoken of, whereby the faithful are assured, as by an earnest, of a larger inheritance reserved in heaven for them (Gal. 4:6; Rom. 8:23; 2 Cor. 5:5). Neither shall we plant ourselves altogether in another circle of images if we further regard the ring as the pledge of betrothal: 'And I will betroth thee unto Me forever: yea, I will betroth thee unto Me in righteousness, and in judgment, and in lovingkindness, and in mercies, and I will even betroth thee unto Me in faithfulness; and thou shalt know the Lord' (Hos. 2:19, 20). Shoes are also put on his feet, to which corresponds the promise, 'I will strengthen them in the Lord, and they shall walk up and down in his name' (Zech. 10:12). The penitent shall be equipped for holy obedience, having his 'feet shod with the preparation of the Gospel of peace' (Eph. 6:51). No needful strength shall be wanting to him (Deut. 33:25).—'*And bring hither the fatted calf* (Gen. 18:7; 1 Sam. 28:24; Amos 6:4; Mal. 4:2), *and kill it; and let us eat and be merry.*' It creates a confusion of images to go back here to the sacrifice of Christ, which was implicitly contained in the giving of the robe.

That sacrifice, moreover, is not a *consequence* of the sinner's return, as the killing of the fatted calf is the consequence of the prodigal's, but the *ground* which renders such a return possible. Nor should we, I am persuaded, see here any special allusion to the Holy Eucharist, but more generally to the festal joy and rejoicing which is in the heavenly places at the sinner's repentance.

As the shepherd summoned his friends (v. 6), and the woman her neighbors (v. 9), so here the householder his servants, to be sharers in his joy. For the very nature of true joy is, that it *runs over*, longs to impart itself: and if this be true of the joy on earth, how much more of the purer and unselfish joy in heaven. And summoning his servants to rejoice, the father announces to them the grounds of the joy in which they are invited to share. Some might naturally be presumed to make part of the household now, who had not belonged to it at the time of the young man's departure. To them, therefore, it is needful to announce that this wanderer, whom they beheld just now in the swineherd's rags, is no other than a son of the house, and as such to be honored. That there may be no doubt upon this matter, the father solemnly reinstates him in the rights and privileges of a son. 'This my son'—so he names him in the presence of all—'was dead';—for the state of sin is a state of death (1 John 3:14; Matt. 8:22; 1 Tim. 5:6; Eph. 2:1; Col. 2:13), 'and is alive again'; for the life in God is life indeed, is the only true life (John 10:28)—'he was lost, and is found' (1 Pet. 2:25); and since thus the lost was found, and the dead was alive again, 'they began to be merry' (Zeph. 3:17; Cant. 2:4).

At this point the parable, like the two preceding, might have ended. But the mention of 'two sons' at v. 11 has already indicated that this has a wider intention; and, complete as is this earlier part within itself, it shall also form part of another and more complex whole, and derive new beauty from the contrast now to be drawn between the large heart of God and the narrow grudging heart of man. For the bringing out of this contrast the elder son, who hitherto has been named and no more, now appears upon the scene. 'Now his elder son was in the field.' While the younger had been wasting his whole portion in excess abroad, he had been engaged at home, on his father's ground; and now, at the close of one among many toilsome days, is returning home, ignorant of all that had befallen; and only receiving the first hint, when, 'as he came and drew nigh to the house, he heard music and dancing.' It would be alien to the manners and feelings of the East, to suppose the guests themselves engaged in these diversions: they would be but listeners and spectators, the singers and dancers being hired for the occasion. Surprised at these unwonted sounds, *'he called one of the servants, and asked what these things meant.'* With what a fine touch the ungenial character of the man is indicated already. He does not at once go in; he does not take for granted that when his father makes a feast, there is matter worthy of making merry about. But, as one already resolved to mislike what is proceeding, he prefers to remain without, and to learn from a servant the occasion of the joy; or, as he himself significantly puts it, *'what these things meant,'* demanding an explanation, as if they required it. *'And he said unto him, Thy brother is come; and thy father hath killed the fatted calf, because he hath received him safe and sound.'* How delicate again is here the observance of the smaller proprieties of the narrative. The father, in the midst of all his natural joy, is yet full of the moral significance of his son's return—that he has come back another person from what he was when he departed, or while he tarried in that far land. He sees into the deep of his joy, that he is receiving him now, a son indeed, once dead, but now alive, once lost to him and to God, now found alike by both. But the servant deals only with the more external features of the case, with the fact that, after all he has gone through of excess and hardship, his father has received him *'safe and sound.'* Even if he could enter more deeply into the matter, he confines himself with a suitable discretion to that which falls plainly under his own and everyone's eye.

The explanation is not satisfactory to the questioner. The contemplation of his father's joy, of his brother's safety, so far from stirring up any gladness in his heart, moves him rather to displeasure; instead of rushing into his brother's arms, *'he was angry, and would not go in.'* Nor even when his father so bore with him that he *'came out and entreated him,'* would he lay aside his displeasure, but loudly complained of the unequal measure dealt out to him and to his brother, of the bounty bestowed upon his brother's misconduct: *'Lo, these many years do I serve thee, neither transgressed I at any time thy commandment; and yet thou never gavest me a kid* (Gen. 27:9; 38:17; Judg. 15:1), *that I might make merry with my friends.'* The word 'father,' it will be observed, does not escape his lips. And then he invidiously compares this treatment of him with that of his brother; *'But as soon as this thy son,'* he says not 'my brother'—*'was come,'* he says not 'was returned,' as of one who had come back to his own,— *'which hath devoured thy living,'* again invidiously, for in a sense it

was his own—*'with harlots,'* most probably, but only a presumption
on his part, though he may have claimed to read backward the
words of Solomon, 'he that keepeth company with harlots,
spendeth his substance' (Prov. 29:3)—*'thou hast killed for him'* not a
kid merely, but *'the fatted calf,'* the choicest calf in the stall. What
would he have said, had he known all? could he have seen his
brother arrayed in the best robe, and with all his other adornments,
when this which alone he mentions, as it is all which he has learned
from his informant, so fills him with indignation

It is too joyful an occasion for the father to take that just exception which he might at the tone and temper of this remonstrance.
There shall not, if he can help it, be a cloud upon any brow; and instead of answering with severity, he expostulates with the malcon-
tent; shows him the unreasonableness of his complaint; warning
him that he is now, in fact, falling into the very sin which his
brother committed when he said, *'Give me the portion of goods that
falleth to me.'* He too is feeling that he does not truly possess what
he possesses *with* his father, but that he must separate something
off from the common stock, before he can count it properly his
own. The same mischief lies at the root of his speech, as spoke out
more plainly in his brother's; and this the father will make him see:
'Son,' or with a still greater tenderness, *'Child, thou art ever with me,
and all that I have is thine'*; and proceeds to show him the unloving
spirit, out of which his discontent proceeded, and the fitness of the
present joy; *'It was meet that we should make merry, and be glad; for this
thy brother'* (not merely *'my son,'* as he ungraciously had put it, but
'thy brother,' kinned to him, and to whom therefore his *kindness* is
due)—*'was dead, and is alive again, was lost, and is found.'*

With this the parable concludes; nor are we told whether the
discontent of the elder brother yielded to these expostulations or
not. This for us will be mainly determined by the interpretation of
the parable with which we have started. It must be admitted that
those who see in the younger brother the Gentile, and therefore in
the elder the Jew, find it encumbered here with fewer difficulties
than such as deny that in its *primary* purpose it sets forth their relations to God and to one another. These last must look elsewhere
for a solution of difficulties, which resemble closely those we have
already met in the parable of the Laborers in the Vineyard. They indeed resolve themselves into this single one,—Is *their* righteousness, whom the elder brother represents, true or false? An answer
either way has its own perplexity. If true, how reconcile this with

his contumacy towards his father, and his unloving spirit towards his brother? What true believer charges God with injustice and partiality? grudges, and does not rather rejoice, when one who may have wandered more widely than himself, is brought home to the true fold? How, too, reconcile this assumption with the scope of this part of the parable, aimed as it is against the Pharisees, whose righteousness in the main was *not* real, but feigned and hypocritical? But on the other hand, if pressed by these embarrassments, we refuse to see in him any true righteousness at all, in what sense shall we understand his having remained ever with his father, or how does an estimate of his character so entirely unfavorable fall in with his uncontradicted assertion of his own continued obedience, or with the need of approbation and assurances of favor, which he receives from his father's lips

Either determination of the question is encumbered with difficulties of its own; theirs certainly with great, though perhaps not with the greatest, who in the elder brother see the Pharisees, with a righteousness altogether feigned and hypocritical. His assertions concerning his own continued obedience are suffered, they say, to pass unchallenged, because, even granting them true, the case would not be altered, the father arguing with him *e concesso:* 'Be it so, that is not the question now in hand; allowing your obedience to have been unbroken, your works always well-pleasing in my sight, yet ought you in love to rejoice that your brother has returned, and to share in this festal gladness with which he is welcomed home.' But is it not possible, by a middle course, to escape the embarrassments which attend this no less than the opposite scheme of interpretation; namely, that we see in this elder brother a low, but not altogether false, form of legal righteousness? He is one whom the law has kept from gross offenses; he has been occupied, though in a servile spirit, in the works of that law. So, no doubt, had it been with not a few of the Pharisees. Some were hypocrites; but some sincerely, though in much blindness of heart, followers after righteousness (Rom. 10:1, 2). The righteousness indeed was of a low sort, in the strivings after which, being mostly external, they attained to no such acquaintance with the plague of their own hearts, as should render them mild and merciful to others, no such insight into the breadth of that law which they professed to keep, as should thoroughly abase them before God. Such may have been the murmurers here; not therefore utterly to be rejected, nor the good in them utterly denied; but requiring to be shown what was deficient, narrow, and loveless in their service;—to be invited to renounce their servile for a filial spirit, and to enter into the nobler liberties of that Church and kingdom which Christ was establishing upon earth. Hitherto the elder son had been laboring *'in the field,'* but now he is bidden to a festival. They whose work for God had hitherto been servile, the hard taskwork of the law, are invited now to *'come in,'* to enter into the joy of the Lord, the freedom of the Spirit. This part of the parable will then be as much a preaching of the Gospel of the kingdom to the legalist, as its earlier part had been to the gross sinner;—as love to the one spoke there, so love to the other here.

But the elder son's reply (vv. 29, 30) to the father's first invitation shows only too plainly that he whom that son represents is ignorant of the nature of that kingdom to which he is invited. He is looking for certain definite rewards of his obedience, to the getting of something *from* God, in preference to possessing all *in* God. Instead of regarding as his true reward, that he had been ever with his heavenly Father, he rather pleads this as establishing his claim to some further reward. In the father's rejoinder (v. 31), we must be careful to place the emphasis on the right word, for without this the meaning will entirely escape us. It is not, 'Son, *thou* art ever with me,' drawing thus a contrast between him and his brother, who for so long a time had *not* been with his father; but 'Son, thou art ever *with me,'* the emphasis resting on the concluding words. 'What need to talk of other friends? thou art ever with a better than them all, with myself. Why shouldest thou feel hurt that a kid was never given thee, when *all that I have is thine?'* To make the first clause of this rejoinder an honorable recognition of his past obedience, the second a promise that the whole inheritance will devolve on him, is a missing and marring of the whole. Rather in the first lies at once the keenest, and the most loving, rebuke: 'Am not I more to thee than all besides?' in the second the most earnest warning: 'What is mine is thine, if only thou wilt so regard it; what can I do for thee, if fellowship in my things fails to make thee rich?' How wonderfully does that *'All that I have is thine,'* when thus understood, declare to us the true nature of the rewards of the kingdom. In the elder son's esteem, whatever was bestowed on his brother was withdrawn from himself; but in the free kingdom of love one has not less, because another has more; all is possessed by each. The fountain of God's grace is no scanty desert spring, round which thirsty travelers need strive and struggle, muddying the waters with their feet, pushing one another away, lest those waters be drunk up by others before their turn shall arrive; but an inexhaustible river, on whose banks all may stand, and where none need grudge lest, if others drink largely and freely, there will not enough remain for themselves. Not to one, but to each of his true servants and children the Lord can say, *'All that I have is thine.'* If any then is straitened, and counts that he has not enough, he is straitened, as the elder son here, not in God, but in himself, and in his own narrow and grudging heart.

It is easy to perceive why nothing should be told us concerning the success or failure of the father's attempt to remove the sullen dissatisfaction of his son; why, as we read the parable, there seems to us a certain abruptness in the close. This was inevitable, for it was still uncertain whether the Scribes and Pharisees might not be won to repentance; which, though of another kind and for other sins, they needed quite as much as the publicans and harlots. The Lord, not distinctly declaring that the elder son obstinately refused *to the last* to enter in, or that he has finally excluded for his contumacy, intimated to these, that the kingdom of God was not yet closed against them; that they too, as well as the publicans and sinners, were invited and summoned to leave their low, poor, and formal service, 'the elements of the world' (Gal. 4:3), and to enter into the glorious liberties of the kingdom of grace; they too guests, if they would esteem themselves such, at that marriage festival where He should manifest his glory, changing the weak and watery elements of that old dispensation into the generous and gladdening wine of the new (John 2:1–11).

For all this, it is impossible to read the parable without an ominous presentiment that the elder brother *does* refuse to the end to go in. Such refusal there was, and on the largest scale, when the Jews in the apostolic age would take no part in the great festival of reconciliation which celebrated the reception of the Gentile world into the Church of the redeemed; nay rather, with all their might set themselves against that reception (1 Thess. 2:14). What a mournful commentary is the whole book of Acts on these words, *'he would not go in'*; *'would not,'* because his brother was received so freely and with such tokens of joy (13:45; 14:19; 17:5, 13; 18:12; 22:21–23). If that younger brother had been submitted first to a painful apprenticeship of the law, if he too had been sent to work *'in the field,'* it might have been another thing (Acts 15:1); but that he should be thus made free of the kingdom, and brought into the festival at once,—this was more than the elder could endure. Numbers stayed openly and sullenly without. Others, as the Ebionites, only pretended to go in, or went in under a mistaken assumption that it should be as in their narrow hearts they desired (Gal. 2:12–14), and, discovering their mistake, presently withdrew themselves again. Yet while all this was then the fact, it behooves us of the Gentile Church never to forget that all the conditions of the parable will be reversed at the end of the present dispensation, and the parts so shifted, that it is *we* who shall at that day be in danger of playing the elder brother's part, and of falling into his sin. And this we shall do, if we repine at the largeness of the grace bestowed upon the Jew, once the son ever with his Father, but now the Prodigal feeding upon husks, far away from his heavenly Father's house (Hos. 3:4, 5; Rom. 11).

25.

The Unjust Steward

Luke 16:1–9

No one, who has seriously considered, will underrate the difficulties of this parable,—difficulties which Cajetan found so insuperable that he gave up the matter in despair, affirming a solution of them impossible. It is nothing wonderful that it should have been the subject of manifold, and those the most singularly diverse, interpretations. I shall make not attempt to render a complete account of all of these; such would be an endless task; but, as I go through the parable, shall note what parts of it those interpreters, who have best right to be heard, have considered its key-words, and the meanings which they have made the whole to render up; I shall at the same time briefly note what seem the weak and unsatisfactory points in those explanations which I reject. For myself, I will say at once that very many of its interpreters seem to me (if one may use a familiar expression) to have overrun their game. I am persuaded that was have here simply a parable of Christian prudence,—Christ exhorting us to use the world and the world's goods, so to speak, against the world, and for God.

Having brought the parable of the Prodigal Son to a close, He did not break off the conversation, but,—probably after a short pause allowed, that his words might sink deeper into the hearts of his hearers,—resumed; not now, however, addressing the gainsayers anymore, but those who heard Him gladly, *'his disciples,'* as we are (v. 1) expressly told. We must not restrict this term to the Twelve (see Luke 6:13); but as little make it embrace the whole multitude, hanging loosely on the Lord, although up to a certain point well affected to Him. By *'his disciples'* we understand rather all whom his word had found in the deep of their spirit, and who, having left the world's service, had taken service with Him. To these the parable was addressed; for them too it was meant; since it is little probable that, as some explain, it was spoken *to* them, but *at* the Pharisees. These last, it is true, were *also hearers* of the Lord's words (v. 14), but the very mention of them as such forbids their being those to whom it was primarily addressed. Christ may have intended,— most probably did intend,—some of his shafts to glance off upon them, at whom yet they were not originally aimed. It will prove important, in relation to at least one explanation of the parable, that we keep in mind for whom first of all it was intended.

'*There was a certain rich man, which had a steward,*'—not a land-bailiff merely, but a ruler over all his goods, such as was Eliezer in the house of Abraham (Gen. 24:2–12), and Joseph in the house of Potiphar (Gen. 39:4). '*And the same was accused unto him, that he had wasted his goods*'; or rather, '*that he was wasting his goods*'; for it is no past scattering, but a present, which is laid to his charge; and this, as we may certainly conclude, not through mere negligence, but himself deriving an unrighteous gain from the loss and wrong which his master's property suffered under his hands. This of the lord needing that his steward's misconduct should reach his ears through a third party, belongs to the earthly setting forth of the truth: yet finds its parallel, Gen. 18:30, 31). There is no warrant whatever for assuming, as some have done, that the steward was calumniously accused; no hint of this conveyed in the word which the Lord employs. Satan is the *accuser* of the brethren (Rev. 12:9), called therefore by this name; but the things of which he accuses them may be only too true. Certain Chaldeans *accused* the Three Children, malignantly indeed, but not falsely, of refusing to worship the golden image (Dan. 3:8); Daniel himself is *accused* (still the same word in the Septuagint as here), and not calumniously, of having knelt and prayed to his God, in defiance of the edict of the king (Dan. 6:24). Those therefore who would clear altogether or in part the character of the steward can derive no assistance here. Indeed his own words (v. 3) contain an implicit acknowledgment of his guilt; he who is so dishonest now will scarcely have been honest before; and assuredly we shall do him no wrong in taking for granted that the accusation, brought against him very probably by some enemy and from malicious motives, was yet founded in truth.

Hereupon his lord '*calleth him, and said unto him, How is it that I hear this of thee?'* or perhaps the question would be better, *'What is this that I hear of thee?'* This is not examination, but rather the expostulation of indignant surprise,—*'of thee,* whom I had trusted so far, to whom I had committed so much.' And then, the man not so much as attempting a defense, his dismissal follows: *'Give an account of thy stewardship; for thou mayest be no longer steward.'* Those who, like Anselm, see in the parable the history of the rise, progress, and fruits of repentance, lay much stress upon this remonstrance, *'How is it that I hear this of thee?'* It is for them the voice of God speaking to the sinner, bringing home to his conscience that he has had a stewardship, and has been abusing it; the threat, *'thou mayest be no longer steward,'* being in like manner a bringing home to him, by sickness or by some other means, that he will soon be removed from his earthly stewardship, and have to render an account. The man feels that he cannot answer God one thing in a thousand; that, once removed hence, there will be no help for him anywhere; he cannot dig, for the night will have come, in which no man can work; and he will be ashamed to beg for that mercy, which he knows will then be refused. Consistently with this view, they see in the lowering of the bills, not a further and crowning act of unrighteousness, but the first act of his righteousness, the dealing of one who will now, while he has time, lay out the things in his power with no merely selfish aims, but for the good of others, will scatter for God rather than for himself, seek to lay up in heaven and not on earth. The dishonesty they get over, either by giving this lowering of the bills altogether a mystical meaning, and so refusing to contemplate it in the letter at all, or in a way presently to be noticed. He is still called, they say, the *'unjust steward'* (v. 8), not because he continues such; but because of his former unrighteousness; and for the encouragement of penitents, who are thus reminded that, unrighteous and ungodly man as he had been before-time, he obtained now praise and approval from his lord. He retained the title, as Matthew the Apostle retained that of 'the publican' (Matt. 10:3), in perpetual remembrance of the grace of God which had found him in that ignoble employment, and raised him to so high a dignity; as Zenas is still *'the lawyer'* (Titus 3:13); Rahab *'the harlot'* (Heb. 11:31); Simon *'the leper'* (Matt. 26:6); not that such they were when receiving these designations, but that such they formerly had been. To all this it may be replied that there is nothing in the man's counsels with himself that marks the smallest change of mind for the better, no acknowledgment of a trust abused, no desire expressed henceforward to be found faithful, but only an utterance of selfish anxiety concerning his future lot, of fear lest poverty and distress may come upon him; and the explanation from analogous instances, however ingenious, of his being still characterized (v. 8) as the *'unjust'* steward, is quite unsatisfactory; neither 'publican' nor 'lawyer' conveyed of necessity a sentence of moral reprobation.

But now follow his counsels with himself; and first his implicit acknowledgment that the investigation of his accounts can only have one issue, and that his definitive dismissal. Had he felt that he could clear himself, he might have hoped that a hasty word uttered by his master might be recalled; but he knows too well that any such clearing is impossible. There is nothing but hopeless penury before him. *What shall I do?* he exclaims. For the same phrase compare Luke 12:17; 20:13; though in curiously different connections. He had scattered his lord's goods, squandered them in reckless profusion on himself; but he had made no purse against that evil day which now all of a sudden had come upon him. His past softness of life has unfitted him for labor; *'I cannot dig';* his pride forbids him to sue for alms; 'better is it,' as the Son of Sirach had long ago exclaimed, 'to die than to beg' (Ecclus. 40:28): *'to beg I am ashamed.'* Yet this sense of utter helplessness and hopelessness endures not long. He knows what he will do; and has rapidly conceived a plan whereby to make provision against that time of need and destitution which is now so near at hand. If his determination is not honest, it is at any rate promptly taken; and this—that he was not brought to a nonplus, but at once devised a way of escape from his distresses—is a part of the skill for which he gets credit: *'I am resolved what to do, that when I am put out of the stewardship, they may receive me into their houses,'* as one from whom they have received kindnesses, and who, therefore, may trust to find hospitable entertainment among them,—a miserable prospect, as the Son of Sirach declares (29:22–28; 40:29); yet better than utter destitution and want.

'So he called every one of his lord's debtors unto him.' Hereupon follows the collusive and fraudulent arrangement between him and them. The two whose cases are instanced, and who must be regarded as representatives of many more,—of those *'all'* whom we just heard of, in the same way as elsewhere only *three* servants are named out of ten (Luke 19:13),—owed to the householder, the one *'a hundred measures of oil,'* and the other *'a hundred measures of wheat.'*

It is not likely that these were tenants who paid their rents in kind, which rents were now by the steward lowered, and the leases or agreements tampered with: the name *'debtor'* seems to point another way. Again, the enormous amount of the oil and the wheat, both costly articles (Prov. 21:17), makes it not less unlikely that they were poorer neighbors or dependents, whom the rich householder had supplied with means of living in the shape of food,—not, however, as a gift, but as a loan, taking from them an acknowledgment, and looking to be repaid, when they had the ability. Rather we might assume the foregoing transactions by which these men came into the relation of his debtors, to have been these,—that he, having large possessions, and therefore large incomings from the fruits of the earth, had sold, through his steward, a portion of such upon credit to these debtors,—merchants, or other factors,—who had not as yet made their payments. They had given, however, their *'bills'* or notes of hand, acknowledging the amount in which they were indebted to him. These, which had remained in the steward's keeping, he now returns to them,—*'Take thy bill,'*—bidding them to alter them, or to substitute others in their room, in which they confess themselves to have received much smaller amounts of oil and wheat than was actually the case, and consequently to be so much less in the rich man's debt than they truly were. To one debtor he remits half, to another the fifth, of his debt; by these different proportions teaching us, say those who justify his conduct, and even some who do not, that charity should be no blind profuseness, exhibited without respect of the needs, greater or smaller, of those who are its objects, but exercised ever with consideration and discretion,—a sowing of the seed by the hand, and not an emptying of it out of the sack's mouth.

In this lowering of the bills, Vitringa finds the key of the parable; his interpretation deserving to be recorded, were it only for its exceeding ingenuity. The rich man is God, the steward the ecclesiastical leaders of the Jewish people, to whom was committed a dispensation of the mysteries of the kingdom. These were accused by the prophets, as by Ezekiel (34:2), by Malachi (2:8), and lastly by Christ Himself (Matt. 2:3), that they abused their stewardship, used the powers committed to them, not for the glory of God, but for purposes of self-exaltation and honor,—that they *'wasted his goods.'* They feel the justice of this accusation, that they are not in their Lord's grace, and only outwardly belong to his kingdom. Therefore they now seek to make themselves friends of others, of the debtors of their Lord, of sinful men; acting as though they still possessed authority in the things of his kingdom. And the device by which they seek to win these friends is by lowering the standard of right-eousness and obedience, inventing convenient glosses for the evading of the strictness of God's law, allowing men to say, 'It is a gift' (Matt. 15:5), suffering them to put away their wives on any slight excuse (Luke 16:18), and by various devices, 'indulgences' in the truest sense of the word, making slack the law of God (Matt. 23:16); thus obtaining for themselves favor and an interest with men, and, however God's grace was withdrawn from them, still keeping their hold on the people, and retaining their advantages, their honors, and their peculiar privileges. In the casuistry of the Jesuits, as denounced by Pascal, we see a precisely similar attempt. This interpretation has one attraction, that it gives a distinct mean-ing to the lowering of the bills,—'Write fifty, write fourscore';—which very few others do. The moral will then be no other than is com-monly and rightly drawn from the parable: 'Be prudent as are these children of the present world, but provide for yourselves not tem-porary friends, but everlasting habitations. They use heavenly things for earthly objects and aims; but do you reverse all this, and show how earthly things may be used for heavenly.'

With this interpretation very nearly agrees that of the writer of an elaborate article in a modern German Review. He too conceives the parable intended for the Scribes and Pharisees—but to contain *counsel* for them,—the unjust steward being set forth for them to copy; while Vitringa found their *condemnation* in it. They were the ministers of a dispensation now drawing to a close; and when in its room the kingdom of Christ was set up, then their much-abused stewardship would be withdrawn from them. The parable exhorts them, in that brief period which should intervene between the an-nouncement and actual execution of this purpose of God's, to cul-tivate such a spirit as would alone give them an entrance 'into *everlasting habitations,'*—the spirit, that is, which they so much lacked, of mildness and love and meekness toward all men, their fellow-sinners. This spirit, and the works which it would prompt, he affirms, are fitly set forth under the image of a remission of debts—and those, debts due to another, since it is against God that primarily every sin is committed. Such a spirit as this flows out of the recognition of our own guilt, which recognition the writer finds in the absence on the steward's part of all attempts to justify or ex-cuse himself. The same temper which would prompt them to these works of love and grace would fit them also for an entrance into the *'everlasting habitations,'* the coming kingdom, which, unlike that dispensation now ready to vanish away, should never be moved. But how, it may be urged, shall this interpretation be reconciled with the words, *'He said also unto his disciples,'* with which the Evangelist introduced the parable? It will then plainly be addressed not to them, but to the Scribes and Pharisees.

With these new acts of unrighteousness this child of the present world filled up the short interval between his threatened and his actual dismissal from office. There is no hint that he attempted to conceal these fraudulent transactions, or that he called his lord's debtors together *secretly,*—whether it was that he trusted they would keep counsel, being held together by a common interest and by the bands of a common iniquity,—or that he thus falsified the accounts, careless whether the transaction were blown abroad or not; being now a desperate man, with no character to lose; at the same time confident that there would be no redress for his lord, when the written documents testified against him. More probably the thing was thus done openly and in the face of day, the arrangement being one which, from some cause or other, when once completed, could not be overturned. Were a secret transaction intended, the lord's discovery of the fraud would hardly be passed over; and the steward would scarcely obtain for a contrivance so clumsy that it was presently detected, even the limited praise which actually he does obtain. Least of all would he obtain such praise, if it depended merely on the forbearance of his master, in the case of discovery, which the event will have proved must have been probable from the beginning, whether the arrangement should stand good or not. Such forbearance could not have been counted on, even though the words of the lord should lead us in the present instance to assume that he did allow the steward to reap the benefits of his dishonest scheming.

But whether the transaction was clandestine or not, that it was fraudulent seems beyond a doubt. Such, on the fact of it, it is; and all attempts to mitigate or explain away its dishonesty are hopeless. It may be, and by some has been said, that this dishonesty is not of the essence of the parable, but an inconvenience arising from the inadequacy of earthly relationships to set forth divine. They must fail somewhere, and this is the weak side of the earthly relation between a steward and his lord, rendering it an imperfect type of the relation existing between men and God,—that in this latter relation, to use Hammond's words, 'the man hath liberty to use the wealth put into his hands so as may be most (not only for his master's, but also) for his own advantage, namely, to his endless reward in heaven, which, though it were an injustice and falseness in a servant here on earth, who is altogether to consider his master's profit, not his own, yet it is our duty and that which by the will and command of God we are obliged to do, in the execution of that steward's office which the rich man holds under God: and is the only thing commended to us in this parable; which is so far from denominating him that makes this advantage of the treasure committed to him an unjust or unrighteous steward in the application, that it denominates him *faithful* (πιστός) in the latter part of the parable, and him only *false* (ἄδικος) that doth it not.' In worldly things there is not, and there never can be, such absolute identity of interests between a master and a servant, that a servant, looking wholly to his own interests, would at the same time forward in the best manner his lord's. But our interests as servants of a heavenly Lord, that is, our true interests, absolutely coincide in all things with his; so that when we administer the things committed to us for Him, then we lay them out also for ourselves, and when for ourselves, for our lasting and eternal gain, then also for Him.

'*And the lord commended the unjust steward, because he had done wisely.*' It is the lord *of the steward*, twice before in the parable called by this name (vv. 3, 5), who is here intended, and not Christ *our* Lord, who does not speak directly in his own person still v. 9, the intermediate verse being the point of transition from the parable to the direct exhortation. The attempt to substitute '*cunningly*' for '*wisely,*' and so by limiting and lowering the commendation given, to evade the moral difficulty of the passage, cannot altogether be justified. '*Wisely*' is not the happiest rendering, since wisdom is never in Scripture dissociated from moral goodness. But if more commendation is implied in '*wisely*' than the original warrants, in '*cunningly*' there is less; '*prudently*' would best represent the original, and so in Wiclif's Version it stood, though the word has disappeared from all our subsequent Versions.

But concerning the praise itself, which cannot be explained away as mere admiration of the man's cunning, it is true that none but a malignant, such as the apostate Julian, would make here a charge against the morality of the Scripture; or pretend, as he does, to believe that Jesus meant to commend an unrighteous action, and to propose it, *in its unrighteousness*, as a model for imitation. Still the praise has something perplexing in it; though more from the liability of the passage to abuse, unguarded as at first sight it appears, though it is not really so (for see v. 11), than from its not being capable of a fair explanation. The explanation is this: the man's deed has two aspects; one, that of its dishonesty, upon which it is most blame-worthy; the other, of its prudence, its foresight, upon which, if not particularly praiseworthy, it yet offers a sufficient *analogon* to a Christian virtue,—one which *should be* abundantly, but *is* only too weakly, found in most followers of Christ,—to draw from it an exhortation and rebuke to these; just as any other deeds of bold bad men have a side, that namely of their boldness and decision, on which they rebuke the doings of the weak and vacillating good. There are 'martyrs of the devil,' who put to shame the saints of God; and running, as they do, with more alacrity to death than these to life, may be proposed to them for their emulation. We may disentangle a bad man's energy from his ambition; and, contemplating them apart, may praise the one, and condemn the other. Exactly so our Lord disengages here the steward's dishonesty from his foresight: the one can have only his earnest rebuke; the other may be usefully extolled for the provoking of his people to a like prudence; which yet should be at once a holy prudence, and a prudence employed about things of far higher and more lasting importance.

The next verse fully bears out this view of the Lord's meaning: *'For the children of this world are in their generation wiser than the children of light.'* We must find the same fault with *'wiser'* here as with *'wisely'* of the verse preceding; as *'prudently'* should replace it there, so *'more prudent'* here. *'The children of this world'* are the Psalmist's 'men of the earth,' those whose portion is here, and who look not beyond; who, born of the world's spirit, order their lives by the world's rule. The phrase occurs only here and at Luke 20:34; *'children of light'* he has in common with St. John (12:36) and St. Paul (1 Thess. 5:5; Eph. 5:8). The faithful are called by this rather than any other of the many names of honor which are theirs; for thus their deeds, which are deeds of light, done in truth and sincerity, even as they are themselves sons of the day and of the light, are contrasted with the 'works of darkness,' the 'hidden things of dishonesty,' wrought by the children of this present world, and of which he who plays the foremost part here has just given a notable specimen.

The declaration itself has been differently understood, according as the sentence has been differently completed. Some complete it thus: *'The children of this world are wiser in their generation,'* namely in worldly things, *'than the children of light'* are in those same worldly things; that is, Earthly men are more prudent than spiritual men in earthly matters; these earthly are their element, their world; they are more at home in them; they give more thought, bestow more labor upon them, and therefore succeed in them better: though it be true that this is only as owls see better than eagles—in the dark. But it is hard to perceive how a general statement of this kind bears on the parable, which most are agreed urges upon the Christian, not prudence in earthly things by the example of the worldling's prudence in the same, but rather, by the example of the worldling's prudence in these things, urges upon him prudence in heavenly.

Others, then, are nearer the truth, who complete the sentence thus: *'The children of this world are wiser in their generation'* (in worldly matters) *'than the children of light'* in theirs, that is, in heavenly matters; *'the children of light'* being thus rebuked that they give not half the pains to win heaven which *'the children of this world'* do to win earth,—that they are less provident in heavenly things than those are in earthly,—that the world is better served by its servants than God is by His. If however we would perfectly seize the meaning, we must see in the words, *'in their generation,'*—or rather, *'toward,'* or *'for their own generation'*—an allusion, often missed, to the debtors in the parable. They, the ready accomplices in the steward's fraud, showed themselves men of the same generation as he was; they were all of one race, children of the ungodly world; and the Lord's declaration is, that the men of this world make their intercourse with one another more profitable,—obtain more from it,— manage it better for their interests, such as those are, than do the children of light *their* intercourse with each other. For what opportunities, He would imply, are missed by these last, by those among them to whom a share of the earthly mammon is entrusted,—what opportunities of laying up treasure in heaven, of making to themselves friends for the time to come by showing love to the poor saints, or generally of doing offices of kindness to the household of faith, to those of the same generation as themselves,—whom, notwithstanding this affinity, they yet make not, to the extent they might, receivers of benefits, to be returned hereafter a hundredfold into their own bosoms.

His disciples shall not so miss their opportunities; but, after the example of him who bound to himself by benefits the men of his own generation, bind those to themselves who, like themselves, were *'children of light:'* *'And I say unto you, Make to yourselves friends of the mammon of unrighteousness, that when ye fail, they may receive you into everlasting habitations.'* This *'mammon of unrighteousness' 'of which,'* or more strictly, *'out of which,'* they shall make themselves friends, has been sometimes explained as wealth unjustly gotten, by fraud or by violence, 'treasures of wickedness' (Prov. 10:2). The words so interpreted would be easily open to abuse, as though a man might compound with his conscience and with God, and by giving some small portion of alms out of unjustly acquired wealth make the rest clean unto him. But plainly the first command to the possessor of such would be to restore it to its rightful owners, as Zacchaeus, on his conversion, was resolved to do (Luke 19:8); for 'he that sacrificeth of a thing wrongfully gotten, his offering is ridiculous' (Ecclus. 34:18; 35:12); and out of such there could never be offered acceptable alms to Him who has said, 'I hate robbery for burnt-offering.' Only when this restoration is impossible, as must often happen, could it be lawfully bestowed upon the poor. Others understand by *'mammon of unrighteousness'* not so much wealth by the present possessor unjustly acquired, as wealth which in a world such as this can hardly have been gotten together without sin somewhere—without something of the defilement of that world from which it was gathered clinging to it;—if not sin in the present possessor, yet in some of those, nearer or more remote, from or through whom he received it: which being so, he that inherits the wealth inherits also the obligation to make good the wrongs committed in the getting of it together. But the comparison with v. 12, where *'unrighteous mammon,'* a phrase equivalent to *'mammon of unrighteousness,'* is set against *'true riches'*—these *'true'* being evidently heavenly enduring goods, such as neither fade nor fail,—makes far more likely that *'mammon of unrighteousness'* is uncertain, unstable mammon, one man's today, and another's tomorrow; which if a man trust in, he is trusting in a lie, in that which sooner or later will betray his confidence (1 Tim. 6:17), which he must leave (Eccl. 2:18, 19; 5:15), or which must leave him (Prov. 23:5). And *'mammon of unrighteousness'* it may in a deeper sense be justly called, seeing that in all wealth a principle of evil is implied; for in a perfect state of society, in a realized kingdom of God upon earth, there would be no such thing as property belonging to one man more than another. In the moment of the Church's first love, when that kingdom was for an instant realized, 'all that believed were together, and had all things common' (Acts 4:32–35); and this existence of property has ever been so strongly felt as a witness for the selfishness of man, that in all ideas of a perfect common-wealth,—which, if perfect, must of course be a Church and a State in one,—from Plato's down to the Socialists', this of the community of goods has entered as a necessary condition. And thus, however the possessor of the wealth, or those who transmitted it to him, may have fairly acquired it, yet it is not less this *'unrighteous* mam-mon,' witnessing in its very existence as one man's, and not every man's, for the selfishness of man,—for the absence of that highest love, which would make each man feel that whatever was his, was everyone's, and would leave no room for a *mine* and *thine* in the world. With all this, we must never forget that the attempt prema-turely to realize this or any other little fragment of the kingdom of God, apart from the rest,—the corruption and evil of man's heart remaining unremoved, and being either overlooked or denied,—has ever proved a fruitful source of some of the worst mischiefs in the world.

The words, *'that when ye fail,'* are an euphemistic way of saying, 'that when ye die.' But indeed there is another reading, *'that when it fails,'* that is, the mammon (cf. Luke 12:33); which is to be pre-ferred. Many have shrunk from referring what follows, *'they may receive you,'* to the friends who shall have been secured by aid of the unrighteous mammon; such reference seeming to them to ascribe too much to men and to their intercession, to imply a right on their parts who had received the benefits, to introduce their benefactors *'into everlasting habitations,'* and so to be trenching on the preroga-tive which is God's alone. For some who have entertained these misgivings *'they'* are the angels, as we find angels (v. 22) carrying Lazarus into Abraham's bosom; others understand that it is God and Christ who will *'receive';* while for others the phrase is imper-sonal (cf. 12:11, 20; 23:31); *'they may receive you'* being equivalent to *'you may be received.'* But if we regard this verse, not as containing an isolated doctrine, but in vital connection with the parable of which it gives the moral, we shall at once perceive why this lan-guage is used, and the justification of its use. The reference to the debtors is plain; they, being made friends, were to receive the de-posed steward into temporary habitations; and the phrase before us is an echo from the parable, the employment of which throws back light upon it, and at once fixes attention on, and explains its most important part. It is idle to press the words further, and against all analogy of faith to assert, on the strength of this single phrase, that even with God's glorified saints, with any except Himself, will reside power of their own to admit into the kingdom of heaven; but idle also to affirm that *'they may receive you,'* in the second clause of the sentence, can refer to any other but the friends mentioned in the first—which no one, unless alarmed by the consequences which others might draw from the words, could for an instant call in question. The true parallel to this statement, at once explaining and guarding it, is evidently Matt. 25:34–40. The heavenly habitations, being *'everlasting,'* are tacitly contrasted with the temporary shelter which was all that the steward, the child of the present world, procured for himself with all his plotting and planning, his cunning and dishonesty,—also, it may be, with the temporary stewardship which every man exercises on earth, from which it is not long before he fails and is removed:—how important therefore, the word will imply, that he should make sure his entrance into a kingdom that shall not be moved (cf. Eccl. 11:2).

In the verses which follow (10–13), and which stand in vital coherence with the parable, it is very noteworthy that not prudence, but fidelity, in the dispensation of things earthly is urged; putting far away any such perversion of the parable, as that the unfaithfulness of the steward could have found a shadow of favor with the Lord. The things earthly in which men may show their faithfulness and their fitness to be entrusted with a higher stewardship, are slightingly called *'that which is least,'* as compared with those spiritual gifts and talents which are *'much'*; they are termed *'unrighteous,'* or deceitful *'mammon,'* as set over against the heavenly riches of faith and love, which are *'true'* and durable *'riches'*; they are *'that which is another man's,'* by comparison with the heavenly goods, which when possessed are our own, a part of our very selves, being akin to our truest life. Thus the Lord at once casts a slight on the things worldly and temporal, and at the same time magnifies the importance of a right administration of them; since in the dispensing of these,—which He declares to be the least,—to be false and with no intrinsic worth,—to be alien from man's essential being, He at the same time announces that a man may prove his fidelity, show what is in him, and whether he can fitly be entrusted with a stewardship of durable riches in the kingdom of God. And in v. 13 He further states what the fidelity is, which in this stewardship is required: it is a choosing of God instead of mammon for our Lord. For in this world we are as servants from whom two masters are claiming allegiance: one is God, man's rightful lord; the other is this unrighteous mammon, given to be our servant, to be wielded by us in God's interests, and in itself to be considered as slight, transient, and another's; but which, in a sinful world, has erected itself into a lord, and now challenges obedience from us. This if we yield, we shall not any longer lay out according to God's will that which He lent us to be merely a thing beneath us, but which we shall then have allowed a will and voice of its own, and to speak to us in accents of command. We shall not any longer be stewards and servants of God; for that usurping lord has a will so different from his will, gives commands so opposite to his commands, that occasions must speedily arise when one will have to be despised and disobeyed, if the other be honored and served; God, for instance, will command a scattering, when mammon will urge to a further heaping and gathering; God will require a laying out upon others, when mammon, or the world, a laying out upon ourselves. Therefore, these two lords having characters so different, and giving commands so contrary, it will be impossible to reconcile their services (James 4:4); one must be despised, if the other is held to; the only faithfulness to the one is to break with the other: 'Ye cannot serve God and mammon.' Such appears to me the connection between v. 13 and the two which go before, and between all these and the parable of which they are intended to supply the moral.

26.
The Rich Man and Lazarus
Luke 16:19–31

The first question in the treating of the Scripture which is now before us is this, namely, Have we here a parable at all? Is it not of the essence of such that in it things heavenly should be set forth by aid of things earthly, that there should be, so to speak, an earthly rind and a heavenly fruit, and that we should pierce through the one to arrive at the other? But in this pregnant little history, as commonly, and I believe rightly, understood, there is nothing of the kind; and assuredly in strictness it does not fulfill the conditions of a parable. As much has been acknowledged by many in old times as in new. There is indeed an interpretation of this passage, which has found a certain amount of favor, and which, if accepted, would restore it to its rights as a parable, but one which even for the sake of this gain I am not disposed to adopt. To this I shall again recur before leaving this Scripture altogether. Setting for the present the question of parable or no-parable aside, and not further calling in question this title which is commonly given to it, I proceed to its nearer consideration. It is addressed to the Pharisees (see vv. 14, 15), and thus a difficulty presents itself at once. 'Covetous' no doubt these were; the Evangelist expressly declares as much (v. 14; cf. Matt. 23:14), but prodigal excess in living, like that of the rich man in the parable, is nowhere, in sacred history or profane, imputed to them. So far from this, their manner of life was sparing and austere; many among them were rigid ascetics. Our Lord Himself allowed all this; his model Pharisee fasts twice in the week (Luke 18:12). Their sins were in the main spiritual; and what other sins they had were compatible with a high reputation for spirituality, which covetousness is, but not a profuse

591

self-indulgence and an eminently luxurious living. Mosheim feels the difficulty so strongly, that he supposes the parable directed against the Sadducees, of whose selfish indulgence of themselves, and hard-hearted contempt for the needs of others (for they had wrought into their very religious scheme that poverty was a crime, or at all events an evidence of the displeasure of God), we shall then, he says, have an exact description. But the parable cannot be for them; there is no mention of Sadducees present, neither can there be any change between vv. 18 and 19 in the persons addressed; as is still more evident in the original than in our Version.

We may, perhaps, explain the matter thus. While it is quite true that covetousness was the sin of the Pharisees, and not prodigal excess, an undue gathering rather than an undue scattering, yet hoarding and squandering so entirely grow out of the same evil root, being alike the fruits of unbelief in God and in God's word, of trust in the creature more than in the Creator, are so equally a serving of mammon (though the form of the service may be different), that when the Lord would rebuke their sin, which was the trust in the world rather than in the living God, there was nothing to hinder his taking an example from a sin opposite in appearance to theirs,—but springing out of exactly the same evil condition of heart,—by which to condemn them. For we must never forget that the primary intention of the parable is not to teach the dreadful consequences which will follow on the abuse of wealth and on the hard-hearted contempt of the poor,—this only subordinately,—but the fearful consequences of unbelief, of a heart set on this world, and refusing to give credence to that invisible world here known only to faith, until by a miserable and too late experience the existence of such has been discovered. The sin of Dives in its root is unbelief: hard-hearted contempt of the poor, luxurious squandering on self, are only the forms which his sin assumes. The seat of the disease is within; these are but the running sores which witness for the inward plague. He who believes not in an invisible world of righteousness and truth and spiritual joy, must place his hope in things which he sees, which he can handle, and taste, and smell. It is not of the essence of the matter, whether he hoards or squanders: in either case he puts his trust in the world. He who believes not in a God delighting in mercy and loving-kindness, rewarding the merciful, punishing the unmerciful, will soon come to shut up his bowels of compassion from his brethren, whether that so he may put more money in his chest, or have more to spend upon his lusts.

This was the sin of Dives, and source of all his other sins, that he believed not in this higher world which is apprehended by faith,— a world not merely beyond the grave,—but a kingdom of truth and love existing even in the midst of the cruel and selfish world; and this too was the sin of the worldly-minded Pharisees: and his punishment was, that he made discovery of that truer state of things only when the share in it, once within his reach, was irrecoverably gone. That his sin at the root is unbelief shows itself again in his supposing that his brethren would give heed to a ghost, while they refused to give heed to the sure word of God, to *'Moses and the prophets.'* For it is of the very character of unbelief, to yield to portents and prodigies that credence which it refuses to God and his truth. Caligula, who mocked at the existence of the gods, would hide himself under a bed when it thundered; superstition and unbelief being as twin births of the corrupt heart of man, and of the number of those extremes, whose nature it is to meet. We must ever keep in mind that this, the rebuke of unbelief, is the main intention of the parable; for if we conceive its primary purpose to warn against the abuse of riches, it will neither satisfactorily cohere with the discourse in which it is found, nor will it possess that unity of purpose, which so remarkably distinguishes the parables of our Lord: it will divide itself into two parts, only slightly linked together,—having not a single but a double point. But when we contemplate unbelief as the essence of the rich man's sin, his hard-heartedness towards others, with his prodigality towards himself, being only forms of its manifestation, we shall then at once admire the perfect unity of all parts of the parable, the intimate connection of the conversation with Abraham in the later part, with the luxurious living of the earlier.

'There was a certain rich man, which was clothed in purple and fine linen, and fared sumptuously everyday.' The *'purple and fine linen'* are named often together (Esth. 1:6; Rev. 18:12; Prov. 31:22); both being in highest esteem, and the combination of colors which they offered, blue and white, greatly prized. The extreme costliness of the true sea-purple of antiquity is well known. It was the royal hue; and the purple garment then, as now, a royal gift (Esth. 8:15; Dan. 5:7; 1 Macc. 10:20; 11:58; 14:43); with it too the heathen idols were clothed (Jer. 10:9); there was as much, therefore, of pride as of luxury in its use. The byssus, or *'fine linen,'* was hardly in less price or esteem. It is with a vesture of this that Pharaoh arrays Joseph (Gen. 41:42); the coat and the miter of the High Priest are of the same (Ex.

28:39); even as the wife of the Lamb and the armies of heaven are said to be clothed in white linen (Rev. 19:8, 14). All then of rarest and costliest he freely bestowed upon himself. Nor was it on some high days only that he so arrayed himself and feasted. The *'purple and fine linen'* were his ordinary apparel, the sumptuous fare his everyday's entertainment. Yet with all this, as we cannot be too often reminded, he is not accused of any breath of the law,—not, like those rich men by St. James (vv. 1–6), of any flagrant crimes. 'Jesus said not, a calumniator; He said not, an oppressor of the poor; He said not, a robber of other men's goods, nor a receiver of such, nor a false accuser; He said not, a spoiler of orphans, a persecutor of widows: nothing of these. But what did He say?—*"There was a certain rich man."* And what was his crime?—a lazar lying at his gate, and lying unrelieved.' Nor is he,—though sometimes so called, as in the heading of the chapter in our Bibles,—'a glutton.' To regard him as this, as a 'Sir Epicure Mammon,' serves only to turn the edge of the parable. He was one of whom all may have spoken well; of whom none could say worse than that he was content to dwell at ease, would fain put far from himself all things painful to the flesh, and surround himself with all things pleasant.—His name Christ has not told us, but the poor man's only: 'Seems He not to you,' asks Augustine, 'to have been reading from that book where He found the name of the poor man written, but found not the name of the rich; for that book is the book of life?' 'Jesus,' says Cajetan, 'of a purpose named the beggar, but the rich man He designated merely as *"a certain man,"* so to testify that the spiritual order of things is contrary to the worldly. In the world, the names of the rich are known, and when they are talked of, they are designated by their names; but the names of the poor are either not known, or, if known, are counted unworthy to be particularly noted.'

'And there was a certain beggar named Lazarus, which was laid at his gate, full of sores, and desiring to be fed with the crumbs which fell from the rich man's table.' In the porch or vestibule of the rich man's palace, whose name, though well known on earth, was unrecognized in heaven, the beggar Lazarus was flung. Such friends and familiars as he once had may have grown weary of him, and at length have laid him there, and with this released themselves of their charge, counting they had done enough, when they cast him under the eye, and thus upon the pity, of one so abundantly able to relieve him. How long he had lain there is not recorded; but long

enough for the rich man, as he passed in and out, to have grown so familiar with him, that in Abraham's bosom he recognizes him at once. Ignorance, therefore, of the beggar's needs he could not plead. This excuse it was left for another to plead for him; who, in his eagerness to fasten charges of unreason or injustice on Scripture, affirms that he is punished without cause, 'his only crime having been his wealth.' But he could not help knowing, and, if he had not known, that ignorance itself would have been his crime; for, with the leisure of wealth, he should not have remained unacquainted with the want and woe at his doors.

As the rich man's splendid manner of living was painted in a few strokes, in a few as expressive is set forth the destitution of Lazarus. We have been already implicitly told that the use of his limbs was gone from him. Like Job (Job 2:7), he was *full of sores*; hungry, and no man gave to him,—for, though these last words have no proper place in the text, doubtless we should understand that he desired, *but in vain, 'to be fed with the crumbs which fell from the rich man's table'* (Judg. 1:7); even these were not thrown to him, or in measure insufficient to *satisfy* his hunger. Shut out from human fellowship and human pity, he found sympathy only from the dumb animals; *'the dogs'*—such probably as wander without a master through the streets of an Eastern city (Ps. 59:14, 15; 2 Kgs. 9:35, 36)—*'came and licked his sores.'* Chrysostom, and others after him, see here an evidence of the extremity of weakness to which disease and hunger had reduced him; there was not in him strength enough even to fray away the dogs, which, licking his sores, aggravated their pain. But scarcely so; medicinal virtue has been popularly ascribed to the tongue of the dog; which, moist and smooth, would rather assuage than exasperate the smart of a wound. More probably the neglect and cruelty of the rich man are thus enhanced and set in the strongest light. Man had no pity for his fellowman, no alleviations for his woe; which yet the dogs could feel for, and would have assuaged, if they might. We have thus stroke for stroke. Dives is covered with purple and fine linen, Lazarus covered only with sores. One fares sumptuously, the other desires to be fed with crumbs. One has hosts of attendants to wait on his every caprice; though this circumstance is left to our imagination to supply; only the dogs tend the sores of the other.

It has been often said that nothing is expressly told us of the moral condition of Lazarus, of his faith, his patience, his hope. Such is not exactly the case; for as names are realities in Christ's kingdom of truth, he who received the name Lazarus, or 'God is my help,' from his lips, must have had faith in God; and it was this his faith, and not his poverty, which brought him into Abraham's bosom. In all homiletic use of the parable this should never be forgotten. How often Augustine, having brought home to the prosperous children of the world the tremendous lessons which are here for them, turns round to the poor, warning them that something more is wanting than sores and rags and hunger to bring them into a conformity with Lazarus, and into the place of his rest. With this outward poverty another poverty, even poverty of spirit, must go hand in hand; for that other does not in itself constitute humility, though an excellent help to it; even as the riches of this world do not of necessity exclude humility, but only constitute an enormous temptation, lest they that have them be high-minded, and trust in those uncertain riches rather than in the living God: and he often reminds his hearers how that very Abraham into whose bosom Lazarus was carried, had on earth been rich in flocks and herds and in all possessions (Gen. 13:2).

But this worldly glory and this worldly misery are alike to have an end: they are the fleeting shows of things, not the abiding realities. *'And it came to pass that the beggar died'*; and then how marvelous the change! he whom but a moment before no man served, whom only the dogs tended, *'was carried by the angels into Abraham's bosom.'* Some have by this understood 'an eminence and privilege of joy which Lazarus had' (Jeremy Taylor); that he was brought into the *chiefest* place of honor and felicity, such as the sons of Zebedee asked for themselves (Matt. 20:23); not admitted merely to sit down among the rest of the faithful with Abraham at the heavenly festival, but to lean on his bosom, an honor of which only one could partake, as the beloved disciple leaned upon Jesus' bosom at the paschal supper (John 13:23). Not so, however; the image underlying these words is not that of a festival at all; in Hades there is no place for such, nor till the actual coming of the kingdom. *'Abraham's bosom'* must find its explanation not from Matt. 8:11; Luke 13:29, 20; but rather from John 1:18. It is a figurative phrase to express the deep quietness of an innermost communion. Besides, the Jews, to whose theology the phrase belongs, spoke of *all* true believers as going to Abraham, as being received into his bosom. The phrase was equivalent for them to the being 'in the garden of Eden,' or 'under the throne of glory,' gathered, that is, into the general receptacle of happy, but waiting souls (see Wisd. 3:1–3). Christ by using has been rightly considered as sanctioning and adopting the phrase; it has thus passed into the language of the Church; which has understood by it the state of painless expectation, of blissful repose, to intervene between the death of the faithful in Christ Jesus, and their perfect consummation and bliss at his coming in his kingdom. It is 'paradise' (Luke 23:43); the place of the souls under the altar (Rev. 6:9); it is, as some distinguish it, blessedness, but not glory. Thither, to that haven of rest and consolation, Lazarus, after all his troubles, was safely borne.

'The rich man also died, and was buried'; we naturally conclude, from the course of the narrative, *after* Lazarus, the mercy of God being manifested in the order of their deaths: Lazarus more early delivered from the miseries of his earthly lot; Dives allowed a longer space for repentance. But his day of probation comes also to an end. Possibly the setting of Lazarus under his eye had been his final trial; his neglect of him the last drop that had made the cup of God's long-suffering to run over. Entertaining him, he might have unawares entertained angels; but having let slip this latest opportunity, on the death of Lazarus follows hard, as would seem, his own. There is a sublime irony, a stain upon all earthly glory, in this mention of his burial, connected as it is with what is immediately to follow. The world, loving its own, followed him no doubt with its pomp and pride, till it could not follow any further. There was not wanting the long procession of the funeral solemnities through the streets of Jerusalem, the crowd of hired mourners, the spices and ointment very precious, wrapping the body; nor yet the costly sepulcher, on which the genial virtues of the departed were recorded. This splendid carrying of the forsaken tenement of clay to the grave is for him what the carrying into Abraham's bosom was for Lazarus; it is his equivalent; which, however, profits him little where now he is. For death has been for him an awakening from his flattering dream of ease and self-enjoyment upon the stern and terrible realities of eternity. He has sought to save his life, and has lost it. The play in which he acted the rich man is ended, and as he went off the stage, he was stripped of all the trappings with which he had been furnished that he might sustain his part: there remains only the fact that he has played it badly, and will therefore have no praise, but uttermost rebuke, from Him who allotted to him this character to sustain.

From this verse the scene of the parable passes beyond the range of *our* experience into the unknown world of spirits; but not beyond the range of *his* eye, to whom all worlds, visible and invisible, are equally open and manifest. He appears as much at home there as here; He moves in that world as one perfectly familiar with it: speaking without astonishment as of things which He knows. He continues, indeed, to us the language of men, for it is the only language by which He could make Himself intelligible to men. Yet it is not always easy now to distinguish between that which is merely figure, vehicle of the truth, and that which must be held fast as itself essential truth. We may safely say that the form in which the sense of pain, with the desire after alleviation, embodies itself (v. 24), is figurative. Olshausen will have it that the entire dialogue between Abraham and Dives belongs in the same way to the parabolical clothing of the truth; that it is nothing else than the hope and longing after deliverance, which alternately rises and is again crushed by the voice of the condemning law speaking in and through the conscience. But we are left in such entire ignorance of all the conditions of existence in that mysterious world of Hades, that it seems as impossible to affirm this as to deny it.

But to return; he that had that splendid funeral on earth is now *'in hell,'*—or *'in Hades'* rather; for as *'Abraham's bosom'* is not heaven, though it will issue in heaven, so neither is Hades *'hell,'* though to issue in it, when cast with death into the lake of fire, which is the proper hell (Rev. 20:14). It is the place of painful restraint, where the souls of the wicked are reserved to the judgment of the great day; it is 'the deep,' whither the devils prayed that they might not be sent to be tormented before their time (Luke 8:31); for as Paradise has a foretaste of heaven, so has the place where he is a foretaste of hell. Dives, being there, is *'in torments,'* stripped of all wherein his soul delighted; his purple robe a garment of fire; or as he himself describes it, he is *'tormented in this flame.'*

For a while he may have been quite unable to realize his new condition, to connect his present self with his past; his fearful change seeming to him only as some ugly dream. But when convinced at length that this was indeed no dream, but an awaking, then, that he might take the measure of his actual condition, *'he lift up his eyes, and seeth Abraham afar off, and Lazarus in his bosom'* (cf. Is. 65:13, 14; Luke 13:28). If this is merely a figure, yet assuredly a figure of the true, conveying to us the fact that the misery of the lost will be aggravated by a comparison which they will be ever making of their estate with the blessedness of the saved. *'And he cried and said, Father Abraham,'*—for he still clung to the hope that his fleshly privileges would profit him something; he would still plead that he has Abraham to his father (Matt. 3:9; Rom. 2:17; John 8:41), not perceiving that this, his glory once, is now the very stress of his guilt. That he, a son of Abraham,—the man of that liberal hand and princely heart, in whom, as the head of the elect family, every Jew was reminded of his kinship with every other, of the one blood in the veins of all, of the one hope in God which ennobled them all from the least to the greatest—should have so sinned against the mighty privileges of his high calling, so denied through his life all which the name 'son of Abraham' was meant to teach him,—it was this which had brought him to that place of torment. Poor and infinitely slight is the best alleviation which he looks for: *'Have mercy on me, and send Lazarus, that he may dip the tip of his finger in water, and cool my tongue; for I am tormented in this flame.'* And this is all which he ventures to ask! so shrunken are his desires, so low the highest hope which even he himself presumes to entertain. It has been observed that his prayer of his is the only invocation of saints whereof the Scripture knows; and it is far from being an encouraging one (Job 5:1). He can speak of *'father Abraham'* and his *'father's house'*; but there is another Father of whom he will know nothing— the Father whom the prodigal had found; for he is as far as hell is from heaven from the faith of the prophet: 'Doubtless *Thou* art our Father, though Abraham be ignorant of us, and Israel acknowledge us not' (Is. 63:16).

'*But Abraham said, Son, remember that thou in thy lifetime receivedst thy good things, and likewise Lazarus evil things; but now he is comforted, and thou art tormented.*' In the answer of the Father of the faithful there is no harshness, no mocking at the calamity of his unhappy and guilty descendant. He addresses him as *'Son,'* while at the same time coupling an allowance of the relationship which the other claimed, with a denial of his request, he rings the knell of his latest hope. And first he brings home to his conscience that all which is happening to him now is just, and that if he will only consider, he must consent to it that it is so. *'Thou in thy lifetime receivedst thy good things.'* I cannot accept the interpretation which by the *'good things'* of Dives would understand certain good actions which in some small measure he had wrought, and the reward of which he had in this present life received; even though it can claim such supporters as Chrysostom in the Greek Church, Gregory the Great in the Latin, and Bishop Sanderson in our own. The following paraphrase of the words is from a sermon of Sanderson's: 'If thou hadst anything good in thee, remember thou hast had thy reward in earth already, and now there remaineth for thee nothing but the full punishment of thine ungodliness there in hell: but as for Lazarus, he hath had the chastisement of his infirmities [his *"evil things"*] on earth already, and now remaineth for him nothing but the full reward of his godliness here in heaven.' Presently before Sanderson had said, 'For as God rewardeth those few good things that are in evil men with these temporal benefits, for whom yet in his justice he reserveth eternal damnation, as the due wages, by that justice, of their graceless impenitency, so He punisheth those remnants of sin that are in godly men with these temporal afflictions, for whom yet in his mercy He reserveth eternal salvation, as the due wages, yet by that mercy only, of their faith and repentance and holy obedience.' Whether there be such a dealing of God with men as this or not, it is very far-fetched to find it here; and the more obvious explanation of the words agrees much better with the general scope of the parable, and of Abraham's discourse in particular. The *'good things'* of the rich man were his temporal felicities, his purple and fine linen, and his sumptuous fare. These, which were *'goods'* to him, in his esteem the highest or indeed the only *'goods,'* and besides which he would know no other, he had *'received.'* He had his choice, the things temporal or the things eternal, to save his life here, or to save it there; and by the choice which he had made he must abide.

This lesson the words, either way interpreted, will contain, namely, that the receiving of this world's good with no admixture of its evil, the course of an unbroken prosperity, is ever a sign and augury of ultimate reprobation (Ps. 17:14; Job 21:7–21; Luke 6:24, 25; Heb. 12:8). Nor is it hard to see why. There is in every man dross in abundance, needing to be purged away, and which can only be purged away in the purifying fires of pain. He therefore whom these purifying fires come not near, is left with all his dross in him, is no partaker of that holiness, without which no man shall see God. Thus Dives, to his endless loss, had in this life received good things without any share of evil. But now all is changed: Lazarus, who received in this mortal life evil things, *'is comforted'* (Matt. 5:4; 2 Cor. 4:17; Acts 14:22), but he is *'tormented.'* He had sown only to the flesh, and therefore, when the order of things has commenced in which the flesh has no part, he can only reap in misery and emptiness, in the hungry longing and unsatisfied desire of the soul (Gal. 6:8). The pity too which he refused to show, he fails to obtain;

so that we have here the severe converse of the beatitude; 'Blessed are the merciful, for they shall obtain mercy' (Judg. 1:7; Jer. 51:49; Matt. 18:32–34; James 2:13; Rev. 16:6; 18:6). The crumbs which he denied have issued in the drop of water which is denied to him. Having failed to make 'himself friends of the mammon of unrighteousness,' now when he has failed, he has none to receive him into everlasting habitations.

Nor is this severe law of the divine retaliations the only obstacle to the granting of his request. There is further brought home to the conscience of this man, once so rich, and now so poor, that with death an eternal separation of the elements of good and evil, elements in this world mingled and confounded, begins (Matt. 13:40, 41). Like is gathered to like, good by natural affinity to good, and evil to evil; and this separation is permanent: *'Beside all this, between us and you there is a great gulf fixed,'* not a mere handbreadth only, as the rabbies fabled, but *'a great gulf,'* and this *'fixed'*—an eternal separation, a yawning chasm, too deep to be filled up, too wide to be bridged over;—*'so that they which would pass from hence to you cannot; neither can they pass to us, that would come from thence.'* The latter statement contains no difficulty; it is only natural that the lost should desire to pass out of their state of pain to the place of rest and blessedness; but it is not so easy to understand the other—*'they who would pass from hence to you cannot'*; for how should any desire this? Not, of course, with a purpose of changing their own condition, but they cannot pass, Abraham would say, even for a season; they have no power to yield even a moment's solace to any in that place, however earnestly they may wish it.

But though repulsed for himself, he has still a request to urge for others. If Abraham cannot send Lazarus to that world of woe, at least he can cause him to return to the earth which he has so lately quitted; between these worlds there is no such gulf interposed: *'I pray thee therefore, father, that thou wouldest send him to my father's house; for I have five brethren, that he may testify unto them, lest they also come into this place of torment.'* He and they, Sadducees at heart, though perhaps Pharisees in name, may oftentimes have mocked together at that unseen world, and by Lazarus he would fain warn them now of the fearful reality which he had found it. *He* could testify at once of heaven and of hell. In this anxiety for the welfare of his brethren, which he, who hitherto had been merely selfish, expresses, some have seen the evidence of a better mind beginning, and the proof that suffering was already doing its work in him, and awakening the slumbering germ of good. With this, were it so, would of necessity be connected his own ultimate restoration, and the whole doctrine of future suffering not being vindicative and eternal, but corrective and temporary. But the rich man's request grows out of another root. There lies in it a secret justifying of himself, and accusing of God. What a bitter reproach against God and against the old economy is here involved: 'If only I had been sufficiently warned, if only God had given me sufficiently clear evidence of these things, of the need of repentance, of this place as the goal of a sensual worldly life, I had never come hither. But though I was not, let, at any rate, my brethren be duly warned.' Abraham's answer is brief and almost stern; rebuking, as was fit, this evil thought of his heart: they *are* warned; they have enough to keep them from that place of torment, if only they will use it: *'They have Moses and the prophets: let them hear them'* (John 5:39, 45–47). Christ putting these words into Abraham's mouth, evidently gives no countenance to them who see an entire keeping back of the doctrine of life eternal and a future retribution in the Pentateuch; but to *'hear Moses,'* is to hear of these things; as elsewhere more at length He has shown (Matt. 22:31, 32; Luke 20:27).

But the suppliant will not so easily be put to silence: *'Nay, father Abraham; but if one went unto them from the dead, they will repent.'* We are told of the faithful, that 'their works do follow them'; their temper here is their temper in heaven; not otherwise does the contempt of God's word, which this man manifested on earth, follow him beyond the grave. That word, as he deems, is not sufficient to save men; they must have something more to lead them to repentance. We have here reappearing in hell that 'Show us a sign, that we may believe,' so often upon the lips of the Pharisees on earth. They will believe, or flatter themselves that they would believe, signs and portents: but they will not believe God's word (Is. 8:19, 20). A vain expectation! *'If they hear not Moses and the prophets, neither will they be persuaded, though one rose from the dead.'* Every word in this reply, with which we may profitably compare Is. 8:19, demands to be accurately weighed. Dives had said, *'they will repent'*; a moral change will be wrought in them; Abraham replies, they will not even *'be persuaded.'* Dives had said, *'if one went unto them from the dead'*; Abraham, with a prophetic glance at the world's unbelief in a far greater matter, makes answer. 'No, not *though one rose from the dead.'* He in fact is saying: 'A far mightier miracle than you demand would be ineffectual for producing a far slighter effect; you imagine that wicked men would *repent* on the return of a spirit,'—the history of the last days of Saul might have taught him better (1 Sam. 28),—'I tell you they would not even *be persuaded* by the rising of one from the dead.'

This reply of Abraham is most important for the insight it gives us into the nature of faith as a moral act; not therefore to be forced by signs and wonders: for where there is a determined alienation of will and affections from the truth, no impression which miracles will make, even when accepted as genuine, will be more than transitory. There will not fail to be always a loophole somewhere or other by which unbelief can escape; and this is well, else we should have in the Church the faith of devils, who believe and tremble. When the historical Lazarus was raised from the dead, the Pharisees were not by this mightiest of all miracles persuaded of the divine mission and authority of Him who had raised him; and this though they did not deny the reality of the miracle itself (John 11:47; 12:10). A greater too than Lazarus has returned from the world of spirits; nay, He has risen from the dead; and what multitudes, who acknowledge the fact, and acknowledge it as setting a seal to all his claims to be heard and obeyed, are not brought by this acknowledgment a whit nearer to repentance and the obedience of faith. And it is very observable, how exactly in the spirit of Abraham's refusal to send Lazarus, the Lord Himself acted after his resurrection. He showed Himself, not to the Pharisees, not to his enemies, 'not to all the people, but unto witnesses chosen before of God' (Acts 10:41), to his own disciples alone. It was a judgment upon others, that no sign should be given them but the sign of the prophet Jonas (Matt. 12:39); and yet it was mercy too, for they would not have been persuaded even by one that had risen from the dead. A satisfaction of the longing, in itself most natural, that one should return from the world beyond the grave, and assure us of the reality of that world,—a satisfaction which Abraham could not give,—was by Christ granted to those who were seeking the confirmation of faith, and not an excuse for unbelief.

I have alluded already to an interpretation of this portion of Scripture, which, if admitted, would restore it at once to its full rights as a parable, even according to the strictest definition of such; for the purely historical or narrative character of it would quite disappear, an allegorical and prophetic taking the room of this. The interpretation of which I speak, though never the predominant one, has frequently made itself heard, having found more or less favor with Augustine, with Gregory the Great, and with more modern commentators than one. Should it obtain allowance, the parable, like so many others which we owe exclusively to St. Luke, will set forth the past and future relations of the Jew and the Gentile. Dives will in this case represent the Jewish nation, clad in the *'purple'* of the king, and the *'fine linen'* of the priest—the kingdom of priests, or royal priesthood (Ex. 19:6; 1 Pet. 2:9). Of this elect people it might be truly said that they *'fared sumptuously everyday,'* being furnished to the full with all things necessary for life and godliness. Salvation was of the Jews (John 4:22); to them pertained 'the adoption, and the glory, and the covenants, and the giving of the law, and the service of God, and the promises' (Rom. 9:4). But while all this was so richly their portion, they, instead of sharing it with those who needed it the most, were at all pains that none of it should reach any other; or if they did make a proselyte, they made him not for God but for themselves, and he exaggerated all which was worst in themselves (Matt. 23:15). Making their boast of God (Rom. 2:17), they did nothing to spread among the heathen the true knowledge of his name. There would not have fallen, if they could have helped it, so much as a crumb from their table for these. Lazarus, the beggar, lay untended at their gate—at their gate and without it; for the Gentiles were 'aliens from the commonwealth of Israel, and strangers from the covenants of promise' (Eph. 2:12):—*'full of sores,'* for their sins and their miseries were infinite. St. Paul, at Rom. 1:23–32, gives us a fearful glimpse of some of the worst among these sores, though indeed we must include in them not sins only, but all the penal miseries consequent on sin. *'And the dogs came and licked'* these *'sores,'* and this was all the alleviation which they had. They were slight and miserable assuagements of its want and woe, in effectual medicine for its hurts, which the heathen world obtained from its legislators, philosophers, and poets. 'Physicians of *no* value' we must not call them; for the moral condition of the world would have been far worse without them; but yet they could only heal slightly at the best the hurt of their people.

The desire of the beggar to be fed with the crumbs that fell from the rich man's table, finds no exact counterpart in any longing on the part of the Gentiles for the satisfaction of their spiritual hunger from the table of the Jews. Such longing there might have been, if these had held, and held forth, the truth as they ought. But, whether from the repulsive aspect under which they presented it, or from some other causes, this desire did not in any large measure exist; though, indeed, the spread of Judaism, and the inclination, especially among women of rank, to embrace it, is more than once noted by Roman writers about the time of the first emperors. Still the yearning of men's souls after a truth which they had not, was a yearning after something which the Jew had, and had richly; and which, had he been faithful to his position, he would have imparted to them, and they would have been willing to receive of him. Christ was 'the Desire of *all* nations'; and thus there was no yearning after deliverance from the bondage of corruption which was not in truth a yearning after Him; so that *implicitly* and unconsciously the nations of the world were desiring to live upon truth which had been entrusted to the Jew, and entrusted to him that he might share it with them.

The dying of Lazarus, with his reception into Abraham's bosom, will find their counterpart in the coming to an end of that economy in which the Gentile was an alien from the covenant, and in his subsequent introduction by *'the angels,'* or messengers of the covenant, into all the immunities and consolations of the kingdom of God;—'which in time past were not a people, but are now the people of God; which had not obtained mercy, but now have obtained mercy' (1 Pet. 1:10; Eph. 2:11–13). But Dives dies also; the coming to an end of that preparatory economy, being life to the Gentile, is death to the Jew, who had desperately clung to this, and who would know of no other. And now Dives is in torments,—*'in hell'*; surely not too strong a phrase to describe the anguish and despair, the madness and astonishment of heart, which must be their portion who, having once known God, refuse to know Him anymore. Who can read the history, as given by the great Jewish historian, of the final agony of his nation,— when turning fiercely upon its foes, it turned with a yet more deadly fierceness upon itself; like a scorpion, which, girdled with fire, fixes its sting in its own body,—and not feel that all which constitutes hell was already there? And ever since have they not been *'tormented'*? What a picture of their condition as the apostate people of God does the sure word of prophecy supply (Lev. 26:14–39; Deut. 28:15–68). What gnashing of teeth, what madness of heart, does Christ announce shall be theirs, when they shall see the despised Gentiles sitting down in the kingdom of God, from which they themselves are excluded (Luke 13:28–30). Nor has history failed to justify these pictures to the full. What a commentary on all this does the whole medieval history, with its record of all the ignominy and shame, all the frightful indignities and outrages, inflicted on the Jewish race during all those ages, supply.

But as Dives looked for some consolation from Lazarus, whom before he despised, so the Jew is looking for the assuagement of his miseries through some bettering of his outward estate,—some relaxation of severities, inflicted upon him,—some improvements in his civil condition:—expecting from the kingdoms of the world that which, even if they gave, would be but as a drop of water on the burning tongue. For it is the wrath of God which constitutes his misery; and till this is removed, till he turns from Abraham to Abraham's God, he is incapable of true consolation. The alleviation which he craves is not given; it had been useless to give it. There is but one true alleviation, that he should be himself received into the kingdom of God, that he should bewail his guilt, and look on Him whom he pierced, and mourn because of Him. The consolations would abound to him. Whatever is short of this is nothing. The upholders of this interpretation urge, and with reason, that the absence of any allusion in the parable to a future time, when the *'great gulf'* of unbelief which now separates the Jew from his blessings shall be filled up, makes nothing against it. The same silence observed in the parable of the Wicked Husbandmen (Matt. 21:33). No hint is there given that the vineyard shall one day be restored to its first cultivators, which yet we know will be the case (Rom. 11:26; 2 Cor. 3:16).

By the *'five brethren'* of Dives will be set forth to us, according to this scheme, all who hereafter, in a like condition and with like advantages, are tempted to the same abuse of their spiritual privileges. The Gentile Church is in one sense Lazarus brought into Abraham's bosom; but when it sins as the Jewish Church did before it, glorying in its gifts, but not using them for the calling out of the spiritual life of men, contented to see in its very bosom a population outcast, save in name, from its privileges and blessings, and beyond its limits millions upon millions of heathens to whom it has little or no care to impart the riches of the knowledge of Christ,— then, as it thus sins, it only too much resembles the five brethren of Dives, who are in danger of coming, and for sins similar to his, to the same *'place of torment.'* Nor are we to imagine that, before judgment is executed upon a Church thus forgetful of its high calling, it will be roused from its dream of security by any startling summonses,—any novel signs and wonders,—any new revelation,—

any Lazarus rising from the dead and bidding it to repent. It has enough to remind it of its duty; its deposit of truth, its talent wherewith to trade till its Lord's return. The parable thus contemplated, speaks to us Gentiles in the very spirit of those awful words which St. Paul addressed to the Gentile converts at Rome: 'Behold, therefore, the goodness and severity of God: on them which fell severity; but towards thee goodness, if thou continue in his goodness; otherwise thou also shalt be cut off' (Rom. 11:22).

Those who uphold this allegorical interpretation maintain that the parable will not, through admitting it, lose any of its practical value. Whatever, according to the more usual interpretation might be drawn from it of solemn warning for the children of this present world, who have faith in nothing beyond it,—for all who forget, in the fullness of their own earthly goods, the infinite want and woe of their fellowmen, the same may be drawn from it still. Only, superadded to this warning to the world, it will yield another and still more solemn warning to the Church, that it do not shut itself up in selfish pride; glorying in the multitude of its own privileges, but at the same time with no feeling sense of the spiritual wants and miseries of those who know not God, with no earnest effort to remove them; that on such forgetfulness a terrible judgment must follow.

27.
Unprofitable Servants

Luke 17:7, 10

It has been much debated whether there be any connection at all, and if any, what connection, between this parable and its immediate context. Expositors not a few have either expressly denied that any such existed, or have, at all events, been at no pains to trace it. Those, on the other hand, who assert a connection, do not trace the same. Thus Augustine, who acknowledges the difficulty which meets him here, has a singular scheme for linking on the parable with that which went before it, and one very forced and unnatural. I must be content to give a reference to it, as fairly to state it would occupy more space than its merits warrant. Theophylact finds the following link between the parable and the verse preceding. The Lord had there declared the mighty works which a living faith would enable his disciples to perform; but then, lest a knowledge of this should entangle them in a snare of pride, a parable which should keep them humble is added. Olshausen suggests as follows. The Apostles by that account of the hindrances they would meet (vv. 1, 2), of the hard duties, hard as they then seemed to them, which were required of them (vv. 3, 4), had a longing awakened in them after a speedier rest and reward. The Lord will make them understand that their work, difficult or not, welcome or unwelcome, must be done; that they are not their own, but his, and to labor for Him: if they found their labor a delight, well; but if not, it was not the less to be accomplished. Instead of looking for recompense and release from toil at once, they should take example of the servant, who, albeit he had strenuously laboring all the day long in the field, 'plowing or feeding cattle,' yet not the less, when he returned to the house, resumed his labors there. Doubtless this is an important truth, and one involved in the parable; but that, 'Lord, increase our faith,' or, 'Lord, give to us more faith,' which calls it out, involves no such meaning as Olshausen traces in it; I cannot recognize in this petition the voice of those desirous of escaping a dispensation committed to them, or snatching prematurely at a reward.

Altogether different from these interpretations, and suggesting a quite different connection, is one first proposed by Grotius; and by Venema taken up and strengthened with additional arguments and illustrations. The parable, they say, does not represent at all the standing of the faithful under the New Covenant or 'perfect law of liberty,' but the merely servile standing of the Jew under the old; and it grew in this manner out of the discourse preceding. The disciples had asked for increase of faith. The Lord, who will grant their request, will at the same time magnify the value of the gift which they ask. That value is so transcendent that all works done without this living principle of obedience are merely servile, and justly recompensed with a merely servile reward; God taking no pleasure in them, and counting that He owes no thanks for them; they who bring such to pass being *unprofitable servants* after all. They object to any other interpretation, that it sets in a light which is not that of the New Covenant the relations of Christ and his people. Is it likely, they ask, that the same gracious Lord who elsewhere has said, 'Henceforth I call you not servants,. . .but I have called you friends,' should here seek to bring them under bondage again? should put them in relations with Himself not filial but servile: beforehand declaring that, however much they might labor for Him, He would owe them no thanks for all? How, they demand, does this agree either with the spirit or the letter of words such as these, 'Blessed are those servants, whom the lord when he cometh shall find watching: verily, I say unto you, *that he shall gird himself*, and make them sit down to meat, and will come forth and serve them' (Luke 12:37)? But all these embarrassments, they affirm, disappear, so soon as the parable is regarded as setting forth the relation of the Jewish people to God. They were hired to do a certain work, which if they did, they were, like servants, free from stripes; they ate and drank; they received their earthly reward. But advancing no further than to this bare fulfilling of things expressly enjoined them, and fulfilling even these without love or zeal or the filial spirit of faith, stopping short so soon as ever they dared, and serving in the oldness of the letter, they were *unprofitable servants,* in whom their Lord could take no pleasure, and who could look for no further marks of favor at his hands.

All this is ingeniously and plausibly urged; and yet does not carry such conviction with it as need compel us to go back from the ordinary exposition. I shall attempt in the interpretation to meet the difficulties which have thus been urged. It is thus that the parable commences: *'But which of you, having a servant plowing or feeding cattle, will say unto him by and by, when he is come from the field, God and sit down to meat?'* Before proceeding any further let me observe that *'by and by'* doest not at this present mean exactly the same which it meant when our Version was made. It was then equivalent to 'straightway' (thus compare Mark 6:25; Luke 21:9); and is used with this meaning here. The purpose of the verse is obscured from the English reader by this change in the force of the phrase, as becomes evident, if we substitute *'straightway'* for it. But to attain the exact sense of the original it will need further to join this *'by and by,'* or this *'straightway,'* with the command which follows it, *'Go straightway, and sit down to meat,'* and not with *'say,'* which went before. *'And will not rather say unto him, Make ready wherewith I may sup, and gird thyself, and serve me, till I have eaten and drunken, and afterward thou shalt eat and drink?'* To wait at table with the dress succinct or girded up, was a mark of servitude, which to keep in mind makes more wonderful the condescension of the Son of God in his saying, Luke 12:37; and in his doing, John 13:4. *'Doth he thank that servant because he did the things that were commanded him? I trow not. So likewise ye, when ye shall have done all those things which are commanded you, say, We are unprofitable servants; we have done that which was our duty to do.'*

To recur to the objections of Grotius and Venema; no doubt the relations of the faithful to their Lord are set forth here under a severer, we might venture to say a less gracious, aspect than is usual in the New Covenant. And yet this word of our Lord need not be opposed to such other words of his, as that which was just now urged (Luke 12:37). It should rather be accepted as furnishing the counterweight of all such. This is the way a God *might* deal; for it is not asserted that thus He *will* deal; since rather that other is the manner in which He will actually bear Himself towards his faithful servants. One relation according to the strictness of justice He *might* assume; the other, according to the riches of his grace, He *will* assume. We, to keep us humble, are evermore to acknowledge that upon that footing He might put all our service done to Him, having at the same time this assurance, that so long as we put it upon this footing, He will not; because so long, we, continuing in our humility, are capable of receiving his favors without being corrupted by them. And assuredly the experience of every heart will attest how necessary this aspect of the truth, as well as the other; how needful that in hours when we are tempted to draw back, to shun and evade our tasks, we should then feel that a necessity is laid upon us; that, indeed, while we do them willingly, we do them also the most acceptably; yet whether willingly or not, they must be done; that we are servants, who are not to question our Master's will, but to fulfill it. Good for us it is to be reminded of this in such moments, and thus kept in the way of duty, till the time of a more joyful and childlike obedience again comes round. When too, because we have accomplished some little work, we count that we may straightway take our ease, and regard out 'Well done' as already gained, very profitable will be then the warning of the parable, the example of the hind, who having labored all day in the field, resumes his labors in the house, and only looks to rest and refresh himself, when his master has no further need of his service; good for us that, in the words of the Son of Sirach, we learn to 'wax old in our work' (11:20), and, so long as we are here, see in one task completed but a stepping-stone to another which shall be begun; ever as we have surmounted one hill of labor, perceiving a new one rising above it, and girding ourselves for the surmounting of that as well. Well for us, too, is it to know and to confess that we are not doing God a favor in serving Him, but He the highest favor to us in enabling us to this service; and that He graciously accepting our work and rewarding it, does this solely out of the freedom and riches of his grace; adding to it a worth which of itself it does not possess; that there is another footing, that namely of the parable, upon which He might have put all—yea, upon which, though *He* does not, yet *we* must evermore put it, so far as this may be needful for the subduing of every motion of pride and vain-glory, every temptation to bring in God as our debtor—which we evermore are doing, or are on the point of doing.

More effectual medicine against this disease of pride and vain-glory, the words which Christ here places in the mouth of his disciples will supply; for if, when they have *'done all,'* they shall still confess, *'We are unprofitable servants'* (cf. Job 22:2, 3; 35:7, 8; Ps. 16:2), how much more, and with how far deeper self-abasement and shame, when their consciences bear them witness, as the conscience of every man enlightened by the Spirit of God must bear witness to him, that so far from having done all that was commanded, they have in innumerable things grievously failed and come short of their duty, of what they might and ought to have done.

28.

The Unjust Judge

Luke 18:1–8

This parable, addressed to the disciples, stands in closest relation with all which has just gone before; with the announcement of those times of tribulation, when even the disciples 'should desire to see one of the days of the Son of man, and should not see it' (17:22). Then, according to the deeply significant language of the Jewish schools, allowed and adopted by our Lord (Matt. 24:8; cf. John 16:21; Rom. 8:22), will be the birth-pangs of the new creation; and the distresses which shall then come to a head, and which, always felt, shall then be felt more intensely than ever are here set forth as the motive for persevering prayer. 'He spoke a parable unto them to this end, that men ought always to pray,' that it behooved them always to pray, if they would escape the things coming on the earth. It is not so much the duty, as the absolute necessity, of instant persevering prayer that is here proclaimed; while in the further words, 'and not to faint,' there are opened to us many glimpses into the inmost mystery of prayer.

We shall scarcely err, I think, in taking these words as words of Christ Himself, rather than of the Evangelist commenting by way of preface on the parable which he is about to record. Christ spoke the parable, and at the same time announced the object with which He spoke it; namely, *'that men ought always to pray, and not to faint.'* But, some will ask, is there not some exaggeration here? Must not this command be taken with very large abatements indeed? Not when we understand of prayer as the continual desire of the soul after God; having, it is true, seasons of an intenser and more concentrated earnestness, but by no means restricted to these seasons; since the whole life of the faithful should be, in Origen's beautiful words, 'one great connected prayer,'—prayer, as St. Basil expresses it, being the salt which should salt everything else. 'That soul,' says Donne, 'that is accustomed to direct herself to God upon every occasion, that, as a flower at sunrising, conceives a sense of God in every beam of his, and spreads and dilates itself towards Him, in a thankfulness, in every small blessing that he sheds upon her,. . .that soul which, whatsoever string be stricken in her, bass or treble, her high or her low estate, is ever turned towards God, that soul prays sometimes when it does not know that it prays.' Admirable are Augustine's utterances on this matter, drawn from the depths of his own Christian experience. Thus in one place: 'It was not for nothing that the Apostle said, "Pray without ceasing" (1 Thess. 5:17). Can we indeed without ceasing bend the knee, bow the body, or lift up the hands, that he should say, "Pray without ceasing"? There is another interior prayer without intermission, and that is the longing of thy heart. Whatever else thou mayest be doing, if thou longest after that Sabbath of God, thou dost not intermit to pray. If thou wishest not to intermit to pray, see that thou do not intermit to desire; they continual desire is thy continual voice. Thou wilt be silent, if thou leave off to love; for they were silent of whom it is written, "Because iniquity shall abound, the love of many shall wax cold." The coldness of love is the silence of the heart; the fervency of love is the cry of the heart.'

With this introduction, indicating the drift of the parable, the Lord proceeds: *'There was in a city a judge, which feared not God, neither regarded man.'* Two strokes describe the reckless and desperate character of the man. He *'feared not God'*; all that God's law had spoken of the awfulness of the judge's charge, of the guilt and punishment of the unrighteous judge, he set at nought (Ex. 23:6–9; Lev. 19:15; Deut. 1:16, 17; 2 Chr. 19:6, 7). Nor was it only that higher motive, the fear of God, which he wanted, but its poor and miserable substitute, respect for the opinion of the world, was equally inoperative with him. Some rise above this respect for the opinion of men; others fall below it, and he was one of these; and, worst sign of all, he dared to avow all this to himself (see v. 4). And it is with such a judge as this that the Judge of all the earth is likened here! None might have ventured upon this comparison, it would have been overbold on the lips of any, save only of the Son of God. Yet with all this we must beware of seeking to extenuate his unrighteousness,—as some by various forced constructions have sought to do. So far from this, the worse that we think of him, the more encouragement does the parable contain, the stronger the argument for unwearied persistency in prayer becomes. If a bad man will yield to the mere force of the importunity which he hates, how much more certainly will a righteous God be prevailed on by the faithful prayer which He loves. The unrighteousness of the judge is not an accident, cleaving to the earthly form under which the heavenly truth is set forth, such as would have been got rid of, if it conveniently might; but is rather a circumstance deliberately chosen for the stronger setting forth of that truth,—which truth indeed, would not have been set forth at all without it.

'And there was a widow in that city; and she came unto him, saying, Avenge me of my adversary.' We have heard the character of the judge; we may conceive therefore how hopeless the case of a suppliant at once weak and poor,—weak, so that she could not compel him to do her justice,—and poor, with no bribe to offer which should induce him to brave for her sake the resentment of formidable adversaries. Such, no doubt, is the widow of the parable, one 'that is a widow indeed and desolate.' The exceeding desolation of the state of widowhood in the East has been often noticed, and the obviousness of the widow, as one having none to help her, to all manner of oppressions and wrongs; from hence the numerous warnings against such oppression with which Scripture abounds (Ex. 22:22; Deut. 10:18; 24:17; 27:19; Job 22:9; Is. 1:23; Prov. 15:25; Mal. 3:5). Very fitly does a widow such as this represent the Church under persecution, under that persecution which never ceases, the oppression from an adverse element in which she draws her breath. Nor is it only the Church at large which by this widow is represented here, but every single soul in conflict with those spiritual powers which are arrayed against the truth. The *'adversary'* will in either case be the prince of the darkness of this world, the head of all which is fighting against the manifestation of the kingdom of God, either in a single soul, or in the world; the spiritual Herod, who is ever seeking to destroy the heavenly child. But the elect, who, having the first-fruits of the Spirit, groan within themselves, waiting their perfect redemption, are here represented as struggling with those adverse powers, as oppressed by them; under the sense of this oppression, and of their helplessness to effect their own deliverance, crying mightily for aid, for the revelation of the Son of man in his glory,—exclaiming with the prophet, 'Oh, that Thou wouldest rend the heavens, that Thou wouldest come down' (Is. 64:1); for they know that not till then shall the

wicked fall and not rise again, and the Church be set free forever from all her foes. We apprehend too slightly those cries for deliverance whereof Psalms and prophets are full, when we restrain them to special outward afflictions or persecutions which the Church or any of its members are enduring. The world is *always,* consciously or unconsciously, by flattery or by hostile violence, oppressing the Church; and Satan evermore seeking to hinder the manifestation of the life of God in everyone of its members; and prayer is the cry *de profundis* which the elect utter, the calling in of a mightier to aid, when the danger is urgent, lest the enemy should prevail. And the widow's prayer, *'Avenge me of mine adversary,'* wonderfully expresses the relation in which we stand to the evil with which we contend;—that it is not our very self, but an alien power, holding us in bondage,—not the very 'I,' as St. Paul (Rom. 7) is so careful to assert, for then redemption would be impossible, but sin which, having entered in, would now keep us in bondage. It is the Spirit's work to make men feel this distinctness between themselves and the evil which is in them; the new creation in this resembling the old, that it is a separating and disengaging of the light from the darkness in the soul of man,—that so the light, brought into direct relation with the fountain of all light, may disperse the darkness and overcome it. The renewed man, knowing that he has an adversary, knows also that this adversary is not his very self, but another; who, resisted, will flee from him; that all dominion by the other exercised upon him is an usurped dominion, which it will be a righteous thing for God to bring to an end; and thus is able to cry, with the widow in the parable, *'Avenge me of mine adversary,'* or rather, since men seek of a judge not vengeance, but justice,—*'Do me right on mine adversary,'* being, as this is, no other than our daily petition, 'Deliver us from evil,' or 'from the Evil *One,'*—from him who is the source and center of all evil.

   'And he would not for a while.' When it was asserted just now that the strength of the parable lay in the *unlikeness* between the righteous judge of the world, and this ungodly earthly judge, it was not intended to deny that to man God often *seems* as this unjust Judge, with an ear deaf to the prayers of his people. For even the elect are impatient in affliction; they expect a speedier deliverance than He always wills to vouchsafe them; and count that they have a claim to be delivered so soon as ever their voices are heard on high. Left long, as they count length, to the will of their enemies, in the furnace of affliction, they are tempted to hard thoughts of God, as

though He took part with the oppressors, at any rate was contented to endure them, while the cry of his afflicted people was as nothing in his ears. They are ready to exclaim, they do exclaim, with the storm-tossed disciples, 'Carest Thou not that we perish?' It is this very temptation, to which the faithful in hours such as these are exposed, that the parable is intended to meet. There is recorded for us next, not of course what the judge spoke aloud, scarcely what he spoke in his own hearing, but the voice of his heart, as it spoke in the hearing of God. *'But afterward he said within himself, Though I fear not God, nor regard man, yet because this widow troubleth me, I will avenge her, lest by her continual coming she weary me';* or *'wear me out,'* as it might be rendered. Stirred to do her right by no other motive than a selfish regard for his own interrupted ease, he yet *'will avenge her,'* if so to be quit of her importunities, and not plagued by her more. The same motive, and not that they were more pitiful than their Lord, moved the disciples to intercede for the woman of Canaan, that she might obtain what she asked: 'Send her away; for she crieth after us' (Matt. 15:23). This parable and that miracle serve each as a commentary on the other (cf. Ecclus. 35:17).

Between it and the lesson of encouragement which it contained the Lord may have paused for a little, and then resumed: *'Hear what the unjust judge saith. And shall not God avenge his own elect, which cry day and night unto Him, though He bear long with them?'* In the first clause of the sentence the emphasis should be laid on *'unjust'*; in the other, the epithet of goodness or righteousness, which should complete the antithesis, is omitted, as being of necessity included in the name, God. If the *'unjust judge'* is moved by prayer to do right at last, shall not the just *'God avenge his own elect'*? And the antithesis should be carried through all the members of the sentence. As the righteous God is opposed to the unrighteous judge, so the *'elect,'* the precious before God, to the widow, the despised among men; their might crying to her mere clamor; and the *'day and night'* which these prayers of theirs fill, to the time, short by comparison, during which her importunities beset the judge. The certainty that they will be heard rests not, however, on their mighty crying as its ultimate ground, but on their election of God; which is, therefore, here urged, and they named *'his elect,'* this being here, among their many names, the most appropriate: compare Dan. 12:1: 'At that time thy people shall be delivered, *every one that shall be found written in the book.'*—When God is said to *'bear long'* with men, the phrase generally sets forth his patience in giving to them time and space for repentance; this however is not intended here. It might be better therefore here if the words were rendered, *'though He bear them long in hand?'*—long, that is, as men measure length. He may be slack in avenging his people, as 'men count slackness' (Rev. 6:10; Ps. 35:17; 74:10; 94:3), as compared with their impatience; but, indeed, *'He will avenge them speedily,'* not leaving them a moment longer in the fire of affliction than is needful, delivering them from it the instant that patience has had her perfect work; so that there is, and is meant to be, an apparent contradiction, which yet is no real one, between vv. 7 and 8. The relief, which to man's impatience tarries long, indeed arrives speedily; it could not, according to the loving counsels of God, have arrived a moment earlier. Not while Lazarus is merely sick, not till he has been four days dead, does Jesus obey the summons of the sisters whom He loved so well (John 11:6). The disciples, laboring in vain against a stormy sea, must have looked often to that mountain where they had left their Lord; but not till the last watch, not till they have toiled through a weary night, does He bring the aid so long desired (Matt. 14:24, 25).

The concluding words, *'Nevertheless when the Son of man cometh, shall He find faith on the earth?'* are perplexing, for they appear to call in question the success of his whole mediatorial work. But though we have other grounds for believing that the Church will, at that supreme moment, be reduced to a little remnant, yet the point is here, not that the faithful then will be few, but that the faith even of the faithful will have almost failed. The distress will be so urgent when the Son of man shall at length come forth for deliverance, that even the hearts of his elect will have begun to fail them for fear. The lateness of the help Zechariah describes under images of the old theocracy,—Jerusalem shall be already taken, and the enemy within its wall, spoiling and desolating, when the Lord shall come forth, his feet standing on the Mount of Olives, to fight against its enemies (14:1–5). All help will seem utterly to have failed, so that the Son of man at his coming will hardly *'find faith,'* or rather, *'that faith upon earth'*—the faith, namely, which hopes against hope, and believes that light will break forth even when the darkness is thickest, and believing this, does not faint in prayer. The words throw light on other words of our Lord's; and receive light from them again: 'for the elect's sake,' lest their faith also should fail, and so no flesh should be saved, 'those days shall be shortened' (Matt. 24:22).

29.

The Pharisee and the Publican

Luke 18:9–14

S ome interpreters have found in this parable, as in that of Dives and Lazarus, a prophecy of the rejection of the Jews, with the reception into God's grace of the Gentiles; the Pharisee representing for them that whole nation which would assuredly have accepted him as embodying its ideal—the publican representing the Gentiles, with whom these hated ministers of Roman oppression were commonly classed. They see in the one the Jew, glorying in his own merits, and proudly extolling himself in these, but through this very pride and self-righteousness failing to become partaker of the righteousness of God; in the other the Gentile, who meekly acknowledging his vileness, and repenting his sins, obtains the grace which the Jew has missed. So long as no more is claimed by the advocates of this interpretation than that Jew and Gentile illustrated on the largest scale the solemn truths which are here declared, it may very fairly pass. But the words which introduce the parable, 'And He spoke this parable unto certain which trusted in themselves that they were righteous, and despised others,' words which must give the law to its interpretation, refute this when made the primary intention with which it was spoken. For who were these 'certain which trust in themselves that they were righteous?' Assuredly not Pharisees, nor any who avowedly admired Pharisees, as did the great body of the Jews. What profit would it have been to hold up to such the spectacle of a Pharisee praying as this one prays in the parable? They would have seen nothing unseemly in it; they would have counted it the most natural and fittest thing in the world that he should pray exactly in this fashion. But a disciple, one already having made some little progress in the school of Christ, yet in danger, as we are all in danger, of falling back into pharisaic sins, such a one would only need his sin to be plainly shown to him, and he would start back at its deformity; he would recognize the latent Pharisee in himself, and tremble and repent. It was in some of his own disciples and followers, that the Lord had detected symptoms of spiritual pride and self-exaltation, accompanied, as these will be ever, with a contempt of others; and it is to their disease that He proceeds in the parable to apply a remedy.

'*Two men went up into the temple to pray,'* at one, no doubt, of the stated hours of devotion (Acts 3:1; Is. 56:7), '*the one a Pharisee, and the other a publican:'* a Brahmin and a Pariah, as one might say, if preaching from this Gospel in India—the Pharisee, representing all those who, having made clean the outside of the platter, have remained ignorant of all the uncleanness within—have never learned to say, 'Deliver me from mine adversary,' do not so much as know that they have an adversary; the publican, an example of all those who have found their sins an intolerable burden; and now yearn after One who shall deliver them from these and from the curse of God's broken law. Christ will make his disciples understand how much nearer the kingdom of God is such a man than the self-complacent Pharisee, or than any who share in his spirit and temper; that he *may be* within that kingdom, while this other is certainly without.

'*The Pharisee stood and prayed thus with himself.'* It is a mistake, growing out of forgetfulness of Jewish and early Christian customs, to urge this *standing* of the Pharisee in his prayer as an evidence already displaying itself of his pride. The parable itself contradicts this, for the publican, whose prayer was a humble one, stood also (v. 13). But to pray standing was the usual manner of the Jews (1 Kgs. 8:22; 2 Chr. 6:12; Matt. 6:5; Mark 11:25); however, in moments of a more than ordinary humiliation or emotion of heart, they may have exchanged this attitude for one of kneeling or prostration (Dan. 6:10; 2 Chr. 4:13; Acts 9:40; 20:36; 21:5). The Church owes this, as so much in the external features of its worship, to the Synagogue. Its *stations* of prayer were so called, because *standing* the Christian soldier repelled the attacks of his spiritual enemy. At the same time, when we weigh the word of the original, this '*stood'* may very well be emphatic, indeed we may confidently assert that it is. It implies that he, so to speak, took his stand, planted and put himself in a prominent attitude of prayer; so that all eyes might light on him, all might take note that he was engaged in his devotions (Matt. 6:5). The words are not always combined as our Translators have combined them, but rather as follows: *'The Pharisee stood by himself, and prayed thus:'*—separatist in spirit as in name, and now also in outward act, he desired to put a distance between himself and all unclean worshipers (see Is. 65:5). The other construction, however, it is generally agreed, should be adhered to.

His prayer at first seems to promise well; *'God, I thank Thee'*; for the Pharisees, as Grotius well observes, 'did not exclude the divine help. But they who allow it and use this language are frequently ungrateful to it, allotting, as they do, to themselves the first share in virtuous actions, to God the second; or so recognizing common benefits, as to avoid fleeing as suppliants to that peculiar mercy which their own sins require.' Thus it was with this man; while a due recognition of God's grace will always be accompanied with deep self-abasement, confessing, as we must, how little true we have been to that grace, how short we have fallen of what we might have been, with such helps at command. And thus the early promise of the Pharisee's prayer quickly disappears; for under the pretense of thankfulness to God, he does but thinly veil his exaltation of self; and he cannot thank God for the good which he fancies that he finds in himself, without insulting and casting scorn upon others for the evil which he sees, or fancies that he sees, in them. He thanks God, but not aright; thanks Him that he is *'not as other men are,'* distributing the whole of mankind into two classes, putting himself in a class alone, and thrusting down everyone else into the other. And as he cannot think too good things of himself, so neither too bad of others. They do not merely fall a little short of his perfections, but are *'extortioners, unjust, adulterers,'*—and then, his eye alighting on the publican, of whom he may have known nothing but that he *was* a publican, he drags him into his prayer, making him to furnish the dark background on which the bright colors of his own virtues shall more gloriously be displayed;—finding, it may be, in the deep heart-earnestness with which the contrite man beat his breast, in the fixedness of his downcast eyes, proofs in confirmation of the judgment which he passes upon him. *He,* thank God, has no need to beat this breast in that fashion, nor to cast his eyes in that shame upon the ground.

So perfect is he in the fulfillment of the precepts of the second table. He now returns to the first; in that also he is faultless. *'I fast twice in the week.'* He has his works of supererogation. Moses ap-

pointed but one fast-day in the year, the great day of atonement
(Lev. 16:29; Num. 29:7); but the devouter Jews, both those who
were, and those who would seem such, the Pharisees above all,
kept two fasts weekly, on the second day and the fifth. *'I give tithes
of all that I possess'*; or rather, *'of all that I acquire.'* He, another Jacob,
has made the same promise to God as the patriarch of old: 'Of all
that Thou shalt give me, I will surely give the tenth unto Thee'
(Gen. 28:22; cf. 14:20). The law commanded only to tithe the fruits
of the field and increase of the cattle (Num. 18:21; Deut. 14:22; Lev.
27:30); but he, no doubt, tithed mint and cummin (Matt. 23:23;
Luke 11:42), *all* that came into his possession (Tob. 1:7, 8), down to
the trifles about which there was question, even in the Jewish
Schools, whether it was obligatory to tithe them or not (Hos. 12:8).
He will thus bring in God as his debtor; misusing those very precepts concerning fasting and paying of tithes, given to men, the
first to waken in them the sense of inward poverty and need, the
second to remind them that whatever they had was *from* God, and
should therefore be *to* God, making even these to minister to his ar-
rogance and pride. Acknowledgment of wants, or confession of sin,
there is none in his prayer,—if that can be called prayer, which has
nothing of these. 'Had he then,' asks Augustine, 'no sins to confess?
Yes, he too had sins; but, perverse and knowing not whither he had
come, he was like a sufferer on the table of a surgeon, who should
show his sound limbs, and cover his hurts. But let God cover thy
hurts, and not thou: for it, ashamed, *thou* seekest to cover them, the
physician will not cure them. Let Him cover and cure them; for
under the covering of the physician the wound is healed, under the
covering of the sufferer it is only concealed; and concealed from
whom? from Him to whom all things are known.'

It will aggravate our sense of the moral outrage involved in the
Pharisee's contemptuous reference to his fellow-worshiper, if we
keep in mind that in him we behold one who at this very moment
was passing into the kingdom of God, who had come, in the fullness of a contrite heart, to make, as seems evidently meant, the first
deep confession of his sins past which had ever found utterance
from his lips, in whom amid sore pangs the new man was being
born. How ugly a thing does the Pharisee's untimely scorn appear,
mingling as a harshest discord with the songs of angels, which at
this very moment hailed the lost who was found, the sinner who
repented. For let us turn now to him. *'And the publican, standing afar
off,'* not afar off from God, for the Lord is *nigh* unto them that are of

a contrite heart, *'would not lift up so much as his eyes unto heaven,'* much less then his hands and his face (1 Tim. 2:8; 1 Kgs. 8:54; Heb. 12:12; Ps. 28:2), to that dwelling of the Holy One; for, like the prodigal, he had 'sinned against heaven' (Luke 15:18), would have exclaimed like Ezra, 'O my God, I am ashamed, and blush to lift up my face to Thee, my God; for our iniquities are increased over our head, and our trespass is grown up unto the heavens' (9:6). He stood *'afar off,'* not that he was a proselyte or a heathen, or had not full right to approach, for he also was a Jew, but in reverent awe, not venturing to press nearer to the holy place; for he felt that his sins had set him at a distance from God, and until he had received the atonement, the propitiation which he asks for, he could not presume to draw nigher. Moreover, he *'smote upon his breast,'* an outward sign of inward grief or self-accusation (Nah. 2:7; Luke 23:48), as one judging himself, that he might not be judged of the Lord; acknowledging the far heavier strokes which might justly light upon him; at the same time crying, *'God be merciful to me a sinner,'* or *'to me, the sinful one'*; for as the Pharisee had singled himself out as the most eminent of saints, or indeed, as the one holy in the world, so the publican singles himself out as the chief of sinners, the man in whom all sins have met—a characteristic trait! for who, when first truly convinced of sin, thinks any other man's sins can equal his own (1 Tim. 1:15)

And he found the mercy which he asked. His prayer, like incense, ascended unto heaven, a sacrifice of sweet savor, while the prayer of the Pharisee was blown back like smoke into his own eyes; for 'God resisteth the proud, and giveth grace to the humble:' *'I tell you, this man went down to his house justified rather than the other.'* Not merely was he justified in the secret unsearchable counsels of God, but he *'went down to his house justified,'* with a sweet sense of forgiveness received shed abroad upon his heart; for God's justification of the sinner is indeed a *transitive* act, and passes from Himself to its object. The Pharisee meanwhile went down from the temple, his prayer ended, with the same cold dead heart with which he went up. By that *'rather than the other'* Christ does not mean that the publican *by comparison with the Pharisee* was justified, for there are no degrees in justification, but that he absolutely was justified, was contemplated of God as a righteous man, and the other not; that here the words were fulfilled, 'He hath filled the hungry with good things, and the rich He hath sent empty away; 'Though the Lord be high, yet hath He respect unto the lowly; but the proud He knoweth afar off' (Ps. 138:6; Is. 57:15; Job 5:11; 40:11, 12; 1 Pet. 5:5, 6). And the whole parable fitly concludes with words not now for the first time uttered by the Lord, for see Luke 14:11, but which would well bear repetition: *'For every one that exalteth himself shall be abased, and he that humbleth himself shall be exalted'* (cf. Prov. 29:23). The saying constitutes a beautiful transition to the bringing of the children to Jesus, the next incident recorded by the Evangelist.

30.
The Pounds

Luke 19:11–27

Much that might have been fitly said upon this parable has been anticipated in treating that of the Talents. The reasons for affirming them to be, not different reports of the same parable, but parables altogether distinct from one another, were then given, nor shall I, save very briefly, repeat these reasons here. The words with which St. Luke introduces the parable are important for its right understanding: 'He added and spoke a parable, because He was nigh to Jerusalem, and because they thought that the kingdom of God should immediately appear.' It was uttered then to repress impatience, to teach the need of a patient waiting for Christ; and, as we further find, an active working for Him till the time of his return. Such was its aim as regarded those who had yielded themselves without reserve to Him, as servants to their Lord. But He had also other hearers on this occasion, such as had not indeed thus attached themselves to Him, but a multitude drawn together by wonder, by curiosity, and by other mingled motives. These, with a certain good will toward Him and his doctrine, and so long as in his presence acknowledging his influence, were not the less exposed to all the evil influences of their age, and in danger of being drawn into the great stream of hostility now running so fiercely and so fast against Him. To this danger they would be exposed still more when his personal presence should be withdrawn from them, when his ignominious death should have seemed to give the lie to all his lofty pretensions. For them is meant that part of the parable (vv. 14, 27) concerning the citizens, who would not have one of their fellows set over them as their king, followed him with their hate, disclaimed obedience to him even while it was yet uncertain whether he should be set over them or not; but who at his return paid the fearful penalties of their guilt.

'He said therefore, A certain nobleman went into a far country, to receive for himself a kingdom, and to return' (cf. Mark 13:34). In the great Roman empire, where the senate of Rome, and afterwards its emperors, though not kings themselves, yet made and unmade kings, such a circumstance as this can have been of no unfrequent occurrence. Thus Herod the Great was at first no more than a subordinate officer in Judea; flying to Rome before Antigonus, he was there declared by the senate, through the influence of Antony, king of the Jews. In like manner his son Archelaus must personally wait upon Augustus, before inheriting the dominions left him by his father; and then did not inherit them as king but only as ethnarch. Spoken as this parable was at or in the neighborhood of Jericho, where stood the magnificent palace which Archelaus built, his example may very easily have presented itself to the Lord. History furnishes many other examples, for it was felt over the civilized world, in the striking words of the historian of the Maccabees;— 'whom they [the Romans] would help to a kingdom, those reign, and whom again they would, they displace' (1 Macc. 8:13).—That this claimant of a crown was one well born, a 'nobleman,' is only what we should naturally expect. No other would be likely to lift his hopes so high; or would give sufficient promise of maintaining himself on his throne, to render the higher authority willing to install him there. The epithet has its fitness here; for who was of such noble birth as He who, even according to the flesh, came of earth's first blood,—was the Son of Abraham, the Son of David (Matt. 1:1); who, besides all this, was the eternal and only-begotten Son of God

The kingdom which this nobleman goes to receive can scarcely be, as some understand it, another and a distant kingdom; but rather he goes to receive the investiture of that kingdom, whereof before he was one of the more illustrious citizens, and which after a while he returns to reign over, as its king. Either supposition, it is true, would suit his case, whom this nobleman represents: He went to be enthroned in his heavenly state, and in heaven to rule over all as the Son of man (Heb. 2:7, 8; Phil. 2:9–11). But it may with equal truth be affirmed that He went to receive solemn investiture of that earthly kingdom which He had purchased with his blood, and which hereafter He shall return and claim as his own, sitting on the throne of his father David; and the parable itself suggests this last as the kingdom intended here. It is over fellow-citizens that the

nobleman departs to obtain a dominion; else would there be no meaning in their message, *'We will not have this man to reign over us.'* It is among fellow-citizens that we find him on his return exercising kingly functions; setting his servants over five cities, and over ten (vv. 17, 19); having power of life and death, and executing extreme judgment on those that had sent messages of defiance after him (v. 27).

Before, however, he went, *'he called his ten servants,'*—or rather, *'ten servants of his,'*—*'and delivered them ten pounds, and said unto them, Occupy,'*—or, as in the margin, *'Employ in trading,'*—*'till I come.'* The sum which they shall thus *'occupy'* is very much smaller than that which, in St. Matthew, the man traveling into a far country committed to *his* servants there; though I do not know that we need seek any explanation of this. How remarkable is this *still* ministry, these occupations of peace in which the servants of the future king shall be engaged, and that while a rebellion is raging. A caviler significantly enough demands, 'Why did he not distribute *weapons* to his servants? Such under the circumstances would have been the most natural thing to do.' Doubtless *the most natural,* as Peter felt, when he cut off the ear of the servant of the high priest; as all have felt, who have sought to fight the world with its own weapon, and by the wrath of man to work the righteousness of God. Such identifying of the Church with a worldly kingdom has been the idea of the Papacy, such of the Anabaptists. Men in either case feeling strongly that there must be a kingdom of God, have supposed that it was immediately to appear (v. 11), and that they, and not Christ Himself, were to bring it into outward form and subsistence; instead of seeing that their part was, with the diligent but silent occupation of their talent, to lay the rudiments of that kingdom, and so to prepare the world for the outbreaking of it; which yet should only be when the King Himself returned in his glory.

'But his citizens hated him, and sent a message after him, saying, We will not have this man to reign over us.' Many understand here that his fellow-citizens, aware of his purpose, give him notice beforehand that they, however he may receive at other hands the dominion over them, will own no allegiance to him. The words describe more probably an embassage which these despatch to the court whither he is gone, to anticipate and counterwork him there, to proclaim how unwelcome his exaltation will be;—'We do not desire that this man should be made our king.' It was exactly thus that a faction of

the Jews, in the case of Archelaus, sent ambassadors to the court of Augustus to accuse him there, and if possible to hinder his elevation over them. The Jews were especially Christ's fellow-'*citizens*,' for according to the flesh, He was of the seed of Abraham, a Jew (Rom. 9:5; John 4:22), and a member of the Jewish polity; and they '*hated Him*' not merely in his life, and unto death; but every persecution of his servants, the stoning of Stephen, the beheading of James, the persecutions of Paul, and all the wrongs done to his people because they were his, these each and all were messages of defiance sent after Him, implicit declarations upon their part that they would not have Him for their king. Twice before yet He had gone to receive his kingdom, this very declaration found formal utterance from their lips,—once when they cried to Pilate, 'We have no king but Caesar'; and again, when they remonstrated with him, 'Write not, The King of the Jews' (John 19:21; cf. Acts 17:7). But the strictest fulfillment of these words is to be found in the demeanor of the Jews after his Ascension, their fierce hostility to Christ in his infant Church (Acts 12:3; 13:45; 14:18; 17:5; 18:6; 22:22; 23:12; 1 Thess. 2:15). When we give this parable a wider range, and find its full and final accomplishment, not at the destruction of Jerusalem, but at the day of judgment,—and it is equally capable of the narrower and the wider interpretation,—then these rebellious citizens will be all, Gentiles and Jews alike, who have denied their relation and subjection to Jesus, as their Lord and King (in this different from the unfaithful servant, for he allows the relation, and does not openly throw off the subjection, but yet evades the obligation by the false glosses of his evil heart), and this message will embody itself in the great apostasy of the last days, which shall be even as this is, not an evading of the subjection due unto Christ; but a speaking of proud things against Him (Rev. 13:5, 6; Dan. 7:25; 2 Thess. 2:1–10); not merely disobedience but defiance, such as, not content with resisting his decrees, shall provoke and challenge Him to the conflict (Ps. 2:2).

On the following verses (15–23) there is little to say which has not been said already (see p. 276). At his return, the nobleman, now a king, distributes praise and rewards to as many as have been faithful to him while he was away,—punishments more or less severe to them who have abused the opportunity and taken advantage of his absence. The rewards are *royal*, and this consistently with the royal dignity wherewith he is now invested; he sets them over cities. In the other parable it is otherwise (Matt. 25:14–30);

there the master, being but a private man, claims no such power of putting his servants in high places of authority: each parable being thus in perfect keeping and harmony with itself through all its minor details, which is another evidence of their original distinctness. The rewards too, as they are kingly, so are they also proportioned to the fidelity of the servants. To him whose pound had made ten pounds it is said, *'Because thou hast been faithful in a very little, have thou authority over ten cities:'* to him whose pound had made five it is said, *'Be thou also over five:'* to one a Decapolis, to the other a Pentapolis assigned. Surely there is vouchsafed to us here a glimpse of the beneficent *activity* of the glorified saints, a commentary on the συμβασιλεύσομεν of St. Paul (2 Tim. 2:12). We hear nothing of the other seven servants, but need not therefore conclude that they had wholly lost or wasted the money entrusted to them. Three are adduced as representatives of classes, and the rest, since all that we are to learn is learned from these, for brevity's sake are passed over.—*Those who stood by,'* and are bidden to take his pound from the slothful servant, and give it to him that had shown himself the faithfullest, or, at all events, the ablest of all, are the angels, who never fail to appear and take an active part in scenes descriptive of the final judgment (Matt. 13:41; 16:27; 24:31; 2 Thess. 1:7; Jude 14; Dan. 7:10). Their wondering remonstrance, *'Lord, he hath ten pounds,'* with the manner in which this is at once overruled, so that the lord proceeds without so much as seeming to hear it, while yet he refutes it, is intended to fix our attention on the paradox and seeming unfairness of that law of the kingdom, which decrees that the poor should become poorer still, and the rich become ever richer. It is a law which Christ here, by this remonstrance and the inattention with which it is received, will with all emphasis declare to be the law of highest righteousness, the everlasting law of his kingdom (Prov. 9:8, 9).

When the king had thus distributed praise and blame, rewards and penalties, to those who stand in the more immediate relations of servants to him, to his own household, he proceeds to execute vengeance on his enemies, on all who had openly cast off allegiance to him, and denied that they belonged to his house at all (Prov. 20:8). *'But those mine enemies, which would not that I should reign over them, bring hither, and slay them before me.'* In the Marriage of the King's Son the vengeance on the open enemies goes before that on the hypocritical friend or servant (Matt. 22:7, 11); here it follows after. This slaying of the king's enemies *in his presence*, is not